The

There are few – if any – significant issues in, or aspects of, contemporary sport that do not raise ethical questions. From on-field relationships between athletes, coaches and officials, to the corporate responsibility of international sports organisations and businesses, ethical considerations permeate sport at every level.

This important new collection of articles showcases the very best international scholarship in the field of sports ethics, and offers a comprehensive, one-stop resource for any student, scholar or sportsperson with an interest in this important area. It addresses cutting-edge contemporary themes within sports ethics, such as gene doping, as well as introducing classic ethical debates that define our understanding of sport, sporting (mis)conduct and sporting practices. The book is arranged into seven thematic sections, each of which includes an introduction by the editor that highlights the key themes and places each article in the contexts of the literature.

The Ethics of Sports sheds new light on a wide range of issues within contemporary sports studies, including doping, disability, gender and ethnicity; the practice of physical education and sports coaching; and sports media, sports business and sports medicine. It is essential reading for all students with an interest in sport or applied ethics.

Mike McNamee is Professor of Applied Ethics in the Department of Philosophy, History and Law in Healthcare, Swansea University, and is also a member of the Clinical Ethics Committee at Cardiff and Vale National Health Service Trust, UK. He is Series Editor of *Ethics and Sport* and Editor of the journal *Sport, Ethics and Philosophy*. His most recent book, *Sport, Virtues and Vices: Morality Plays*, was published in 2008 by Routledge. He is a former President of the International Association for the Philosophy of Sport and the Founding Chair of the British Philosophy of Sport Association.

The Ethics of Sports

A Reader

Edited by
Mike McNamee

Routledge
Taylor & Francis Group

LONDON AND NEW YORK

First edition published 2010
by Routledge
2 Park Square, Milton Park, Abingdon, Oxon, OX14 4RN

Simultaneously published in the USA and Canada
by Routledge
711 Third Avenue, New York, NY 10017

Routledge is an imprint of the Taylor & Francis Group, an informa business

Typeset in Galliard and Frutiger by Glyph International

British Library Cataloguing in Publication Data
A catalogue record for this book is available from the British Library

Library of Congress Cataloging-in-Publication Data
The ethics of sports: a reader / edited by Mike McNamee. – 1st ed.
p. cm.
Includes bibliographical references and index.
(pbk.: alk. paper) 1. Sports–Moral and ethical aspects. I. McNamee, M. J. (Mike J.)
GV706.3.E87 2010
175–dc22

2009050150

ISBN10: 0-415-47860-X (hbk)
ISBN10: 0-415-47861-8 (pbk)

ISBN13: 978-0-415-47860-1 (hbk)
ISBN13: 978-0-415-47861-8 (pbk)

For Mam

Contents

Acknowledgements

This Reader would not be possible without the kind permission of the publishers and authors noted below, to whom I am grateful. I also wish to express my gratitude for the considerable encouragement and support offered by a succession of friends and colleagues at Routledge (Taylor & Francis) in more than a decade of collaboration. I wish to thank Samantha Grant, who initially proposed the project to me, and Simon Whitmore, who saw it through. Both they and I were ably supported by Brian Guerin and Joshua Wells. I happily record my considerable thanks to Professor Steve Edwards and Professor Graham McFee for their many and helpful discussions along the way. Final thanks and love to Cheryl, Megan and Ffion without whom ...

Permissions

Gunnar Breivik, 'Can BASEjumping Be Morally Defended?', from *Philosophy, Risk and Adventure Sports*, Mike McNamee ed., © 2007 Gunnar Breivik. Reprinted by permission of Routledge.

David Carr, 'What Moral Significance Has Physical Education? A Question in Need of Disambiguation', from *Ethics and Sport*, Mike McNamee and Jim Parry eds, © 1998 David Carr. Reprinted by permission of Routledge.

Paolo David, 'Sharp Practice: Intensive Training and Child Abuse', from *Human Rights in Youth Sport*, © 2004 Paolo David. Reprinted by permission of Routledge.

Philip Ebert and Simon Robertson, 'Adventure, Climbing Excellence and the Practice of "Bolting"', from *Philosophy, Risk and Adventure Sports*, Mike McNamee ed., © 2007 Philip Ebert and Simon Robertson. Reprinted by permission of Routledge.

Warren P. Fraleigh, 'The Ends of the Sports Contest', from *Right Actions in Sport: Ethics for Contestants*, © 1984 Warren P. Fraleigh.

David Fraser, 'It's Not Cricket: Underarm Bowling, Legality and the Meaning of Life', from *Cricket and the Law: The Man in White is Always Right*, © 2005 David Fraser. Reprinted by permission of Routledge.

Michael Gard and Hayley Fitzgerald, 'Tackling *Murderball*: Masculinity, Disability and the Big Screen', from *Sport, Ethics and Philosophy*, Vol. 2, Issue 2, pp. 126–141, © 2008 Michael Gard and Hayley Fitzgerald. Reprinted by permission of Taylor & Francis.

Raimond Gaita, 'Sacred Places', from *The Philosopher's Dog*, © 2003 Raimond Gaita. Reprinted by permission of Routledge.

Søren Holm, 'Doping Under Medical Control: Conceptually Possible but Impossible in the World of Sports?', from *Sport, Ethics and Philosophy*, Vol 1., Issue 2, pp. 135–145, © 2007 Søren Holm. Reprinted by permission of Taylor & Francis.

Johan Huizinga, 'Nature and Significance of Play as a Cultural Phenomenon', from *Homo Ludens*, © 1951 Johan Huizinga. Reprinted by permission of Routledge.

Thomas Hurka, 'Games and the Good—I', from PASH/*Proceedings of the Aristotelian Society*, Supplementary Volume 80, pp. 217–235, © 2006 Thomas Hurka. Reprinted by permission of Wiley-Blackwell.

Jesús Ilundáin-Agurruza, 'Kant Goes Skydiving: Understanding the Extreme by Way of the Sublime', from *Philosophy, Risk and Adventure Sports*, Mike McNamee ed., © 2007 Jesús Ilundáin-Agurruza. Reprinted by permission of Routledge.

Carwyn Jones and Scott Fleming, 'I'd Rather Wear a Turban Than a Rose: A Case Study of the Ethics of Chanting', from *Race Ethnicity and Education*, Vol. 10, Issue 4, pp. 401–414, © 2007 Carwyn Jones and Scott Fleming. Reprinted by permission of Taylor & Francis.

R. Scott Kretchmar, 'From Test to Contest: An Analysis of Two Kinds of Counterpoint in Sport', from *Journal of the Philosophy of Sport*, II, pp. 23–30, © 1975 R. Scott Kretchmar. Reprinted by permission of Human Kinetics.

Christopher Lasch, 'The Degradation of Sport', from *The New York Review of Books*, Vol. 24, Issue 7, © Christopher Lasch 1977. Reprinted by permission of Nell Lasch.

Sigmund Loland, 'Fairness in Sport: An Ideal and Its Consequences', from *Performance-Enhancing Technologies in Sports: Ethical, Conceptual and Scientific Issues*, Thomas H. Murray *et al.* eds, © 2009 Sigmund Loland. Reprinted by permission of The Johns Hopkins University Press.

Graham McFee, 'The Project of a Moral Laboratory; and Particularism', from *Sport, Rules and Values*, © 2004 Graham McFee. Reprinted by permission of Routledge.

Graham McFee, 'Spoiling: An Indirect Reflection of Sport's Moral Imperative', from *Values in Sport*, T. Tännsjö and C. Tamburrini eds, © 2000 Graham McFee. Reprinted by permission of Routledge.

Mike McNamee, 'Whose Prometheus? Transhumanism, Biotechnology, and the Moral Topography of Sports Medicine', from *Sport, Ethics and Philosophy*, Vol. 1, Issue 2, pp. 171–180, © 2007 Mike McNamee. Reprinted by permission of Taylor & Francis.

Mike McNamee, 'Racism, Racist Acts, and Courageous Role Models', from *Sport Virtues and Vices: Morality Plays*, © 2008 Mike McNamee. Reprinted by permission of Routledge.

Mike McNamee, '*Schadenfreude* in Sports: Envy, Justice and Self-Esteem', from *Sport Virtues and Vices: Morality Plays*, © 2008 Mike McNamee. Reprinted by permission of Routledge.

Andy Miah, 'Why Not Dope? It's Still About the Health', from *Genetically Modified Athletes*, © 2004 Andy Miah. Reprinted by permission of Routledge.

Mary Midgley, 'The Game Game', from *Heart and Mind*. © 1981 Mary Midgley. Reprinted by permission of Routledge.

Verner Møller, 'The Athletes' Viewpoint', from *The Ethics of Doping and Anti-Doping*, © 2009 Verner Møller. Reprinted by permission of Routledge.

William Morgan, 'The Moral Case Against Contemporary American Sports', from *Why Sports Morally Matter*, © 2006 William Morgan. Reprinted by permission of Routledge.

Christian Munthe, 'Ethical Aspects of Controlling Genetic Doping', from *Genetic Technology and Sport: Ethical Questions*, C. Tamburrini and T. Tännsjö eds, © 2005 Christian Munthe. Reprinted by permission of Routledge.

Jim Parry, 'Sport, Ethos and Education', from *Sport and Spirituality*, Jim Parry *et al*. eds, © 2007 Jim Parry. Reprinted by permission of Routledge.

Heather L. Reid, 'Athletic Virtue: Between East and West' from *Sport, Ethics and Philosophy*, Vol. 4, Issue 1, pp. 16–26 © Taylor & Francis 2010. Reprinted by permission of Taylor & Francis.

J. S. Russell, 'The Value of Dangerous Sport' from *Journal of the Philosophy of Sport*, Vol. 33, Issue 1, pp. 1–19, © 2005 J. S. Russell. Reprinted by permission of Human Kinetics.

Michael J. Sandel, 'Bionic Athletes', from *The Case Against Perfection: Ethics in the Age of Genetic Engineering*, © 2007 Michael J. Sandel. Reprinted by permission of The Belknap Press of Harvard University Press.

Angela Schneider, 'On the Definition of "Woman" in the Sport Context', from *Values in Sport*, T. Tännsjö and C. Tamburrini eds, © 2000 Angela Schneider. Reprinted by permission of Routledge.

Anthony Skillen, 'Sport: An Historical Phenomenology', from *Philosophy*, Vol. 68, pp. 344–368, © 1993 Anthony Skillen. Reprinted by permission of Cambridge University Press.

Giselher Spitzer, 'Sport and the Systematic Infliction of Pain: A Case Study of State-Sponsored Mandatory Doping in East Germany', from *Pain and Injury in Sport: Social and Ethical Analysis*, S. Loland *et al*. eds, © 2005 Giselher Spitzer. Reprinted by permission of Routledge.

Bernard Suits, 'Construction of a Definition', from *The Grasshopper*. © 2005 Bernard Suits. Reprinted by permission of Broadview Press.

Bernard Suits, 'Introduction to the Appendices', from *The Grasshopper*. © 2005 Bernard Suits. Reprinted by permission of Broadview Press.

Torbjörn Tännsjö, 'Against Sexual Discrimination in Sports', from *Values in Sport*, T. Tännsjö and C. Tamburrini eds, © 2000 Torbjörn Tännsjö. Reprinted by permission of Routledge.

Claudio Tamburrini, 'The "Hand of God"?', from *The Hand of God: Essays in the Philosophy of Sports*, © 2000 Claudio Tamburrini. Reprinted by permission of The University of Gothenburg Press.

John Tasioulas, 'Games and the Good—II', from PASH/*Proceedings of the Aristotelian Society*, Supplementary Vol. 80, pp. 237–264, © 2006 John Tasioulas. Reprinted by permission of Wiley-Blackwell.

Ivo van Hilvoorde and Laurens Landeweerd, 'Disability or Extraordinary Talent: Francesco Lentini (Three Legs) versus Oscar Pistorius (No Legs)', from *Sport, Ethics and Philosophy*, Vol. 2, Issue 2, pp. 97–111, © 2008 Ivo van Hilvoorde and Laurens Landeweerd. Reprinted by permission of Taylor & Francis.

Adrian Walsh and Richard Giulianotti, 'Moral Philosophy Out on the Track: What Might Be Done?', from *Ethics, Money and Sport: This Sporting Mammon*, © 2006 Adrian Walsh and Richard Giulianotti. Reprinted by permission of Routledge.

Introduction to sports ethics

Mike McNamee

In some earlier historical times, such as in ancient Greece or Victorian Britain, sports have flourished. The global pervasiveness of sports is, however, a very modern phenomenon. Fuelled, not unproblematically, by the media–commodification–marketing complex, sports are ubiquitous. Their expansion pays little heed to differences in cultural, economic, religious or political order. Sports are now everywhere around us. And this is not, as the public health fraternity are keen to tell us, because we are all participating in them. While billions of children and young people participate in sports in their early years, most people consume sports passively. Is this necessarily a problem from the perspective of sports themselves? Not necessarily: it could be said that sport is Janus-faced. Sport has always involved both play and display. The privileging of display over play is problematic in its own right, and many of the authors of this collection sing a loud hymn to sports internal values and goods. Yet it is undeniably true that sports form a kind of social glue. If nothing else, sports give us something to talk about: whether our home town or city will win the league; whether the latest act of cheating represents a new low in human aspirations; whether sports stars really deserve to be paid so much; whether this or that sport and its spectators are racist, sexist and/or xenophobic; whether sports coaches are good role models; whether officials have been taking bribes; whether Jesse Owens should be thought of as superior to

Usain Bolt all things considered; whether the latest 100 metre record will ever be broken – and whether it was legitimately or illegitimately secured. Such debates are to be found in the media, in newspapers, television and blogs, but also in bars and pubs, at the bus stop or the train station, on the factory line, in the gym or the classroom. And, increasingly, they are also discussed more formally in universities too.

To what extent does this seepage of sport into our ivory towers represent a barbarian intrusion? The great nineteenth century educational theorist and Headmaster of Rugby School (a much venerated private school for young English gentlemen) Matthew Arnold certainly thought it had value in developing what became known as 'muscular Christianity'. Nevertheless, others in Arnold's day and in the nearer present have thought that the very presence of sport in an establishment of learning to be highly suspect. And that was before sport attempted to gain educational credibility as a curricular subject. The Dean of Yale Law School, Robert Hutchins, is widely credited with the quotation that sums up the educational disregard of sport: 'Every time I feel like exercising, I lie down til the feeling goes away'. Equally, in more recent times, sports in American universities have been derided as an educationally dubious incubator of talent for highly commercialised franchises. Undeniably, there are facts and arguments in favour both of critics and supporters alike. However, this book is not a historical or sociological title. Its authors

1

do not set out to describe the rise of sports, or sports scholarship, in universities. Nevertheless, it is undeniable that the broadening of university curricula has opened up new subjects such as sports studies or sports sciences. And in the processes of their development it was inevitable that they would draw upon established curricular disciplines, from philosophy to physiology and psychology. If we accept and support the notion that our dominant cultural practices should be studied critically at the highest educational levels it follows that the study of the ethics of sports is valuable.

In the following pages, readers are invited to reflect critically upon the range of ethical issues that surround sports participation, and the ethical character of sports themselves. In this way they may decide for themselves upon an answer based upon the depth and value of the wisdom contained herein. The aim of this brief introduction is to outline the rise of sports ethics, as a sub-branch of applied philosophy generally and applied ethics in particular, and to offer a selective sketch of its contours. The account presented is not given from the standpoint of an impartial spectator. The mode of working is not like that of a physiologist who might record levels of carbon dioxide in the expired breath of an athlete on a laboratory treadmill. Nor is it to be conflated with the quantifications of a biomechanist who calculates precise measurements of forces and angles as athletes propel themselves in time and space. Students of sports and sports sciences are well aware of the differences of modes of investigation that comprise their curricula. They are not always so sensitive to the contested ideologies that attend these ways of operation (McNamee, 2005). Being neither impartial in the manner of the physiologist, nor quantificationist in the manner of the biomechanist, their reflections are often tagged as 'subjective' or as mere 'opinion'. This loose (and, to put it frankly, sloppy) labelling serves both to mischaracterise philosophical discussions of sports, and to relegate them to the lower ranks of supposedly scientific enquiries into sports.[1]

A brief historical sketch of the emergence of sports ethics

While a number of university courses had been offered in certain American universities during the early 1980s, there was little by way of a developed literature until the last decade. What had been published was in the only journal dedicated to the field at that time, *The Journal of the Philosophy of Sport* (from 1974 onwards), or in multidisciplinary journals in sport and physical education. In the nascent studies of sport, and the many academic subject areas that grew out of it, the philosophy of sport can rightly claim to be among the earliest. While essays in ethics had been published there, the *Journal* had been dominated largely by debates around the conceptual relations between games, play and sport. There was also a significant amount of scholarship in the 1970s and 1980s that was devoted to the aesthetic, and the social and political aspects of sport.[2] Like all fields of scholarship, the philosophy of sport reflected a fashion that was largely dependent upon the predilections of its leading authors. One of those leading authors, indeed one of the founding fathers of the subject, Warren Fraleigh, had broken new ground in the early 1980s with his own architectonic working out of the ethics of sports based upon his conception of the duties that sports contestants owed each other (Fraleigh, 1984).

Despite the emergence of that ground-breaking book, the field continued to grow in various directions across the philosophy of sport. It was not until later in the 1990s that a critical mass of scholars and scholarship emerged in sports ethics. This prompted a conference held in Wales, UK, in 1995 and a subsequent edited international collection by McNamee and Parry *Ethics and Sport*, the success of which spawned a book series of the same name[3] that explored issues as diverse as commodification and corruption of sports; elitism, professionalism and nationalism; fair play, the heterogeneity of rules and their uses in sports; sports medicine and the rise of genetic and other medical technologies; the place and significance of pain and injury in sports; the ethics of eating disorders within athletic populations. Based upon the original collection and subsequent volumes,[4] courses in the ethics of sports arose throughout the UK and then on a wider international basis, fuelled by further scholarship written predominantly – but not exclusively – in English across the Anglophone academic world. In 2002 the British Philosophy of Sport Association was formed and developed a new journal,

Sport, Ethics and Philosophy, which was established in 2007. Sports ethics is now an established feature of undergraduate and postgraduate courses in Kinesiology, Sports Studies, and Sports Science departments around the world, and also increasingly in philosophy departments where scholars have been able to transform their personal interest in sports participation into a professional one through the presence of an established literature.

The conceptual foundations of sports ethics

A crude, but pedagogically useful, way of introducing newcomers to the field of sports ethics might be to commit what is sometimes referred to as the 'fallacy of composition'. It would be a logical mistake to reduce the term sports ethics to its constituent parts, for the field connotes more than the sum of the meanings of the individual parts. Nevertheless, something must be said of both concepts to get the reader started.

In the first instance, what is commonly called 'sport' in the West draws upon a rich history of Greek and Roman athletics (Reid, 2002), on through to the modern incarnation of educational sports in Victorian Britain and on to the re-birth of the Olympic Games under Baron Pierre de Coubertin and others. While across Europe the paradigmatic sports we recognise as Olympic ones were practised and promoted, so too were alternative movement cultures including fitness and health related activities groups, folk games and sport for all organisations (Eichberg, 2010), which bore only a family resemblance to the rule-governed and competitive activities we typically think of and classify as 'sports' in the West.

There is a deeper and philosophically interesting difference at play here. In the West, there has been a tendency for one philosophical tradition to dominate: analytical philosophy. This is not to deny that continental philosophy has not developed a sport philosophical literature, including important contributions to sports ethics (e.g. Ortega y Gassett, in Lenk, 1975). The labels themselves, as Bernard Williams (1995) once noted, are somewhat misleading – and both, being traditions of Western philosophy, take no significant account of Eastern

philosophy, which in Japan (at least) has spawned a significant volume of literature. Given that philosophical research is always and everywhere internally related to the expression of ideas, the idiom of that expression somewhat shapes the boundaries of what can be said.

In contrast to the biomedical sciences of sport, which represent a near universal language housed in technical rationality ('the' scientific method), philosophers working in the continental tradition have largely developed research within the fields of existentialism, hermeneutics, ontology and phenomenology. Although the label 'continental' is itself driven by geographical considerations (the work emanated from communities of scholars in France, Germany and more generally in Continental Europe), one finds philosophers of sport right across the globe drawing upon those traditions. Similarly, analytical philosophy, although the dominant tradition in the Anglo-American tradition of Western philosophy, is misleadingly named in the sense that some of its founding fathers were indeed from Continental Europe. Nevertheless, the drawing of distinctions to represent our experience of the world is common to all schools or traditions of philosophical and sports philosophical endeavour, and thus of sports ethics too. It is with some regret then, that although the present volume is intended to be as comprehensive as possible, it works within the constraints of language and inevitable word limitations imposed by (albeit supportive) publishers.

To what does 'sports ethics' or the 'ethics of sport' refer?

Nothing much hangs upon whether one refers to the field as 'sports ethics' or the 'ethics of sports'. Thus they are used interchangeably in this volume. Typically, however, some confusion surrounds the precise nature and scope of the concept 'sports ethics' itself, irrespective of its designation. The book series, 'Ethics and Sports', has promoted scholarship that is both philosophical and social scientific. Sometimes the latter of these has been referred to as 'descriptive' or more recently 'empirical' ethics. This reflects academic trends elsewhere. Although, certain fields of applied ethics, such as medical ethics, have tended to include both types of enquiry within their field, this has not traditionally been the case in sports ethics.

The most common examples of 'ethics' in sport that spring up in casual conversations, as well as the academic literature, are matters of equity (i.e. social justice in terms of unequal pay for male and female sports stars) and/or of access (for example, with respect to racism or disabled sportspersons), deviant sub-cultures and practices (for example, so-called football 'hooliganism' and cheating, sexual abuse/harassment or doping), the corruption of sports by powerful stakeholders (such as awarding of lucrative contracts to potential host cities of the Olympic games, or the allocation of tickets to events therein); the distortion of sport as a site of child abuse and exploitation, homophobia, and so forth. Within this literature, 'sports ethics' is simply social science by another name. We understand these enquiries to be 'social scientific descriptions of ethically problematic practices, persons or policies', although that is hardly a snappy shorthand. The older label 'descriptive ethics' was designed to capture precisely such enquiries. Here researchers seek critically to describe that portion of the world that is ethically problematic by the received methods of social science whether by (c)overt observation, interview, questionnaire or some combination of them as in anthropology and ethnography.

While philosophical contributors to this collection frequently draw upon data from descriptive ethics, this volume comprises only sports ethics literature drawn from philosophical scholarship. It is both difficult and undesirable to police language and to prescribe usage that dissipates conceptual confusion effectively. Nothing whatever is to be gained by withholding the term 'sports ethics' from the foregoing empirical research. Yet it is important to articulate the conceptual and methodological differences between both forms of sports ethics. It will therefore be useful to observe some important distinctions before describing the work of philosophers in the field of the 'ethics of sport' that is collected here.

In the first instance, the words 'ethics' and 'morality' are used interchangeably in everyday language. Many mainstream philosophers have come to question a pervasive understanding of the concept 'morality'. They note that, as widely understood, it is a peculiarly Western convention whose aim to universalise guides to right conduct is overly ambitious. Along with the project of modernity, philosophers were looking to cast the contours of ethics along the lines that scientists had so powerfully done in discovering natural laws. A number of traditions of moral thinking emerged, which shared certain features in their development of systems of thought and that ought to guide the conduct of citizens of the globe wherever they existed.

In this modern philosophical vein, then 'ethics' was used to refer to the systematic study of morals; i.e., universal codes or principles of right conduct. The distinction between the rules, guidelines, mores or principles of living ('morality') that exist in time and space and the systematic reflection upon them ('ethics') is still worth observing. Under this conception of ethics, academics are engaged in the systematic conceptual enquiry using reflective questions regarding how we ought to live our lives. This entails the analysis of central concepts such as duty, right, harm, pain, pleasure and promise within (often ignored) theoretical perspectives such as Contractarianism, Deontology, Utilitarianism, Virtue Ethics, and so forth. Each of these moral philosophical traditions aims to systematise thinking about the nature of ourselves in the contexts of good living and right conduct. Nevertheless, their nature and scope differ widely. At some points they are coherent and comparable, at other times, and pressed into particular questions, they throw up radically divergent norms for conduct.

The distinction between descriptive ethics (which was originally thought to be a scientific and thus value-free endeavour) and normative ethics (where philosophers advanced a particular action, policy or program that was supposed to have authoritative status) is a contentious one. Again, it is conceived of differently according to how one understands the nature of 'ethics' itself. Questions such as whether there are moral facts; whether there is a clear distinction between facts and values; how the fact/value relationship is to be characterised; whether moral obligations override considerations of virtue and so on, are not answerable from outside a given theoretical perspective. However, there are difficulties with any attempt to distinguish one programme that sets out to describe the world, from another that prescribes a programme for action; the two are intertwined in complex ways. Most philosophers working in mainstream ethics and in the ethics of sport have given up the idea of a neutral, descriptive, ethics (of sports) and pursue normative programmes for which they attempt to give reasonable support in terms of the clarity and coherence of their developed positions. Nonetheless, the distinction need not be sharp to be important.

Ethical theories in the ethics of sport: duties, rules, contracts and virtues

In most writings in the ethics of sport, three families of theories have been adopted; two modern and one ancient. Modern moral philosophy was dominated by the universalistic ethics of either consequentialism or deontology. Over the last 20 years or so (a relatively recent time period in philosophical thought) there has been a revival of virtue-theoretical work in mainstream ethics and in the ethics of sports. Some introductory remarks and references to indicative sources in the literature must suffice here.

Deontology (from the Greek word 'deon'; roughly, duty), is the classical theory of the right action. Before we act, deontologists (the German philosopher Kant is the key figure here) argue that we must consider those duties (usually in the form of principles or rights), which we owe others in our transactions with them. The system of principles is usually thought to have its foundation in a super-rule (often called the Golden rule – enshrined in Christian thought among others) that one ought always to treat others with respect. To cheat, deceive, harm, or lie to people is to disrespect them. Warren Fraleigh's classic *Right Actions in Sport* (1984) is a beautiful statement of the deontological ethic in sport. It attempts to cash out a system of guides to right conduct for participants and coaches engaged in sports. In other cases (see, for example, Lumpkin, Beller and Stoll, 1999) philosophers have assumed a deontological framework and applied it to good effect without necessarily interrogating the theoretical basis upon which their sports ethics is based.

Of course, philosophically troubling questions can be posed to every ethical theory as it applies to sport as to any other social practice. Thus scholars have asked, precisely 'what is meant by respect?'; 'does respect always trump other moral values?'; 'does respect entail not harming others even when they consent to it?'; and so on. These questions trouble deontological ethicists and are posed by their own advocates as well as by those committed to opposing theories. Equally, it is commonly held that for every duty there is a corresponding right and vice versa. If, therefore, children's rights to play, or to be free of abuse or exploitation pertain, then there must be persons such as coaches, parents or teachers, who have duties to preserve, protect and promote them. Fraleigh (1984), for example, argues that boxing is immoral since it involves the intentional harming of another – even though boxers consent to the possibility of harm arising fairly from the contest. It can be argued, though, that athletes, like others, have a right to pursue their own life plans and activities insofar as they do not harm others. Thus, while deontology (whether promoting rights and/or duties) remains a commonsense ethic for many people, there are others who think it simply starts from the wrong place.

In apparent contrast, consequentialism is a teleological theory (from the Greek word 'telos'; roughly nature/purpose). Rather than looking backwards to considerations of duty or rightness, it projects moral attention forwards. Like deontology it is comprised not of a single position but rather a family of theories of the good, which justify actions according to their yielding the most favourable and least unfavourable consequences. The dominant member of the family is 'utilitarianism', which itself has produced a variety of more subtle variations. Each of them is based upon the maximising of a good such as 'pleasure', 'welfare' or (as in their original conception) 'utility'. In distinguishing good from bad we merely need to add up the potential consequences of different courses of action and act upon that which maximises good outcomes.

While utilitarianism is the dominant theory in certain fields of applied ethics such as medical ethics, there are very few sustained efforts at utilitarian thinking in sports. Inspired by the thought that the general good is served by allowing persons to freely chose what is in their best interests based on consequential grounds, philosophers such as Savulescu (2007), adopting a harm-minimisation approach from public health ethics, have argued that boxers should be offered health screening to facilitate their informed decision making, or that professional cyclists ought to be allowed to compete until such time as their drug-induced performances are not deleterious in terms of consequences to their health (Foddy and Savulescu , 2007). Similarly, Claudio Tamburrini (2000) has defended the Argentinian football (soccer) player Diego Maradona's infamous 'Hand of God' incident. During the 1986 World Cup, Maradona deceived the referee into thinking he had headed the ball over the on-rushing England goalkeeper, Peter Shilton, despite the fact that video replays showed he had illegally punched the ball into the net. Tamburrini argued, on utilitarian grounds, that the good consequences of increased rivalry, television coverage, sponsorship agreements and so on, outweighed (and therefore morally justified) Maradona's action. Utilitarians have also argued for counter-intuitive conclusions to the acceptance of doping and gender segregation of sports, where they do not consider rights to equality of opportunity to be as important as the good consequences brought about by enhanced performances and open competition.

It is easy to see why people consider consequentialism and deontology as diametrically opposed moral theories that supply competing foundations for the justification of moral action in sports, as elsewhere in life. Yet, in an important sense, they also share certain conceptual features. In the first instance they are universal in scope: moral rules apply in all places and times and to all persons – it's just that they have different foundational moral principles: respect and utility. Equally important is the idea that they enshrine impartiality. In considering which course of action is morally obligatory or permissible or optimal, they insist that no one person or group must be favoured over another. Bias or caprice is ruled out from the beginning. Everyone is equally deserving of respect, just as everyone should be counted in the decisions as to which course of action should be taken (not just whether to commit a strategic foul in terms of good consequences for my team, but the effect on the opposition and on the good of the game). Finally, they share the idea that the moral rules have genuine imperatival force: once you understand the moral rule as it applies in any given situation, you must act in a manner that brings the conclusion to life in your actions. Failure, to do so – on both sets of accounts – would not merely be immoral but irrational.

For scholarly purposes, contractarianism is typically divided into two parts by philosophers: political and moral. Clearly the parts share many resemblances. Notably they reject appeals both to a divine will, and to perfectionist models of humanity, as the foundation of moral legitimacy. Nevertheless, only moral contractarianism is of present concern. In the kinds of communities exemplified by Western Liberal Democracies much is made of individual rational autonomy and the need for it to be respected (usually captured in terms of a human right). In modern times, Rawls (1972) developed a contractarian theory that attempts to secure the agreements as to the conduct of individuals each seeking their own conception of the good in so far as it does not unreasonably impinge upon others freedoms to do so, with minimal state interference. Sport is commonly held up as a metaphor for his model: (sports) persons join together, recognising their abilities and limits, to enjoy the fruits of co-operation under an agreed framework of rules and norms. Additionally, the legitimate authority, whether the state or the sports official(s), plays only a procedural role in determining the actions of citizens (players) therein.

Within the philosophy of sport, Warren Fraleigh (1984) first explored this idea in his blending of a social contract of sport with the moral duties of contestants into normative guides to action. After him both Robert Simon (2004) and Sigmund Loland (2002) developed substantive contractarian positions. Loland, unlike Fraleigh or Simon, draws on utilitarian rather than deontological support. His is a theory of norms ascribed to by autonomous and rational sports participants who are committed to right and good competitions. He articulates these would-be rational agreements in norms for fair play that maximise individuals' equality of opportunity to secure the goods of sports.

In addition to the differences and similarities noted above, contractarianism, consequentialism and deontology each place great emphasis on the intimate relation between morality and rationality. While it is difficult to imagine any theory of ethics which did not make such a claim (although they have existed in moral history: emotivism and intutionism are their names) quite what is meant by morality and rationality have been radically contested by virtue theorists or ethicists in particular.

It has been a commonplace to distinguish between virtue ethics and virtue theorists after Driver (1996). The latter articulate what virtue consists in while the former is thought to be a theory of right and good action and in that sense virtue ethicists oppose vices that are thought to issue in wrongful or bad choice and action, and consequently to form bad character. While deontological and utilitarian theories have dominated the philosophical landscape of ethics over the last century, the recent revival of virtue ethics has usually taken the form of a resuscitation of Aristotle's work. Here ethics is based upon good character and the good life will be lived by those who are in possession of a range of virtues such as courage, co-cooperativeness, sympathy, honesty, justice, reliability, and the absence of vices such as cowardice, egoism, dishonesty and hubris. The language of virtue ethics has an immediate application in the contexts of sports in theory. In practice, however, hubris, greed, *schadenfreude*, spitefulness and violence often characterise sports, and not just at elite levels. Moreover, we often question the integrity of certain coaches or officials, just as we chastise players who deceive the officials, in the language of vices and the absence of virtue. Both the language of virtue and of excess, and deficit of desirable character traits seems to find as natural home in modern sports just as it did in the ancient Greek myths.

This sketch of underlying ethical theories and their application to sports is merely suggestive and readers are encouraged to follow the footnotes and advice found in the following essays if they wish to explore more deeply the sources that nourish ethical discussion of sports at a more fundamental level.

Sports ethics as applied ethics

In this volume, despite the foregoing section, there is little discussion of metaethics. By metaethics is meant, roughly, the theoretical exploration of the very nature of ethics itself. The remarks above are intended principally to help the reader contextualise the essays that follow. An extremely useful collection of essays that situate sports in a metathetical frame can be found in Morgan (2007: 1–102). It is assumed here, however, that substantive and sophisticated debate can and does proceed relatively innocent of these more abstract philosophical disputes. This view is not to be confused with the view, held in positivistic science, that one's observation and discussion of ethical disputes is theoretically innocent or neutral. That is not the case. Some justification is therefore called for. Were the present collection to be intended exclusively for researchers or established scholars of the field, the omission of metaethical discussion would be a significant one. Determining whether duty or rules, contracts or virtue is the primary concept of ethics, or whether the central question(s) housed in each of these theories are the most salient or truthful is no small nor insignificant matter. But I take it that these discussions operate at a level that is more appropriately addressed by the journals of the field (the *Journal of the Philosophy of Sport* and *Sport, Ethics and Philosophy*) and relevant journals in applied philosophy and moral philosophy that occasionally publish valuable articles shedding light not just upon particular issues in the ethics of sports, but regarding the very possibility of such a subject as a philosophically credible one. The present volume caters for a broader audience, and consciously attempts to reach across the undergraduate/postgraduate student divide. Each of the essays here – although challenging in its own right – is accessible to that reader who is committed to see what is there in them.

When I wrote the first university curriculum module in sports ethics in the UK in 1988 I was responding to a pragmatic pedagogical need. The sports students whom I then taught compulsorily studied an introduction to philosophy at level 1 and aesthetics at level 2. Perhaps due to the compulsion or their natural inclinations they were – perhaps unsurprisingly – not attracted to the subject matter in any substantial way. Their curricula comprised an introduction to conceptual analysis, the nature of sports-related knowledge, and the aesthetics of sports, which never really caught and developed their interest beyond the question of whether sports may also be considered art, or the epistemological question of whether the elite performer was the possessor of some unique knowledge that was denied the informed spectator. What lectures were given on drugs, equality or violence genuinely elicited passionate debate. This response, it turned out, was not a local phenomenon. Nowadays, the interest in sports ethics demands greater attention within and beyond universities, and this is witnessed in the very rapid growth of literature in the field over the last decade or so. I hope the present volume serves to further stimulate that interest and provides a temporary summing up of the state of play of sports ethics – albeit from my own particular vantage point.[5]

Notes

1. It also mischaracterises and improperly promotes a value-laden picture of the nature of 'sport science'. See McFee (2010); McNamee (2005) and Parry (2005) for critical essays on the rise of positivistic sport science and its prejudices.
2. Many of its best early articles have been collected in two editions by William Morgan and Klaus Meier (1988, 1995) which attempted to chart the entire field of philosophy of , not just sports ethics.
3. McNamee and Parry (1998). The series editorship was expanded to include Heather Reid in 2009.
4. Notably the edited collection Morgan, Schneider and Meier (2001), and the second volume edited solely by William Morgan (2007). A fuller introduction to the extant literature can be found in Culbertson, McNamee and Ryall (2008).
5. I happily record my thanks to Andrew Bloodworth, Steve Edwards, Scott Kretchmar, Sigmund Loland, Jim Parry, the anonymous reviewers for Routledge, and especially to Graham McFee for their various advice on the introductory essays of this volume, and/or for discussion on the selection of essays herein. The usual admission of responsibility for errors, oversights, and so on applies certainly to me.

References

Culbertson, L., McNamee, M. J. and Ryall, E. (2008) 'Resource Guide to the Philosophy of Sport and Ethics of Sport'. Available online. http://www.heacademy.ac.uk/assets/hlst/documents/resources/philosophy_ethics_sport.pdf. Accessed 4.10.09.

Driver, J. (1996) 'The Virtues and Human Nature', in R. Crisp and M. A. Slote (eds.) (1997) *Virtue Ethics*, Oxford: Oxford University Press.

Eichberg, H. (2010) *Bodily Democracy; Towards a Philosophy of Sport for All*, London: Routledge.

Foddy, B. and Savulescu, J. (2007) 'Performance Enhancement and the Spirit of Sport: Is There Good Reason to Allow Doping?', in R. E. Ashcroft, A. Draper, J. R. Dawson and J. McMillan (eds.). *Principles of Healthcare Ethics,* 2nd edn, Chichester: John Wiley & Sons, pp.511–20.

Fraleigh, W. P. (1984) *Right Actions in Sport*, Champaign, IL: Human Kinetics.

Huizinga, J. (1951) *Homo Ludens*, London: Routledge & Kegan Paul.

Lenk, H. (1975) *Social Philosophy of Athletics*, Champaign, IL: Stipes.

Loland, S. (2002) *Fair Play; a Moral Norm System*, London: Routledge.

Lumpkin, A., Beller, J. and Stoll, S. K. (1999) *Sport Ethics*, New York: McGraw-Hill.

McFee, G. (2009) *Ethics, Knowledge and Truth in Sports Research: An Epistemology of Sport*, London: Routledge.

McNamee, M. J. (2005) *Philosophy and the Sciences of Exercise, Health and Sports*, London: Routledge.

McNamee, M. J. and Parry, S. J. (1998) (eds) *Ethics and Sport*, London: Routledge.

Morgan, W. J. and Meier, K. V. (1988/1995) (eds) *Philosophic Inquiry in Sport* 1st and 2nd edns, Champaign, IL: Human Kinetics.

Morgan, W. P. (2007) *Ethics in Sport*, Champaign, IL: Human Kinetics.

Morgan, W. P., Schneider, A. and Meier, K. V. (2001) *Ethics in Sport*, Champaign, IL: Human Kinetics.

Parry, S. J. (2005) 'Must Scientists Think Philosophically about Science?' in M. J. McNamee (ed.) *Philosophy and the Sciences of Exercise, Health and Sport*, Abingdon: Taylor & Francis, pp. 20–31.

Rawls, J. (1972) *A Theory of Justice*, Oxford: Oxford University Press.

Reid, H. (2002) *The Philosophical Athlete*, NC: Carolina Academic Press.

Savulescu, J. (2007) 'Compulsory Genetic Testing for APOE Epsilon 4 and Boxing', in C. Tamburrini and T. Tännsjö (eds) *Genetic Technology and Sport*, London: Routledge, pp.136–46.

Simon, R. (2004) *Fair Play: The Ethics of Sport*, second edition, Colorado: Westview Press.

Tamburrini, C. (2000) *The Hand of God*, Gothenburg: University of Gothenburg Press.

Williams, B. A. O. (1995) *Making Sense of Humanity*, Cambridge: Cambridge University Press.

Part 1

The roots of sports ethics

Games, play, sports

Introduction

Mike McNamee

It was noted in the introductory essay that this text contains no section on metaethics, or moral theory and sport, but it is necessary to reflect on the philosophical antecedents of sports ethics. It is reasonable to assume that if one is to adopt or advance nuanced positions in sports ethics, it should be done on a basis informed by the broader conceptual discussions of sports and its closely related cousins 'games' and 'play'. Therefore, some early and important work, both within and outside the field of philosophy of sport, is selectively reflected in Part 1. These essays help to lay the conceptual groundwork for substantive ethical discussions which comprise Parts 2–7. A conceptual background and introduction is offered in the following pages.

Analytical philosophy, which emerged in the twentieth century, conceives of the philosopher's task as an essentially conceptual enquiry. Philosophers were trained to use analytical tools of dissecting concepts for constituent criteria, to seek fine-grained differences in their employment, and to draw conceptual distinctions by their logical grammar. The discipline of philosophy reduced in some quarters to the detailing of ordinary linguistic usages, and necessary and sufficient conditions, in order to detect the proper meaning of concepts others had to operate with and between. Despite this 'new' direction, there remained a strong sense of continuity with the ancient past. Philosophers such as Plato and Aristotle too were concerned with marking

distinctions, bringing clarity where before there was puzzlement or, worse, commonsensical acquiescence.

This approach certainly dominated the first 20 years of scholarship in the *Journal of the Philosophy of Sport*. Much of it revolved around the triad of concepts indicated in the title of this Part, that were central to the study of sports. The work emanated from Bernard Suits's original essay on the definition of 'game' published in 1967 and later forming part of his classic monograph on the nature of games, game playing and their place in the good life. This Part, while taking its cue from Suits's analytical argument, and presenting his widely reproduced essay on the nature of game playing, looks also to work before and after it was published. It moves from an early classic on the nature of play (Huizinga, 1951[1]) and a closely related article by Mary Midgley (1974) on games and play.[2]

Both articles have a heavy ethnological/ anthropological leaning. Indeed, there is a sense in which the work of Huizinga is not philosophical at all but rather an essay in cultural history. Yet he, and Midgley after him, draw out and amplify the the thesis that humans are game playing animals both naturally and culturally speaking. From there we move on to Suits's latterly published appendix responding to his critics' comments. Following Huizinga's account, three essays appear that offer more or less different strategies of tying games to conceptions of play, work and the good life beyond merely articulating the boundaries of the analytic triplex that represent the roots of sports ethics.

The opening lines of Huizinga's essay, and his book *Homo Ludens*, are like a manifesto: 'Play is older than culture, for culture, however inadequately defined, always presupposes human society, and animals have not waited for man to teach them their playing. We can safely assert, even, that human civilization has added no essential feature to the general idea of play.' (1951: 1) And later 'Play cannot be denied. You can deny, if you like, nearly all abstractions: justice, beauty, truth, goodness, mind, God. You can deny seriousness, but you cannot deny play.' (1951: 3). Now of course non-human animals are not self-conscious of their play. They form no conception of it. The extent to which their consciousness, non-linguistic as it must be, is present in playing is an open question.[3] Nevertheless, Huizinga identified properties of play that he thought represented its essence: play is freely engaged in; it is free from seriousness; it has its own order. Huizinga's remarks about play being somehow separate from the serious business of living[4] are worth pausing on. 'Play lies outside the antithesis of wisdom and folly, and equally outside those of truth and falsehood, good and evil. Although it is a non-material [i.e. non-productive] activity it has no moral function. The valuations of vice and virtue do not apply here.' (1951: 6). Were this posture true then the ink spilt on sports ethics in academic journals and newspapers would represent so much hot air. And in the West at least, the historical function of moral education that has been tied to game playing would be considered what philosophers call a 'category mistake': applying the terms of one discourse inappropriately or mistakenly to another. Nevertheless, these remarks about the space of play must be understood in their context[5] – before sports became big business there was something to the idea that they were somehow self-contained worlds or even thought of by some as 'moral holidays' as Reddiford (1981) once remarked. Nowadays, this view is not widely held. But at its heart is a point about ritual that is still apposite and is picked up by Mary Midgley in the next essay: 'The game game'.

The concept of 'game' has been no stranger to mainstream philosophical debates. In Wittgenstein's *Philosophical Investigations* (Wittgenstein, 1967), the concept was used as a foil against an earlier theory of language and its relation to the world. On this view, words were thought to stand for things existing in the world. The example could be taken as a hinge of an ancient debate: could all games have nothing in common other than the fact that they were called games, or was there some substantial essence shared by them all? The attack on the realist position, is attributed to Wittgenstein's writings in *Philosophical Investigations* which were intended as a foil against those who craved generality in meaning:

> Consider for example the proceedings that we call 'games'. I mean board-games, card-games, ball-games, Olympic games, and so on. What is common to them all? – Don't say: 'There must be something common or they would not be called "games"' – but look and see whether there is anything common to all. For if you look at them you will not see something that is common to *all*, but similarities, relationships and a whole series of them at that. To repeat: don't think, but look! ...
>
> And the result of this examination is: we see a complicated network of similarities overlapping and criss-crossing: sometimes overall similarities, sometimes similarities of detail.
>
> (1967: §66)

Midgley takes on board Wittgenstein's insight that the many different uses of the word games only bore 'family resemblances' to each other and that there was no essence to be found by conceptual analysis. But Midgley, although critical of Wittgenstein's conclusions, has a quite different path to tread that shows an aspect of their unity that is worth taking seriously. In part her argument has to be understood as a criticism of a suggestion by the Oxford philosopher R. M. Hare, that the act of promising was like a game that, logically speaking, we could drop at any time. Clearly for him, games did not matter: they were discontinuous with life around them in the same way that an enclave is somehow not part of the city to whose geography it belongs. Midgley's response is a sharp one:

> Now this is a distinctly queer account of promising. First, if there were no promising there could be no games. As many of us have found, consenting to play, say, cricket usually turns out to have involved promising not to go to sleep while fielding deep, or stomp off in a fury if

one is bowled, etc. In this way, rejecting the promising game might make all other games and institutions impossible as well.

(1974: 137)

One of Midgley's chief moves in this essay is to point to the connectedness of human reasons and motivations to play games with the surrounding scenery of living. And, games and their playing being integral to matters of human association, such as promising, rule following, ritualising conflict and so on, they can scarcely be disconnected from the catalogue of virtues and vices either.

If Midgley takes Wittgenstein's insight charitably and looks at the heterogeneity of games (whether as poker or prostitution: the oldest game?) while holding on to their formal unity, Bernard Suits's challenge to Wittgenstein's thesis is more direct. He had suggested one merely needed to 'look and see' if there was an essence to games. Suits claimed that if one looks and sees one can recognise the features that he (Suits) offers. Suits argues that games can be defined and that the definition would allow all such things we know of as games to be included in that logical class, and would exclude non-games properly too.

Suits argues that an activity may properly be called a game if it has (i) a *pre-lusory goal* (that is to say a goal specified prior to the contest such as scoring more goals, jumping the furthest, and so on); (ii) a set of *means* that limited the ways in which the goal could be legitimately achieved; (iii) *rules* which define the activity and specify permissible and impermissible means in the achievement of the pre-lusory goal; and (iv) a disposition that game players must adopt in their attempt to achieve the pre-lusory goal. This disposition to achieve the pre-lusory goal (as opposed to any further goals the sportsperson may individually hold) is called the 'lusory attitude': the knowing acceptance of constitutive rules in order that the activity made possible by such rules can occur.

Suits (1973) later argued that all sports are games, but that they are games of a special kind. Thus, anyone failing to hold such a disposition is simply not *playing* the game (or sport) even where they share the same field, or court, or track with others so engaged. In a beautifully pithy summary Suits holds that playing a game is the voluntary attempt to overcome unnecessary obstacles. Moving from this logical basis, his account of sports draws upon four criteria that necessarily apply: He argues that in addition to being games that there are four necessary conditions for sports that, taken together, are sufficient:

1 That the game be a game of skill;
2 That the skill be physical;
3 That the game have a wide following;
4 That the following achieve a wide level of stability.

While there are few who would doubt the presence of the first two criteria, there has still been dispute about how they are to be interpreted. In Cuba, chess, an activity widely classified as a board game, is considered a sport. As scholars in the philosophy of sport have noted, there is room for argument here.[6] Additionally, the final two criteria are more vague and more readily open to interpretation. It might be argued that bog snorkelling, moving through the water in a peat bog without traditional swimming strokes, should be considered a sport (McNamee, 2008) even if it does not conform to the criterion of a wide following.

Criticism notwithstanding, Suits's groundbreaking thesis in *The Grasshopper* (1978) was so influential that the following decade of the *Journal of the Philosophy of Sport* seemed scarcely to discuss much else. The second edition of Suits's *The Grasshopper* (2005) came with a laudatory introduction by Thomas Hurka. Subsequently Hurka developed his ideas into a full blown essay 'Games and the Good' which comes as a pair with John Tasioulas's essay of the same title. Both papers were presented as part of a symposium at the joint conference of the Aristotelian Society and Mind Association in the UK (one of the relatively few occasion when subject matter central to the philosophy of sport was the object of scrutiny at such an august philosophical gathering). The format at that conference requires two papers with opposing views. The essays serve to exemplify the commentary and debate that is characteristic of philosophy. They also provide original contributions to the philosophy of sport and sports ethics in their own right. Hurka and Tasioulas find much to admire in Suits's reflections on ideas of the good in relation to games and play. Only Hurka, however, draws upon it in a fulsome way and,

13

as we shall see, Tasioulas finds the groundwork laid out by Huizinga to be more philosophically fruitful.

Hurka's account is based on two values that give game playing its ethical significance: achievement and commitment to ludic activity as worthwhile in itself. In particular Hurka gives a detailed account of how the value of achievement underwrites what is a common understanding of sports. It had been laid out clearly by Robert Simon (1991) that sports entail the mutual pursuit of excellence between competitors. Hurka acknowledges the widespread (modern) admiration for sportsmen and sportswomen and states that he takes this to rest 'on the judgement that excellence in games is good in itself' (2006: 217). Furthermore, he adds the original dimension that this admiration 'rests on the perfectionist judgement that skill in games is worth pursuing for its own sake and can add value to one's life'. While other spheres of life contain activities admired for skill, it is excellence which marks the reason why we admire our athletes and games players.

In spelling out the nature of athletic and game playing achievement, Hurka argues that many of the activities we call good are based on their very difficulty. It follows then, for Hurka, that the less difficult, narrow and varied their contents, the less precision required for successful performance in them, the less we value activities and achievement therein. But these, he observes, 'are precisely the aspects of difficulty found in *good* games' (2006: 225, emphasis added). Note that not all game playing confers achievement in any meaningful sense. Hurka, therefore, develops Suits's account. It is not just the overcoming of unnecessary obstacles that confers the value of achievement and thus admiration. By specifying the kinds of games in which admiration is properly founded, and ruling out more basic activities (like the children's game 'rock, paper, scissors') on grounds of the absence and thus their lack of complexity, even where they require and reproduce the lusory attitude. He writes: 'When you play a game for its own sake you do something good and do it from a motive that fixes on its good-making property' (2006: 228). And he acknowledges that, based on the criteria that give activities their depth, the trivial ends of game playing necessarily require us to withhold the highest admiration that we reserve for more internally

complex and thus more inherently valuable human endeavours.

Tasioulas is less sympathetic than Hurka to Suits's general account of the nature and value of games. He argues that Suits's account is too open so as to allow other pursuits such as war and the infliction of unnecessary punishment to be included. Unsatisfied with Hurka's attempt to articulate the value to be found in achievement, Tasioulas points to less complex games in which we find value but not because of their internal demands. Rather, the games of lower cognitive complexity still afford opportunities for playful pleasure and the enjoyment of contingency. What Tasioulas attempts is the uncoupling of admiration/excellence in achievement that is the foundation of Hurka's account of the ethical significance of game playing. Part of this manoeuvre is shown in Hurka's delimitation: he discusses 'good' games and has selected for illustration just those activities that instantiate cognitive complexity which heighten our regard for the excellent players of them. Underwriting this move is Tasioulas' commitment to a more basic and more democratic good that unites and drives the ethical significance of games: play.

Tasioulas takes us back to the first reading of this volume and takes Huizinga, not Suits, as the ground-breaking theorist of the value of games. Having argued that Suits's account of game playing is so broad that it could include the justified infliction of punishment or the waging of a lawful war, he then moves on to a critique of achievement as the basis of ethical value in game playing. While Hurka does not deny that it is proper to admire athletes and games players for their achievements, Tasioulas's support for that viewpoint is qualified. He argues that difficulty, in and of itself, does not confer value on an activity. Developing ideas found elsewhere in ethical writings (notably those of another Oxford philosopher, James Griffin, 1986; 1991) Tasioulas notes that values such as complexity, precision and breadth of content, are 'intensifiers of the good of achievement' (2006: 252). Moreover, he also recognises that our admiration of achievement may be in relation to either 'deep' and/or 'wide' achievements.

To die, for example, fighting nobly or heroically in the pursuit of some noble end may be considered an achievement of some depth.

Equally, one may achieve 'widely' without depth over the course of a life comprised of everyday activities done well with self-direction, forbearance, dedication and so on. On neither of these axes is our admiration based on the achievement of excellence thought of under the headings of 'complexity' or 'intensity'. The 'bare' achievement model, of the kind Hurka endorses, lacks normative authority for Tasioulas, who argues that we can see complexity in affairs that we despise (such as strategically co-ordinated terrorist attacks). What achievement needs, he argues, is a framing value. And he argues that the framing value of games, and thus of sports, will be that of play.

The last essay of Part 1 brings together many of the previously discussed concepts but illuminates them in a historically sensitive way and connects them distinctly to sports. Tony Skillen's 'Sport: An Historical Phenomenology' attempts to show that as far as the values attending and enshrined in sports go, there is nothing new under the sun. In demonstrating the continuity of virtue and vice in sport he considers both participants and spectators alike. He does this since sport, considered as a spectacle, is always both play and display. The audience thus are constitutive of the sport as spectacle and not merely an adjunct or an accretion. Skillen draws upon the lineage of ancient sports and shows how admiration for athletic heroes was a natural extension of admiration for military prowess and how both, for participants eager to distinguish themselves, were a path to what appears to be the greatest of goods: glory. Skillen, with an eye to the politics of admiration and envy, draws attention to the exclusivity of glory and athletic success. He shows how exultation and significant economic rewards were present in athletic events in ancient Greece, competitors were still driven to achievement for what it conferred in and of itself and even amid cheating and hubris filled ambition, there was some semblance of balance and giving one's due to others.

Skillen is especially sensitive to the role of the audience in athletic contests and modern day sports. Just as the Romans manufactured their 'bread and circuses' routine as a policy of social control, he warns against the dumbing down of athletic contests into mere entertainment of the masses such as the Chariot races had descended to. This diminishes both the notion of informed spectatorship (where the audience both recognise and properly admire excellence) and the athlete who becomes a hired hand uncommitted to the excellences of their craft. Yet, he notes that certain virtues did remain in Roman culture that attended gladiatorial and military contests, and that the courageous and the noble suffered no shame in loss – an idea redolent of todays' heroic failures in sports. Skillen notes the extension of this idea in the very masculine virtues of muscular Christianity that suffuses not merely Victorian sport but also the attendant literature of the day. He shows how a concern for athletic excellence cannot be distinguished from a deep and ongoing concern for excellence of the (public) character of the Christian gentleman.

Skillen too returns to the value of play:

> It was not an arbitrary focus that led Piaget [the distinguished Swiss developmental psychologist] to observe children's unrefereed games as the best index of the spontaneous growth of moral sense. With its dialectic of skill, co-operation, forbearance, courage, enterprise and luck, sport is a microcosm of life in man of its major aspects, nor is its moral dimension reducible to being a good sport in victory or defeat.
>
> (1993: 366)

Though he is therefore an able critic of the potential elitism or exclusivity of athletic excellence, and of the excesses of conduct and character, Skillen offers an idealisation of sport as properly committed rule-governed play.

This introduction serves to conclude the essays of Part 1 and open the door more specifically to sports as athletic contests, and to consider the moral values enshrined in the rules that define and regulate activity therein in the remainder of the volume.

Notes

1. Note that the version reproduced here is the Routledge imprint originally published by Paladin.
2. Note that the version reproduced here is the revised and shorter version that appeared in Midgley's *Heart and Mind* and is from the Routledge imprint of that book originally published by Harvester.
3. One which Gaita (2003) has much to say about. And in his philosophical elegy to animals generally

(and his pets in particular) he also remarks on other aspects of nature and our place within it. Fittingly, while the first essay alerts us to our playful nature so the last essay of this collection elaborates the playful in nature as expressed in mountaineering (an activity Suits would surely not have called a game).

4. A hived-offness that the philosopher of education Richard Peters (1966) once argued was the basis of denying games their status as educative.

5. For a sophisticated defence of the values of play see Hyland (1984).

6. For criticisms of different parts of the thesis see the *Journal of the Philosophy of Sport* generally, though for a full-scale critique of Suits's essentialism see McFee (2004: 15–32). Suits's responses to the general criticisms regarding his definition of games, included as an appendix in his second edition, are reprinted in this Part.

References

Griffin, J. (1986) *Wellbeing: Its Meaning and Measurement*, Oxford: Blackwell.

Griffin, J. (1991) *Value Judgement*, Oxford: Blackwell.

Huizinga, J. (1951) *Homo Ludens*, London: Routledge & Kegan Paul.

Hurka, T. (2006) 'Games and the Good', *Proceedings of the Aristotelian Society*, 80: 217–35.

Hyland, D. (1984) *The Question of Play*, Lanham; MD: University Press of America.

McFee, G. (2004) *Sport, Rules and Values*, London: Routledge.

McNamee, M. J. (2008) *Sports, Virtues and Vices*, London: Routledge.

Midgley, M. (1974) 'The Game Game', *Philosophy* 49: 231–53.

Midgley, M. (1981) *Heart and Mind; the Varieties of Moral Experience*, London: Routledge.

Peters, R. S. (1966) *Ethics and Education*, London: Allen & Unwin.

Reddiford, G. (1981) 'Morality and the Games Player', *Physical Education Review*, 4: 8–16.

Simon, R. (1991) *Fair Play: Sport, Values and Society*, Boulder; CO: Westview Press.

Skillen, A. (1973) 'Sport: An Historical Phenomenology', *Philosophy*, 68: 344–68.

Suits, B. (1973) 'The Elements of Sports', In R. Osterhaudt (ed), *The Philosophy of Sport*, Springfield, IL: C.C. Thomas Publisher Ltd: pp. 48–64.

Suits, B. (1978) *The Grasshopper: Games, Life and Utopia*, Toronto: University of Toronto Press.

Suits, B. (2005) *The Grasshopper: Games, Life and Utopia* (2nd edn), Toronto: Broadview Press.

Tasoulias, J. (2006) 'Games and the Good', *Proceedings of the Aristotelian Society*, 80: 237–64.

Wittgenstein, L. (1967) *Philosophical Investigations*, trans. Anscombe, G. E. M. (3rd edn), Oxford; Blackwell.

Construction of a definition

Bernard Suits

Here the Grasshopper arrives at a definition of games by two different routes.

Game playing as the selection of inefficient means

Mindful of the ancient canon that the quest for knowledge obliges us to proceed from what is more obvious to what is less obvious [began the Grasshopper], let us start with the commonplace belief that playing games is different from working. Games therefore might be expected to be what work, in some salient respect, is not. Let us now baldly characterize work as 'technical activity,' by which I mean activity in which an agent seeks to employ the most efficient available means for reaching a desired goal. Since games, too, evidently have goals, and since means are evidently employed for their attainment, the possibility suggests itself that games differ from technical activities in that the means employed in games are not the most efficient. Let us say, then, that games are goal-directed activities in which inefficient means are intentionally chosen. For example, in racing games one voluntarily goes all round the track in an effort to arrive at the finish line instead of 'sensibly' cutting straight across the infield.

The following considerations, however, seem to cast doubt on this proposal. The goal of a game, we may say, is winning the game. Let us take an example. In poker I am a winner if I have more money when I stop playing than I had when I started. But suppose that one of the other players, in the course of the game, repays me a debt of a hundred dollars, or suppose I hit another player on the head and take all of his money from him. Then, although I have not won a single hand all evening, am I nevertheless a winner? Clearly not, since I did not increase my money as a consequence of playing poker. In order to be a winner (a sign and product of which is, to be sure, the gaining of money) certain conditions must be met which are not met by the collection of a debt or by felonious assault. These conditions are the rules of poker, which tell us what we can and what we cannot do with the cards and the money. Winning at poker consists in increasing one's money by using only means permitted by the rules, although mere obedience to the rules does not by itself ensure victory. Better and worse means are equally permitted by the rules. Thus in Draw Poker retaining an ace along with a pair and discarding the ace while retaining the pair are both permissible plays, although one is usually a better play than the other. The means for winning at poker, therefore, are limited, but not completely determined, by the rules. Attempting to win at poker may accordingly be described as attempting to gain money by using the most efficient means available, where only those means permitted by the rules are available. But if that is so, then playing poker is a technical activity as originally defined.

Still, this seems a strange conclusion. The belief that working and playing games are quite different things is very widespread, yet we seem obliged to say that playing a game is just another job to be done as competently as possible. Before giving up the thesis that playing a game involves a sacrifice of efficiency, therefore, let us consider one more example. Suppose I make it my purpose to get a small round object into a hole in the ground as efficiently as possible. Placing it in the hole with my hand would be a natural means to adopt. But surely I would not take a stick with a piece of metal on one end of it, walk three or four hundred yards away from the hole, and then attempt to propel the ball into the hole with the stick. That would not be technically intelligent. But such an undertaking is an extremely popular game, and the foregoing way of describing it evidently shows how games differ from technical activities.

But of course it shows nothing of the kind. The end in golf is not correctly described as getting a ball into a hole in the ground, or even, to be more precise, into several holes in a set order. It is to achieve that end with the smallest possible number of strokes. But a stroke is a certain type of swing with a golf club. Thus, if my end were simply to get a ball into a number of holes in the ground, I would not be likely to use a golf club in order to achieve it, nor would I stand at a considerable distance from each hole. But if my end were to get a ball into some holes with a golf club while standing at a considerable distance from each hole, why then I would certainly use a golf club and I would certainly take up such positions. Once committed to that end, moreover, I would strive to accomplish it as efficiently as possible. Surely no one would want to maintain that if I conducted myself with utter efficiency in pursuit of this end I would not be playing a game, but that I *would* be playing a game just to the extent that I permitted my efforts to become sloppy. Nor is it the case that my use of a golf club is a less efficient way to

achieve my end than would be the use of my hand. To refrain from using a golf club as a means for sinking a ball with a golf club is not more efficient because it is not possible. Inefficient selection of means, accordingly, does not seem to be a satisfactory account of game playing.

The inseparability of rules and ends in games

The objection advanced against the last thesis rests upon, and thus brings to light, consideration of the place of rules in games: they seem to stand in a peculiar relation to ends. The end in poker is not simply to gain money, or in golf simply to get a ball into a hole, but to do these things in prescribed (or, perhaps more accurately, not to do them in proscribed) ways; that is, to do them only in accordance with rules. Rules in games thus seem to be in some sense inseparable from ends, for to break a game rule is to render impossible the attainment of an end. Thus, although you may receive the trophy by lying about your golf score, you have certainly not won the game. But in what we have called technical activity it is possible to gain an end by breaking a rule; for example, gaining a trophy by lying about your golf score. So while it is possible in a technical action to break a rule without destroying the original end of the action, in games the reverse appears to be the case. If the rules are broken the original end becomes impossible of attainment, since one cannot (really) win the game unless one plays it, and one cannot (really) play the game unless one obeys the rules of the game.

This may be illustrated by the following case. Professor Snooze has fallen asleep in the shade provided by some shrubbery in a secluded part of the campus. From a nearby walk I observe this. I also notice that the shrub under which he is reclining is a man-eating plant, and I judge from its behaviour that it is about to eat the man Snooze. As I run across to him I see a sign which reads KEEP OFF THE GRASS. Without a qualm I ignore this prohibition and save Snooze's life. Why did I make this (no doubt scarcely conscious) decision? Because the value of saving Snooze's life (or of saving a life) outweighed the value of obeying the prohibition against walking on the grass.

Now the choices in a game appear to be radically unlike this choice. In a game I cannot disjoin the end, winning, from the rules in terms of which winning possesses its meaning. I can, of course, decide to cheat in order to gain the pot, but then I have changed my end from winning a game to gaining money. Thus, in deciding to save Snooze's life my purpose was not 'to save Snooze while at the same time obeying the campus rules for pedestrians.' My purpose was to save Snooze's life, and there were alternative ways in which this might have been accomplished. I could, for example, have remained on the sidewalk and shouted to Snooze in an effort to awaken him. But precious minutes might have been lost, and in any case Snooze, although he tries to hide it, is nearly stone deaf. There are evidently two distinct ends at issue in the Snooze episode: saving Snooze and obeying the rule, out of respect either for the law or for the lawn. And I can achieve either of these ends without at the same time achieving the other. But in a game the end and the rules do not admit of such disjunction. It is impossible for me to win the game and at the same time to break one of its rules, I do not have open to me the alternatives of winning the game honestly and winning the game by cheating, since in the latter case I would not be playing the game at all and thus could not, *a fortiori*, win it.

Now if the Snooze episode is treated as an action which has one, and only one, end – (Saving Snooze) *and* (Keeping off the grass) – it can be argued that the action has become, just by virtue of that fact, a game. Since there would be no independent alternatives, there would be no choice to be made; to achieve one part of the end without achieving the other part would be to fail utterly. On such an interpretation of the episode suppose I am congratulated by a grateful faculty for my timely intervention. A perfectly appropriate response would be: 'I don't deserve your praise. True, I saved Snooze, but since I walked on the grass it doesn't count,' just as though I were to admit to carrying the ball to the cup on the fifth green. Or again, on this interpretation, I would originally have conceived the problem in a quite different way: 'Let me see if I can save Snooze without walking on the grass.' One can then imagine my running as fast as I can (but taking no illegal short cuts) to the Athletic Building, where I request (and meticulously sign out) a pole vaulter's pole with which

I hope legally to prod Snooze into wakefulness, whereupon I hurry back to Snooze to find him disappearing into the plant. 'Well,' I remark, not without complacency, 'I didn't win, but at least I played the game.'

It must be pointed out, however, that this example could be misleading. Saving a life and keeping off the grass are, as values, hardly on the same footing. It is possible that the Snooze episode appears to support the contention at issue (that games differ from technical actions because of the inseparability of rules and ends in the former) only because of the relative triviality of one of the alternatives, This peculiarity of the example can be corrected by supposing that when I decide to obey the rule to keep off the grass, my reason for doing so is that I am a kind of demented Kantian and thus regard myself to be bound by the most weighty philosophical considerations to honour *all* laws with equal respect. So regarded, my maddeningly proper efforts to save a life would not appear ludicrous but would constitute moral drama of the highest order. But since we are not demented Kantians, Skepticus, a less fanciful though logically identical example may be cited.

Let us suppose the life of Snooze to be threatened not by a man-eating plant but by Dr. Threat, who is found approaching the snoozing Snooze with the obvious intention of murdering him. Again I want to save Snooze's life, but I cannot do so (let us say) without killing Threat. However, there is a rule to which I am very strongly committed which forbids me to take another human life. Thus, although (as it happens) I could easily kill Threat from where I stand (with a loaded and cocked pistol I happen to have in my hand), I decide to try to save Snooze by other means, just because of my wish to obey the rule which forbids killing. I therefore run towards Threat with the intention of wresting the weapon from his hand. I am too late, and he murders Snooze. This seems to be a clear case of an action having a conjunctive end of the kind under consideration, but one which we are not at all inclined to call a game. My end, that is to say, was not simply to save the life of Snooze, just as in golf it is not simply to get the ball into the hole, but to save his life without breaking a certain rule. I want to put the ball into the hole fairly and I want to save Snooze morally. Moral rules are perhaps

19

generally regarded as figuring in human conduct in just this fashion. Morality says that if something can be done only immorally it ought not to be done at all. 'What profiteth it a man,' etc. The inseparability of rules and ends does not, therefore, seem to be a completely distinctive characteristic of games.

Game rules as not ultimately binding

It should be noticed, however, that the foregoing criticism requires only a partial rejection of the proposal at issue. Even though the attack seems to show that not all things which correspond to the formula are games, it may still be the case that all games correspond to the formula. This suggests that we ought not to reject the proposal but ought first to try to limit its scope by adding to it an adequate differentiating principle. Such a principle is suggested by the striking difference between the two Snooze episodes that we have noted. The efforts to save Snooze from the man-eating plant without walking on the grass appeared to be a game because saving the grass strikes us as a trifling consideration when compared with saving a life. But in the second episode, where KEEP OFF THE GRASS is replaced by THOU SHALT NOT KILL, the situation is quite different. The difference may be put in the following way. The rule to keep off the grass is not an ultimate command, but the rule to refrain from killing perhaps is. This suggests that, in addition to being the kind of activity in which rules are inseparable from ends, games are also the kind of activity in which commitment to these rules is never ultimate. For the person playing the game there is always the possibility of there being a non-game rule to which the game rule may be subordinated. The second Snooze episode is not a game, therefore, because the rule to which the rescuer adheres, even to the extent of sacrificing Snooze for its sake, is, for him, an ultimate rule. Rules are always lines that we draw, but in games the lines are always drawn short of a final end or a paramount command. Let us say, then, that a game is an activity in which observance of rules is part of the end of the activity, and where such rules are non-ultimate; that is, where other rules can always supersede the game rules; that is, where the player can always stop playing the game.

However, consider the Case of the Dedicated Driver. Mario Stewart (the driver in question) is a favoured entrant in the motor car race of the century at Malaise. And in the Malaise race there is a rule which forbids a vehicle to leave the track on pain of disqualification. At a crucial point in the race a child crawls out upon the track directly in the path of Mario's car. The only way to avoid running over the child is to leave the track and suffer disqualification. Mario runs over the child and completes the race. I submit that we ought not, for this reason, to deny that he is playing a game. It no doubt strikes us as inappropriate to say that a person who would do such a thing is (merely) playing. But the point is that Mario is not playing in an unqualified sense, he is playing a *game*. And he is evidently playing it more whole-heartedly than the ordinary driver is prepared to play it. From his point of view a racer who turned aside instead of running over the child would have been playing *at* racing; that is, he would not have been a dedicated player. But it would be paradoxical indeed if supreme dedication to an activity somehow vitiated the activity. We do not say that a man is not really digging a ditch just because his whole heart is in it.

However, the rejoinder may be made that, to the contrary, that is just the mark of a game: it, unlike digging ditches, is just the kind of thing which cannot command ultimate loyalty. That, it may be contended, is precisely the force of the proposal about games under consideration. And in support of this contention it might be pointed out that it is generally acknowledged that games are in some sense non-serious undertakings. We must therefore ask in what sense games are, and in what sense they are not, serious. What is believed when it is believed that games are not serious? Not, certainly, that the players of games always take a very light-hearted view of what they are doing. A bridge player who played his cards randomly might justly be accused of *failing* to take the game seriously – indeed, of failing to play the game at all just because of his failure to take it seriously. It is much more likely that the belief that games are not serious means what the proposal under consideration implies: that there is always something in the life of a player of a game more important than playing the game, or that a game is the kind of thing that a player could always have reason to stop playing. It is this belief which I would like to question.

Let us consider a golfer, George, so devoted to golf that its pursuit has led him to neglect, to the point of destitution, his wife and six children. Furthermore, although George is aware of the consequences of his mania, he does not regard his family's plight as a good reason for changing his conduct. An advocate of the view that games are *not* serious might submit George's case as evidence for that view. Since George evidently regards nothing in his life to be more important than golf, golf has, for George, *ceased to be a game*. And this argument would seem to be supported by the complaint of George's wife that golf is for George no longer a game, but a way of life.

But we need not permit George's wife's observation to go unchallenged. The correctness of saying that for George golf is no longer merely a form of recreation may be granted. But to argue that George's golf playing is for that reason not a game is to assume the very point at issue, which is whether a game can be of supreme importance to anyone. Golf, to be sure; is taking over the whole of George's life. But it is, after all, the game which is taking over his life, and not something else. Indeed, if it were not a game which had led George to neglect his duties, his wife might not be nearly as outraged as she is; if, for example, it had been good works, or the attempt to formulate a definition of game playing. She would no doubt still deplore such extra-domestic preoccupation, but to be kept in rags because of a game must strike her as an altogether different order of deprivation.

Supreme dedication to a game, as in the cases of the auto racer and George, may be repugnant to nearly everyone's moral sense. That may be granted – indeed, insisted upon, since our loathing is excited by the very fact that it is a game which has usurped the place of ends we regard as so much more worthy of pursuit. Thus, although such behaviour may tell us a good deal about such players of games, I submit that it tells us nothing about the games they play. I believe that these observations are sufficient to discredit the thesis that game rules cannot be the object of an ultimate, or unqualified, commitment.

Means, rather than rules, as non-ultimate

I want to agree, however, with the general contention that in games there is something which is significantly non-ultimate, that there is a crucial limitation. But I would like to suggest that it is not the rules which suffer such limitation. Non-ultimacy evidently attaches to games at a quite different point. It is not that obedience to game rules must fall short of ultimate commitments, but that the means which the rules permit must fall short of ultimate utilities. If a high-jumper, for example, failed to complete his jump because he saw that the bar was located at the edge of a precipice, this would no doubt show that jumping over the bar was not the overriding interest of his life. But it would not be his refusal to jump to his death which would reveal his conduct to be a game; it would be his refusal to use something like a ladder or a catapult in his attempt to clear the bar. The same is true of the dedicated auto racer. A readiness to lose the race rather than kill a child is not what makes the race a game; it is the refusal to, *inter alia*, cut across the infield in order to get ahead of the other contestants. There is, therefore, a sense in which games may be said to be non-serious. One could intelligibly say of the high-jumper who rejects ladders and catapults that he is not serious about getting to the other side of the barrier. But one would also want to point out that he could be deadly serious about getting to the other side of the barrier *without* such aids, that is, about high-jumping. But whether games as such are less serious than other things would seem to be a question which cannot be answered solely by an investigation of games.

Consider a third variant of Snooze's death. In the face of Threat's threat to murder Snooze, I come to the following decision. I choose to limit myself to non-lethal means in order to save Snooze even though lethal means are available to me and I do not regard myself to be bound by any rule which forbids killing. (In the auto racing example the infield would *not* be filled with land mines.) And I make this decision even though it may turn out that the proscribed means are necessary to save Snooze. I thus make my end not simply saving Snooze's life, but saving Snooze's life without killing

Threat, even though there appears to be no reason for restricting myself in this way.

One might then ask how such behaviour can be accounted for. And one answer might be that it is unaccountable, that it is simply arbitrary. However, the decision to draw an arbitrary line with respect to permissible means need not itself be an arbitrary decision. The decision to be arbitrary may have a purpose, and the purpose may be to play a game. It seems to be the case that the lines drawn in games are not really arbitrary at all. For both *that* the lines are drawn and also *where* they are drawn have important consequences not only for the type, but also for the quality, of the game to be played. It might be said that drawing such lines skilfully (and therefore not arbitrarily) is the very essence of the gamewright's craft. The gamewright must avoid two extremes. If he draws his lines too loosely the game will be dull because winning will be too easy. As looseness is increased to the point of utter laxity the game simply falls apart, since there are then no rules proscribing available means. (For example, a homing propellant device could be devised which would ensure a golfer a hole in one every time he played.) On the other hand, rules are lines that can be drawn too tightly, so that the game becomes too difficult. And if a line is drawn very tightly indeed the game is squeezed out of existence. (Suppose a game in which the goal is to cross a finish line. One of the rules requires the contestants to stay on the track, while another rule requires that the finish line be located in such a position that it is impossible to cross it without leaving the track.) The present proposal, therefore, is that games are activities in which rules are inseparable from ends (in the sense agreed to earlier), but with the added qualification that the means permitted by the rules are narrower in range than they would be in the absence of the rules.

Rules are accepted for the sake of the activity they make possible

Still, even if it is true that the function of rules in games is to restrict the permissible means to an end, it does not seem that this is by itself sufficient to exclude things which are not games. When I failed in my attempt to save Snooze's life because of my unwillingness to commit the immoral act of taking a life, the rule against killing functioned to restrict the means I would employ in my efforts to reach a desired end. What, then, distinguishes the cases of the high-jumper and auto racer from my efforts to save Snooze morally, or the efforts of a politician to get elected without lying? The answer lies in the reasons for obeying rules in the two types of case. In games I obey the rules just because such obedience is a necessary condition for my engaging in the activity such obedience makes possible. In high-jumping, as we have noted, although the contestants strive to be on the other side of a barrier, they voluntarily rule out certain means for achieving this goal. They will not walk around it, or duck under it, or use a ladder or catapult to get over it. The goal of the contestants is not to be on the other side of the barrier *per se*, since aside from the game they are playing they are unlikely to have any reason whatever for being on the other side. Their goal is not *simply* to get to the other side, but to do so only by using means permitted by rules, namely by running from a certain distance and then jumping. And their *reason* for accepting such rules is just because they want to act within the limitations the rules impose. They accept rules so that they can play a game, and they accept these rules so that they can play this game.

But with respect to other rules – for example, moral rules – there is always another reason – what might be called an external or independent reason – for obeying whatever rule may be at issue. In behaving morally, we deny ourselves the option of killing a Threat or lying to the voters not because such denial provides us, like a high-jumper's bar, with an activity we would not otherwise have available to us, but because, quite aside from such considerations we judge killing and lying to be wrong. The honest politician is not honest because he is interested primarily in the activity trying-to-get-elected-without-lying (as though he valued his commitment to honesty because it provided him with an interesting challenge), but for quite different reasons. He may, for example, be a Kantian, who believes that it is wrong, under any circumstances whatever, to lie. And so, since his morality requires him to be truthful in all cases, it requires him to be truthful in this case. Or he may be a moral teleologist, who believes that the consequences of dishonesty (either in this case or in general) work against practical possibilities which are in the long run more desirable than the possibility of being elected to office. But the high-jumper does not accept rules for either of these kinds of reason. He does not on principle always make things harder for himself; he does not even on principle always make surmounting physical barriers harder for himself. He does these things only when he wants to be engaged in high-jumping. Nor does the high-jumper, *qua* high-jumper, deny himself the use of more efficient means for clearing the bar because of higher priority moral claims (the catapult is being used to defend the town just now, or the ladder is being used to rescue a child from a rooftop), but just because, again, he wants to be high-jumping. In morals obedience to rules makes the action right, but in games it makes the action.

Of course it is not moral rules alone which differ from game rules in this respect. More generally, we may contrast the way that rules function in games with two other ways that rules function. 1/ Rules can be directives useful in seeking a given end (If you want to improve your drive, keep your eye on the ball), or 2/ they can be externally imposed limitations on the means that may be chosen in seeking an end (Do not lie to the public in order to get them to vote for you). In the latter way a moral rule, as we have seen, often functions as a limiting condition upon a technical activity, although a supervening technical activity can produce the same kind of limitation (If you want to get to the airport in time, drive fast, but if you want to arrive safely, don't drive too fast). Consider a ruled sheet of paper. I conform to these rules, when writing, in order to write straight. This illustrates the first kind of rule. Now suppose that the rules are not lines on a piece of paper, but paper walls which form a labyrinth, and while I wish to be out of the labyrinth I do not wish to damage the walls. The walls are limiting conditions on my coming to be outside. This illustrates the second kind of rule. 3/ Now returning to games, consider a third case. Again I am in the labyrinth, but my purpose is not just to *be* outside (as it might be if Ariadne were waiting for me to emerge), but to *get* out of the labyrinth, so to speak, labyrinthically. What is the status of the walls? It is clear that they are not simply impediments to my being outside the labyrinth, because it is not my purpose to

(simply) be outside. For if a friend suddenly appeared overhead in a helicopter I would decline the offer of a lift, although I would accept it in the second case. My purpose is to get out of the labyrinth only by accepting the conditions it imposes, that is, by responding to the challenge it presents. Nor, of course, is this like the first case. There I was not interested in *seeing whether* I could write a sentence without breaking a rule, but in using the rules so that I could write straight.

We may therefore say that games require obedience to rules which limit the permissible means to a sought end, and where such rules are obeyed just so that such activity can occur.

Winning is not the end with respect to which rules limit means

There is, however, a final difficulty. To describe rules as operating more or less permissively with respect to means seems to conform to the ways in which we *invent* or *revise* games. But it does not seem to make sense at all to say that in games there are always means available for attaining one's end over and above the means permitted by the rules. Consider chess. The end sought by chess players, it would seem, is to win, which involves getting chess pieces onto certain squares in accordance with the rules of chess. But since to break a rule is to fail to attain that end, what other means are available? It was for just this reason that our very first proposal about the nature of games was rejected: using a golf club in order to play golf is not a less efficient, and therefore an alternative, means for seeking the end in question. It is a logically indispensable means.

The objection can be met, I believe, by pointing out that there is an end in chess analytically distinct from winning. Let us begin again, therefore, from a somewhat different point of view and say that the end in chess is, in a very restricted sense, to place your pieces on the board in such an arrangement that the opponent's king is, in terms of the rules of chess, immobilized. Now, without going outside chess we may say that the means for bringing about this state of affairs consist in moving the chess pieces. The rules of chess, of course, state how the pieces may be moved; they distinguish between legal and illegal moves. Since the

23

knight, for example, is permitted to move in only a highly restricted manner, it is clear that the permitted means for moving the knight are of less scope than the possible means for moving him. It should not be objected at this point that other means for moving the knight – e.g., along the diagonals – are not really possible on the grounds that such use of the knight would break a rule and thus not be a means to winning. For the present point is not that such use of the knight would be a means to winning, but that it would be a possible (though not permissible) way in which to move the knight so that he would, for example, come to occupy a square so that, according to the rules of chess, the king would be immobilized. A person who made such a move would not, of course, be playing chess. Perhaps he would be cheating at chess. By the same token I would not be playing a game if I abandoned my arbitrary decision not to kill Threat while at the same time attempting to save Snooze. Chess and my third effort to save Snooze's life are games because of an 'arbitrary' restriction of means permitted in pursuit of an end.

The main point is that the end here in question is not the end of winning the game. There must be an end which is distinct from winning because it is the restriction of means to this other end which makes winning possible and also defines, in any given game, what it means to win. In defining a game we shall therefore have to take into account these two ends and, as we shall see in a moment, a third end as well. First there is the end which consists simply in a certain state of affairs: a juxtaposition of pieces on a board, saving a friend's life, crossing a finish line. Then, when a restriction of means for attaining this end is made with the introduction of rules, we have a second end, winning. Finally, with the stipulation of what it means to win, a third end emerges: the activity of trying to win – that is, playing the game.

And so when at the outset we entertained the possibility that games involved the selection of inefficient means, we were quite right. It is just that we looked for such inefficiency in the wrong place. Games do not require us to operate inefficiently with respect to *winning*, to be sure. But they do require us to operate inefficiently in trying to achieve that state of affairs which counts as winning only when it is accomplished according to the rules of the game. For the way in which those rules function is to prohibit use of the most efficient means for achieving that state of affairs.

The definition

My conclusion is that to play a game is to engage in activity directed towards bringing about a specific state of affairs, using only means permitted by rules, where the rules prohibit more efficient in favour of less efficient means, and where such rules are accepted just because they make possible such activity.

'Well, Skepticus,' concluded the Grasshopper, 'what do you think?'

'I think,' I replied, 'that you have produced a definition which is quite plausible.'

'But untested. I shall therefore ask you, Skepticus, to bend all of your considerable sceptical efforts to discrediting the definition. For if the definition can withstand the barrage of objections I believe I can count upon you to launch against it, then perhaps we shall be justified in concluding that the account is not merely plausible, but substantially correct. Will you help me with that task?'

'Gladly, Grasshopper,' I replied, 'if you will give me a moment to collect myself. For I feel as if we, too, had just succeeded in finding our way out of a complicated maze. I know that we have finally got clear, but I am quite unable to say how we managed to do it, for our correct moves are hopelessly confused in my mind with the false starts and blind alleys which formed so large a part of our journey. Just trying to think back over the twists and turns of the argument makes me quite lightheaded.'

'What you are describing, Skepticus, is a chronic but minor ailment of philosophers. It is called dialectical vertigo, and its cure is the immediate application of straightforward argumentation. In terms of your metaphor, you need to be suspended, as it were, over the maze, so that you can discriminate at a glance the true path from the false turnings. Let me try to give you such an overview of the argument.'

'By all means,' I said.

A more direct approach to games [continued the Grasshopper] can be made by identifying what might be called the *elements* of game-playing. Since games are goal-directed activities which involve choice, ends and means are two of the elements of games. But in addition to being means-end-oriented activities, games are also rule-governed activities, so that rules are a third element. And since, as we shall see, the rules of games make up a rather special kind of rule, it will be necessary to take account of one more element, namely, the attitudes of game players *qua* game players. I add '*qua* game players' because I do not mean what might happen to be the attitude of this or that game player under these or those conditions (e.g., the hope of winning a cash prize or the satisfaction of exhibiting physical prowess to an admiring audience), but the attitude without which it is not possible to play a game. Let us call this attitude, of which more presently, the *lusory* (from the Latin *ludus*, game) attitude.

My task will be to persuade you that what I have called the lusory attitude is the element which unifies the other elements into a single formula which successfully states the necessary and sufficient conditions for any activity to be an instance of game playing. I propose, then, that the elements of game are 1/ the goal, 2/ the means of achieving the goal, 3/ the rules, and 4/ the lusory attitude. I shall briefly discuss each of these in order.

Goal We should notice first of all that there are three distinguishable goals involved in game playing. Thus, if we were to ask a long-distance runner his purpose in entering a race, he might say any one or all of three things, each of which would be accurate, appropriate, and consistent with the other two. He might reply 1/ that his purpose is to participate in a long-distance race, or 2/ that his purpose is to win the race, or 3/ that his purpose is to cross the finish line ahead of the other contestants. It should be noted that these responses are not merely three different formulations of one and the same purpose. Thus, winning a race is not the same thing as crossing a finish line ahead of the other contestants, since it is possible to do the latter unfairly by, for example, cutting across the infield. Nor is participating in the race the same as either of these, since the contestant, while fully participating, may simply fail to cross the finish line first, either by fair means or foul. That there must be this triplet of goals in games will be accounted for by the way in which lusory attitude is related to rules and means. For the moment, however, it will be desirable to select just one of the three kinds of goal for consideration, namely, the kind illustrated in the present example by crossing the finish line ahead of the other contestants. This goal is literally the simplest of the three, since each of the others presupposes it, while it does not presuppose either of the other two. This goal, therefore, has the best claim to be regarded as an elementary component of game playing. The others, since they are compounded components, can be defined only after the disclosure of additional elements.

The kind of goal at issue, then, is the kind illustrated by crossing a finish line first (but not necessarily fairly), having x number of tricks piled up before you on a bridge table (but not necessarily as a consequence of playing bridge), or getting a golf ball into a cup (but not necessarily by using a golf club). This kind of goal may be described generally as *a specific achievable state of affairs*. This description is, I believe, no more and no less than is required. By omitting to say *how* the state of affairs in question is to be brought about, it avoids confusion between this goal and the goal of winning. And because any achievable state of affairs whatever could, with sufficient ingenuity, be made the goal of a game, the description does not include too much. I suggest that this kind of goal be called the *prelusory* goal of a game, because it can be described before, or independently of, any game of which it may be, or come to be, a part. In contrast, winning can be described only in terms of the game in which it figures, and winning may accordingly be called the *lusory* goal of a game. Finally, the goal of participating in the game is not, strictly speaking, a part of the game at all. It is simply one of the goals that people have, such as wealth, glory, or security. As such it may be called a lusory goal, but a lusory goal of life rather than of games.

Means Just as we saw that reference to the goal of game playing admitted of three different (but proper and consistent) interpretations, so we shall find that the means in games can be of more than one kind – two, in fact, depending upon whether we wish to refer to means for winning the game or for achieving the prelusory goal. Thus, an extremely effective way to achieve the prelusory goal in a boxing match – viz., the state of affairs consisting in your opponent being 'down' for the count often – is to shoot him through the head, but this is obviously not a means for winning the match. In games, of course, we are interested only in means which are permitted for winning, and we are now in a position to define that class of means, which we may call *lusory* means. Lusory means are means which are permitted (are legal legitimate) in the attempt to achieve prelusory goals.

It should be noticed that we have been able to distinguish lusory from, if you will, illusory means only by assuming without analysis one of the elements necessary in making the distinction. We have defined lusory means as means which are *permitted* without examining the nature of that permission. This omission will be repaired directly by taking up the question of rules.

Rules As with goals and means, two kinds of rule figure in games, one kind associated with prelusory goals, the other with lusory goals. The rules of a game are, in effect, proscriptions of certain means useful in achieving prelusory goals. Thus it is useful but proscribed to trip a competitor in a foot race. This kind of rule may be called constitutive of the game, since such rules together with specification of the prelusory goal set out all the conditions which must be met in playing the game (though not, of course, in playing the game skilfully). Let us call such rules *constitutive* rules. The other kind of rule operates, so to speak, *within* the area circumscribed by constitutive rules, and this kind of rule may be called a rule of skill. Examples are the familiar injunctions to keep your eye on the ball, to refrain from trumping your partners ace, and the like. To break a rule of skill is usually to fail, at least to that extent, to play the game well, but to break a constitutive rule is to fail (at least in that respect) to play the game at all. (There is a third kind of rule in some games which appears to be unlike either of these. It is the kind of rule whose violation results in a fixed penalty, so that violating the rule is neither to fail to play the game nor [necessarily] to fail to play the game well, since it is sometimes tactically correct to incur such a penalty [e.g., in hockey] for the sake of the advantage gained. But these rules and the lusory consequences of their violation are established by the constitutive rules and are simply extensions of them.)

Having made the distinction between constitutive rules and rules of skill, I propose to ignore the latter, since my purpose is to define not well-played games but games. It is, then, what I have called constitutive rules which determine the kind and range of means which will be permitted in seeking to achieve the prelusory goal.

What is the nature of the restrictions which constitutive rules impose on the means for reaching a prelusory goal? I invite you, Skepticus, to think of any game at random. Now identify its prelusory goal: breasting a tape, felling an opponent, or whatever. I think you will agree that the simplest, easiest, and most direct approach to achieving such a goal is always ruled out in favour of a more complex, more difficult, and more indirect approach. Thus, it is not uncommon for players of a new and difficult game to agree among themselves to 'ease up' on the rules, that is, to allow themselves a greater degree of latitude than the official rules permit. This means removing some of the obstacles or, in terms of means, permitting certain means which the rules do not really permit. On the other hand, players may find some game too easy and may choose to tighten up the rules, that is, to heighten the difficulties they are required to overcome.

We may therefore define constitutive rules as rules which prohibit use of the most efficient means for reaching a prelusory goal.

Lusory attitude The attitude of the game player must be an element in game playing because there has to be an explanation of that curious state of affairs wherein one adopts rules which require one to employ worse rather than better means for reaching an end. Normally the acceptance of prohibitory rules is justified on the grounds that the means ruled out, although they are more efficient than the permitted means, have further undesirable consequences from the viewpoint of the agent involved. Thus, although nuclear weapons are more efficient than conventional weapons in winning battles, the view still happily persists among nations that the additional consequences of nuclear assault are sufficient to rule it out. This kind of thing, of course, happens all the time, from the realm of international strategy to the common events of everyday life; thus one decisive way to remove a toothache is to cut your head off, but most people find good reason to rule out such highly efficient means. But in games although more efficient means are – and must be – ruled out, the reason for doing so is quite different from the reasons for avoiding nuclear weaponry and self-decapitation. Foot racers do not refrain from cutting across the infield because the infield holds dangers for them, as would be the case if, for example, infields were frequently sown with land mines. Cutting across the infield is shunned solely because there is a rule against it. But in ordinary life this is usually – and rightly – regarded as the worst possible kind of justification one could give for avoiding a course of action. The justification for prohibiting a course of action that there is simply a rule against it may be called the *bureaucratic* justification; that is, no justification at all.

But aside from bureaucratic practice, in anything but a game the gratuitous introduction of unnecessary obstacles to the achievement of an end is regarded as a decidedly irrational thing to do, whereas in games it appears to be an absolutely essential thing to do. This fact about games has led some observers to conclude that there is something inherently absurd about games, or that games must involve a fundamental paradox. This kind of view seems to me to be mistaken. The mistake consists in applying the same standard to games that is applied to means-end activities which are not games. If playing a game is regarded as not essentially different from going to the office or writing a cheque, then there is certainly something absurd or paradoxical or, more plausibly, simply something stupid about game playing.

But games are, I believe, essentially different from the ordinary activities of life, as perhaps the following exchange between Smith and Jones will illustrate. Smith knows nothing of games, but he does know that he wants to travel from A to C, and he also knows that making the trip by way of B is the most efficient means for getting to his destination. He is then told authoritatively that he may *not* go by way of B. 'Why not?' he asks. 'Are there dragons at B?' 'No,' is the reply, 'B is perfectly safe in every respect. It is just that there is a rule against going to B if you are on your way to C.' 'Very well,' grumbles Smith, 'if you insist. But if I have to go from A to C very often I shall certainly try very hard to get that rule revoked' True to his word, Smith approaches Jones, who is also setting out for c from A. He asks Jones to sign a petition requesting the revocation of the rule which forbids travellers from A to C to go through B. Jones replies that he is very much opposed to revoking the rule, which very much puzzles Smith:

SMITH: But if you want to get to C, why on earth do you support a rule which prevents your taking the fastest and most convenient route?

JONES: Ah, but you see I have no particular interest in being at C. *That* is not my goal, except in a subordinate way. My overriding goal is more complex. It is 'to get from A to C without going through B.' And I can't very well achieve that goal if I go through B, can I?

S: But why do you want to do that?

J: I want to do it before Robinson does, you see?

S: No, I don't. That explains nothing. Why should Robinson, whoever he may be, want to do it? I presume you will tell me that he, like you, has only a subordinate interest in being at c at all.

J: That is so.

S: Well, if neither of you really wants to be at C, then what possible difference can it make which of you gets there first? And why, for God's sake, should you avoid B?

J: Let me ask you a question. Why do you want to get to C?

S: Because there is a good concert at C, and I want to hear it.

J: Why?

S: Because I like concerts, of course. Isn't that a good reason?

J: It's one of the best there is. And I like, among other things, trying to get from A to C without going through B before Robinson does.

S: Well, *I* don't. So why should they tell me I can't go through B?

J: Oh, I see. They must have thought you were in the race.

S: The what?

I believe that we are now in a position to define *lusory attitude*: the acceptance of constitutive rules just so the activity made possible by such acceptance can occur.

The definition

Let me conclude by restating the definition together with an indication of where the elements that we have now defined fit into the statement.

To play a game is to attempt to achieve a specific state of affairs [prelusory goal], using only means permitted by rules [lusory means], where the rules prohibit use of more efficient in favour of less efficient means [constitutive rules], and where the rules are accepted just because they make possible such activity [lusory attitude]. I also offer the following simpler and, so to speak, more portable version of the above: playing a game is the voluntary attempt to overcome unnecessary obstacles.

'Thank you, Grasshopper,' I said when he had finished speaking. 'Your treatment has completely cured my vertigo, and I believe I have a sufficiently clear understanding of your definition to raise a number of objections against it.'

'Splendid. I knew I could rely upon you.'

'My objections will consist in the presentation of counter-examples which reveal the definition to be inadequate in either of the two respects in which definitions can be inadequate; that is, they will show either that the definition is too broad or that it is too narrow.'

'By the definition's being too broad I take it you mean that it erroneously includes things which are *not* games, and by its being too narrow you mean that it erroneously excludes things which *are* games'

'That is correct,' I answered.

'And which kind of error will you expose first, Skepticus, an error of inclusion or an error of exclusion?'

'An error of exclusion, Grasshopper. I shall argue that your account of the prelusory goal has produced too narrow a definition.'

Nature and significance of play as a cultural phenomenon

Johan Huizinga

Play is older than culture, for culture, however inadequately defined, always presupposes human society, and animals have not waited for man to teach them their playing. We can safely assert, even, that human civilization has added no essential feature to the general idea of play. Animals play just like men. We have only to watch young dogs to see that all the essentials of human play are present in their merry gambols. They invite one another to play by a certain ceremoniousness of attitude and gesture. They keep to the rule that you shall not bite, or not bite hard, your brother's ear. They pretend to get terribly angry. And—what is most important—in all these doings they plainly experience tremendous fun and enjoyment. Such rompings of young dogs are only one of the simpler forms of animal play. There are other, much more highly developed forms: regular contests and beautiful performances before an admiring public.

[...]

Since the reality of play extends beyond the sphere of human life it cannot have its foundations in any rational nexus, because this would limit it to mankind. The incidence of play is not associated with any particular stage of civilization or view of the universe. Any thinking person can see at a glance that play is a thing on its own, even if his language possesses no general concept to express it. Play cannot be denied.

You can deny, if you like, nearly all abstractions: justice, beauty, truth, goodness, mind, God. You can deny seriousness, but not play.

[...]

To our way of thinking, play is the direct opposite of seriousness. At first sight this opposition seems as irreducible to other categories as the play-concept itself. Examined more closely, however, the contrast between play and seriousness proves to be neither conclusive nor fixed. We can say: play is non-seriousness. But apart from the fact that this proposition tells us nothing about the positive qualities of play, it is extraordinarily easy to refute. As soon as we proceed from "play is non-seriousness" to "play is not serious", the contrast leaves us in the lurch—for some play can be very serious indeed. Moreover we can immediately name several other fundamental categories that likewise come under the heading "non-seriousness" yet have no correspondence whatever with "play". Laughter, for instance, is in a sense the opposite of seriousness without being absolutely bound up with play. Children's games, football, and chess are played in profound seriousness; the players have not the slightest inclination to laugh.

[...]

The more we try to mark off the form we call "play" from other forms apparently related to it, the more the absolute independence of the play-concept stands out. And the segregation of play from the domain of the great categorical antitheses does not stop there. Play lies outside the antithesis of wisdom and folly, and equally outside those of truth and falsehood, good and evil. Although it is a non-material activity it has no moral function. The valuations of vice and virtue do not apply here.

If, therefore, play cannot be directly referred to the categories of truth or goodness, can it be included perhaps in the realm of the aesthetic? Here our judgement wavers. For although the attribute of beauty does not attach to play as such, play nevertheless tends to assume marked elements of beauty. Mirth and grace adhere at the outset to the more primitive forms of play. In play the beauty of the human body in motion reaches its zenith. In its more developed forms it is saturated with rhythm and harmony, the noblest gifts of aesthetic perception known to man. Many and close are the links that connect play with beauty. All the same, we cannot say that beauty is inherent in play as such; so we must leave it at that: play is a function of the living, but is not susceptible of exact definition either logically, biologically, or æsthetically. The play-concept must always remain distinct from all the other forms of thought in which we express the structure of mental and social life. Hence we shall have to confine ourselves to describing the main characteristics of play.

Since our theme is the relation of play to culture we need not enter into all the possible forms of play but can restrict ourselves to its social manifestations. These we might call the higher forms of play. They are generally much easier to describe than the more primitive play of infants and young animals, because they are more distinct and articulate in form and their features more various and conspicuous, whereas in interpreting primitive play we immediately come up against that irreducible quality of pure playfulness which is not, in our opinion, amenable to further analysis. We shall have to speak of contests and races, of performances and exhibitions, of dancing and music, pageants, masquerades and tournaments. Some of the characteristics we shall enumerate are proper to play in general, others to social play in particular.

First and foremost, then, all play is a voluntary activity. Play to order is no longer play: it could at best be but a forcible imitation of it. By this quality of freedom alone, play marks

itself off from the course of the natural process. It is something added thereto and spread out over it like a flowering, an ornament, a garment. [...]

Be that as it may, for the adult and responsible human being play is a function which he could equally well leave alone. Play is superfluous. The need for it is only urgent to the extent that the enjoyment of it makes it a need. Play can be deferred or suspended at any time. It is never imposed by physical necessity or moral duty. It is never a task. It is done at leisure, during "free time". Only when play is a recognized cultural function—a rite, a ceremony—is it bound up with notions of obligation and duty.

Here, then, we have the first main characteristic of play: that it is free, is in fact freedom. A second characteristic is closely connected with this, namely, that play is not "ordinary" or "real" life. It is rather a stepping out of "real" life into a temporary sphere of activity with a disposition all of its own. [...] Any game can at any time wholly run away with the players. The contrast between play and seriousness is always fluid. The inferiority of play is continually being offset by the corresponding superiority of its seriousness. Play turns to seriousness and seriousness to play. Play may rise to heights of beauty and sublimity that leave seriousness far beneath. Tricky questions such as these will come up for discussion when we start examining the relationship between play and ritual.

As regards its formal characteristics, all students lay stress on the *disinterestedness* of play. Not being "ordinary" life it stands outside the immediate satisfaction of wants and appetites, indeed it interrupts the appetitive process. It interpolates itself as a temporary activity satisfying in itself and ending there. Such at least is the way in which play presents itself to us in the first instance: as an intermezzo, an *interlude* in our daily lives. [...] It adorns life, amplifies it and is to that extent a necessity both for the individual—as a life function—and for society by reason of the meaning it contains, its significance, its expressive value, its spiritual and social associations, in short, as a culture function. The expression of it satisfies all kinds of communal ideals. It thus has its place in a sphere superior to the strictly biological processes of nutrition, reproduction and self-preservation.

Now, does the fact that play is a necessity, that it subserves culture, or indeed that it actually becomes culture, detract from its disinterested character? No, for the purposes it serves are external to immediate material interests or the individual satisfaction of biological needs. As a sacred activity play naturally contributes to the well-being of the group, but in quite another way and by other means than the acquisition of the necessities of life.

Play is distinct from "ordinary" life both as to locality and duration. This is the third main characteristic of play: its secludedness, its limitedness. It is "played out" within certain limits of time and place. It contains its own course and meaning.

Inside the play-ground an absolute and peculiar order reigns. Here we come across another, very positive feature of play: it creates order, *is* order. Into an imperfect world and into the confusion of life it brings a temporary, a limited perfection. Play demands order absolute and supreme. The least deviation from it "spoils the game", robs it of its character and makes it worthless. The profound affinity between play and order is perhaps the reason why play, as we noted in passing, seems to lie to such a large extent in the field of aesthetics. Play has a tendency to be beautiful. It may be that this aesthetic factor is identical with the impulse to create orderly form, which animates play in all its aspects. The words we use to denote the elements of play belong for the most part to aesthetics, terms with which we try to describe the effects of beauty: tension, poise, balance, contrast, variation, solution, resolution, etc. Play casts a spell over us; it is "enchanting", "captivating". It is invested with the noblest qualities we are capable of perceiving in things: rhythm and harmony.

The element of tension in play to which we have just referred plays a particularly important part. Tension means uncertainty, chanciness; a striving to decide the issue and so end it. The player wants something to "go", to "come off"; he wants to "succeed" by his own exertions. Baby reaching for a toy, pussy patting a bobbin, a little girl playing ball—all want to achieve something difficult, to succeed, to end a tension. Play is "tense", as we say. It is this element of tension and solution that governs all solitary games of skill and application such as puzzles, jig-saws, mosaic-making, patience, target-shooting, and the more play bears the character of competition the more fervent it will be. In gambling and athletics it is at its height. Though play as

such is outside the range of good and bad, the element of tension imparts to it a certain ethical value in so far as it means a testing of the player's prowess: his courage, tenacity, resources and, last but not least, his spiritual powers—his "fairness"; because, despite his ardent desire to win, he must still stick to the rules of the game.

These rules in their turn are a very important factor in the play-concept. All play has its rules. They determine what "holds" in the temporary world circumscribed by play. The rules of a game are absolutely binding and allow no doubt. Paul Valéry once in passing gave expression to a very cogent thought when he said: "No scepticism is possible where the rules of a game are concerned, for the principle underlying them is an unshakable truth. ..." Indeed, as soon as the rules are transgressed the whole play-world collapses. The game is over. The umpire's whistle breaks the spell and sets "real" life going again.

The player who trespasses against the rules or ignores them is a "spoil-sport". The spoil-sport is not the same as the false player, the cheat; for the latter pretends to be playing the game and, on the face of it, still acknowledges the magic circle. It is curious to note how much more lenient society is to the cheat than to the spoil-sport. This is because the spoil-sport shatters the play-world itself. By withdrawing from the game he reveals the relativity and fragility of the play-world in which he had temporarily shut himself with others. He robs play of its *illusion*—a pregnant word which means literally "in-play" (from *inlusio, illudere* or *inludere*). Therefore he must be cast out, for he threatens the existence of the play-community. The figure of the spoil-sport is most apparent in boys' games. The little community does not enquire whether the spoil-sport is guilty of defection because he dares not enter into the game or because he is not allowed to. Rather, it does not recognize "not being allowed" and calls it "not daring". For it, the problem of obedience and conscience is no more than fear of punishment. The spoil-sport breaks the magic world, therefore he is a coward and must be ejected. In the world of high seriousness, too, the cheat and the hypocrite have always had an easier time of it than the spoil-sports, here called apostates, heretics, innovators, prophets, conscientious objectors, etc. It sometimes happens, however, that the spoil-sports in their turn make a new

31

community with rules of its own. The outlaw, the revolutionary, the cabbalist or member of a secret society, indeed heretics of all kinds are of a highly associative if not sociable disposition, and a certain element of play is prominent in all their doings.

[…]

Summing up the formal characteristics of play we might call it a free activity standing quite consciously outside "ordinary" life as being "not serious", but at the same time absorbing the player intensely and utterly. It is an activity connected with no material interest, and no profit can be gained by it. It proceeds within its own proper boundaries of time and space according to fixed rules and in an orderly manner. It promotes the formation of social groupings which tend to surround themselves with secrecy and to stress their difference from the common world by disguise or other means.

The function of play in the higher forms which concern us here can largely be derived from the two basic aspects under which we meet it: as a contest *for* something or a representation *of* something. These two functions can unite in such a way that the game "represents" a contest, or else becomes a contest for the best representation of something.

Representation means display, and this may simply consist in the exhibition of something naturally given, before an audience.

[…]

The game game

Mary Midgley

Some people talk about football as if it were life and death itself, but it is much more serious than that.

(Bill Shankly, manager of Liverpool
Football Club)

Some time ago, an Innocent Bystander, after glancing through a copy of *Mind*, asked me, 'Why do philosophers talk so much about games? Do they play them a lot or something?'

Well, why do they? Broadly, because they are often discussing situations where there are rules, but where we are not sure why the rules have to be obeyed. Treating them as Rules of a Game fends off this problem for the time. And should it turn out that the reasons for playing games are in fact perfectly simple, it might even solve it completely. This hope shines through numerous discussions. I shall deal here with one of the simplest; namely Hare's on *The Promising Game*,[1] which suggested that our duty to keep promises was simply part of the game or institution of promising, and that if we decided not to play that game, the duty would vanish. That suggestion is the starting-point of this paper. It has made me ask, all right, what sort of need is the need to obey the rules of games? Why start? Why not cheat? What is the sanction? And again, how would things go if we decided tomorrow *not* to play the Promising game, or the Marriage Game or the Property Game? What is gained by calling them games? What, in fact, *is* a game?

Problems about definition and generality come up here. Can such general questions be asked at all? They come up with special force, because of two diverging elements in the philosophic talk of games. On my right, apparently, games are things we can say very little about; on my left, they are things we can talk of boldly. On my right, that is, Wittgenstein used 'game' as the prime example of a word which we cannot define by finding a single feature common to all its instances: they are linked only by a meandering string of family resemblances. He is attacking the idea of a fixed, given essence which language seeks out and definition can capture. There is, he says, no underlying unity; all that games have in common is that they are games. On my left we have a number of philosophers (including Wittgenstein himself) who suggest that we do have a firm grasp of the underlying unity, by using the word in metaphorical phrases like 'language game'. Now metaphor is hardly possible where we don't have a pretty clear, positive idea of the root notion. To give a parallel, when the early Church spoke of Christ as the Light of the World, the metaphor succeeded because people knew very well what lights have in common, namely a

Mary Midgley 'The Game Game', from *Heart and Mind*. © 1981 Mary Midgley. Reprinted by permission of Routledge.

certain relation to the things and people lit—although if you think about the differences between lights you might find they varied as much in detail as games do. Or again, to pick up the point about family resemblances, it is possible to use the term BORGIA as a metaphor because we take the Borgias to have something in common apart from being linked by their family resemblances. If I say 'for goodness sake don't go to supper with him: he's a sort of a Borgia', my metaphor works, but if I substitute Jones or any other surname where we do know only a string of family resemblances, it won't work. In the same way, philosophers must, I think, know what the underlying unity linking things called 'games' is if their constant use of this metaphor is to be justified. When Wittgenstein considered the problem of finding 'one thing in common' between all the various games, he noted the shifting network of surface similarities, and said:

> I can think of no better expression to characterize these similarities than 'family resemblances'; for the various resemblances between members of a family, build, features, colour of eyes, gait, temperament, etc., etc. overlap and criss-cross in the same way—And I shall say, 'games' form a family.
>
> (*Philosophical Investigations*, 67, cf. *Blue Book* p. 17–18)

But to form a family is quite a different thing from having a family resemblance. Elliots need not have the Elliot countenance at all; they may be quite untypical, and plausible-looking Tichborne Claimants need not be Tichbornes. A family is a functional group with a concentric structure, a centre, and well-understood rules governing the claims of outlying members. This difference becomes still clearer with Wittgenstein's next simile of the thread:

> And we extend our concept (of number) as in spinning a thread we twist fibre on fibre. And the strength of the thread does not reside in the fact that some one fibre runs through its whole length, but in the overlapping of many fibres.
>
> (*Philosophical Investigations*, 67)

But threads must end somewhere; how do we know when to cut them off? This argument proves too much. As Kovesi remarks:

> I do not see any foundation for a claim that we call both football and chess 'games' because football is played with a ball, and so is tennis, while tennis is played by two people, and so is chess. Not only is this insufficient to explain that connection between football and chess which makes both of them games, but this way we could connect everything to everything else. We could turn off at a tangent at every similarity and what we would get in the end would not be a rope but a mesh. Balls, cannonballs, were used to bombard cities, and duelling is a matter for two people. What we need in order to understand the notion of a game or the notion of murder is what I call the formal element. This is what enables us to follow a rule.
>
> (*Moral Notions*, p. 22)

If we could not follow the rule, we would never know where to draw the line. But this is just the kind of concept where drawing the line is most crucial. Is it oppression? Is it exploitation? Is it murder? This type of question is what brings 'common elements' and 'underlying unities' into the limelight. We need them. '*Is it a game?*' asks the anxious mother listening to the yells upstairs, the eager anthropologist watching the feathered figures round the fire, the hopeful child or dog watching the surveyors place their chains, the puzzled reader of *Games People Play*. They can all *use* the concept, because it does have some principle of unity, because it is not infinitely elastic. They all take their stand, not on the same point, but on the same small island of meaning—a firm island with a definite shape. By contrast, anyone asking today, 'Is it a work of art?' may simply find himself floundering over ankles in water, because that island has been shovelled off in all directions into the sea, in a set of deliberate attempts to extend it for propaganda purposes. 'Don't think, but look!' says Wittgenstein. But we need to think in order to know what to look for.

I am not now going to take on the whole enormous subject of Wittgenstein's general attack on generality, nor even ask his reasons for speaking of a 'craving for generality' as something morbid, when one does not so speak of a craving for fragmentation. I do not think that he meant, what many philosophers have assumed, that there are *no* limits to the conventions human language might adopt; that in principle anything goes. But I shall investigate only this single concept of a game. I want to look at the sense in which we *do* know what is in common between games, the sense in which there is an underlying unity. I hope both that this may be a helpful example when we wonder about other examples of seeing something in common, and that the concept itself may be a more important one than it seems, and may cast some light on the serious.

What, then is meant by such moves as calling promising a 'game'? I shall follow up R. M. Hare's case of the Promising Game because I think it is a typical, though unusually clear, example of the suggestion that anything might go. Hare was answering John Searle's suggestion that the duty of keeping promises might simply follow from the fact of having made them. Hare replied 'that depends on whether you have agreed to play the Promising game or not'. He wanted, that is, to treat promising as one of the many dispensable games or institutions which people could adopt or not as they chose. Only our narrow-mindedness, said Hare, made us assume that promising or any other institution is particularly basic; people with different views might choose different ones, just as they might prefer poker to bezique.

Obviously, the game parallel is very useful to Hare here, because it makes it easy to treat promising as optional. Of course, we think, a game is a self-contained system, an enclave which can be dropped without upsetting the surrounding scenery, an activity discontinuous with the life around it. It wouldn't matter whether we played baseball or cricket, poker or scrabble: it wouldn't matter if we invented a new game or didn't play any of them at all. That, we reflect, is part of the meaning of game. We really seem to have that rare thing, so precious to Hare, a pure decision without reasons. Games, in fact never matter.

Now this is a distinctly queer account of promising. First, if there were no promising, could there be games? As many of us have found, consenting to play, say, cricket, usually turns out to have involved promising not to go to sleep while fielding deep, or stomp off in a fury if one is bowled, etc. In this way, rejecting the 'promising game' might make all other games and institutions impossible as well. (Other examples given are marriage and property, which do involve promising, and speech, which seems involved in the whole lot.) We may be no better off than those who derived the duty of keeping promises from the Social Contract—no promising; no contract, and in the same way, no promising, no game.

Second and converging, Hare doesn't say anything about what the promiseless world would be like. Philosophers are rather prone to throw out claims like 'I can imagine a tribe which ...' without going to the trouble of actually doing it. I suspect this has happened here from certain of Hare's casual remarks, e.g., 'Suppose that nobody thought that one ought to keep promises. It would then be impossible to make a promise; the word 'promise' would become a mere noise, except ... for anthropologists.' (p. 124.)

When nobody keeps promises anymore, how will there be any anthropologists? Who is paying them? What does he use for money? (Note the wording on a pound note.) What ship did they travel out on? How will they publish? Who will believe them? This is no more understandable than the equally inspiring converse suggestion made by Phillips and Mounce, who say, 'Let us consider a people who have the practice of promise-keeping, *and let us suppose that this is their sole moral practice*' (*Moral Practices* p. 10, my italics). Thus a botanist might ask us to consider a plant which has fruit, and to suppose that is all it has—no roots, stem, leaves or flower. What follows? Until you tell us more, anything you please. Nietzsche, no great enthusiast for moral dogmatism, gave a better account of the position of promising at the head of his essay on 'Guilt, Bad Conscience and the Like':

> The breeding of an animal that *can promise*— is not this just that very paradox of a task which nature has set itself with regard to man? Is not this the very problem of man? ... At the end of this colossal process ... we find ... the man of the personal, long and independent will, *competent to promise*.
> (*Genealogy of Morals*, Essay 2, Section 1)

Taking this with the importance given to commitment in existentialist thinking, we can see that not everyone who treats the morality of custom lightly thinks that promising is part of it.

Perhaps then, promising is not very like a game. It may be more like the institution of playing games in general, if by chance there is such a thing. In fact, it is not *an* institution at all; it is a condition of having institutions. And this point would have been much more obvious, were it not for the plausible parallel of the game.

I do not want here to pursue the question about the basis of promising so much as to investigate the notion of games as closed systems. This, I suggested, means that they are discontinuous with the life around them. That seems to be how the term is used in mathematics; the theory of games deals with a certain set of closed systems. In this sense, no question arises about the reasons or motives for playing; there is no suggestion of playfulness or jollity in the ordinary sense. But of course, when you bring the term into moral philosophy and apply it to people's *actual* activities, the reasons and motives begin to matter. Any actual activity has motives, and it won't be a closed system, optional and removable, unless the motives are of a special kind. They must not be very strong, or it will begin to matter whether we play or not; they must not be very specific, or it will begin to matter *which* game we play. If they are strong or specific, the system will not be self-contained.

I want to suggest that some quite complex points about motives and reasons for playing are part of the ordinary meaning of game; that the philosopher's use to denote simply a closed system (abstracting from these) is most misleading. Both Manser and Khatchadourian[2] have brought this up, and so far as they go I agree with them. But each of them stresses just one point about games (Khatchadourian pleasure, Manser the separation from common life) and not even the two together are enough to distinguish games from the surrounding scenery. For instance, both these points apply also to art, telly-watching, wine-fancying or the miser's delight in his gold, and none of these are games. We know a lot more about games than this, and there is nothing to be said for affecting ignorance.

I should like to examine the concept further, and see how complete the separation of games from common life is.

First, then I want to say that even *actual* games, normally classed as such, do not keep themselves to themselves in this way but flow over in a perfectly recognized way into the rest of life. Secondly, I want to mention some extended, but still perfectly proper, uses of 'game' and related concepts, like 'playing'. These uses may be metaphorical, but they are quite natural and familiar and tell us a lot about why people play. If Hare's notion of the Promising Game has a place it is among these extended uses, so they are highly relevant. Until we understand the reasons for playing, I do not think we understand the bindingness of the rules.

I turn, then, first to actual existing games, called so without metaphor. How far is it true that they are closed systems, discontinuous with the rest of life?

In a simple way, this looks obvious; in fact it looks like *the* characteristic point about a game. You buy little books of the rules for a given game, and they will tell you how to start and stop playing, but not how to fit these procedures into the rest of your life. What happens in a game can be contrasted with what happens in (as we say) 'real' life, and a person taking his game animosity too strongly may be checked with the reminder. 'Relax man, calm down, remember it's only a game.' This is true where the motives for playing are weak and largely negative, which they often are: we want the simple rewards of play as a change from the strains of serious life. But often there are positive motives. If you say to a grandmaster, 'Calm down, chess is only a game' your point will be obscure. Chess is the business of his life; he may have no other. This may also be true of children. Similarly when Rangers play Celtic, not only may people get killed, but the event is central to the lives of many people present. (I have seen a press report of someone interviewing boys from the Gorbals, who asked them, 'Which is the best of these four things: Drink, Sex, Fighting and Celtic?' and got the answer, 'Celtic every time.') Should we say that this concern attached to a game is accidental; it just happens to have become hitched on to it? But Russian Roulette is a game, and death is an essential part of it, and the same insistence on real danger shows up in many forms of gambling ('it isn't poker if you play for love') and indeed of cheating.

In the case of football or chess, to treat the traditional concern as accidental would mean that it could just as well be attached to something else; that the pattern of life surrounding them demands *some* game, but is quite indifferent what game it is. Well then, we will try substituting halma for chess and lawn tennis for football. Will there be any difficulties? There will. These rituals *will not be suitable forms for the conflicts they are designed to ritualize.* Halma cannot stand in for chess because it is too simple; were the change imposed by law, the result would be an inconceivable complication of the rules of halma. Lawn tennis will not do instead of football for some quite interesting reasons. It is not a team game; it involves no physical contact and does not make the payers dirty. Moreover there are rackets, which, if used in the spirit of football, might kill people. Any attempt to substitute it would result, either in changing lawn tennis past recognition, or (more likely) in the public's abandoning tennis and inventing instead some much more primitive ritualized contest of the kind from which football originally sprang.

These games are continuous with the life around them, and their selection is not at all optional or arbitrary. The Rule Book is misleading; or rather, it misleads those few unhappy people who expect to see the whole truth about anything written down in a book. Books take obvious points for granted. For instance, the book does not mention spectators, nor the reasons for playing and the kind and degree of friendliness called for between players: nor does it mention the choice of teams and opponents, but every game makes quite complicated demands here. Nor does it mention how you give up playing, but that doesn't show there are no proper or improper ways of doing it. (Anyone giving up chess in Russia or football in Glasgow would soon find out about that.) It is just these unwritten parts of a game which are distorted when games are played in schools under compulsion. Compulsion can kill the game stone dead, which shows how much they matter.

Games, in fact, spring from the life around them, because games are, among other things, *ritualized conflict*, and the type of ritual is by no means arbitrary, but must fit the kind of conflict which is already going forward. Such ritual proceedings are not at all an optional extra, a froth on human life, peculiar to advanced and leisurely cultures. They are extremely widespread, if not universal, throughout the human race, and are also found in a wide variety of animals. The lower the animal, the more standardized the proceedings; higher mammals and particularly primates have a much richer repertoire. But throughout the animal kingdom quite elaborate rituals surround a fight, as well as other social occasions, entirely discrediting the traditional notion of formless and uncontrolled savagery in Nature.

Actual games, then, are not closed systems in the sense of being arbitrary, optional and discontinuous with the life around them. They are systems, but not closed ones. What about metaphorical games?

Moralists have used the metaphor of a game rather widely, which is not surprising since it is widely used in common life ('So that's your game?', 'The game's up', 'Playing a waiting game', 'a deep game', etc.) I want to look at some of these uses, along with those of related ideas like 'sport' and 'play', so as to throw some light on what we are doing when we say that something is or is not a game.

One notable and familiar use is the one in which the sour fatalist calls All Life a Game, or something like it, in the sense that it is futile, pointless or absurd. Thus, in Hardy: 'The President of the Immortals had ended his sport with Tess'. Or Gloucester in *King Lear* 'As flies to wanton boys are we to the Gods. They kill us for their sport.' Or Omar Khayyam:

Tis all a chequer-board of Nights and Days
Where Destiny with men for pieces plays.
Hither and thither moves, and mates, and slays.
And one by one back in the closet lays.

Now, this does come close to the notion of a closed and arbitrary system. But then it is a use you cannot rest in if you think beyond your first, hasty comment, because games are not arbitrary in this way. Someone plays them; he has a purpose in playing whether the pawns understand it or not. Thus Hardy would have done better not to turn our attention from Tess to the President of the Immortals, a subject on which he is much less convincing. This use of the concept may be meant in the first place to stress the arbitrariness and disconnection of our life, but if we put any weight on it, it will do something quite different and give it a context; pointing to a purpose beyond our ordinary aims and possibly much more important than them. (Compare the curiosity about Godot roused by *Waiting for Godot*).

There are other ways in which the notion of games can be used to enforce seriousness. Even without the thought of a divine player or spectator, the figure is common in Stoic morality. Epictetus, for instance, uses it when he finds a difficulty in explaining his concept of seriousness. He indicates by it that he wants us to be detached from ordinary life so far as to despise its rewards, but does not want us to drop back with a sigh of relief into the Cynic's barrel or the Epicurean's garden seat, to be strenuous yet not anxious, committed yet free. Again, to our surprise, we find that very serious character Plato telling us that 'human affairs are not worth much serious attention' (Laws 803b), but that since we have unfortunately got to consider them, the only important question is, what sort of play are we to spend our time on? What life is really about, Plato explains, is playing to amuse God. God is our central business and also our most satisfying play. À modern writer who is still more interested in such motives, and who seems to me to throw a lot of light on them is Jan Huizinga in his book *Homo Ludens*. Huizinga's point is that play is an essential element in all highly regarded human activities, and may in some sense be called the basis of all of them. Stylized patterns akin to play are found in the rituals of religion, in lawsuits and court ceremonial, in the formal feuds of politics, in family life and in the play of lovers, in war, and above all in art. All these activities have rules which matter greatly and yet do not really matter at all, in much the same paradoxical manner as the rules of a game. None of them would be as they are without the taste for certain definite kinds of *ritualized conflict*.

It does not follow that this taste is perverted or frivolous. It is a mistake to think that what is regulated must be trivial, that the needs involved must be weak or they would be stronger than the rule. The restraining rules are not something foreign to the needs or emotions involved, they are simply the shape which the desired activity takes. The chess player's desire is not a desire for general abstract intellectual activity, curbed and frustrated by a particular set of rules. It is a desire for a particular kind of intellectual activity, whose channel is the rules of chess. Similarly, human love is not a general need, curbed and frustrated by the particular forms offered to it. It is a need for a specific kind of relation—say a permanent one—with a particular person, and for this purpose only some kinds of behaviour will do. The football player similarly does not just want to rush about kicking things. He wants to do so in a special context of ordered competition with companions; he needs to know what sort of response he will get and who has won. Similarly, as Huizinga points out, rituals like court ceremonial are not arbitrary restrictions clogging personal intercourse. In their origin, when courts meant something, they were forms, and suitable forms,

by which subjects could express their loyalty and kings their kingliness. Forms can die, but formality is not deadness. Huizinga's remarks stress the value of play in human life, the profound and complex need there is for it. Because this need is complex, the things which satisfy it will not share any obvious simple characteristic, like being painted green, but because it is strong and universal, they will share structural characteristics which are easily recognised, not only by others of their own species but even by outsiders, (This successful signalling can be studied for instance in the dealings of people with dogs, and in the pleasing situation where zoo visitors, observing the animals, are themselves observed by keepers and ethologists.)[3] Where a need is shared, we know what marks to look for. The need for play is subtle and complex. We do not fully understand it. Huizinga exalts play by 'stressing the links between this need and what are generally supposed to be man's most important activities'. Eric Berne, on the other hand, points out, in *Games People Play*, its strength and thereby something rather more sinister about it, namely its obsessiveness, the way in which a taste for play can get the better of us, entangling us and frustrating our other needs. But both points of course suggest that the need is no trivial one, and both equally, if accepted, tell against the suggestion that games as such do not matter.

Berne's point converges with Huizinga's. Play is found pervading our most important concerns; play insists on being taken seriously. We need it. Can we say why? I think Huizinga is perfectly right to connect this issue with the equally mysterious question of the purpose or value of art. Whatever that purpose or purposes may be, art does share with play the paradoxical property of being somehow set aside from the prodding practical purposes of life, and yet asserting at times a mysterious right to predominate over them. If one says that art cannot affect life, one is liable to be brought up by the thought of someone who has jumped off the Clapham omnibus and gone away to devote his life to it, or by the reflection that nobody's life will be quite the same again after he has read the *Agamemnon* of Aeschylus properly. Apart from that, the activities used in art—singing, dancing, drawing etc.—do not belong to a select minority, they are all prominent in the play of children, and a taste for them can be detected in young apes as well. One could look here towards the peculiar biological characteristic of man called Neoteny, that is, the extension of infantile characteristics into adult life.[4] This is a device by which a species often exploits a possibility already present in its genetic make-up, but previously limited to an early phase, by prolonging that phase. People resemble baby apes, and even embryo apes, much more strongly than they resemble adult apes, on a number of points of physical development, but of course most notably in their large and quick-growing brain. An ape or monkey brain completes its crown in 6–12 months from birth; a human brain goes on growing for about 23 years. And a related pattern can be seen in the development of behaviour. Playing at all is behaviour confined to relatively intelligent, active, big-brained, non-specialist animals, and where it occurs, it occurs mostly in the young. Now the free, enquiring use of the intellect belongs originally in this context of play. Nearly all the experiments on primate learning and intelligence are done with ape babies and children; once an ape is adult he gets above such things, loses interest and refuses to co-operate—he may even turn nasty. But in man, it is just this use of the intellect which is prolonged into adult life. Does it carry play patterns with it? Is the taste for problem-solving, for ritual, for constantly formalizing disputes and taking sides a relic of the matrix within which exploratory thought emerged? And is the aesthetic approach another? (Apes show the rudiments of dance forms, continuing even into adult life, and have in childhood a pronounced taste for painting.)[5] This seems to me a real and perplexing issue. Perhaps a *mature* pattern of behaviour, suitable for a creature possessing a mature human brain, is something that has not yet been evolved. That might explain more than one of our difficulties.

I return now to Hare's suggestion about the Promising Game. My point in surveying the extended uses of game has been to draw the meanings that emerge from it when you use it metaphorically. Metaphor, I suggested, is an epidiascope projecting enlarged images of a word's meaning; turn the word round and you get different pictures, but where we don't grasp an underlying unity we can get no metaphor at all, and where the meaning isn't what we hope, the metaphor will fail. Now if anyone thinks that all the people I have quoted fail in their metaphors—that they are simply misusing 'game' and 'play', he will of course reject my argument. My own impression about this is that Plato and Huizinga *are* somewhat paradoxical; they do make a rather startling use of the word 'play' but justify it by the clearness and fertility of their point; they make us see after a moment's thought that *play* might really not be a bad word for the things they apply it to, and they thereby throw a new light on the notion of seriousness. Berne and the Stoics on the other hand don't seem to me to use the word *game* surprisingly at all, only to extend and enlarge perfectly normal uses along the lines already laid down. The Stoic notion about playing the game has been good common morality down to our own day, and until the public schools got hold of it there was nothing ridiculous about it at all. And what Berne says about chronic quarrelling or scenes of remorse might well occur to any experienced bystander; calling these a game is hardly a metaphor, it is one in a vigorous series of extremely common uses—he's taken up the con game, honesty's his game at present, daughters of the game. These uses are hardly more metaphorical than 'seeing' or 'grasping' a point in argument. There is no more literal phrase available. And as all these uses stress in the end the importance of games, not-mattering cannot be the central point about them. But there is of course a sense in which games do not matter, in which they are considered as cut off from other activities, and there would be nothing to stop Hare making successful use of the concept from this angle—it is the beauty of a rich concept like this that you *can* get a lot of metaphors out of it. Has he done so?

If we examine that sense, we are struck at once by its failure to fit Hare's point. Games, for instance, are shut off from *each other*, far more sharply than they are shut off from the rest of life—you cannot play cricket and football at the same time. But these metaphorical games are closely interwoven. Marriage cannot be played without other games like promising, and can generate an indefinite number of further games, all in definite relations to it. A married, religious, liberal, promise-keeping physicist plays his five games, not only simultaneously but in a pretty closely-ordered structure because—a point which seems to have been overlooked—he has only got one life to live, and he needs to make sense of it, Therefore he has to try all the time to fit them together and work out his priorities. Of course he will often fail and get confused, which is what makes the suggestion of separating them seem plausible. *But if he gave up the attempt entirely, he would be making it his policy to let his personality disintegrate.* This cannot be treated as an optional further game, because it is negative and ruleless; moreover, it means losing the capacity for any further human enterprise whatsoever. To press the point, has this man now one game or five games? And could these games possibly fail to involve others—teacher, truth-teller, pupil, citizen, property-owner, colleague, friend, Jew, customer—you name it? And the involvement is deep. This man's marriage will be a *different kind of marriage* from that of a man without religion, and his religion a different kind of religion from that of a man with no knowledge of science. This is not just an external relation, like that between a grandmaster's chess and the football he may play to keep in training. It is more like that between marriage and parenthood, or between my political views and and my view of history. They *must* be congruent to work at all, and where they change they must change together. Certainly we often fail to relate aspects of our lives; we become dishonest, hypocritical and confused. But these are the names of faults, not of the norm. Where we do this (to repeat the obvious) we pay for it in confusion of life, in ineffectiveness and disintegration of the personality. *We do not actually have the option of splitting ourselves into a viable batch of coral polyps.* And it is just in the necessary business of relating these aspects that most of our moral problems arise, so that a philosopher who rules that nothing can be said about it has shown his uselessness pretty thoroughly. Thus the *game* metaphor dissolves in confusion.

We see this again if we try to imagine the transaction of 'stopping playing'. Unless we can point to some kind of possible world without (say), promising, calling it 'just an institution' will be rather like calling the world we actually live in 'just a dream.' (It might have a meaning, but not for us.) Hare describes the *invention* of promising as taking place among a people whose language is already so far advanced in abstraction as to include the word 'obligation' in its modern general sense (a sense which has only emerged in European thought in the last two centuries), and describes it as consisting in linking that idea with a speech ritual. But how did they get that far without any promising? Is their language supposed to have contained no performative words before? If it did, are they supposed not to have minded when people using them then went on to act as if they had not done so? The resulting confusion and difficulty must be at least as great as that where people constantly tell lies; is the objection to *that* supposed to be also an optional institution? This need is at least as old as the need for speech itself; it is the first condition of co-operation. Animals like wolves have other ways of holding a dialogue like, 'I'll go round and drive the antelope into the valley'. 'Right, I'll wait for them under this tree.' Men, developing speech, could not fail to use it for this very important purpose. How could it *not matter*, not be objected to, if one of the speakers then went off to sleep instead? How could this fail to be a concern for morality as it develops?

To give some positive evidence—Ruth Benedict, emphasizing the very wide variations there can be in human habits, remarks that there are 'very few traits that are universal or near-universal in human society. There are several that are well known. Of these everyone agrees on … the exogamous restrictions upon marriage.' But marriage after all involves promising. Actually, the most hopeful example I know of an almost non-promising society is Ruth Benedict's Dobu, who she says, 'put a premium on ill-will and treachery and made of them the recognized virtues of their society'. '*Behind a show of friendship, behind the evidences of co-operation*, in every field of life, the Dobu believes he has only treachery.'[6] But (as the words I have italicized make clear) this happy state of affairs is, of course, parasitical on promising. The show of friendship, the evidences of co-operation, must be there and must still largely be believed in, for treachery to flourish. 'Only treachery' has to be a gross exaggeration, like 'a world consisting only of exceptions'. That Dobu culture-hero, the successful con-man, is doomed to defeat himself unless he remembers this. As one of them sadly says: 'I cannot [bilk creditors] for too long, or my exchanges will never be trusted by anyone again. I am honest in the final issue.' In effect, both he and the Machiavellian politician mentioned by Hare are small-time operators tinkering within an established pattern, not Nietzschean supermen who have invented something quite different. They differ from ordinary promisers only in the relative importance they give to the obligation of promising as against other motives. On top of this the Dobu is of course operating at a very primitive level, in a shame-culture which could make nothing of Hare's abstract notion of 'obligation', and the Machiavellian politician may be doing that too. But whatever sense they do give to obligation, promising has to carry it.

Thus it is hard to see what a promiseless society would be like, and the burden of argument seems to lie on those who claim the thing makes sense. If it does not, it is misleading to call promising, or any other very general moral form, a game or an institution, assimilating it to particular local forms like Freemasonry or driving on the left of the road. What misleads us here is, of course, that *a* game, and *an* institution, are terms used for systems of varying sizes, often for concentric ones, such as speech, promising and trial by jury, and Hare has assumed that, because you can readily change the smallest example of each, you can change all the others in the same way. Thus your picking up a rock proves that you could pick up the Bass Rock, and your taking off your coat and jacket proves you can take off your skin as well. Speech is not really an institution at all, nor is sex, nor is playing games, nor walking upright, nor weeping nor laughing, nor loving one's children, nor marriage, nor property, nor promising, though the forms all these things take in different societies will of course be so. The word 'institution' would be best saved for things which were once instituted and could at a pinch be disinstituted again without taking the entire human race with them.

So much for the philosopher's misuse of this particular concept, *game*. I return to the wider point about definition, of which I have suggested this case is an instance—the need to look for 'underlying unities'.

Why does this matter? Because, as I have suggested a great number of the concepts that actually do the work in moral discussion today are general ones which are in the same sort of trouble as 'game'. Since they do a lot of work we *must* try to define them and look for underlying unities (here they are unlike 'family resemblance', an idle concept if ever there was one) and yet we shall certainly not be able to give a single plain litmus-paper test for them because their point is structural, and not at all like that of colour-words. Such concepts are— exploitation, oppression, sanity, disease, pollution, fulfilment, justice, freedom, art form, escapism, obscurity, sexual, serious, normal. Suppose we took Wittgenstein's line about one of these—suppose we said for instance that the only thing all cases of exploitation had in common was that they were cases of exploitation— should we be better off or worse when we have to decide whether something is a case of exploitation or not, than we are when we constantly look for an underlying unity? As things are we may indeed employ a number of different marks, but only on the assumption that they have some sort of connection with one another and are aspects of an underlying structure. Otherwise the concept falls to pieces, as indeed, the concept of art has already done. We do assume a unity in such concepts, and we are not silly to do so, because they all deal with human needs, which certainly do have a structure. Man is an animal given to exploitation, and he is also a game-playing animal. The business of moral philosophy starts with the analysis of such concepts. If all we had to do in moral philosophy was to wait for people to pronounce moral judgements like 'x is good', life might perhaps be simpler, but far less interesting. And we would certainly be members of a so far unknown species, not Homo sapiens.

Notes

1. *Revue Internationale de Philosophie*, no. 70 (1964). Reprinted in *Theories of Ethics*, ed. P. Foot, O.U.P., 1967. I shall call it henceforth PG, with pages as in *Theories of Ethics*. My objections obviously extend to the rather more subtle uses of 'game' by writers like Winch, and in part also to Phillips and Mounce's notion of a 'Moral Practice'.
2. A. R. Manser, 'Games and Family Resemblances', *Philosophy*, 42, 1967. H. Khatchadourian, 'Common Names and Family Resemblances', in

Philosophy and Phenomenological Research, XVIII (1957–8).

3. See an excellent paper by C. Loizos on 'Play Behaviour in Higher Primates', in *Primate Ethology,* ed. D. Morris, Weidenfeld and Nicolson, 1967.

4. See D. Morris, *The Naked Ape,* p. 32; C. Loizos, op. cit., pp. 185, 214.

5. See D. Morris, *The Biology of Art, passim.*

6. Ruth Benedict, *Patterns of Culture,* pp. 95, 123, 115 (my italics).

Introduction to the appendices

Bernard Suits

The following two essays [only the vast majority of the first Appendix is reproduced here] arose from both spoken and published responses to *The Grasshopper's* definition of games. The first essay uses that definition as the reference point for a discussion of definition in general. The second essay addresses itself to a game offered in evidence against the definition. There is of course nothing remarkable in that; *The Grasshopper* is full of such challenges, But the challenge here, I am confident the reader will agree, has a special claim to be made and to be met.

Appendix I

The fool on the hill

Not long after *The Grasshopper* was published I was invited to present a paper to a university audience, and it was suggested that I might want to talk about some issue raised in my book. I replied that I would like to do that, and sat down at my typewriter (*sic*) to address myself to the question of what issue I would like to address. If the book had been reviewed in some

scholarly journal, I mused, I could take the occasion to reply to one of the objections, exceptions, or outright refutations such reviews can be counted upon to provide. But since the book had been out for only a year or so, it was much too soon to expect any response from the laid back – indeed Grasshopper-like – editors and reviewers it is the practice of such periodicals to employ. Still, I reflected, it had been reviewed in a number of publications capable of moving a bit faster than the glacial pace set by traditional academic presses. So I hauled out a review of the book published in the *Ottawa Citizen* and re-read its opening sentence: 'Bernard Suits has written a pleasing, unusual book with an odd texture – something like a sandwich of gravel and jam.' But this critical response, far from giving me an issue for my paper, simply set my teeth on edge. So I got up from my machine and its blank sheet of paper and went out to a cocktail party on the thin pretext that something might come to me with a change of scene.

Oddly enough, it did. For at the party a friend from out of town informed me that Professor So-and-so was even then engaged in preparing a review of the book, and that he would raise, with the review's publication, a very damaging point indeed. I pressed him for further details.

'Well,' my friend responded, 'he finds highly questionable, to put it mildly, your use of certain types of races as examples of games.'

'Why should he question that?' I asked with some disappointment at what appeared to be an exceedingly jejune point.

'Because it is far from clear,' was the answer, 'that races *are* games.'

'What nonsense,' I replied. 'It is perfectly obvious that the hundred yard dash, for example, is a game.'

'No,' my friend replied, 'it is not. As Professor So-and-so asks, how often have you heard people use the expression "the hundred yard dash game"?'

Oddly, this comment had very much the same effect upon me as had my reading of the observation in the *Ottawa Citizen*: it too set my teeth on edge.

'Does Professor So-and-so,' I asked with some impatience, 'suppose that only things *called* games are games?'

'I really don't know,' said my friend, 'but it seems to me that he, or anyone else, might expect that examples you use in constructing your definition of games with as great frequency and with as great weight as you do various kinds of racing events ought at least to be among the things commonly acknowledged to be games. You seem to be using as a paradigm of game something that is not even called a game.'

'Thank you, my friend, thank you!' I cried and, continently declining a fifth martini, I raced home, just noting on the way that by 'racing home' I understood no more than that I was moving quite rapidly.

Wittgenstein and Plato

Seated once more at my typewriter (*sic*) I discovered that I was in something of a sweat, but whether because of my exertions in returning speedily home or because of anxiety over the possibility of having committed an egregious methodological blunder I preferred not to examine too carefully. *Had* I chosen as a virtual paradigm of game something that is not a game at all? And if I had, how could I have made so supremely stupid a mistake? This led me to think, in quick succession, of Wittgenstein and then of Plato.

Why was it so important, I asked myself, that true instances of games be *called* games? Placing a good deal of importance on what things are called made me think of Wittgenstein and of the well-known passage in *Philosophical Investigations* that I had, in fact, quoted in the Preface of my book: 'Don't say "There must be something common or they would not be called games," but look and see whether there is anything common to all.' I saw that this way of putting the question is quite literally guaranteed to lead the seeker after knowledge away from definitions and towards something quite different. For the question whether all things *called* games have something in common is very different from the question whether all things that *are* games have something in common. If, obviously, some of the things called games are called games metaphorically or carelessly or arbitrarily or stupidly, then there will predictably be nothing importantly common to all of them. So the fact that certain kinds of races are not *called* games seemed no embarrassment to me.

But then I found myself sweating again, and this time I was quite sure that it was not due to my exertions in returning home from the party. For it struck me that I had escaped Wittgenstein's frying pan only to find myself in Plato's fire. Small wonder I was sweating! For what was my position? I had persuaded myself that in defining games I need not be expected to provide a formula that would cover all things *called* games, but only things that really were games. But if, in constructing my definition, I permitted myself to use as data things that were games, but were not called games, then I must already have known which things were, in fact, games and which were not. But how could I possibly know these things in the absence of the very definition I imagined myself to be seeking? Had I really had one tucked up my sleeve all along, and was my supposed search for a definition simply a cynical charade?

So I naturally thought of Plato, for my trouble appeared to be the same kind of trouble that Meno tried to make for Socrates: 'A man cannot enquire either about that which he knows or about that which he does not know; for if he knows, he has no need to enquire; and if not, he cannot; for he does not know the very subject about which he is to enquire.'

44

It is true that Socrates did not remain in trouble for long. In proposing the doctrine of recollection as a solution of the dilemma, he simply admitted that seekers of definitions do have the definitions they are seeking already tucked up their sleeves, and that philosophic inquiry after definitions is a kind of retrieval system for shaking them into view again. Certainly not many philosophers have accepted such legerdemain as a solution of the problem. But I would like to suggest that there would be reason to continue seeking definitions even at the price of having to live in some intellectual discomfort with Meno's dilemma if the only alternative were a life of thought confined to mapping linguistic usages. Socrates makes something like this point in responding to Meno's objection: '... we ought not to listen to this sophistical argument about the impossibility of inquiry; for it will make us idle, and is sweet only to the sluggard; but the other way [that learning is recollection] will make us active and inquisitive.'

Still, Meno's dilemma is an entirely sensible one to raise against the search for definitions, and name-calling, even if justified, is still name-calling. The question remains, can anyone define anything, and more particularly can I define games, without begging the question? How did I know the hundred yard dash was a game unless I already knew what a game was? And more generally, how did I choose my examples? How did I select my data?

The fool on the hill

I began with a group of what may be called hard core games, by which I mean that if the members of this group are not games, then nothing is. In this group I included bridge, baseball, golf, hockey, chess, Monopoly – things everyone calls games. So far then, evidently, so good. But next I did something that is perhaps not so evidently so good. I included some things that are not called games and I excluded some things that are called games. I included the hundred yard dash (if it is indeed true that it is not called a game), and I excluded Ring Around the Rosie (which is called a game by small children and by Wittgenstein). How can I justify such a procedure? If I subscribe to the principle that naming must be a decisive criterion for selecting my data I cannot justify it.

But I do not and cannot subscribe to that principle – not if I am quite sure that some things called games are not games and that some things not called games are. For of the entire class of things called games, where could I make a start?

Very well, where do I make a start? Why am I so sure in the cases of the hundred yard dash and Ring Around the Rosie? Because I can more convincingly assign Ring Around the Rosie to a class other than the class *game*, and I cannot do the same with the hundred yard dash. Despite the fact that Ring Around the Rosie is sometimes called a game, it seems clear to me that Ring Around the Rosie is much more like certain kinds of theatrical performance than it is like chess or golf. It is a kind of dance to vocal accompaniment, or a choreographed song, so that it appears to be no more a game than *Swan Lake* is. Similarly, even though no individual racing event as such may be called a game, it seems clear to me that the hundred yard dash is more like golf and chess than it is like any non-game I can think of, for example, Ring Around the Rosie, or *Swan Lake* or the insurance game or confidence games.

Still, the case for including racing events in my select data appears to be weaker than does the case for excluding Ring Around the Rosie. For I excluded the latter by finding another class to put it into, whereas I evidently included the hundred yard dash only by *failing* to find another class to put it into. In fact, however, I have a much better reason than that for including the hundred yard dash among games. For I put to myself the following question: How do I distinguish between races that are run at the Olympics and at Indianapolis from such things as the following: a race between a police constable and a felon, a race among homesteaders when new land is opened up, a race with death on the part of an ambulance driver? How do we, I asked myself, distinguish between what are obviously two very different kinds of racing? And in attempting to answer that question I put to myself another: Is the hundred yard dash more like the race between a police officer and a burglar, or is it more like chess? Now this is, upon examination, a somewhat more tricky question than it appears to be. For one superficially plausible answer is that the hundred yard dash is patently more like a race between a cop and a robber than it is like chess. For in the former case both people are running and one is trying to overtake the other, whereas in chess neither player is trying to do either of those things. This is what may be called the dim answer to the question. I disdain the dim answer, with its reliance upon surface similarities, and give a different answer. I distinguish the hundred yard dash from the constable sprinting about his lawful occasions precisely by recognizing that the former is a game and the latter is not. This method is clear, it is decisive, and it is completely convincing – as it is in the following illustrative tale.

'Halt!' cries a police constable to a man who is being hotly pursued by another. 'In the name of the law.'

'Why?' responds the runner who is in the lead.

'Because,' the constable replies, drawing abreast of the runner and beginning to puff a bit, 'you appear, *prima facie*, to be some kind of felon.'

'Well, I am not,' answers the lead runner. 'I am Roger Bannister, and the man rapidly closing the gap between us is another miler.'

'Ah!' says the constable, and goes about his business.

The fact, therefore, that there is no event called 'the hundred yard dash game' does not make me at all uncomfortable. To call something the hundred yard dash is a very different matter indeed from calling the pursuit of a robber by a cop over a distance of one hundred yards a race. And I will not accept the response that 'dash' is just another name for 'race.' For when Smith, expecting a call from his broker, dashes to the phone, he is not competing with anyone (or any thing) – he just wants his anxieties allayed forthwith.

Still, the foregoing considerations do not quite show that foot races are games – only that they are quite different from some activities that can look very much like them. So let me propose the following general principle. I submit that when some activity or enterprise not initially included in the hard core group (e.g., because it is not called a game) is seen, upon examination, to conform to the group's definition, then there exists a good *prima facie* reason for granting that that activity or enterprise is a game, despite the fact that it is not called one. It seems to me that now the burden of proof shifts to the critic, and that he must show cause why that additional activity should *not* be acknowledged to

be a game. And this showing cause, I suggest, must consist in his identifying a property of the additional activity that is sufficient to include it in a class different from, and exclusive of, the class specified by my definition. Now the required property, I further suggest, cannot be simply the property of being *called* something else, because that is not a feature of the thing but of our language about things, and one of the chief purposes of definition is to make our referential language more exact.

I believe that the general principle here at issue can be illustrated quite convincingly by the following example. Let us identify the following class of activities: watching things dip. This class includes watching the boat dip against the background of the horizon, watching dancers dip against the background of the ballroom, watching a dipper dip through the water in the bucket, and so on. Now I want to include one additional item in this class: watching the earth dip – which anyone can do by facing east at dawn on a clear day. But we find that this activity is never called, nor is it customarily thought of as, watching the earth dip. It is always called, and almost always thought of as, watching the sun rise. So very often we call things by the wrong names because of culture lag: our ancestors, who formed this part of our language, thought the sun moved. It is true, of course, that we also call things by the wrong names simply because it is useful to do so: since it *looks* as though the sun is rising, we are calling attention to a common experience by using the expression 'sunrise.' I am not, accordingly, calling for a reform of our language. I am not recommending, for example, that we begin saying things like 'That was a beautiful earth-dip this morning,' quite aside from the fact that earth-dip suggests something an environmentalist might serve at a cocktail party. For even astronomers use the expression 'the sun is rising' while knowing full well that it is really the earth that is revolving. And the fool on the hill sees the sun going down, but the eyes in his head see the world spinning round.

So I am not insisting that races of the kind under consideration be called games, only that, in the absence of some further distinguishing property, they be acknowledged, upon reflection, to *be* games.

Furthermore, to return for a moment to matters linguistic, one might question, using the same kind of standard whereby it is denied that races at games, whether the hundred yard dash is even a race, since no one uses the expression 'the hundred yard race' either. In point of fact, the word 'race' is hardly ever used in referring to the kind of athletic event under consideration. 'The high hurdles' is not a shortened form of the expression 'the high hurdle race.' (Is the reply that 'race' is here *understood* without being expressed? Then why is 'game' not understood in the expression 'the hundred yard dash'?) Nor does the generic expression used for referring to these events include the word 'race.' These events are customarily called 'track' events, though it is clear that their being run on a track is hardly an exclusive description of what they are. Locomotives are also run on tracks. 'Hurdles' and 'dash' seem not to be shortened forms of any expression whatever. They appear to be specifications of things that are, indeed, races, and they are called track events because that is a sufficient characterization of them in contrast to *field* events and, especially when taken together, *track* and *field* are specifications of athletic *games* – as in the expressions 'the Olympic games,' 'the Commonwealth games,' and so on.

My purpose, however, is not to score a victory over Professor So-and-so by showing that certain races are indeed called games, because the point I wish to argue is that not all members of my hard core group need to be called games. (As I understand it, Professor So-and-so's attention was called to the familiar usage 'Olympic Games' as evidence for the fact that races are sometimes called games. His response, I am told, was that this is a deviant use of the word 'game.' Coming from a Wittgensteinian, one can only wonder, deviant from *what*?)

Still, it may be asked why I use racing as a kind of paradigm among paradigms – as I certainly seem to do, since I make so many appeals to racing to illustrate or, more seriously, to nail down a point. Why single out to bear such a heavy load of evidence things that are not even called games?

For two reasons. 1/ Racing events are exceedingly simple, and thus more readily lay bare their forms than do more complex games. I would not normally use chess as a clarifying example because just getting clear on the form of chess itself requires quite a bit of additional analysis. In fact, quite unintended by me, there is a kind of interplay or tension in the book between chess and racing events. Chess presents some of the greatest difficulties to my analysis and racing many of my most comforting solutions. 2/ The second reason is that racing is, perhaps of all games, the kind of game that is closest to a corresponding type of event in ordinary life, and so racing examples are much more useful in contrasting games with activities that are not games than other examples would be. If one considers a very complex, highly artificial game like chess, it is misleadingly easy to say why chess is a game and not some activity in ordinary life. Chess involves a curious board, and oddly carved bits of wood, and the latter are pushed about on top of the former, and things like that go on in life hardly at all. But that is not what makes chess importantly unlike ordinary life, any more than what distinguishes poetry from prose is the fact that in poetry the right-hand margin is usually uneven. But a game like the hundred yard dash, which is so similar to real life cops and robbers behaviourally, is not likely to lead us astray. Since practically all of their behavioural features are identical we are forced to look elsewhere for the real difference between them.

(It is instructive in this regard to notice that many of the properties of games that Wittgenstein calls to our attention in *Philosophical Investigations*, in order to reveal the lack of commonality among the things *called* games, are precisely such directly observable behavioural properties.)

Still, even if these considerations justify the inclusion of racing events in my hard core group, they do not resolve Meno's paradox. For the question remains, even granting that certain racing events have as much claim to be identified as games as do chess, golf, and so on, how can I begin my quest by identifying *any* of these games without begging the question? So I turn from the Wittgensteinian objection to the more serious objection raised in the *Meno*.

The doctrine of recollection revisited

The answer to Meno's dilemma, I suggest, is that the same considerations are at work in selecting the original group as are at work in getting at the essence of that group. This is, it seems to me, the kernel of truth in the doctrine of recollection. If it is possible to construct definitions, then perhaps there is, and must be, some sense in which we do know and some sense in which we do not know the definition beforehand. And I submit that an explanation of that seeming oddity less fanciful than Plato's is available to us. Consider, once more, my treatment of Ring Around the Rosie and the hundred yard dash. I excluded Ring Around the Rosie from my select group, as I said, because it was more like a ballet than it was like a game. That is, I felt justified in excluding from or including within my select class items which could or could not more aptly be referred to other classes. In other words, the search for definitions does not proceed in a vacuum, nor even in a universe of randomly distributed observable properties. When, in selecting our initial data, we throw out some contender (like Ring Around the Rosie or the confidence game) we do so not by giving it the wholesale or gross denomination 'non-game.' That would indeed be to beg the question, and is the way a callous saloon-keeper handles drunks; he removes them from his saloon not because he believes that they belong in some other particular place – at home, for example – but because, from his point of view, they belong *anywhere* except in his establishment. But judicious definition-makers treat unwanted members of their select group not like unruly drinkers, simply by throwing them out, but like émigrés whom a solicitous government will encourage to emigrate only if they have been accepted as immigrants elsewhere.

Still, it might be objected that such a procedure, far from getting us out of the woods, only gets us deeper into it. For whereas originally we had only the problem of identifying *one* class, we now have the problem of identifying a great many classes – as many, evidently, as there are unsuccessful contenders for inclusion in the original class, since the only standard for exclusion that we can apply is their properly belonging to a different class. And so the original problem we were trying to solve by the introduction of this technique seems to remain as knotty as ever, with the added horror that in place of one problem we are now faced with an indefinitely large number of them, thus committing the Sorcerer's Apprentice fallacy: I seem to be arguing that the way to avoid begging the question once is to beg it many times.

Well, I am in fact suggesting something that can, from a certain point of view be parodied in just that way. And the point of view to which I am suggesting an alternative is that when we set out to define something we are working, conceptually speaking, in a kind of classless society. If that *were* the case, then of course the problem of how to define one class could not be solved by appealing to other classes which would not, by hypothesis, yet exist. It was, perhaps, a consideration of this kind that prompted Aristotle to remark that all knowledge is acquired on the basis of pre-existent knowledge. And Socrates, in the *Cratylus*, more specifically to my point, likens the world as conceived by a definition-phobe like Protagoras to a sieve through which all meaning leaks, and even more picturesquely, to a man with a running nose.

We do not, every time we seek to define something, have to start from scratch, as though we were required to define everything else before we could define *this*. We do not begin at the beginning of time or at the beginning of knowledge but in *medias res* – in the midst, that is, of a network or community of other definitions.

One might of course still pose the question whether these other definitions that one is relying upon are *correct*. The reply to this is that if very many of them are *not* correct, then the construction of a new definition on the basis of these incorrect definitions would not be very successful. But refraining from attempting to define anything whatever on the ground that none of the distinctions available may have been drawn with sufficient accuracy is, it seems to me, to exhibit a nearly pathological degree of taxonomic insecurity. Most of us, at any rate, may be presumed to know, for example, our ass from our elbow, and a good deal more besides.

To take a rather more polite example, consider Aristotle's distinction between the following two classes of things: the kind of thing that has its principle of motion internal to it in contrast to the kind of thing that has its principle of motion external to it. I submit that without knowing (or at least without being conscious of knowing) anything as relatively sophisticated as that distinction, we are perfectly capable of telling a hawk from a handsaw. Aside from the fact that I do not take special care to protect my chickens from handsaws, nor try to saw boards with a hawk, it does not seem particularly fanciful to surmise that something like the difference between natural objects and artefacts operates in this bit of minor knowledge most of us share with Hamlet. Similarly, I suggest, when I discern an important difference between things somewhat less easily distinguishable from one another than hawks are from handsaws, that the same kind of an intimation of a difference in meaning is at work.

Yes, but how do I *get* these intimations? Shall we say with Plato that I have a dim but sufficiently guiding recollection of what the meaning will turn out to be? Or shall we take a tip from Aristotle's treatment of a similar problem and simply avoid any explanation at all, as when he observes laconically that we perceive the universal in the particular because the mind is so constituted as to be able to do that kind of thing? The answer lies, I am suggesting, in the pre-existence in our experience (that is to say, in our post-natal experience) of a great many distinctions, and this necessary condition for any definition whatever enables us to rein in Plato's flight of fancy in attempting to answer the question, and at the same time to give Aristotle's laconic observation its head. An intimation of definitional meaning is like recollection in that it is based on past experience, and the mind is able to perceive the universal in the particular also by past experience. What makes Plato's doctrine of recollection and Aristotle's account of the induction of a universal appear to be, respectively, fanciful and evasive is, I believe, that both Plato and Aristotle have (or perhaps it is just that their readers have understood them to have) treated definition and induction as though those operations proceeded one at a time, in isolation from that community of classes that makes induction and definition possible.

In order to illustrate how the community of classes works, let us go back to racing once more and look at it. I was quite sure when I began in earnest to look for a definition of games that the hundred yard dash was a game and that Ring Around the Rosie was not. Refusing to be misled by superficialities, I was putting a hawk-shaped handsaw in the workshop where it belongs and not in the aviary, where it doesn't. How was I able to do this kind of thing? First, I had ready to mind the difference between a competitive and a scripted performance. (How did it come about that I had this difference ready to mind? From observing, among other things, the difference between

genuine wrestling matches and those produced for television.) In one of these, for openers, the outcome is (or ought to be) known beforehand, and in the other the outcome is not (or ought not to be) known beforehand. But is a competition necessarily a game? No. Some competitions are and some are not. The ambulance driver's race with death is not a game (or at least it ought not to be), but the hundred yard dash is, although both (as well as civil service examinations and wars) are types of competition. Well, why is the hundred yard dash competition a game but the race with death not a game? Because games are things that are (or properly can be) valued as ends in themselves, but races with death of the kind under consideration are not (or ought not to be). These dichotomies, or something very much like them, are at work right at the start of my search for definitions. I have not been describing the results of a careful, exacting step-by-step process, but a number of distinctions that came to mind faster than pell-mell but more ordered than higgledy-piggledy, much like an instant revelation, as though I were calling up some forgotten but now wholly retrieved past knowledge. Of course, to call it 'forgotten' is too strong. It was, to use another Aristotelian distinction, knowledge in possession in contrast to knowledge in use. For I already knew that it was possible to distinguish between competitive and non-competitive events, and between autotelic and instrumental activities, and this pair of distinctions was sufficient for me to include the hundred yard dash within, and to exclude Ring Around the Rosie from, my earliest data.

Polemically ornamented summary

In summary I would like to raise and briefly answer three questions [...]

In constructing a definition, how do I select my data?

As a practical problem of method the question hardly arises. If one is on a promising line of inquiry (that is, a line of inquiry that is likely to succeed), the data largely selects itself, and if it does not select itself that may be a good reason to conclude that one is not on a promising line of inquiry. And this is as it should be, for we do not construct definitions *in vacuo*. The already apprehended classes and the network of differentiae which they exhibit and depend upon are the conditions upon which successful definition itself depends.

There is, of course, a bit more to it than that, since not everyone is equally successful in the search for definitions even when they are there to be found. Such lack of success, I believe, comes down in the end to a certain kind of insensitivity – insensitivity, that is, to the way in which human experience has classified the objects that arise in human discourse and inquiry. And such insensitivity, where it exists, is roughly one or the other of two kinds – natural or induced. By a natural insensitivity of this kind I mean simply a constitutional inability to apprehend definitions. It is analogous in music to being tone deaf. By an induced insensitivity of this kind I mean that a bias is at work in the person which actively prevents him from apprehending definitions that he *would* apprehend in the absence of the bias. What I am calling a bias is the kind of thing Francis Bacon called an idol, and one of the idols at issue here is the idol of family resemblance, which I would class as an Idol of the Academy. It might be thought that this idol ought to be classed as an Idol of the Market Place, since Wittgenstein's appeal to ordinary usage can be understood as an appeal to the verbal commerce carried on by the *anthropos* in the *agora*. But I submit that the man in the street is not a Wittgensteinian. He is a working essentialist, like the constable in the street who was able to correct his mistake about the behaviour of Roger Bannister.

Having distinguished constitutional insensitivity to definitions from idolatrous insensitivity, it should be noted that the behaviour that arises from these two different causes can be very much the same in outward appearance. Thus, when Wittgenstein seeks to explain why a number of *prima facie* disparate things are called games in terms of family resemblance he appears to be simply dim, as though he were functioning under the handicap of a temperamental incapacity. It is only when we realize that he is behaving this way on principle that

we are able to identify him as a professional philosopher at work.

What is the relation between language and definition?

It is not necessary to presume (a presumption Wittgenstein is inclined to attribute erroneously to all essentialists) that all things called by the same name have the same definition. But if a great many things in a great many cases do not, then it would follow, I should think, that naming was so unsuited to the task of describing the world in any useful way, or of communicating with one another to any intelligible purpose, that referential language would be an entirely futile institution.

Accordingly, I do not claim that it would be tolerable for my definition to command an extension containing only a very few of the things commonly called games – say hopscotch and bridge and no others. I am not saying that I can disregard usage – just that I am not obliged to conform to every bit of it. And so I claim that my definition of games better explains general usage of the word 'game' than does Wittgenstein's family resemblance thesis. In *Philosophical Investigations* Wittgenstein writes:

> Consider for example the proceedings that we call 'games.' I mean board-games, card-games, ball games, Olympic games[!], and so on. ... Compare with noughts and crosses. Think of patience [and of the game where] a child throws his ball at the wall and catches it again. ... [Think of] tennis. Think of games like ring-a-ring-a-roses.

Wittgenstein asks, about these diverse proceedings, 'What is common to all of them?' by which he means, of course, that nothing is common to all of them. But I believe that with the exception of his last example there *is* something common to all of them. Furthermore, I claim that the commonality I detect is a good explanation of why they are all, or very nearly all, called games, and that family resemblance is not a good reason. For if family resemblance were the reason they are nearly all called games, then it would be puzzling, I submit, that a cop chasing a robber is *not* called a game.

What does the foregoing have to do with the question whether the definition of games I advance is a good one?

Nothing – though if the definition is a good one, that would have a great deal to do with the foregoing, I should think. For it would mean that the proper question to ask about definitions is not *whether* they are possible – not if the question has been answered in the affirmative by producing one – but *how* they are possible.

[…]

Games and the good—I

Thomas Hurka

Our societies attach considerable value to excellence in sports. In Canada hockey players are named to the highest level of the Order of Canada; in Britain footballers and cricketers are made MBE and even knighted. And this attitude extends more widely. Sports are a subclass of the wider category of games, and we similarly admire those who excel in non-athletic games such as chess, bridge, and even Scrabble.

I take this admiration to rest on the judgement that excellence in games is good in itself, apart from any pleasure it may give the player or other people, but just for the properties that make it excellent. The admiration, in other words, rests on the perfectionist judgement that skill in games is worth pursuing for its own sake and can add value to one's life. This skill is not the only thing we value in this way; we give similar honours to achievements in the arts, science and business. But one thing we admire, and to a significant degree, is excellence in athletic and non-athletic games.

Unless we dismiss this view, one task for philosophy is to explain why such excellence is good. But few philosophers have attempted this, for a well-known reason. A unified explanation of why excellence in games is good requires a unified account of what games are, and many doubt that this is possible. After all, Wittgenstein famously gave the concept of a game as his primary example of one for which necessary and sufficient conditions cannot be given but whose instances are linked only by looser 'family resemblances'.[1] If Wittgenstein was right about this, there can be no single explanation of why skill in games is good, just a series of distinct explanations of the value of skill in hockey, skill in chess, and so on.

But Wittgenstein was not right, as is shown in a little-known book that is nonetheless a classic of twentieth-century philosophy, Bernard Suits's *The Grasshopper: Games, Life and Utopia*. Suits gives a perfectly persuasive analysis of playing a game as, to quote his summary statement, 'the voluntary attempt to overcome unnecessary obstacles'.[2] And in this paper I will use his analysis to explain the value of playing games. More specifically, I will argue that the different elements of Suits's analysis give game-playing two distinct but related grounds of value, so it instantiates two related intrinsic goods. I will also argue that game-playing is an important intrinsic good, which gives the clearest possible expression of what can be called a modern as against a classical, or more specifically, Aristotelian, view of value.

But first Suits's analysis. It says that a game has three main elements, which he calls the prelusory goal, the constitutive rules, and the lusory attitude. To begin with the first, in

Thomas Hurka 'Games and the Good—I', from PASH/*Proceedings of the Aristotelian Society*. Supplementary Volume 80, pp. 217–235, © 2006 Thomas Hurka. Reprinted by permission of Wiley-Blackwell.

playing a game one always aims at a goal that can be described independently of the game. In golf, this is that a ball enter a hole in the ground; in mountain climbing, that one stand on top of a mountain; in Olympic sprinting, that one cross a line on the track before one's competitors. Suits calls this goal 'prelusory' because it can be understood and achieved apart from the game, and he argues that every game has such a goal. Of course, in playing a game one also aims at a goal internal to it, such as winning the race, climbing the mountain, or breaking par on the golf course. But on Suits's view this 'lusory' goal is derivative, since achieving it involves achieving the prior prelusory goal in a specified way.

This way is identified by the second element, the game's constitutive rules. According to Suits, the function of these rules is to forbid the most efficient means to the prelusory goal. Thus, in golf one may not carry the ball down the fairway and drop it in the hole by hand; one must advance it using clubs, play it where it lies, and so on. In mountain climbing one may not ride a gondola to the top of the mountain or charter a helicopter; in 200-metre sprinting, one may not cut across the infield. Once these rules are in place, success in the game typically requires achieving the prelusory goal as efficiently as they allow, such as getting the ball into the hole in the fewest possible strokes or choosing the best way up the mountain. But this is efficiency within the rules, whose larger function is to forbid the easiest means to the game's initial goal.

These first two elements involve pursuing a goal by less than the most efficient means, but they are not sufficient for playing a game. This is because someone can be forced to use these means by circumstances he regrets and wishes were different. If this is the case—if, for example, a farmer harvests his field by hand because he cannot afford the mechanical harvester he would much rather use—he is not playing a game. Hence the need for the third element in Suits's analysis, the lusory attitude, which involves a person's willingly accepting the constitutive rules, or accepting them because they make the game possible. Thus, a golfer accepts that he may not carry the ball by hand or improve his lie because he wants to play golf, and obeying those rules is necessary for him to do so; the mountaineer accepts that he may not take a helicopter to the summit because he wants to climb. The restrictions the rules impose are adhered to not reluctantly but willingly, because they are essential to the game. Adding this third element gives Suits's full definition: 'To play a game is to attempt to achieve a specific state of affairs [prelusory goal], using only means permitted by the rules ... where the rules prohibit the use of more efficient in favour of less efficient means [constitutive rules], and where the rules are accepted just because they make possible such activity [lusory attitude].' Or, in the summary statement quoted above, 'playing a game is the voluntary attempt to overcome unnecessary obstacles.'[3]

This analysis will doubtless meet with objections, in the form of attempted counterexamples. But Suits considers a whole series of these in his book, showing repeatedly that his analysis handles them correctly, and not by some ad hoc addition but once its elements are properly understood. Nor would it matter terribly if there were a few counterexamples. Some minor lack of fit between his analysis and the English use of 'game' would not be important if the analysis picks out a phenomenon that is unified, close to what is meant by 'game', and philosophically interesting. But the analysis is interesting if, as I will now argue, it allows a persuasive explanation of the value of excellence in games.

Suits himself addresses this issue of value. In fact, a central aim of his book is to give a defence of the grasshopper in Aesop's fable, who played all summer, against the ant, who worked. But in doing so he argues for the strong thesis that playing games is not just an intrinsic good but the supreme such good, since in the ideal conditions of utopia, where all instrumental goods are provided, it would be everyone's primary pursuit. The grasshopper's game-playing, therefore, while it had the unfortunate effect of leaving him without food for the winter, involved him in the intrinsically finest activity. Now, I do not accept Suits's strong thesis that game-playing is the supreme good—I think many other states and activities have comparable value—and I do not find his arguments for it persuasive. But I will connect the weaker thesis that playing games is one intrinsic good to the details of his analysis more explicitly than he ever does.

Consider the first two elements of the analysis, the prelusory goal and constitutive rules.

53

By forbidding the most efficient means to that goal, the constitutive rules usually make for an activity that is reasonably difficult. They do not always do so. Rock, paper, scissors is a game whose prelusory goal is to throw rock to one's opponent's scissors, scissors to his paper, or paper to his rock, and the rules forbid the easiest means to this goal by forbidding one to make one's throw after he has made his. But though the rules make achieving this goal more difficult than it might be, they do not make it by absolute standards difficult; rock, paper, scissors is not a challenging activity. But then rock, paper, scissors is not a very good game, and certainly not one the playing of which has much intrinsic value. It is characteristic of good games to be not only more difficult than they might be but also in absolute terms reasonably difficult. They cannot be so difficult that no one can succeed at them, but also cannot lack all challenge; they must strike a balance between too much and too little difficulty. In what follows I will defend the value only of playing good games, because they realize what seems an internal goal of the design of games. If the constitutive rules of a game make achieving its prelusory goal more difficult than it might be, this is surely because they aim at making it simply difficult.

If the prelusory goal and rules of a good game make succeeding at it reasonably difficult, they will also give it one ground of value if difficult activities are as such intrinsically good. And I believe that difficult activities are as such good. Though not often explicitly affirmed by philosophers, this view can be defended in at least two ways.

Many contemporary philosophers include among their intrinsic goods achievement, by which they mean not just moral but also nonmoral achievement, for example, in business or the arts.[4] But what exactly is achievement? It clearly involves realizing a goal, but not every such realization counts as an achievement; for example, tying one's shoelace does not unless one has some disability. And among achievements some are more valuable than others; thus, starting a new business and making it successful is a greater achievement than making a single sale. If we ask what explains these differences—between achievements and non-achievements, and between greater and lesser achievements—the answer is surely in large part their difficulty: how complex or physically

challenging they are, or how much skill and ingenuity they require. It is when a goal is hard to bring about that doing so is an achievement. So reflection on our intuitive understanding of the value of achievement suggests a first reason for holding that difficult activities are as such good.

A second reason, which is complementary but more abstract, is suggested by Robert Nozick's fantasy of an 'experience machine'.[5] This machine, which can electrically stimulate the brain to give one the pleasure of any activity one wants, is intended as a counterexample to the hedonistic view that only pleasure is good, but it also makes a positive point. If life on the machine is less than ideal, this is largely because people on it are disconnected from reality. They have only false beliefs about their environment and never actually realize any goals: they may think they are discovering a cure for cancer or climbing Everest, but in fact they are not. This suggests that an important good is what we can call 'rational connection to reality', where this has two aspects, one theoretical and one practical.[6]

The theoretical aspect is knowledge, or having beliefs about the world that are both true and justified. The beliefs' truth means there is a match between one's mind and reality; their being justified means the match is not a matter of luck but something one's evidence made likely. But a full account of this good must explain which kinds of knowledge are most worth having. Classical philosophers like Aristotle thought the best knowledge is of the intrinsically best objects, such as the divine substances, but the more plausible view is that the best knowledge has the most of certain formal properties that are independent of its subject matter. More specifically, the best knowledge is explanatorily integrated, with general principles that explain middle-level principles that in turn explain particular facts. This integration results in an explanatory hierarchy like that represented in Figure 1.6.1, where items of knowledge higher up in the hierarchy explain those below them. And this hierarchy embodies more intrinsic value than if one knew only isolated unexplanatory facts, like the number of grains of sand on seven beaches (Figure 1.6.2). We can give an artificial but illustrative model for measuring this value if we imagine that each item of knowledge initially has one unit of value in itself, but gains an extra unit for every other

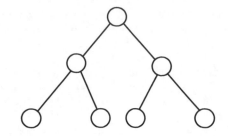

Figure 1.6.1.

item of knowledge subordinate to it in a hierarchy. Then the seven isolated items in Figure 1.6.2 have just one unit of value each, for a total of seven units. But in Figure 1.6.1 the middle items have three units, since they each explain two further facts, and the top item has seven units, for a total of seventeen units in the hierarchy as a whole. The explanatory relations between them give an integrated set of beliefs more value than ones that are unconnected.

This model can be enriched. We may think it especially valuable to give unifying explanations of diverse facts, or to make surprising connections between what seemed unrelated phenomena. If so, we can count not just the number of individual items a given item of knowledge has subordinate to it, but the number of items of different kinds, so there is more value in explaining more types of fact. We may also value precision of knowledge, such as knowing that the constant of gravitational acceleration is not just somewhere between 5 and 15 m/s² but exactly 9.8 m/s². And we can capture this view both by giving more value to precise knowledge in itself and by giving it more additional value for explaining further precise truths.

Finally, we may think that knowing truths concerning many objects is better than knowing highly particular ones, even apart from the former's explanatory role; thus, knowing a scientific law is better than knowing the number of grains of sand on some beach even if one has not used the former to explain anything else.

The practical parallel to knowledge, and the other value missing on the experience machine,

Figure 1.6.2.

is achievement, or realizing a goal in the world given a justified belief that one would do so. Here again there is a match between one's mind and reality, though now reality has been made to fit one's mind, and a justified belief that makes the match not just lucky. Again we must specify which achievements are best. A classical view might say they are of the goals that are independently best, but we can maintain the parallel with knowledge, and give a better account of achievement as achievement, if we say they are of the goals with the most of certain formal properties that again centre on hierarchical integration. This time, however, the integrating relation is not explanatory but means–end. Thus, in Figure 1.6.1 we achieve the goal at the top of the hierarchy by achieving the two middle-level goals as means to it, and each of those by achieving the two below them. And if each non-luckily achieved goal has one unit of value in itself plus an additional unit for every other goal achieved as a means to it, the achievements in this hierarchy again have seventeen units of value as against the seven in seven unrelated achievements. Just as more complex explanatory relations make for more value in knowledge, so more complex means–end relations make for more value in achievement.

Again this model can be enriched. We may think achievements are especially valuable if they require subsidiary achievements of varied kinds, and can capture this view by counting the number of goals of different types a given one has subordinate to it. More strongly, we may deny significant value to achievements that involve only subordinate goals of the same repetitive type. We may also value precision in achievement—hitting a particular target rather than just some vague area—and can give achievements additional value for that. And we can think that, apart from means–end relations, achieving goals whose content extends more widely, through time or in the number of objects they involve, is likewise more valuable.

This model deepens the value of achievement by showing it to be parallel to knowledge and, with it, one aspect of a more abstract good of rational connection to reality. It also makes many difficult activities good for the very properties that make them difficult. First, the more complex the means–end hierarchy an activity involves, the more places there are where one can fail at something crucial and the harder success in the activity becomes. Second, the more complex the hierarchy, the more deliberative skill it requires, since one has to monitor one's progress through a more elaborate sequence of tasks. There is a further increment of difficulty if the hierarchy involves a greater variety of subordinate goals, since then it requires a greater variety of skills, and likewise if the activity demands more precision. And it is more difficult to achieve goals with more extended contents, both because holding them in one's mind is more difficult and because achieving them requires changing more of the world.[7]

Moreover, these are precisely the aspects of difficulty found in good games. These games usually require one to go through a complex sequence of tasks rather than do one simple thing such as throw rock, paper or scissors. The tasks in question often demand varied skills: thus, golf requires one not only to drive the ball a long distance but to drive it accurately, play from bunkers, putt, and make strategic decisions. Good golfers are also precise, hitting their approach shots to a particular part of the green rather than just somewhere near it. And many games, such as chess, hockey and basketball, require players to grasp an extended content, including all the pieces on the board or all the players on the ice or court, in a single act of consciousness. That again is difficult, and requires years of practice to master.

Not all the difficulty in games involves this complex ratiocination. Weightlifters have to go through a precisely ordered sequence of moves in order to lift their weights, but also need brute strength: if one of two lifters has less perfect technique but is stronger and therefore lifts more, he wins the competition. Boxing, too, depends in part on raw power. These purely physical forms of difficulty do not instantiate the value of rational connection, and their role in making game-playing good is unclear. Why do we value the physical aspects of weightlifting and boxing but not those found in, say, pie-eating contests? Does this reflect just the historical accident that weightlifting and boxing began long enough ago that we can value them now for their traditions? Or do we value physical difficulty only when it accompanies more rational forms of challenge but not on its own? I will not pursue this issue, taking the rational connection model to capture what

makes purely cerebral games such as chess difficult, and also much of what makes sports such as golf and hockey difficult.

I have argued that the prelusory goal and constitutive rules make playing a good game difficult, and have given two reasons to believe that difficulty is as such good. But I have not yet used the third element in Suits's analysis, the lusory attitude. Let us examine it more closely.

In his 1907 book *The Theory of Good and Evil* Hastings Rashdall remarked that '[s]port has been well defined as the overcoming of difficulties simply for the sake of overcoming them'.[8] This definition is close to Suits's, but differs on one point. It in effect takes the lusory attitude to be one of accepting the rules because they make the game difficult, whereas Suits takes it to be one of accepting the rules because they make the game possible. For Rashdall, the golfer accepts the rule against improving one's lie because it makes golf harder; for Suits, it is because it makes golf. Which view is correct?

Suits's view is preferable if we are analysing the generic concept of playing a game. Consider what we can call a pure professional golfer, who plays golf only as a means to making money and with no interest in the game for itself. He does not cheat as a means to making money; he knows that to make money he must play golf, which means obeying all its rules. But his only reason for accepting the rules is to make money. If we used Rashdall's view to define the generic concept, we would have to say the pure professional is not playing golf, which is absurd. But on Suits's view he is playing golf: though he accepts the rules only as a means to money, he does accept them in order to play golf and so has the lusory attitude.

But though Suits defines the generic concept of game-playing, this is not what he defends as the supreme intrinsic good. His argument, recall, is that in utopia, where all instrumental goods are provided, game-playing would be everyone's primary activity. But this description of utopia implies that it would contain no professional players; since no one would need to play a game as a means to anything, all players would be amateurs who chose the game for itself. But then they would have Rashdall's lusory attitude of accepting the rules because they make the game difficult, and Suits explicitly agrees. He describes how one utopian character decides to build houses by carpentry rather than order them up telepathically because carpentry requires more skill. And he starts his discussion of utopia by saying he will defend the value of game-playing as a specific form of play, where he has earlier denied that playing a game necessarily involves playing: to play is to engage in an activity for its own sake, and a pure professional does not do that.[9] So the activity Suits defends as supremely good is game-playing that is also play, or what I will call 'playing in a game'. And that activity involves accepting the rules not just because they make the game possible, but also because they make it difficult.

I will follow Suits here and narrow my thesis further: not only will I explain the value only of playing good games, I will explain the value only of playing *in* these games, or of playing them with an at least partly amateur attitude. But this is not in practice much of a restriction, since most people do play games at least partly for their own sakes. Consider Pete Rose, an extremely hard-nosed baseball player who was disliked for how much he would do to win. Taking the field near the end of the famous sixth game of the 1975 World Series, and excited by the superb plays that game had involved, he told the opposing team's third base coach, 'Win or lose, Popeye, we're in the fuckin' greatest game ever played'; after the game, which his team lost, he made a similar comment about it to his manager. Intensely as he wanted to win, Pete Rose also loved baseball for itself.[10]

So the game-playing whose value I will explain involves accepting the rules of the game because they make it difficult. But then the elements that define this type of game-playing are internally related: the prelusory goal and constitutive rules together give it a feature, namely difficulty, and the lusory attitude chooses it because of this feature. More specifically, if difficulty is as such good, the prelusory goal and rules give it a good-making feature and the lusory attitude chooses it because of that good-making feature. This connects the lusory attitude to an attractive view that has been held by many philosophers, namely that if something is intrinsically good, the positive attitude of loving it for the property that makes it good, that is, desiring, pursuing and taking pleasure in it for that property, is also, and separately, intrinsically good. Thus, if another person's happiness is good, desiring, pursuing and being pleased by her happiness as happiness is a further

good, namely that of benevolence; likewise, if knowledge is good, desiring, pursuing and being pleased by knowledge is good. Aristotle expressed this view when he said that if an activity is good, pleasure in it is good, whereas if an activity is bad, pleasure in it is bad,[11] and it was accepted around the turn of the twentieth century by many philosophers, including Rashdall, Franz Brentano, G. E. Moore, and W. D. Ross. And it applies directly to playing in games, which combines the good of difficulty with the further good of loving difficulty for itself. The prelusory goal and constitutive rules together give playing in games one ground of value, namely difficulty; the lusory attitude in its amateur form adds a related but distinct ground of value, namely loving something good for the property that makes it so. The second ground depends on the first; loving difficulty would not be good unless difficulty were good. But it adds a further, complementary intrinsic good. When you play a game for its own sake you do something good and do it from a motive that fixes on its good-making property.

This two-part explanation deepens Suits's claim that playing in games is an intrinsic good, by connecting it to more general principles of value with application beyond the case of games. At the same time, however, it makes playing in games a derivative rather than a fundamental intrinsic good. It would not appear on a list of basic goods, since it combines two other, more fundamental, goods in a particular way.

But a good that is not fundamental can nonetheless be paradigmatic because it gives the clearest possible expression of a certain type of value. If difficult activities are as such good, they must aim at a goal: it is achieving that which is challenging. But their value does not derive from properties of that goal considered in itself, depending instead on features of the process of achieving it. Yet this can be obscured if the goal is independently good, since then the activity, if successful, will be instrumentally good, and this can seem the most important thing about it. If the farmer who works by hand successfully harvests a crop, his work contributes to the vital good of feeding his family, and this can distract us from the value it has in itself. But there is no such danger if the goal is intrinsically valueless, as it most clearly is in games. Since a game's prelusory goal—getting a ball into a hole in the ground or standing atop a mountain—is intrinsically trivial, the value of playing the game can depend only on facts about the process of achieving that goal. And this point is further emphasized by the lusory attitude, which chooses that process just as a process, since it willingly accepts rules that make achieving the goal harder. Game-playing must have some external goal one aims at, but the specific features of this goal are irrelevant to the activity's value, which is entirely one of process rather than product, journey rather than destination. This is why playing in games gives the clearest expression of a modern as against an Aristotelian view of value: because modern values are precisely ones of process or journey rather than of the end-state they lead to.

The contrary Aristotelian view, which denigrates these values, was expressed most clearly in Aristotle's division of all activities into the two categories of *kinēsis* and *energeia*, and his subsequent judgements about them.[12] An Aristotelian *kinēsis* — often translated as 'movement'—is an activity aimed at a goal external to it, as driving to Toronto is aimed at being in Toronto. It is therefore brought to an end by the achievement of that goal, which means that a *kinēsis* can be identified by a grammatical test: if the fact that one has *X*-ed implies that one is no longer *X*-ing, as the fact that one has driven to Toronto implies that one is no longer driving there, then *X*-ing is a *kinēsis*. But the main point is that a *kinēsis* aims at an end-state separate from it. By contrast, an *energeia*—translated variously as 'actuality', 'activity', or 'action'—is not directed at an external goal but has its end internal to it. Contemplation is an *energeia*, because it does not aim to produce anything beyond itself, as is the state of feeling pleased. And *energeiai* do not pass the above grammatical test, and therefore, unlike *kinēsis*, can be carried on indefinitely: that one has contemplated does not imply that one is not contemplating now or will not continue to do so. Contemplation, like driving to Toronto, is an activity, but it does not aim to produce anything apart from itself.

Now, Aristotle held that *energeiai* are more valuable than *kinēsis*, so the best human activities must be ones that can be carried on continuously, such as contemplation. This is because he assumed that the value of a *kinēsis* must derive from that of its goal, so its value is subordinate, and even just instrumental, to that of the goal. As he said at the start, of the

Nicomachean Ethics, 'Where there are ends apart from the actions, it is the nature of the products to be better than the activities.'[13] But it is characteristic of what I am calling modern values to deny this assumption, and to hold that there are activities that necessarily aim at an external goal but whose value is internal to them in the sense that it depends entirely on features of the process of achieving that goal. Suits cites expressions of this modern view by Kierkegaard, Kant, Schiller, and Georg Simmel,[14] but for an especially clear one consider Marx's view that a central human good is transforming nature through productive labour. This activity necessarily has an external goal—one cannot produce without producing some thing—and in conditions of scarcity this goal will be something vital for humans' survival or comfort. But Marx held that when scarcity is overcome and humans enter the 'realm of freedom' they will still have work as their 'prime want', so they will engage in the process of production for its own sake without any interest in its goal as such. Or consider Nietzsche's account of human greatness. In an early work he said the one thing 'needful' is to 'give style to one's character', so its elements are unified by 'a single taste', and that it matters less whether this taste is good or bad than whether it is a single taste.[15] Later he said the will to power involves not the 'multitude and disgregation' of one's impulses but their coordination under a single predominant impulse.[16] In both discussions he deemed activities good if they involve organizing one's aims around a single goal whatever that goal is. So for both Marx and Nietzsche a central human good was activity that on the one side is necessarily directed to a goal but on the other derives its value entirely from aspects of the process of achieving it. This is why the type of value they affirm is paradigmatically illustrated by playing in games; when one's goal is trivial, the only value can be that of process. Marx and Nietzsche would never put it this way, but what each valued is in effect playing in games, in Marx's case the game of material production when there is no longer any instrumental need for it, in Nietzsche's the game of exercising power just for the sake of doing so.

Playing in games also clearly straddles Aristotle's division between *kinēsis* and *energeiai*. It has the logical structure of a *kinēsis*, since it aims at a goal external to itself, and passes the relevant grammatical test: if one has parred a golf hole or climbed a mountain, one is no longer doing so. But it also has value in itself, as an *energeia* does, based on properties internal to it as an activity. We can show this more precisely using our formal model of the value of achievement, on which the value of any goal depends in part on the number of other goals achieved as means to it. In Figure 1.6.1 the lower-level goals are pursued as means to higher-level ones, and contribute to those goals' value only if they are both successfully achieved and contribute causally to them. And the higher-level goals must themselves also be successfully achieved. Since the hierarchy is precisely one of *achievements*, a highest-level goal that is not achieved does not qualify for inclusion in the hierarchy, and so does not gain any value from having other goals achieved as attempted means to it. This means that if two people go through the same complex process as a means to a given goal, and the first achieves the goal while the second through bad luck does not, the first's activity has more intrinsic value: his hierarchy contains his highest-level goal, which has his greatest value, but the second's does not. (If Pete Rose's opponents played as well as he did but Rose's team won the World Series, his play was intrinsically better.) So the activities valued by our formal model are directed at an external goal, as *kinēsis* are, and have their full value only if that goal is achieved. But their value does not depend on properties of the goal considered by itself; if the same goal were achieved without complex means, it might have just one unit of value. Instead, their value depends on means–end relations between their components, and so depends on internal features of the activity as does that of an *energeia*.

If playing in games is the paradigm expression of modern values, it helps us see similar value in other activities not normally associated with games. One, emphasized by Nietzsche, is a life organized around a single goal; it embodies through a longer stretch of time the same hierarchical structure present in individual difficult activities. The relevant activities also include ones in business and the arts. Business activity sometimes aims at an independent good such as relieving others' suffering or increasing their comfort. But often its goal is just to win market share and profits for one company, which is morally trivial; there is no intrinsic value in

people's drinking Coke rather than Pepsi or using Microsoft rather than Apple. Aristotle should therefore deny this activity value, and he did, arguing that if money has no intrinsic value, the activity of money-making must likewise have no value.[17] But if winning market share is difficult, requiring a complex series of finely balanced decisions, a modern view can grant it significant worth. And its pursuit can also involve something like the lusory attitude, since business people who aim partly for profits can also value the exercise of business skill just as skill, or for its own sake. Artistic creation too, to cite a different activity, has an independently good product if it aims, say, at communicating truths that cannot be communicated by non-artistic means. But a distinctively modern view (which is not to say the only view held nowadays) says that art aims only at beauty, where that consists in organic unity, or having the different elements of a painting, novel or piece of music form a coherent, dynamic whole. This view makes the value of artistic production rest on its intentionally creating all the complex relations that define its product's beauty, that is, on its itself being complex. And its value will be greater if it has more of the supplementary qualities mentioned above: if it unifies more varied elements, if it requires more precise brushstrokes, notes or words, and if it involves grasping more extended contents in a single act of consciousness, as Henry Moore could see his sculptures from all sides at once.[18] And of course artistic creation can involve a lusory attitude, if the artist enjoys and values the skill his work involves for its own sake.

But playing in games is also in one respect a lesser good, and I want to close by explaining why. Imagine two activities that are equally complex and difficult, one of which produces an intrinsically good result while the other does not. Perhaps one is political activity that liberates an entire nation from oppression while the other involves winning a high-level chess tournament. The first activity will, of course, be instrumentally better, because it produces a separate intrinsic good. But it will also arguably be on that basis intrinsically better. Consider Derek Parfit's example of a person who spends his life working for the preservation of Venice. Parfit claims, plausibly, that if after this person's death Venice is preserved, and in a way that depends crucially on his efforts, that will make his life and activities intrinsically better than if Venice had been destroyed.[19] This conclusion already follows from our formal model of achievement, since any realization of a topmost goal adds value to a hierarchy. But I think there is an extra ground for its truth if, as Parfit clearly intends, the preservation of Venice is independently good. Whatever additional value there is in achieving a goal just as a goal, there is further value in achieving one that is good. When an activity aimed at a valuable end successfully achieves that end and therefore is instrumentally good, its being instrumentally good is an extra source of intrinsic goodness.[20]

Now, because game-playing has a trivial end result, it cannot have the additional intrinsic value that derives from instrumental value. This implies that excellence in games, though admirable, is less so than success in equally challenging activities that produce a great good or prevent a great evil. This seems intuitively right: the honour due athletic achievements for themselves is less than that due the achievements of great political reformers or medical researchers. Whatever admiration we should feel for Tiger Woods or Gary Kasparov is less than we should feel for Nelson Mandela. It also implies that, whatever their other merits, Suits's utopia and Marx's realm of freedom would lack an important intrinsic good. Their inhabitants could play the game of, say, farming or medicine by going through the same complex procedures as farmers and doctors today. But if food could be produced and diseases cured by pushing a button, as they can in Suits's vision, their activity would not have the additional intrinsic value that comes from actually feeding or curing people and that is found in present-day farming and medicine.[21] The very perfection of Suits's and Marx's Utopias prevents them from containing the distinctive good of producing intrinsic goods that would not otherwise exist.

The point that an ideal world may exclude certain intrinsic goods should not be unfamiliar: G. E. Moore noted that the best possible world could not contain compassion for real pain, which he plausibly held was a greater good than compassion for merely imaginary pain.[22] And Suits's and Marx's utopias can still contain, alongside such goods as pleasure and knowledge, the distinctively modern good of achieving a difficult goal regardless of its value. Moreover, their doing so can help make them

better on balance than any world in which successful instrumental activity is possible. Many philosophers have assumed, with Aristotle, that the value of a process aimed at producing some end-state must derive entirely from the end-state's value, so if the latter is negligible so is the former. But there is no reason to believe this. Even if some of the process's intrinsic value depends on its instrumental value, in the way just described, there can also be intrinsic value in its properties just as a process and apart from any value in its product. To return again to Figure 1.6.1, this value will depend not on any qualities of the topmost goal considered in itself, but only on the means–ends relations between the various goals whose sequential achievement constitutes the process. I have argued that this distinctively modern value is illustrated most clearly by playing in games, especially when that is analysed as in Bernard Suits's wonderful book *The Grasshopper*.[23]

Notes

1. Ludwig Wittgenstein, *Philosophical Investigations*, 3rd edn, trans. G. E. M. Anscombe, Oxford: Blackwell, 1972, Sect. 66.
2. Bernard Suits, *The Grasshopper: Games, Life and Utopia*, Toronto: University of Toronto Press, 1978; repr. Peterborough, ON: Broadview Press, 2005, p. 41/55 (page references are first to the University of Toronto Press edition, then to the Broadview Press edition).
3. Ibid., p. 41/54–5.
4. See, for example, James Griffin, *Well-Being: Its Meaning, Measurement and Moral Importance*, Oxford: Clarendon Press, 1986, p. 67.
5. Robert Nozick, *Anarchy, State, and Utopia*. New York: Basic Books, 1974, pp. 42–5.
6. I give a fuller account of this value in my *Perfectionism*, New York: Oxford University Press, 1993, Chs 8–10.
7. Some may deny that difficulty is as such good, on the ground that an activity aimed at evil, such as genocide, is not in any way made good by its difficulty. The issue here is complex (see my *Virtue, Vice, and Value*, New York: Oxford University Press, 2001, pp. 144–52), but those moved by this objection can retreat to the weaker claim that only activities with good or neutral aims gain value by being difficult. This weaker claim is sufficient to ground the value of games.
8. *The Theory of Good and Evil*, 2 vols, London: Oxford University Press, 1907, vol. 2, p. 105.

9. Suits, *The Grasshopper*, pp. 166/149, 144/130.
10. Tom Adelman, *The Long Ball: The Summer of '75—Spaceman, Catfish, Charlie Hustle, and the Greatest World Series Ever Played*, New York: Back Bay Books, 2003, p. 313.
11. Aristotle, *Nicomachean Ethics*, trans. W. D. Ross and J. O. Urmson, Oxford: Oxford University Press, 1980, 1175b24–30. I discuss this view at length in *Virtue, Vice, and Value*.
12. *Nicomachean Ethics*, 1094a1–7, 1174a13–b8, 1176b1–8, 1177b2–4.
13. Ibid., 109414–5.
14. Suits, *The Grasshopper*, pp. 93–94/92.
15. Friedrich Nietzsche, *The Gay Science*, trans. Walter Kaufmann, New York: Vintage, 1974. Sect. 290.
16. Nietzsche, *The Will to Power*, trans. Walter Kaufmann and R. J. Hollingdale, New York: Vintage, 1968, Sect. 46.
17. *Nicomachean Ethics*, 1096a5–10. An obvious suggestion is that an activity like money-making can be a *kinēsis* when described in one way and an *energeia* when described in another. But, plausible though it is, this does not seem to have been Aristotle's view. He seems to have treated the distinction as a metaphysical one, between types of activities as they are in themselves. Nor could he have accepted the suggestion and continued to give his arguments about the inferiority of money-making and the superiority of contemplation, however described, based on then-properties as *kinēsis* or *energeia*.
18. Howard Gardner, *Frames of Mind: The Theory of Multiple Intelligences*, New York: Basic Books, 1983, p. 188.
19. Derek Parfit, *Reasons and Persons*, Oxford: Clarendon Press, 1984, p. 151.
20. On this see Shelly Kagan, 'Rethinking Intrinsic Value', *Journal of Ethics*, 2, 1998, pp. 277–97; and my 'Two Kinds of Organic Unity', *Journal of Ethics*, 2, 1998, pp. 299–320.
21. This claim is defended, with specific reference to Suits, in Shelly Kagan, 'The Grasshopper, Aristotle, Bob Adams, and Me' (unpublished ms.).
22. G. E. Moore, *Principia Ethica*, Cambridge: Cambridge University Press, 1903, pp. 219–21.
23. I am grateful for helpful conversations to my former student Gwendolyn Bradford, whose essay 'Kudos for Ludus' first linked the value of games and the details of Suits's definition of a game.

References

Adelman, Tom 2003: *The Long Ball: The Summer of '75—Spaceman, Catfish, Charlie Hustle, and the Greatest World Series Ever Played*. New York: Back Bay Books.

Aristotle 1980: *Nicomachean Ethics*. Trans. W. D. Ross and J. O. Urmson. Oxford: Oxford University Press.

Gardner, Howard 1983: *Frames of Mind: The Theory of Multiple Intelligences*. New York: Basic Books.

Griffin, James 1986: *Well-Being: Its Meaning, Measurement and Moral Importance*. Oxford: Clarendon Press.

Hurka, Thomas 1993: *Perfectionism*. New York: Oxford University Press.

—— 1998: 'Two Kinds of Organic Unity'. *Journal of Ethics*, 2, 1998, pp. 299–320.

—— 2001: *Virtue, Vice, and Value*. New York: Oxford University Press.

Kagan, Shelly 1998: 'Rethinking Intrinsic Value'. *Journal of Ethics*, 2, 1998, pp. 277–97.

—— unpublished: 'The Grasshopper, Aristotle, Bob Adams, and Me'.

Moore, G. E. 1903: *Principia Ethica*. Cambridge: Cambridge University Press.

Nietzsche, Friedrich 1968: *The Will to Power*. Trans. Walter Kaufmann and R. J. Hollingdale. New York: Vintage.

—— 1974: *The Gay Science*. Trans. Walter Kaufmann, New York: Vintage.

Nozick, Robert 1974: *Anarchy, State, and Utopia*, New York: Basic Books.

Parfit, Derek 1984: *Reasons and Persons*. Oxford: Clarendon Press.

Rashdall, Hastings 1907: *The Theory of Good and Evil*, 2 vols. London: Oxford University Press.

Suits, Bernard 1978/2005: *The Grasshopper: Games, Life and Utopia*. Toronto: University of Toronto Press. Repr. Peterborough, ON: Broadview Press, 2005.

Wittgenstein, Ludwig 1972: *Philosophical Investigations*, 3rd edn. Trans. G. E. M. Anscombe. Oxford: Blackwell.

Games and the good—II

John Tasioulas

Thomas Hurka endorses three arresting claims in his contribution to this symposium: (a) that game-playing can be defined as 'the voluntary attempt to overcome unnecessary obstacles',[1] where the obstacles are created by constitutive rules with respect to a goal that can be specified and achieved independently of those rules; (b) that this definition enables us to identify the two intrinsic or non-instrumental goods internal to game-playing: they consist, primarily, in the good of engaging successfully in difficult activity (achievement), and, derivatively, in loving (that is, desiring, enjoying, and so on) such activity for its own sake; and (c) that the primary good realized through game-playing—success in achieving a difficult goal regardless of its value—is a distinctively modern, as opposed to classical, type of authentic good. In this paper, I take issue with all three claims. In the course of doing so, I put forward the rival hypothesis that the primary intrinsic good internal to game-playing—a good worth pursuing for its own sake and so capable of making one's life go better in so far as one participates in it—is that of play itself.

Games and their value

Hurka's thesis (a) invokes Bernard Suits's definition of game-playing, according to which

To play a game is to attempt to achieve a specific state of affairs [prelusory goal], using only means permitted by the rules ... where the rules prohibit the use of more efficient in favour of less efficient means [constitutive rules], and where the rules are accepted just because they make possible such activity [lusory attitude].[2]

Yet this definition seems wildly over-inclusive. Neither the justified infliction of punishment nor the waging of a lawful war is the playing of a game. But consider a Hartian understanding of the former. Here the 'prelusory' goal is to prevent criminal behaviour and the rules that make its attainment more difficult include those that forbid punishing the innocent or punishing the guilty disproportionately. Moreover, officials of the criminal justice system may adopt a 'lusory attitude' towards its rules, voluntarily accepting them just so that, they can engage in the activity thereby made possible, i.e. the justified punishment of offenders. Whatever the defects of Hart's theory of punishment, that it turns punishment into a game is not plausibly among them. A similar verdict holds in the case of a war, aimed at repelling an attack by another state, which is conducted in accordance with humanitarian law, since the latter prohibits such potentially efficient means as the torture of enemy soldiers and the terror bombing of civilians.[3]

John Tasioulas 'Games and the Good–II', from PASH/*Proceedings of the Aristotelian Society*. Supplementary Vol. 80, pp. 237–264, © 2006 John Tasioulas. Reprinted by permission of Wiley-Blackwell.

Perhaps these intended counterexamples mis-fire because they do not involve 'intrinsically trivial' goals (p. 285), unlike the prelusory goals of golf (putting a ball in a hole) or chess (bringing about a certain arrangement of chessmen). But it is not obvious what the requirement of 'triviality' amounts to, nor that all the activities Hurka considers to be games meet it. Are the prelusory goals of poker (increasing one's money) or boxing (incapacitating or outpunching one's opponent) also trivial? The answer is unclear, partly because the goals admit of a variety of descriptions that seem to differ in point of triviality. In any case, other activities with more obviously trivial goals may serve as counterexamples. Consider a goal-involving ritual, such as a pilgrimage. Here, a trivial goal (being present in location X at time t) is to be achieved only by complying with certain rules (such as travelling on foot via a circuitous route) that make the accomplishment of the goal more difficult. Moreover, the rules may be complied with for the sake of the activity they make possible, e.g. a pilgrimage.

Not only is Suits's definition over-inclusive in so far as it appears to be satisfied by activities that Hurka himself would not count as games, it is also over-inclusive by virtue of embracing activities that he implausibly considers to be games. The problem here is with the unqualified contention that sports are 'a subclass of the wider category of games' (p. 273). Some of the sports Hurka mentions, such as golf, baseball and hockey, are unquestionably games, whereas others, such as sprinting, weightlifting and mountaineering, would not ordinarily be so described. Naturally, this observation is hostage to the vagaries of linguistic usage, but an underlying rationale can be adduced in its favour.[4] Sports are activities the successful pursuit of which characteristically invites the display of some kind of physical prowess; indeed, having the opportunity to display such prowess is part of the point of engaging in sporting activities. This is why many jib at awarding unathletic indoor games such as tiddlywinks, darts or billiards the honorific description 'sport'. And just as not all games are sports, so too not all sports are games. Sports that are not games tend to be institutionalized—or rule-governed—versions of some form of activity that involves the display of physical prowess, and in which one might intelligibly engage, or take an interest,

pre-institutionally. Thus, boxing is a rule-governed fist fight, the 100 metres sprint a rule-governed foot race, weightlifting a rule-governed trial of strength of a certain kind, and so on. The goings-on in a cricket match, by contrast, notoriously cannot be understood without pervasive reference to a system of 'arbitrary' rules, that is, rules that do not essentially structure and facilitate the realization of some fairly specific pre-institutional activity. Of course, this leaves the distinction between sports that are games and those that are not occasionally indeterminate, but that is as it should be.

The reply might now be that even if true, everything I have said so far is innocuous to the success of Hurka's project. And this because the concept of 'game-playing' he deploys is a term of art, one that captures what is importantly common to participating in both games and sports. Perhaps so; but this reply skates over the dialectical significance of treating all sports as games and concentrating heavily, as Hurka does, on sports in elucidating the value of game-playing. The overall effect is to confer far greater plausibility on thesis (b) than would have been the case had a different set of examples been employed, since most people are inclined to believe that sporting success is a genuine form of achievement. This tendency to skew the dialectic in (b)'s favour is compounded by three other features of Hurka's discussion.

The first is his brisk dismissal of many games, for instance, rock-paper-scissors, as not 'good games' because they are not 'challenging' or 'reasonably difficult' (p. 276). Yet, like snakes-and-ladders, this is a perfectly good game when played by or with a child, and its goodness has little to do with any form of achievement as opposed to the fun of playing it. And there are, of course, adult analogues: games that involve no significant room for skill in meeting difficult challenges. The most conspicuous category, which is entirely absent from Hurka's discussion, is games of chance such as bingo or roulette.[5] Of course, even these can be played in a way that eliminates or curtails the influence of chance on the outcome (for example, one might buy up all the tickets in a lottery). But to play them in this spirit is to miss their distinctive appeal. Moreover, many games combine skill with luck, and one of the determinants of the extent to which the latter figures may be the players' comparative levels of competence.[6] Still, the presence of luck seems to be a valuable feature of many games despite having nothing to do with striving and achievement, and everything to do with the thrill of surrendering to fate and delighting in good fortune.

Relatedly, Hurka focuses on 'excellence' manifested in skilful game-playing and the 'admiration' it merits. Yet there are innumerable instances of game-playing in ordinary life that we judge worthwhile even though they do not, and often cannot in virtue of the nature of the relevant game, realize the excellence/admiration pairing. Here, the perspective of those who participate in games, and not merely that of potential spectators, needs to be taken into account. Consider, for example, young children playing blind man's bluff, factory workers engaged in an impromptu football match during their lunch break, or an Old Age Pensioner enjoying a weekly game of bingo. One would be hard-pressed to deny that these activities have value for those engaged in them, and so are properly desired by the latter. But the realization of this value is typically no cause for admiration on the part of onlookers. Instead, what seems to be at stake is an interest, like our interest in autonomy or freedom from pain, the meeting of which makes a person's life go better. In so far as this interest is fulfilled, some attitude of approval other than admiration is usually in order; conversely, its non-fulfilment may rightly provoke frustration and indignation.[7] It is primarily under this decidedly non-elite aspect that our interest in play is protected by various human rights instruments, such as Article 31(1) of the United Nations Convention on the Rights of the Child and Article 24 of the Universal Declaration of Human Rights. But it is a dimension of the value of game-playing that is screened from view by Hurka's analysis.

Finally, not everyone accepts the claim that engaging in games and sports can manifest a form of excellence that merits admiration. Indeed, some take a dim view of the widespread adulation of leading sporting figures in contemporary society—a phenomenon Hurka invokes in order to lend credence to this claim—attributing it to some such cause (or complex of causes) as the distorting influence of nationalist sentiment, the commodification of sport under capitalism or the cultural 'levelling-down' wrought by democratization. George Orwell, for example, diagnosed the modern preoccupation with

sporting success as 'merely another effect of the causes that have produced nationalism', and he went on to ridicule those spectators and nations 'who work themselves into furies over these absurd contests, and seriously believe—at any rate for short periods—that running, jumping and kicking a ball are tests of national virtue'.[8] Such scepticism is not obviously perverse, especially when recast as the less uncompromising claim that modern culture grossly overvalues sporting success. But an approach that simply deems it a platitude that the primary good internal to sport is a form of excellence that merits admiration is scarcely well-placed to counter it.

Play as a basic good

The provisional upshot of our discussion is that, in so far as there is a good 'internal' to game-playing, that is, one in terms of which the nature and point of that activity is primarily to be elucidated, it is not best thought of as a kind of 'excellence' that rightly evokes 'admiration'. So, *contra* (b), it is not achievement which is presumably a good of that sort. Someone might respond that this conclusion is vitiated by a failure to distinguish between intrinsic and instrumental value: Hurka aimed to elucidate the intrinsic value of game-playing—the good accruing to game-playing as such, independently of its consequences—whereas the supposed counterexamples identify aspects of its instrumental value. Of course, claims about the instrumental value of game-playing are well-rehearsed. According to Herodotus, the Lydians purported to have invented all games common to them and the Greeks as a way of mitigating the effects of a famine. And evolutionary psychologists in our day attribute adaptive value to play as preparation for coping with future challenges, both expected and unexpected.[9] So, it might be said in connection with our illustrative cases, that the bingo player's weekly game is a means to enjoyment and friendship; that the factory workers' football match affords a period of recreation and diversion that helps them go back to work with renewed vigour; and so on.

Without disputing that game-playing can be instrumentally valuable in myriad ways, in this section I contend that the primary intrinsic value internal to game-playing is play itself.

Moreover, one can affirm this without first having defined game-playing, so to that extent Hurka's thesis that a unified account of the value of game-playing must be erected on the back of a definition of that activity is mistaken. Achievement in game-playing is also a good, and when instantiated it typically constitutes a form of excellence that merits admiration; but in the next section I argue that it is a relational good. In other words, although achievement is an intrinsic value that can be realized through game-playing, when it is so realized it is typically dependent on the value of play itself.

The thesis that play is a basic good opposes the contention that playing in games is 'a derivative rather than a fundamental intrinsic good', combining the two goods of difficult activity and the love of such activity. Still, it is a claim with a notable pedigree, even if its proponents have not usually accorded it the benefit of a sustained defence.[10] Of course, it faces the immediate objection that there seems to be a world of difference between, say, chess and football; so much so, it will be said, that it is highly artificial to suppose that the same good is instantiated by both activities. The first line of response must be that the value of play is a determinable, one that assumes different determinate shapes in the context of the various activities instantiating it. After all, subscribers to an objective list of goods will have to make some such claim about other items on it. Notice, too, that play need not be any more definable than other putative goods, such as enjoyment, friendship and knowledge. But we can be satisfied with this response only if an informative characterization of the value of play can be given at a fairly high level of generality, one that confirms its status as a distinct and irreducible value.

The most promising way to formulate such an account is by adopting a bottom-up approach that identifies characteristic features of instantiations of the value of play. Such an approach contrasts sharply with Hurka's subsumption of game-playing under a pre-established theory of value, according to which pleasure, achievement and knowledge are basic goods. An important source for this enterprise is Johan Huizinga's classic study *Homo Ludens*, in which play is characterized as follows:

[A] free activity standing quite consciously outside 'ordinary' life as being 'not serious', but at the same time absorbing the player intensely and utterly. It is an activity connected to no material interest, and no profit can be gained by it. It proceeds within its own proper boundaries of time and space according to fixed rules and in an orderly manner. It promotes the formation of social groupings which tend to surround themselves with secrecy and to stress their difference from the common world by disguise or other means ... The play-mood is one of rapture and enthusiasm, and is sacred or festive in accordance with the occasion. A feeling of exaltation and tension accompanies the action, mirth and relaxation follow.[11]

It is worth elaborating some of the elements, whether explicit, or implicit, in this formulation. (1) *Free activity*. At its best play is a free activity, voluntarily entered upon (and exited) and without any sense of material or moral compulsion. Of course, sometimes play is not engaged in freely, or not straightforwardly so—for instance, compulsory sport at school—but, to the extent that this is so, it lacks an important, dimension of the good of play. Leaving aside any instrumental concern with health, discipline or the prevention of delinquency, a key justification for dragooning schoolchildren into sports and other worthwhile forms of play is that they may eventually acquire a liking for them and engage in them freely in their own time.

(2) *Separation from ordinary life*. Play takes place outside the routine of 'ordinary' life, especially those aspects concerned with reproducing the material and moral conditions of our existence. It typically unfolds during one's leisure or 'free' time, often within spatial boundaries marked out in advance (court, stage, field, etc.) and sometimes with participants wearing distinctive attire. Its separation from ordinary life lends it a quality of being 'not serious' or 'only pretend', which is related to the fact that what takes place in play is not supposed to have significant (especially, significantly *negative*) repercussions for the rest of life. The inconsequential nature of play explains our disinclination to classify duelling or any other activity that involves the deliberate infliction of serious harm, or even a very high risk of severe injury, as a form of play.[12] It also explains the familiar denunciations of the commercialization of sport as a corruption of play. Ordinary life, in these cases, oversteps the boundaries that separate it

from play. Hence also the tendency of play to lose its value when it becomes an obsession, so all-pervading that the player loses touch with ordinary life, or when participation in games of chance fosters a superstitious or fatalistic attitude to life as a whole, or when players of mimetic games come to identify with their fictional persona. Play in these cases is corrupted by invading ordinary life. None of this, of course, prevents play from interposing itself benignly into even the most serious activities, from the administration of justice to philosophical disputation, as Huizinga's work famously showed.

(3) *Significant order.* Play tends to be ordered by rules, roles or expectations that confer a point on the activity for those engaged in it. This is certainly true of sports, with their formally defined rules, but it applies equally to chess, dancing, the telling of jokes, etc. Two dimensions of the order exhibited by play are worth stressing. The first is the aesthetic character of play, which is evident in the vocabulary often used to describe it: tension, balance, variation, harmony, grace, rhythm, resolution, and so on. The second is the important role that uncertainty, and the tension it creates, assumes within this order. Resigning one's will to an uncertain outcome, beyond one's control, belongs to the essence of games of chance. But uncertainty is also a significant factor in competitive games that call for intellectual or physical skill. Here, the rules set difficult challenges for the participants, which they might fail to meet. Indeed, were they assured of meeting them without too much effort, the game would lose much of its appeal.

(4) *Valued for its own sake.* Play is activity (capable of being) valued and engaged in exclusively for its own sake, as opposed to any instrumental benefit, such as the meeting of needs or desires of the player or of others in society. This marks a basic contrast with activity that counts as 'work', which is typically directed at the creation of a product or outcome that has intrinsic or instrumental value, where this value in turn provides at least a partial basis for the intrinsic value of engaging in work. Yet despite not being 'serious' in the sense discussed under (2), play is capable of being taken seriously in virtue of its perceived intrinsic value, and in its most worthwhile manifestations it absorbs the player 'intensely and utterly'.

(5) *Enjoyment.* The enjoyment of playful performances for their own sake is an important source of their intrinsic value. There is a temptation to think that in the absence of being enjoyed, such performances lack intrinsic value. But this claim is too strong. Many instances of play, especially of the sporting variety, are imbued with a kind of tension, concentration or physical exertion that renders enjoying them whilst one is whole-heartedly engaged in them very difficult, if not impossible.[13] But this does not mean that they have no value when engaged in without enjoyment. Where enjoyment is not incompatible with being whole-heartedly engaged in play, the absence of enjoyment can diminish the value of a particular instance of game-playing. Still, we should not discount the possibility that, as John Finnis has suggested, 'participation in basic goods which is emotionally dry, subjectively unsatisfying, nevertheless is good and meaningful as far as it goes.'[14] The obvious caveat is that in the case of play it might not go very far at all, since with many kinds of play it is virtually unintelligible why anyone should choose to engage in them if they do not enjoy them (leaving aside any instrumental benefit, such as exercise or sociability). This seems especially true of games that are in no sense challenging. At this point one might be attracted to a disjunctive account of the intrinsic value internal to games and sports, with achievement and enjoyment as the two disjuncts (but, unlike Hurka's theory, the latter not being dependent on the former). Although not without its merits, this account fails to capture the strong sense that play often involves participation—whether enjoyed or not—in an independently valuable activity, where the independent value is not plausibly characterized as achievement. Thus, someone might think that a low-grade game of football was intrinsically worthwhile, even though they did not enjoy it because they were upset at missing a 'sitter' early on or were anxious throughout about the outcome of the match. This, however, is not to exclude the possibility that some forms of play need to be enjoyed if they are to have value, or at least if they are to contribute to the well-being of those participating in them.

(6) *Social dimension.* A component of the value of many forms of play is their being socially acknowledged, at least potentially so, as valuable. In the passage quoted above, Huizinga

characterizes the social dimension of play in terms of the propensity of devotees of various forms of play to establish clubs and associations. Equally, we have noted that play often depends on rules, roles and expectations, and these are typically socially generated. But the deeper point is that it can belong to what makes a form of play worthwhile that there are spectators or competitors who can or do 'play along', engaging in or valuing the activity as worthwhile in itself. The goodness of games can consist, in part, in the fact that their goodness is—and is generally known to be—acknowledged by others who engage in or with the playing of it as fellow participants or as spectators. This is especially so with games of skill, which have a natural tendency to become competitive and seek out an audience, but it also applies to games of chance, which explains why many prefer gambling at a casino or racetrack to the solitary activity of placing their bets by telephone or through the Internet. The phenomenon of fads for certain games, puzzles and toys, which suddenly flare up and just as quickly peter out only to be replaced by the latest craze, is partly to be understood by reference to the social dimension of play.

The recognition of play as the basic good internal to games yields a number of advantages over Hurka's account. First, it remedies one way in which Suits's definition is over-inclusive. If the primary intrinsic value internal to games is play—that is, if games are activities that are characteristically worth engaging in for the sake of play—this suffices to distinguish them from activities that involve the pursuit of goals subject to voluntarily accepted constitutive rules, such as punishment, lawful warfare and pilgrimages, which are engaged in for the sake of goods other than play. This way of distinguishing game-playing seems preferable to Hurka's suggestion that games can be engaged in with a 'pure' lusory attitude, one whereby the rules in question are accepted because they make the resultant activity difficult, and not just possible. One reason is that this attitude is inapplicable to games that do not pose a reasonably difficult challenge; another is that the attitude seems to be present in difficult rule-bound and goal-directed activities that are not the playing of a game: for example, an adult who teaches himself Russian in his spare time might decide to sit the A level examination in the subject, as a test of his competence, but no game is being played as a result.

Second, it corrects Hurka's tendency to focus on games in which there is scope for the realization of excellence, or instances of game-playing in which excellence is realized, thereby depriving an implausibly large number of everyday instances of game-playing of any significant intrinsic value. Instead, acknowledging play as a basic good brings to light the intrinsic good internal to the four broad, and overlapping, categories of games: competitive games (e.g. chess), games of chance (e.g. roulette), games of simulation (e.g. charades), and those of vertigo (e.g. drinking games).[15] Moreover, we are equipped to identify the key feature that unites game-playing with activities that do not count as games because they are not governed by (arbitrary) rules. We can thus keep hold of the common-sense idea that when a child, in the course of an afternoon, moves from playing in his sandpit, to playing with his toy animals, to bouncing a ball, to playing hide-and-seek, and so on, he is, throughout, ultimately engaged in the same kind of activity, one that broadly realizes the same intrinsic value.

Third, specifying the nature of games by reference to the value of play preserves the valid insight buried in the misleading claim that sports are a sub-class of games. This is the idea that play is the primary good internal to both games and sports. Indeed, one might understand (I do not say define) the concept of a game, in its focal sense, as an activity that is characteristically engaged in for the sake of play, the rules of which tend to be pervasively 'arbitrary', that is, not primarily facilitative of some pre-institutionally meaningful form of activity. The 'arbitrariness' of the rules is perfectly compatible with their being purposely adapted to facilitate enjoyable, imaginative, intellectually or physically challenging, etc., instantiations of the good of play. Sports are activities in which this good is realized indirectly, in a way intended to manifest the participants' physical prowess. This potentially unstable combination of play and physical prowess is reflected in the uneasiness many feel about classifying as sports activities in which the relevant form of prowess essentially involves the deliberate infliction of severe pain or the assumption of a significant risk of injury, since these features threaten to crowd out anything obviously recognizable as play. Some observations in Joyce Carol Oates's *On Boxing*, although perhaps going too far in denying that boxing is a form of play and insufficiently attentive to the distinction between sports and games, help bring out the tension:

> I have no difficulty justifying boxing as a sport because I have never thought of it as a sport … There is nothing fundamentally playful about it; nothing that seems to belong to daylight, to pleasure. At its moments of greatest intensity it seems to contain so complete and so powerful an image of life—life's beauty, vulnerability, despair, incalculable and often self-destructive courage—that boxing *is* life, and hardly a mere game. During a superior boxing match (Ali–Frazier I, for instance) we are deeply moved by the body's communion with itself by way of another's intransigent flesh. The body's dialogue with its shadow-self—or Death. Baseball, football, basketball—these quintessentially American pastimes are recognizably sports because they involve play: they are games. One *plays* football, one doesn't *play* boxing.[16]

The point is not simply about the negation of enjoyment by pain, fear and despair, but also the blurring of the boundary between 'ordinary' life and 'non-serious' play. It is worth observing that Hurka also registers the problematic status of boxing as an exemplification of the good internal to sport. But he ascribes it to the influence of 'raw power' (and also, presumably, speed, endurance, etc.) in determining the outcome of a bout, since this sits uncomfortably with his emphasis on a 'rational connection to reality' in specifying the value of achievement. In other words, whereas I have suggested boxing's problematic character *qua* sport stems from its being all too consequential for 'real life', Hurka attributes it to a lack of 'complex ratiocination'. But not only is this a curiously intellectualized account of the good internal to sport, one that implausibly ranks golf (or sailing, lawn bowls, etc.) above boxing (or swimming, sprinting, etc.) despite the limited role of physical prowess in the former. It is also a questionable explanation of the problematic status of boxing as an exemplification of the good internal to sport, since the importance of raw power and other non-rational capacities is

also a feature of swimming, weightlifting, javelin-throwing, sprinting, and other sports that are quite properly found unproblematic on this score.

Fourth, the good of play provides a general, albeit not exhaustive, account of the intrinsic good internal to games and sports that neatly sidesteps—or, at least, postpones—a confrontation with Orwellian scepticism regarding the presence of admiration-meriting excellence in such activities. However things may stand with respect to achievement in sports and games, engagement in both can have intrinsic value in so far as it instantiates the value of play itself. Even Orwell did not deny that sports can be played in a way that is (intrinsically?) valuable for their participants: 'On the village green, where you pick up sides and no feeling of local patriotism is involved, it is possible to play simply for the fun and exercise.'[17]

Finally, we can respect an intuitive distinction between play and work activities, one that survives the complication that for some, such as professional sportspeople, their work consists in a form of play. For Hurka, presumably, achievement is the key intrinsic value internal to both games and sports, on the one hand, and work, on the other, even though it is only in the latter case that the activity's value derives in significant measure from its product or outcome. But whereas lack of personal achievement, or of any prospect of it, is always a good *pro tanto* reason for dissatisfaction with one's work, the same is not true of one's play. From this perspective, Hurka's argument for (b) is a sophisticated manifestation of a problematic trend in modern life, one that has been aptly described as 'the invasion of play by the rhetoric of achievement'.[18] As such, it is a defence of games in the spirit of the work ethic, and so yet another expression of the imperialist tendencies of the latter in our culture.[19]

Achievement and difficulty

There are two reasons why we still need to examine Hurka's account of achievement. I have disputed (b) in part by relying on a common-sense grasp of the nature of achievement, one according to which it is instantiated by activities characterized by certain kinds of excellence that merit admiration. But Hurka's account of achievement might be compelling, and so provide a basis for affirming (b), even though it deviates from this ordinary notion. Second, even if play is the primary value internal to games and sports, it is plausible to suppose that achievement is also an important intrinsic good that can be realized through playing them. So it is worth considering whether Hurka offers a compelling account of achievement independently of its use to support (b).

On Hurka's construal, achievement involves 'realizing a goal in the world given a justified belief that one would do so' by means of a process that is 'reasonably difficult' in absolute terms, for example, one that involves complexity, physical prowess, skill and ingenuity. In contrast to a supposed 'classical' or Aristotelian view, which would assess the value of goal-directed pursuits exclusively by reference to the independent value of the goal they realize, Hurka claims that the intrinsic value of such activities *qua* achievements is fundamentally dependent on certain 'formal properties' that make them difficult. On this view, the intrinsic value of difficult activity is increased to the extent that its goals, and the hierarchical means–end relations that obtain among them, exhibit, properties such as *complexity* (which relates not just to the number of goals to be achieved, but also their diversity and the complexity of their interrelations), the level of *precision* required in achieving the goals, and the *breadth of content* of the goals, for example, across time or in the number of objects they involve. The important point is that these intensifiers of the good of achievement are among the very properties that make an activity— including every kind of 'good game'—difficult: achievement is successful engagement in difficult activity as such.

Now, Hurka's 'formal model' contrasts with two other plausible accounts of achievement, which I shall label the 'deep' and the 'wide'. According to the former conception, achievement is one prudential value among others, so that its instantiation in a person's life can enhance their well-being by conferring weight or point on it.[20] A person's life can contain deep achievements, and to that extent be admirable, despite not going well for them overall—for example, they might have fought heroically in a just cause, but died tragically young—and also despite not being admirable overall. The other, 'wide' conception of achievement is instantiated

when a person's life as a whole *does* go well for them. On an objectivist construal of well-being, one according to which a good life is not ultimately or predominantly a life in which certain mental states obtain, this is a life in which the person living it is active, and to a significant degree successful, in pursuing worthwhile goals, both shorter-term and longer-term in character, that make up an overarching network of goals. A good life will involve self-direction, choice, discipline, etc., on the part of the person whose life it is, and so can be thought of as an achievement of theirs, something actively secured through their efforts, rather than a condition that might have come into being primarily through the benevolent actions of others, the workings of a Nozickian 'experience machine', etc.[21] On a wide, as opposed to a deep, conception of achievement, its presence in someone's life does not necessarily merit admiration.

Success in difficult activity as such is not achievement in either of these senses. One must go beyond the bare fact of an activity's difficulty, and its possession of the formal qualities mentioned earlier, to see it as instantiating either deep or wide achievement; some other value, or combination of values, must be appropriately related to difficult activity if engaging in it is to be an achievement. Since the dependence of 'wide' achievement on other values is fairly obvious, let me concentrate on 'deep' achievement. Regarding the latter, James Griffin denies that even very difficult activities, such as flagpole-sitting of 'Guiness-Book-of-Records duration', constitute accomplishments: 'bare, even rare, achievement' does not suffice.[22] I think this denial is best understood as reflecting the following thesis: whether an activity is a deep achievement depends on its being appropriately related to evaluative qualities that make it worth overcoming the difficulties it involves, and so capable of conferring weight or point on one's life. In this connection, Griffin mentions Darwin as someone who accomplished great things; yet his accomplishment consisted not just in the bare fact that he surmounted difficulties, but that in doing so he made a momentous scientific break-through. Here the value of understanding needs to be registered for the very fact of Darwin's achievement, not just its magnitude, to come into view. Similarly, a poor immigrant's achievement may consist in the great sacrifices he made to secure the welfare of his children, but again only because both his relationship with them and their welfare are independently valuable.

This last example brings out the limitations of specifying difficulty in terms of formal properties and achievement as the display of skill in overcoming them. For we can elaborate it in such a way that the difficulties in question essentially consist in the *substantive* costs that the father willingly bore—for example, many years of mind-numbingly repetitive and physically draining factory work that seriously impaired his own self-development, to the extent perhaps that his own life did not go well overall—rather than the complexity, precision, etc., of the means–end reasoning required to attain his goal. Some of the finest achievements combine skill or ingenuity with a willingness to incur considerable substantive costs in realizing an objective. For instance, the magistrate protagonist in the Costa-Gavras film *Z* displays both investigative prowess and moral courage in bringing to justice the high-ranking officials complicit in the murder of a left-wing politician. Nor does this exhaust the kinds of difficulty the overcoming of which can make for achievement without any skill being displayed. To give one more example: it is an achievement for a victim of serious crime to overcome powerful feelings of anger and resentment, and the incomprehension and suspicion of their community, in coming to forgive their attacker. The difficulty here consists in retaining or coming to an appreciation of the value of forgiveness in such circumstances, and having the compassion and courage needed to forgive despite countervailing pressures, both internal and external. In the last three cases I have described, the overcoming of difficulty manifests not (or not merely) the agent's skill, but their possession of a moral virtue. Moral virtues contrast with skills in always being directed towards the realization of a good end. One consequence of this is that an agent's voluntary error within a domain of decision-making governed by a virtue would undermine the ascription to him of that virtue; by contrast, an agent's possession of a skill is fully compatible with his making voluntary errors within its domain: for example, a master-builder might deliberately use the wrong technique for a job in order to test an apprentice's understanding of the craft.[23]

The phenomenon of dependence exhibited in these cases involves an intentional relation: the agent engages in difficult activity in order to realize one or more values. The mode of realization is not confined to situations in which difficult activity acquires intrinsic value through bringing about, in an instrumental manner, an independently valuable outcome, for instance in the way that a physician's activities cause his patients' improved health. It is also possible for the relationship to be constitutive, such that engagement in an independently valuable activity (e.g. being a good friend) inherently involves overcoming certain difficulties. Notice, further, that the relevant value to which difficult activity is related need not itself be a manifestly 'prudential value', that is, one that constitutes some aspect of human flourishing. On the contrary, the relevant value may be moral (e.g. justice), and so only indirectly related to individual flourishing, or even non-anthropocentric—someone's achievement might consist in helping preserve a rainforest from destruction, but the value of the latter's existence is not exhausted by its instrumental or constitutive bearing on human interests.

Both deep and wide achievement, I contend, have a relational character, in that some other value must appropriately characterize a difficult activity before it can be an achievement. Activity that amounts to an achievement is always a difficulty-overcoming mode of participation by an agent in some value, such as deep personal relations, knowledge, justice, beauty, and so on, one that rightly commands our admiration. Although a necessary element, overcoming difficulty by itself does not suffice to constitute achievement. Let us call the relevant other value(s) the 'framing value(s)'.[24] By contrast, goods such as play or understanding seem to be relatively self-standing, in that they can be instantiated independently of any instrumental or constitutive relationship to another good. Against this view, Hurka grounds achievement in difficult activity as such, independently of its connection to any other intrinsic value, although of course he also allows that such a connection can *enhance* the value of the activity (but presumably not *qua* bare achievement). How might the bare account of achievement be defended against the relational view?

Two lines of defence emerge in Hurka's article. The first is to countenance, at least *arguendo*, a negative version of the relational thesis: in order for an activity to be valuable by virtue of its difficulty it must not (exclusively?) aim at producing a (very) bad or evil outcome.[25] This blocks the inference that, on a bare account of achievement, the complex planning and execution of a terrorist atrocity has intrinsic value (even if it is bad overall, and so appropriately condemned, in light of its evil goal). This is a welcome result, since it is reasonable to suppose that the terrorists' success in overcoming difficulties, instead of possessing any intrinsic value (let alone the sort of intrinsic value that merits admiration), only serves to aggravate both the heinousness of their crime and the blight it casts on their lives. This is partly because an agent who deliberately surmounts difficulties in order to realize an evil end is typically more volitionally identified with that end, and hence more morally culpable, than someone who does not. Presumably something similar must be said about the adoption of evil yet difficult means to the attainment of a neutral or good objective.

But Hurka's second line of defence resists the apparently plausible flip side of the negative thesis, that is, the positive claim that for achievement to be instantiated the overcoming of difficulty must exhibit an appropriate connection to some framing value. Instead, he believes that defenders of the relational view of deep achievement are mistaken, and that their error is best exposed through reflection on game-playing, since a game's prelusory goal lacks value. Game-playing shows us, on this view, that the essence of achievement is success in difficult activity as such. Now, a defender of the relational view should readily agree that the prelusory goal of valuable instances of game-playing, even those that manifest achievement, is usually neutral considered by itself. But it does not follow that game-playing does not instantiate framing values that are capable of entering into the right kind of relation with difficult activity to ground deep achievement. Drawing on the discussion in the previous section, he should say that these values include the good of play itself. After all, my aim in playing golf is not simply to put the ball in the hole; on the contrary, I have that aim precisely because I want to participate in the good of play (specifically, the determinate version of that good instantiated by playing the game of golf). Overcoming the difficulties imposed by the rules of golf is a constitutive means of pursuing the framing good of play, in the specific version of that good represented by the playing of golf.

To adjudicate between the bare and the relational accounts of achievement, consider an exemplar of perversity familiar from recent value theory: let us call him Joe, a man whose dominant pursuit in life is counting blades of grass in various well-delineated lawns. We can describe his activity in such a way that it involves considerable difficulty and, moreover, constitutes a Suitsian game. The prelusory goal is to count the exact number of blades of grass in as many lawns of a certain size as possible within a given calendar year, remembering at the end of the year how many blades each area contained and also accurately describing its general condition. The constitutive rules that make the attainment of this goal more difficult include that the counting must be done manually and without assistance, that it must continue uninterrupted for twelve hours per day, that on every other day the player must entirely abstain from food, that no resort may be had to aide-mémoires, etc. Moreover, Joe accepts these rules because of the very difficulties they create, so he manifests a 'pure' lusory attitude. Let it also be the case that the grass-counting game is his own creation, that it affords him a sense of fulfilment but little pleasure, and that no one else engages in or sees the point of this activity; on the contrary, others in his society treat Joe as an object of ridicule, pity or bewilderment.

Let us suppose that Joe becomes highly proficient at the grass-counting game, able to count and accurately recall the details of ten times as many lawns of a given size annually as the average hypothetical amateur. Does this amount to an achievement on his part? It seems Hurka must say so. Joe's game demands great physical stamina and mental concentration, it also requires some fairly impressive feats of memory. Over the years, he attains rare levels of manual dexterity and perfects a very effective counting technique. His activity exhibits a significant degree of complexity, precision and breadth of content—certainly as compared with sports such as weight-lifting or sprinting. And yet, we

71

should rightly judge it an appalling waste of time, hence as utterly devoid of achievement. Perhaps it will be countered that *some* intrinsic value is realized in Joe's life as a result of this activity, since even a life of grass-counting is preferable to a supremely indolent existence. This suggestion may be correct, but then it seems we are according value to activity informed by practical and theoretical reasoning *per se*, rather than to anything recognizable as an achievement. For surely there is nothing to be admired in what Joe does.

How might achievement come to grace this dismal scene? Well, although I said Joe's activity was a game on Suits's definition, it is hardly a clear-cut instantiation of the good of play as understood in the previous section. But imagine now grass-counting transformed into play: not only freely engaged in, but enjoyed by Joe for its own sake, yet regarded by him as not serious, so that it takes place in his free time, filling no more than seven days in a year and imposing no health-endangering burdens. Imagine also that others take part in it competitively, for instance, that it is an all-day event during an annual community festival. Now the elements of play are more obviously present, and as a result playing the game seems to acquire real value—the value of play itself. And this value, in characterizing the point of the activity, provides a framework within which some performances might conceivably be judged genuine achievements, that is, admirable displays of skill, physical dexterity, speed, endurance, memory, and so on. It need not be (exclusively) the good of play that performs this framing role; it might have been some other good, such as friendship, religion or deep personal relations. Even flagpole-sitting, or some comparable feat of endurance, might qualify as an achievement if appropriately framed by other values. St Simeon Stylites, who spent thirty-six years on a column as an expression of religious devotion, is venerated for his spiritual achievement, whereas a present-day imitator who did the same thing simply because it is difficult would rightly be judged perverse.

Of course, not any connection between difficult activity and a framing value grounds achievement. Whether the overcoming of specific kinds of difficulty is an achievement depends on the nature of the framing value in question. The point is especially compelling

regarding difficulties that impose what I called substantive costs. Thus, it is an achievement for a mother to sacrifice her life in order to save her child's life; but someone who is prepared to lay down their life purely in order to secure victory in a football match has a distorted grasp of the value of playing games, and therefore also a distorted grasp of what counts as achievement in playing them. Notice, in this connection, that scope for achievement was created in the grass-counting game precisely through the activity being made in certain respects *less* difficult—in particular, less consequential in its potentially negative impact on players' interests—since this was necessary for it to be seen as a genuine instantiation of the value of play.

Consider, finally, how the two opposing views of achievement bear on the proposal that the use of performance-enhancing drugs be permitted in athletic competitions. Abstracting from moral or public policy considerations, this proposal might be advanced as a way of making athletics more challenging; for example, athletes might be required to determine and administer their own dosage, thus necessitating some chemical and medical expertise on their part. On the bare view of achievement, this seems to be a way of increasing the difficulty, hence also the potential level of achievement, in sports such as sprinting or weight-lifting, adding an element of ratiocination to pursuits that Hurka believes to be overly dominated by 'raw power'. On the relational view, by contrast, the proposal works to diminish the scope for achievement. This is because sports realize the good of play through displays of physical prowess, and the introduction of performance-enhancing drugs strikes against both framing values: the health risks of drug-taking contravene the inconsequentiality that characterizes the good of play, and the artificial enhancement of performance is inimical to the kind of physical prowess that sport is traditionally concerned to elicit. The relational view thus provides a means of justifying the plausible and widely held view that legalizing drug use would be corrosive of sporting achievement.

To sum up: the bare account denatures achievement by reducing it to the counterfeit intrinsic good of success in difficult activity as such, thereby ignoring its relational character. Since this account collapses, it cannot be used to prop up thesis (b).

A comment on 'modernity'

If modern goods are a subset of authentic goods, then achieving a difficult goal regardless of its value cannot be a modern good, since it is not an authentic good.[26] Thesis (c), therefore, is false. Is the value of play, as I have described it, a modern good, at least when realized by the playing of games? If we follow Hurka in using Aristotle's notoriously slippery distinction between *energeia* and *kinēsis* as a touchstone for the classical/modern divide—so that distinctively modern goods are realized by activities that have an external goal and satisfy the Aristotelian grammatical test for *kinēsis*, but which resemble *energeiai* in deriving intrinsic value from properties internal to the activity itself—then the good of play may well be no less modern than the putative good of bare achievement.

Assuming we retain the structure of prelusory goal, constitutive rules and lusory attitude in characterizing game-playing, we can still describe instances of it as *kinēsis* that possesses intrinsic value not derived from the value of their prelusory goal, since in the case of games the latter is typically valueless. Instead, the intrinsic value of game-playing derives from the fact that the process of achieving the prelusory goal is a way of participating in the good of play. But it also seems that game-playing can be redescribed as a form of *energeia* if the adoption of the prelusory goal, and the activity aimed at achieving it, are treated as constitutive means to the good of play itself. Now, the goal of the activity is no longer external to it, in so far (for example) as it is not possible to specify the goal of playing golf (a determinate form of the determinable good of play) without reference to activities such as teeing off, putting, etc. Moreover, the grammatical test for an *energeia* is also satisfied: from the fact that I have played golf (that is, realized this particular form of the good of play) at *t*, it does not follow that I am not still playing golf at *t*. More generally, a particular phase or instance of play will always come to an end, but an agent's potential engagement with the basic value of play itself is inexhaustible.[27] But presumably something similar may be said about the putative good of overcoming difficulty: from the fact that I have already overcome difficulties at *t*, it does not follow that I am not still doing so at *t*. This is an instance of the well-known problem that whether an activity counts as an instance of *energeia* or *kinēsis* seems worryingly sensitive to apparently insignificant variations in its description.

Given among other things its malleability, it is doubtful that the hybrid Aristotelian criterion tracks a historically resonant distinction between classical and modern conceptions of value. And yet the bare account of achievement *is* unmistakably 'modern' in a way that both the basic good of play and the relational account of achievement are not, since it displays the hallmarks of large-scale cultural tendencies associated with modernity. These include the exaltation of considerations of efficacy, form and procedure in evaluating an agent's adoption, ordering and realization of their goals, whatever their content—hence the significance that instrumental reasoning, consistency, integrity, skill, power, and so on assume in modern thought—and a corresponding down grading of substantive concerns about the worth of those goals. But we are now in the shadow of one of modern ethical thought's dark sides, a fact to which Hurka's invocation of Nietzsche's conception of human greatness as a distinctively modern good should alert us. The idea that there is value, let alone supreme value, in subordinating one's impulses to an overarching master-impulse irrespective of the latter's content,[28] amounts to a *reductio ad absurdum* of the modernist tendencies just described. Indeed, Charles Taylor's critique of the prevailing modernist, essentially Nietzschean, conception of authenticity on the grounds that it fatally detaches creativity, originality, opposition to convention, and so on from 'horizons of significance' nicely parallels my argument that the bare account of achievement ignores its inherently relational character by severing the overcoming of difficulty from framing values.[29]

Lest it be thought that I have simply adopted a neo-Aristotelian party line, one that is hopelessly nostalgic in its antipathy to certain features of modernity and disquietingly illiberal in its focus on the value of ends, let me conclude by quoting a philosopher whose modernist and liberal credentials are unassailable:

> [I]n times of social doubt and loss of faith in long established values, there is a tendency to fall back on the virtues of integrity: truthfulness

and sincerity, lucidity and commitment, or, as some say, authenticity ... Now of course the virtues of integrity are virtues, and among the excellences of free persons. Yet while necessary, they are not sufficient; for their definition allows for most any content: a tyrant might display these attributes to a high degree, and by doing so exhibit a certain charm, not deceiving himself by political pretenses and excuses of fortune. It is impossible to construct a moral view from these virtues alone; being virtues of form they are in a sense secondary. But joined to the appropriate conception of justice ... they come into their own.[30]

What Rawls says about the virtues of integrity applies *mutatis mutandis* to personal achievement. Achievement only comes into its own—in other words, admirable activity that confers weight or point on a person's life only exists—when the overcoming of difficulty is appropriately joined to some framing value or other. It is a characteristically modern illusion, not an insight, to suppose otherwise.[31]

Notes

1. B. Suits, *The Grasshopper: Games, Life and Utopia*, Boston, Godine, 1990, p. 41.
2. Ibid. pp. 54–5, quoted in T. Hurka, 'Games and the Good', p. 275.
3. Suits would presumably seek to exclude these putative counterexamples on the grounds that those who engage in the practices of punishment and legal warfare accept the rules for general and independent *moral* reasons (op. cit., pp. 31–2). But players often accept the rules of paradigmatic games for moral reasons, for example, rules disallowing dangerous tackles in football. More importantly, from the fact that there are independent moral reasons for accepting the rules of a practice, it does not follow that those who engage in it accept them for those reasons. Some may simply wish to be judges or soldiers and therefore accept the rules that apply to these roles.
4. There is a Wittgensteinian irritant here, but not the thesis that 'game' is indefinable that irritates Hurka. Instead, it is the mistranslation of 'Kampfspiele' as 'Olympic games' in the English-language edition of the *Philosophical Investigations* (see L. Wittgenstein, *Philosophical Investigations*, 3rd edn, trans. G. E. M. Anscombe, Oxford: Blackwell, 1972, §66). Greeks continue to call them '*agones*', which is best rendered 'contests'. On the view I am advancing, 'games' in the expression 'Olympic games' operates as a metonym.
5. For the observation that, notwithstanding the dominance of the rhetoric of skill and achievement over that of fortune or fate among the professional classes, the amount of money spent annually on games of chance in the United States ($400 billion) exceeds that spent on all others combined, as well as the defence budget, see B. Sutton-Smith, *The Ambiguity of Play*, Cambridge, MA: Harvard University Press, 1997, p. 66.
6. Mae West: Is poker a game of chance? W. C. Fields: Not the way I play it.—*My Little Chickadee*.
7. For an attempt to understand human well-being itself in terms of the enjoyment of excellence, see R. M. Adams, *Finite and Infinite Goods: A Framework for Ethics*, Oxford: Oxford University Press, 1999, Ch. 3. This thesis faces the difficulty that 'excellence', if it is not simply identical with goodness, is either a high level of (attainable) goodness or else a type of goodness, for example, that which merits admiration. Either way, it is radically incomplete as an account of well-being, since engagement with good (but not excellent) things can enhance one's life. Moreover, Adams makes strained judgements—both about the source of an activity's value and the presence of excellence—that only confirm this incompleteness, for example, that physical pleasure is 'normally an enjoyment of healthy life, which ... is an excellence', or that 'bad' art can enhance our lives only because the latter 'typically has excellences, in some degree' (op. cit., pp. 100–1).
8. George Orwell, 'The Sporting Spirit', in *George Orwell: Essays*, London: Penguin, 2000, pp. 322, 324.
9. Herodotus, *The Histories* I.94; Sutton-Smith, op. cit., Ch. 2.
10. For some examples from English-language philosophy in recent years, see J. Finnis, *Natural Law and Natural Rights*, Oxford: Oxford University Press, 1980, p. 87 (listing play as a basic form of human good); G. Grisez and R. Shaw, *Beyond the New Morality: The Responsibilities of Freedom*, 3rd edn, Notre Dame, IN: University of Notre Dame Press, 1988, Ch. 7; M. Nussbaum, *Women and Human Development: The Capabilities Approach*, Oxford: Oxford University Press, 2000, p. 80 (listing play as a 'central human functional capability'); and M. Oakeshott, 'Work and Play', in *What is History? and Other Essays*, Exeter; Imprint Academic, 2004.
11. J. Huizinga, *Homo Ludens: A Study of the Play Element in Culture*, Boston: Beacon Press, 1955, pp. 13, 132. I have also benefited from R. Caillois, *Man, Play and Games*, Urbana, IL: University of Illinois Press, 2001.

12. By contrast, on Suits's definition, a fight to the death (provided it is governed by at least one constitutive rule, e.g. one that sets a start time, that is accepted by the fighters in order to engage in the activity made possible) is just as much a game as chess (op. cit., Ch. 6).

13. 'There are no pleasures in a fight but some of my fights have been a pleasure to win' (Muhammad Ali).

14. Finnis, op. cit., pp. 96–7.

15. Here I invoke Roger Caillois's fourfold classification of games according to the characteristic attitude that animates them: 'the desire to win by one's merit in regulated competition (*agôn*), the submission of one's will in favor of anxious and passive anticipation of where the wheel will stop (*alea*), the desire to assume a strange personality (*mimicry*), and, finally, the pursuit of vertigo (*ilinx*)' (op. cit., p. 44; see also pp. 14–26).

16. J. C. Oates, *On Boxing*, New York: Harper Collins, 2002, pp. 18–19.

17. Orwell, op. cit., p. 322.

18. C. Lasch, *The Culture of Narcissism: American Life in an Age of Diminishing Expectations*, New York: Norton, 1978, p. 65.

19. 'Instead of regarding "work" and "play" as two great and diverse experiences of the world, each offering us what the other lacks, we are often encouraged to regard all that I have called "play", either as a holiday designed to make us "work" better when it is over, or merely as "work" of another sort' (Oakeshott, op. cit., p. 313).

20. It is in this vein that James Griffin defends the value of 'accomplishment', which he describes as 'roughly the sort of value that gives life weight or point'—see J. Griffin, *Value Judgement: Improving our Ethical Beliefs*, Oxford: Oxford University Press, 1996, p. 24.

21. This understanding of happiness or well-being as achievement is explicitly presented in J. Annas, 'Happiness as Achievement', *Daedalus*, Spring 2004, pp. 44–51. However, it can also be found (without explicit reference to achievement) in J. Raz, *Ethics and the Public Domain*, Oxford: Oxford University Press, 1994, Ch. 1.

22. Griffin, op. cit., p. 20.

23. Cf. Aristotle, *Nicomachean Ethics*, 1140b.

24. The relational view is thus anticipated by Aquinas: 'When something is more difficult, it is not for that reason necessarily more worthwhile, but it must be more difficult in such a way, as also to be at a higher level of goodness' (*Summa Theologiae* II-II, Q.27, a.8, ad 3um).

25. Hurka's concession here is grudging (see p. 225, n. 7): 'Some may deny that difficulty is as such good, on the ground that an activity aimed at evil, such as genocide, is not in any way made good by its difficulty. The issue here is complex,

... but those moved by this objection can retreat to the weaker claim that only activities with good or neutral aims gain value by being difficult.' In the end, he would not allow the concession to stand, because achievement figures as a 'base-level value' in his recursive theory of virtue, and it is essential to its having that status that it can be specified independently of both (a) other base-level values, and (b) any reference to morally good or evil attitudes. See, T. Hurka, *Virtue, Vice, and Value*, New York: Oxford University Press, 2001, pp. 144–52. One way of reading my argument in this section is as denying that achievement is a 'base-level value' in this sense.

26. It is not the good of achievement; and I leave aside the possibility, that overcoming of difficulty may have some intrinsic value *qua* expression of practical and theoretical reasoning.

27. Cf. '[W]e must recall the distinction between, on the one hand, values in which we participate but which we do not exhaust and, on the other hand, the particular projects we undertake and objectives we pursue (normally, if we are reasonable, as ways of participating in values) and which can at a given point of time be said to have been fully attained, or not, as the case may be' (Finnis, op. cit., p. 155).

28. F. Nietzsche, *The Will to Power*, trans. W. Kaufmann and R. J. Hollingdale, New York: Vintage, 1968, Sect. 46.

29. '[W]e can say that authenticity (A) involves (i) creation and construction as well as discovery, (ii) originality, and frequently (iii) opposition to the rules of society and even potentially to what we recognize as morality. But it is also true ... that it (B) requires (i) openness to horizons of significance (for otherwise the creation loses the background that can save it from insignificance) ... That these demands may be in tension has to be allowed. But what must be wrong is a simple privileging of one over the other ... This is what the trendy doctrines of "deconstruction" involve today. They stress (A.i), the constitutive, creative nature of our expressive languages, while altogether forgetting (B.i) ...' (C. Taylor, *The Ethics of Authenticity*, Cambridge, MA: Harvard University Press, 1991, pp. 66–7).

30. J. Rawls, *A Theory of Justice*, revised edn, Oxford: Oxford University Press, 1999, pp. 455–6.

31. I wish to thank Roger Crisp, James Griffin, John Ma, Joseph Raz, Helen Steward, Christopher Taylor, David Wiggins and Susan Wolf for helpful comments and discussion. I am also grateful to Constantine Tasioulas for the valuable insights into this topic that he has afforded me.

References

Adams, R. M. 1999: *Finite and Infinite Goods: A Framework for Ethics*. Oxford: Oxford University Press.

Annas, J. 2004: 'Happiness as Achievement', *Daedalus*, Spring 2004.

Aquinas; *Summa Theologiae*.

Aristotle: *Nicomachean Ethics*.

Caillois, R. 2001: *Man, Play and Games*. Urbana, IL and Chicago: University of Illinois Press.

Finnis, J. 1980: *Natural Law and Natural Rights*. Oxford: Oxford University Press.

Griffin, J. 1996: *Value Judgement: Improving our Ethical Beliefs*. Oxford: Oxford University Press.

Grisez, G. and R. Shaw 1988: *Beyond the New Morality: The Responsibilities of Freedom*, 3rd edn. Notre Dame, IN: University of Notre Dame Press.

Herodotus, *The Histories*.

Huizinga, J. 1955: *Homo Ludens: A Study of the Play Element in Culture*. Boston: Beacon Press.

Hurka, T. 2001: *Virtue, Vice, and Value*. New York: Oxford University Press.

—— 2006: 'Games and the Good'. *Proceedings of the Aristotelian Society*, Supplementary Volume 80, pp. 217–35.

Lasch, C. 1978: *The Culture of Narcissism: American Life in an Age of Diminishing Expectations*. New York: Norton.

Nietzsche, F. 1968: *The Will to Power*. Trans. W. Kaufmann and R. J. Hollingdale. New York: Vintage.

Nussbaum, M. 2000: *Women and Human Development: The Capabilities Approach*. Oxford: Oxford University Press.

Oakeshott, M. 2004: 'Work and Play'. In *What is History? and Other Essays*. Exeter: Imprint Academic.

Oates, J. C. 2002: *On Boxing*. New York: Harper Collins.

Orwell, G. 2000: 'The Sporting Spirit'. In *George Orwell: Essays*. London: Penguin.

Rawls, J. 1999: *A Theory of Justice*, rev. edn. Oxford: Oxford University Press.

Raz, J. 1994: *Ethics and the Public Domain*. Oxford: Oxford University Press.

Suits, B. 1990: *The Grasshopper: Games, Life and Utopia*. Boston: David R. Godine.

Sutton-Smith, B. 1997: *The Ambiguity of Play*. Cambridge, MA: Harvard University Press.

Taylor, C. 1991: *The Ethics of Authenticity*. Cambridge, MA: Harvard University Press.

Wittgenstein, L. 1972: *Philosophical Investigations*, 3rd edn. Trans. G. E. M. Anscombe. Oxford: Blackwell.

Sport

An historical phenomenology

Anthony Skillen

Sport often seems to teeter on the edge, on one side of the entertainment industry, on the other of cheating violent aggression: from a make-believe simulacrum of serious play to a nasty chemically enhanced descent into a Hobbesian state of nature. Such perversions lend credibility to reductive views of sport itself as a metonymic feature of capitalism. But that sport as entertainment means fixing it to produce exciting outcomes and amplifying capacities to superhuman proportions, while sport as aggression means treating rules as mere obstacles to brute dominance, shows how far we in fact are from these abysses, even in the days of the Coca Cola/Nike Olympics, Vinny Jones and cricket sledging. In this essay, I try to delineate through history—from Homer to … Gomer?—a common culture of sport and sportsmanship that, with its excesses and perversions, continues to operate as one, albeit complex, ideal of human excellence.

George Carey set off a ripple of laughter at his enthronement as Archbishop of Canterbury by quoting Liverpool Football Club's old manager, Bill Shankly's 'Football is not a matter of life or death; it's more important than that'. But he was in the highest tradition:

> You know, do you not, that at the sports all the runners run in the race, though only one wins

the prize. Like them, run to win! But every athlete goes into strict training. They do it to win a fading wreath, win a wreath that never fades … I am like the boxer who does not beat the air.[1]

We have more than one model and there is more than one way of sport's distinctness from the normal run of life. 'Only a game' suggests an appropriate lack of serious purpose. 'It's not cricket' assumes cricket as a paradigm of human worth.

Greatness, games and the Greeks

Hannah Arendt, learning, she claimed, from the Ancient Athenians, divided life into three main areas: 'labour', 'work' and 'action'.[2] *Labour*, the lowest category and the lot of the lowest in society, was the necessary drudgery whose aim is biological survival. Animal in aim, labour is, as she conceives it, animal, even 'mechanical' in form: mindless and repetitive and, like any biological process in that its outcome is lost in consumption or disposal. This is servile activity under the thumb of necessity. *Work*, the next level, consists in the more or less skilled production of more or less durable artefacts—the vessels made from the

Anthony Skillen 'Sport: An Historical Phenomenology', from *Philosophy*, Vol. 68, pp. 344–368. © 1993 Anthony Skillen. Reprinted by permission of Cambridge University Press.

labour-extracted clay, in which the labourer's produce is served. This is the realm of craft, of the making of a distinctively human world out of the materials nature yields. Though reflecting the individual skill of their producers, work's creations are, like the outcomes of labour, subordinated to ends beyond themselves: shelter, nourishment, warfare—to utility. *Action*, the highest realm, consists of what might more idiomatically be called 'deeds', of public and publicly esteemed actions of individuals living in or stepping into the 'arena' or 'stage' of decisions, enterprises, struggles, whose outcome is seldom predictable and whose consummation is glory. Achilles, 'doer of great deeds and speaker of great words', is a paradigm, his heroics immortalized in popular tradition as well as in Homer's *Iliad*. Whereas the workman's creation may survive for ages, his own position tends to anonymity. But the hero, the participant in great affairs, constitutes his public identity through his conduct, and it is in the public eye and ear that such actions are embarked on. Hence, whatever their objective consequences, actions do not outlive their completion unless they are recounted, remembered and commemorated. The man of action lives in the realm of honour and glory. Insignificance, neglect, dishonour, derision are what he fears more than the destruction of objects (work's products) or of life (labour's concern).

In *On Revolution*, Arendt gives a wonderful illustration of what she means by the spirit of 'action'. She quotes the American revolutionary John Adams:

> The poor man's conscience is clear; yet he is ashamed ... He feels himself out of sight of all others, groping in the dark. Mankind takes no notice of him ... In the midst of a crowd, at church, in the market ... he is in as much obscurity as he would be in a garret or a cellar. He is not disapproved, censured or reproached; he is only not seen ... To be wholly overlooked and to know it are intolerable.[3]

Arendt's categories are open to criticism. 'Labour' and 'work' for example are defined by their goals, yet she assumes that they are characterized equally by their modes—mechanical against skilled. (In this context, by the way, she draws a superbly illuminating contrast between craft specialization and Adam Smith–Henry Ford type 'division of labour'.) But artefacts can

be produced 'mechanically' and amazing skill can go into the struggles of survival, let alone that most 'immediately consumable' good, a meal. Arendt tends to assume that labour, being under the rule of necessity ('enslavement to nature'), is by the same token under the thumb of masters ('enslavement to man'). But these dimensions should be kept analytically separate. The position of the artist, even if we confine our attention to the ancients: of the famous sculptors, architects and poetic singers of deeds, is anomalous in a scheme which counts art 'work'. Arendt valorizes Athenian democracy and the public forum of speeches as 'conversation'. But she plays down the decisive role of 'great' demagogues in whipping up the assembly to fervent militarism; she writes shy of the invidious harshness of the 'agonistic' struggle for greatness and of the bloody heartlessness of much of the aristocratic action most bathed in glory at the time. Plato's critique of the corruptibility inherent in the 'timarchic' life:[4] of the tendency to deceit, and of the way reputation becomes a means to material advantage rather than a sacred trust, is underplayed in Arendt's urge to contrast ancient glory with modern servility. Arendt's trio might be thought of as possible dimensions of many activities: there is labour, and work, involved in the most consummate actions. None the less, as a framework within which to develop an Olympian perspective on the modern world, labour-work-action are invaluable categories. But it is sport, unmentioned by Arendt, that is action par excellence.

Although warfare and political debate take place in the pursuit of 'policies', of concrete objectives, it is as constituents of a culture, of a way of life and of the self-identity of an individual and of a people that actions, for Arendt, have their primary meaning. Homer voices this vision: Achilles, eager to avenge Patroclus,

> made sign to the Achaean host and shook his head to show that no man was to aim a dart at Hector, lest another might win the glory of having hit him and he himself might come in second (*Iliad* 367).

Hector, realizing himself outmatched, responds (to the inevitability of a fight—in full view of the Gods and the Trojans):

> My doom has come upon me; let me not die ingloriously and without a struggle, but let me

first do some great thing that shall be told among men hereafter (*Iliad* 369).[5]

Achilles is determined not only to defeat Hector but to dishonour him. Having refused Hector's plea for an agreement about due treatment of the vanquished's body, and having killed his rival champion, with vengeful viciousness and in contempt of the dying man's last prayer, he seeks (unsuccessfully) to render Hector's body unrecognizable and fit only as meat for dogs and vultures, by dragging it ostentatiously around behind his chariot. As a further mark of the Homeric hero's preoccupation with honour, he elects, though Troy is at his mercy, to devote a day to games in celebration of Patroclus' funeral. No Francis-Drake-like demonstration of nonchalance, these games are an appropriate and necessary tribute. No time out from the real struggle, they have their own stature as part of the realm of action. The gods, indeed, watch and intervene just as they do in the Trojan war itself.

That heroic excellence is some distance from Socratic virtue is manifest from the fifth century Pindar:

> Whensoever a man who hath done noble deeds descendeth to the abode of Hades without the meed of song, he hath spent his strength and his breath in vain and winneth but little pleasure by his toil, whereas thou hast glory shed upon thee by the soft-toned lyre and by the sweet flute, and thy fame waxeth widely (Olympic Ode X).

Again:

> When toilsome contests have been decided the best of healers is good cheer and songs that are the sage daughters of the muses are wont to soothe the victor by their touch. Nor doth warm water soothe the limbs in such welcome wise as praise that is linked with the lyre. Louder than deeds liveth the word, whatsoever it be that the tongue,—by the favour of the Graces, draweth forth from the depth of the heart (Nemean Ode IV).[6]

I have passed from the heroism of war to the heroism of the athletic contest. It ought also to be noted that Pindar not only sees his commemorative odes as constitutively establishing the champion's glory, ('one thing thirsts for another, but victory loves song best') but, contrary to Arendt's placings, accords his own lyric an equal status to that of the magnificent athlete's performance. For the ode shares divinity-seeking perfection with the bodily action of the victor. It is not only a matter of action's dependence on words for its fame, nor as if the poem belonged alongside scalps and armour as a lasting trophy; the poetic celebration appropriately matches the athlete's glory in another mode and thereby lays its own claim to greatness.

Werner Jaeger expressed this intimate union in the following terms:

> The athlete whom these sculptures portray in the harmonious strength and nobility of this utmost perfection, lives, feels and speaks for us again in Pindar's poetry, and through his spiritual energy and religious gravity, still affects us with the strange power which is given to the unique and irrecoverable achievements of the human spirit. For it was a uniquely precious moment when a god-intoxicated but human world of Greece saw the height of divinity in the human body and soul raised to a perfection high above earthly powers and when in those Gods of human shape the effort of man to copy that divine model through which artists had realized the law of perfection, unattainable yet imperious, found its purpose and its happiness.[7]

To the extent that man seeks to partake of divine excellence, the earthly ambitions of territory or wealth, let alone of mere property and material comfort, are set at low value. Thus does the hero, whether in war or wrestling match, pray for victory or death. By the same token then, the sort of greatness alluded to by Arendt, the military and the political, is inherently compromised by its utilitarian dimension. Sport, games, play, then, stand out in relief, and not just as relief, in the purity of their pointlessness. They take place in the arena of the exhibition for its own sake of heroic virtue: strength, courage, skill, stamina, patience, judgment, quickness of mind, style, and enterprise: of the struggle to attain one's potential and to excel. Shorn of the mythic lineage of Greek theology whereby the Gods themselves admire the attainments of their mortal descendants, such besting requires social acknowledgement, recognition. We are not now talking only of the 'Aristotelian Principle' of John Rawls, according to which:

> other things being equal, human beings enjoy the exercise of their realized capacities (their innate or trained abilities) and this enjoyment increases the more the capacity is realized, or the greater its complexity.[8]

Such ('workmanlike') pleasures consist in their possibly private exercise. Action's happiness is in fact closer to Robert Nozick's more Pindaric principle:

> People generally judge themselves by how they fall along the most important dimensions in which they differ from others.[9]

Indeed, Aristotle himself has a more public and aristocratic vision of the happy life than Rawls' cheerful craftsman model allows, for his 'magnificent' gentleman is 'properly' concerned to display his qualities and to receive due praise.[10]

There is a salutary contemporary backlash among historians against the 'mythic' elevation of the Ancient Games by the Victorians and their inheritors of the ideology of amateurism, of sport for love.[11] These illusions are thought to be immortalized in the utopian words of the modern Olympics' founder, Baron de Coubertin:

> The important thing in the Olympic Games is not to win but to take part, as the most important thing in life is not the triumph but the struggle. The essential thing is not to have conquered but to have fought well.[12]

On the contrary, such was the attitude to 'taking part' that, not only did the winner in the Ancient Olympics alone receive a prize, the loser had to endure such ignominy as this from Pindar:

> Alicimedon, by heaven-sent good fortune, but with no slackness in his own prowess, thrust off from himself on the bodies of four boys, a most hateful return amid jibes of contempt, while they slink to their homes unseen ... Ye know that the grave is forgotten by him who has won befitting fame (*Olympian Ode* VIII).[13]

And Epictetus says:

> In the Olympic Games, you cannot just be beaten and then depart, but first of all, you will

be disgraced, not only before the people of Athens or Sparta or Nikopoulos but before the whole world.[14]

Such, moreover, was the attitude to the intrinsic rewards of athletic prowess, that contests were for big prizes, for which the laurel wreath is said to have been a mere token. Payment, says Donald Kyle, was taken for granted,[15] while our distinction between amateur and professional was merely the difference between those in part and those in full-time training. David Young tells us that a sprinter's income from a major win in the fifth century was the equivalent of three full years' wages for a skilled worker, enabling him to buy a fine house and slaves to go with it.

There was no prize for second at the ancient Olympics. But historians are rash to assume that, in the inevitably lost oral culture, no honour attached to good losers, that there was no conception of a bravely lost fight or race well fought or run. In an event which we shall examine in more detail below, the paradigmatic funeral games for Patroclus in the *Iliad*, Achilles offers not only a first prize for the chariot race, but a fifth prize, and that in a five man contest. So it would be unwise to assume that Olympic prizes and Pindar's odes are an accurate reflection of the distribution of honour. Imagine someone from your village winning the right to compete in the first place! Nor should the revisionists be allowed to have all their own way on the issue of 'professionalism' or 'payment'. For we ought not to assume that the magnificent prizes offered stood to the successful performance simply as mere 'payment' for a win, as if the magnificence of the prize were a matter, not of pride, but only of avarice. In a culture that is both materialistic and emulative, material 'recognition' was a visible and durable form of esteem—if a champion athlete is a demigod, he deserves to live and to be seen to live like one. If, from the other side, the rich patron of a contest is a great man capable of recognising greatness in athletic achievement, he had better offer prizes appropriate to the esteem proclaimed.

If more recent historians are to be trusted, then the fathers of sports history, such as H. A. Harris[16] and E. Norman Gardiner,[17] allow idealism to generate their vision of an amateur aristocratic golden age replaced only after many decades by the 'Nemesis' of an hitherto creeping 'professionalism', reaching its peak with the replacement of Greek athletics by the stadium spectacles of Rome. But the idealists' fault may have lain more in their chronology than in their sense of ancient values at play. For it is surely important that, although from the sixth century BC an Olympic victor could expect to be not only famous but rich, these riches came to him as triumph from his own city patrons and from appearance money at 'Prize' Games. The Olympics themselves retained the aura of the 'sacred', with the laurel wreath as the official prize. So 'prize' was conceptually distinct from 'reward'. Moreover, as I have suggested, 'reward' itself was honorifically bestowed and should itself be distinguished from the more 'alienated' phenomenon of 'income' seen in abstraction from honour. This abstraction had its concrete expression in athletes' pursuit of the wealth the many games' prizes offered and in the transfer for gain of athletes' allegiance from one place to another. But, however frequent, such contempt for honour was contrary to the norms and ideals of the time: when the reigning champion Astylus switched nationalities for the 480 Olympics,

> His fellow citizens, indignant at what must have seemed an act of sacrilege, destroyed the statues they had erected in his honour and turned his house into a common prison.[18]

This is not the response of a public inured to what we think of as professionalism. We might expect then that, as today, the most mercenary performers would know that their bread was buttered by maintaining and even exaggerating the trappings of glory as an end in itself, in preserving the Homeric mystique. The hero's contempt for mere gain is superbly expressed in the *Odyssey*. Entertained as an unknown guest in a royal household, the mighty Odysseus is invited to join the athletic contest:

> I hope, Sir, that you will enter yourself for one or other of our competitions if you are skilled in any of them—and you must have gone in for many a one before now. There is nothing that brings any one so much credit all his life long as the showing of himself a proper man with his hands and feet.[19]

Trying to excuse himself from what would be an embarrassing and revealing pushover, Odysseus pleads that grief make acceptance disagreeable. He is, however, successfully goaded by this worst of insults:

> I gather then that you are unskilled in any of the many sports that men generally delight in. I suppose you are one of those grasping traders that go about in ships as captains and merchants, and who think of nothing but of their outward freights and homeward cargoes. There does not seem to be much of the athlete about you.[20]

But it is on the *Iliad* that I want to concentrate:

> He brought prizes from the ships—cauldrons, tripods, horses and mules, noble oxen, women with fair girdles, and swart iron.[21]

Thus in commemorating Patroclus does Achilles set up the stakes as he summons the contenders from among his athletic military elite. It is unnecessary to labour the fierce competitiveness of the proceedings. I want rather to emphasize the dimension of 'sportsmanship' that current writings are prone to deny. I would go further: Achilles has just gone over the limit in his revenge against the more roundedly heroic Hector. He has thus risked the Gods' anger. It seems to me that these games, strategically placed in the epic, have almost literally the status of a play-within-the-play, with heroic values being asserted here against the hubristic ambitions of the participants.[22]

Early on in the major event, the chariot race,[23] Antilochus dangerously crowds Menelaus, 'Cheat', cries the latter 'You'll not bear away the prize without sworn protest on my part'. Eumelus, his yoke broken by Minerva's intervention, finishes at the tail. But Achilles says 'The best man is coming in last. Let us give him a prize for it is appropriate.' So he awards him second place, thereby relegating to third place Antilochus, who protests that Minerva's sabotage was due punishment for Eumelus' lack of prayer. Antilochus urges Achilles not to deny him his second prize but, if he must, give Eumelus gold from his own tent, worth if he likes, as much or more than the coveted prize itself. 'But I will not give up the mare and he that will fight me for it let him come on'. Achilles, moved by the argument, gives Eumelus a trophy breastplate. At that point Menelaus voices his protest against Antilochus' deliberately cutting him and challenges him to swear by Neptune to the contrary. Antilochus admits his foul. 'I would rather yield [the mare] to you at once than fall from your good graces and do wrong in the sight of heaven'. Honour satisfied, Menelaus 'freely grants' his rightful prize to Antilochus—'the people will then see that I am neither harsh nor vindictive'—and accepts the third prize of the cauldron. To complete this particular contest of anomalies, the uncompeted-for fifth prize goes to old Nestor, Antilochus' father, in honour of his former eminence. Thereafter, in the boxing, the winner helps support the hurt loser, the wrestling match is declared a tie as it seems so evenly balanced, the third-placed runner accepts his prize with humble laughter and the spear fight is called off for fear of a death, the prize going to the superior combatant. All in all then, these games display a range of paradigms around the theme of sportsmanship and make a mockery of the idea that Greek athletic values scarcely rose above the brutal or commercial. And, given the pedagogic authority of Homer, we can say that sporting ideals existed. This is not to deny the permanent reality of mere pot-hunting or of cheating. It is, however, to assert the reality of 'sportsmanship' as a recognized virtue, as a cultural fact.

Onlookers, partisans and the Romans

I want to bring out some aspects of this ethos that have been only implicit in the discussion so far.

To be 'glorious' one must stand out, not only against vanquished or disgraced rivals but against those who are not even 'in the race'; the ordinary run of mankind, at least in terms of that event. Moreover, one must stand out to an 'audience', first of observers, second of those for whom the event is mediated by reporters—whether bards, chroniclers or humbler eyewitnesses. The realm of 'action' as a public realm requires a 'public'. This is evident in Homer: Achilles' battle with Hector is watched, not only by the gods (hence 'the gods' at the theatre), who 'take our places on some hill off the beaten track and let mortals fight it out' (*Iliad* XX, 133), not only by the Achaean host, but also, from the city walls, by the alarmed Trojan citizens, especially Priam and Hector.

Andromache, as befits a wife, is not present to see the horrible action. She is within her proper, private realm, 'at her loom, in an inner part of the house, weaving a double purple web, and embroidering it with many flowers' and having a bath prepared for the return of the already killed and violated Hector (*Iliad*, 437). 'Watching' all this is the omniscient poet, bestowing human immortality on the whole proceedings. At the funeral games, in addition to the mythic presence of the gods, the presence 'in spirit' of Patroclus ('Farewell, Patroclus!') and the metaphoric presence of the poet, there is of course the Achaean crowd. Standing out in that crowd is Achilles himself, the games' great and in this context truly noble patron, capable, were he to condescend, of beating any of the contestants at their own games. For the great chariot race, as if he were scripting a great movie, Homer moves partly into direct speech, relating the progress through a spectator's running commentary ... 'Come up and see for yourselves, I cannot make out for certain but the driver seems. ...'He is brusquely interrupted by a rival commentator:

> You are not one of the youngest, nor are your eyes among the sharpest, but you are always laying down the law. You have no right to do so, for there are better men here than you are. Eumelus' horses are in front now.

His rival-in-judgment angrily meets the challenge with a big bet on himself. But Achilles majestically silences the 'unseemly' and 'scandalous' row and focuses attention back on the real event.

If this passage shows up the normal spectators, Homer gives them a different status after the race. Then, in the controversy over prizes, they assume the right, as an assembly rather than as a mere crowd, to influence on Achilles' decisions. And when Menelaus returns the second prize to the remorseful cheat Antilochus so that, as we have seen, 'the people will see that I am neither harsh nor vindictive', Antilochus for his part confesses his misdemeanour rather than proclaim the propriety of his driving conduct on oath before the judgment of Neptune. So not only do earthly spectators adopt a variety of roles, the gods themselves pass without much apology from race-riggers to justices.

Why be concerned with the spectator? As we have seen, Arendt's account of action entails an audience. But to return to her paradigmatic 'hero' John Adams, quoted already,

> the poor man … is ashamed. He feels himself out of sight of all others, groping in the dark. Mankind takes no notice of him … To be wholly overlooked and to know it are intolerable.

If a culture sets the glory of victory in conspicuous exploits as a pinnacle of excellence, then, by the same token as they share that valuation and bestow glory on the Great Men, the many who, by definition, cannot themselves be part of this aristocracy of the body, are in the position of implicit acknowledgment of their own inglorious defectiveness and invisibility—'intolerable'. To the extent that the culture is one of competition for honour and one shares that culture, then, in so far as one is not honoured one is not only not a success, one is a failure. Whether on a seat or standing, the average spectator is a bum—yet he jeers at the loser in the game itself.

This constitutive unpleasantness was perhaps pre-empted in fully aristocratic cultures where you had to be an aristocrat to enjoy the privilege of participating in 'action' and where the lack of utilitarian motivation defined the activity as proper to the free man. It is precisely in this context that, in his great *Theory of the Leisure Class*, the American sociologist Thorstein Veblen in 1899 located sport. His account casts a critical shadow on 'action' that is foreign to Arendt's glorying account:

> The rule holds with but slight exception that, whether warriors or priests, the upper classes are exempt from industrial employments and this exemption is the economic expression of their superior rank …
>
> Under this ancient distinction, the worthy employments are those which may be classed as exploit; unworthy are those necessary everyday employments into which no appreciable element of exploit enters …
>
> These manifestations of the predatory temperament are all to be classed under the head of exploit. They are partly … expressions of an attitude of emulative ferocity, partly activities deliberately entered upon with a view to gaining repute for prowess … Sports shade off from the basis of hostile combat, through skill, to cunning and chicanery, without it being possible to draw a line at any point. The ground of an addiction to sports is an archaic spiritual constitution—the possession of the

predatory emulative propensity in a relatively high potency … A strong propensity to adventuresome exploit and to the infliction of damage is … especially pronounced in … sportsmanship.[24]

So if athletics, like generalship, is the aristocracy's own god-like game, the mass can admire, even shower glory, in the secure sense that they are not in the class of their betters through the divine providence that determines their 'ascribed' social status, not through their failing to match up to an ideal that properly regulates their lives.

In more democratic cultures whose elite of sporting heroes are not confined to an hereditary aristocracy, the sense of failure is opposed by the possibility of identification: to the extent that an audience 'identifies' with its heroes it shares in their glory. If 'we' won, I through my 'representative' won. I am proud, I can look down, not only on the vanquished athlete but on the 'them' that he represents. This identifying capacity, which in young children is part of the imitation that is at the heart of Plato and Aristotle's conception of art. ('Trabert lobs but Hoad jumps and smashes it away!' Mutters the Australian tennis tyro in a magnificent self-commentary as he swipes clumsily at the ball rebounding from the wall. 'The Australian has won! The crowd goes mad!')

I may identify with an individual champion. But if, as since the ancient Olympics, athletes have regional and local identities, then this is no mere personal fantasy. Rather it becomes a constitutive part of the imagining of community, of the affective unity of a collectivity. And to the extent that this unity is a matter of 'sharing' in victories, whether military or sporting, the 'rant and swagger' which Veblen[25] found pervasive among sportsmen filters down to non-participants who, more than 'fans', become intoxicated as if they themselves had drunk from the victory cup rather than from the beer can. And so instead of feeling a 'wholly overlooked' nobody in the civic street, the individual, himself perhaps an utter incompetent, exults in a fantasy of triumphal 'active' citizenship. So the proudest moment of *his* life may be 'the time when Stan McCabe hit Larwood all around the Sydney Cricket Ground'. And so although it is indeed the case that just because the few are gloriously successful the many are humble failures, it is also the case that the many are flushed with pride through their champions' achievements and when glory is denied this unstably narcissistic identification projects itself in vengeful derision on to the 'clowns', 'mugs', 'girls' in whom all hopes had been placed.

A third refuge from the pain of the not-even-also-ran, given again, a shared sporting culture, is a consequence of 'professionalism'. For if the athlete is a professional his excellence passes from one any one might-but-does-not share to one that is a product of a specialized aptitude and dedication requiring the abandonment of other work and, for that matter, other pleasures. The professional then, can be admired without the admirer having to endure a sense of humiliation, by those with a different 'job'.

There is a huge distinction between the background necessity for an audience of lesser mortals to constitute a champion's glory and the champion's being there only because there are people to applaud and financially maintain him. Similarly, there is a huge distinction between the privilege that an audience feels in being present at a great contest and the sense a crowd might have that it has a right to be impressed and entertained. None the less the conceptual link that I have been stressing between 'action' and audience exposes the deep but fine line between sport and entertainment, or show business. And, although the spectator at professional sports is likely to be aware of his own frailty as a physical actor, he is compensated by the sense that, as part of the public, he has the power to shape, if not this particular game, then the fate of the game itself—it exists after all *for* his pleasure.[26] Consumer sovereignty means that, except as a gimmick, the athlete had better 'respect' the public and not disdain the common man in the manner of an aristocratic Pindaric hero.

As the charioteers charged around the field at the games for Patroclus, spectators as we saw had to be restrained by Achilles from an unseemly verbal brawl. 'Hooliganism' appears to have been characteristic of spectators from the start. It represents, arguably, a fourth balm for the witnesses of excellence. Begotten by imitative identification out of envy, this ugly near-universal, occasionally redeemed by bardic wit, guarantees a punk piece of the 'action' to people otherwise beyond its perimeter. The hooligan, in other words, both apes and competes for attention with the champions. At the same time, he asserts his identifying attachment to this against that country, region, town, district, club or colour, an attachment which may well be deeper than that felt by professional sportsmen kitted out far from any soil that may be native to them in the colours of the highest bidder. In a fashion, albeit ritualized and sometimes restrained, the hooligan expresses the militaristic aggression in the sport itself, but unsublimated by its rules and unanswerable to its referee. Local explanations of hooliganism ought to be qualified by the thought not only of its relative ubiquity, but of its ancient, even divine lineage: Homer's gods, as we have seen, orchestrated ancient wars as mortal proxies of their own immortal rivalries, using human beings 'for their sport'.

Bobby Moore, who had captained England's victorious World Cup soccer team in 1966, wrote in the *Daily Mail*:

> I've a simple message to that moronic minority who do not go to watch football and its great players, but go to fight, throw missiles at policemen, invade the pitch and make an utter nuisance of themselves. Clear off.[27]

But, in his study of the great Roman crowds two thousand years ago, *Roman Factions*, Alan Cameron offers reasons for doubting the efficacy of Moore's message:

> The games can serve as a field where the youth who lives an otherwise ordinary and unexciting life can prove himself a man by fighting and destroying, hunting in a pack with his peers; for an hour or two he can be an object of fear to all who cross his path.[28]

So timocratic cultures, I am arguing, have a conflict built into their ego-tripping core which shows itself in a range of options for the common man. Hence, it seems to me, what we might think of as the 'ideal' spectator: the appreciative admirer of 'great play', must himself have a measure of grounding independent of the sport's honorific culture itself such that his modesty of achievement is matched by personal humility, enabling him to resemble the second-century Roman writer Lucian:

> No one can describe in mere words the extraordinary pleasure derived from [Greek games] ... feasting your eyes on the prowess and stamina

of the athletes, the beauty and power of their bodies, their incredible dexterity and skill, their invincible strength, their courage, ambition endurance and tenacity. You would never stop applauding them.[29]

In the Roman world the spectator and the colossal circuses that housed him (and her),[30] came into their own. Not only was sport, especially chariot racing, big business, its significance in political life was recognized. The 'factions', supporters of the various racing 'colours' competing for glory, more materially sought to influence political decisions. Meanwhile, it seems, their focus on the make-believe world of the circus made them distractable from the harder realities of life. The cultural decadence inherent in all this is not something I wish to contest. Suffice it here to say that the 'moment' of spectatorial 'fan' consumerism and surrogate power-assertion has already been prefigured in our account of sport in its 'classical' phase.

Given the above, though, it is interesting that among the Roman elite there was widespread contempt for what was seen as the specifically Greek way of sport.[31] First, their near-naked wrestling was seen as tending to homosexuality and narcissism, to an 'unmanliness' that belied the military values thought to be expressed and reinforced in proper sporting activity. Secondly, and perhaps more interestingly, the Greek mania for victory and intolerance of defeat was seen, again, as unmanly and dishonourable. The Roman gentleman was to compete, as he was to fight, virtuously. His virtues, indeed, were manifested in defeat as much as in victory, for they were qualities of character as much as proficiencies of art. Here though, and again, the rules and conduct of Homer's funeral games again prefigure this, it is central that sport is an activity constituted and regulated by rules, reverence for which is therefore a part of the sportsman's ethos. So profoundly does this attitude appear to have embedded itself in Roman culture that generals on condition that their nobility and courage in the face of the enemy was attested, suffered no shame, loss of credibility or power, at home through defeat.[32] Character rather than craft had such priority that public criticism of what we would call 'generalship' regarding strategy and tactics was an extreme rarity.

So it is wrong to rubbish the Romans as merely wine-soaked addicts of the circus.

The Roman sporting culture was Janus-faced and so that culture 'points forward' with both cheeks to the Victorians and their successors.

Christian muscularity and the Victorians

'You say you don't see much in it at all; nothing but a struggling mass of boys, and a leather ball, which seems to excite them to a great fury, as a red rag does a bull. My dear Sir, a battle would look much the same to you, except the boys would be men and the balls iron; but a battle would be worth your while looking at for all that, and so is a football match. You can't be expected to appreciate the delicate strokes of play, the turns by which a game is lost and won—it takes an old player to do that, but the broad philosophy of football you can understand if you will. Come along with me a little nearer and let us consider it together.'

'As endless as are boys' characters, so are their ways of facing or not facing a scrummage at football.'

'And Tom and Slogger shook hands with great satisfaction and mutual respect. And for the next year or two, whenever fights were being talked of, the small boys who had been present shook their heads wisely, saying, "Ah but you should first have seen the fight between Slogger Williams and Tom Brown."'

'Come, none of your irony, Brown', answers the master. 'I'm beginning to understand the game scientifically. What a noble game it is too.'

'Isn't it? But it's more than a game. It's an institution', said Tom.

'Yes', said Arthur, 'the birthright of British boys, old and young, as *habeas corpus* and trial by jury are of British men'.

'The discipline and reliance on one another which it teaches is so valuable, I think', went on the master, 'it ought to be such an unselfish game. It merges the individual in the eleven, he doesn't play that he may win, but that his side may'.

'That's very true', said Tom, 'and that's why football and cricket, now that one comes to think of it are much better games than fives or hare-and-hounds, or any others where the object is to come first or to win for oneself, and not that one's side may win'.

'And then the captain of the eleven!' said the master. 'What a part is his in our school world. Almost as hard as the Doctor's; requiring skill and gentleness and firmness, and I don't know what other rare qualities.'

(On a technicality, Rugby loses).

'But such a defeat is a victory: so think Tom and all the school eleven, as they accompany their conquerors to the omnibus and send them off "with three ringing cheers".'[33]

In Hughes' conception and in the Victorian age, sport reaches its apotheosis. The pursuit of excellence is, by becoming a team thing, moralised into a microcosm of communal virtue. By its closely representative tie to house and school, moreover, the team becomes the very image of a wider communal unity, where yet that community is constituted of distinctive characters and talents. We are, via Newbolt's *Vitai Lampada*, on the way to that stunning and perverse moment on the first day of the Battle of the Somme, when Captain D. P. Nevill, five minutes from his own death, produced four footballs and led his Surrey regiment in a dribbling charge towards the German trenches:

The fear of Death before them is but an empty name
　True to the land that bore them the Surreys play the game (*Daily Mail*).

There had been team ball games from the start. The big Roman chariot events were team efforts, with the lesser drivers' task to wreck the danger men's chances. But the Victorians' inventiveness should not be underrated. The Public School not only standardized popular collective sports, and invented new ones. They placed them in an arena to be viewed, marrying participatory with spectatorial dimensions in such a way as to cement the bond of player with the represented institution.

There is no lack of the craze for victory in *Tom Brown*.[34] But, as the quotations show, disinterested reverence, with both ethical and aesthetic constituents, for the game itself, is central. Slogger Williams' 'sportsmanship' in accepting that he has been bested (even though Tom has used some village tricks) needs to be emphasized here. Clearly, if the 'human excellence' that I am claiming for the sporting ideal is to be worthy of full respect, this dimension, present as I have mentioned in the 'Roman' outlook (Shakespeare's Mark Antony: '... a Roman by a Roman valiantly vanquished') must be central. Yet, if you read through the 'Boys' Own' literature of the period it is almost universally the

case that 'we' win, while Tom Brown himself never loses an important contest, so that we do not get an imagined presentation in Hughes of what that means to a hero. Rather, what we usually find is the villainization of the opponent as a sometimes murderous cheat whose machinations fail in the face of the superior qualities of 'our' fair-playing heroes. So, we need to dig for this vein, this quality that, as children, we are taught makes a 'good sport'.

Shakespeare's Hector, in *Troilus and Cressida* is such. With Achilles helpless, he shows what Troilus derides as the 'vice of mercy':

'You bid him rise and live'
'O, 'tis fair play'
'Fool's play, by heaven, Hector.'[35]

And in the final battle, before Achilles has his henchman hack down the 'unarmed' Hector, he again offers Achilles a 'pause if thou wilt'.[36] Such an outlook permeates the chivalric legends of the Christian era in which we can include those of Robin Hood. The true knight fights fair, and if in no position to show himself magnanimous in victory, rejoices appreciatively in his opponent's excellence. And so it was in the later more democratic literature of the fist fight. Hazlitt's fighters' courage and thirst for victory is matched by their fairness, mutual admiration and acknowledgement:

'What's the matter?' asks the dazed and battered Gasman Hickman after failing to come out for the nineteenth round.
　'Nothing is the matter, Tom, but you, you are the bravest man alive. You have lost the battle.' '... Neate (the victor) instantly went up and shook him cordially by the hand', celebrating 'in all good humour and without any appearance of arrogance'.[37]

Pip in *Great Expectations* is challenged by Herbert Pocket, fetishistically but ineffectually devoted to the noble art, who finally throws in the sponge:

... I said 'Can I help you?' and he said, 'No thankee', and I said 'Good afternoon', and *he* said 'Same to you'.[38]

But it is in Horace Annesley Vachell's late-Victorian Harrow stories *The Hill* and its sequel *John Verney* that the idealization of the good sport is most clearly seen. For the main thing here is that it is the hero, Verney, who suffers defeat and takes it properly, whereas the 'ill-bred' Scaife, wonderfully talented, lacks all the attributes of sportsmanship: he is selfish, greedy, gives up under pressure, blames every one else, and cheats when he thinks he can get away with it. As 'Caterpillar' puts it:

> One doesn't pretend to be a Christian, but as a gentleman, one accepts a bit of bad luck without gnashing one's teeth. What? That Spartan boy with the fox was a well bred 'un, you take my word for it. Scaife isn't.[39]

By contrast, the Eton captain at the Lord's match, having been caught out by the glorious (and beautiful) 'Caesar', pauses on his way back to the pavilion:

> 'That was a glorious catch' he says with the smile of a gallant gentleman. As the sound judge Caterpillar remarks 'That Eton captain is cut out of the whole cloth; no shoddy there, by Jove!'.[40]

Caesar, still a boy, takes his Harrovian attributes to the Transvaal where, 'cheering on his fellows' as he leads the assault on 'a small hill', he 'ran—so the Special Correspondent reported— as if he were racing for a goal … aflame with ardour'. He is found 'shot through the heart, and dead, and smiling at death'.[41]

In the sequel, Vernon and Scaife, now politicians, continue, crucially, to show in the world of affairs their qualities as schoolboy cricketers.

Kipling modulates his imperial triumphalism, not only in 'If':

> If you can meet with triumph and disaster
> And treat these two impostors just the same,

but in 'Fuzzy Wuzzy' a salute from the Soudan Expeditionary Force to a foe who 'played the cat an' banjo with our forces'.

Reference to Kipling is a reminder of *Recessional*'s deeper theme:

> Lo, all our pomp of yesterday
> Is one with Nineveh and Tyre.

and this suggests a perspective from which to look at the sporting morality I have been lately stressing. We have seen that the Pindaric

outlook is one of 'victory or death'. But for the 'Roman' and the 'Christian' gentleman, earthly death is itself the ultimate antagonist. In that respect, earthly victory is in many ways a temptation and it is in defeat that the sportsman confronts the deeper truth. Though they verge on necrophilia and masochism, Vachell's books are important in bringing home these chivalric depths, in which coming to terms with losing, with defeat, are seen, not just as fundamental to decency in life but to an ability to face a loss that is inevitable, whether or not, with Paul, one sees such loss as only a stingless preliminary to victory in the Grand Final Analysis.

The complexity and importance of play

Arendt's sphere of 'action', we saw, was a realm of glory, and on the other side of the same token was the mute inglory either of defeat or of non-participation. We are in Nozick's realm of invidious esteem here, where one person's pride is another's humiliation. Rawls' 'Aristotelian Principle', on the other hand, is one of satisfaction in the 'exercise of realized capacities.' Such satisfactions require encouragement and training, the cultivation of capacities; but the person absorbed in their constituent activities, is neither looking over her neighbour's fence to see if she is being out-done, nor glancing at the surrounding windows in the expectation of being the object of admiration. If sport approaches, or can approach this model, de Coubertin's ideal of 'taking part' is not an empty fantasy.

I criticized Arendt for conflating distinct dimensions in her way of demarcating 'action' from 'work' and 'labour'. But this was not a mere analytical confusion. It reflects a conceptual tension at the heart of the 'Greek' culture. For, as Aristotle says, the things 'valued for their own sake' are, being 'that for the sake of which other things are done', necessarily valued more highly than the means to them (which is not the same as their being more worthwhile than the means to more important ends). These are the highest, hence the most esteemed, praised and glorified pursuits. But this produces a timocratic echo of 'Psychological Egoism', the doctrine that when we do something for its own sake we do it for the sake of the satisfaction we get out of it. For the valorization of activities, entails their cultural recognition and celebration. Hence excellence in such activities is praised to the point where it is the praise that can seem to be their very point. This slippage is visible even in those purest of performances in the realm of the intrinsically valued, the Socratic dialogues, where Socrates is as often presented as sending off his interlocutory rivals with their tails between their legs, whipped by an irony the more painful for the putative purity of its motivation, and where only a pious reading can fail to notice that Socrates is scoring 'eristic' points and rubbing noses in their own excretions.

But as we saw in Patroclus' funeral games, the pleasure in praised achievement is glory, and Antilochus demands his second prize, not a material compensation for being denied it. Glory's satisfaction is in recognized achievement, not in its material reward considered in abstraction from it. The cheat, who otherwise would have lost, is denied that sense of triumph just as much as is someone given a prize through mistaken identity. This is a conceptual, not a moralistic point, and can be evaded only by self-deception. The ego tripper, in modern terms, must actually make that trip, he cannot get his high simply through drugs! Were Socrates to think, as the audience scoffs at Euthyphro, that he had seen the fool off through a sophistic cheat, he would indeed be the 'Socrates dissatisfied' of Mill's phrase. Yet the more detachable are the satisfactions and rewards from the activities that merit them: valuable trophies, money, admiration, sexual and other favours, power, the more are they capable of being the objects of unprincipled pursuit. And so enters the continuum from gamesmanship to sabotage: the perversions familiar throughout sporting history. And they are 'perversions', rather than mere anomalies, because of their intimate connection with the very ennobling of sport as valuable 'in itself'.

There are other tensions in the idea of Action being 'for its own sake'. Gilbert Ryle, for example, used as a paradigm his much-loved activity of gardening. The true gardener is not a utilitarian about his plants—he would not stop growing them if he could get as good blooms or vegetables more cheaply from the shop. He loves gardening for its own sake. But would he be as happy to go on with this activity if annually the flowers and vegetables were stolen? Hardly. Gardening, unlike going for a walk, has, like a journey, its 'ends' built into it. Its constituent activities, preparing the soil, digging, even weeding, are enjoyed, but partly because of their yield. And yet the yield is enjoyed, partly because it is an index and measure of those lead-up activities—their 'prize'.

Vegetarianism not withstanding, nothing so resembles gardening in these respects as the blood sports, hunting and fishing, whose victims are also trophies which would lose that meaning if they were bought or, for that matter, if they were brought down by poisoning or dynamite without a 'sporting chance'.

Drawing a veil over these delinquent members of the sporting family, however, we find the same structure in all competitive sports. Ryle writes hyperbolically:

> The absorbed golfer … would at no moment of it have welcomed an interruption; he was never inclined to turn his thoughts or his conversation from the circumstances of the game to other matters … he had enjoyed the whole game.[42]

But the fullest enjoyment of 'the whole game' is not, again, as much like the fullest enjoyment of a walk as it is like the fullest enjoyment of a journey. For the game has an aim: to go a round with the lowest score. If you are not aiming at that you are not really playing. Other games' targets are different. But in all those with proper names, to talk of a target is to talk of what counts as winning, hence of at least doing well.

Does this reduce games' activities to mere means to victory? Are games Rylean 'tasks'? Our comparison with the multi-layered activities of gardening and journeying rightly suggests not. 'Whole games' break down into indefinite component sequences and outcomes at various levels. Winning entails the intermediate achievement of goals, tries, holings, runs, dismissals, points. These entail moves, passes, shots, tackles, pitches, bowls, throws, sidesteps, dribbles, charges, jumps. Cerebral activity is entailed in co-ordinating with team-mates in strategic and tactical planning and switching, in feints, in spotting weaknesses, in anticipating and exploiting conditions. At the other ('laborious') end of the mind-body unity essential to sports, the physical heart-lung-and-muscle end, we have the dimensions of speed, strength and endurance. And it should not be forgotten that all these dimensions have, in addition to their intrinsic joys and distresses, their aftermaths, from retrospective exultations and miseries, from delicious or agonized weariness, and from friendly and respectful embraces and exchanges 'when it's all over', to convivial relaxation with fellow players—or gloating, depression, back-biting and complaint, whether collective or individual.

Any one-track view of sport, whether it focuses with Arendt and Pindar on public glory, or with more private individual or team pursuit of a victory whose delights are confined to the victors, will miss the multi-dimensional pleasures internal to sporting activity. Such views, while avoiding the outright utilitarianism of seeing sport solely in terms of getting fit or training for 'life' (whose own point is left unclear), are in many ways as reductive. The pleasures and pains of sport are multiple and many-layered. Sports and games exercise and test all sorts though by no means all of physical, mental and moral capacities. The keen player of what occupy most playing time in the world, informal games, will try his or her hardest, even though the final result—which may be the score when the lights, or the sun provides insufficient illumination to continue—is of little moment, especially when teams are chosen and re-shuffled to even things up and to pre-empt an easy winner ('Only nine of them turned up so we lent them one of ours'). Pindar, in whose odes is to be found no interest whatever in the description of component activities, would read a book while such playing was going on. Yet you will hear 'good shot', 'bad luck', in every real field of informal play just as much as in Vachell's Harrovian idyll. And, whether or not such recognition is forthcoming, let alone from absent spectators, the pleasures in games' activities, in the harmonious, even beautiful, exercise of 'psycho-physical' 'sensory-motor' capacities, is attested in the universal delight in 'aimless' ball-playing—testing but relaxing, competitive but co-operative, serious but playful, in which, while one might be better than the other, no one 'wins', because no one keeps score or because there is no score to keep.

Games and sports, as the above analysis displays, can be engaged in from a variety of motives. For the seeker of exercise they may function equivalently to mowing the lawn.

For the pursuer of victories, other avenues of personal triumph are available. At every level there are virtues and vices, obsessions and slacknesses. There is no general rule governing all this except that most adaptable one of 'appropriateness'. These are matters of cultural nuance.

In the last few paragraphs I have slipped surreptitiously between talking of games and sports. One could add the complication that when people play, say, catching and throwing a ball to each other, it is artificial to say there is *a* game they are playing. As Wittgenstein's remarks at *Investigations* 66 and 67 suggest, the tangle and multicentred clustering here are connected with the historical and cultural nature of these terms. It seems to me for example that 'sport' becomes consolidated as a quasi-institutional concept with the use of this term for school games in the nineteenth century. Its earlier meaning had been more 'playful'. Why is clay-pigeon shooting a sport and not a game? Why is a sprinter a sportsman but the hundred metres dash not a game? In these cases the competitor simply strives to attain a target. Even where the path between start and finish is strewn with obstacles, as in steeple-chasing or rock-climbing or, saving decency, fox-hunting, there are not the ingredient interactive contestations characteristic of, say, football, tennis, cricket or even snooker. (How about golf?) At the other end, chess and Monopoly are games all right, but hardly sports. They are competitive and cerebral, but lack a physical, sensory-motor, dimension. Why, then, is boxing, despite being called 'the fight game', not what we would, in another tone of voice, call a game? Or wrestling?—'Let's play boxing' would be an invitation to a shadow-spar with theatrical grunts. Ordinary, living language, which is capable of seeing that some games are not 'just games' to the professional or for that matter, to that quite different animal, the fanatical addict of victory, is sensitive to nuances that defy ready categorization.

Though practice often lends it weight, the view of competitive sport as essentially a vicious rage for conquest is a jaundiced and superficial one, sustained by a bogus historicism attaching sport intextricably to cut-throat capitalism or militarism. It was not an arbitrary focus that led Piaget to observe children's unrefereed games as the best index of the spontaneous growth of the moral sense[43]. With its dialectic of skill, co-operation, forbearance, courage, enterprise and luck, sport is a microcosm of life in many of its major aspects, nor is its moral dimension reducible to that of being a good sport in victory or defeat. At any level, sporting activity involves the pursuit of quality, the struggle to do well, a 'technical' achievement requiring a measure of dedication, enterprise, attention to detail, capacity to relax,[44] and self-subjection, not only to hard work, misfortune and defeat, but to criticism. Hannah Arendt's Homeric men of 'action' were, of necessity, an aristocracy, and there is, as far as I can see, no getting away from some sort of hierarchy, grades, levels or divisions, in sport, as long as it is taken seriously. But it is a travesty to ignore, not only the delights and achievements at every level of sport, but the non-Nozickian satisfactions intrinsic to sporting achievement, in victory or defeat, through doing one's best in a competitive context. Now of course this sort of satisfaction presupposes a culture in which such self-excellence is recognized and validated (I still remember my high school sports master, Brian Downes, whose best athletes at one stage held the half-mile record in every age division in the New South Wales Schools Championships, shouting with excitement as the slowest runner in the class broke three minutes for the first and only time). In a culture in which only the (boys') first team gets an outing and only victory counts, you are scarcely going to get the sort of thing I am advocating. Nor, to look at the other side of the decadent coin, are you going to get it in environments where sport is reduced to non-competitive exercises, for fear of 'creating losers'.[45] This approach is the ludic equivalent of preventing one's children from mixing in case they should be on either end of bullying, or of banning discussions in case someone has to endure the 'humiliation' of being shown to be wrong. It is a protection from reality and an excuse for avoiding the task of developing a culture which is as tough and tender as a decent human culture has to be. At the other extreme, populist swimmers with contemporary soda streams deride de Coubertin's 'aristocratic' and 'elitist' celebration of the 'amateur ideal'. These pro-sport buffs do not seem to appreciate that only an elite can make money out of a few spectacular sports and that, if sport is to be a central part

of a worthwhile and active popular culture its '*age quod agis*' ethic has to be amateur and sustained by sporting ideals in according priority to doing one's best within the letter and spirit of the code—who, after all, can afford referees and linesmen and appeal committees?

There is a tendency to think that because sport is properly peripheral to the main businesses of life and because its achievement is pleasure, it is humanly and morally unimportant. But it is precisely because of its contrast with the more utilitarian side of things that it has the importance in people's attention that it has. In sports we have arenas where human qualities are not subordinated to other ends but are expressed, tested and exhibited to be enjoyed, judged and admired for their own sake. In suggesting this humanist and implicitly universalist account, I am of course, taking issue with reductive forms of historicism and utilitarianism for which sports are seen essentially as functional ancillaries of ruling orders and as instances of statist, capitalist, racist and sexist regulation of life. In this article, with no apologies for an 'idealism' which a longer account would seek to knit back into a more material account of their evolution, sport's universal claims have been urged through a demonstration of the continuity of its organizing values, from Homeric to modern times. In assuming a living familiarity with sporting ideologies in the present century, then, I am appealing to a recognition of continuity.

Only a fanatic would elevate sport into a be-all-and-end-all, and the world is littered with depressed crocks seeking drearily to maintain a dreamy after-glow of 'glory days'.[46] Similarly, the viciousness associated with winning at all costs, exacerbated but not originated by professionalism,[47] and the thuggish sexism consequent on the historical exclusion of women from the very field of the public pursuit of excellence as physically active beings, present ugly faces of the dominant culture of sport. At the same time, while today more and more couch-potatoes plant themselves in front of televised images of sporting excellence, fewer and fewer, young or old, play sport. This implies a substitution of fantastic images for genuine practice,[48] a replacement of sport as popular culture by sport as identificatory spectacle. Sport is an arena of freedom and beauty that is part of the forces resisting the reduction of pleasure to consumption and compensatory dream. This article has 'assembled reminders', however, that the very fantasy-energy invested in sport is rooted in its actually enduring practical ideals.[49]

Notes

1. *Epistle of St. Paul*, I Corinthians, 9, 24–27.
2. *The Human Condition*, (Chicago University Press, 1958).
3. *On Revolution* (London: Faber and Faber, 1963), 63.
4. *Republic*, 547–550. But see *Laws* 795–8, for Plato on the significance of games.
5. The translation is Samuel Butler's (1898). (London: Jonathan Cape, 1936).
6. Translations from Moses Finley's *The Olympic Games, the First Thousand Years* (London, Chatto & Windus, 1976), pages 1191 and 347. It wasn't Pindar who composed the doggerel by which the teams at the 1992 Winter Olympics were introduced:

   'Stand now and sing if you're a fan o'
   The wonderful team from beautiful Canada'.

7. *Paedeia. The Ideals of Greek Culture* transl. G. Highet. (Oxford: Blackwell, 1965), 205.
8. *A Theory of Justice* (Harvard University Press, 1971), 426.
9. *Anarchy, State and Utopia* (UK: Blackwell, 1974), 243. I criticize Nozick's ignoring of intrinsic pride in *Ruling Illusions* (UK: Harvester, 1978), 48–52.
10. *Ethics*, Book IV.
11. See Finley, op. cit., Donald G. Kyle's *Athletics in Ancient Athens* (Leiden: E. S. Brill, 1987) and Waldo E. Sweet's *Sport and Recreation in Ancient Greece* (Oxford University Press, 1987).
12. The Baron's quote does not foresee the impact of nationalism on the Olympics, let alone the move to professionalism, and show business.
13. Finley, op. cit., 91.
14. *Discourses* 3.22.52 (quoted in Sweet).
15. See also 'Professionalism in Archaic and Classical Greek Athletics' David C. Young. *Ancient World* 7 (1983) pages 44–5.
16. Harris, *Greek Athletes and Athletics* (UK: Hutchinson, 1964) and *Sport in Greece and Rome* (London: Thames and Hudson, 1972).
17. Gardiner, *Athletics of the Ancient World* (UK: Oxford, 1930). It seems to me that the Trinidadian Marxist C. L. R. James's great book on cricket, *Beyond a Boundary* (UK: Hutchinson, 1963), is much closer in spirit to these humanist and Christian historians than to the economic reductionists.
18. Gardiner, op. cit., page 99f.
19. Book VIII. 143; translation of Samuel Butler (1900) (London: Jonathan Cape, 1922).
20. Op. cit. 158.
21. Iliad 23, 256ff.
22. The values here are deeper and more complex than the 'hopeless tangle' unearthed by Adkins in *Merit and Responsibility* (Oxford: Clarendon Press, 1960), 56.
23. 470–486.
24. (1899) (New York: B. W. Huebsch, 1919), pages 1, 8, 253. But see C. L. R. James' aptly horrified observations on American sport, op. cit. pages 52–53.
25. Veblen, op. cit., page 256.
26. This non-participatory 'democratization', notorious in Ancient Rome's blood sports, has been revived in Spain where the crowd can now 'vote' for a 'brave' bull to be spared and retired to the stud. Whether electronics will eventually include television viewers in the plebiscite remains to be seen.
27. Quoted in 'Understanding Aggro', by Peter Marsh, *New Society*, Vol 32, April 3, 1975. Gambling is a non-aerobic form of secondary participation. Punters put their money where their mouths are and commit themselves so that they, and not only the contestants, stand to win or lose. The proper analysis of gambling and of games of chance would need to go beyond talk only of greed or masochism to look at the expressive dimensions of the gambler's plunge.
28. *Circus Factions, Blues and Greens at Rome and Byzantium*, Alan Cameron, (Oxford: Clarendon Press, 1976), 294.
29. *Anarcharsis II* quoted by Judith Swaddling in *The Ancient Olympic Games* (London: British Museum, 1980), 12.
30. There is a poem of Ovid in which the young lover, failing to distract his Stadium companion from the chariot race, seeks to channel her passion for her champion towards himself. Ovid likened exile to an athlete's being-sidelined and able only to watch from outside the arena.
31. See, for example, Harris, *Sport in Greece and Rome*, page 48. One must of course make allowances for petty racism in all such attributions.
32. Treated in Nathan Rosenstein's *Imperatores Victi* (USA: University of California, 1990).
33. *Tom Brown's Schooldays* (1857) (Dublin: Educational Company of Ireland, 1929), 79, 80 (Part I Chapter 5), 219 (Part II, Chapter 5), 257, 260 (Part II, Chapter 8).
34. James Fitzjames Stephen in the *Edinburgh Review*, Vol CVII. No. CCXVII, January 1858, reviews Hughes' story as veiling some hideous barbarism. J. A. Mangan's researches emphasize the vicious Social Darwinism of the Victorians' sporting ideology (*See* 'The Grit of our Forefathers' in *Imperialism and Popular Culture*

J. M. MacKenzie (ed.) (UK: Manchester, 1986), pages 113–140. A mellower but critical perspective is found in the tenth chapter of Morris Marples, *A History of Football* (London: Secker and Warburg, 1954).

35. Act V, Scene 3.
36. Act V, Scene 6.
37. 'The Fight', in *Selected Essays of William Hazlitt* Geoffrey Keynes (ed.) (London: Nonesuch Press, 1948) pp. 98–99. Hazlitt had likened the Gasman Hickman to Achilles in his swaggering arrogance).
38. Chapter XI (London: Everyman, 1907), 86.
39. *The Hill* (London: John Murray, 1920). 'Fellowship' page. 68.
40. Op. cit., 'Lord's', 202.
41. Op. cit., 'Good Night', 235.
42. *The Concept of Mind* (UK: Hutchinson, 1949), 108.
43. *The Moral Judgement of the Child* (London: Routledge & Kegan Paul, 1932). Chapter I: 'The Rules of the Game'.
44. See William James' lecture 'The Gospel of Relaxation' in *Talks to Teachers* (London: Longmans, Green & Co., 1917), 37.
45. Even in aerobics sessions the public acknowledgement of pulse-rate changes functions to foster among pounding hearts a gentle emulation.
46. A Bruce Springsteen song about wallowing in such memories.
47. 'Professionalism' conceals a great variety in ethos. Some professional clubs tend towards mere business outfits imposing purely monetary incentives, while others are more deeply permeated by a spirit of solidarity and tradition. A 'tourist's' account of English Rugby League clubs, *Simply the Best*, by Adrian McGregor, (Australia: University of Queensland 1991) is revealing of this issue of 'true professionalism'. I, for example, am frequently struck by the respect and understanding among professionals in contrast with an adolescent triumphalism common among amateurs.
48. In *Brave New World* 'experience surrogates' that prefigure 'virtual reality' machines give fantastic adventure experiences to citizens whom real risks would reduce to a wreck.
49. Colin Radford, Michael Irwin, Walter Chamberlain and Jack Kyriaco have helped in the preparation of this article, as has Radford's 'Utilitarianism and the Noble Art', *Philosophy*, 63, 1988. This article addresses from a different perspective themes discussed in Mary Midgley's 'The Game Game' [this collection, Chapter 1.4].

Part 2

Fair contests

Rules, spoiling and cheating

Introduction

Mike McNamee

While Part 1 laid out some of the essential conceptual foundations of sports ethics, Part 2 discusses the structure of game playing, its rule-based framework, and the thorny issues of rule-breaking in general and cheating and spoiling in particular. The first two essays build directly on the early work of Suits, while the latter essays draw heavily upon areas beyond the philosophy of sport to nourish ideas in sports ethics. In particular Loland and Fraser draw upon contractarian ethics and work in political philosophy and jurisprudence. Equally, Tamburrini's discussion, although explicitly utilitarian also addresses ethics in a political context, while McFee's essay draws upon and develops work in jurisprudence and the philosophy of rules. This Part therefore shows most clearly how sports ethics has developed in part through iteration with other branches of applied philosophy. Not only are the particular issues and examples, such as rule-following, free-riding and the possibility of cheating, illuminated by these related branches of philosophy, but discussion of the sports contexts themselves serve to bring new problems to those other areas of philosophy too.[1]

Part 2 begins with an early classic essay in the philosophy of sport: Scott Kretchmar's 'From Test to Contest'. Kretchmar aims to clearly distinguish 'tests' from 'contests'. In his discussions he reveals both differences and similarities between them. Irrespective of win, draw (tie) or loss, sports participants attempt to demonstrate superiority of some range of athletic action.

While we may acknowledge qualitative differences in the ways in which people perform skills, it is only through a certain agreed structure that the demonstration of superiority can be displayed.

Kretchmar articulates two conceptual features of tests: impregnability and vulnerability. 'Impregnability is the facet of a test which indicates that a person might "get it wrong". Vulnerability allows for the possibility that one may "get it right"' (1975: 224). Moreover, he argues, these two facets allow for the possibility of uncertainty of outcome, a 'sweet tension' (a phrase which Warren Fraleigh is credited with capturing) which enriches the phenomenological enjoyment of the activity. Success and failure are thus permitted by these facets and the better tests and contests are designed and played so as to suspend the resolution of this sweet tension optimally. Tests, as their etymology reveals, are a basis of sports contests. The transition marks the move between self and other, singularity and community. Victory and defeat, rather than success and failure, depend upon the presence of an opponent. Kretchmar observes two steps in the move: the recognition of a fellow tester, and the striving to better them. The success of the contest is in part a function of the ability of the rules to allow for a distinction to be drawn between winner and loser.

Both Kretchmar and Fraleigh, although working independently, have much in common, not least of all because much of their early work was produced at a time when they worked in what was the engine room of the philosophy of sport, Brockport University in the USA. Fittingly, then, the next essay is Fraleigh's 'The Ends of the Sports Contest'. Recognising that contestants or sports competitors come together to test each others skill, he nevertheless observes that discussion often conflates the ends (or goals, or purposes) that participants have with those that are properly internal to the sports contests themselves. Building upon both Suits and Kretchmar, Fraleigh notes that the end of winning, although constitutive of the sports contest, cannot be the personal end of all contestants because winning and losing are exclusive. This enables us to see how a third end, 'exerting one's best effort in the requisite ways towards the specific state of affairs' (1984: 36–7). And this is a widely shared intuition captured in the phrase that if one is not *trying* to win, then one simply isn't playing the game.

Fraleigh points out that participants frequently have as ends the securing of other social goods such as admiration or adulation, health, prizes or trophies that are logically speaking externally related to sports contests. He argues that where these personal aims predominate over the end of trying to win, the outcome is not a good sports contest. He goes on to say that the rules of sports preserve its ends in that they 'provide a equitable opportunity for contesting of the relative abilities of the participants to move in mass in space and time within the confines prescribed by an agreed upon set of rules' (1984: 42). In articulating what he calls 'the purpose of the sports contest' Fraleigh goes on to set out explicitly the feature of equal opportunity as the framing value – a foundation for the duties contestants owe each other in sports contests.

While calls are made that this or that action in sport was unfair, it is rare that the precise grounds for the normative judgement are made explicit. Fraleigh's discussion is extended and deepened in the work of Loland (2002, 2009). The next essay is his 'Fairness in Sport: An Ideal and Its Consequences' which is an attempt to chart the benefits and burdens individual sportspersons ought morally and rationally to expect from playing sports. Voluntary participation in sports, he argues, demands obligations of the players. Anyone who wishes to enjoy the benefits ought not to be what economists call a

'free rider', on the backs of the efforts and commitments of others, without doing their fair share.

Loland views sports as meritocratic practices where rewards should be distributed according to distinctions in performance. The best ought to win, and to achieve this outcome, or state of affairs, requires that sports are configured justly. One important part of his overall thesis is the appeal to principle that all contestants have 'equality of opportunity to perform' (2009: 163), assuring, for example, that they share the same test as Kretchmar (Chapter 2.2) had noted. According to this principle, everyone is treated equally within the sporting contest. If handball is wrong for outfield players of one football team, it must be wrong for all; if one athlete must run 100 metres in the sprint, so must all contestants. He recognises that natural inequalities in innate talent exist and are important in the achievement of sporting excellence and that these are not typically to be eradicated (notwithstanding 'handicapped events' such as horseracing, which are designed to create a spectacle that makes sense for gambling). Nevertheless, he wishes, following the 'fair opportunity principle', to remove irrelevant obstacles, or those for which the sportsperson is not deemed responsible for, that contaminate the attempt to distinguish the better sportsperson or team in their pursuit of victory. Exploring the limits of this thesis will challenge some existing classification systems both in relation to disability sports and able-bodied sports, and also some single sex sports, where membership of fe/male categories is irrelevant to the test and therefore do not raise questions of fairness.

There are relatively few full book length treatments of the ethics of particular sports. David Fraser's 'It's Not Cricket' is an excellent example of such an approach in his working through of the relevant ethical ideals and practices within a legal framework. In the sporting history of the UK the phrase 'It's not cricket' has entered into the general language as a metaphor to express revulsion at the failure of a person to act in accordance with a widely shared and lauded ideal of conduct. As is well known, one may break the rules overtly, or one may do it covertly. But these acts of rule breaking do not exhaust the catalogue of blameworthy conduct. Fraser discusses a case notorious in cricket history where the underdog nation (in this case

New Zealand) were on the brink of a famous victory over their neighbours (Australia) who have a long history of being far superior to them in cricketing terms.

At the end of the game, the New Zealanders needed six runs to win, but had only one delivery (pitch) from which to score it. The 'magic' stroke that achieves six runs is the hitting of the ball clear over the boundary rope without its bouncing first. This cannot, of course, be done unless the batter can get sufficiently underneath the ball to hit it with a mighty blow and make it sail over the boundary rope without meeting *terra firma* first. Cognisant of this fact, as any cricketing schoolboy or girl would be, the Australian captain ordered his bowler (pitcher) – who happened to be his brother – to roll the ball along the ground to the batter in order to prevent (or at least to reduce the possibility to nearly nil) their losing the match.

In bowling thus, no formal rule was broken. There is no constitutive rule that outlaws underarm deliveries nor is their a regulative rule that forbids it on grounds of (e.g.) harm or disrespect to the opponent. Neither could a pre-competition or 'auxiliary rule' (Meier, 1985) apply mid-contest. Nevertheless, a conventional tacit agreement regarding what counts as a fair (note: not lawful or unawful) delivery had been fallen well short of. Moreover, the sweet tension of uncertainty of outcome had been rendered both sour and certain – indeed sourly certain it might be said. What this essay raises, is the dominance of the formal rules over the ethos in the adjudication of the game. While informal agreements, or informal rules if you prefer, clearly guide players actions, Fraser explores the limits of the Umpire (the official) to act against unethical (one might describe it as base, ignoble, shameful and the like) though not unlawful action. Can an official at one and the same time intervene to preserve the best practices of the sports, or will this compromise his or her judicial neutrality?[2] In one way the problem represents an excellent case study for the dominance of certain ethical theories to explain our intuitions, since fairly compelling accounts can be offered in terms of the officials' duties, or their virtue, or indeed the utility of their actions for the greater good of the game. These intuitions and theories not only supply different descriptions of the problem but supply potentially different solutions too. Fraser revels

in the irony that the phrase 'it's not cricket' appears to date to the time when the techniques of bowling were limited to underarm deliveries. He argues for an interpretivist framework, which recognises that practices evolve over time and whose criteria of normative evaluation change accordingly. He argues, therefore, that appeal to some former and purer sporting times is so much hot air.

Tamburrini's 'The "Hand of God"?' discusses a famous case of rule-breaking. During soccer's 1986 World Cup, Maradona, one of the world's greatest ever footballers punched a ball into the net. Needless to say, the act broke one of football's regulative rules. Only the goalkeeper is permitted to handle the ball, and even then only in a well defined area surrounding his or her goal. No outfield player may handle the ball during play without being penalised. And in this case, Maradona punched the ball into the net so artfully, that he deceived nearly everyone (but most importantly, all the officials) into thinking that he had actually headed the ball.[3] He later claimed (surely tongue in cheek) that it was the 'hand of God'. Tamburrini discusses the case to highlight that any act of cheating is not merely one of rule-breaking but must exhibit both intentionality and deception.

While all this is relatively uncontroversial, Tamburrini uses the case as a springboard to discuss praise and blame in sports. He argues that sportspersonship, loosely defined as an act over and above one's duties (referred to in moral philosophy as supererogation) is praiseworthy but not demanded by fairness nor fair play. He then asks the question of when we should blame players who engage in foul play. His answer is that where it is uncertain what is and is not permissible, violations may not be blameworthy. The conventionality of sport, raised in Fraser's writings above, rears its head again. Nevertheless, Tamburrini insists that the ethos of sports is a compound notion of norms shared by the participants and not the ruling authorities or institutions of sports. In doing so he rejects Loland's contractualist reading of fair play. Tamburrini concludes:

> In the light of this wider, compound ethos notion, it is pretty obvious that Maradona's 'handball' does not run counter to the way football is played today. Particularly among

97

football players, handling the ball is not an exceptional fault; when the occasion demands it, they resort to hand touches, and they do so often.'

(2000: 19)

Maradona's 'hand of God' is thus an act of blameless wrongdoing for Tamburrini. He leaves open the possibility that Maradona's action was indeed not wrongful but 'right' under indirect utilitarian thinking, if it was an action performed from optimific motives (even if the act itself produced some negative consequences that are not to be condoned) – in order to bring about a greater good. He invites the reader to consider all the beneficial outcomes of the cheating; including the added spice to the remainder of the game, and all subsequent England/Argentina sports contests. He sums up by saying that since Maradona's act was not motivated by optimific considerations, but rather by the cheat's characteristic motivatation of deceptively achieving an illicit advantage, we should characterise the goal as an act of 'blameful right doing' (2000: 32).

The concluding essay to Part 2, Graham McFee's article: 'Spoiling: An Indirect Reflection of Sport's Moral Imperative?', adopts a posture directly contrary to Tamburrini's. McFee draws upon Ronald Dworkin's work in jurisprudence concerning the relationship between legal principles and legal rules and shows how his analysis is pertinent to the spoiling cricketing example above. To spoil is to act contrary to the spirit of sport, although not its rules. Perhaps the most famous UK example is what is referred to as the voluntary suspension of play (VSP).[4] Under VSP, players voluntarily kick the ball off the field to suspend play and allow a seriously injured player to receive treatment. In an act of reciprocity, that allows a measure of restorative justice, the opposing team throw the ball back to the opposition voluntarily. It is the presence of such a convention that McFee calls a principle and the violation of it that constitutes spoiling.

It is in the nature of principles, thus conceived, that they form the background for judgements of how to proceed in sports. Equally the rules are abstract in the sense that they always need to be particularised in relation to a given context. Initiation into sports principles,

as it were, often goes hand in hand with learning to play the game, and is often tacit. It is often said that players and officials need to respect the integrity of their sports. This for McFee means, effectively, that we should interpret the rules in order to show sports in their best light and thus to preserve their principles (under his account of them). On his more sophisticated reading, McFee holds that spoiling is not simply upholding the spirit of the unwritten rule, but rather interpreting the written rule in the right spirit (i.e. in keeping with said principles) And this, following Wittgenstein, he argues is not a matter of simply learning more rules, but rather developing a certain interpretive sensitivity towards them.

Notes

1. On the particular issue of interdependence, McFee (1998) argues that only the ethics of sport makes a unique contribution to philosophy, the other aspects of the philosophy of sports being derivative upon discussion in the parent discipline.
2. For an extensive deliberation of this and related questions see Russell (1999).
3. In order to forestall a legion of abuse from my Argentinian friends, I am obliged to say that Maradona later went on to score one of the most sublime goals in World Cup history, beating half the England team in the process (without a hint of bad character).
4. See for example, Loland and McNamee (2000) and Hardman (2009).

References

Fraleigh, W. P. (1984) *Right Actions in Sport: Ethics for Contestants*, Champaign; IL: Human Kinetics.

Hardman, A. R. (2009) 'Sport, Moral Interpretivism, and Football's Voluntary Suspension of Play', *Sport, Ethics and Philosophy*, 3: 49–65.

Kretchmar, R. S. (1975) 'From Test to Contest: An Analysis of Two Kinds of Counterpoint in Sport', *Journal of the Philosophy of Sport*, II: 23–30.

Loland, S. (2002) *Fair Play: A Moral Norm System*, London: Routledge.

Loland, S. (2009) 'Fairness in Sport: An Ideal and Its Consequences', in T. H. Murray *et al.* (eds) *Performance-Enhancing Technologies in Sports: Ethical, Conceptual and Scientific Issues*, Baltimore: Johns Hopkins University Press.

Loland, S. and McNamee, M. J. (2000) 'Fair Play and the Ethos of Sports: An Eclectic Philosophical Framework', *Journal of the Philosophy of Sport*, 27: 63–80.

McFee, G. (1998) 'Are There Philosophical Issues with Respect to Sport (Other than Ethical Ones)?' in M. J. McNamee and S. J. Parry (eds) *Ethics and Sport*, London: Routledge, 3–18.

Meier, K. V. (1985) 'Restless Sport', *Journal of the Philosophy of Sport*, XII: 64–77.

Russell, J. (1999) 'Are Rules All an Umpire Has to Deal With?' *Journal of the Philosophy of Sport*, 26: 27–49.

Tamburrini, C. (2000) 'The "Hand of God"?', in *The Hand of God: Essays in the Philosophy of Sports*, Gothenburg: University of Gothenburg.

From test to contest

An analysis of two kinds of counterpoint in sport

R. Scott Kretchmar

Sport thrives on contraries. Where point and counterpoint, thesis and antithesis, and more or less stand out most clearly, sport appears to be its richest. Think of the common sport milieu where East is pitted against West, North against South, the "haves" versus the "have-nots." There is this side and that, home and away, opponents and teammates, winners and losers. Athletes strive to be in contact or apart, here rather than there, now rather than then, and so on. One can barely speak of sport without filling his language with contraries.

Moreover, in sport there appears to have been an invention of new counterpoints. "Shirts," which went for centuries without a clear logical opposite, now have one—"skins." And notions which were thought to have obvious contraries now traffic in the world of sport with new counterpoints. For the opposite of winning is building character; the counterpoint of cheating is stupidity; there is the successful play and its contrary, practice.

But taking language as a primary clue to present hunches about the blood kinship of sport and oppositional relationships is dangerous. Just as the English language allows one to say, "I love you," at least four times without being redundant, an athlete may be able to say quite sensibly, "I meet opposition in sport, and what is more, I meet opposition in sport." Indeed, in the present paper it is suggested that sport entails two very different kinds of point-counterpoint. It is further maintained that one set of opposites is presupposed by the other.

One basic kind of point-counterpoint,[1] as described by Ogden (2: pp. 53–66), is opposition by scale. This involves one phenomenon ranging in degree from 0 to 100. There is no juxtaposition of logical opposites anywhere between the extremes, but simply more and less of some element as one moves up the scale and down, respectively. Common examples of such opposition are black-white, empty-full and poor-rich. Black, for instance, is the total absence of white and is given a position at the zero end of this hypothetical scale. Black becomes charcoal, gray, light gray, and so on as one moves "up" this scale toward absolute white or the 100 point.

A second kind of point-counterpoint, which is of interest here, is opposition by "cut." (2: pp. 53–66) This places two phenomena on opposite sides of a zero point. When this point is crossed in either direction, a phenomenon immediately changes to its opposite. Opposition by "cut" is characteristic of all logical opposites which, by nature, exclude one another. Opposite direction and two of its bases, attraction and repulsion, involve opposition by "cut." Sense-nonsense, possible-impossible, true-false and

R. Scott Kretchmar 'From Test to Contest: An Analysis of Two Kinds of Counterpoint in Sport', from *Journal of the Philosophy of Sport*, II, pp. 23–30, © 1975 R. Scott Kretchmar. Reprinted by permission of Human Kinetics.

A-not A exemplify this kind of contrariety. It may be the case that a scale exists on one or both sides of the "cut." For example, different actions are thought to be more or less possible while impossibility would seem to admit of no variation. But the fact remains that the zero point separates two exclusive opposites and does not stand at one extreme of a distinction by degree. While there is some variation on the side of possibility, to continue with the same example, it is *all not* impossibility; the "cut" remains intact.

Sport and the test

It is commonly recognized that winning and losing are essential to sport. In sport contests one bears witness to his comparative physical prowess. An attempt is made to perform more impressively than another. If successful in this venture, the participant wins; if not, a loss or tie must be recorded.

But there could be no *superior* performance without the possibility for variance in quality among the feats of different performers. One cannot win unless his actions are different *and* noticeably better than another's. While any two human acts would be different (i.e., they occur at separate times and/or places and involve, at least minimally, unique styles), they may not be discernibly superior or inferior to one another. Surely two normally coordinated adults, for instance, who pick up motionless baseballs from the ground do so differently. One person moves more deliberately than the other; one has more rhythm in his movements, and so on. But a person would be hard-pressed to determine who picked up his ball better. Both succeeded quite well.

Thus, while it appears difficult not to do things differently than another, acting in a superior or inferior fashion occurs only in particular situations. It will be argued, in the remainder of this section, that a genuine test provides such minimal (necessary) conditions. The comparisons inherent in the sport contest are unintelligible in the absence of a true test.

A test is an ambiguous phenomenon which is seen as both impregnable and vulnerable. A test "defies" one to solve its riddles. Yet, it "invites" one to try. It offers the challenger both a "yes" and a "no." Its contrariety appears to be an opposition by "cut," not degree.

While tests do vary in their degree of difficulty, each test itself is grounded in an opposition by "cut." Of extreme importance here is the recognition that impregnability and vulnerability are not extremes on a single scale. Impregnability is the facet of a test which indicates that a person might "get it wrong." Vulnerability allows for the possibility that one might "get it right." While an individual could be wrong or right to different degrees, the "cut" remains intact. A mountain climber, for example, who on his first attempt made it halfway to his objective, the summit, and on his second effort traversed three quarters of the distance, failed both times. While his failures differed in degree, they were *both not* successes. The mountain was, in this case, not vulnerable.

Were one to trade this opposition by "cut" for one of degree, a test would become something which is more or less vulnerable or more or less impregnable. But if a "test," to examine the prior possibility, were wholly vulnerable (albeit to different degrees), one's objective would become wholly a foregone conclusion (albeit to different degrees). The climber *will* reach the top of the mountain.

But if a climber tries to reach an easily attainable summit "as fast as possible," a test shows itself once again. To scale this mountain in four hours, for instance, is neither to meet something which is simply more or less vulnerable nor to have a project which is more or less a foregone conclusion. One might fail. The stark opposition by "cut" shows itself clearly.

The testing opposition by "cut" produces an irrevocable sense of uncertainty on the part of the performer. He lives ambiguously toward his test, acting on the one hand as if his project were destined for success but knowing on the other that his gestures may be ineffectual. This uncertainty is an acknowledgement of the twin truths of taking tests —that of the may and may not, making progress and being stymied, solving and trying futilely. The performer's act, then, correlates directly with its object, the test. One lives an expectation of success toward the test's vulnerability and an awareness of possible failure toward the test's impregnability.

Tests simply become unthinkable or unintelligible in the absence of such opposition. As suggested, if something were merely vulnerable, the "test" would become gratuitous facilitation and one's project a foregone conclusion.

Nothing would be tested. This is the case with any project which can be done simply, automatically, or without any trouble. On the other hand, if something were merely impregnable, the "test" would become a "state of affairs," and one's project would be wholly futile. Again, nothing would be tested. Immortal feats are not tests for mere mortals.

Thus, neither vulnerability nor impregnability can stand by itself if the test is to exist. To redefine a current cliche, one truly has "no problem" when *either side* of the present oppositional schema is absent, not only when difficulty has fled. Surely an impregnable state of affairs is "no (human) problem."

Yet, the discord created by logical opposites standing, as it were, side by side is bothersome. How can an object reveal itself as both vulnerable and impregnable? And how can the correlating testing act be lived toward both success and failure?

Toward a resolution of this apparent conflict, it can be suggested that a test involves an alternation of vulnerability and impregnability rather than a simultaneity of these factors. This at once avoids the problem of contradiction and retains the contrast offered by the opposites. But this can be no solution. An alternation of vulnerability and impregnability is but an alternation of the foregone conclusion and impossible feat, respectively. Any acceleration of the process only produces a more stroboscopic alternation. The test can never appear. Any revision of this "alternation thesis" which would include overlapping "after effects" is a fatal concession to the present point, for the door to simultaneity and full discord thereby has been reopened.

If an alternation of contraries does not give one a test, there may be some philosophic future in attempting to average the two together. But the mean in this case is a zero point and thus, neither vulnerability nor impregnability. And a test cannot appear at the nil. In other words, a test cannot be described by avoiding references to both "yes" and "no."

In a final argument it could be suggested that the true contraries in this matter are the test and oneself, not elements of the test itself or reflections in the testing act itself. In this schema the actor would constitute the "yes" and the test the "no." Indeed, one often hears talk, for example, about a person confronting a mountain. This would be, supposedly, an individual's

courageous affirmation of possibility against the mountain's intransigence. In this case neither the test nor the testing act is internally contradictory, and the sharp opposition by "cut" is preserved.

Yet, this common talk about men and mountains is misleading. If the mountain were simply impregnable, the climber must be (to preserve the opposition) vulnerable. But these attributes both characterize objects, neither one of which, incidentally, is a test. And, of course, the climber wants to take a test, not be one.

The same difficulties obtain on the side of the act. If the climber were to live possibility toward the mountain, the latter must be supposed somehow to exemplify impossibility. But a mountain, of course, cannot live impossibility toward anything, and these two characterizations of acts are individually not those of taking a test. One is the anticipation of a foregone conclusion, the other resignation to the status quo.

Further difficulties are encountered when one tries to match an act's possibility with a mountain's impregnability. In addition to not providing logical opposites, this produces at best a stalemate and at worst a wholly irrational act. In this situation one's capabilities have no arena for their exercise. This supposed testing other cannot be of service, for, as impregnable, it is unable to receive one's skillful thrusts in any way. More to the point, a person who lived simple possibility toward what *he himself* saw to be an unchangeable state of affairs is not obeying the most basic laws of correct thinking. The act and object do not match up. This individual is not just a dreamer, for a dreamer's goals are seen by him as somehow attainable, if only through imaginary acts. This climber, on the other hand, is simply not thinking correctly.

If there is any synthesis to be found "above" the testing thesis (an act's possibility lived toward (an object's vulnerability) and antithesis fan act's impossibility lived toward an object's impregnability), it may be described by Fraleigh's terms "sweet tension."[2] Tension on the side of the testing act shows itself as uncertainty. One's testing gesture is forever tentative. It "aims" for success but is never assured of it. The testing act is lived in the mood of "will it happen?"

However, the objective of one's act is not uncertain. Indeed, the very recognition of a test presupposes a *specific, unambiguous act* in virtue of which something is a test. For example, a mountain may show itself as a test, but only against the implicit background of the act of climbing in a certain way to its summit. Without the presence of this specific project, there could be no uncertainty about whether or not *it* can be done.

Tension on the side of the object is encountered as ambiguity. In the manner of an ambiguous figure, the test has two faces. In this case they can be thought of as identical and pointed in opposite directions. The ambiguous profiles at once reveal Ogden's attraction and repulsion. (2: pp. 63–65) As *one* ambiguous object,[3] they are both facing and facing away from one another. They are opposed. But again, the ambiguity is met as a "sweet tension." It is compelling, attractive. The tester is silently called to engage it.

The moment that a mountain climber, for instance, sees an imposing edifice, it can present itself in its full testing ambiguity. There is usually no need on the part of the climber to first measure his own skills and subsequently deduce the testing or non-testing nature of the mountain. One's finite skills *are* one's perspective; they are implicit in meeting the mountain immediately as a test or no test.

As the climb is begun in the face of a true test, one anticipates success in pursuing promising avenues of access. Yet, it is also understood that these very paths may truly be no way to the summit. This "sweet tension" of uncertainty lived toward an ambiguous environment may be resolved momentarily as a particular path is successfully traversed. But uncertainty emerges again as one's gaze falls upon new testing ambiguities in the form of a snow field, steep incline or loose rock. The moment that the discord disappears, the test dissolves. For example, the last half of a mile to the peak may present no problems. One's test disappears in this case precisely one half mile from the summit. The rest of the climb is "exercise."

It may be clearer now why the loss of *testing* uncertainty and ambiguity precludes any possibility for *contesting*. Variance in the quality of two person's performances (thus, permitting victory and defeat) is virtually assured in testing situations. Each "inch" of success is difficult to gain. A person can reveal precisely what he can do, ranging from utter failure to complete success.

So long as the testing ambiguity survives, a vast field of potential accomplishment stretches out before the performer. When this ambiguity is lost, the full range of possible success is diminished to just two collecting pools of non-differentiation—the "foregone conclusion" (wherein *everyone* can succeed) and the "state of affairs" (wherein *nobody* can succeed).

While the test provides a basis for contests, it is, in principle, independent from competitive acts. In other words, a test permits intelligible activity in its own right. When one takes a test he learns "X" about his own skills. This "X" need not stand in relation to another's "X" for it to indicate the state of one's skill. It surely makes sense to talk of someone being successful or unsuccessful without making reference to victories or defeats. One need not lose in a baking contest, for instance, to know that a badly burned pie was unsuccessfully baked.

Billy Jean King, to cite a second example, reported that at times she becomes totally involved with the *test* of tennis and forgets about the relative status of her opponent as an opponent. To paraphrase a portion of her statement, "The ball never comes across the net the same way twice. It is terrifically interesting to deal with the forever new features of the problem." How her opponent is faring is, at least momentarily, irrelevant. Ms. King's "opponent" in such circumstances is providing her with a very rich test, whether or not a contest is being lived between them.

Sport and the contest

The transition from test to contest is the change from human singularity to community. Simply, it is finding someone with whom one can share a test. In addition, a commitment is made by each side to attempt to better the other's performance. Victory is always victory over someone, defeat is forever suffered "at the hands of," minimally, a second individual.

If a second person and a commitment to excel one another is characteristic of contests, in contrast to tests, it is not difficult to see that a second point-counterpoint is at work here. The contraries in this polarity would appear to be the opponents themselves. One player wants to do this, his adversary that. One team moves east, the other west. There are the winners and the losers. Or as it is sometimes put in contests, "It is either you or me."

This appears to be a second opposition by "cut," a matching of true opposites. But a closer inspection reveals something else. If one wanted to do the opposite of his adversary's efforts to score points, for example, he would *not* be committed to score points, be committed *not* to score points or perhaps, committed to score *non*-points. Of course, this is not the case. Each side wants to score points, more points than the other. Opponents try to do the same thing as one another, only more so. They attempt to pass the same kind of test better, to a greater degree, higher on the scale, than another. Opponents are not essentially opposites but rather very much alike. Their difference is by degree, and it is often slight.

This is not surprising when one considers the derivation of the term "contest" itself. Coming from *com* plus *testari*, meaning to bear witness together, it suggests both human plurality and a common testimony. A minimal two persons must be doing the same kind of thing for valid comparisons of success to be made. It would sound strange for a person to claim victory in a running race to the store even though his adversary used a car or, worse yet, drove to another place. But this contesting "togetherness" is not a community project toward one end, as it would be if two or more persons were trying collectively to pass a test. It is doing the same kind of thing in an attempt to show difference in the direction of superiority.

Thus, contesting opposition would be one of scale. This is a continuous scale running from a hypothetical zero point (utter failure on the test) to 100 (total success on the test). The greatest distinction in the contest is that which exists, for example, between one who "could not get to first base" and another who scored runs as a "matter of habit." Interestingly, the polarity black-white, which is Ogden's archetype for opposition on a continuous scale (2: p. 66), finds its way into such a loser's vocabulary when he complains of being "whitewashed."

Yet it is the subtle distinction between two hues of white, gray, or black which typifies the close contest. So delicate is the distinction that it is often difficult to discern. The exact nature of differences in performance (if any) may be left in doubt until the last moment of the contest. Paradoxically, many behemoths of sport spend hours sending the resounding shock waves of their collisions into the air to symbolize what they see as the great mutually exclusive opposites of the universe—victory and defeat. Yet they may produce but a whisper of difference by degree, only the most subtle of distinctions between themselves. The would be quest for "A" rather than "not-A" or at least white rather than black turns out to be one for a slightly lighter shade of off-white.

There appear to be two steps taken in moving from test to contest. The first is the development of testing families. It is one tester recognizing another individual as a like tester. It is grounded in the ability to see that someone else can encounter the same test as oneself.

This does not mean that one merely identifies other golfers, swimmers, or mountain climbers as members of a general category. Testing families are much more specific, for golf courses, swimming pools and mountains offer a multitude of different tests. An advanced golfer sees his test, for example, in much different terms than the beginner. A high rough, a heavy cross wind, or a 225 yard distance which must be traversed in a single shot with the ball moving from left to right provides testing ambiguity for the excellent golfer. These same phenomena may be seen by the beginner as impossible situations. The novice cannot exercise his skill in relationship to these situations. In short, the beginner and advanced golfers do not see themselves as members of the same testing family.

This identification of family membership often occurs without knowledge of another's scores or record. There are certain "signs of the family" which serve to identify communities of like testers. The quality of another's equipment, the clothes he wears, the stories he tells, and mannerisms in speech, gait, and other body gestures often announce quite loudly the specific testing fraternity to which he belongs. More telling yet is the manner in which another individual approaches his test. The preparation, deliberation, positioning, and focus of concentration are all family specific. In golf, for example, one can generally watch another merely walk onto the tee and address his ball and thereby recognize the specific community to which he belongs. The eventual swing and result are superfluous for these purposes.

Again, one's own skill is implicit in identifying other members of his testing community.

There is usually no need to recall recent scores or otherwise assess one's own skill at taking the test to make this identification. An athlete lives his skill (even if it had changed recently) toward other potential members of his testing family. Their welcome or non-welcome is immediate and is not the end result of a chain of deductions which begin with the measurement of one's own athletic prowess.

The second step in moving from test to contest is making a commitment within a testing family to better one another's performances. This step succeeds the formation of a testing family simply because in the absence of such a community one has at worst no basis for a comparison (two individuals are engaged in taking two different tests) or at best a poor basis for contesting (one side will be "whitewashed").

Such a commitment to do better than another is often difficult to observe and, at times, exists only tenuously. One's supposed opponent may become so fascinated with the test itself that the contest is ignored. Or a counterfeit opponent may play for his health, relaxation, or being "in the great outdoors." Victory and defeat, in such situations, are not shared. The contest is not mutually held.

But if two family members are truly contesting, they are interested in each other's progress in taking the test. Their own strategies, rhythms, their very relationship to the test is, in part, dictated by the *other's* performance. Contestants watch one another. The contestants cannot be concerned merely with passing the test, for an opponent may pass it in a superior fashion. The test itself cannot give a contestant sufficient information on what is required of him.

Conclusions

Sport is diverse, even in its basic structure. The two kinds of point-counterpoint examined in this essay undergird two very different kinds of activity. Both are captivating; both have their own "sweet tension." The radical ambiguity of the test, its strident vulnerability and impregnability, as well as the contest's more subtle opposition by degree, the shadings of a little more and a little less, call to those who like to move in an aura of uncertainty.

Notes

1. Point-counterpoint is defined as opposite points, themes, or courses and is used interchangeably with opposition and contrariety in this paper.
2. A phrase used to describe human fascination with sport from Warren P. Fraleigh of the State University College at Brockport, New York.
3. They can be neither back to back nor face to face, for this would eliminate the ambiguity.

Bibliography

1. Kretchmar, R. Scott. "A Phenomenological Analysis of the Other in Sport." Unpublished doctoral dissertation, University of Southern California, 1971.
2. Ogden, C. K. *Opposition: A Linguistic and Psychological Analysis.* Bloomington: Indiana University Press, 1967.
3. Suits, Bernard. "The Elements of Sport," *The Philosophy of Sport.* Robert G. Osterhoudt (ed.). Springfield, Illinois: Charles C Thomas, 1973.

2.3

The ends of the sports contest

Warren P. Fraleigh

Certain ends must be pursued to have the sports contest. These ends are therefore necessary for the good sports contest when the reference point of view is the nature of the sports contest. Sports participants pursue different personal intended ends which may or may not be supportive of the ends necessary for the good sports contest. Also, the sports contest has an institutionalized purpose, which is a common understanding of the nature of the event called the sports contest. These three kinds of ends and their relationships will be examined to see which are necessary for, which are consistent with, and which are inconsistent or incongruent with the good sports contest. Finally, a certain set of relationships between these ends is necessary for all participants and is for the good of everyone alike. Thus, this set of relationships is necessary for the good sports contest from the moral point of view.

The ends in the sports contest

The ends in the sports contest are those that exist because of the contest itself; in fact, no contest can occur without them. Therefore, sports participants must adopt some of these ends as their personal intended ends or a contest cannot exist – good or not. Suits[1] identifies these ends as the end of achieving a specific state of affairs, the end of winning, and the end of playing the game. This last end will be called the end of contesting, since we are now restricting its use to the sports contest.

Achieving a specific state of affairs may be understood, in the language used previously, as bringing about a change in a state of affairs as a result of an agent's action. In the present context this means realizing some specific result for an action – a result which the sport so specifies. For instance, as Suits provides, the specific state of affairs achieved in any race is having the racers reach a designated point. The designated point is common to all race contests and includes many variations such as crossing a finish line drawn on a track, touching a wall at the end of a swimming pool, or rowing under a certain bridge on the river Thames. In a badminton game the specific state of affairs sought by both players is hitting the shuttlecock in the air with the racket.

The end of winning, a necessary end of any sports contest and therefore of the good sports contest, is constituted by achieving the specific state of affairs adopted using the means specified and within the restrictions set by the accepted rules of the sport. If I am to achieve the end of winning a race, I must arrive at the designated point, not necessarily by the shortest

Warren P. Fraleigh 'The Ends of the Sports Contest', from *Right Actions in Sport: Ethics for Contestants,* © 1984 Warren P. Fraleigh.

and the most efficient means, but certainly by those defined by the rules. For instance, to win a running race of 200 meters around a curved track I must start on a given signal from point A, run within marked lanes around the track to the designated point B 200 meters away, and arrive there before anyone else who follows the same regulations. If I am interested only in arriving at the designated point B, I could run across the infield to get there, or ride a turtle, or use any means and routes that suit my fancy. But if I am interested in achieving the end of winning I must adopt, at the least, the mode of transport and the route specified. Furthermore, I must achieve the same state of affairs, the means and routes to which are rule-determined, by engaging an opponent and achieving that same state of affairs better than the opponent.[2] Accordingly, in our description of a good sports contest in badminton, John alone wins because he has hit the shuttlecock with his racket legally in the air more often, over the net within the prescribed boundaries, against the opposition of Bob, who was also attempting to hit the shuttle more often and within the rule-determined prescriptions.

In the good sports contest, all participants must achieve the end of the specific state of affairs. Yet it is clearly not necessary to the sports contest, good or bad, that all participants achieve the end of winning. As a matter of fact, in zero sum or negative sum games, only one of the opponents can win. Thus, the end of winning is a constitutive feature of any sports contest but cannot be a necessary personal intended end of all participants.

If the above statement appears to be contradictory, it is because of an unfortunate conflation of our common language about winning. But this may be clarified by discussing the third end in the sports contest, namely, the end of contesting or trying to win. This end means exerting one's best effort in the requisite ways toward the specific state of affairs. Exerting one's best effort is trying to win better than an opponent is winning. Please note that there is a real difference between the end of winning as a factual condition, which is achieved by only one participant, and the end of trying to win, or contesting, which is necessary for all participants. Thus all participants must adopt, as their personal intended end, the end of trying to win – the end of contesting.

We may summarize the ends in the sports contest in a way that will anticipate further discussion, and three generalizations are appropriate. In order for the good sports contest to occur:

1 The ends of achieving a specific state of affairs, of winning and of trying to win, or contesting, are all necessary.
2 All participants must adopt as personal intended ends the end of achieving a specific state of affairs and the end of trying to win.
3 It is not necessary that all participants adopt the end of winning as their personal intended end.

The intended ends of the participants

The intended ends of participants in sports contests range from very specific states of affairs intended as ends within the contest to states of affairs intended as ends resulting from the contest. In the badminton game one participant executes a smash and the intended end of this action is to hit the shuttle to the floor on the opponent's side and to score the point or to win the serve. One action is often instrumental in achieving an end which helps achieve another end. Thus, smashing the shuttle with the intended end of scoring the point is useful, along with other actions, in pursuing the end of trying to win or contesting. The action of smashing and its intended end of scoring the point is congruent (alike in characteristics) with the end of trying to win, or contesting. Now it is conceivable that any sports participant may adopt, as a personal intended end of actions, an intended end that does not anticipate any state of affairs beyond itself. This is to say that we can, in Chisholm's words, "define an *ultimate end* as one that is intended but not intended in order that some *other* end be realized."[3] In short, trying to win can be all that a participant is doing in the sports contest and, accordingly, intended ends are contained wholly within the sports contest itself. As indicated, a sports participant does not need to adopt the end of winning as a personal intended end.

This understanding is important. First, it is important to distinguish between winning and trying to win in the sense of what agent participants in sports contests do, that is, the actions which they perform. Agent participants perform actions that intend the end of trying to win – they do not perform winning. Winning is not an action; it is an achievement verb, whereas trying to win or contesting is an activity verb for an action.[4] Second, the end of winning is properly understood, not as the personal intended end of an agent participant but as the description of the point of termination of the sports contest, good or bad. In other words, winning is a constitutive element of the complete sports contest,[5] as is its opposite, losing. As terms describing termination, winning and losing are the partners of those terms that describe the beginning of the sports contest such as serving, where we have servers and receivers.

Trying to win can be a sports participant's personal intended end, adopted not because it is sufficient in itself but because it is instrumental in achieving a state of affairs outside the contest. Trying to win becomes a means to another intended end such as earning money or prizes, achieving social recognition, or improving one's physical fitness. These are not ends within the sports contest itself but are external ends. The adoption of personal intended ends external to a sports contest sometimes effectively negates one of the ends which must be intended by all participants, namely, the end of trying to win. For example, in American college football we observe situations in which the participants have chosen an action that intended an end of trying to achieve a tie game, or even avoiding a defeat, both of which negate the end of trying to win. Kicking a point after a touchdown rather than trying a two-point conversion by the losing team in the last seconds of a 7–6 game is trying to achieve a tie, not trying to win. Trying to tie negates exerting one's best effort except in unusual circumstances. For instance, if a basketball player whose team is behind by two points attempts a field goal in the last second of a contest, he/she is exerting the best effort.

Spectators react negatively to an action that intends the end of trying to tie but they cheer an action that intends an end of trying to win, such as trying to run for two points in the football game. The reason is evident. Choosing to tie negates the end of trying to win – and trying to win is an end that all participants must intend in order for the contest to be the good contest. But the "experts" among the sports participants, the athletes, or coaches, always claim good reasons for trying to tie. The reasons they give are that achieving a tie is instrumental for some external intended end such as attaining or maintaining a national ranking, maintaining their standing in an athletic league, or qualifying for a postseason bowl game. When such intended ends predominate over the end of trying to win, this is not a good sports contest.[6] Exerting one's best effort is essential to determining who is better in a contest; such a determination is what the contest is about.

Sports participants may also adopt intended ends external to the sports contest that do not negate the end of trying to win but reduce its significance so that the good sports contest cannot occur. For instance, entertaining spectators with unusual and indirect clowning methods of trying to win may emphasize the external end of entertainment. Exhibitions by organizations such as the Harlem Globetrotters is a good illustration of this. Clearly, the intended end of these actions is to entertain the audience by obviously hilarious antics, not to determine which team plays better basketball. No aspersion on the basketball skills of these players is intended; obviously they are well-skilled. The point is that these skills are used to provide laughs for the audience, not for good sports contests.

Individual sports participants can also adopt personal intended ends that are external to the contest and reduce the significance of trying to win so that the good sports contest cannot occur. For instance, a tennis player may deliberately play in a haphazard or a less skillful manner, or perhaps deliberately and unnecessarily execute unusual strokes such as hitting the ball between the legs, behind his/her back, or with the racket held by the nondominant hand. Such actions may be taken for the fun of it, to embarrass the opponent, to get the game over with, and so on, all of which indicate a personal intended end external to the contest itself. By assuming priority, these actions reduce the significance of the end of trying to win so that the contest is not the good sports contest but is a farce instead.

Finally, sports participants may intend personal ends external to the contest but yet consistent with the personal intended end of trying to win or contesting. This occurs when the personal intended end can be realized only by trying to win. For instance, when the external end is a consequence of a participant being declared a winner because he or she has tried to win, that external end can happen only if the participant indeed does try to win. A golfer who adopts the personal intended external end of earning a $60,000 first-place prize in a tournament, for example, must adopt the end of trying to win as a personal intended end. Inasmuch as intending one of these ends entails intending the other end as its necessary instrumental means, the two intended ends are consistent with one another.

In summary, we may now make some general conclusions about the various possible relationships of the participants' own intended ends to those constituted by the sports contest.

1 If a participant intends ends that are realized wholly within the sports contest, such as trying to win, then personal intended ends are congruent with the ends in the good sports contest.

2 If a participant intends ends that are realized externally to the contest, but are realized only if the participant intends the end of trying to win the contest, then his/her external personal intended ends are consistent with the ends in the good sports contest.

3 If a participant intends ends that are realized externally to the contest, but are realized by the participant intending an end which negates the end of trying to win, then his/her external personal intended ends are incongruent with the ends in the good sports contest.

4 If a participant intends ends that are realized externally to the contest, but are realized by the participant intending an end which assumes priority over the end of trying to win, then his/her external personal intended ends are inconsistent with the ends in the good sports contest.

The purpose of the sports contest

The purpose of the sports contest is the reason for its existence.[7] [...], the purpose of the sport contest can be understood as the collective intended end of those participants who voluntarily enter into the institution of sport. As a collective intended end it is an institutionalized purpose, the establishment of and maintenance or destruction of which can occur only through the actions of many agent participants. The ends in the sports contest are those that occur within a specific sports contest, while the purpose of the sports contest is the reason why any sports contest exists.

I have stated elsewhere that if sport has an institutional purpose, it comes from someone or somewhere. There seem to be three logical possibilities: the existential thesis, the metaphysical thesis, and the historical thesis. The existential thesis contends that each individual who engages in the sports contest is the source of the purpose of the contest. "This view considers purpose as the conscious choice of what the participant wants to get out of his participation. Sport becomes an instrumentality to a diversity of individual purposes."[8] The metaphysical thesis contends that, "the purpose of sport is supplied by God, or whatever agent you wish, who is the originator of all that is. In short, there is a metaphysical essence of sport which contains a true purpose in its given structure."[9] The historic thesis states that "the purpose of sport is supplied by the historic institutionalized structure of sport as it has developed over thousands of years by millions of individuals and by hundreds of societies. That is to say that the structure of sport itself as it has evolved carries within itself a sense of purpose."[10]

In viewing these three possibilities I have chosen the historical purpose, for it seems to me that historical human consciousness intends a phenomenal structure for sport that includes an awareness of the purpose of the institution of sport. Sport has been initiated and developed by humans through history so that, as with all human institutions, value may be available to human beings that would not be available to individuals in a state of nature – that is, without institutions. A historical phenomenal structure for sport may not give us the clear and precise definitions of sport that the language analyst would prefer,[11] but it can provide, rather, a description of what the substantial content of human consciousness of sport carries. Since our primary focus is to establish a moral point of view for sport which will be the reference source for moral actions in the sports contest, that reference point must portray what human consciousness intends as sport so that the result may make sense to sports participants.

We may describe the purpose of a sports contest by first providing a phenomenal description of what the sports contest is.

> A sports contest is a voluntary, agreed upon, human event in which one or more human participants opposes at least one human other to seek the mutual appraisal of the relative abilities of all participants to move mass in space and time by utilizing bodily moves which exhibit developed motor skill, physiological and psychological endurance and socially approved tactics and strategy.[12]

It is the claim here that when human consciousness focuses upon the concept of the sports contest (not sport), this description, or something very near to it, has been embodied in our collective, historical consciousness. In short, this phenomenal structure of the sports contest has become institutionalized. Given the description above, we may readily describe the sports contest's purpose, remembering that purpose is understood to mean the reason for the existence of the sports contest. It follows that:

> The purpose of the sports contest is to provide equitable opportunity for mutual contesting of the relative abilities of the participants to move mass in space and time within the confines prescribed by an agreed-upon set of rules.[13]

This is what sport participants are about, in common, when they enter the sports contest. It is the common purpose, shared by its institutionalization, which provides for value that would be otherwise unattainable for agents acting without sports contests. It is the specification of the reason for the sports contest's existence, as distinguished from the personal intended ends of the participants and from the ends in the sports contest.

This normative concept of the purpose of the sports contest is helpful in several ways. First, "it allows us to conceive of the activity itself as having a purpose as distinct from whatever intentions individuals or societies bring to the activity."[14] In this book such a conception will

allow the necessary moral perspective, which is in principle superior to either the perspective of self-interest or that of convention. "Second, this description of purpose serves to individuate sport from other human activities which appear to be at the same level of generalization ...Third, because this individuation of purpose occurs at less than the cosmological level of generalization, it allows for possibilities of relating the purpose of sport to other more general purposes without confusing levels of generality."[15] In differentiating the purpose of the sports contest from that of, say, the dance performance, we have a reference point that allows us to differentiate actions appropriate in one context from the same actions as less or not appropriate in the other. This allows us to appraise actions concerning sport itself without, in certain cases, importing external standards that are inappropriate at least and misleading at worst. On the other hand, differentiating the purpose of sports contests from broader conceptions allows the application of general concepts of purpose to sport which are appropriate to all human activities, and to realize that such occurs precisely because some broader conceptions of purpose are relevant to all human activity and not simply to sport.

Finally, establishing the concept of the sports contest's purpose, along with the idea of the participants' intended ends and the ends in the sports contest, allows us to relate these three distinct conceptions of the ends of the sports contest to ascertain, in particular conflict situations, which idea is of highest priority. Furthermore, these three concepts may be related to each other in sports-relevant language that is necessary in developing the moral guides for action.

Notwithstanding the above perspective, that the purpose of the sport contest is best expressed as the reason for its existence, some other views relevant to this discussion have appeared. In an earlier work[16] I reviewed briefly the ideas of Vanderzwaag in his *Toward a Philosophy of Sport*, Slusher in *Man, Sport and Existence*, Metheny in *Movement and Meaning*, and Weiss in *Sport, a Philosophic Inquiry*. Vanderzwaag interprets purpose in sport by discussing it as the motive that impels individuals to participate. Slusher states that sport is not purposeful itself but that human beings have purpose, and their entry into the purposeless activity of a sport can be understood as a way of pursuing their purpose of actualization. Metheny speaks of the intention of sport performers as directed at moving mass in space and time in a specified way, and appears to conceive of purpose as the intention of the performer within sport. She also says sports rules provide an opportunity for concentration of the performer's energies into performing a self-chosen task or the actions of sport. Finally, Weiss interprets sport purpose in terms of the deep satisfaction it provides humans in their realization of the desire to be self-complete through testing and extension of the body.

All these explanations of sports purpose are interesting and illuminating but, with the exception of Metheny, are not too useful for developing moral guides for the sports contest. Except for Metheny, the ideas of the purpose of sport are not derived from the nature of the sports contest and do not speak directly to sports actions. Also, the motive or the pursuit of actualization does not necessarily consider other sports participants and is probably similar to what was discussed earlier here as the intended ends of the participants. Because such intended ends are for individual participants, they do not in principle meet the characteristic of being for the good of everyone alike. Accordingly, although Weiss, Slusher, or Vanderzwaag do not necessarily contradict the concept of the sports contest's purpose stated here, none of them speaks directly to sport itself nor pays specific attention to the characteristics of the moral point of view. Metheny's ideas and the purpose of the sports contest presented by this work focus upon sport as sport and provide a base for moral principles of action that are sports relevant.

The purpose of the sports contest as stated here qualifies as the purpose of a just institution. First, it embodies a collective intended end which guarantees that sport's unique value is available to all participants. It does so by prescribing equitable opportunity for contesting to all participants. Prescribing such opportunity guarantees that the unique value is available to all participants because these goods are a direct result of contesting; and equitable opportunity for contesting therefore guarantees access to those things which are a direct result of contesting.

In the description of a good sports contest we can see manifestations of the normative purpose of the sports contest, discussion of which will serve two important functions. First, it will show different instances in how such an institutional purpose becomes evident in the actions of sports participants. Second, it will illustrate the earlier claim that this institutional purpose is a result of historic human consciousness of the purpose of sports contests in that the actions taken in the badminton game are not unusual but normal. John and Bob act in the certain ways because they, as sports participants, already know that the purpose of the sports contest is to provide equitable opportunity for mutual contesting of the relative abilities of the participants to move mass in space and time within the confines prescribed by an agreed upon set of rules, as stated earlier.

First we notice that John and Bob have agreed to play a game of singles and, following their game, reiterate their agreement by the brief interchange "See you next week, then?" "Yes, let's do it again!" This agreement has two aspects relevant to the normative concept of the purpose of the sports contest: first, to pursue the purpose of the contest together by both adhering to the rules of badminton; second, to choose an opponent of one's own caliber to try to guarantee an even contest so that the relative abilities of the participants will be contested in this particular contest. Indeed, in examining what occurs in sport where participants have a choice of opponent, we find almost invariably that they choose opponents who will provide an equal contest. Sport is replete with examples of the attempt to assure equal opportunity for contesting of the participants' relative abilities. Within sports we specify weight classes, novice or open competitive groups, age groups, and all other divisions which intend to equalize the contest before it occurs. In American professional football, a player draft is one way of trying to develop more equal opponents by allowing the poorer teams earlier player choices.[17] American professional football also attempts to equate competition by its scheduling policy.

The next thing we note is the action of spinning the racket to determine who will serve and who will occupy which court. This is so each player has equal opportunity to have the slight advantage of serving first, a slight advantage not

111

given by a procedure that provides a better chance to one player. Rather, the opportunity is 50% for each player. This assures equal opportunity to all participants so that the contest is between their relative performance abilities, and the determination of who displays better relative ability is not unduly influenced by arbitrary and privileged advantage. Normal sports actions illustrate this: Coins are flipped to determine who will kick off and who will receive. Captains of opposing teams guess odd or even number of fingers that the official conceals. And in some instances, a player earns the right to serve first by winning a rally for service or by throwing a ball to see who will come closer to a predetermined mark.

To strengthen the case, we see that if one player loses the spin of the racket or the coin flip, that player is compensated by having the right to choose which half of the badminton or tennis court he/she will play on, or which goal he will defend in American football. These actions illustrate the continued effort of trying to maintain equal opportunity for all participants; they are not simply conventional actions but are actions exhibiting the historic consciousness of the purpose of the sports contest.

A third thing to be noted in the badminton game is what occurs when Bob, who is the server and is behind 12–13 at the time, executes a smash that lands very close to the sideline on John's side. John, who saw the shuttle clearly land on the line, immediately calls the shot "good." Bob asks "are you sure?", to which John replies affirmatively. John calls the shot good because he knows that Bob has earned a point within the agreed rules, and if he were to deny Bob that earned point, then he would be putting Bob into an unfair disadvantageous position that would contradict the purpose of the sports contest. The same kind of consciousness is illustrated in those two previous occasions when neither player was sure whether the shuttle was in or out. In those instances, they agreed to play the point over. This illustrates consciousness of contesting the participants' relative abilities, which refers to ability to perform the skills of the sport itself and not the players' abilities to guess at the landing point of the shuttle or for either player to use the situation to his/her own advantage.

One more illustration will reinforce the argument that human consciousness in the sports contest displays awareness of the purpose of the sports contest. The option of setting or not setting the badminton game when a tie occurs at either 13 or 14 points indicates this consciousness at work in the rules. Badminton rules provide this option because in any contest that becomes tied either one or two points away from its normal completion, it is obvious that neither player has demonstrated markedly greater ability to that point and, since only the server may score points in badminton, being the server is a distinct advantage. Therefore, the option is available to extend the contest by either two or three points in order to diminish the advantage which the server has at this time. If I am the player who has an option, I will now calculate what choice is to my advantage since my opponent has the advantage of service. If I choose to set the game at five points I must then play a longer contest which, if my endurance is less than my opponent's, could work to my disadvantage. If I set the game at five points and my endurance is greater than my opponent's (of which I cannot be positive), I nonetheless still must overcome the opponent's advantage of having the service and being able to score several points quickly. This will diminish the chance of my being able to score five before my opponent does. If I choose not to set the game because my opponent now appears exhausted and I believe I can win the service quickly, I run the risk that my opponent may summon a reserve of perseverance and win two points by sheer determination. These points show that the consciousness displayed in the rules and in the player's calculations show awareness of the purpose of equitable opportunity for contesting the relative abilities of the participants.

Let us now summarize the major points on the purpose of the sports contest. This will anticipate the task of relating the purpose of the sports contest to the personal intended ends of participants and to the ends in the sports contest. Relating these three will then allow for a clear and normative exposition of the ends of the good sports contest.

1 The purpose of the sports contest, when conceived as the reason for its existence, is to provide equitable opportunity for mutual contesting of the participants' relative abilities to move mass in space

and time within the confines prescribed by an agreed-upon set of rules.

2 This purpose of the sports contest is understood as the collective intended end established by historic human consciousness of why sports contests exist.

3 This purpose of the sports contest is specific to sport as a distinct form of human action but may be related to general human purposes that are applicable to all human activities.

4 Establishing this purpose indicates that, as an institution, sport has a purpose distinguishing it from the personal intended ends of participants and the conventional ends established within any particular social group.

5 This stated purpose of the sports contest is a just purpose because it guarantees equal opportunity to the good(s) of the institution of sport by all participants.

The ends of the good sports contest

The ends of the good sports contest may now be established by describing the necessary relationships among the ends in the sports contest, the personal intended ends of the participants, and the purpose of the sports contest, and by giving reasons why such relationships are necessary.

The ends of the good sports contest are a composite of certain relationships of those ends of the sports contest that must exist in order for the good sports contest to be possible. Such a condition does not guarantee that the good sports contest will occur, but only that it is now possible because the ends pursued will allow it. As we shall see in subsequent chapters of this section, elements other than the ends pursued are necessary for the good sports contest. Those kinds of ends needed for the good sports contest to occur are summarized as:

1 The institutionalized purpose of the sports contest expressed as the reason for the existence of any sports contest;

2 The ends in the sports contest, namely, the end of achieving a certain state of affairs, the end of winning, and the end of trying to win or contesting;

3 Those personal intended ends of the participants which are, at best, congruent, and at the least, consistent with both the institutional purpose of the sports contest and with the ends in a sports contest of achieving a certain state of affairs and of trying to win, or contesting.

The purpose of the sports contest is necessary for a good sports contest for several reasons. It is that goal which the participants have in common and which guarantees access to the value(s) of the sports contest for all participants. It is what binds people together in a common endeavor; the sports contest cannot have any social meaning without it. For if a person wants to have a sports contest and a sports contest necessarily involves at least one other person, neither can have the sports contest unless the other is guaranteed equal opportunity to do the task. Neither John nor Bob can have a badminton game unless the other is there to hit the shuttle over the net. Furthermore, there is no contest, no test which is shared,[18] unless both have equal opportunity to hit the shuttle over the net. Equal opportunity to perform that task is the presupposition of satisfying the desire to contest relative ability. So, the purpose of the sports contest is not only necessary for the good sports contest but has priority over the ends in a contest or the personal intended ends of the participants.

The ends in the sports contest come into being when the participants begin a particular contest that is constituted by the purpose of the sports contest. Achieving a specific state of affairs, such as arriving at a designated point in a race, has no relevant sports meaning independent of the purpose of the sports contest. Without the purpose of the sports contest, arriving at a designated point remains just that. Arriving at a designated point, however, when observed in relation to the purpose of the sports contest, is now either crossing the finish line or completing the race. Likewise, the ends of winning and of contesting derive their sports-relevant meaning from the purpose of the sports contest. The term winning cannot be sports meaningful until it is seen in relation to equitable opportunity for mutual contesting of the participants' relative abilities within the confines prescribed by an agreed-upon set of rules, since winning means the result of the mutual contesting. Also, contesting as an end receives its meaning from the purpose of the sports contest since contesting means testing the relative abilities of the participants to do the same task.

The ends in the sports contest then come into being and depend for meaning upon the existence of a sports contest, which itself comes into being when the participants accept the purpose of the sports contest. However, the personal intended ends of the participants need careful analysis in relation to both the ends in the sports contest and the purpose of the sports contest. We have seen earlier in this chapter that participants may adopt ends either within the contest or external to the contest. If a participant adopts as his/her final ends the achievement of a state of affairs relevant to that sport and trying to win in that contest, his/her personal intended ends are wholly within a sports contest. In our badminton game John and Bob may both adopt as their final ends the achievement of hitting the shuttle in the air and trying to win, or contesting, by hitting the shuttle in such a way that it falls to the floor on the opponent's side. The adoption of these as personal intended ends by John and Bob means that their personal intended ends are meaningful only in relation to the purpose of the sports contest.

In such cases, the personal intended ends of these participants are congruent with the purpose of the sports contest since they are exactly equivalent to ends which participants must pursue in any contest and because their meaning as ends depends upon the purpose of the sports contest. Personal intended ends that are congruent with the purpose of the sports contest are one way to enhance the possibility of the good sports contest because what the participants intend is for the sake of the contest alone. Accordingly, the particular actions actually performed are most likely to be actions that will sustain the good sports contest. If all the participants in the sports contest intend nothing more than contesting, it is most likely that the actions they choose will result in the good sports contest, along with other elements yet to be discussed, since their practical reasoning will select the most appropriate actions (means) to those ends.

The personal intended ends of participants may be consistent with the purpose of the sports contest when they adopt as a personal intended end trying to win in order to achieve an end external to the specific sports contest. For instance, either John or Bob can intend the ends of hitting the shuttle in the air in such a way that it falls to the floor on the opponent's side in order to win a beer or increase cardiovascular endurance. If all the participants adopt personal intended ends external to the sports contest, ends that, however, may only be achieved by adopting the end in the contest of contesting, then it is more likely that the actions they choose, along with other elements yet to be discussed, will result in the good sports contest.

Participants' personal intended ends may be inconsistent with the purpose of the sports contest if they adopt an external end that reduces the significance of contesting to a level whereby it is not deemed necessary. For example, either John or Bob could try hitting the shuttle over the net by striking it consistently behind the back, even though the opponent struck the shuttle with normal badminton strokes. The participant who performs in this way is not pursuing the end of contesting as a necessary end. Hitting the shuttle consistently behind one's back, after all, is not the kind of action which ensures a contest but, rather, decreases its possibility. A participant who acts in this way may be pursuing a personal intended end of being funny, which relegates the end of contesting to a subordinate role. And since such an end is a necessary one that all participants must pursue, the actions thus performed are less likely to produce the good sports contest.

Finally, the personal intended ends of the participants may be incongruent with the purpose of the sports contest. This occurs when a participant adopts an external personal intended end that negates pursuit of the end in the contest of contesting. Trying to tie a football game in order to achieve the external end of attaining or maintaining a national rating is a good illustration here. Again, the pursuit of this end negates the necessary end in the game of trying to win, and trying to win derives its meaning from that part of the sports contest's purpose which mentions contesting. Contesting is by nature "a commitment ... made by each side to attempt to better the other's performance"[19] and trying to tie is one form of denial of trying to better the other's performance.

Thus, a personal intended end that is incongruent with the purpose of the sports contest is the source of those actions which, if performed, are unlikely to produce the good sports contest.

We may now see that those personal intended ends which participants adopt may foster actions that maintain the integrity of the sports contest by being either congruent or consistent with the purpose of the sports contest. Conversely, those personal intended ends that are inconsistent or incongruent with the purpose of the sports contest compromise its integrity by detracting from it or negating it.

In conclusion, the good sports contest is one in which the personal intended ends of actions are congruent with or consistent with the purpose of the sports contest and necessary for the establishment of one condition from which a good sports contest may grow. Other conditions are also necessary foundations for a good sports contest.

Notes

1. Bernard Suits, "What is a Game?" *Philosophy of Science* 34 (June 1967), pp. 148–156.
2. R. Scott Kretchmar, "From Test to Contest: An Analysis of Two Kinds of Counterpoint in Sport," *Journal of the Philosophy of Sport* II (September 1975), pp. 28–29.
3. Roderick Chisholm, "The Structure of Intention," *Journal of Philosophy* LXVII, No. 19 (October 8, 1970), p. 639.
4. Nicholas Rescher, "On the Characterization of Actions," in *The Nature of Human Action*, ed.

Myles Brand (Glenview, IL: Scott, Foresman & Co., 1970), p. 248.
5. A tie describes the incomplete sports contest, and the lack of general human satisfaction with a tie is probably why various means have been adopted to complete tie contests: tie breakers, overtimes, sudden death, sudden victory, and so on.
6. In some sports, the constitutive rules virtually prevent the problem of trying to tie. The rules prescribe either that winning is always achieved at a specific time, such as in badminton, volleyball, or handball, or that if the game is tied at the end, winning will be achieved by using overtimes, tie breakers, and so forth. Those who formulate the constitutive rules of a sport should note that rules against trying to achieve a tie would benefit that sport by producing more good sports contests.
7. Warren P. Fraleigh, "Sport-Purpose," *Journal of the Philosophy of Sport* II (September 1975), p. 78.
8. Ibid., p. 76.
9. Ibid., p. 77.
10. Ibid., p. 77.
11. See Frank McBride, "Toward a Non-Definition of Sport," *Journal of the Philosophy of Sport* II, (September 1975), pp. 4–11.
12. Adapted from an earlier version in Fraleigh, "Sport-Purpose," p. 78.
13. Ibid., p. 78.
14. Ibid., p. 79.
15. Ibid., p. 79.
16. Ibid., pp. 74–76.
17. The idea of trying to guarantee more equal contests before any particular sports contest occurs is very important and will be discussed below in relation to the element of winning/losing and of quality of play.
18. Kretchmar, "From Test to Contest," pp. 28–30.
19. Ibid., pp. 27–29.

Fairness in sport

An ideal and its consequences

Sigmund Loland

Ideas of fairness play an important role in sport. The classical challenge to fairness is intentional rule violations or cheating. Cheaters search for exclusive advantages not available to rule-abiding competitors, and most people consider the results of cheating invalid and unfair. But issues of fairness arise in many other circumstances as well. Outdoor competitions are exposed to changing external conditions. When, in ski jumping, an increase in wind makes conditions more difficult for the last 20 jumpers, people talk of an unfair competition. Sometimes individual differences between competitors also give rise to discussions of fairness. In 2003, eminent professional golfer Annika Sörenstam's debut among male players caused heated public debate. Among the arguments was the view that Sörenstam was placed at an unfair physical disadvantage. Moreover, fairness easily becomes an issue when there are great inequalities in resources in the support of competitors and teams. Technologically advanced sports, such as Formula One car racing or alpine skiing, are sometimes considered unfair due to inequalities among competitors in equipment and technical support.

In this chapter, I examine the fairness ideal in sport and its consequences for practice. I first suggest an interpretation of fairness in terms of two interconnected moral principles, then provide a critical and systematic discussion of actual and possible procedures for realizing these principles in sport. After spelling out an interpretation of fairness in sport, I examine its possible implications for the use of performance-enhancing technologies, including doping.

Fairness

With etymological roots in the old English *fæger*, the term *fair* can mean, among other things, "attractive," "beautiful," "unblemished," "clean," "just and honest," and "according to the rules."[1] From a review of the philosophical literature, Carr lists a series of more or less overlapping moral accounts of *fairness*:

- not disadvantaging others
- being unbiased, impartial, or neutral in our treatment of others
- sharing burdens and benefits equally, or maintaining a proper proportion between benefit and contribution
- treating equal or similar cases equally or similarly
- adhering to the rules
- treating others with the concern and respect they deserve.[2]

Sigmund Loland 'Fairness in Sport: An Ideal and Its Consequences', from *Performance-Enhancing Technologies in Sports: Ethical, Conceptual and Scientific Issues*, Thomas H. Murray *et al.* eds, © 2009 Sigmund Loland. Reprinted by permission of The Johns Hopkins University Press.

As is evident, from the examples, in my introductory paragraph, most of these accounts are relevant in the discussion of fairness in sport. For the sake of precision and to narrow the discussions somewhat, I will try to be more specific.

In Rawls's influential *A Theory of Justice* (1971), *fairness* is understood in two ways.[3] First, it is seen as an individual obligation that arises as a result of voluntary engagement in rule-governed practices. Rawls's argument, drawn from the writings of C. D. Broad and H. L. A. Hart, among others, goes as follows: "when a number of persons engage in a mutually advantageous cooperative venture according to rules and thus restrict their liberty in ways necessary to yield advantages to all, those who have submitted to these restrictions have a right to a similar acquiescence on the part of those who have benefited from their submission." In short, the intuitive idea is that it is wrong to benefit from the cooperation of others without doing one's fair share. Rawls makes explicit mention of games in this respect. Voluntary engagement in games gives rise to an obligation of fairness prescribing the need "to play by the rules and to be a good sport."[4] Here, then, is a background for the common understanding of cheating as a classic case of unfairness. Cheaters search for an exclusive advantage that depends on others' adherence to the rules. Cheaters are "free riders" benefiting from the cooperation of others without doing their fair share.

The second interpretation is to see fairness as certain structural characteristics of a particular situation of choice between moral principles. As a methodological tool, Rawls proposes she thought experiment of the "original position."[5] Here, free and equal persons concerned to further their own interests are to choose the basic structure or principles of the just society. However, they do not have free access to all relevant information in this regard. To eliminate reasoning based on pure self-interest and to ensure impartial decisions, a "veil of ignorance" is lowered before the decision makers. Behind this veil, they are blind to particular information about themselves and their position in society, such as their sex, race, and intelligence, their psychological profile, and their special talents or handicaps. However, they are given knowledge of general, relevant facts about human societies, such as facts about political affairs, economic theory, organization, and human (moral) psychology and well-being. The "original position" is considered a paradigmatic example of an impartial and informed setting—it is fair. The principles of justice arrived at here are seen to gain authority by the fairness of the procedures by which they arise.[6]

Rawls indicates that the idea of the original position can be a methodological tool of relevance in the examination of more general issues of the morally right, including, I assume, the morally right in sport.[7] In what follows, behind an imagined veil of ignorance that screens out self-interest but with access to relevant facts, I will search for an understanding of fairness in sport.

Fairness in sport

In the many and diverse social practices and institutions of modern societies, a variety of schemes of local justice can be found, depending on the goals of the practice or institution under examination.[8] In a lottery, we cultivate chance and rely on pure procedural justice. Physical education in school includes evaluation of students on the basis of a combination of effort, motivation, and skill. Fair procedures for evaluation have to include all these elements in an impartial manner.

To a larger extent, competitive sport builds on a meritocratic scheme of distributive justice. Goods, such as competitive advantages and victories, are distributed based on distinction in performance. Burdens, such as competitive disadvantages, penalties, and losses, are distributed based on lack of performance or violation of performance standards. The characteristic, structural goal of sports competitions is to measure, compare, and rank competitors according to performance of relevant skills within the framework of the rules.[9] The critical question here is how this goal can be reached in fair ways.

As demonstrated by the chapter's introductory examples, challenges to fairness can come from rule violations and cheating and from inequalities in external conditions, in competitors' individual characteristics, and in the strength of their support systems. A key principle to reach fair and valid outcomes seems to be that of *equality of opportunity to perform*.

117

However, as a formal principle, this is of little help in resolving dilemmas arising from the various procedures for evaluating performance in practice. For instance, where are we to draw the line in outdoor sports for degree of climatic inequalities? What is a fair classification of competitors in golf? To what extent are inequalities in technology and equipment acceptable in sport? There is a need here for substantial criteria for what should count as relevant and nonrelevant equalities and inequalities.

In this regard, sports vary. Each sport has its distinctive rules that define a local interpretation of the requirement on equality of opportunity to perform. In soccer, catching and throwing the ball with the hands is strictly forbidden, whereas in U.S. football this is a critical skill. In boxing, knocks to the head are rewarded, whereas in wrestling the same kind of conduct leads to disqualification. However, on closer inspection, and above local accounts of relevant and nonrelevant equalities and inequalities, we can find some more general ideas.

The "equality of opportunity to perform" premise can be given a Kantian underpinning. As potentially autonomous and rational moral agents, persons ought to be treated never merely as means but always as ends in themselves. This by no means indicates equal or identical treatment in all settings. On the contrary, in most human practices, certain inequalities are considered relevant, acceptable, and even admirable, whereas others are considered nonrelevant and/or problematic and should be eliminated or compensated for. The point is to treat everyone as equals.[10]

Inequalities in natural talents or circumstances of birth are not just or unjust in themselves. However, social interpretations and regulations (or the lack thereof) of the consequences of such inequalities can be problematic indeed. A principle of relevance here is the so-called *fair opportunity principle* (FOP).[11] FOP has been formulated in various ways in various ethical theories, but the following version seems to encapsulate the key points: we should eliminate or compensate for essential inequalities between persons that cannot be controlled or influenced by individuals in any significant way and for which individuals cannot be deemed responsible.

In sport, FOP has particular relevance as an operationalization of the "equality of opportunity to perform" principle, where "essential inequalities" are to be understood as inequalities with a significant Impact on sporting performance. In what follows, and from behind the imagined Rawlsian veil of ignorance, I test this assumption by discussing actual and possible procedures to ensure equal opportunity to perform in practice.[12]

Inequalities in external conditions

Let me start with the most obvious example of challenges to fairness: inequalities in external conditions, such as in arena and weather conditions during competitions. These are not within the sphere of control of individuals, and in line with FOP they ought to be eliminated and compensated for. In direct competitions in which participants compete simultaneously, there seem to be few problems. In track and field, all competitors run identical distances on identical surfaces. In ball games, the size of courts and pitches is more or less accurately given in the rules, and players and teams change positions regularly. Inequalities in climatic conditions that cannot be controlled, such as a sudden gust of wind on a tennis court or a sudden clearing of the sky and a low evening sun in the second half of a soccer match, are distributed by chance in a drawing of positions. In this way, possible inequalities linked to surface or weather conditions are eliminated or at least minimized.

These procedures are generally accepted and uncontroversial. However, some sports pose more difficult challenges and call for additional procedures. In outdoor indirect competitions in which participants compete partially or fully separated in time, uncontrollable climatic inequalities may have a strong impact on performance. In skiing, temperature changes can significantly affect the gliding of the skis; in speed skating, sun and wind can make conditions very different from one pair of skaters to another. In most of these sports, the solution is to have seeded groups in which competitors at similar levels of skill compete close in time and, within each group, to draw starting numbers in a lottery. Competitors of similar levels of performance are given as equal conditions as possible. Within each seeded group, uncontrollable inequalities are distributed by chance.

Hence, the impact of these inequalities on the evaluation of performance is minimized.

To sum up, the primary procedure for ensuring equal external conditions is standardization of arenas. Additional procedures, used in cases of uncontrollable inequalities in climatic conditions, are chance (by a drawing of positions) combined with a seeding of competitors.

Inequalities linked to persons

As the introductory example of the golfer Annika Sörenstam demonstrates, issues of fairness arise in discussions of individual differences, too. In line with FOP, the critical criterion will be that if there are inequalities in person-dependent factors that will have an impact on performance that individuals cannot control or influence in any significant way, then these inequalities should be eliminated or compensated for.

This ideal is followed in sport in many ways. Obvious inequalities here are linked to sex, age, and, to a certain extent, body size. Competitors are classified according to sex and age in most sports. Moreover, in sports in which body mass is important to performance, such as in the martial arts, boxing, and weightlifting, there are weight classes.

However, a critical look at a variety of sports demonstrates a lack of consistency in classification matters. In many sports, sex and age classifications are not relevant.[13] Think of a continuum here. At one end we find sports such as the 100-meter sprint in which biomotor abilities such as explosive strength and speed are crucial.[14] Statistically, men are genetically predisposed to develop these abilities to a significantly larger extent than women, and the development of such abilities is at its peak in young men. In other words, in these sports, most young men have a significant advantage over women. Sex classification seems justified. Other sports, such as archery, shooting, sailing, and curling, are at the other end of the continuum. Here, technical and tactical skills are far more important. Such skills are not dependent to the same extent on biomotor abilities but must be learned through years of training and social interaction.[15] Performances are less dependent on genetic predispositions and more dependent on factors over which the individual has influence and control. Moreover, performances are usually more complex and open to a variety of genetic predispositions, or a variety of talents. A moderately fast soccer player can compensate for a lack of speed by strong tactical skills. Similarly, a player with moderate endurance can make up for this with brilliant speed and technique. In principle, in many of these sports, women can compete on an equal level with men, and older people with younger people. Inequalities in sex and age do not have a significant effect on performance. Today's classification patterns are expressions of traditional gender and age roles and seem hard to justify from a systematic, normative point of view such as that of FOP.

In other instances, classification does not seem to be taken far enough. Unlike sex classes, which are based on statistical generalizations, classification according to body size is based on individual characteristics—that is, according to each individual competitor's body composition. In boxing, in the martial arts, and in weightlifting, weight classes are part of the tradition and are uncontroversial. In the shot put or the discus, however, body mass (or rather mass velocity) is crucial to performance, too, but there is no classification by weight. Moreover, in sports such as basketball and volleyball, height is significant to performance. In gymnastics, being small is of decisive importance to master the many technical challenges of the apparatus. On the basis of FOP, when inequalities in body height and/or mass have a significant effect on performance, these inequalities are nonrelevant and should be eliminated or compensated for by height and weight classes. This would make sports such as basketball, volleyball, and gymnastics fairer.[16]

An additional comment is needed here. Athletic performances are the result of a large number of factors and inequalities in both genetic predispositions and environmental stimuli. One person with a good genetic predisposition for swimming may grow up next to a public pool with a good coach, whereas another person with identical predisposition never gets the chance to develop swimming skills. Two persons with different genetic predispositions for swimming may grow up side by side in a fortunate environment and with the same environmental stimuli but end up with significant inequalities in performance. Should we not, then, eliminate or at least compensate for far

119

more inequalities between persons than those in sex, body size, and age? What about inequalities in muscle fiber composition, or in the potential for developing strong cardiovascular capacity and endurance, or in environmental stimuli?

My response would be as follows: FOP does not prescribe the elimination of or compensation for *any* inequality with a significant impact on performance, only those "that cannot be controlled or influenced by individuals in any significant way." Inequalities in sex, body size, and age are biological and physical invariables, and these inequalities qualify for elimination or compensation. Inequalities in genetic predispositions for strength or endurance, or in mental capacities such as willpower and determination, or in environmental factors, are not outside the sphere of individual effort and control and can be compensated for by hard training and effort. Moreover, as I argue below, extensive inequalities in background variables can be compensated for by standardization procedures in the competitions themselves. Restrictions on the application of FOP seem justified.

The broader ethical question is whether this fairness ideal holds water in a larger scheme of socioethical values. What is the value of competitive sport in society? Is it possible to defend ethically a ranking of persons in absolute hierarchies that, at least in part, depend on fortunate genetic predispositions? Eric Juengst (2009) explores these questions in more depth. My brief response here is that as long as elite sport does not represent the norm for the distribution of basic goods and burdens in society (and I do not believe anyone seriously holds that this should be the case), and as long as athletes are voluntarily engaged and competitions meet the fairness requirements proposed in this chapter, sport can be an acceptable and also an admirable practice in society.

Sport expresses an absolute perfectionist ideal in which individuals are evaluated and compared in exact and objective ways. Who is the fastest 100-meter sprinter in the world? What is the best football team ever? Although absolute perfectionism does not seem to carry strong ethical value, it offers fascinating stories of human possibilities (and limitations!) and can play an acceptable role, among a variety of other practices with other ideals, in modern, complex societies. In addition, sport can be a carrier of what we might call relative perfectionist ideals. The field is full of examples and narratives of how individual and team success grows from doing one's best with one's own particular talents and predispositions. The ideal plays a substantive role in strong sporting cultures and in the coaching and psychology of performance. Moreover, and more important in this respect, the striving for one's "personal best" seems to have significant bearing and value outside the sporting context.[17] In this sense, sport can become, in Thomas Murray's (2009) phrase, a sphere for the "virtuous perfection of natural talents" and thus be a strong and concrete expression of a general moral ideal of perfectionism. Here, then, is a possible justification of competitive sport on moral grounds.

Inequalities in system strength

The fair opportunity principle has consequences for inequalities in support systems, that is, in the economic, technological, human, and scientific performance-enhancing support for an athlete or a team. Inequalities in system strength depend to a large extent on the cultural, national, and socioeconomic context in which one is born and raised and in which one lives. Such contexts cannot easily be controlled or influenced by the individual According to FOP, if system inequalities exert a significant effect on performance, they ought to be eliminated or compensated for. How can this be done? What procedures can be of relevance here?

The idea of eliminating or compensating for inequalities in background and resources has a long and troubled history in sport, not least with the ruling on amateurism in the Olympic movement. The origins of the idea are found in the British aristocracy in the eighteenth century. By banning people as sports professionals who earned money by manual labor, the upper classes were able to keep sport an exclusive sphere. Moreover, with rules on amateurism it was possible to emphasize the ideology of an aristocratic, noninstrumental, noble attitude toward life. Although there might be philosophically interesting ideals in the amateur ethos, its practical-political consequences have been repressive for the majority of sports participants.[18] Instead of trying to control and regulate athletes' background, we should look at possibilities of reducing unfair inequalities in system strength with procedures linked to the competitions themselves.

First, based on FOP, equipment and technology should be identical for all competitors, or at least standardized as far as possible, and all competitors should be given equal access. Standardization procedures are found in sailing and in the throwing events in athletics, but they are more or less absent in other sports, such as skiing. There seems to be no acceptable justification for these inconsistencies. In tight skiing competitions, the quality and preparation of skis has a significant effect on the outcome. These inequalities are the responsibilities of ski manufacturers and support systems, not of athletes, and they should be eliminated or at least compensated for by standardization routines.[19]

Second, as seen, for example, in international soccer—in which a few wealthy clubs, such as Spain's Real Madrid, England's Manchester United, and Italy's Juventus, control the market of star players—inequalities in economic strength significantly affect performance. Again, according to FOP, these are inequalities for which teams and players have little or no responsibility. They are unfair. And again, there are alternative procedures. For instance, for every season within the same series, economic resources could be distributed equally among all participating teams. The challenge thus becomes sport-relevant and within the sphere of responsibility of the players and the coach. In a situation of scarce but equal resources, the coach must make sport-specific analyses of what kind of players he or she needs and prioritize among them. Moreover, together with the players, the coach's task becomes to realize the collective potential of the group of players—that is, to make a well-playing team out of them.

Third, the fairness ideal requires elimination of, or at least compensation for, inequalities in scientific know-how. These, too, are inequalities for which the individual cannot be held responsible. In line with a general norm of democratic science, procedures should be installed to secure open publication of all findings on performance enhancement. Knowledge is a public good, and all parties involved ought to be able to enjoy the fruits of it. This does not necessarily mean that those who invest and succeed in sports research give away advantages for free and that those who benefit from the openness of knowledge are free riders who enjoy the efforts of others without doing their fair share. Whether we are talking of new physiological insights in endurance training or new waxing techniques in alpine skiing, selection and practical implementation of knowledge would still require sport-specific knowledge, experience, and skills. The crucial point here is that the main effect of procedures to open up knowledge would be to reduce unfair inequalities between competitors.

Fairness and the use of performance-enhancing technologies

This chapter is part of a larger project on ethical, conceptual, and scientific issues in the use of performance-enhancing technologies in sport. Two aims of the project are to attempt to conceptualize and distinguish between acceptable and unacceptable performance-enhancing technologies and to provide a thorough evaluation of the ethical arguments concerning the use of such technologies. I believe that FOP can contribute to this project.[20]

In general, technology can be understood as a human-made means to serve human interests and goals.[21] Sports technology can be defined as a human-made means to serve human interests and goals in or related to sport. The logic of competitive sport is the evaluation and comparison of performance. And indeed, the most powerful and radical kind includes those technologies designed to have performance-enhancing effects.

Performance-enhancing technologies can be categorized in many ways. A prime category is enhancement of body techniques, or the instrumental use of bodily movement patterns to execute sporting skills and perform. Sometimes, innovations in body techniques cause value conflicts. New technical moves and movement patterns, such as Dick Fosbury's flop in the high jump or the so-called V-style in ski jumping, gave the innovators a competitive advantage over their opponents at the time of their introduction. Critical arguments are often linked to contingent esthetic viewpoints ("the Fosbury flop is ugly" or "the V-style is ugly") or to essentialist views on the traditional "nature" of a sport. Such arguments tend to be short lived.

The predominant view is to see technical innovations as the results of trial-and-error processes among talented athletes and coaches and as creative and valuable developments of a sport. In line with FOP, the advantage of an innovative technique is considered a fair advantage because it is within the sphere of individual influence and control.

A more common understanding of sports technology is to see it as the material means with which athletes perform—that is, sports equipment. The interaction between athlete and equipment is crucial to good performances in all sports. To the good skier, the skis and poles become prolongations of the body with which she feels and interacts with the environment. In bicycling, the master racer and his bike appear as one unified, balanced whole. However, and perhaps more often than with body techniques, innovations in sports equipment are controversial from a fairness point of view. If one athlete has exclusive access to superior technology, he or she has an advantage over others that, according to FOP, should be eliminated or compensated for. As noted above, the key procedure here is standardization of, or at least equal access to and free choice between, various kinds of equipment.

A third category of sports technology consists of all kinds of performance-enhancing means used outside competition, in training, that require athletes' effort to have effect. Examples are weights and strength-training regimens and machines, treadmills for running, and wind tunnels for finding aerodynamic positions in speed sports such as cycling and downhill skiing. Again, controversies may arise. The introduction of systematic, daily training in the early 1900s was met by criticism and skepticism by proponents of amateurism and was considered an expression of a simple, instrumental attitude and as "unnatural" and unhealthy. Similar reactions occurred with the introduction of weight training in the 1950s.[22] Today, such views are seen as historical anachronisms. To the modern sports community, most training technologies that require athletes' effort and control are considered valuable and/or acceptable, at least as long as they do not represent unreasonable risks of harm.

The most radical ethical challenges to sport today are often linked to what can be called *expert-administered technology*. Expert-administered technology differs from training technology, as the category includes means that do not require athletes' effort and control but depend for their efficacy on external experts. I am talking now of everything from rather uncontroversial nutritional regimens, to high-altitude chambers to enhance oxygen transport and endurance, to doping, and perhaps to, in the future, genetic technology. The most powerful forms of expert-administered technology, such as doping and genetic technology, may have radical consequences for the welfare and health of the individual athlete and, in fact, for ideas of what sports performance and sport are all about. How far can FOP take us in this respect?

The underlying premise of the fairness principles defended here is the Kantian idea of persons as potentially autonomous moral agents who are to be treated, never merely as means, but always as ends in themselves. A minimum requirement for fairness in sport is equality of opportunity to perform in competitions. All competitors ought to compete under equal conditions and to be given equal access to the same kind of technology. But this is not enough. According to FOP, athletes and teams should be able to influence and control key aspects of their performances: performances should be within their sphere of responsibility. Expert-administered performance-enhancing technology tends to reduce the significance of athletes' effort, control, and responsibility. From the perspective of FOP, this is problematic. Sport is easily turned into a moral risk zone in which the welfare of individuals becomes increasingly dependent on the moral standards of their support systems and in which athletes can be exploited and treated as means toward system survival. From the perspective of FOP, what are thought to be harmless expert-administered technological variants, such as the high-altitude chamber, should be met with skepticism. Potentially harmful technologies such as doping should be banned.

These arguments do not suggest that FOP provides clear-cut distinctions between the acceptable and unacceptable in this regard. First of all, in a situation with mature and rational athletes who can make free and informed choices of the use of technology, the argument about athletes' vulnerability and exploitation seems without merit. However, such a scenario is unlikely to arise. Athletic performances are the result of many years and even decades of hard training from a young age, and few athletes have the necessary knowledge to make their own choices along the way. Second, there are gray zones here, and there is a need for continuous ethical examination of the nature of performance-enhancing technologies and their consequences. Thus far I have mentioned only briefly one of the main technological challenges to current sport—the possible use of performance-enhancing genetic technology. Scenarios of manipulation of genetic predispositions for sports performances—or sporting talent—raise a series of new questions.[23] Popular images of the genetically modified superathlete simplify the matter. A sports performance is an extremely complex result of a high number of interactions between genetic potential and environmental influence and can probably never be fully controlled and manipulated. Still, the technological possibilities are radical enough. For instance, there is a possibility for genetic manipulation toward both better-performing and healthier athletes. In such a setting, traditional arguments in the doping debate on the potential harm to athletes do not hold. Moreover, use of genetic technologies may challenge radically the idea of athletes as autonomous moral agents and turn sport into a moral front zone in which general ethical questions on the status of agency, freedom, and responsibility are tested and rethought. I cannot pursue these questions further here, but I assume that principles such as FOP, with their Kantian underpinnings, may contribute in interesting ways to the development of sound ethical positions.

Conclusion

I have proposed here an interpretation of fairness in sport in terms of the principle of equality of opportunity to perform and its operationalization: the fair opportunity principle that prescribes the elimination of or compensation for essential inequalities that individuals cannot control or influence in any significant way and for which they cannot be held responsible. Furthermore, and inspired by Rawls's thought experiment on the original position, I have discussed systematically and critically some actual

and possible procedures for realizing FOP in sporting practice.

Another question that I have touched on but not discussed is whether my interpretation represents a realistic ideal. Is it reasonable to assume that the principle and procedures suggested in this chapter can be implemented in today's competitive sports?

The requirement of equality in external conditions is uncontroversial. Competitors and organizations usually have an open mind toward improving their procedures here. When it comes to the consequences of the fairness principles for individual differences and system inequalities, however, practices and attitudes seem more ambiguous. Reclassification strategies, such as fewer sex and age classes and more classifications by body size, challenge traditional gender roles and conceptions of equality and would no doubt meet resistance. In elite sport, the great potential for payoff in terms of profit and prestige intensifies the hard quest for exclusive advantages. Regulative regimes designed to decrease system inequalities, whether standardization of equipment in international skiing or an equal distribution of economic resources in professional soccer leagues, require grand cooperation in a social setting that is dominated by short-term self-interest. The possibilities for implementation of fairness ideals and procedures look rather grim.

This pessimistic scenario, though, is built on a traditional vision of competitive sport. But the development of sport can go in other, newer directions. In a series of new activities that are growing in popularity in the younger generations, a change in the nature of performance may make the ethical questions discussed here less pertinent. In the so-called board sports—skateboarding, surfing, wind-surfing, and snowboarding—the focus is not so much on objective performance measurements under standardized conditions as on technical and tactical skills, expressiveness, and esthetic values. The significance of strict, classification and inequalities in system strength decreases, and the significance of nonmanipulative factors such as complex skills and expressive qualities increases. Requirements on fairness are less rigid and more easily met. Perhaps we are witnessing the emergence of a new sports paradigm that is less vulnerable to the ethical challenges faced by more traditional sports today.

Notes

1. *Webster's New World Dictionary of the American Language* (New York: Warner Books, 1984).
2. C. L. Carr, *On Fairness* (Aldershot, UK: Ashgate, 2000), 2.
3. J. Rawls, *A Theory of Justice* (Cambridge, MA: Harvard University Press, 1971).
4. Ibid., 112, 113.
5. Ibid., 136–37.
6. The distinction between two interpretations of fairness in Rawls's work must not be understood as rigid. In Rawls's contractualist approach, the two interpretations are interconnected. Fair decision procedures are thought of as giving just outcomes. Agreements between rational decision makers under fair conditions are considered to have a morally obligating force. For further discussion, see C. Kukathas and P. Pettit, *Rawls: A Theory of Justice and Its Critics* (Cambridge, UK: Polity Press, 1990), 18ff.
7. Rawls, *Theory of Justice*, 17.
8. For a discussion of "local justice" or of the many and diverse schemes of justice found in various social practices and institutions, see J. Elster, *Local Justice: How Institutions Allocate Scarce Goods and Necessary Burdens* (Cambridge: Cambridge University Press, 1992).
9. S. Loland, "Technology in Sport: Three Ideal-Typical Views and Their Implications," *European Journal of Sport Sciences* 2, no. 1 (2002): 1–11.
10. For further discussion and justification of the concept of equality used here, see R. Dworkin, "What Is Equality?" *Philosophy and Public Affairs* 10 (1981): 185–246.
11. Rawls, *Theory of Justice*, 40, 100ff.; T. Beauchamp, *Philosophical Ethics* (New York: McGraw-Hill, 1991), 372ff.
12. The following discussion is based on S. Loland, *Fair Play in Sports: A Moral Norm System* (London: Routledge, 2002).
13. T. Tännsjö, "Against Sexual Discrimination in Sport," in *Values in Sport*, ed. T. Tännsjö and C. Tamburrini (London: F & F N Spon 2000).
14. T. O. Bompa, *Theory and Methodology of Training: The Key to Athletic Performance*, 3rd ed. (Dubuque, IA: Kendall/Hunt, 1994), 259ff.
15. R. A. Schmidt, *Motor Learning and Performance: From Principle to Practice* (Champaign, IL: Human Kinetics, 1991).
16. Elsewhere I have proposed a variety of procedures for eliminating inequalities of this type. Loland, *Fair Play in Sports*, 56. In volleyball, basketball, and gymnastics, there could be two leagues for men with the critical height of 180 centimeters, and similarly for women with the critical height of 170 centimeters. In addition, changes could be made in equipment and arenas to make sure that competitors meet the same relative challenges; basket and net height could be adjusted in relation to the critical height that defines the class. In the shot put there could be similar classes, with average body mass, for each sex, as the differentiating criterion. Indeed, the specific classification criteria could be discussed and, based on experience and statistical information, other solutions might be better. However, these are discussions about the appropriateness of the procedures, not about the principle of classification (FOP) itself.
17. W. M. Brown, "Personal Best," *Journal of the Philosophy of Sport* 22 (1995): 1–10.
18. L. Allison, *Amateurism in Sport: An Analysis and a Defence* (London: Frank Cass, 2001); E. A. Glader, *Amateurism and Athletics* (West Point, NY: Leisure Press, 1978).
19. An original procedure to ensure equality of equipment is found in the so-called folk races—motorcar rallies with participation open to all. Inequalities in car quality are regulated by a rule that the winning car must be open to purchase by any other competitor for a low sum of money, say, $2,000. If a competitor races with a car worth much more, this is considered an expression of vanity and a possible win gives little or no prestige.
20. Much of the discussion here is based on Loland, *Fair Play in Sports*.
21. D. E. Cooper, "Technology: Liberation or Enslavement?" in *Philosophy and Technology*, ed. D. Fellows (Cambridge: Cambridge University Press, 1998).
22. J. M. Hoberman, *Mortal Engines: The Science of Performance and the Dehumanization of Sports* (New York: Free Press, 1992).
23. A. Miah, "Bioethics, Sport and the Genetically Enhanced Athlete," *Journal of Medical Ethics and Bioethics* 9, no. 3–4 (2002): 2–6.

References

Juengst, E. (2009) in *Performance Enhancing Technologies in Sports*, T. H. Murray *et al.* (eds), Baltimore, The Johns Hopkins University Press, Ch. 9.

Murray, T. (2009) in *Performance Enhancing Technologies in Sports*, T. H. Murray *et al.* (eds), Baltimore, The Johns Hopkins University Press, Ch. 7.

It's not cricket

Underarm bowling, legality and the meaning of life

David Fraser

No other case in recent cricket memory has so epitomized the conflict between law and morality than the infamous underarm incident at Melbourne in Feb. 1981. In a One-Day match with New Zealand, with the visitors needing six from the last ball for a tie, Australian captain Greg Chappell ordered the bowler, his brother Trevor, to deliver a 'mullygrubber', that is an underarm delivery rolled along the ground. Trevor complied and 'A stunned New Zealand batsman blocked it.'[1]

Australia won and the battle was on. On television, former Australian captain Richie Benaud called the Chappells' action 'the most gutless thing I have ever seen on a cricket field'.[2]

Kiwi Prime Minister (Sir) Robert Muldoon called the underarm delivery an 'act of cowardice' and stated he now understood the reason Australia's One-Day uniform is 'yellow'. The ACB condemned and censured Chappell for not meeting the duty of an Australian captain to uphold the spirit of the game. Australian Prime Minister Malcolm Fraser bemoaned the loss of the good and decent tradition of cricket. The incident became part of Australian and New Zealand popular cultural history and is compared in terms of jurisprudential and cultural importance with Bodyline.[3]

The underarm incident continues to serve as an almost universal signifier in Australian–New Zealand sporting contacts. Some of the metaphors and social translations are humorous, others filled with a more serious sense of national outrage at the triumph of legal formalism over cricket's (and society's) higher values. The manager of the New Zealand blind cricket team complained that Australia had an advantage in such competitions because all bowling was underarm. During a One-Day match played at Hobart, the Kiwi PM's Christmas Party focused on the television coverage of the game.[4] As Australia approached the New Zealand total and required two runs off the last ball to win

> … underarm bowling jokes swept the room. New Zealanders have not forgotten Trevor Chappell's final, unplayable ball on his brother Greg's orders, that ended a 1981 Melbourne one-day final so sourly, denying New Zealand a chancy six off the last ball.[5]

While these references are clearly accompanied with good humour, and the text of the underarm bowling incident takes on a different meaning with the passage of time, another adoption of the referent offered a chance to combine a seemingly 'neutral' legal formalism with a strong personal and social desire for revenge. During a trans-Tasman Test in netball, the Australian team was late coming on to the floor after the half-time break, and the New Zealand team restarted the game without their opponents. In other words a contest between two teams was actually briefly occurring with only one team present. For the Kiwis it was clear what sporting interpretive context informed their reaction to Australian tardiness. The incident had evened the score for cricket's infamous underarm delivery.

Reaction at the time of the Chappell brothers' incident was, as might be expected, heated. Television and radio stations were inundated with telephone calls, some seeking the number of the Kiwi's Melbourne Hotel in order to apologize, others calling for Greg [but interestingly not Trevor] Chappell's scalp.[6] New Zealanders were equally vociferous in their complaints. A local judge said 'I hope there are no Australians coming up before me this morning.'[7] New Zealand feeling remained heated one year later when Chappell led the Australians to Auckland.[8] Editorial writers bemoaned not only Chappell's poor sportsmanship, but branded him a traitor to his country. His action, it was said, was 'an act that will sour anyone who ever held sportsmanship dear. It was contrary to the Australian spirit.'[9]

The incident itself was cast in the broader context of Australia–New Zealand relations. Like Australian Prime Minister John Howard's frequent invocation of cricket metaphors to explain and clarify political questions, Chappell's mullygrubber was itself placed in the broader socio-political context of Australia's condescending attitude towards its trans-Tasman neighbour. Instead of limiting itself to the cricket pitch – it's just a game – the underarm delivery, precisely *because* it took place on the cricket pitch, took on a broader interpretive political function. As the editorial writer for the *Sydney Morning Herald* put it the next day:

New Zealanders will however, undoubtedly use the 'underarm' incident for years to come as a metaphor for the way Australians continue to show lack of consideration to a trans-Tasman relative and friend. This is a disregard that transcends everything that has happened this cricket season – all the controversial LBW decisions, the undue protection by umpires of Australian tail-end batsmen and the non-granting of legitimate catches.

The editorial writers and politicians were not the only ones to see a broader social and political hermeneutic at work. For the cricket fans, Chappell's decision symbolized and embodied other broader issues from capitalism: 'Maybe Manning Clarke is right when he says that Mammon has taken over in this fair country of ours', to class: 'Cricket, the game loved by many kinds of people from judges to housewives, actors to building workers, appears to have died. In its place is cricket, a sport for boozing ockers and yobbos …', to literary criticism: 'Test cricket is drama. Limited over cricket is farce. Mr Chappell introduced into the farce a further dash of comedy', to religion: 'Sadly, we have seen our national sporting reputation sold for the proverbial 30 pieces of silver', to the counternarrative of formalism: 'Greg Chappell's action but places him on a sparsely populated pedestal of "thinking" captains who have brains as well as just co-ordination.'

Finally, at least two readers saw parallels with another significant and signifying social, political and legal text, the 1975 Constitutional Crisis in Australia when the lawfully elected Whitlam government was dismissed by the Governor-General's use of the reserve power and replaced by Malcolm Fraser's Liberals: 'Mr Fraser approached the zenith in hypocrisy with his denunciation of Chappell's methods. Surely the Prime Minister used the rules of the game to his own advantage in 1975' and 'Has there been a more sensational event in Australia since Sir John Kerr sacked Mr Whitlam?'[10]

Other members of cricket's interpretive community also jumped into the hermeneutic circle. Former Australian bowler, noted journalist and iconoclast, Bill O'Reilly, joined in on the side of morality. His feelings of private and public outrage were clearly stated:

As a patriotic Australian, influenced by all the tough spots through which my Test career took one, I felt humiliated. It was an injury to all the great players who have played over the past 100 years.[11]

O'Reilly here seeks to utilize and invoke a classic interpretive and legal strategy. His appeal, yet again, is to the past, to the historically constituted community of players, its morality and its internal rule of law. By making this appeal in these circumstances he is clearly seeking to exclude Chappell (and his team) from the community of Australian cricketers ('I implore the selectors to brush this team aside', id), to banish them from the group of those who may impose an authentic meaning on what is for O'Reilly, an exclusive, elite and private text. Like those who seek to cherish and preserve the sacred traditions of the Bench and the Bar, to confirm them as guardians of the Ark, O'Reilly wishes under the guise of a universal and public moral code to impose a limited and private morality. This does not necessarily mean that the content of this morality is one which is not shared by other interpretive sub-communities in cricket. It does mean, however, that we must always guard against those who seek to legitimate private moral codes by imbuing them, by mere assertion, with a broader public status, especially given O'Reilly's position on *Mankading* and his reputation as an aggressive, if not intimidatory, appellant. This does not mean that it is not possible to construct an ethically and legally consistent position which adopts these interpretations of various moral and legal questions. It does mean however, that each element of that position needs to be clearly articulated and interrogated without any elevation to Truth status simply because O'Reilly played for Australia.

Finally, authoritative representatives of another interpretive sub-community, umpires, jumped into the fray. Don Oslear, the English Test umpire condemned Greg Chappell for violating the spirit of the game. Asked how he could have reacted had been standing in the match, he replied: 'I might have said, "Come on Greg, It's been a tremendous game. Let's bowl it up".'[12]

Here we have a rather surprising addition to the interpretive canon. Rather than relying on the traditional ideals of rule formalism and judicial neutrality and invoking standards of passivity, Oslear takes the position that umpires must play an active role in upholding the spirit of the game. That entity must dominate and take precedence over the letter of the *Law*. Perhaps Oslear, looking at events from a distance, is speaking from principle, perhaps he is simply being disingenuous, but whatever the case, it is interesting to note that nothing he says indicates that he could or would have intervened beyond mere imprecation. Had he been present, had Chappell rejected his imprecations and bowled underarm, whatever his own moral view, he *could* not, as an umpire, have acted any

differently than did the two umpires who were actually present. At that actual practically real point of obedience to the letter of the law, personal morality must be set aside. Unless, again, Oslear is willing to argue that the umpire's jurisdiction of 'fair and unfair' play, for example, could be extended to allow him to assert an injunctive power to prohibit an act which is legally permissible and permitted but ethically suspect. This idea, that the spirit of the game is superior to strict adherence to the formal content of the *Laws of Cricket*, whatever its moral, deontological status, has never, in such circumstances, had an actual legal consequence or effect.

The issues surrounding the underarm incident are myriad. At the surface level, the conflict is a straightforward one of rule formalism confronting an unwritten ethical norm, for, needless to say, at the time, Chappell's underarm delivery was perfectly 'legal'. At the same time, however, something deeper and more contextually important arises from even a cursory analysis of the 'case'.

First, like all events to which we attribute significance and which we imbue with meaning, the underarm bowling affair occurs in a particular context. For example, the Chappell incident takes on importance only because of a conflict, yet again, between the *Law* and convention. But there is in the debate around this case, as in all cases where it is convenient or necessary, a tendency to forget history and grant one's position the status of a universal and transcendent epistemological basis. The 'it is legal' argument from this position appears much less problematic than the conventional 'it's not cricket' argument. As a matter of historical fact, for example, until 1864, it was illegal to bowl *overarm* and any bowler attempting to do so was no-balled. It was not until 1878 that Australia became the first team to use a specialist overarm attack.[13] Appeals to the *absolute* ontological immorality of Chappell's decision lose their argument with the history of the game and its *Laws*.

Secondly, again perhaps mostly as an historical curiosity, is the phrase 'it's not cricket' which embodies the argument of the proponents of anti-formalist ethical versions of the game in general and of those who condemn the Chappells in particular. The phrase was apparently originally coined by Rev. James Pycroft to express his displeasure at and disapproval of *overarm bowling*. In a neat historical, contextual flip, 'it isn't cricket' has left its original place in the interpretive community to stand as moral armament for those on the opposite end of its historical positioning. Truth and falsehood shift as time and community practices and texts shift.

Historical counter-facts to one side however, it is obvious that the underarm bowling incident raises many questions. First, as in other instances we have seen, it was *legal*, and for the sake of brevity, *immoral*. Unlike other types of 'sharp practice', however, there was something special enough about this affair that the *Laws* of One-Day Cricket were changed so that it could not be repeated. Why was outrage so great and the weight of ethical norms so powerful that the formalist trend was turned on its head and traditional practice enshrined in the rules?

A first and most plausible reason for the reaction and outrage also finds, in a bizarre way, its sources in the historical or perhaps mythological, origins of the game. Overarm, roundarm bowling was, according to cricket legend, first developed by a woman. As Frindall explains:

> The first woman technically to assist the development of cricket was Christina Willes, later Mrs Hodges. It is generally accepted that she originated round-arm bowling *c* 1807 when she practised with her brother John in the barn of their home at Tonford, near Canterbury. Her full skirt of the period made the legitimate bowling style of the times impossible. John, who was to become a squire and sports patron, found round-arm bowling difficult to play, adopted it himself, was the first to be no-balled for employing it in a major match ... and had the satisfaction of seeing the style made legal six years later in 1828.[14]

While it was originated by a woman, overarm bowling, especially fast bowling, is now clearly associated with virility and manliness, which are essential elements (*infra*) of the moral and social nature of cricket. The contest between bat and ball which characterizes and defines the game is embodied for many in the confrontation between a batter and a bowler capable of delivering the ball at high speed. Fast bowlers are the big, virile men of the team and the ability to stand up to a 'barrage' or 'attack' of bouncers from these big men is a sign of the courage and virility of batters. What happened

in the underarm bowling incident was that Greg Chappell, in the words of one writer 'failed the virility test',[15] or as Richie Benaud put it, he was 'gutless'. As Australian captain in an international match, he represented all Australians (read Australian men) as weak, wimpish, hiding behind the rules, rather than facing destiny 'like a man', a fact exacerbated by traditional Australian attitudes of superiority towards New Zealanders, especially in cricket. The decision to change the rule was a decision in favour of masculinity. No longer could an Australian hide behind the skirts of the Law, he would have to put his manhood on the line.

Connected with the virility explanation is the fact that Chappell might have achieved the same result in a masculine and virile way, and in a way which would both conform with the *Laws* and the spirit of the game. As McVicar pointed out: 'If the same result could have been effected by Lillee rocketing down a bouncer, everyone would have preened.'[16]

Even Harold Larwood, the fast bowler who followed Douglas Jardine's orders to such devastating effect in the Bodyline series (*infra*), condemned Chappell's actions: 'It was a bloody stupid thing to do and I hope it will never happen again.' When asked if he would have acted like Trevor Chappell, following his captain's order to bowl underarm, he replied: 'No, definitely not. No one in my time would have done anything like that.'[17]

It is immediately difficult to characterize Larwood's response as anything but disingenuous or at best evasive. Jardine never hesitated to stand on the letter of the *Law* to achieve victory and it is impossible to believe that he would by definition have seen anything 'immoral' about underarm bowling if it would achieve the desired result. This was the very nature of Bodyline and the legal and moral conflict which arose as a result. Jardine insisted that his tactics were perfectly legal and the Australians claimed that what England were doing, 'just wasn't cricket'. Nor is it possible to imagine the working-class bowler Larwood disobeying an order from his captain, Mr Jardine. Again, there is ample proof that legal formalism and sharp practice have a continuous presence in the practice of cricket so that Larwood's invocation of the 'good old days' can hardly be persuasive.

Yet beneath this text which seemingly refutes Larwood's position, there lies an equally, if not more, persuasive argument to strongly support his view that he would not have been faced with such a situation (or even if faced with such an order he might have refused). The text which supports Larwood is one which arises frequently in discussions of the underarm incident, that is once more the cult of virility.

One reason Chappell is condemned for the mullygrubber incident is that his action is seen as unmanly, as violating a strong social imperative, and an even stronger cricket imperative, that a man should be a man and not hide behind the letter of the *Law* and use a weak, feminine underarm delivery. Larwood, Jardine and Bodyline cannot be placed in the same interpretive matrix. While standing on the letter of the *Law*, Bodyline does so from the other side of the hermeneutic circle. In its very essence, Bodyline is manly, virile, masculine. It is about fast bowlers bowling fast. It is about assault and attack, it is war on the oval. If it stands on the letter of the *Law*, it stands against a weaker, more feminine 'gentle'-manly spirit of the game. Bodyline points out and underlines the androgynous (*infra*) nature of cricket – both the *Laws* and the spirit – because it demonstrates when contrasted with the underarm incident, that one can stand by the *Law* and still be a man, or one can stand by the *Law* and be regarded as a wimp. Larwood, then, is right when he says that no one, not even Jardine, would have ordered him to bowl underarm because such an action, while legal would have violated the spirit of Bodyline, which *was* legal but more especially and more essentially it was masculine.

Another possible explanation, not at all inconsistent with the virility thesis, is that the public outrage over Chappell's actions arose as a result of a deep disquiet about the newly evident and growing commercialization of cricket. Chappell's action was seen as a public manifestation of all that was wrong with this phenomenon. For supporters of the Denningesque tradition, Chappell's decision demonstrated the nefarious impact of the Other, with its own, contraindicated code of 'professionalism', 'gamesmanship' and 'win at all costs'. For supporters of the 'new' cricket, Chappell's order and his brother's compliance (as a good wage-slave?) constituted perhaps an embarrassing display of the Emperor's new clothes.

But neither explanation is completely satisfactory, nor is it total or holistic. To explain away the underarm delivery as the result of commercialization overlooks and ignores a strong connection between the interests of capitalism and the interests of patriarchy. Commonly, weak, wimpish behaviour is unacceptable under both. It is also to ignore the historical (*infra*) connections between commercial interests and cricket. If there has always been such a connection, commercialization cannot have been the only reason or explanation for the underarm bowling incident, for such actions would have been common and acceptable. Again, any attempt to explain anything about cricket by an appeal to a one-dimensional master referent must always fall victim to the inevitable and inherent complexities both of the practice of the game and the practice of talking about the game.

At the same time, the virility thesis is not, and cannot be, universally acceptable or applicable, even in these apparently clear circumstances. After the game, Geoff Howarth, the New Zealand captain 'wondered whether he would have had the guts to do what Chappell did'.

Is it gutless to hide behind the *Law* or does it take guts to use the letter of the *Law*, knowing that in 'standing up for your rights', you will be roundly condemned for doing so? For example, when Javed Miandad of Pakistan hit a six off the last ball in the final of the Australasian Cup of 1986 against India, at least one journalist from that country chided the team for not being 'professional enough' to have bowled the ball so short it would have rolled to the batter.[18] In the domain of legal and ethical discourse, judgements about the moral infirmity of Greg Chappell appear to rest in the shifting and uncertain sands of ethical indeterminacy, part of a situation in which even the construction of the dominant trope of masculinity in a phallogocentric world (see *infra*) is more and more uncertain. If capitalism, law and cricket all demanded that Chappell act like a man, how can each be blamed for his failure to do so?

It is easy, in the underarm incident as in all other aspects of cricket, *Law* and life, to tell other stories from other perspectives. While the dominant and lasting canon, relates to the immorality of Greg Chappell's order to his brother, other sub-texts, albeit slightly tongue in cheek, permit us either to place blame on Chappell from another perspective, or, in a unique twist, to put the moral culpability purely on Brian McKechnie, the New Zealand batter who faced the final and fateful delivery from Trevor.

In the first instance, Chappell can be faulted not from the point of view of some moral condemnation of his insistence on legal formalism or by assaulting his 'manhood', but more particularly on 'the facts'. On this view, Chappell must be criticized because he made a bad utilitarian calculation. McKechnie could not have hit even a regular delivery for six.[19] Chappell's decision to bowl underarm was therefore *wrong* on the facts because a 'normal' cricket delivery would have had the same result. He then could have avoided all the moral outcry which followed his action and achieved exactly the same result. This is confirmed not only by Larwood's analysis but *ex post facto* by Trevor Chappell. As his brother Ian relates the story, some years after the incident Trevor was invited to New Zealand to compete in a double-wicket competition. 'Someone with a sense of humour' partnered him with McKechnie. Upon his return home, Trevor was heard to complain that not only had McKechnie not hit a six, he had not been able to manage a single boundary during the entire competition. Greg Chappell could have, and should have avoided all the controversy surrounding the underarm incident if only he had known.

At the same, it is possible to tell a story about what a skilled batter could have done even against an underarm delivery. In this narrative matrix, the moral culpability falls not on either of the Chappells but on McKechnie for failing to be a good batter. Ian Chappell tells a story of the great Australian batter Doug Walters' reaction to the incident. Walters simply expressed his disgust at McKechnie's inability to hit the mullygrubber for six. As his teammates shook their heads in disbelief, Walters offered to prove his theory. At net practice at the SCG, someone rolled an underarm delivery at Walters. Walters moved down the wicket, kicked the ball into the air with his front foot and hit the ball onto Driver Avenue. While his teammates pointed out his theoretical vulnerability to an LBW appeal, Walters nonetheless 'proved' once again that in cricket any number of stories, from any number of perspectives, can be told, each as 'valid' as every other. Legal

formalism and ethical debate can never be simply or crudely deployed or asserted as complete explanations.

Notes

1. Jack Pollard, *Australian Cricket*, op. cit., at p. 267. The incident continues to haunt Trevor Chappell. He points out, however, that at one level, the incident has a different epistemological status than that attributed to it generally. He says that 'Most people did not realise that you had to tell the umpire, and he tells the batsman, that you were going to bowl underarm…'. Thus, the 'active' participants 'knew' what was about to occur. This is confirmed by contemporaneous press accounts which indicate clearly that '… the Umpires Don Weser and Peter Cronins, having been told by Greg Chappell of his intention and having in turn advised the batsmen, were powerless.' Rex Mossop, 'One ball dents Australia's image as a sports nation', *Sydney Morning Herald*, 2 Feb 1981. See also Greg Growden, 'Trevor Chappell reflects: Why I bowled Underarm', *Sydney Morning Herald*, 25 March 1986.

> 'I was probably disappointed to the extent that it was against the spirit of the game. That was the most disappointing aspect, particularly as it was such a good game of cricket.' Chappell loses some power in his response however when he continues '… it was in the rules anyway'. Greg Growden, 'Face to face with Trevor Chappell', *Sydney Morning Herald*, 27 Oct. 1990. For the perspective of the other active participant, New Zealand batter Brian McKechnie, see Mike Coward, 'The batsman has forgiven, but is not allowed to forget', *Sydney Morning Herald*, 27 March 1986, 'I don't think I had a grudge against Greg Chappell. It was in the rules at the time and what is in the rules is fair.'

2. Id., at p. 268.
3 'The Ins and Outs of Bad Sportsmanship', *Good Weekend*, 9 Dec. 1989. It has also been immortalized by Australian cultural icons Roy and H.G., see John Huxley, 'Face to Face with H.G. and Roy', *Sydney Morning Herald*, 16 Dec. 1989.

> Now, I was one of those who thought cricket was bound for a burton. The jig's up. They'd tried everything. Privatisation. One-day games. But within minutes of the decade opening, there was that marvellous incident with the underarm delivery.

4. *Sun Herald*, 30 Dec. 1990. Anthony Hay, 'When the sound of bat and ball is all that's needed for a great day's cricket', *Sydney Morning Herald*, 13 March 1997. The 'case' also continues to influence legal discourse. When describing a position of unfair advantage or dominant position in Section 36A of the Commerce Act (N.Z.) 1986, the authors chose to highlight the issue in the trans-Tasman market by using the title, 'Section 36A: Underarm Bowling?', The Interface Between Amended Section 36 of the Commerce Act 1986 and Intellectual Property Law, Competition Law and Policy Institute of New Zealand (Inc.), Aug. 1990 Workshop, at p. 16.

5. Paul Whelan, *Sydney Morning Herald*, 19 Dec. 1990. References to the incident continue to inform Australian/New Zealand relations and to haunt Greg and Trevor Chappell. See e.g., 'Underarm: Chappell admits he was mental', *Weekend Australian*, 13–14 Jan. 1996; Phillip Derriman, 'The ball that changed NZ', *Sydney Morning Herald*, 1 Feb. 1996; Ray Kershler, 'Under not over', *Daily Telegraph*, 1 Feb. 1996; Phil Wilkins, 'Incident that has echoes in Eden', *Sydney Morning Herald*, 14 Feb. 1998; Don Cameron, 'Trevor Chappell: The pain goes on forever', *CricInfo*, 2 Dec. 2001.

6. 'Ashamed to be an Aussie', *Sydney Morning Herald*, 2 Feb. 1981.

7. 'Irate New Zealanders had plenty to say', id.

8. 'NZ wants Chappell's blood', *Sydney Morning Herald*, 2 Feb. 1982.

9. 'Sports Opinion', *Sydney Morning Herald*, 2 Feb. 1981.

10. Letters found in 'The Great Underarm Controversy', *Sydney Morning Herald*, 4 Feb. 1981. It is interesting to note that on the day following the incident, that newspaper received 111 letters. Superstitious English cricketers and cabalists might find ever greater hermeneutic significance in that number. See Harold Bloom, *Kabbalah and Criticism* (New York: Continuum, 1984) and Umberto Eco, *Foucault's Pendulum* (London: Secker and Warburg, 1989).

11. 'As a patriotic Australian, I felt humiliated', *Sydney Morning Herald*, 2 Feb. 1981. Hugh Lunn tried to put events in a broader context by pointing to the public, and therefore *moral* nature of Chappell's actions when compared to other cricketing practices. He wrote:

> Yes Greg Chappell you may be a great man who doesn't sledge, never unnecessarily appeals when bowling and never shows disapproval of the decision of umpires. But in a game surrounded by fine sportsmen intent only on playing the game, you dared to publicly display that you were prepared to win without actually cheating. You should have been more underhanded.

'Greg's critics sniping from glass houses', *Australian*, 3 Feb. 1981

12. 'English Umpire lashes us', *Sydney Morning Herald*, 3 Feb. 1981.

13. Bill Frindall, *Cricket Facts and Feats*, op. cit., at pp. 12–13.

14. Op. cit., p. 192.

15. 'How Greg Chappell failed the virility test', *New Statesman*, 13 Feb. 1981. It is interesting to note that while Trevor is still 'famous' as the man who bowled underarm, Greg, as captain, was the one who was singled out for moral disapproval for *ordering* his brother to act in that manner.

16. Id.

17. 'Chappell: Skipper whose ship died of shame', *Times*, 3 Feb. 1991.

18. Ashis Nandy, op. cit., at p. 29.

19. Harold Larwood, of Bodyline fame pointed out at the time that it would have been possible to prevent a six simply by bowling the ball up and at the wicket. See 'Chappell's Skipper whose ship died of shame', *Times*, 3 Feb. 1991.

The "hand of God"?

Claudio Tamburrini

When Maradona scored his famous – or, depending on the geographical context, infamous – 'handball' goal against England at the Mexico Football World Cup in 1986, the whole world of sport – except for the Argentineans – accused him of cheating.

Maradona, however, showed no repentance. As a matter of fact, he added even more fuel to the controversy by ascribing his goal to "the hand of God". Some interpreted his expression as a sign of lack of contact with reality. Others, as a reference to the recent war between Argentina and England for the possession of the Falkland/Malvinas Islands. Still others saw in the argument on divine agency a wider political statement on the historical economic gap between the Northern and Southern hemispheres, and welcomed his goal as supreme compensatory justice. Whichever interpretation we like, the fact remains that Maradona cheated. Indeed, he flagrantly violated the rules of football.

Most sports-interested people – and the vast majority of sports philosophers – believe cheating to be *wrong*. For them, the 'handball' goal embodies a regretful tendency of sports at present, with athletes resorting to whatever means they might deem necessary to achieve victory. These pessimistic voices underline that cheating, doping scandals, unsporting conduct and even violence have become common ingredients of current sport practices. And they concur on where the root of all these evils can be found: *widespread professionalisation and commercialisation of sports are made responsible for all the excesses above.*

In this chapter, I will question the objection to elite sports that says that commercialism and professionalism encourage (1) cheating, and (2) unsporting behaviour, to the point of spoiling the game. Regarding the former, I will try to show that not all cases of cheating can properly be labelled as wrongful. Particularly regarding "the hand of God", I intend to show that Maradona as a matter of fact acted *rightly* when he scored his goal, from a universalistic moral point of view.

Unsporting conduct is often stigmatised by sport critics almost as strongly as cheating. I believe this to be unreasonable. Though at the limit of what is permitted by the rules, this sort of strategic behaviour is part of an extended normative framework – a sort of sport practitioners' ethos – within which sport rules are interpreted and applied, and should therefore not be considered as reprehensible. As a matter of fact, I will argue that some violations of the code of good sportspersonship should even be encouraged, as they enhance the quality of the game.

I will first proceed to characterise cheating, in order to distinguish it from unsporting behaviour. Following that, I will try to determine when cheating and unsporting behaviour (in short, 'foul play') are blameable and, therefore, deserve to be discouraged, as part of my intent to delimit the idea of game-enriching strategic behaviour. Finally, my defence of certain forms of cheating and unsporting behaviour in sports will be presented in more detail.

What is cheating?

Cheating is usually characterised as the intentional violation of the rules of the game, in order to gain an unfair advantage over competitors. In the next sections, I will argue that intentionality is neither a necessary nor a sufficient condition for cheating, and that the advantage obtained by the cheater needs not be unfair either.

Intentionality

Let us begin by discussing the place of intentionality in the evaluation of sporting conduct. Is it the intention *to break the rules* that is relevant here? Suppose Maradona, after touching the ball with his hand, had openly signalled his fault to the referee, before the fault was even noticed. Would we really call his action cheating, simply because the 'handball' was intentional? On the contrary, we would rather judge that intentionality was not a sufficient condition for characterising this particular rule violation as cheating.

By the same token, provided the player committing a fault tries to get away with it, even unintentional rule violations could be said to constitute cheating. Suppose, for instance, that Maradona had no intention of touching the ball with his hand. Nonetheless, we would consider him guilty of concealing the 'handball' to the game authorities, particularly to the referee. We would call his action cheating, and rightly so. That means that the intentional violation of a rule is not a necessary condition for cheating either.

It could be argued that such cases might be dealt with simply by postulating intentionality at a previous point of time. As the player now tries to hide her fault, intentionality could be retrospectively ascribed to the (originally unintentional) rule violation. This, however, would be to stretch common language too much. Rather, what these arguments suggest is that it is the intentionality to *deceive*, rather than merely to break the rules, that is relevant here, in a moral sense.

This, however, is only half the truth. As a matter of fact, not all cases of cheating imply intentionally deceiving the game authorities. Consider the so called 'good fouls'. As the term has been defined by Warren Fraleigh, a good foul (which also goes under the name of 'professional' or 'rational foul') is a rule violation that "occurs when a participant knowingly violates a rule to achieve what would otherwise be difficult to achieve, but violates the rules so as to expect and willingly accept the penalty".[1]

A football player, for instance, might intentionally and overtly commit an infraction against a rival who is in a position to score, in order to neutralise the danger at the reduced cost of a free-kick. In the good foul, the player does not intend to escape the penalty. There is no deceitful intention in her action. However, Fraleigh – and our intuitions – still tell us that good fouls constitute cheating. How can we support this intuition, in the absence of intentional deception?

In my opinion, good fouls show that the intention relevant for cheating is not so much the intention to deceive (the good fouler commits her fault openly, often in front of the referee), but the intention of obtaining a game advantage.[2] What is the nature of this game advantage? Is the advantage obtained by the cheater *unfair*? That will depend on the context in which the game is being played, and on what kind of rule violation we have in mind. Suppose a player indulges in a type of rule-infringing behaviour, B1, and that B1 is, when given the proper occasion, generally performed by game practitioners. Everybody has the opportunity of doing B1, and – more important – everybody actually does it. So, it could be asked, where does the unfairness lie? Rather, the advantage obtained by the cheater has to be characterised as *illicit*, instead of unfair. Thus, good fouls are cheating simply because they (are supposed to) yield an advantage to the fouling player through an action which is proscribed in the written code of rules. When illicit behaviour is incorporated in the way game practitioners play the game, when 'everybody does it', it does not seem justified to speak of unfairness.

Cheating, fair play and sportspersonship

The upshot of the discussion above might then be summarised in the following characterisation of cheating. *Cheating is a violation of the written rules of a game, performed in order to gain an illicit advantage for oneself, or for one's team, over rival players.*[3] The "hand of God" and Mike Tyson's biting of Evander Holyfield's ear are examples of cheating.

The opposite of cheating is *fair play*. We practise fair play when we abide by the rules of the game. Unlike cheating (which is prohibited by the rules and considered as noxious for the game), fair play is demanded by the rules and expected to enhance its quality. Fair play demands subjection to the letter of current regulations. It implies a ready acceptance of the rules, and a willingness to abide by them. But it need go no further than that.

Another pair of opposites is that constituted by *good* and *bad sportspersonship*. Good sportspersonship is conduct that goes beyond the requirements of fair play, as it demands more than simply abiding by a rule code. Good sportspersonship differs from fair play, not in terms of whether it is good for the game or not (it often is), but rather by not being formalised in the rules of the game. Recall the Maradona situation. He scored a goal with his hand. As he did gain an advantage through his fault, and did it intentionally, he can rightfully be said to have cheated. But what about his team mates, who chose not to tell the referee that Maradona's goal was unfairly scored? By keeping silent, they might be said to accept the advantage granted to them by the cheater's action. Maradona's team mates violated no rule. There is no rule in football stating that players are under an obligation to denounce a cheating team mate. Therefore, they cannot reasonably be charged with cheating. Nonetheless, through their omission, these players violated a tacit rule of good sportspersonship. Good sportspersonship requires that Maradona's team mates address the referee and ask him to annul the 'handball' goal. They did not. Thus, they are guilty of unsporting behaviour.

Another example of good sportspersonship is, for instance, when a player voluntarily refrains from provoking psychic instability in a rival player, even when that could be done within the limits of the rule framework (for instance, by coughing on purpose at a particular tense moment, or altering the pace of the game by doing up one's shoe-laces when not needed).

Good sportspersonship, then, belongs to the class of *supererogatory acts* in professional sports. Professional players who live up to it deserve to be praised. But, if they fail to do so, it is at least not evident that they should be blamed. The good sportsperson is generous and magnanimous with her rivals. But generosity and magnanimity are not included in the notion of fair play. Nor are they part of any known secularised professional ethics.[4] Though it sometimes might be reasonable to encourage sport practitioners to honour the precepts of good sportspersonship, it is not always reasonable to blame them if they fail to reach its standards.

Bad sportspersonship, in its turn, is considered to affect the quality of the game negatively. But, unlike cheating, bad sportspersonship, though certainly discouraged, is not a course of action forbidden by the rules of the game. In football, 'diving' and 'deterrent interventions' are considered to be bad sportspersonship. [While this chapter was being written, 'diving' became formally proscribed by FIFA regulations and is now sanctioned with yellow card. Nevertheless, my arguments below are still valid: if there is no reason to criticise diving as unsporting behaviour, it should not be proscribed either.] Diving consists in simulating that one has been fouled by a rival in order to get a free kick or a penalty awarded to one's team. An example of a deterrent intervention – also labelled 'intimidating actions' – is the tight marking of a rival player that, though performed within the limits of what is allowed by the rules, is intended to intimidate her from further action.

The English national football team provided us with another example of bad sportspersonship. I will call it 'the persecution of Schwartz'. In the second half of the match against Sweden at Wembley on June 13th 1999, the Swedish midfielder Schwartz was given a yellow card by the referee. Some English players began then to play more aggressively against Schwartz every time he got the ball, although without fouling him. Obviously, their intention was to get him to lose his temper, get a second yellow card and thus be sent off the field.[5]

English football has recently added another case to the bad sportspersonship repertoire. During a match between Sheffield and Arsenal, a Sheffield player intentionally threw the ball out so that medical attention could be provided for a rival injured player. When the game started again, an Arsenal player intended to return the ball to the rivals by kicking it long into Sheffield's field half. One of his team mates, however, caught the ball and scored a goal. The referee condoned the goal, as no formal rule had been violated. The great majority of the public, however, strongly disapproved of the Arsenal player's action.

The question that occupies us is whether these cases of foul play are reprehensible and should for that reason be discouraged in sports. Are we justified in condemning Maradona's 'handball' goal? Should we really do our best to try to eradicate such cases of unsporting behaviour as diving, deterrent interventions, putting off a rival player and 'the persecution of Schwartz' from the world of sports? Does the Arsenal goal differ in any relevant sense from the previous examples of unsporting behaviour?

When is foul play blameable?

Foul play (i.e., cheating or bad sportspersonship) deserves condemnation, and should therefore be discouraged, when at least one of the following conditions is fulfilled:

(a) it introduces unfairness in competition;
(b) it spoils the game;
(c) it exposes sport practitioners to (an increased risk of) unnecessary physical injury.

Do the examples of foul play listed in the previous section satisfy any of these conditions? Let us discuss them one by one.

Unfair competition

According to a common view on rule-breaking advanced by Gunther Luschen:

Cheating in sport is the act through which the manifestly or latently agreed upon conditions for winning such a contest are changed in favor of one side. As a result, the principle of equality of chance beyond differences of skill and strategy is violated.[6]

Randolph M. Feezell has also formulated this contract idea as a kind of promise-breaking. According to him, "... cheating is a kind of promise-breaking or violation of a contractual relationship, which implies that the cheater "has attempted to gain an unfair advantage by breaking a rule."[7]

We have then two different ideas here, usually combined in the discussion of rule-breaking in sports. First, there is the notion of a *contract* supposedly agreed to by game participants, and that the cheat breaks.

Secondly, in Luschen's and Feezell's definitions of cheating we also find the idea of an *unfair advantage*. The cheat not only fails to honour the previous agreement to respect the rules of the game she has freely and voluntarily engaged in. She also disrupts the equal conditions of competition "beyond differences of skill and strategy" that existed before the rule violation. While other participants abstain from using proscribed means to attain victory, the argument runs, the cheat resorts to more effective, illicit means to win the contest. A sanction is therefore required to *annul* the unfair advantage obtained through rule-breaking, and to *restore* competitive balance between players. I will discuss these two different aspects of the contractarian view of sports in the following two subsections.

Cheating as a contractual breach What kind of agreement is it that the cheat supposedly breaks? This agreement is obviously not always explicit. Rather, by entering the game, a player is (most often, implicitly) taken to accept submitting herself to the formally sanctioned norms of the sport discipline in which she engages. This acceptance, it is argued, makes respect for the rules mandatory. Thus, by the very action of playing, a sport practitioner puts herself under an obligation to honour the contract she has undertaken, and to abide by its rules. Sigmund Loland has formulated this idea as follows:

When we voluntarily engage in a rule-governed practice, we enter a more or less tacit social contract in which a moral obligation arises: keep the formal playing rules of the game! Here, then, we have the core justification of the fairness ideal.[8]

Against this contract view on fair play, Oliver Leaman stated that "(n)on-compliance by some players makes the problem of identifying precisely what the latent agreement is allegedly about insoluble".[9] Uncertainty about what the contract actually entails also casts a shadow of doubt on its validity. The strategy of supporting contractual obligation in sports on the notion of 'latent' or 'implicit' agreements made by the players is obviously weakened by the fact that many (even a majority) of them do not act in accordance with what supposedly has been agreed upon.

Put in this light, our initial question can now be reformulated: Has Maradona broken the implicit agreement among football players, when he scored his goal against the English national football team? The answer to this question will depend on whether touching the ball with one's hands runs counter to the prevailing ethos of football.

Now, according to the traditional understanding of a game ethos, it certainly does. In Fred D'Agostino's view, besides the formal, written rules of a game, there is "an unofficial system of conventions which determines how the official rules of the game will be applied in various concrete circumstances."[10]

On the basis of this notion, D'Agostino distinguishes three different kinds of sporting behaviour: *permissible* (that is, in accordance with the formal rules); *impermissible but acceptable* (that is, proscribed though not penalised conduct; and *unacceptable* behaviour (proscribed and penalised conduct). There is no question that handling the ball in football belong to the third category. When discovered, this is without exception penalised by referees.

The classical notion of a game ethos is, however, too narrow. It refers only to the way in which officials interpret sporting behaviour. *It is the ethos of game authorities, rather than the ethos of game practitioners.* It leaves aside the conventions, group norms, etc., upon which other participants in the sporting game base their understanding of the sporting activity in which they engage. Parallel to D'Agostino's official ethos, there are, for instance, the ethoses of the public, the media and the players, all different

from each other, which together render a comprehensive understanding of what the game is about. *D'Agostino's ethos is a set of conventions regulating how rule violations are to be penalised, rather than how the game is to be understood, much less how it has to be played.*

In the light of this wider, compound ethos notion, it is pretty obvious that Maradona's 'handball' goal does not run counter to the way football is played today. Particularly among football players, handling the ball is not an exceptional fault: when the occasion demands it, they resort to hand touches, and they do so often. It is true that, normally, these rule violations do not take place under the same spectacular and dramatic circumstances under which Maradona scored his goal. But hands faults are nonetheless relatively common in football games.

This does not mean that handling the ball in football should be tolerated by game officials, not even that it should not be criticised. In Maradona's case, for instance, it would be far-fetched to say that the fact that many football players actually commit that kind of infraction turns his fault into a permissible action. But the fact that handling the ball is relatively widespread among football practitioners at least weakens the rule formalist objection that hand touches are not part of the normative framework of football. If "handballing" is relatively frequent in football, then it ought to be seen as part of the reality of the game, as a practice sanctioned by the way in which football is played. *If everyone does it – or if everyone would do it, given a suitable occasion – the cheater simply acts as if she (reasonably) expects others to act in similar circumstances. No contractual breach can be derived from that.*

Against this realistic approach, it could be objected that, unlike Maradona's goal, hands faults – though indeed common – are often accidental and performed with no intention to deceive the authorities and obtain a game advantage. This move, however, will not do. Even if unintentional at the moment of being performed, the failure to signal one's fault to the referee turns the (originally unintended) action into an intentional strategy to obtain an illicit game advantage. From a contractual point of view, there is no morally relevant difference between trying to get a game advantage through a voluntary infraction, or through concealing an involuntary one. Committing an intentional hands fault is on a moral par with doing it unintentionally and failing to acknowledge it.

Finally, it could be objected that my argument unwarrantably takes for granted that the players' ethos should be given priority to the authorities' or the public's. However, *in the present context of fairness*, I believe this is as it should be. Fairness is a relational concept, it requires reciprocity: in the absence of reasons that could justify acting differently, it demands that you treat others as you are treated by them. The public's ethos pays most attention to how the way the play is played affects its quality, particularly its entertainment value. The authorities' ethos is concerned with how to penalise rule violations. The players' ethos, instead, is mainly concerned with how players treat each other, and how they fairly compete with each other within a commonly accepted rule set, rather than with how to preserve the quality (or entertainment value) of the game, or how infractions are to be penalised. Therefore, when fairness is on the focus, among all the complementary ethoses of the game, the players' ethos is the one with most relevance.

Cheating as unfair advantage According to a wider notion of game ethos, then, handling the ball in football is no contractual breach. And, as a matter of fact, it yields no unfair advantage either. Fairness in competitive conditions is not affected if, according to the prevailing ethos (unwritten rules and conventions) of the game, a certain cheating behaviour is accepted and generally performed. Everyone is allowed to proceed according to this (expanded) rule framework. Equal conditions of competition are thereby achieved. There is no unfair advantage in cheating, *provided it is (somehow) considered as part of the game by regular practitioners, and everyone has that option open for herself.*

According to the same line of reasoning, it becomes even more evident that the above mentioned cases of bad sportspersonship constitute no contractual breach or unfair advantage either. They are committed much more frequently than handling faults.

But, it could be retorted to this, why should the fact that sport practitioners seldom abide by a regulation have any bearing on whether or not its violation should be accepted, or

even tolerated? Think, for instance, of Mike Tyson's biting of Evander Holyfield's ear. Even if that practice were to become generalised (as a matter of fact, it is more common in boxing than one might think), would not such a practitioners' ethos be a perverted one? And, if so, does not this fact speak against giving any consideration whatsoever to the general level of compliance of a rule?

There is, in my opinion, a relevant difference between Maradona's and Tyson's illicit actions. Tyson's bite harmed the physical integrity of his opponent. Thus, it runs counter to one of the basic goals that the rules of the game are designed to achieve: preventing injuries to other players.

That is not the case regarding Maradona's goal. Obviously, a 'handball' goal still might be said to affect, if not the physical integrity, at least the interests of rival players negatively. But that is exactly what the game is about! Even in cases when the advantage is the result of an action proscribed by the formal rules of the game, that circumstance is tempered by the fact that the action is included in the enlarged ethos adopted by *sport practitioners*.

Thus, the examples of bad sportspersonship discussed in this chapter are not cases of unfair sporting behaviour. As a matter of fact, not even handling the ball in football (including the most famous instance, the "hand of God"), implies unfairness towards rivals, as handling is widely accepted (at least, in the weak sense of being indulged in, in given circumstances) among football players.

But does this decide the question whether foul play is acceptable? Could we not reject such sporting behaviour on other grounds than unfairness? To see that, let us now discuss condition (b) above.

Spoiling the game

An essentialist interpretation of (b) would establish that rules must be followed because only then can the true nature or essence of the game be preserved. Obviously, this amounts to game Platonism: there are no such entities as 'games', which remain unchangeable and immune to outer influence or transformation. Rather, condition (b) should be understood as a requirement that games be decided exclusively on grounds of differences in *skills* that are relevant for the actual discipline, and which the competition is expected to measure as objectively as possible. Thus, it could be argued, one reason to have rules in sports, and to discourage rule-breaking, is that without them sport contests would be decided on other grounds – by displaying other abilities – than those considered relevant for the game.

Though appealing, however, this approach does not fully meet the objection from game Platonism. Even skills central to a particular sport discipline evolve. And so does our view on them. At the turn of this century, runners were said to compete in the ability to get to the finish line as fast as possible without any training or preparation. Today, it is obvious that, in spite of superficial similarities, runners excel in quite another type of abilities, both physical and mental.

Besides, regarding certain examples of bad sportspersonship (for instance, putting off a rival player), it is not evident that the skill a sport practitioner has to display to avoid becoming a victim of that kind of action actually is so irrelevant to sport excellence as the present argument seems to assume. *There is no doubt that psychological make-up (particularly the capacity to resist pressure) also forms part of the skills repertoire tested by the contest.* Björn Borg was admired not only for his tremendous tennis abilities. We also admired him for his coolness of mind in the decisive moments. Other things being equal, this quality makes him superior to other, more temperamental players as, for instance, John McEnroe. At least, that is the way we reason in other professions. Good entrepreneurship is defined not only by the capacity to perform well in business, but also by the possession of a strong character to confront tough, *though licit*, competition. So, putting off a rival player might reasonably be seen as *expanding, rather than distorting*, the skills repertoire required by sporting games. By similar reasons; the English football team goes free from the accusation of unsporting behaviour in its encounter with Sweden. They were, so to speak, testing Schwartz's psychological excellence.

Perhaps we could, in order to avoid game or skill Platonism, reformulate (b) in terms of the *quality* of the game. On this view, rules – and the sanctions (formal and informal) attached to them – aim at preserving the quality of sport

competitions. Cheating, and sometimes even bad sportspersonship, as they are violations of the normative code of a game, lowers its quality and should therefore be discouraged.

The notion of the quality of a sporting game is usually referred to in a rather loose way in the literature on sports, and it has seldom been assessed in a stringent manner.[11] The difficulty of the task suggests such an enterprise probably will not be entirely successful. But this fact can hardly justify the surprisingly few attempts made to characterise the idea of a 'good game'. A tentative characterisation will have to include the following elements:

(i) Flow: a good game cannot be interrupted too often, it needs to have a certain fluidity to allow different game combinations to arise, and the development of game skills to flourish.

(ii) Skill: a good game has to attain a relatively high level in the display of the relevant skills. In a game frequently interrupted by rule violations, in a game with no flow, skills will have difficulty to flourish.

(iii) Challenge: a good game has to be a (roughly) even competition between rivals. An uneven match is not a good match, as it will lack intensity and the outcome will almost be given in advance.

(iv) Excitement: if the outcome is uncertain, and if the skill level is high, then the game will probably turn out as exciting. When the excitement rises above a certain degree, the game might even become dramatic.

(v) Drama: in very disputed and even games, the outcome could be decided only in the final moments of the competition, thus adding drama to the game.

(vi) Joy: when the game has flow, skill level is high and the contest even and exciting, both competitors and the public will experience joy, a sensation of having fun as a consequence of being engaged in a practice of great hedonic quality. Joy, however, is a rare quality in today's professional sports. Athletes need victory too badly to experience any fun in competing: their prestige and economic future are sometimes at stake on the field. And, often, spectators are not dispassionate enough to be able to enjoy a sport contest without suffering the agony of not knowing how their own team or their favourite athlete will do in the competition. In that sense, there is a tension between elements (v) and (vi): the more dramatic a contest is, the less fun the (passionate) spectator will experience.

To return to our previous question, there is no reason to assume a priori that keeping the rules of a game necessarily has a quality-enhancing effect, as characterised in (i)–(vi) above. As a matter of fact, there are several cases in which violations of the rules of a game have led to technical improvements of the discipline.[12] Further, even when no technical adjustments will follow, some cases of rule-breaking are sometimes 'game-enriching', in the sense of enhancing the challenge and excitement of the competition, without necessarily affecting the skills or the flow of the game negatively. Take, for example, deterrent interventions in football. Tougher play style will probably increase the heat of the game. As long as they stay within the limits of fair play (that is, of what is permitted by the written rule code), we have no reason to regret more aggressive contests. Granted that better skills will be required to elude tougher marking. But that means that players will develop the skill repertoire further.

The same applies to diving. A goal scored by a simulated penalty no doubt adds to the excitement of the game, as it compels the wronged team to play offensively to even the score. The match will then become more disputed and challenging. The flow of the game is not much affected either, as the situations in which it is rational to dive do not occur so often as to yield frequent interruptions in the game.

Further, diving seems to further, not only the excitement of the game, but also offensive playing skills. Diving, no doubt, obliges defending players to play in a more cautious manner. Thus, indirectly, it rewards offensive football styles. Dribbling skills will flourish, more goals will be scored, all this adding to the enjoyment of the public.

Spoiling and cheating as free-riding But perhaps the above discussion of spoiling behaviour

renders us another sense in which the above examples of foul play could be seen to be unfair. A condition for not spoiling the game is that, if not all, at least a great majority of players abide by the regulations. Otherwise, the play would become too dull, as a consequence of frequent interruptions, and the different skills and abilities of the players would have no opportunity to unfold and flourish. That means that the reason why cheats do not spoil the game is that others respect the regulations. As Sigmund Loland stated, "[t]he general idea is that it is wrong to benefit from the co-operation of others without doing our fair share".[13] Does not this then turn cheats into free-riders?

I do not think so. The kind of foul play we are discussing here (the examples of unsporting behaviour quoted above and such rule violations as handling the ball) are indeed so commonly practised that no player can reasonably be said to profit from other players' obedience to the rules. There is so to speak a fluent 'rotation' in playing dirty among the players. This, in my view, erases any unfair advantage cheaters might get and neutralises the free-rider argument.

Preventing injuries to others

Finally, could it not be argued that, if not all, at least some unsporting behaviour (for instance, deterrent interventions and the Sheffield–Arsenal incident) need to be discouraged, perhaps even formally forbidden, on the grounds that those actions increase the risk of physical injury for sport practitioners?

I do not think this argument affects deterrent interventions. Obviously, intimidating interventions increase the risk of harm, as they imply playing 'on-the-limit'. That risk, however, does not exceed what can reasonably be demanded from a professional player. Performing a professional activity is always related to the risk of being harmed by the strategies of one's competitors. So is also the case in professional sports.

Things are different regarding the Arsenal goal. If generalised, that action will have the consequence that no team will be prone to throw out the ball in order to provide for the medical attention of an injured rival player. This will increase the risk of injury for football players beyond what can be reasonably required from game participants. It is not part of any ethos of the game that, when injured, you will have to manage on your own without any medical attention, in particular, this is totally contrary to the player's ethos. The Arsenal team's action is thus blameable. It actually deserves the condemnation it met from football fans at the stadium.

What's wrong with cheating?

At the beginning of this chapter, I addressed the argument that commercialism and professionalism in elite sports encourage cheating and unsporting behaviour to the point of spoiling sport games. According to this criticism, these instances of foul play are wrong or, alternatively, an undesirable element in sport competitions. Such actions, it is said, give an athlete an unfair advantage over others, sometimes lowering the quality of the game or even jeopardising the physical integrity of sport practitioners. Against this, I suggested that at least some instances of cheating and unsporting behaviour do not fit within this description. They might, for example, increase the excitement of the competition, thereby enhancing its hedonic quality for spectators. Further, some of the risks involved in these infractions or unsporting actions must be accepted as part of the sport profession.

The realistic approach to sport practices advanced in this chapter also answers the criticism that originates in the contract view of fair play. According to this position, by making an agreement to compete, the athlete binds herself with self-imposed rules and conditions. By entering the game, then, she would be accepting, albeit implicitly, the imposition to abide by its rules, even those latent or not overtly formulated, if the athlete then fails to live up to this self-imposed obligation, it is argued by these critics, she might justifiably be accused of cheating, as she obtains an unfair game advantage over other players, an advantage that they have renounced by sticking to the rules.

I reject this view. If those actions are open for all practitioners, in the sense of being a part of the enlarged ethos of the players, no contractual breach takes place and no unfair advantage is obtained by the athlete who indulges in them.

Obviously, in Maradona's case, the fact that many football players actually commit that kind of rules violation is not sufficient to turn his fault into a permitted action. But at least it neutralises the objection that handling gives an unfair advantage to some players. If everyone does it – or if everyone would do it, given a suitable opportunity – the cheater simply acts as she (reasonably) expects others to act in similar circumstances. No unfair advantage can be derived from that.

From an (indirect) utilitarian point of view, it could even be argued that Maradona's action was right. Indirect utilitarianism states that an action is right when it is performed for optimific motives, even if its direct consequences are not condoned from an act-utilitarian point of view. Derek Parfit has provided an enlightening example of what indirect utilitarianism amounts to. In his *Reasons and Persons*,[14] he tells us about Claire, an act-utilitarian girl who has to decide between giving money to a charity organisation (and thereby saving many children from death in a foreign country), or using the money to cure her own child from a serious, though not life-threatening, disease. The disease will cause a handicap to her child, but will not turn the child's life into one that is not worth living. Claire decides to cure her child. In doing so, she fails to save the lives of the children who depended on her aid to survive. From an act-utilitarian point of view, it is evident that Claire acts wrongly. She fails to maximise welfare for all those concerned by her action, and chooses instead to actualise a lesser good. However, according to Parfit, her action, though wrong, is nonetheless blameless, as it is performed for a set of motives (taking care of one's offspring) that, in the long run and indirectly, will make the world a better place to live.

By the same token, we could say that Maradona's 'handball' goal became a *right, though blameworthy*, action. Blameful right doing stands for an action that, though stemming from a wrong motive, still turns out to be right because of the positive effects that, albeit indirectly, follow from it. Maradona's cheating is to blame, because it stems from the wrong set of motives. Normally, being driven by the motive of getting an advantage over others by circumventing the rule framework tends to produce negative consequences for the game or even for society as a whole. But, some of these actions, although contrary to the formal, written rules of the game, turn out nonetheless to be right, because, in the end, they have a positive impact on the game, either by being innovative for sport techniques, or by enhancing the quality and the excitement of the game, or for all these reasons together.

This is particularly true of the "hand of God". After it took place, football matches between England and Argentina acquired a special agonistic flavour, that seems to have overshadowed the tragic inheritance of the Falkland/Malvinas war. Thus, his goal had positive effects not only for the game of football, but even for the international community at large.

Further, the unfair advantage view also confronts the problem that not all the sanctions actualised by the regulatory rules can properly be described as restoring the previous competitive balance between athletes. Some of them obviously fit under this description. Thus, when a player plays the ball outside the physical limits of the football field, she loses the possession of the ball and the rival team regains it through an out-goal. But take, for instance, a red card for violent fouling. If the game is allowed to continue after the fault is committed, the fouler gets the ball from the fouled player. This is no doubt an illicit game advantage and should therefore be sanctioned. But the game advantage is the same, regardless of the harshness of the fouling. Why then send her out? If the aim is to erase the illicit advantage, why not sanction this one foul, like any other, with a free kick for the rival team?

Another example is the newly introduced rule of football that requires sending out a player who fouls, or simply holds, a rival player in a goal position. Even if the game advantage obtained by the fouler (or, rather, the disadvantage she avoided through her fault) seems to justify a more severe sanction than a free kick, there is nonetheless a lack of proportionality between the type of fault (often, explicit and innocuous), and the sending out of the fouler. Why such harshness?

Similar difficulties arise regarding another rule of football sanctioning the suspension from the next match of a player who is booked twice during a tournament. He/she is allowed to finish the match in which the second card is awarded. The team against which the second fault is committed is not benefited by the suspension. Instead, it is the next rival team which is benefited. A highly counter-intuitive situation (from a fairness point of view) arose in the World Football Cup, in France 98. The Nigerian national team was not allowed to field some of its best players in the last match of the classificatory group against Paraguay, because they had got a second yellow card in the previous match against Spain. By winning over the weakened Nigerian team, Paraguay qualified for the next round, thereby leaving Spain out of the competition. Not only did Spain not benefit from the yellow cards its performance provoked in the Nigerian team: they were even harmed by it! In that sense, sending out a cautioned player for a period of time during the same match (as, for instance, is done in ice-hockey) seems a more reasonable way to act. At least, the team benefited by the sanction would be the one against which the fault was committed.

In my opinion, these examples suggest that certain sanctions in football (and in other sports as well) are designed to operate as deterrents, rather than as restorative measures for infringements that yield game advantages. In the goal-position example, the severity of the sanction is intended to protect the quality of the game by keeping occurrence of this kind of fouling at a low level. Goals make the game more exciting. So, red cards for fouling a player who is about to score can be justified in terms of (a) above, understood as a quality-enhancing condition.

Red cards for violent fouls, instead, seem appropriate for discouraging actions that risk the infliction of physical injury on the players. That means that their justification will have to be formulated in terms of (c) above.

However, protecting sport practitioners from injury should not be confused with trying to eliminate reasonable professional risks at all costs. In professional football, for instance, dangerous fouls are still prohibited, and so they are in recreational football. But while so called intimidating interventions (tough actions 'on the edge' of what is permitted by the rules, intended to instil respect for one's physical strength in rival players) definitely do not belong in the latter, they seem to be, not only acceptable, but even recommendable in the professional field. At least, one positive consequence which might follow from them is the increased excitement of a tough match.

141

Towards an enlarged sport ethos

The arguments above suggest that, in sports, besides the traditional and already established ethos of the game, there is a wider normative framework, directly stemming from the evolving practice of the game, that condones a set of acceptable actions (*even unsporting or rule-infringing ones*) that are open for sports practitioners. In this practical, 'down-to-game' normative framework, the sport practitioners' ethos – the particular understanding of the game entertained by players – is the most relevant indication of how the game should be played.

This *extended* ethos, I would like to underline, should be clearly distinguished from a perverted one as, for instance, the general acceptance of actions similar to Tyson's bite would amount to. The reason is that, with the exception of the Sheffield–Arsenal incident, the examples of foul play discussed in this chapter are no hindrance to achieving the goals of the rule system. They do not spoil sports. The examples of bad sportspersonship advanced above are not necessarily negative for the quality of the game. Often, they might even be expected to increase its excitement, by furthering the agonistic element of the contest. This is particularly true in professional sports, where so many material gains are at stake.

Bad sportspersonship does not violate the requirement of fairness in competition either. Diving, deterring interventions, persecuting a booked rival player, or the possibility of obtaining a game advantage by disturbing the concentration of one's opponent, are strategies open to everyone who chooses to engage in sport activity. Nor can such conduct be said to deprive individuals from an equal chance to enter the game. At least, not more than in the legitimate sense of putting higher demands on the skills to be mastered by the contestants.

The argument for the idea on an evolving ethos has obvious implications for the issue of fair play and good sportspersonship. Not only the attitudes of sport participants towards the rules of the game will change over time. Also what was previously seen as fair play, and the character qualities associated with it, will be submitted to a transformation, along with changes in values and the concrete situation of the community of sport practitioners. An example of these transformations is the commercial character acquired by sports during the last decades. The prospect of economic rewards and public acknowledgement put athletes under a pressure to increase performance standards. An expected consequence of this process is the relaxation of the system of rules governing sporting activities. Needless to say, the rules and traditions of the practice, as well as current notions of fair play, will have to undergo changes along with such a major transformation. These changes are not necessarily negative for sports. As a matter of fact, many of them can be said to increase competitive tension and the excitement of the game.

The picture of blameworthy actions in professional sports that finally emerges is that of a continuum. At one extreme, we have licit and non-blameable actions. At the other extreme, we see those examples of cheating that clearly have a negative effect on the game, as well as on sports practitioners. In between, there is strategic behaviour that, though unsporting, can neither be properly labelled as cheating (as it does not violate the written rules of the game), nor rightfully blamed (as it does not jeopardise the physical integrity of rival players, is not unfair, and might even increase the excitement of the game).

Finally, within the cheating domain, we find a special type of conduct that, though overtly violating the written normative code, constitutes nonetheless *blameful right doing*. Examples of blameful right doing, it should be underlined, are very exceptional. Maradona's 'handball' goal, I have argued, is one of them. After its occurrence, encounters between the Argentinean and the English national football teams are marked by enhanced competitive character, and the aggressive postwar atmosphere between the teams was definitely eliminated. Therefore, his goal should be placed on a moral par with other actions (such as diving, intimidating interventions, and others), that – though performed from morally suspect motivations – add to the hedonic quality of the sport performance and increase the enjoyment of the public.

If my arguments are correct, it then follows that certain cases of bad sportspersonship and (though in very exceptional cases) cheating should be tolerated and even lauded, rather than discouraged, in professional sports. In my opinion, this is exactly what is happening in elite sports at present. Obviously, that encouragement has not been formally sanctioned by rule changes: the rule system is always behind the reality of the practice it purports to regulate. Nonetheless, I believe it is possible to perceive a more condescending attitude towards cheating and bad sportspersonship in at least some professional sports. Is that negative? Traditionally, this laxity has been interpreted as an evident sign of the perversion of sports by commercialism and professionalism. And, indeed, professional elite sports are practised at the intersection of fair play and bad sportspersonship. If the game becomes more exciting, with no increased risks for the physical integrity of the players, I think we should revise that negative judgement. Or, at least, we should think twice before making categorical pronouncements on these matters.

Notes

1. In "Why the Good Foul is not Good", in Morgan, William J. and Meier, Klaus V. (eds.), *Philosophic Inquiry in Sport*, Human Kinetic Publishers, Champaign, IL., 1995 (2nd edition), pp. 185–7, quotations from p. 186. Immediately after this definition, Fraleigh exemplifies a 'good' foul in basketball as follows: "… a defensive player, moving behind an offensive player with the ball who is dribbling for an easy lay up shot, intentionally holds the player, forcing him to shoot two free throws to make the same number of points". According to him, what makes such faults *good* is that it is "in the prudent self-interest of the fouling player to force the opponent to shoot twice from a greater distance to make the same number of points as would have been made by shooting once for a lay up". Incidentally, it should be noticed that, after Fraleigh wrote his article, basketball regulations had undergone changes in this respect. At present, situations as those exemplified in the good foul render three, instead of two, shoots. A similar tendency can be noticed in football. Recent rule changes sanctioning fouls from behind (even innocuous ones, like holding) to rival players in a goal position with a red card are intended to outweigh the beneficial effects for the fouler and her team of such violations of the rules. Notwithstanding these changes, Fraleigh's argument could be restated by resorting to other examples of good fouls gathered from other sports.
2. Or, in Peter McIntosh's terms, the intention 'to beat the system' by gaining a game advantage even when the violation is sanctioned according to the rules. In *Fair Play: Ethics in Sport and Education*, he says that "Cheating … need be no more than breaking the rules with the intention of not being found out … Cheating, however, implies an intention to beat the system even although the penalty, if the offender is found out, may still be acceptable". (Heinemann, London, 1979, quoted in Leaman, Oliver. "Cheating and Fair Play in Sport", in Morgan, William J. and Meier, Klaus V. (eds.), op. cit., pp. 193–7, quotation on p. 193.
3. Strictly speaking, the advantage to be gained might also be the fulfilment of one's desire to benefit another competing athlete or team. Suppose, for instance, that a football team that already classified for the final instances of a tournament confronts a match that, if lost, can help the other team to classify. And suppose there is a long tradition of friendship between both teams. If the first team plays to lose, that would be a case of cheating, even if, properly speaking, the advantage they would thereby be getting is not a *game* advantage, but merely a preference satisfaction.
4. For more on the distinction between 'fair play' and a 'sportspersonlike attitude', see, for instance, James W. Keating, "Sportsmanship as a Moral Category", in Morgan, William J. and Meier, Klaus V. (eds.), op. cit., pp. 144–51, particularly p. 147.
5. A distinction should be drawn here between: (a) provoking a rival player by fouling him (that is, through cheating); (b) provoking by playing at the limit of what is permitted by the rules (that is, through bad sportspersonship); and (c) provoking by displaying outstanding dribbling abilities in front of a warned rival player (which is a licit and often game-enriching action). It is (b) that will be discussed in this chapter.
6. "Cheating in Sport", in Landers, D. (ed.), *Social Problems in Athletics*, University of Illinois Press, Urbana, 1977, quoted in Leaman, Oliver, "Cheating and Fair Play in Sport", in Morgan and Meier (eds.), op. cit., pp. 193–197, quotation on p. 193.
7. In "Sportsmanship", in Morgan, William J. and Meier, Klaus V. (eds.), op. cit., pp. 152 60. Quotations on p. 153.
8. "Fair play: historical anachronism or topical ideal?", in McNamee, Mike and Parry, Jim, *Ethics and Sport*, E & FN Spon (Routledge), London–New York, 1998, pp. 79–103 (quotation on p. 93).
9. Op. cit., in Morgan, William J. and Meier, Klaus V. (eds.), op. cit., pp. 193–7, quotation on p. 195.
10. "The Ethos of the Game", first printed in *Journal of the Philosophy of Sport* VIII, 1981, pp. 7–18. Reprinted in Morgan, William J. and Meier, Klaus V., op. cit., pp. 42–9 (quotation from page 47).

11. An exception is Sigmund Loland's characterisation of the 'good game' in his previously mentioned article.

12. Underwater breast swimming, for instance, though not fully allowed after its appearance, amounted to a technical paradigm shift in the discipline. The skyhook (in basketball) and the 'Boklöv jump' (in ski jumping) are other examples.

13. Op. cit., p. 99.

14. Clarendon Press, Oxford, 1984, on pp. 32–7. Parfit's indirect utilitarianism might be seen as an attempt to reconcile a consequentialist approach with virtue ethics.

Spoiling

An indirect reflection of sport's moral imperative?

Graham McFee

The moral imperative sometimes located within sport (and rightly so, in my opinion) is often not a direct consequence of the rules or laws of particular sports, and this fact is recognised when appeal is made, not to those rules themselves, but to the *spirit* of the rules, or to considerations of *fair play*, or some such. But how do these matters manage to impinge on sport performance? In this chapter, I argue that they stand to the rules of sport roughly as Ronald Dworkin's (legal) *principles* stand to his (legal) *rules*: recall that it is the *principle* that one should not benefit from one's crime that prevents the grandfather-killer, Elmer, from inheriting his grandfather's wealth – there is no *rule* here (Dworkin 1978: 22–28, 71–80).[1] In just this way, the principles underlying a sport provide a *learned* background essential for appropriate participation in that sport. But this seems rendered problematic once the *constitutive* role of the rules of particular sports is granted.

In Dworkin's own example, that of the rule in baseball, '… that if a batter has had three strikes, he is out' (Dworkin 1978: 24), a sporting case illustrates human situations (especially legal ones) where there are *rules* but no *principles*, and (therefore?) one where such moral considerations do not apply.[2] Or so Dworkin thinks.

For the decision to select *three* strikes (rather than, say, four) is arbitrary: if so, there would be no need for further justifications. But this is misleading if we view sport more realistically: these moral(ish) principles do apply in at least some sports, as illuminated by the possibility of contravening the 'spirit of the rules' (for example, by what I shall call 'spoiling'). Even in Dworkin's example, there are many factors. For instance, one motivation for the rule must relate to the proposed/intended duration of a game – the rule '300 strikes and you are out' would make a typical game too long – but even here there might be *some* consideration of fairness; that one strike did not give the batter a *fair* chance to display prowess, for example. So there is an implicit appeal to (principled) fairness.

To say this is to stress the importance of the *possibility* of winning (etc.) where this means more than just the logical possibility. I use the term 'spoiling' to characterise approximately behaviour that, while not contrary to the rules of a game/sport, is nonetheless not how one *ought* to play it, for 'participating in the game/match' should mean participating in ways that respect one's opponents, showing due regard for them.[3] Plays which involve spoiling do not permit opponents the possibility of playing the

Graham McFee 'Spoiling: An Indirect Reflection of Sport's Moral Imperative', from *Values in Sport*, T. Tännsjö and C. Tamburrini eds, © 2000 Graham McFee. Reprinted by permission of Routledge.

game according to its spirit, a possibility one *must* grant to opponents taken seriously. Although permitted by the rules, such plays are recognised – at least by knowledgeable audiences – as inappropriate ways to play the game/sport: an arena where players who 'spoil' may legitimately be criticised by the audience, teammates and the media, but not by referees.

Nor should we think of this as an impossible burden on referees – their problems are not the key ones here. One of Dworkin's own examples to illustrate this point runs as follows:

> Suppose some rule of a chess tournament provides that the referee shall declare a game forfeit if one player 'unreasonably' annoys the other in the course of play. The language of the rule does not define what counts as 'unreasonable' annoyance ...
>
> (Dworkin 1978: 102)

His example could readily be replaced by one about sport; about cricket or soccer, for instance. And his point would be ours – that the rules do not circumscribe the exact behaviours they permit or prohibit.

In referring to the need for what, following Dworkin, I am calling 'principles', my point is not one about the completeness/incompleteness of rules as represented by rule-formulations (the kind of thing better drafting might be thought to cure) – there is always an element of judgment in the application of a rule, and in 'knowing how to go on'[4] on the basis of a rule. Rather this distinction is employed to highlight a species of more general constraint on *appropriate* sporting behaviour (for some sports, at least), but one not required (nor prohibited) by that sport's rules.

As Dworkin (1978: 103) continues, such rules '... are not incomplete, like a book whose last page is missing, but abstract ...' This means that they must be filled in, *particularised*,[5] to a given context. And that immediately licenses disputes about the appropriateness of the various cases offered. For how exactly do the rules apply – and how should they be applied – in this (testing) case? There will always be room for dispute here, since no application of a rule is uniquely determined by the rule-formulation. Nor should we think of such disputes as rare, for they are driven by questions of *principles*. And, as Dworkin remarks, 'Once we identify

legal principles as separate sorts of standards, different from legal rules, we are suddenly aware of them all around us' (1978: 28). For we see the normativity of such principles in many of the social behaviours of human beings.

A crucial thought here is that one learns at least *some* of the principles through learning how to '... *construct* the game's character' (Dworkin 1978: 103) when we learn the *rules*. Dworkin's exposition takes the acquiring of principles as somehow prior to, and the basis for, such learning of rules; as he puts it, the principles provide a '... gravitational force' (1978: 115) operative within the rule. But, in sporting cases, this cannot be quite right. The interlock between the moral metaphors of justice – 'level playing field', 'fair play', etc. – and the specifics of sport mean that, in learning how to make sense of these ideas *as they apply in particular sports*, one is learning the general moral principles, by learning how to apply these key metaphors more exactly. (If this is true, it places a particular obligation on teachers of sport: they can be teaching the 'rules' of a moral laboratory – see below.)

Through a consideration of cases of 'spoiling' plays, this chapter defends both the thesis that, properly understood, such principles offer essential moral constraints on (some) sports and the idea that, *for this reason*, some sports have the capacity to provide examples of those concrete particulars that alone permit the learning, and learning to apply, of moral concepts; in short, that some sport can function – as I put it earlier – as a *moral laboratory*, in which moral concepts are acquired, but with less risk than in genuine moral confrontations.

Key differences between principles of this kind and typical rules constitutive of sport highlight the 'framework' character of those principles. And, since the principles regulate human interactions (in the sense of headlining what one ought or ought not to do), it cannot be far off the mark to call them 'moral'.

Since my argument is for the *intrinsic* moral possibilities of sport, as we will see, it is interesting to note a typical explanation of spoiling: for example, the case of someone bowling underarm and along the ground the last delivery of a limited-over cricket match – to preclude the *possibility* of the opponents winning. For – as later – these explanations point to the externality or extrinsic-ness of the counter-forces here, thereby suggesting the internality of the principles against which spoiling (etc.) offends. And my concern is with the *nature* of sport (what is intrinsic to it) rather than what is extrinsic – for example, its ability to make money.

In this way, one sees how sport's claims to be genuinely beneficial to human beings (in an *intrinsic* fashion) might be sustained, and thus how a commitment to sport's (broadly) educative potential, which *parallels*, say, that of Pierre de Coubertin, might be defended – although in a more realistic version.

Yet arguments for particularism in morality (here accepted) might make us doubt the possibility of acquiring *moral* principles through learning in *sporting* situations. For, surely, particularism emphasises the *sporting* character of these situations. But a more realistic account of the relation of the particular to the abstract can resolve this tension.

Before returning to these abstract considerations, it is useful (perhaps essential) to have a concrete example in front of us. As my central example is from cricket, I will spell it out at some length, drawing rough parallels to baseball. The situation is the end of a limited-over cricket match: there is one delivery (one 'ball') to go and the batting side needs *six runs* to win. Now while, in principle, six runs might be scored in a large number of ways from one delivery, in practice these runs can only be scored by the batsman hitting the ball over the boundary rope without its bouncing; 'on the fly', as people say. Typically the bowler in cricket delivers the ball overarm, where it bounces *roughly* in front of the batsman. Such a delivery might be hit for six, hit over the boundary rope, 'on the fly'; and this is especially likely, given that the relevant batsman is a *good* hitter of sixes.

To give names to the players (fictional names), let us call the bowler 'Trevor Chappell'. What he does – following the instructions of his captain (who we will call 'Greg Chappell', and designate to be his brother) – is to bowl underarm, along the ground. This facilitates the batsman's *hitting* the ball, but effectively precludes his hitting it 'for six'. As a result, Chappell's side wins the match.

Now, one *is* permitted to bowl underarm in cricket – there is no rule precluding it. Further, one is permitted to bowl along the ground; again, there is no rule prohibiting it.[6] But the net effect of the action is to win the match with a technique which – as people say – 'is not cricket': it is a *spoiling* gesture.

Notice that this is not a technique one could always use: first, it would not always be necessary. But it is effective in this case partly because here one is trying to preclude (exactly) *six* runs, and would be quite happy to concede, say, *four* runs: that would still leave the Chappell team winners! Second, it would be counterproductive if all teams used it, either *throughout* the game (which would destroy much of the excitement) or *at the end*, where its predictability would make it useless as a *match-winner* – everyone would be doing it!

This example is powerful *partly* because cricket is regularly offered as a model of fair play – although today's high-class game, with its 'sledging' (that is, behaviour designed to unsettle the opposing player by, say, commenting on his skill or his mother's virtue) is often far from that.

It is granted on all sides that spoiling behaviour in cricket is permitted by the rules of the sport. But if this spoiling behaviour really were acceptable, why not do it *all* the time? The idea of only doing it on this (strange) occasion is tacit acknowledgment that it is not OK. (Also, as noted above, there are practical issues about the effectiveness of it as a long-term strategy, one consequently to be adopted by one's opponents, say.)

This is an example of *spoiling* because bowling in that fashion at that point in the game does not give the opposing side a *fair chance*. So spoiling has a direct connection to the 'spirit of the game' idea – to the *essence* of a sporting contest, as we might put it. But here there is a pun on the term 'sporting', both to mean conforming to the rules of the game (and hence part of that sport) and to mean played appropriately!

Spoiling comes about when there is a *conflict* between the letter of the rules (the written rule/statute) and the *spirit* of the rules – that is, the principles (for instance, of fairness) on which the rules rest.

In determining the relevant principles here, notice the (*conceptual*) importance, within cricket, of the idea of a 'wide', a delivery beyond where the batsman can plausibly hit the ball. Here we see the commitment, within cricket, to the bowling of deliveries from which the batsman *can* score, if he is sufficiently skilled. That its rules allow the concept of a *wide* therefore indicates something about the principles underlying cricket. Further, the penalty for bowling a *wide* is twofold: first, the bowling side automatically gains one run for the wide and, second, the ball is delivered again. In this way, the bowling side *simply* loses one run and *still* has to bowl that delivery. Its importance here, though, lies in the connection of sport's rules to its principles being visible here – as the case of spoiling identifies. In recognising the place of (effectively) moral principles here – and thereby of the preservation of the integrity of the sport – we begin to see how the hoped-for connection of sport to the moral might be defended. (Notice, though, that this concerns what sport can do, not what it must, or inevitably will, do.)

But need there be *one* account here for sport in general? Suppose that we resolve this case: how far *need* that commit us? To what degree are there *precedents* being set here? Well, we began from the interpenetration of moral notions with our lives – what we are adding is the thought that they (also?) have a role in sport – a role recognised in the moral metaphors from which we began.

Of course, this parallel also makes plain a limitation of the moral laboratory – not a problem for the theory but for the practice. For, just as someone might be a master of pure mathematics but unable to 'manage' elementary applied maths (say, unable to check one's change quickly after buying a round of drinks), so one might be a master of the moral concepts in the sporting context but unable to apply them outside the 'laboratory'. There is no theoretical safeguard here, no guarantee that generalisability won't be thwarted (*pace* de Coubertin) – although eternal vigilance might work against this being a regular occurrence; and valuing sport partly as a moral laboratory might make such vigilance easier to organise!

But those 'moral metaphors' are either *not* metaphorical or are *less* metaphorical in the sporting context, where there really can be fair playing and the levelness of actual playing fields. Seeing how these ideas interact with the rules (and spirit) of sport can show us how such notions might *apply* – and hence, perhaps, how they might be applied more generally. And saying this is acknowledging a kind of generality

of *application*, which is *very different* from simply generalising – as we might put it, it is the generalisability of the particularist (see Travis 1996).

If particularism in morality is granted (i.e. true), principles could only be acquired ('learned') in concrete situations: that is, learned 'concretised'. This is one reason why one cannot (usefully) write down such principles. Or, we can write them down, but not helpfully. The principle against spoiling might be, 'Play the game' or, more exactly, 'Do not act so as to impede your opponent's playing to the spirit of the rules'.

Of course, one is here formulating *in the abstract* the objection to spoiling, but this simply reflects the contours of the relevant principle – it certainly would not be exceptionless. So that if I render the principle against spoiling as 'Play the game', I do not give useful guidance as to what to *do* in a particular situation, nor how to judge what someone else does. And this is especially true when the principle applies to more than one sport, as well as to different situations *within* a sport. But, if I am an experienced cricketer, being told 'play the game' may be informative – it might highlight ways in which my behaviour to date was less than exemplary. Even more revealing is when I am told, say by my captain and older brother, to *not* 'play the game': I might know what to do *then* just because I *do* know 'how to go on' without contravening this principle – although on this occasion I do not do so. The point, though, is that formulating the abstract principle is doubly unhelpful. Of course, like any 'rule'-formulation, the application of my principle-formulation is a matter of judgment (as noted above). But, more crucially, the application here is circumscribed by the specific nature of the sport itself. Unsurprisingly, this conclusion reinforces the particularism (explicitly) assumed earlier.

A good question here will be how we learn such (sporting) principles, and this will be especially important *for me*, given my account of the connection between understanding and explaining.[7] For what is involved in *learning* X surely has a bearing on *explaining* X. So how does this happen? How do we (typically) learn sporting principles? My most general answer is that this happens in *appropriate* teaching of the sporting activity. It follows that what one learns is not – and could nor be – just a formulation of the principle (a principle-formulation), but how to *behave* in accordance with the principle; for instance, how to manifest 'fair play' (which is, of course, no guarantee that one will then actually play fairly). In effect, then, my thought is that principles are taught when rules are properly taught – where the term 'properly' makes just that point!

We have a sense how, in teaching the rules of a game (for example, cricket), a teacher sensitive to the principles might inculcate those principles too; indeed, those of us who were well taught can remember this process. So, if we cannot *say* how to teach these principles, we do at least know. But now a further issue intrudes. How, given the teaching and learning of sporting principles, does this apply to morality? The model here is of an abstract principle learned from (and in) concrete instances in sport, then applied to concrete moral situations where – perhaps for theoretical reasons – we might also formulate abstract moral principles.

Notice the way principles of (roughly) rule-application are moral: for instance, there is a moral obligation to mean what one says, in two senses: first, that one *does* mean what one says, because (other things being equal) one means what one's words mean – to put it roughly; and second, because the alternatives are lying or frivolity (or self-deception) – that is, they are moral failings.[8]

Of course, one must acknowledge the limitation of my argument here: spoiling is at best *one* such index of moral connection; moreover, it is for some sports only.[9] But it is not for that reason a useless or trivial index. For these cases illustrate why someone might misconceive the relation of sport to moral development as well as offering some 'fixed points' for many discussions (although not all). As we might say, they point to answers to *particular* perplexities. The particularism thus exposed – that there are no wholly general problems here – reinforces a conception of philosophy on which the concerns that philosophy should address are the philosophical puzzlements of particular individuals: that is, a therapeutic conception of philosophy.

To return to the main thread, it was noted earlier that there is something 'fishy' about spoiling procedures: for, otherwise, only tactical considerations would preclude their being used throughout the game – and this is not so. Might we make some more of this, by asking whether such a procedure is as obviously within the rules of the game as it appears? Here we would be looking at the nature of rules or statutes.

At first sight, this behaviour is certainly permitted by the rules of the sport – in the sense of not being explicitly excluded. But a more radical solution might be considered. In line with some of Dworkin's remarks, we might ask whether the behaviour is actually excluded by the 'real' rules – that is, the rules on their 'best' interpretation, the interpretation that maintains the 'integrity', as Dworkin puts it (1986: 94) of those rules; what he elsewhere calls the *principles* underlying it (typically moral/political principles and, for games at least, concerned with fairness/justice). For Dworkin illustrates how, in legal disputes over the correct decision in a difficult case, the opposing judges are disagreeing about the correct interpretation of the law – over *what the law is* (Nagel 1995: 196). For instance, they might dispute '… how to construct the real statute in the circumstances of that case' (Dworkin 1986: 17). The point, of course, is that if this were also true of the statutes of our game, we might with justice argue that the rules of the game, its *real* rules, do have a bearing here – and find against the legality of spoiling!

As Dworkin says, one is here recognising '… implicit standards between and beneath the explicit ones' (1986: 217). And these standards – enshrined in the *principles* – will typically be moral ones. Preserving *integrity*, in this sense, amounts to 'reading' the rules of the practice so as to show that practice in its best light – thereby preserving its principles – in the light of what has gone before in that practice. Here, as Dworkin (1986: 227) records, 'History matters because … [the] scheme of principles [appealed to] must justify the standing as well as the content of … past decisions'. We need such integrity 'all the way up'!

Three points are of interest for us. First, as Nagel (1995: 197) notes, *integrity* in this sense is '… an ambiguous virtue', so construing the law and its purposes '… makes decisions flow from a coherent set of principles, even when those principles are not your own'. So, in this idealised version, we have an explanation of consistency requirements as well as a basis for disputes about what counts as consistently interpreting a rule of sport. Second, such a model of integrity fits practices like sport, where the rules (and even some of the principles) have explicit formulation, at least as well (and perhaps better) than it accords with Dworkin's preferred case, municipal legal systems. And this is revealing, since it cannot be far off the truth to say that the *integrity* being preserved is the integrity of the sport itself – and this accords with earlier talk of its *spirit*. Third, we know where to look for the 'interpretative' acts here; namely, to the decisions of umpires and referees, as well as to appeals concerning those decisions. Here, a crucial *difference* is that, in contrast to typical judicial decisions, the decisions of umpires (etc.) will always be required in a fairly brief time span: the players (etc.) cannot wait for ever ... (This just places yet more importance on the umpires as *informed* judges, and hence places yet greater weight on their appropriate training.)

In the context of Aristotle's discussion of rule/case thinking, McDowell (1998: 26–27) considers the possibility that, if one has the rule, that only leaves open questions of 'interpretation'. But, first (as above), one must acquire the rule via cases; second, as Dworkin (1986: 20) illustrates, the general separation between cases and rules is spurious – finding out how to treat *this case* can be finding *what the rule is.*

Dworkin urges that legal rules, as regularly conceived, '... are not themselves programmes *of* interpretation' (1986: 226). As Nagel (1995: 197) notes, this constitutes a *substantive* theory of law; and we could, of course, reject it.[11] But suppose – at least for the sake of today's argument – that we do not. What follows about the rules (the *laws*, as they are often rightly called) of sports?

First, we should have to rephrase our account of spoiling – it would be contrary to the rules on their real interpretation (that is, roughly, with the principles imported), although not on a more conservative or literalist interpretation.

Second, and more important, Dworkin is here offering a different perspective on the fact that any *written* statute requires 'interpretation' (that is, understanding) for its implementation in *this* case. But it invites us to see this as an *essential*, and as a *productive*, feature of such law. We have already noted that – on pain of regress – the applications of rules cannot themselves be a matter of rules. Here we see its

weirder sister: that what is and what is not a *real* rule is an *essentially* 'interpretative' process, such that pointing to *the wording* of some statute cannot (typically) decide the matter. And if this were true of the statutes of a legal system (*any* legal system, as a matter of logic), how much more likely that these points apply ('in spades') to the rules of sports?

This, then, addresses two points: first, as others have recognised,[12] one cannot resolve *all* of the moral problems (potentially) occurring in a particular sporting situation by tinkering with the sport's rules; and second, the *pressure* here genuinely is pressure from the *principles* (in Dworkin's sense) that drive those rules – and that is a way of asserting that these genuinely are moral concerns.[13]

A crucial point here is hard to get *exactly* right: on the one hand, there is a sense in which the fact that no rule (or law) can deal with *all* cases must be acknowledged. So one cannot, for instance, resolve *all* difficulties in a particular sport by making new rules for that sport (or new codes of professional ethics, for that matter),[14] rules which deal with every situation unequivocally. Now, one way to make *that* point would be to emphasise the role of judges (say, referees) in *interpreting* rules in real cases. Equally, and on the other hand, we must recognise (as Dworkin does)[15] that what can *look like* the making of law by judges is in fact the kind of judicial discussion that determines *what the law is*; at the least, judges are not *free* to 'make the law' – say, in these 'hard cases'. And one way to articulate this point would be to see judges as *looking for* the law. The difficulty, of course, is that these two images of legal practice (and legal decision) *seem* to run in opposite directions. And what is true of law generally conceived is – by extension – true of the laws of particular sports. Some might say 'So what?' Our reply is that we want (or perhaps need) to say both of these things, on different occasions; that the same form of words can be different questions in different mouths, with each being resolvable, taken case by case – yet without there being some *general* resolution! So there will be some occasions when the revealing answer will point in one direction, and other occasions when it will point in the other. As Gordon Baker and Peter Hacker comment, of a similar difficulty, '... The question is misleading but the facts are clear' (Baker and Hacker 1985: 47n.).

A key question (one *you* may have been asking for some time) is 'Can one spoil in sports other than cricket?' The crucial characteristics of spoiling – as I have characterised spoiling here – might make one doubt this. The spoiling behaviour must be *within* the rules of the sport (so attracting no penalty, nor gaining censure from the governing body) yet contrary to that sport's *spirit*; and this will mean, roughly, contrary to how it *is* played, rather than to how it *might* be. And the activity must give the perpetrators an advantage – at least in that context. I do not know enough about *all* sport to answer with confidence the question of whether it applies elsewhere.[16] Nor can we produce some 'transcendental argument' to determine the matter once and for all. But we progress by, first, considering the *upshot* of spoiling for our view of sport (roughly, the insight it provides) and, second, considering cases which are *not* spoiling.

My suggestion is that spoiling – in illustrating the place of (roughly) *principles* in sport – illuminates some of the ways sport might be thought generally valuable. But that suggestion turns on sport's use as moral laboratory, an idea made concrete through consideration of spoiling but not (of course) limited to it.

Now consider some cases which are *not* spoiling. If I waste time in soccer (say, by kicking the ball away prior to a free kick), I may be penalised; at the least, a competent referee will simply add on the time wasted. So I will have gained nothing. Thus what I do *is* contrary to the rules, and is recognised as such. Therefore this is not spoiling as I have explained it, since this is contrary to the letter of the law. (Still, given that there was no penalty ... well, there is *really* no advantage either, if the referee is 'on the ball'.) Correspondingly, a quarterback who 'throws the ball away' to avoid being sacked is not *spoiling*, because his behaviour is *not* censured (by players or officials). But a basketball player who fouls an opponent in the act of shooting is doing something both *expected* of him and (as the rules are 'read' by referees) not contrary to the rules – as the imposition of fixed penalties for this behaviour is taken to illustrate; indeed, to call this *foul* is to use the term 'foul' in a way quite different from its everyday use. For, far from being a behaviour censured, it is behaviour *applauded* (or at least required) within the contemporary playing of the game.

What we learn, then, – if we attend to the contemporary version – is that sport retains the possibility of an engagement with morality (in line with the *moral laboratory* concept); the spoiling cases both show this to us and give us insight into its basis in what, following Dworkin, have been called 'principles' – a moral underpinning not divorced from the contexts of realisation in sports practice.

Notes

1. See Dworkin (1978: 72) for his own comments on the distinction, and its importance. See also Dworkin (1986: 15–20) for a discussion of Elmer.
2. Dworkin is, of course, alive to the number of exceptions which must be recorded for a 'full' statement of this rule.
3. This may be cashed out in terms of *lusory goals* (if it were clear what that expression amounted to). See Suits (1978: 36–37). Notice that the pre-lusory goal is there characterised as '... a specifically achievably state of affairs' (1978: 36); we might see this as a discussion of its achievability!
4. See Wittgenstein (1953: 151, 179).
5. See Dancy for particularism as including the view '... that no set of principles will succeed in generating answers to questions about what to do in particular cases' (1993: 56), but also '... that the moral relevance of a property in a new case cannot be predicted from its relevance elsewhere' (1993: 57) with 'predicted' the key term. See especially the discussion (and rejection) of switching arguments (1993: 64–66), attempts '... to determine what to say here by appeal to what we say about something else' (1993: 64). Particularism is opposed to *substantial* moral principles, not to moral principles *as such*.
6. A subsequent rule change, arguably as a result of the events described, simply made a different (and more complex) way of spoiling possible.
7. See Baker and Hacker (1980: 76–85).
8. See Cavell (1969: 32).
9. If one thought that the summer Olympics were too large, one might use this as a basis for selecting Olympic sports: those with a role in the moral laboratory are in; the others are out. In this way, some of de Coubertin's commitments might be maintained.
10. See Wittgenstein (1953: §309). I explored this topic in my inaugural lecture, 'A Nasty Accident with One's Flies', University of Brighton, May 1996.
11. See, for instance, 'Postscript' to Hart (1994: 238–276).

151

12. See, for instance, McNamee (1995: 166–167).
13. For what sports can there be spoiling? Certainly not all ... for it requires conflict between letter and spirit of the sport's law. (Does basketball lack such a spirit? Or consider chess, a sport in Cuba – we do not need face-to-face contact *at all*, so is there no necessary *moral* contact?)
14. See McNamee (1995).
15. In both Dworkin (1978) and Dworkin (1986); see McDowell (1998: 62, especially n.).
16. One might think of 'walking' a batter in baseball as akin to (or as quasi-) spoiling. As Haugeland (1998: 162n.) explains: 'Generally, the opposing pitcher would try to avoid giving a batter a free "balls on base" (also called a "walk"); but in certain threatening situations, especially when the current batter is on a "hot streak", then that batter is "walked" intentionally'.

References

Baker, G. and Hacker, P. (1980) *Wittgenstein: Understanding and Meaning – An Analytical Commentary on the Philosophical Investigations*, Oxford: Blackwell.

Baker, G. and Hacker, P. (1985) *Wittgenstein: Rules Grammar and Necessity – Volume 2 of an Analytical Commentary on the Philosophical Investigations*, Oxford: Blackwell.

Cavell, S. (1969) *Must We Mean What We Say?*, New York: Scribners.

Dancy, J. (1993) *Moral Reasons*, Oxford: Blackwell.

Dworkin, R. (1978) *Taking Rights Seriously*, Cambridge, MA: Harvard University Press.

Dworkin, R. (1986) *Law's Empire*, Cambridge, MA: Harvard University Press.

Hart, H. L. A. (1994) *The Concept of Law*, 2nd edition, Oxford: Clarendon Press.

Haugeland, J. (1998) *Having Thought*, Cambridge, MA: Harvard University Press.

Nagel, T. (1995) *Other Minds: Critical Essays 1969–1994*, Oxford: Clarendon Press.

McNamee, M. (1995) 'Theoretical Limitations in Codes of Ethical Conduct', in *Leisure Cultures: Values, Genders, Lifestyles*, ed. Graham McFee, Wilf Murphy and Garry Whannel, Eastbourne: Leisure Studies Association, pp. 145–147.

McDowell, J. (1998) *Mind, Value, and Reality*, Cambridge, MA: Harvard University Press.

Suits, B. (1978) *The Grasshopper: Games, Life and Utopia*, Toronto: Toronto University Press.

Travis, C. (1996) 'Meaning's Role in Truth', *Mind* 105: 451–566.

Wittgenstein, L. (1953) *Philosophical Investigations*, trans. G.E.M. Anscombe, Oxford: Blackwell.

Part 3

Doping, genetic modification and the ethics of enhancement

Introduction

Mike McNamee

There is little question that the issue for which sports ethics has become most widely known is the issue of doping. The problems that comprise doping ethics sharply divide devotees of sports within the philosophical community. While the subject has a history which stretches back as far as to the ancient Greeks and their ingestion of alcohol and mushrooms believed to enhance their powers,[1] there is little sign of accord among scholars or sportspersons and their support systems. Part 3 attempts to frame the more general ethical issues surrounding performance enhancement, whether pharmacological or genetic. In particular it articulates the shared terrain between sports and medical ethics because of the manner in which the sports medicine communities have come to shape doping itself.

But first a word about terminology. Those new to the field often talk a little loosely about the use of 'drugs in sports'. But the uses of pharmacology are varied and not, in themselves, necessarily problematic. Many of us, from novices to seniors, regularly use anti-inflammatory drugs either to help heal an injury or to allow us to participate in sport while reducing risks of further harming ourselves. Even at the elite level, athletes are awarded Therapeutic Use Exemption Certificates to allow them to receive medical treatments for conditions, such as asthma, which they suffer from and which may be performance enhancing. It is widely acknowledged, then, that the use of pharmacology in sport is not merely widespread but properly so,

since the access to healthcare is thought to be a right more fundamental than the strictures of sports rules. So 'doping' and 'drug use' are not to be used as synonyms. It is worth noting that some commentators object to the use of 'doping' because it is pejorative (Fost, 2008), arising from negative historical descriptions of opium users. It can be argued then that referring to the use of certain pharmacologies as 'doping' already predisposes people (without fair argument) against those who use them. While there is value in attending to this point, the call for value-neutral characterisations is in itself problematic in a debate that is itself inherently normative and where the linguistic currency of the debate is so well established.

The first essay in this Part addresses what is, perhaps surprisingly, a lacuna in much of the debate. Verner Møller's 'The Athletes' Viewpoint' sets out a more complex and ambiguous terrain of the motivations of athletes to dope. It takes little insight to recognise that labelling doping athletes as cheats may be accurate but hardly explains anything beyond the labelling. After all, we admire athletes who willingly make huge sacrifices in order to achieve absolute excellence. Ought we not to admire them when the risks they take are to themselves? Møller draws attention to the relations between athlete, sports medicine and the sport's support system in order to contextualise doping choices. He quotes testimony from doping users who have discussed their entry into the world of doping, how it was facilitated, supported and promoted, whether implicitly (by introduction and gestures as to what is and is not necessary to achieve one's ultimate sporting goals) or explicitly (how senior professional cyclists were part of a socialisation process that taught junior ones how and when to inject themselves). Ambition, he argues, is the driving motive. Møller's picture is to an extent one of Nietzschean sport: the strongest and those willing to sacrifice all will set themselves apart from the herd. Nevertheless, he also raises the issue of de-sensitisation. How culpable are athletes who are merely initiated into a social milieu that is at odds with the world-wide anti-doping regime but consistent with a vision of elite sports that is myopically focussed on external goals? Athletes are aware of grey areas, such as the use of hypoxic chambers to promote greater oxygenation, the abuses of Therapeutic Use Exemption Certificates to allow medications that are themselves performance enhancing, and so on. Møller's discussion warns against essentialising the doping athlete as simply 'the cheat'. Some feel guilty, others reluctant, others still press ahead with a clear conscience in the belief that they are doing no more than submitting themselves to what they perceive to be the dominant norm of elite sports: achievement (at whatever cost). In the midst of this ambiguity athletes often feel themselves caught between a rock and a hard place. They are damned if they dope and (so it is said) doomed to failure if they do not.

Moving beyond the athlete's perspective to the specific arguments of the debate itself, Andy Miah's essay 'Why Not Dope?' is a useful summary of the standard arguments of the debate. These arguments hinge singly or in combination on factors such as coercion; unfairness, harms to health, and their opposition to the rules and spirit of sport. Miah draws attention to the media-politics of the debate and attempts to show how it has subtly framed a negative posture on doping. He all but rejects sports-specific arguments about the condemnation of doping. He also suggests that sports administrators and policy makers have not thought through the consistency of their postures to other technologically driven enhancement, implying that doping has wrongly been singled out for public scrutiny and the resultant moral panic. Miah discusses what he takes to be indefensibly exaggerated or loosely applied claims

regarding the consequent harms associated with doping. He concludes, however, that espousing some ethical essence to sports which justifies the bans on doping practices is inadequate. Rather, it is the harm to athletes themselves which is the strongest ground on which to legitimate anti-doping practices.

Of course, the extent to which harm is or is not consequent on doping practices will depend crucially on how such regimes are developed and administered. One recent technological advance is the development of 'hypoxic chambers' that facilitate faster injury recovery times and force physiological adaptations in the body of the athlete that mimic training at oxygen-starved altitude (Spriggs, 2005; Tamburrini, 2005; Tännsjö, 2005). This appears to provide a borderline case of a sophisticated medical technological means that achieves ends which arise naturally in certain countries of the world with the required geology. Some commentators worry about the increasing power of expert-administered systems that can control the lifestyle of the athlete. Clearly borderline cases like the hypoxic chamber give rise to arguments that are not at all clear cut. Yet it is often said by detractors of anti-doping that, insofar as doping is medically supervised to minimise risks to harm, it ought to be permitted (Foddy and Savulescu, 2007; Kayser and Smith, 2008; Kayser et al., 2005; Savulescu, 2007; Tamburrini, 2006). Søren Holm, a doctor and medical ethicist, argues to the contrary in 'Doping under Medical Control'. He notes that the forms of arguments utilised are either based on grounds of inconsistency of anti-doping rationales, supporting the norms (or conventions) of elite sports, or on grounds of athlete's freedoms. Using an approached referred to as 'Game Theory' he works through the motivations (and perceived benefits and risks) of all parties involved based upon a general assumption that those involved act in rational self-interest while calculating the probabilities of different outcome scenarios.

Holm considers the catalogue of options for the athlete once the bans have been lifted to allow medical supervision where athletes still seek a competitive advantage over others. He also considers the ranges of influence over athletes' decision making and information gathering as to risks and benefits of drug usage. However, even under medical supervision, side effects of cutting-edge drugs will not reliably be known. He argues that the rational athlete will take minor, not major, health risks. The rationally self-interested athlete's choices are to: (i) take and hide; (ii) take and tell; (iii) reject and hide; and (iv) reject and tell. Keeping secret the use of the drug for as long as possible will help to secure competitive advantage. The most positive choice will be to take and hide the usage of the new performance-enhancing drug.

Holm then goes on to explore why this decision is problematic. He considers how the secrecy would prevent any recourse to a club or doctor should serious harm arise. He also considers the difficulty of the athlete achieving impartial advice unless they themselves are paying the healthcare team, thus overriding any interest that third parties have in maximising the athlete's performances for their own (e.g. commercial) ends. He notes how problematic it will be to gain an accurate picture of drug usage in order to better understand potential side effects and thus better understand risk and benefit analysis. Restrictions on drug usage, he concludes, are therefore in everyone's best interest.

Christian Munthe brings to the forefront the discussion regarding biotechnology's potential in elite sports when he considers 'Ethical Aspects of Controlling Genetic Doping'. Like Holm, he too is sceptical of the global benefits of banned technologies in sports, although his focus is on genetics not performance-enhancing drugs. Having noted that the World Anti-Doping Agency, which regulates doping at the elite level of sports, has banned genetic manipulation in order to enhance performance, he sets out some forms gene doping could take and the prospects for its detection.

Munthe notes the need for any genetic testing regime to be able to distinguish an athlete's natural genetic constitution from any deviations. Moreover, it must be able to distinguish naturally caused variations from artificial ones that are the object of bans. Given that elite athletes are almost by definition abnormal specimens, the detection of artificial variants is not easy, because the statistically derived norms are difficult to apply to such an atypical population. Nor would any testing regime be able to rule out prenatal genetic selection of athletic excellence (an analogue of what already happens in certain healthcare situations where the presence – in the foetus – of certain disabling conditions allows

parents to terminate the pregnancy under certain conditions). In health care generally, somatic genetic modification is thought superior to germ line modification, since the former affects only the individual while the latter alters the genetic make up of all future generations of that person. In the former it may be that certain modifications will enhance muscular strength, power or blood properties that would enhance performance, and Munthe is sceptical that current testing will feasibly be able to detect such with efficiency. He then goes on to articulate ethically problematic aspects of genetic testing, from risk evaluation, to the reliability of the results, the difficulty of interpreting them in a valid way, and how to deal with adverse findings that may come out of tests and the potential need for subsequent counselling for the athlete. He finally notes the issue of consent. In sports policy if an athlete refuses to give a sample he has committed a doping offence, whereas in healthcare the patient always has the right to give or withhold consent. He concludes somewhat sceptically about the justification of genetic testing in sports under these constraints.

While genetic testing is the object of Munthe's essay, genetic and pharmacological enhancement is the focus of Michael Sandel's 'Bionic Athletes'. Sandel's critical focus is on the apparent narcissistic aspect of perfectionism, which neglects the fact that some means are ethically superior to others in the pursuit of our goals. The use of illicit performance-enhancing substances, he argues, diminishes the achievements of those who use them. Responsibility for performance, to a given degree, shifts to the inventor or technologist who supplants human effort and giftedness with more efficient artificial means. He is critical of these developments which 'undermine effort and erode human agency' (2007: 26) by reinforcing a picture of superhuman or Promethean aspiration. Acknowledging the giftedness of life, by contrast, involves a recognition that even the greatest of athletes are – just like the rest of us recreational sportspersons – not wholly of their own making and thus not accountable solely to their powers.

Sandel is sensitive to the line-drawing problem. Similar ends may be brought about by means (such as the altitude training athlete versus the one in a hypoxic chamber noted above) that are not always obviously superior or inferior: 'It hardly seems nobler' (he writes) 'to thicken the blood by sleeping in a room with thin air than by injecting hormones or altering one's genes' (2007: 33). Despite the presence of rules for doping, he argues that these by no means account for all the ways in which sports may be debased. Sandel argues that the integrity of the sports may be at stake when means are adopted that undermine the traditional excellences that the activity enshrines. These excellences can be accounted for by an examination of the *telos* or internal purpose of the activity promoted in, and preserved by, their framework of rules. But far from wanting to ossify sports, he concludes, that 'technologically enhanced versions of a practice seldom leave old ways undisturbed; norms change, audiences become rehabituated, and spectacle exerts a certain allure, even as it deprives us of unadulterated access to human talents and gifts.' (2007: 41–2).

In the final essay of Part 3, McNamee also considers the Promethean promise of biotechnology for sports, and the relations between sports ethics and sports medicine ethics. The liberal/libertarian argument for allowing athletes as individuals to enhance their capabilities through technologies of their choice is how some envision the future of sports. An important social movement known loosely as 'Transhumanism' advocates such a position, and McNamee gives an account of it. He discusses whether Transhumanism provides a model for the future of sports. He uses two contrasting lenses that are drawn from the same ancient Greek myth.

While Mary Shelley's Frankenstein is often referred to in public debates about genetic, robotic and other medical technologies, the root of the story goes back to the ancient Greek myth of Prometheus who goes against the Gods' command by bringing fire to human kind. Whether this act of cunning and intelligence is to be celebrated (as it is in Aeschylus' account of Prometheus) or denigrated as an hubristic defiance of the Gods (as in Hesiod's version) is open to argument. McNamee concludes that Aeschylus' account is more akin to the brave new world of the Transhumanists and should be viewed in a very sceptical light. It involves a denial that there are limits to human nature and capabilities that those committed to sports, as athletes or physicians, ought to observe and respect. The myth(s) of Prometheus

thus draw our attention not merely to the ends of sports and the proper limits of human desire to overcome all (natural) impediments, it also invites reflection upon the proper ends of sports medicine as a social practice, and the boundaries of interventions by team doctors and other athlete-centred physicians.

What is at stake in each of the essays in Part 3 is the permissibility and desirability of employing pharmacological and other medical technologies to enhance sporting performance. Under the surface of these arguments about the vision of sports are more or less explicit arguments about deeper moral phenomena, such as human nature, personhood and sportspersonship, and the normative appeal of the natural in human living. One of the reasons why the ethics of enhancement, broadly considered, are so appealing to so many is the connection between the value of achievement and the means that are fitting in the pursuit of it. In that regard they serve as a metaphor for many ideas about our striving after the good life itself.

Note

1. Various accounts are well worth reading for critical historical perspective: Dimeo (2007), Hoberman (1992), Møller (2008) and Voy (1991).

References

Dimeo, P. (2007) *A History of Drug Use in Sport 1876–1976*, London: Routledge.

Foddy, B. and Savulescu, J. (2007) 'Ethics of Performance Enhancement in Sport: Drugs and Gene Doping', in R. E. Ashcroft, A. Dawson, H. Draper, J. McMillan (eds.), *Principles of Healthcare Ethics* (2nd edn), London: Wiley, 511–20.

Fost, N. (2008) 'Doping is Pejorative and Misleading', *British Medical Journal*, 337: a910.

Hoberman, J. (1992) *Mortal Engines*, New York: Free Press.

Kayser, B. and Smith, A.C.T. (2008) 'Globalisation of Anti-doping: The Reverse Side of the Medal', *British Medical Journal*, 337: a584.

Kayser, B, Mauron, A. and Miah, A. (2005) 'Viewpoint: Legalisation of Performance Enhancing Drugs', *Lancet*, 336: S21.

Møller, V. (2008) *The Doping Devil*, Odense: University of Southern Denmark Press.

Sandel, M. J. (2007) 'Bionic Athletes', in *The Case Against Perfection: Ethics in the Age of Genetic*

Engineering, Cambridge, MA: The Belknap Press of Harvard University Press.

Savulescu, J. (2007) 'Doping True to the Spirit of Sport', *Sydney Morning Herald*, 08.08.2007. Available Online http://www.smh.com.au/news/opinion/doping-true-to-the-spirit-of-sport/2007/08/07/1186252704241.html. Accessed 18.05.09.

Spriggs, M. (2005) 'Hypoxic Air Machines: Performance Enhancement through Training – or Cheating?', *Journal of Medical Ethics*, 31: 112–13.

Tamburrini, C. (2005) 'Hypoxic Air Machines: Commentary', *Journal of Medical Ethics*, 31: 114.

Tamburrini, C. (2006) 'Are Doping Sanctions Justified? A Moral Relativistic View', *Sport in Society* 9: 199–211.

Tännsjö, T. (2005) 'Hypoxic Air Machines: Commentary', *Journal of Medical Ethics*, 31: 113.

Voy, R. (1991) *Sport, Drugs and Politics*, Champaign, IL: Leisure Press.

The athletes' viewpoint

Verner Møller

The former Italian athletics trainer, Alessandro Donati, who has since become one of the world leading doping experts, has provided significant insights into the complex psychology of doping use and in the following I am drawing heavily on his work. In 1981, Donati was contacted by Professor Dr Francesco Conconi, who had a proposal to make. Conconi had become familiar with a performance-enhancing technique in Finland, which he had then developed further. By using a 'transfusion of selected red blood cells, in which these cells were stored at −90°C, enriched with particular substances and then transfused into the athlete two or three days before a major event' (Donati 2004: 46), it was possible to achieve performance improvements of 3–5 seconds over 1500 metres, 15–20 seconds over 5000 metres and 30–40 seconds over 10,000 metres. This improvement was hugely significant, and the technique was not yet on the doping list.

Donati just did not find the idea very appealing. He chose to present the proposal to the seven athletes he was responsible for without concealing the fact that he was against the idea. It would, however, be up to them to decide whether they wished to collaborate with Conconi. There was no doubt that their chances of winning would improve. And if they chose to opt for Conconi's programme, then Donati would withdraw as trainer without making a fuss and return to his position on CONI, the Italian Olympic Committee. The athletes were training with an eye on the Olympic Games in Los Angeles three years later. Nevertheless all of them expressed the view that they would never dream of going along with the transfusion technique. After a few weeks had passed, Conconi wrote to Primo Nebiolo, who was President of both the Italian Athletics Association and the International Association of Athletics Federations, to say that Donati was refusing to cooperate. Shortly afterwards Donati was contacted by the chief trainer of the national athletics team, who attempted without success to put pressure on him to change his position. Donati replied that he would have to find a new trainer, if he insisted on using the programme. And there the matter rested. For a time. Once the Olympic Games started to loom closer, the association became more aggressive. The athletes were now called to a meeting and asked directly whether they would be prepared to increase their performance levels in the run-up to the Games with the assistance of the blood transfusion technique. Donati was also present but was obliged to keep his opinions to himself. Once again the athletes declined.

Incitements to doping

Donati's account gives the impression that the attitude of the trainer has a decisive influence on the choice of the athletes. If the key people around the athletes clearly distance themselves from illegal or dubious medication and methods for enhancing performance, athletes will follow their lead and stay away from them. There is no doubt that trainers and managers often share the responsibility for their athletes' use of doping. Nevertheless we should beware of drawing the conclusion that, if only trainers and other key individuals would one and all keep the moral flag aloft (which is at least a theoretical possibility), then the use of doping in sport would disappear. The pressure of expectations, tacit acceptance and naïve enthusiasm at sudden and unexpected progress can be enough encouragement to make an athlete turn to the needle. The inner driving forces of sport are so strong that some athletes will under any circumstances regard doping substances as an irresistible temptation to go that extra mile. Athletes way down the sporting league tables can get to experiment with caffeine tablets, ginseng and such substances that are taken orally out of sheer curiosity.

When athletes include medical performance boosting as part of their preparations for a competition, however, they do not do so lightly. Weighty considerations precede the decision. This can be seen from an interview study of cycling undertaken by my colleague, Ask Vest Christiansen. One cycle rider, for example, talks about the first time he was to do something so taboo as to give himself a completely legal vitamin injection:

> I was shit scared. I sat in my hotel room and stared at the needle for half an hour before I stuck it into my arm … The sweat was pouring off me. All of a sudden I was going to stick a needle into my own arm. Hell, it feels almost like running into a wall or hitting yourself. It's like doing an injury to yourself. That's how I felt anyway.
>
> (Christiansen 2005: 81ff)

Later, once he had got used to it, he taught a friend how to give himself an injection:

> He did fine really … He pulled the needle out and put a piece of cotton-wool on. Then he got

up and said, 'I feel rather dizzy now'. And then he walked over towards the bedroom, and halfway there his knees suddenly gave way and he fell forwards, his head hitting the stone floor … That was an unpleasant experience, I can tell you.
>
> (ibid.: 82)

It subsequently became a matter of course for his friend, too. It is only at the start that sticking a needle through your skin seems to be breaking a taboo. Even though the injection only contained vitamins, it gave the impression of being on the verge of doping. He had had vitamin injections before, but they were given by a doctor and that was not the same thing. No doubt because the ministrations of doctors are associated with healing and health promotion, the injection the doctor gave seemed to be a help and support, something not essentially different from a vaccination. Doctors who agree to give athletes vitamin injections do so because they have a more powerful effect than vitamin pills. In doing so, such doctors are in effect recognising performance-enhancing medication. Since doctors are not always on hand, it is naturally an advantage for athletes to be able to treat themselves. And even though it evidently requires them to overcome serious reservations on the first occasion they do it, the doctors' recognition of the method makes self-administration easier to manage. It is clearly still far from easy. But once they have got used to injecting themselves, however, and felt that it benefits their performance, the transition to doping boils down to a question of what substance is contained in the syringe. The rider explains further:

> It was a huge relief to be able to do it yourself. And then it just becomes a routine. I wouldn't say that it becomes so much a routine that you become indifferent to what runs through the syringe, but it was still the business of sticking a needle in yourself that was the big barrier to overcome.
>
> (ibid.: 86)

As an athlete at the highest level, you live with a huge pressure on you to perform. The competition is colossal. Among the very best the distance between average and excellent performances is only marginal. Tiny things can decide the outcome. A career does not begin with doping. If an athlete needs that extra boost from the very start in order to get on, it stands to reason that, as competition becomes sharper, you will fall by the wayside. Most people begin to practise a sport in all innocence because they enjoy it, and they continue because they find it fun. Sooner or later they may discover that they have exceptional talent, which can arouse an ambition that makes sport much more than mere fun. It also becomes ruthless training directed at more or less clear goals. Those of them who as seniors even get anywhere near the absolute elite are super-talents who have succeeded in cultivating their skills with intensity and focus. These are people who physically and mentally are totally geared to achieving their sporting ambitions and are tuned to do so. They do not live like the majority. Their perception of their body is different. This is what we have to appreciate if we are to understand the temptation to use doping.

When an athlete is optimally prepared in the traditional way and still finds it insufficient to allow him to fulfil the goal of his dreams, then he is only human if he looks to less traditional means that promise renewed progress. As one of the riders in the study says:

> I have wanted to be a professional cycle rider since I was a boy, and now I have got the chance. If the consequences are that I have to take medication, that does not make me stop pursuing the dream. I have not ridden for so many years just to stop now that I have reached a point when the dream can be lived out in reality.
>
> (ibid.: 105)

Here, too, ambition is the driving force behind the use of doping. As long as a rider can get by among the top flight of their peers without using medicine, it is no temptation. But once he becomes aware that this is what is required if he is to stay up with the field at the highest level, he perceives it simply as the next necessary step in his career development. The motive is, then, somewhat different from the official explanations given by riders like David Millar, for example, who after they have been caught claim that, for no reason at all really, they chose to take doping in a weak moment to secure themselves a chance of winning.

Doping is not something athletes suddenly clutch at in a moment of uncertainty and return to the shelf once their self-confidence has improved, only to fish it out again when self-confidence nose-dives again. Christiansen's study shows up quite a different scenario, in which doping takes place in a far more calculated manner. Treatments are scheduled just as systematically as training. In some races, riders compete at 'low heat' or, if possible, with no medical assistance. In other events, however, where they are particularly reckoning on making a mark, the 'heat' is turned up. One rider, for example, relates:

> When it really mattered, I might have had slightly higher levels. You could say that I wanted to ensure that my blood count was competitive in comparison to those I was going to compete against.
>
> (ibid.: 114)

The ambition to get out ahead is the principal motive behind the use of performance-enhancing substances. Many people have a tendency to condemn doping users as morally corrupt. This is an easy mistake to make, but nonetheless a mistake. The belief that doping can be put down to weak or immoral character involves an underestimation of the attraction of sport. Some people have pangs of conscience, others do not. But it is not even the case that those who are without scruples are evil individuals without a conscience. If, as is the case with the rider just mentioned, you see nothing wrong in using illegal medicine, the reason lies in the fact that you perceive doping in a different light from those who condemn it. This rider saw it as a step in the process of becoming professional. If what he wanted was to excel, then this was one of the pre-conditions. His own moral code told him that he should do it in a proper fashion. He had no time for those riders who got caught. They were unforgivable losers who deserved their punishment, because they got the sport into disrepute and ruined it for everyone else. In his view a sense of responsibility to the sport went hand in hand with doping. You must not he caught. Seen from the outside, this can easily come to sound like the viewpoint of a 'bad' character, but it is understandable enough given the fact that the increasingly negative way in which doping is seen by the world at large is developing, as far as riders are concerned, into a greater and greater threat. And there is nothing odd about people trying to defend the milieu in which they live and work. It can, of course, be objected that, since riders know that doping is prohibited, defending doping without the least trace of a guilty conscience is still an expression of low moral standards. But in that case we choose to ignore the fact that athletes are encouraged by their sporting environment to perceive doping as acceptable medication in spite of the fact that it is, in reality, illegal.

Kelli White

Kelli White, the American sprinter who tested positive for modafinil and was subsequently banned from competition by USADA, articulated this clearly at the conference Play the Game in 2005, when in the midst of her enforced quarantine she made an appearance to talk about how she had ended up going down the doping road. She started by stating: 'Those who do use drugs are not bad people, we just have made a bad mistake' (White 2005). Her aim was not to absolve herself or other 'doping cheats'. If we want to understand why people begin to dope themselves, however, we have to throw the facile image of rotten apples in sport out of the window.

Her involvement in athletes had started when she was 10. As a 12–13-year-old she started training with the famous Ukrainian-born trainer, Remi Korchemny. He came to play a significant role in her life over the subsequent ten years or so. Having competed in athletics at the University of Tennessee for a period of four years, she decided to go professional and in 2000 returned to California, where she once again started training under Korchemny. Shortly after this, he introduced her to Dr Victor Conte. At that point she did not know what he stood for. Ostensibly the reason for going to him was to seek his advice about legal nutritional supplements that might help her improve her performance. She had no idea that she might get involved in anything illegal. He gave her, she said, flaxseed oil among other things. She used it for some weeks. Then she was invited once again to his office, where he told her that what he had given her was, in fact, not flaxseed oil but a substance that could give rise to a positive doping test if it was not used correctly. She stopped taking it immediately, and did not touch the other things he had given her again either. After a dreadful season in 2002 plagued by injury followed by a subsequent failure to qualify for the world championships in indoor athletics in 2003, she decided to seek out Conte again. He proposed a treatment that would be able to bring her back, which she accepted well knowing that it contained THG and banned substances such as EPO and other stimulants. With Conte's help, she managed within a relatively short space of time to become the world's fastest woman while at the same time undergoing 17 doping tests both during and outside competitions without testing positive. On the one hand, she was pleased with her progress. On the other, she was plagued by feelings of guilt. She explains the psychology behind it:

> It not only took Mr. Conte's help, it took my coach making me believe it was OK, and I think that a lot of the time what happens to athletes is that people make you believe that what you are doing is OK because everyone else is doing it.
>
> (ibid.)

Despite the fact that the feeling of guilt apparently is negligible among cyclists doping, this explanation fits in neatly with the points made above. When doctors sanction the use first of vitamin injections and then later of actual doping substances, athletes can be led to believe that there is nothing wrong with it, that cheating the doping controls is simply part of the professional game. This is, however, far from saying that athletes wish to see the controls done away with in order that they can throw themselves into unlimited experimentation with drugs.

Attitudes of elite athletes to performance-enhancing methods

Elite athletes are not in agreement as to where the boundary between legal and illegal methods should be set. They also disagree as to how the fight against doping should be addressed. Nevertheless there seems to be a general agreement that limits and a system of control are needed if sport is to function in an acceptable fashion.

In an interview study that I conducted with Christiansen into elite athletes' attitudes towards the use of methods for enhancing performance, no athlete advocated the deregulation of doping.

The study was constructed around 19 in-depth interviews with anonymised athletes competing at the highest levels in a variety of sports. A similar kind of study carried out by Christiansen into cycling (mentioned above) which comprised both young talents and senior riders in the national and international elite, also found no athletes who were sympathetic to the idea of lifting the doping ban although some expressed the opinion that the doping controls and their implied suspicion were a nuisance they ideally would rather be without. Combined, the two studies involved more than 50 athletes and not a single one, whether they had doped or not, believed that the anti-doping campaign should or could be abandoned in the real world. We cannot, of course, conclude on that basis that there are no athletes in favour of deregulating doping, but these studies allow us to presume that they are clearly in the minority.

Another striking aspect of these interviews was that, regardless of the sport that was represented, the athletes interviewed had almost identical perceptions of what constituted the essence and the ideals of sport – although, it has to be said, without being able to unite these values into a consistent idea of what was sporting. We heard athletes say, for example, that of course sportsmen had to be fair, and then without a pause for breath explaining the next moment how from time to time, as an integral part of the game, they used intimidating tactics against their opponents to gain a psychological advantage. They attempted throughout to unite ideas about what was sporting with their own experiences of sport, which often resulted in glaring inconsistencies and self-contradictions, as ideas and experiences conflicted with each other. The way in which they related to methods for enhancing their performance, too, often resulted in their line of reasoning leading them into dead ends. This was particularly evident with athletes who had a clear sense of right and wrong. The following example from our interviews (italicised to distinguish our own material from other quotes) illustrates the point:

Of course, the basic principles of sport are quite clear. You have to stick to them. Competition has to be on an equal footing. The athlete who has prepared himself best, physically and mentally without the use of artificial stimulants, he is the winner. He is the best.

When the athlete in question is then challenged about his views and asked to specify what he means by 'artificial stimulants', the answer comes:

For me these are substances produced chemically or in other artificial ways that have a passive effect on physical development. To take an injection to get into better shape while you are asleep, that's wrong. And then there is the debate about hypobaric chambers ... In my view, altitrainers [hypobaric chambers] are cheating, because they are a form of passive chemical manipulation that mean you get into better shape. Whether you take EPO in an injection or a tablet or whether you change your blood levels using an altitrainer, it's all one to me.

Since he himself has not at any point felt the need to increase his haematocrit values in order to be competitive, he can easily reject all of the methods mentioned above. However, when asked whether high altitude training was an acceptable method for increasing haematocrit values, he replied:

Then it's not artificially influenced. You can say that it gives the same effect, but it's not artificially produced, and that does not give a competitive advantage to those with the money and the technology. If you have clear limits for what is artificially produced manipulation, then you can get rid of all the grey areas. The athletes will know what they can and cannot do.

There are two things here that are worth looking at more closely. The first is the desire for clear demarcation, so that the discussion about grey zones can be put to rest once and for all and athletes can know what they have to comply with. The second is the desire that everyone should be on an equal footing. Both fall under the heading of the idea of fair play. Unfortunately, reality is not so simple, and attempts to create simplicity, clarity and clear demarcations, as a rule, tend to end up running into paradoxes which is precisely why WADA has chosen to refrain from making a verbal definition of doping. It goes almost without saying, therefore, that the athlete's brave attempt to create clarity ends in self-contradiction.

There are two things about hypobaric chambers that he objects to. They seem to be an artificial method for preparing an athlete for a competition, and they cost money. The use of them is, therefore, unfair on those athletes who wish to compete on natural premises, or those who do not have the money. Taken in isolation, the viewpoint seems reasonable. The problem arises when we try to explain why it is acceptable to live in a hut at high altitude, where the oxygen content is just as low as that set in a hypobaric chamber and where the body's reaction is the same. Athletes who live at sea-level do not get up there free of charge, and they transport themselves by means of technological inventions such as the aeroplane or the car. If the energy consumption were to be compared for these two performance-enhancing methods, the hypobaric chamber would, undoubtedly, have the advantage. Consideration of nature would then dictate that the latter was preferable. In this light, you would have to be fairly uncompromising if you continued to pursue the argument that it is cheating for athletes to spend time in a room in which the concentration of oxygen is artificially kept at the same low level as in a mountain hut, where they could reside without being accused of cheating. Nevertheless, this is what the athlete in question does. In order not to compromise clarity, he sticks *ad absurdum* to artificiality as a demarcation line: '*I have always thought that artificial manipulation in order to gain competitive advantage should be banned. Whether it is tablets, injections or something else is irrelevant. It must be banned.*' What about vitamin pills that are artificially manufactured? Should they also be banned? This was clearly taking the argument too far, but instead of giving up on artificiality, he chooses to sidestep the issue: '*But vitamins are a natural substance. They are not a chemical compound.*'

Here, however, he runs into another problem, namely that EPO is also a natural substance. '*Yes, but it is artificially, chemically produced, and that is banned.*' The athlete is, of course, well aware that vitamin C tablets are also artificially produced, and for that reason he adds in the next sentence: '*You can eat 10 kilos of vitamin C and that won't make you a better sportsman.*' This is doubtless correct. But his argument is no longer directed against artificiality, but against the effect the methods might (or might not) have, and this he immediately acknowledges: '*Yes, it is of course the effect that determines the doping list.*'

If an athlete can be permitted to spend time at high altitudes, then that is only fair if others are permitted to spend time in a hypobaric chamber or take EPO. If EPO is not acceptable, then nor is spending time at high altitudes. There is no way around it, if the requirement is that the rules have to have a consistent basis and are to be designed around the effect of a substance or a method. A similar difficulty would be encountered if we attempted to argue our way out of the problem of 'grey areas', as has already been suggested in the above discussion about hypobaric chambers.

In the discussion of products thought to lie in this 'grey area', we also found that athletes' views were influenced by their need to compete. Those who did not need 'grey area' products were typically critical. Replies to questions as to whether they had used them could, for example, be as follows:

> *Very little … I believe that if I eat the correct food and have a good diet, then nutritional supplements are unnecessary. That is the view I have from my upbringing and from my own experience. I don't think tablets would have raised me any higher. But to take a multivitamin tablet and some fish oil to ensure the quality of your diet, that's OK. It means that you minimise the risk of getting ill.*

On the other hand, those who operated in branches of sports where 'grey area' products might give some advantage did not believe that the 'grey area' concept was of any use. As one of them says:

> *Grey areas and all that stuff, they don't exist in my world. Either it is on [the list] or it is not. If a pill came on the scene that meant that I progressed by 20 kg. and which wasn't a steroid and wasn't on the list, then I would take it. And if it then got banned the next day, then I wouldn't take it any more. That's how I feel. Unless it is something that makes you go crazy. Of course I'm not prepared to risk the rest of my life for that. But if it's not on the list, then it's legal. That's how it is. I don't even think it's open to debate.*

Asked whether he would use it if it was something that corresponded to hypobaric chambers, which could increase his muscle power, he replies without hesitating: '*Yes. There are loads of things where I think they've gone right off the rails.*' He then goes on to elaborate by making a critique of the way elite sport is managed in his country. The organisation in charge has made it a declared aim to make the country the best place in the world to practise sport. At the same time it tries to score cheap points by distancing itself from 'grey area' products. This, in his view, is absurd. No athlete can eat at the same table as the top dogs, if he is subject to special restrictions. There is simply no room for latitude in sport at the highest level.

In his world, things are either black or white. He abides by the list that happens to be in force at the moment. Over and above that he takes anything he can that can provide a performance-enhancing effect and that is not directly damaging to his health. Waving a moralising finger at athletes who use 'grey area' products and setting restrictions for their use is in his eyes 'not on'. But even though there are things on the doping list that, in his opinion, ought not to be there, he still believes that the anti-doping campaign provides indispensable protection. It stands to reason. For his ambition is such that he will follow his fellow competitors to the very limits in risking his health. And he does not want competitive conditions of that kind. They would quite literally be destructive. He believes, therefore – just like the rider cited above – that sportspersons have a moral obligation towards their sport. It is all about not being caught, and the best way to prevent that is to stay on the right side of the line. His reasoning is as follows:

> I think that sports people have a task ahead of them [for] doping ruins sport. No matter how little it is and no matter how stupid it is, if it is on the list, then don't take it. And if some kind of collective understanding of this doesn't emerge – and it won't because this is elite sport and people are egoists – then it is up to WADA and organisations like that to make sure that the rules are so strict that it cannot be done. That's the only way to do it … otherwise these fantastic sports will die.

The athletes who want to see an active anti-doping campaign are, then, not just those who are deeply uncompromising as regards performance-enhancing means. Disagreement arises as to how this campaign should be fought.

The difficult balancing act: too much or too little?

In our studies, the athletes who showed least sympathy for the use of doping were those who also advocated the harshest penalties. Even the

most hardcore opponents of doping, however, were inclined to the view that the testing system had become a pain in the neck and wished that it could be reduced. Many comments ran, for example, as follows:

> The worst time was in 1995, when I was tested 18 times here in [my home country] and 5 times abroad. Long distance runners were tested even more. But I think it ought to be possible to create statistical tools so that they wouldn't have to test that often. Then they could reduce the frequency of the tests and release a load of resources.

This statement comes from an athlete who – even before the anti-doping campaign was intensified under WADA – thought that the frequency of the tests had become such a thorn in the side that he had begun to speculate about how it could be reduced. It bothers him that he, as a clean sportsman time and again has to provide proof of his clean bill of health. In his view it is a waste of resources to test athletes like him over and over again. These resources could be better employed in testing athletes who might be suspicious, those who show sudden, unexpected progress, for example. But even though he is dissatisfied with the way the fight against doping is tackled, he still sees testing as the only path open to sport and will not, therefore, say that recurrent tests are a problem. When asked directly whether he was frustrated at having to submit so many tests, he replied:

> No. It is a necessary evil. I will do anything to make sport clean. And if that means that I have to pee in a cup 20 times a year, then that's a small price to pay. What is frustrating is that we do it, but it isn't done in other places.

He does not have faith in athletes from other countries being monitored just as zealously by their anti-doping organisations, the so-called NADOs, as he is. And on the rare occasion when someone does get caught, he thinks that they get let off too easily. Two years is perhaps a harsh penalty in the Scandinavian countries, for here athletes end up being pilloried as well, stripped, he says, of all honour and glory.

> But for an athlete from Italy or Russia, someone who comes from a culture in which cheating is not met with the same disapproval but is perhaps on the contrary more like the better you are at cheating the more of a popular hero you are – there two

*years suspension, why, that's just a new opportu-
nity to load yourself up and return to the sport
with a big comeback. In the final of the 100m.
women's hurdles a few years ago, eight out of nine
entrants had previously been done for doping.
What's that supposed to be? If you've been done for
doping, you shouldn't be allowed in any final.*

By extension, he feels that a lifelong quarantine
should be introduced, even for first offenders.
This is a view that we find again in a woman
who has even been tested positive herself. This
was, it is true, for a milder drug, and this colours
her opinion:

*I think that in many ways the list is stupid,
because there are so many things on it. I don't
know whether an eardrop is something that has
any effect. But I know that if you have an ear-
ache and can't bear it any longer, then the only
thing you can get is something you aren't allowed
to take. So you don't take it and go round with a
pain in your ear – but why? I have difficulty
imagining that it might have any performance-
enhancing effect. I can't imagine that was the
case. But there are some drugs that really are
hard – EPO and anabolic steroids – and they've
got to have tough penalties. But I can't see why
there should be 400 drugs on the list, for there
aren't that many.*

What she has in mind when she calls the list
stupid is not her own case, but one about two
girls who tested positive for ephedrine. One had
taken slimming pills and the other eardrops that
contained the drug. The interviewee is sure that
they did not try to cheat. She believes, therefore, that penalties should be adjusted according to intention:

*When someone starts out on a course, a body-
builder in a fitness centre, when they are part of
a treatment in a schedule … Things like that
which are planned don't belong in sport and as
far as I'm concerned they should be banned for
life, because then it's not elite sport that they
belong in.*

The example is clear. The problem is just that it
is not possible to determine in every case
whether the drug that the athlete has tested
positive for has been taken as part of a treatment
with the aim of enhancing performance. If
ephedrine is on the doping list, the reason is that
the drug can have a performance-enhancing

effect, and the test cannot tell whether the drug
has been taken for a cough, or an ear-ache
or with a view to improving performance.
And working out which drugs are too trivial
to be on the doping list is not as easy as she
makes it sound when she adds with tautological
conviction:

*Everything that is not performance-enhancing –
and now it's not ear-drops that make you better
or pain-killers I'm talking about – that does not
improve performance. Performance-enhancing
is something which gives you a better performance. This is the sports world, you know, this is.*

Tolerance generally towards doping is at an all-
time low. This has made athletes all the more
vulnerable, and that puts them under stress.
Broadly speaking, athletes believe that the list
includes too much and that monitoring is too
intense, but they accept the regime because it
does not appear that things can be otherwise.
Desperation at the evident difficulties that exist
in putting an end to the problem lead to yet
further controls and yet more tests both during
and outside competitions. WADA are fond of
presenting themselves as the defenders of clean
athletes, but as a result of their professional mistrust of athletes they end up coming across in
practice as something quite different. The more
the anti-doping campaign is intensified, the
more sportspersons come to appear as criminals
who have something to hide. This is tiresome.
Like everyone else, athletes would like to be
respected and to receive recognition for what
they do. To rid themselves of suspicion, a number have, therefore, been talking about even
more extensive control systems.

Paula Radcliffe, the women's world's marathon record-holder, was unable to attend the
WADA conference in Copenhagen in 2003.
She responded, therefore, to the invitation to
attend by sending a statement, in which she
supports WADA with a declaration that what is
needed is to create a worldwide doping control
system that the world can rely upon. Such a system, she goes on to explain, involves out-
of-competition-controls and tests at all events
and competitions in which elite sportspersons
compete in order to avoid some of them keeping to minor, uncontrolled events and then setting spectacular records there. In addition she
supports the idea of an 'athlete's passport',

a system in which athletes regularly have their blood and urine tested. In that way it would be possible to keep an eye on the athletes' physiological parameters and – in the event of the organism showing abnormal biological irregularities that indicate doping – to treat these signs as a positive test:

> To do this we need to have a worldwide scheme so that athletes can be tested regularly and reliably wherever they are based, and all athletes need to cooperate. Samples given could also be built up to help research to establish new tests.
>
> (Radcliffe 2003: 10)

What she is suggesting is a wide-ranging surveillance system, and the crowning glory is a recommendation that doping tests should be frozen with a view to retrospective testing as new test methods evolve. When athletes come up with such a desperate proposal, they pressurise others into following their lead. Sceptical athletes have enormous difficulty in formulating any defence against yet more stringent restrictions of their personal freedoms. The gentlest questioning of the regime easily comes to give the impression that the athlete only supports the anti-doping campaign half-heartedly, and that in turn brings the risk of bringing suspicion on oneself.

It is, however, doubtful whether the wide-ranging system of control proposed by Radcliffe would benefit sport at all in the long term.

There are grounds for supposing that many potential athletes will baulk at entering a field whose conditions demand that they submit to a regime that would be utterly unacceptable outside sport. Attempts to rescue the reputation of sport through further tightening of the anti-doping campaign focused on athletes would appear as a whole only to contribute to making something bad, worse. The use of doping does not seem to have decreased, and since the WADA initiative was launched, the image of sport has only deteriorated. It seems, therefore, as though the time is ripe to consider new strategies – both for the sake of sport and of the athletes involved.

References

Christiansen, A. V. (2005) *Ikke for pengenes skyld* [Money Is Not the Thing], Odense: University Press of Southern Denmark.

Donati, A. (2004) 'The Silent Drama of the Diffusion of Doping among Amateurs and Professionals', in J. Hoberman and V. Møller (eds) *Doping and Public Policy*, Odense: University Press of Southern Denmark.

Radcliffe, P. (2003) 'An Athlete's View', in The World Anti-Doping Agency, *Play True*, issue 1.

White, K. (2005) 'Why I Became a Part of the BALCO Affair (+ Questions and Answers)'. Online. Available at: http://www.playthegame. org/Knowledge%20Bank/Articles/Why_I_ became_part_of_the_BALCO_affair. aspx (accessed 14 August 2006).

Why not dope?

It's still about the health

Andy Miah

One of the initial questions asked about the prospect of genetic manipulation in sport is whether it is conceptually different from drug use or other forms of doping. Even though genetic modification for sport has yet to be firmly realised as a practice of performance enhancement, and even though the technology has not yet been formally conceptualised by sporting authorities, it is already being treated as a form of doping. It is on this basis that genetic modification is currently being rejected by a number of international sporting organisations and becoming part of anti-doping policies. Most recently, the World Anti-Doping Agency (WADA) and the International Olympic Committee (IOC) have each written into their anti-doping codes a note about genetic modification, stipulating that its use is unacceptable, except when therapeutic. The IOC convened a working group that met in June 2001, and concluded the following:

> Gene therapy holds great promise for all people including athletes competing in Olympic sports. We endorse the development and application of gene therapy for the prevention and treatment of human disease. However, we are aware that there is the potential for abuse of gene therapy medicines and we shall begin to establish procedures and state-of-the-art testing methods for identifying athletes who might misuse such technology. This will require investment in modern detection methods including antigen detection, gene chip and proteomic analysis which are now becoming available. We are confident that we shall be able to adequately monitor abuses and establish the procedures for doing so using ethically acceptable methods. We call upon other sports, medical and scientific organisations to endorse our position.
>
> (IOC, 2001: html)

However, the development of anti-doping policy has recently reached a watershed, which should prevent such clear comparisons from being made between other methods of doping and genetic modification. The new anti-doping Code, drafted by WADA, has committed to ensuring that there is a process of rationalisation in respect of varying methods of performance modification. For the first time, the Code now distinguishes between substances or methods that enhance the body – such as steroids – and those that do not – such as nasal decongestants. For this reason, it is reasonable to expect that subsequent versions of the Code will be more rigorous in making distinctions surrounding genetic modification in sport.

A subsequent question – which often quickly follows the previous one – is whether anti-doping policies can be sustained in an era of genetic modification. Some would argue that the possibility of detecting genetic manipulation, together with the cost in time and money that such testing would require, is too big a burden for sport to bear. For this reason, enforcing anti-doping policy would become impossible, and sporting communities would need to reappraise the value of enhancement and, perhaps, ignore the fact that pharmacological enhancements are constitutive of an athlete's performance.

The ability to make meaningful contributions to this discussion will depend largely upon the way in which genetic modification in sport becomes conceptualised by sporting authorities. If genetic modification is treated like any other form of doping, then the ability to sustain anti-doping ambitions will become very difficult, since, I suggest, the ethical issues arising from genetics are very different from other forms of enhancement technology in sport. Anti-doping policy makers need not end up in such a situation, though, in order to explain how this is so, it is necessary to outline the conceptual weaknesses of current anti-doping approaches.

In this context, I will first discuss the discourse surrounding the presentation and representation of performance enhancement in sport, exploring the way in which the media create the moral discourse surrounding so-called drug cheats. My interest is to understand the political context of anti-doping, as a basis for explaining the way in which genetic modification in sport might also be conceptualised. I will suggest that the condemnation of drug users and dopers in sport is manufactured largely by the media, but more specifically from inconsistent methods of reasoning about drugs, enhancement and sporting values. This perspective will be supported by a detailed clarification of the arguments against drug use in sport. I argue that there is currently no unobjectionable argument against many forms of doping and, collectively, such arguments also lack persuasiveness, if – and only if – the basis for rejection relies solely upon some ethical component of *sport*. This caveat is necessary, since there are many reasons why it is sufficient to reject doping on the basis of a concern for *health* alone. One of the key questions to answer is whether *sport ethics* offers anything more meaningful about the ethics of genetic modification in sport, beyond the *medical ethical* concern for health.

The media-political context of anti-doping

The media-political context of anti-doping refers to the varying institutions and forces operating to sustain an anti-doping agenda within sport. It is useful to explain why it is that anti-doping has such symbolic importance and why there is such strong support for believing that doping challenges sporting values. Moreover, it is important to recognise that this is an *explanation* rather than a *justification* for why doping is undesirable. Such ideas reveal very little about the coherence of such perspectives, which will be addressed later in this chapter.

To appreciate the rational and ethical basis for rejecting doping, it is necessary to acknowledge both the culture of doping *and* the culture of anti-doping in competitive sport. People are generally familiar with the former, which describes the problem of doping in cultural terms (Brewer, 2002). For example, one might refer to such a concept by discussing the overwhelming pressure on athletes to surpass human limits and how this creates a climate where there is a need to dope. In contrast, I refer to the *culture of anti-doping* as the overwhelming pressure to embrace international policy in anti-doping, which necessarily pervades sporting and other official organisations.[1]

Currently, it would seem that popular opinion about doping in sport is that it is morally undesirable. This may be a culturally biased perspective and caution may be necessary in making such claims given the varying meanings associated with doping, drug use, and even what constitutes a 'drug' between different cultures. However, within the industry of competitive sport, doping is internationally recognised as being undesirable, at least if one accepts that adherence to anti-doping codes is an indication of expressed values. This presents a very serious challenge to an ethicist who might reject this initial premise about performance enhancement.

One of the most familiar ways in which this perspective is reinforced is through the media, which repeatedly demonise drug-induced athletes. It also instils the idea that using such substances or doping methods is recognised as *cheating* and attributable to a flaw in the athlete's character; a character that should be otherwise (there is an expectation that athletes should uphold morally desirable behaviours). Measuring this alleged public contempt for drug use in sport is both problematic and highly imprecise, though some useful work may be found in Brian Denham's research on this issue (Denham, 1997, 1999, 2000).

Even if one accepts that the content of media productions is reflective of dominant social values, it is not possible to presume that there is a consensus about the ethics of drug use and doping in sport. Indeed, it is possible to identify characteristics of doping stories that suggest the need for caution in making clear conclusions about their relevance. After all, the typical *drug cheat story* has a number of elements that make it inherently interesting and engaging, even if the reader does not care (or know) much about sport. The athlete's endeavour is immersed in strong symbolic meaning related to a host of social values, such as national pride, meritocracy, hard work, talent, ethnicity and individualism. Arguably, it is this rhetoric of doping that sustains the public interest in the drug cheat, rather than it having to do with some coherent ethical or moral perspective. The contempt for drug users conveyed in the media has little to do with what such athletes have actually done to devalue sport. Rather, it is about engaging the public in stories about good and evil or right and wrong, as Denham suggests. Ridiculously, the drug cheat story is analogous to the narrative in such films as *Rocky IV* (or any of the Rocky films), where the naturally gifted and strong-willed athlete overcomes the evil, drug-enhanced, techno-athlete.[2]

Integral to media coverage, as a measure of why drug taking in sport is morally repugnant, is an 'expert' discourse given by *respected* individuals and organisations who regularly condemn drug use and doping through the formation of policy. Thus the IOC President, various governmental and non-governmental agencies such as United Nations Education, Scientific and Cultural Organisation (Unesco) or the Council of Europe, and the vast sporting federations networks, all publicly work towards a similar goal – the elimination of moral badness in sport (usually doping). It is unreasonable to claim that all these people and such trusted institutions have misplaced values or are acting without any morally credible imperative. Yet such claims cannot be taken for granted, and it is also unreasonable to conclude that

improvements cannot be made to the way in which such institutions conceptualise performance enhancement. I have suggested that the mechanisms within international sport prevent this reconsideration about doping, which is detrimental to striving for ethical credibility.

In addition, support for anti-doping relies upon the voices of athletes who express their contempt for use of drugs and other forms of doping in sport. Determining whether this is a representative impression of athletes' feelings about doping specifically and performance enhancement more generally is difficult, since very few athletes receive media attention for what they want to say about such matters. It is unreasonable simply to assume that such athletes reflect the moral majority. Moreover, the very same athletes who criticise doping do not conduct their own training in a manner that reflects a coherent and consistent philosophy of sport or ethical view on performance enhancement. For example, athletes who claim erythropoietin (EPO) is wrong and that it should be banned from sport because it is dangerous and unfair, are also the same athletes who use such technologies as altitude chambers without any moral concerns, even though many athletes cannot have such advantages and even though there may be some dangerous health implications associated with the technology. In this context, while one would not criticise athletes for being inconsistent in their decisions about using different methods of performance enhancement, my point is that it is unreasonable to ignore the fact that this is a complex and difficult distinction to make. It is hard to rationalise the ethical difference between an altitude chamber and blood doping, or an aluminium baseball bat and a neoprene swimming costume. This is why it is important to requestion fundamental premises about anti-doping, since they appeal to some ethical view of sport that is incomplete and question begging.

It is naïve to assume that these various interest groups are apolitical or are acting wholly from a position of striving for moral purity in sport. However, the important point is that the public seems unlikely to suddenly change its opinions about the value of drug use in sport, even if such opinions are more emotive and politically motivated than philosophically grounded. Popular opinion is still very much against the use of drugs and any other kind of innovation in sport that leads to a perception of greater injustice. For this reason, it does not matter whether there is a justification for such arguments. The existence of moral rejection of doping is sufficient for it to be taken seriously and given moral weight, even if the perspective is inconsistent and conceptually flawed.[3]

However, it has yet to be discerned whether these perspectives are conceptually coherent. I have merely suggested that there is a powerful moral discourse surrounding drug use, which influences the way in which the *doped athlete* is morally evaluated and that this might have nothing to do with what is ethically inappropriate for sports. Therefore, the task is to understand whether or not specific kinds of enhancement are unacceptable. It involves not being persuaded by the rhetoric found in media and politics.

These various discourses provide an explanation for why arguments encouraging the use of more forms of doping in sport are not met with sympathy from anti-doping policy makers. Even if it is desirable to approach performance enhancement in sport with an entirely blank page, there is no use in trying to remove the entire infrastructure of anti-doping policy, even if one is wholeheartedly against such work.[4] Thus it is no good to advocate the use of doping and drugs in sport based solely on the idea that the arguments supporting that perspective are inconsistent or weak. Nevertheless, an ethicist can, at least attempt a systematic analysis of the arguments about a matter, in order to try and allow justifiable conclusions to surface and to reveal the weaknesses of inadequate argumentation and flawed conclusions.

While some moral weight may be ascribed to the outrage felt about the acceptance of drugs in sport, this does not constitute a sufficient basis for the rejection. As Tollefsen (2001) recognises, one may argue that a public outcry about a moral issue might have enough weight to make its tolerance impossible. Yet it is not clear that there is such a public outcry felt in relation to drug taking in sport, as might have once been said in the era of the Ben Johnson scandal. It is not even possible to give much credibility to intuitive appeals about the moral badness of drug use in sport. For example, it is common to hear as a defence against drug use that no parent would wish their child to end up a drug enhanced athlete. Supposedly, the very

fact that all parents are united against drug use in sport conveys some credibility to the weight of such arguments. Such appeals are not helpful if the task is to determine whether drugs, doping or any kind of performance modifier is ethically acceptable. While one can acknowledge that the parents of such children are sincere in their belief and wish to prevent their children from getting involved with performance-enhancing drugs, one cannot accept their testimony as a moral rationale for working towards ensuring that drug use is prohibited from sport. Indeed, such views reveal very little about what is valuable in sports.

If importance is given to these parental interests, or any party for that matter (as, indeed, it is), then it is necessary to determine what criteria may be used to conclude that these interests have moral weight. For this, it is necessary to define what constitutes a public outcry. Presumably it may involve protests, lobbying to government, demonstrations and so on. Yet there do not seem to be such protests about drugs in sport. These are the usual criteria for ascribing legal weight to an issue, and it is not that sporting communities are unable to levy such support. The blood sport of fox-hunting has recently caused controversy in the United Kingdom and an interest in this topic did provoke a significant amount of protest, demonstrations and a feeling of grief among the fox-hunting communities about the issue. Such strong feelings are not quite as apparent in respect of doping in sport. There is no public outcry about drugs in sport, aside from the rhetorical media articles and the accompanying institutional lobbying for keeping drugs out of sport. Moreover, even if this lobbying is sincere, it is more tied up with a social concern for drug use and harm deriving from it in general, than a concern for sporting values or performance enhancement. Spectators are, quite reasonably, not particularly concerned about athletes gaining an extra hundredth of a second on their performance by using a banned substance. People have been cajoled into feeling strongly about something that matters little in their lives through what Denham (1999) describes as agenda building.

Yet it is not possible to dismiss the anti-doping arguments so quickly. Most of what has just been said addresses the speculative claims about the public lack of appreciation for drugs.

However, there has been an ethical discourse about drug use and doping for some years, even though it has been confined mostly to academic journals and the media. Consequently it is incumbent to address some of the arguments that are used to sustain anti-doping ambitions. Importantly, it is often the case that many of the sophisticated arguments made within academic literature have had no place in informing anti-doping policy. Even accepting that there is a distinction between policy and ethics, it is still surprising to see the lack of appreciation for academic arguments that have endeavoured to reinforce anti-doping ideals.

[. . .]

Why drugs have no place in sports

A useful articulation of the arguments concerning drug use in sport is provided by Schneider and Butcher's (2000) philosophical overview, which addresses the harms resulting from doping. Their synopsis brings together a number of overlapping perspectives that have been asserted during the past twenty years in the philosophy of sport literature and in anti-doping policy statements.[5] Schneider and Butcher (2000) separate their various arguments thus:

- Cheating and unfairness.
- Harm (to users, clean athletes, society and sport).
- Perversion of sport (against its nature).
- Unnaturalness and dehumanisation.

Their overview encompasses a number of sub-arguments that it is helpful to make more explicit, particularly since some of their advocates may not see them as fitting within the broader categories asserted by Schneider and Butcher. Indeed, I wish to suggest that there are some conceptual flaws with the manner in which Schneider and Butcher have derived these categories.[6] A different kind of categorisation may resemble the following:[7]

1 *Coercion*: The legalisation of drug would create an environment that forces athletes into choosing drugs to remain competitive, thus risking harm to their lives. For this reason, they are unethical since they force athletes to engage with practices they feel strongly against (Gardner, 1989; Lavin, 1987; Murray, 1984, 1986a; Parry, 1987; Simon, 1991; Tamburrini, 2000a).

2 *Unfair*: Permitting drug use has some unfair consequences for either the participating athletes, other members of the sporting community or the sport itself (Gardner, 1989; Lavin, 1987; Parry, 1987; Schneider and Butcher, 2000; Simon, 1991; Tamburrini, 2000a).

3 *Health risk*: Permitting drug use entails a substantial risk to the biological constitution of an athlete, which is unnecessary and undesirable. As such it is unethical to permit drug use, since it would also imply creating circumstances where athletes are at a higher health risk (Brown, 1995; Holowchak, 2000; Lavin, 1987; Parry, 1987; Schneider and Butcher, 2000; Simon, 1991; Tamburrini, 2000a).

4 *Unnatural*: Drugs are unnatural and, for this reason, they are unethical, because sporting performances are valued as natural performances (Hoberman, 1992; Houlihan, 1999; Lavin, 1987; Perry, 1988; Schneider and Butcher, 2000; Tamburrini, 2000a).

5 *Rule breaking/Cheating/Respect*: Drug taking is unacceptable because it is against the rules. Breaking the rules is considered to be cheating and so the use of drugs is also cheating. Cheating is also unacceptable because it demonstrates a lack of respect for other participants and the sport (Arnold, 1997; Houlihan, 1999; Simon, 1985, 1991).

6 *Unearned advantage*: Because drugs make it possible to achieve better performances without additional training, they are unethical; sporting achievements should be earned by the athlete (Carr, 1999).

7 *Contrary to/Does not promote the internal goods of sport*: Sports are valued because of their unique, internal goods. The use of drugs does not contribute to, and is contrary to, such goods. As such, it is unethical (Schneider and Butcher, 1994).

8 *Contrary to the nature of sport*: Sport has an internal essence that is compromised by the use of drugs. As such, their use is unethical (Simon, 1991; Tamburrini, 2000a).

9 *Contract violation*: Entering sporting competition entails making a tacit contract with one's opponent to play under the same conditions. Failure to do this by using means of performance modification that are outside of the agreed means is unethical because it breaks this contract with other participants (Butcher and Schneider, 1998; Eassom, 1998; Feezell, 1986; Loland, 1998; Morgan, 1994; Simon, 1991).

There are some clear overlaps between these nine arguments and Schneider and Butcher's four generic categories, though the reason for making the individual positions clearer is that reducing them to the four categories offered by Schneider and Butcher conflates a number of these quite different positions. For each of these arguments, there is no consensus about whether one or some of them can justify the prohibition of all forms of doping from sport. One of my main criticisms of the approach to ethical issues concerning doping and drug use so far is that it does not distinguish between different methods of performance enhancement, such as sports equipment, drug use, training or doping. Instead, as is common in many discussions concerning doping in sport, the philosophical literature has placed an emphasis upon analysing drugs as the primary method of doping. (Again, one might attribute this to the media-political influence, for which the drug stories have gained such attention.)

Examples of innovation such as blood doping, technological innovation or altitude chambers are not considered as explicit cases aside from their being labelled as methods of doping. It is not entirely surprising that drugs have been a priority. Certainly, blood doping and altitude chambers are quite recent innovations. Nevertheless, it is surprising that technological innovations have not been given much attention, particularly since there is substantial debate about their legitimacy. In addition, the rules are constantly shifting to include or exclude certain kinds of innovation and so they would be a rich source of examples, which could inform arguments about drugs or other methods of doping. However, drug use has been a high priority, largely, it would seem, because drugs are perceived to cause physical and mental harm to the athlete. I will not attempt to develop a theoretical framework for enhancements in sport, which I have anyway done elsewhere (Miah, 2002a), though it is perhaps important to recognise that virtually no overlap exists between the narrow ethical framework on doping and drug use and the similar concern in relationship to other methods of performance modification (Miah and Eassom, 2002).

There is one further conceptual limitation in Schneider and Butcher's (2000) categorisation, which is their interpretation of the concept *harm*. In their categorisation, harm refers to some physical or mental impairment incurred by the athlete, which results from doping, or potential social harms that arise from promoting a culture of doping. The basis for Schneider and Butcher's argument is the idea that *only* living entities can be harmed. On such a view, because harm is something that must be felt, non-living entities cannot be harmed because they are incapable of perceiving such harm. In the context of medicine, Glannon (2001: 10) reflects a similar perspective, arguing that 'only beings with interests can be harmed, and having interests presupposes the capacity for consciousness and other forms of mental life that defines persons'. Thus harm to non-living or abstract entities is understood vicariously, where harm is experienced by entities that *perceive* harm is taking place. Consequently the harm is indirect, but nevertheless has consequences for human beings. For this reason, harm to non-living entities is separated from specific others by Schneider and Butcher (2000).[8]

Yet Schneider and Butcher's admission that harm may also be incurred by sport or society suggests that their view on harm is rather more complex. If they are correct, then it does not make sense that cheating is considered as a separate category from harm. Rather, it should form a subcategory within a broad category of doping harm, where risk of harm is better understood more broadly to encompass harms that are *unrelated* to physical and mental impairment. As such, the effect of doping to create *unfairness* or a *perversion of a sport's nature* can each be understood as forms of harm. This clarification of the problem may be a relatively trivial point, though it is significant because it develops a conceptualisation of technologies in sport within which forms of doping can include other kinds of technologies such as sports equipment.

Thus a more useful categorisation of arguments in relation to the ethics of performance modification must encompass those that are made in Schneider and Butcher's overview, along with a number of their other reasons for banning doping within the general category of harm. The differences between the two approaches may be seen in Table 3.3.1. On the left is Schneider and Butcher's (2000) categorisation of harm, which falls within their broader conceptualisation of arguments against doping. In contrast, the present categorisation of harm reflects these 'other' arguments as also indicative of some form of harm.

Thus the category of harm used here includes harm to people, society and sports, within which Schneider and Butcher's other categories of argument against doping are included. For example, Schneider and Butcher's *cheating and unfairness* category appears in the form of a number of different kinds of harm in various sections of the proposed restructure. The revised framework also encompasses the nine specific arguments raised earlier. With this in mind, it is now possible to examine each of the arguments for why doping and drug use should be banned from sports.

Harm to others

Harm as risk of damage to health

One of the strongest claims about the problem of doping is that it causes unnecessary short-term and long-term harm to the athletes who use them (where necessary risk implies the risk required to accept in order to undertake the sport). For this reason, it is argued that such substances should not be allowed into sports, since they place athletes at *too much of* a risk. Given that this tends often to have been related to the use of drugs, there are additional fears about addiction and the socially debilitating effects of doping. Since such harms might overlap with the *harms to society*, this category will be specific to health-related harm to persons, rather than the social harm of doping, which tends more to be the social harm of drug use.[9]

Within this category, it is also possible to include the subcategory *harms of coercion*, which indirectly have moral weight due to the propensity of the coerced persons to be taking risks with their health as a consequence of being forced into a position of needing doping to remain competitive (Simon, 1984). One might also assert that coercion is problematic not because of the consequence, but because it is an infringement of liberty to be coerced into decisions (Houlihan, 1999). However, this argument does not have such strength in the context of sport, since sport is already a coercive environment. For example, one might protest at being coerced into training seven days a week as a requirement of being an elite athlete, yet have very little ethical concern for such coercion. These practices are deemed necessary if one

Table 3.3.1. A harms-based conceptualisation of arguments against doping and drug use in sport

Schneider and Butcher's (2000) categorisation of harm	Present categorisation of harm

Cheating and unfairness
Harm:
  ▪ to athletes (users)
  ▪ to (clean) athletes
  ▪ to society
  ▪ to the sporting community
  ▪ caused by bans
Perversion of sport's nature
Unnaturalness and dehumanisation
	Harm to others:
	  ▪ athletes (users)
	    unfair advantage, health
	  ▪ athletes (non-users):
	    unfair advantage, contract violation, coercion
	  ▪ members of the sporting community
	    expectation disappointment; role models
	Harm to society
	Harm to the nature of sport:
	  ▪ unfair advantage/de-skilling
	  ▪ rule breaking
	  ▪ compromise of internal goods
	  ▪ unnaturalness

seeks great achievements such as elite sporting status and are considered to be an integral, valued aspect of sport. Consequently, it cannot be coercion in itself that is problematic. Rather, it is the added condition that athletes are coerced into taking significant risks with their health by using banned methods of doping (Holowchak, 2000).

An important point of clarification is required about this argument in relation to the concept of *necessity*. A fairly typical pro-liberal response to doping is that sport is inherently risky. As such, if the basis for banning doping from sport is that it is too dangerous to an athlete's health, then one might question the practice of some sports at all, such as boxing or horse-racing, which are inherently dangerous, whether or not one dopes. On this view, there is no justification for doping on the basis of harm, if such sports as boxing and horse-racing are considered to present acceptable risks. For precisely this reason, the concept of 'unnecessary risk' serves to counter this perspective and assert that there are necessary risks in sport that cannot be removed without preventing or significantly altering the practice of the activity. Such risks, it is argued, must be tolerated. Nevertheless, this does not commit one to taking further risks, such as might be incurred by using drugs or doping.

In summarising the position, if a performance enhancement increases the risk an athlete accepts when competing, then it is likely that discussions will ensue about its ethical status. Yet this does not mean that if no additional risk is incurred, the technology will be ethically acceptable. Such circumstances have recently arisen in relation to altitude chambers and tents, which are argued as enhancing performance, but for which there has been little significant discussion in relation to their increased risk. Instead, the ethical debate about these technologies has been based upon their accessibility, largely because they are very expensive. Thus there are other characteristics of the performance enhancement that might make it unethical besides health risk, though if a performance enhancement is riskful to health, this is often sufficient to make it unethical. In such cases, it is important to recognise that this is a *medical* argument, rather than one which relies upon sporting values.

Harm as being unfairly disadvantaged

A concern for fair play dominates many sports' ethical discussions, and controversies surrounding performance enhancement are no exception. As a guiding normative principle, methods of performance enhancement that are unfair are unethical. However, the basis for determining what counts as 'unfair' is not straightforward to defend. Importantly, these methods of performance enhancement are to be contrasted with 'fair' disadvantages, which are ethical and desirable in sport (Gardner, 1989). The point then is that sport embraces performance enhancement, but only when it is regarded as fair. For example, if one discovers through training that, instead of building endurance capacity by running steadily for a very long time it is better to run at different speeds over a longer period of time, this would be regarded as a 'fair' means towards performance enhancement. Thus a fair advantage implies gaining some additional competitive edge in a competition by means that are considered to be legitimate. Thus, even though the means result in other competitors being disadvantaged, it is *desirable* disadvantage since they are legitimate means.

By articulating unfair disadvantage as a harm in sport, it is possible to identify two arguments that suggest how doping is unfair. The first may be understood as the *contract* argument; the second has to do with unfair disadvantage as failing to *respect* other competitors. Importantly, both arguments rely upon the doped athlete breaking the rules, though precisely what this entails is contested. Suits' (1973) seminal work on games and sport implies that it is sufficient to understand rule breaking precisely and only in terms of what is specified by the constitutive and regulative rules of the sport (see also Suits, 1978, 1988). It is possible to further apply this requirement of rule keeping to a broader 'ethos', which also entails rules that are tacitly understood, even if they are not written into any rule book (D'Agostino, 1981). For example, one might include within the accepted rules of soccer the understanding that, if the opposing team has a player injured on the pitch when one's own team has position, the ball will be kicked out of bounds rather than used to build an attack against the 'injured' team. Moreover, an accepted mode of practice would be for the 'injured' team to return the ball to the other team (who had possession), once the injured player had received treatment and was either removed from the pitch or back on her feet. This example of an underpinning ethos which extends the formal rules of a sport is also considered to be part of the ethical framework within that sport.

Regardless of where one decides to limit the articulation of rules, both perspectives (*formal rules* or *formal rules and ethos*) argue that failing to keep the rules entails failing to play the game (Arnold, 1997; Feezell, 1988; Loland and McNamee, 2000). If rules are not maintained in sports, then the objective of the contest becomes meaningless. For example, if it were acceptable to run a marathon by using a motorcycle or pole vault wearing anti-gravity boots, this would defeat the object of the competitions. The activities would cease to make sense as contests that try to evaluate a particular kind of performance.

Feezell (1986) argues that the sporting competition is analogous to a kind of contract, since competitors agree voluntarily upon the specific conditions in which they will compete. As Arnold (1992: 247) argues,

> when a person voluntarily chooses to enter a sport he or she makes a tacit commitment to abide by the rules that are applicable. To renege upon the agreement is rather like making a promise and then not keeping it.

In addition, Butcher and Schneider (1998: 7) suggest that fair play has meaning precisely because competition is such a contract. However, they also state that:

> Fair play as contract is open on the content of the agreement. On some versions of this view, the content of the contract is created solely by the rules. In other versions, it is the rules as practised and understood by the athletes.

This reinforces the idea that the specific content of the would-be sporting contract is not straightforward to articulate. Moreover, Wertz (1981) argues that the contract analogy is true only metaphorically and that, even if there is some kind of agreement between competitors,

this does not constitute a contract between them.

Alternatively, unfairness may be seen as harmful, since it fails to give value to the interests of others. In short, it fails to *respect* them as ends in themselves, and instead treats them as means to the ends of others (Tuxill and Wigmore, 1998). This view takes its lead from the Kantian maxim to *treat others as ends in themselves, rather than as means to our own ends.* By accepting the former, we recognise individuals as rational agents with their own capacity for intelligence and own volitions. As such, doping and drug use would be considered unethical because it fails to take account of the interests of other athletes.

On each of these views, doping in sport is an instance of unfair play because it is an instance of rule breaking. However, the reason why rule breaking is harmful may be either because it entails breaking a contract or it demonstrates a failure to have respect for other competitors. A variety of people are harmed – conceived either as contract breaking or failing to respect – by doping just because they are placed in a more disadvantageous position than they would be if the doping method were prohibited. Most typically, attention is drawn to the non-users, the so-called *clean* athletes, who are disadvantaged because the *drug cheats* are gaining an advantage over them. However, even *users* could be disadvantaged, if the drugs they use do not confer the kind of enhancement they expect. For example, not all athletes using EPO will incur similar enhancements in their performance – some of the drug users will derive an advantage over other users. This argument is further supported by the claim that there is little certainty about the effects of specific substances – including possible side effects, which would further debilitate the user. Consequently, if our intention is to conclude that some athletes are harmed by the use of drugs in sport, then it cannot stop short of encompassing the drug-using athletes who may be using drugs in a way that is actually ineffective at performance enhancement. This would not be conceived typically as *unfair*, since the risk will have been undertaken voluntarily. Yet clearly the drug-induced athlete, who receives no benefit to his or her performance and, potentially, might be debilitated by using such substances, would also be harmed.

Indeed, one might suggest that this consequence is (or should be) a genuine concern for anti-doping authorities.

A similar kind of claim may be made in relation to the non-using athlete who is also disadvantaged by the doped athlete. This is more typically the athlete for whom people have a moral concern – the *clean* athlete. For the non-user, the harms are rather more transparent. Initially, there is the obvious harm of being disadvantaged in competition as a consequence of the opponent using a performance enhancer that is not available to others. From an ethical perspective the salience of this has been made clear in numerous cases in sport. Innovations are frequently banned on account of their not being available to the whole athletic community. For example, in the 1980s, the development of the fibreglass pole in pole vaulting led to circumstances where some athletes had the benefit of an enhanced pole while others did not. For this reason, the fibreglass pole was prohibited from use until such time that it was available to all competitors (Houlihan, 1999). A similar ruling was made in relation to the superman bicycle design, which assisted the ride by making the seating position more streamlined (Fotheringham, 1996a, 1996b). More recently, Speedo's FastSkin swim-suits raised similar controversies in the approach to the Sydney 2000 Olympic Games (Loland, 2002; Magdalinski, 2000). All of these examples are cases where the technology was seen as ethically problematic by governing bodies largely because it was not available to all participants.

Underlying this judgement is the premise that a sporting contest *should* involve athletes who have an equal opportunity to win – no athlete should have access to means that others do not (Fraleigh, 1982, 1984b). Importantly, this is not to say that athletes should always use the *same* equipment, even though this is the case in some sports. Rather, it is to recognise that all athletes should have the opportunity to maximise their performance capabilities by having access to all legal methods of performance enhancement. In many cases, it might be that the same piece of equipment provides a similar advantage for all athletes. However, in sports such as skiing or even the FastSkin swim-suit, it is not necessarily beneficial for all athletes to have the same equipment, given the diversity of human body types, strategies and techniques. Consequently, the rules are such that some specifications of the skis can be altered to the needs of the individual, within a general framework of what is accepted by the governing bodies. Where such equal opportunities are not ensured, this is harmful because some athletes will be disadvantaged by something that is out of their control. Yet this alone is not sufficient to claim that the harm is unethical. After all, the *fair advantage* is something that gives value to sporting competitions. Consequently, while an advantage does create unequal competition, this kind of inequality is not sufficient to conclude that a performance enhancement is unethical, even if it might be a necessary characteristic for such a conclusion.

Each of these ideas is not without complications. The idea that cheating or rule breaking is determined solely by what is outside of the rules begs the question as to what ought to constitute the rules in the first place. As Brown (1980: 18) argues,

> Another question is if the use of drugs is ever unfair. Yes, if using them is cheating; if one contender uses them against the rules, but others do not. But why should we ever outlaw their use?

Why is it that drug taking is considered to be against the rules and, as such, a form of cheating at all? Presumably, if it were recognised as an acceptable method of performance enhancement, it would not be a form of cheating. Similarly, if all pole vaulters wore anti-gravity boots and such boots were legal, or if there were another event called the *anti-gravity boot pole vault*, then this would make it acceptable and it would neither be cheating nor unfair. Simon (1991: 87) goes even further, suggesting that by

> prohibiting athletes from using performance-enhancing drugs ... we disrespect them as persons ... we deny them the control over their own lives that ought to belong to any autonomous, intelligent, and competent individual.

However, Simon also recognises that the *voluntary* context of competitive sport means that athletes waive their right to such freedoms and accept that they will be subject to certain individual restrictions. He also uses this as a basis for concluding why drug testing is not unethical, though more will be said about this later.

Harm to the nature of sport

Earlier in this chapter, I indicated that Schneider and Butcher also consider there to be possible harm to sports, even though a sport is not a living entity, and therefore cannot, literally, be harmed. Conceivably, this distinction might be merely linguistic, but perhaps speaks more to different notions of harm. To support Schneider and Butcher's analysis, it would be sufficient to consider that persons are harmed indirectly by harm to sports. This leads Schneider and Butcher (2000) to assert a further level of harm, which may be understood as *undermining the value of the sport itself*. This is identified by Schneider and Butcher as *gaining an advantage over the sport*, which they see as a more useful argument to conclude why doping is unethical. For Schneider and Butcher, even if drugs were legal in sports, they would still be unfair because they undermine the challenge of the competition by providing levels of performance that are not attributable to the athlete. In this sense, Carr (1999) argues that such performance enhancements *devalue* the competition because they do not merit praise for the athlete.[10]

Again, Schneider and Butcher's conceptualisation – while inclusive of the various arguments against doping – theorises its categories inappropriately. For example, they include a separate category as *unnaturalness and dehumanisation* which, I suggest, should also be understood as a subcategory of the *harm to sport* section. The arguments of naturalness and dehumanisation both assert that there is something unethical about doping because it is unnatural or dehumanising. However, underpinning this argument is an assumption that sport is an activity that is valued because it involves the natural human athlete. The two arguments assert a theory of sport, albeit rather briefly, arguing that doping challenges some alleged essence of sport.

A different (but related) argument in relation to the concern for *harm to sport* is the claim that doping challenges the prelusory goal of sports (Suits, 1973). This also fits into the unfairness category and asserts that the purpose of sports – the prelusory goal – no longer makes sense if certain means are used to achieve that goal, as is suggested in the example of participating in the pole vault event using anti-gravity boots. In such an activity, the challenge of pole vaulting is to use the pole to vault as high as possible over a horizontal bar. With anti-gravity boots, this challenge becomes simply a matter of how far the boots will power the athlete into the air and requires very little challenge from the athlete. In this sense, the challenge of the sport is made easier and less valuable thereby (Simon, 1991). On this Suitsian perspective on performance, enhancements are seen as unethical if they corrupt some inherent essence, nature or prelusory goal of a sport (Gardner, 1989).

The challenge for each of these arguments based upon an alleged nature of sport is to present an explanation of precisely what this essence or nature entails, but also to provide some way of negotiating conflicting views on this essence. Importantly, this additional requirement of negotiation suggests that it is possible to construct different kinds of sport, each of which could be ethically justifiable (at least in relation to performance modification). Loland (2002) challenges this idea. While recognising that different ethical views on performance modification in sport can be asserted, he argues that they are not each comparably valuable. Specifically, Loland describes three theories of sport – the 'non-theory', 'thin theory' and 'thick theory'. The 'thin theory' argues that sport is valued largely because it is an enterprise concerned with pushing human limits and that this philosophy embraces the use of any kinds of performance enhancement. In contrast, Loland's 'thick theory' argues that sport is a complex social practice 'with its own characteristic norms, values and internal goods that ought to be protected and cultivated'. However, Loland accepts that there are various thick theories in the sport philosophy literature, which may be found in the work of Fraleigh (1984b), Simon (1991) and Morgan (1994). Loland's (2002: 167) own thick theory asserts that:

> an athletic performance is a combination of talent and of cultivation of talent in terms of environmental influence in which our own efforts play the dominant role. Moreover, athletic performances ought to take place within a framework of non-exposure to unnecessary harm.

Clearly, further elaboration is necessary on such ideas as 'talent', 'environment', 'effort' and 'unnecessary harm', though this is a useful basis from which such ideas might be asserted.

An argument to assist the *negotiation* of different ethical theories of using technology in sport is found in Alasdair MacIntyre's (1985) theory of social practices. This approach would also seem to satisfy Loland's requirement for considering sports as social practices.

In the context of sport, Brown (1990) argues that a feature of practices is reflected in the typical relationship of novice to master where becoming an expert necessarily requires a process that is not easily attainable and requires time and commitment. As such,

> the relationship is frequently between novice and coach and includes the transmission of skills and values through the careful application of standards of excellence, which are the product of the sport's own history and the coach's prior experience. It is submission to this learning and the standards that govern it that is a prerequisite to mastery, just as it is the ability to extend and enrich the practice's techniques and goals that is the mark of achievement.
>
> (Brown, 1990: 73)

Moreover, it is only through this process that one realises the valued aspects of the practice, or, as MacIntyre phrases it, the 'internal goods' (1985: 188). It is on this basis that it can be claimed how sport might be harmed if the internal goods are challenged. Yet this perspective does not necessarily imply that performance modifiers that are currently banned contradict the internal goods of a sport. As Brown (1990: 77) argues,

> The constraints of the practice, including the internalising of the virtues are compatible with the use of performance enhancing drugs, novel and risky training regimes and biomedical or surgical treatments of modification or practitioners.

Nevertheless, it is possible to develop a critique of performance modifiers, such as drug use, based upon this argument. For example, one might argue that some enhancements are unethical since they prioritise individualistic values and because they do not foster the acquisition of internal goods, which derive mainly from skill-related abilities. However, it is not really accurate to suggest that methods of performance enhancement in sport necessarily make a practice easier. It might even allow an athlete to perform with greater competence and to enjoy a greater challenge. It must not be inferred, therefore, that the athlete need train any less to achieve such performances.

Harm to other members of the sporting community

Harm may also be incurred upon other members of the sporting community, not *clean athletes*, nor the sport itself, but people who simply care about sports; fans, spectators, enthusiasts. Such harms can be articulated from a number of perspectives, though clarification is needed first on what constitutes the sporting community to understand the limits of this category. Within sports, Morgan (1994) presents the notion of a sporting community in the form of a *practice community*. Defined in this way, a *practice community* draws upon a MacIntyrean concept of practices, which asserts that a practice is:

> any coherent and complex form of socially established co-operative human activity through which goods internal to that form of activity are realised in the course of trying to achieve those standards of excellence which are appropriate to, and partially definitive of, that form of activity, with the result that human powers to achieve excel, and human conceptions of the ends and goods involved, are systematically extended.
>
> (MacIntyre, 1985: 187)

Some confusion has arisen within sports ethics about the scope of MacIntyre's practice account, and how it is to be applied to sport (McNamee, 1995). Arnold (1997) considers that the concept may be used to encompass the practice of sport in general. Conversely, Eassom (1998) argues that the definition provided by MacIntyre delimits that a practice cannot be sport in general, but is reflective of specific sports. Instead, Eassom argues that sport is not a practice but *particular* sports, such as golf, soccer or basketball, are practices.

Returning to Morgan's concept of sporting practice communities, the problem of asserting the existence of a sporting community is more apparent. Accepting Eassom's position, it makes no sense to refer to a sporting *community*, since such an entity does not exist. Sports are far too diverse to lump them altogether as one single community. Doing so would be akin to referring to the community of human beings, who, by virtue of their sharing a species type, might be perceived to be a community. Morgan's practice community argument is useful, since it refers to those individuals who may be described as part of the sport's community, and thus have an interest in the state of their practice. This interest constitutes having a concern for the internal goods of the practice or those goods that are necessarily and exclusively tied to the practice.

Expectation disappointment　In the context of drug use (and doping in general), Schneider and Butcher (2000) describe how the sporting community has an expectation that athletes will be drug free. As such, one kind of harm incurred from athletes using drugs will be the realisation by the specific sporting community that athletes are not. Thus the harm derives from performances that are partly derivative of doping, which collapse the value that is placed into sport by members of the sporting community. A solution, they consider, is to remove the expectation and, consequently, to remove the harm. Yet Schneider and Butcher recognise that the majority of spectators want a drug-free sport and that removing the expectation (legalising the drugs) is not a solution to preserve the value that is invested into sport.

While one might attach moral weight to such a concern, the expectations of the sporting community are perhaps more difficult to discern, as there exist many examples of performance-enhancing technology that are ethically ambiguous. For example, the FastSkin swim-suit that raised controversy at the Sydney 2000 Olympic Games was neither clearly unacceptable nor clearly acceptable. It could not reasonably be claimed that its use challenged spectators' expectations of the sport. Consequently, the basis for claiming that the swimming community would be harmed by the use of this technology is tenuous. In the case of drug use – accepting the media-political argument raised earlier – it might be reasonable to identify clearly defined community expectations, though even here caution is necessary, since it requires reconciling the importance of consensus as the basis for an ethical conclusion.

Role models　A further claim against doping in sport is that it sets a bad example for young children, encouraging the taking of risks with one's body in pursuit of unrealistic and ephemeral aspirations (Houlihan, 1999; Schneider and Butcher, 2000). However, although this may have strength in the context of drug use specifically, it is relatively weak in respect of other technologies. After all, it is not particularly alarming for a child to see that an athlete is using a titanium tennis racket rather than a wooden one. This comparison suggests that the particular theorisation of an innovation as a socially situated technology is what makes it potentially harmful for children to see their role models using it. In the case of drugs, parents are justifiably concerned about their children aspiring to be like the drug-enhanced athlete, specifically because drugs can be harmful in numerous antisocial and unhealthy ways (which, incidentally, also seems reflective of elite sport with or without drugs). Consequently, like the argument based upon a concern for coercion, this argument might be seen as being reflective of the *health risk* argument in disguise. After all, the conclusion that doping athletes sets a bad role model for children relies upon some negative connotation associated with the enhancement. As such, the onus must first be placed upon deciding whether the method of enhancing performance in question is morally problematic in itself. If the technology is not something that would set a bad example for children to follow, then it need not be harmful to children that athletes use such technology or that they also aspire to use it.

Harms to society

Finally, arguments against doping in sport focus upon the potential and actual harms to society. These are perhaps the most difficult harms to assess, largely because they rely upon many contingent facts about how society deals with social problems. Nevertheless, it is possible to make some attempt at describing such harms.

First, the media-political context of drug use and doping places strong emphasis upon the link between the use of drugs and doping inside sport and its use outside of it. Understandably, it is highly problematic for officials and organisations to speak out in favour of tolerating drug use in sport and, at the same time, vilify such use in society. Such a perspective would distort the circumstances within which doping in sport takes place. To suggest that there is no relationship between drug users in sport and outside grossly misrepresents the manner in which drugs are obtained.

As such, the use of specific kinds of drug provokes responses that doping results in significant social harm. However, one might ask why it is that the specific level of harm resulting from the use of some drugs in sport is considered more alarming than the harm resulting from, say, limiting personal freedoms by prohibiting such use (Tamburrini, 2000b). This specific argument has been raised in relation to the consumption of marijuana in the United Kingdom, where its use is currently illegal. Legalisation advocates draw attention to the inconsistency of the argument, using the legal examples of tobacco and alcohol as a basis for arguing that a concern for social harm cannot be the sole justification for prohibition. After all, these legalised drugs are also associated with significant social harms – violence, accidents, health problems and so on – yet they remain legal. While a stronger case may be made for the prohibition of such substances, there is greater strength in the legalisation of such drugs in favour of personal liberty.

Within sport, it is not that all forms of doping or drug use are anything like the examples of tobacco, alcohol or marijuana (although these substances do appear on some anti-doping lists of banned substances). There are specific substances for which there is reason to believe that they are more like hard drugs, insofar as they give rise to significant and life-threatening harms. In such cases, the argument from social harms is much stronger in respect of drug use. However, not all forms of performance enhancement are comparable to such hard drugs and there is a need for distinctions to be made – if, and only if, importance is attached to the health risk incurred by athletes.

athletes and the interest to try to avoid a situation in elite sport where all athletes are taking unnecessary risks with their lives. Yet this argument alone does not tell us what is uniquely valuable about sport. Clearly there are concerns about, say, giving pole vaulters anti-gravity boots, which have nothing to do with health. Equally, it is unfortunate that some athletes deceive others in a way that neglects the value of competition and the assumption that all athletes adhere to a similar rule base. However, sport ethicists have contested such claims, arguing that athletes do not compete on an equal basis, even if all competitors adhere to the rules. Moreover, it is not necessarily the case that failing to maintain the rules implies deceiving competitors (Rosenberg, 1995; Wertz, 1981). If sports are seen as being undermined by a method of performance enhancement, then there might be a better argument for changing the kind of competition that is being tested.[11] Finally, it seems that both a concern for coercion and a concern for social harms only have moral weight when they are also a concern for health.

Each of these positions does not necessarily legitimate the prohibition of all methods of doping. In many situations, there is a reasonable case for arguing in favour of adapting the sport to create a new kind of competition, where performance enhancement is not simply associated with the emotive connotations of drug use. These arguments will be revisited again later in relation to the use of genetic modification for sport performance enhancement. For now, with this ethical context to doping in mind, it is necessary to turn to the philosophical underpinning of anti-doping policy, beyond the specific, ethical reasons for being against doping. The importance of this way of critiquing anti-doping is provoked by a lack of interest to question the manner in which anti-doping is approaching the problem. In addition, it derives from a perception of there being a pervading belief for anti-doping policy makers that there is an answer to the difficult task of making anti-doping a success: the ideology of *harmonisation*.

Summary

Perhaps the strongest argument against doping in sport (and most used by anti-doping policy makers) remains the concern for the health of

Notes

1. There seem to be similar assumptions made about the undesirability of genetic modification as are

made about drug taking in sport. This can help elucidate how genetic modification in sport might become distorted and rejected on similarly questionable philosophical bases.

2. Thanks to Bruce Jennings for a rather fruitful conversation about the moral athlete and for reminding me how useful is the film *Rocky IV*, even if we partially disagree on the precise characteristics of such athletes.

3. However, it might be argued that public opinion in respect of different kinds of performance enhancements might be more difficult to apprehend. For example, while we might expect clear ideas about how drugs are perceived, it may be more difficult to discern reactions to the use of blood transfusions or altitude chambers. Unfortunately, such methods of enhancement are subsumed into the discourse of doping – e.g. blood doping – which makes it difficult to gauge any clear differences in perception.

4. I would like to stress here that I am not entirely dismissing the work of the anti-doping movement. I have many valued colleagues who are involved with anti-doping in various contexts, who are genuinely seeking to develop coherent and justifiable ethical policies. Even those colleagues who I believe are making fundamental errors in their approach to anti-doping are not operating from an interest to do harm to sport, nor lack sincerity in their decisions and conclusions. My concern (and rejection) is for the rather stagnant manner in which such discussions are often made, the inconsistency of policies, and the lack of significance that is given to ethical inquiry in relation to doping. After all, misplaced sincerity is not a sufficient justification for the continuance of poor ethical conduct.

5. It is important to note that Schneider and Butcher (2000) are dealing specifically with doping and that genetic modification is not considered explicitly within their argument.

6. It is not possible here to give a thorough articulation of why I consider Schneider and Butcher's (2000) overview is inconsistent. Specifically, I have difficulties with their category of harms and how this fits in relation to other categories. It would seem that, on many occasions, other categories could also be seen as harms. Thus my tendency is to provide an overview of all arguments departing from a central concept of 'harm'. They use harm more to refer to biological harm, though I consider that a more generic term is relevant, where harm may also be to fail to respect the constitutive elements of a sport. More details of this analysis may be found in Miah (2002a).

7. The authors referenced alongside the different harms provide a picture of where these arguments have been considered in some detail, rather than necessarily reflecting the central argument of the author.

In many cases the authors consider a variety of viewpoints in the analysis of arguments concerning doping, though it is useful as some form of guide to understand how interests have been focused.

8. For more details about the moral consideration of non-living entities see Elliott (1993).

9. I am unaware of any strong concerns about the social harm of blood doping or of using altitude chambers.

10. The implications of Carr's conclusions are far-reaching and pertinent to the ethical discussion about genetic modification. It may be possible to extend Carr's argument to genetic endowment and conclude that genetic modification would be desirable, if it could eliminate differences between athletes based upon genetic luck. For Carr, this characteristic of sport has no value, since it is beyond the influence of the athlete.

11. Such an example is beginning to emerge in male professional tennis, where bigger balls are being piloted to combat the dominance of the strong serve, which is becoming impossible for a human to retrieve (Miah, 2000, 2002b).

References

Arnold, P.J. (1992) 'Sport as a Valued Human Practice: A Basis for the Consideration of Some Moral Issues in Sport', *Journal of Philosophy of Education*, 26 (2): 237–255.

Arnold, P.J. (1997) Sport, *Ethics and Education*, London: Cassell Education.

Brewer, B.D. (2002) 'Commercialization in Professional Cycling 1950–2001: Institutional Transformations and the Rationalization of Doping', *Sociology of Sport Journal*, 19: 276–301.

Brown, W.M. (1980) 'Ethics, Drugs and Sport', *Journal of the Philosophy of Sport*, 7: 15–23.

Brown, W.M. (1990) 'Practices and Prudence', *Journal of the Philosophy of Sport*, 17: 71–84.

Brown, W.M. (1995) 'Personal Best', *Journal of the Philosophy of Sport*, 22: 1–10.

Butcher, R. and Schneider, A. (1998) 'Fair Play as Respect for the Game', *Journal of the Philosophy of Sport*, 25: 1–22.

Carr, D. (1999) 'Where's the Merit if the Best Man Wins?', *Journal of the Philosophy of Sport*, 26: 1–9.

D'Agostino, F. (1981) 'The Ethos of Games', *Journal of the Philosophy of Sport*, 8: 7–18.

Denham, B.E. (1997) 'Sports Illustrated, the "War on Drugs," and the Anabolic Steroid Control Act of 1990', *Journal of Sport and Social Issues*, 21 (3): 260–273.

Denham, B.E. (1999) 'On Drugs in Sports in the Aftermath of Flo-Jo's Death, Big Mac's Attack', *Journal of Sport and Social Issues*, 23 (3): 362–367.

Denham, B.E. (2000) 'Performance-enhancing Drug Use in Amateur and Professional Sports: Separating the Realities from the Ramblings', *Culture, Sport, Society*, 3 (2): 56–79.

Eassom, S.B. (1998) 'Games, Rules and Contracts', in M.J. McNamee and S.J. Parry(eds) *Ethics and Sport*, London and New York: E & FN Spon, pp. 57–78.

Elliott, R. (1993) 'Environmental Ethics', in P. Singer *A Companion to Ethics*, Oxford: Blackwell, pp. 284–293.

Feezell, R.M. (1986) 'Sportsmanship', *Journal of the Philosophy of Sport*, 13: 1–13.

Feezell, R.M. (1988) 'On the Wrongness of Cheating and why Cheaters Can't Play the Game', *Journal of the Philosophy of Sport*, 15: 57–68.

Fotheringham, W. (1996a) 'Cycling: Hour of Pain, Shame or Glory', *Guardian*, London: 14.

Fotheringham, W. (1996b) 'Cycling: Obree Outraged at "Superman" Ban', *Guardian*, London: 23.

Fraleigh, W. (1982) 'Why the Good Foul is not Good', *Journal of Physical Education, Recreation and Dance*, January: 41–42.

Fraleigh, W.P. (1984a) 'Performance Enhancing Drugs in Sport: The Ethical Issue', *Journal of the Philosophy of Sport*, 11: 23–29.

Fraleigh, W.P. (1984b) *Right Actions in Sport: Ethics for Contestants*, Champaign, IL: Human Kinetics.

Gardner, R. (1989) 'On Performance-enhancing Substances and the Unfair Advantage Argument', *Journal of the Philosophy of Sport*, 16: 59–73.

Glannon, W. (2001) *Genes and Future People: Philosophical Issues in Human Genetics*, Oxford: Westview Press.

Hoberman, J.M. (1992) *Mortal Engines: The Science of Performance and the Dehumanization of Sport*, New York: The Free Press (republished in 2001 by Blackburn Press).

Holowchak, M.A. (2000) 'Aretism and Pharmacological Erogenic Aids in Sport: Taking a Shot at the Use of Steroids', *Journal of the Philosophy of Sport*, 27: 35–50.

Houlihan, B. (1999) *Dying to Win: Doping in Sport and the Development of Anti-Doping Policy*, Strasbourg: Council of Europe Publishing.

International Olympic Committee (IOC) (2001) Press Release: 'IOC Gene Therapy Working Group – Conclusion', Lausanne: *International Olympic Committee*. Online. Available: <http://www.olympic.org/uk/news/publications/press_uk.asp?release=179> (accessed August).

Lavin, M. (1987) 'Are the Current Bans Justified?', *Journal of the Philosophy of Sport*, 14: 34–43.

Loland, S. (1998) 'Fair Play: Historical Anachronism or Topical Ideal?', in M.J. McNamee and S.J. Parry (eds) *Ethics and Sport*, London and New York: E & FN Spon, pp. 79–103.

Loland, S. (2002) 'Sport Technologies: A Moral View', in A. Miah and S.B. Eassom (eds) *Sport Technology: History, Philosophy and Policy*, Oxford: Elsevier Science, pp. 157–171.

Loland, S. and McNamee, M. (2000) 'Fair Play and the Ethos of Sports: An Eclectic Philosophical Framework', *Journal of the Philosophy of Sport*, 27: 63–80.

MacIntyre, A. (1985) *After Virtue: A Study in Moral Theory* (2nd edn), London: Duckworth.

McNamee, M.J. (1995) 'Sporting Practices, Institutions, and Virtues: A Critique and a Restatement', *Journal of the Philosophy of Sport*, 22: 61–82.

Magdalinski, T. (2000) 'Performance Technologies: Drugs and Fastskin at the Sydney 2000 Olympics', *Media International Australia*, 97 (November): 59–69.

Miah, A. (2000) '"New Balls Please": Tennis, Technology, and the Changing Game', in S.A. Haake and A.O. Coe (eds) *Tennis, Science, and Technology*, London: Blackwell Science, pp. 285–292.

Miah, A. (2002a) *Philosophical and Ethical Questions Concerning Technology in Sport: The Case of Genetic Modification*, Department of Sport Science, Leicester: De Montfort University.

Miah, A. (2002b) 'Is Bigger Better? A Response to the International Tennis Federation's "Bigger Balls" Proposal', *International Sports Studies*, 24 (2): 19–32.

Miah, A. and Eassom, S.B. (eds) (2002) *Sport Technology: History, Philosophy and Policy*, Oxford: Elsevier Science.

Morgan, W.J. (1994) *Leftist Theories of Sport: A Critique and Reconstruction*, Urbana: University of Illinois Press.

Murray, T.H. (1984) 'Drugs, Sports, and Ethics', in T.H. Murray, W. Gaylin and R. Macklin (eds) *Feeling Good and Doing Better*, Clifton, NJ: Humana Press, pp. 107–126.

Murray, T.H. (1986) 'Guest Editorial: Drug Testing and Moral Responsibility', *The Physician and Sports Medicine*, 14 (11): 47–48.

Parry, S.J. (1987) 'The Devil's Advocate', *Sport & Leisure*, November–December: 34–35.

Perry, C. (1988) 'Blood Doping and Athletic Competition', in W.J. Morgan and K.V. Meier (eds) *Philosophic Inquiry in Sport*, Champaign, IL: Human Kinetics, pp. 307–312.

Rosenberg, D. (1995) 'The Concept of Cheating in Sport', *International Journal of Physical Education*, 32 (2): 4–14.

Schneider, A.J. and Butcher, R.B. (1994) 'Why Olympic Athletes Should Avoid the Use and Seek the Elimination of Performance Enhancing Substances and Practices from the Olympic Games', *Journal of the Philosophy of Sport*, 21: 64–81.

Schneider, A.J. and Butcher, R.B. (2000) 'A Philosophical Overview of the Arguments on

Banning Doping in Sport', in T. Tännsjö and C.M. Tamburrini (eds) *Values in Sport: Elitism, Nationalism, Gender Equality, and the Scientific Manufacture of Winners*, London: E & FN Spon, pp. 185–199.

Simon, R.L. (1984) 'Good Competition and Drug-enhanced Performance', *Journal of the Philosophy of Sport*, 11: 6–13.

Simon, R.L. (1985) *Sports and Social Values*, Englewood Cliffs, NJ: Prentice-Hall.

Simon, R.L. (1991) *Fair Play: Sport, Values, and Society*, Boulder, CO: Westview Press.

Suits, B. (1973) 'The Elements of Sport', in R.G. Osterhoudt (ed.) *The Philosophy of Sport: A Collection of Original Essays*, Illinois: Charles C. Thomas.

Suits, B. (1978) *The Grasshopper: Games, Life and Utopia*, Toronto: University of Toronto.

Suits, B. (1988) 'Tricky Triad: Games, Play and Sport', *Journal of the Philosophy of Sport*, XV: 1–9.

Tamburrini, C.M. (2000a) 'What's Wrong with Doping?', in T. Tännsjö and C.M. Tamburrini (eds) *Values in Sport: Elitism, Nationalism, Gender Equality, and the Scientific Manufacture of Winners*, London: E & FN Spon, pp. 200–216.

Tamburrini, C.M. (2000b) *The 'Hand of God'? Essays in the Philosophy of Sports*, Göteborg: Acta Universitatis Gotoburgensis.

Tollefsen, C. (2001) 'Embryos, Individuals, and Persons: An Argument Against Embryo Creation Research', *Journal of Applied Philosophy*, 18 (1): 65–77.

Tuxill, C. and Wigmore, S. (1998) '"Merely Meat?" Respect for Persons in Sports and Games', in M.J. McNamee and S.J. Parry (eds) *Ethics and Sport*, London and New York: E & FN Spon, pp. 104–115.

Wertz, S.K. (1981) 'The Varieties of Cheating', *Journal of the Philosophy of Sport*, 8: 19–40.

3.4

Doping under medical control

Conceptually possible but impossible in the world of professional sports?

Søren Holm

Introduction

One of the arguments in the debate about whether or not the current blanket ban on doping in sports should be lifted is that if the ban is lifted it will be possible to have doping under medical control. If doping becomes legitimate there is no longer a need for sportspersons to hide that they are using doping and no longer a need for doctors to hide that they are prescribing doping.[1] This would, according to the argument, entail a number of positive consequences: (1) that the sportsperson can access impartial medical advice about the effectiveness and side-effects of different doping methods and can therefore make a more informed decision; (2) that side-effects of doping are picked up more quickly and dealt with more effectively; and (3) that it will be possible to collect reliable information about the effects and side-effects of different doping techniques because sportspersons and sports doctors will be able to share their experiences (Kayser *et al.* 2005).

In this paper I will critically analyse this argument and show that it is very unlikely that these positive effects will occur as a general

phenomenon across all, or even most, sports and doping techniques. I will mainly focus the analysis on the situation facing the professional sportsperson, but some of the arguments and conclusions will also apply to non-professional sportspersons who are part of, for instance, national teams.

The argument that the lifting of the ban on doping will lead to safe doping under medical control is usually not the main argument put forward to justify changing the doping rules. The main arguments are usually either liberal/libertarian, conventionalist or consistency arguments, or some combination of these (Spriggs 2005, 112–13; Tännsjö 2005, 113; Tamburrini 2000; 2006). The liberal/libertarian arguments claim that unless doping can be shown to harm other people than the people doping themselves it should not be prohibited in a liberal society, since prohibition would then be paternalistic. The conventionalist arguments point out that the rules of sports are conventions and that they therefore ought to reflect what really happens in the sport, not what outsiders would ideally want to happen. So if active sportspersons regularly take doping substances, that should be allowed by the rules. And finally the consistency arguments rely on showing that we cannot draw a line between doping and other performance-enhancing activities and procedures in sport (e.g. no justifiable line between EPO use and the use of hypoxic air machines or high-altitude training). These arguments are not analysed in this paper, but as we shall see they constrain what actions we can justify to ensure that legal doping is also safe doping under medical control.

Some initial distinctions

Initially it is necessary to make some distinctions concerning different sports and different doping techniques. Sport is usually defined as 'institutionalized competitive activities that involve vigorous physical exertion or the use of relatively complex physical skills by individuals whose participation is motivated by a combination of internal and external factors' (Coakley 1994, 21).

But, as we are all aware, this leaves a very large range of human activities within the concept of sport, and a huge range of distinctions can be applied to this set of activities. The distinctions that are important here are not so much distinctions concerning the different types of sports but distinctions concerning the contexts in which sports take place and professional sportspersons are employed, because those contexts influence their ability to act in relation to doping.

The first important distinction is a distinction concerning the degree to which the sportsperson is employed and controls his or her income stream. Is the sportsperson self employed with income mainly from prize money, self-employed with income mainly from sponsorship, employed but with income mainly from sponsorship or employed with income mainly from the employer? (Similar distinctions apply to sportspersons who are technically amateurs but who sustain their sports activities by income generated by these activities.)

The second distinction concerns the degree of control the sportsperson has over the decision to play. Does the sportsperson have personal control over both the decision to play, and the decision not to play in a given instance?[2] There are in reality two issues here. The first is an issue of formal control. In many team sports a considerable degree of control over who plays is exercised by the coach of the team, or a committee of selectors. The same is the case for a number of individual sports where a sportsperson is only allowed to compete if chosen by his or her association. In these cases the sportsperson can decide not to play, but he or she cannot decide to play if he/she is not selected. The second is an issue of informal control: 'stars' may well be able to demand to play, and sportspersons may, on the other hand, also be leaned upon to compete even if they don't want to.

The third distinction concerns the degree of control the sportsperson has over the choice of medical adviser and the medical adviser's employment status.[3] Is the medical adviser chosen and employed by the sportsperson, or is he or she chosen and employed by the sportspersons' employer?

We also need to make distinctions concerning different forms of doping. I will here mainly focus on doping with pharmaceutically active substances, but I think the arguments can be extended to other forms of doping techniques as well. We can distinguish between:

1 Well known drugs with well known doping effects (e.g. beta-adrenergic antagonists for the removal of hand tremor in shooting sports);
2 Well-known drugs with not generally known doping effects;
3 Well-known drugs with doping effects outside the normal clinical dosing range;[4]
4 Experimental drugs developed by the mainstream pharmaceutical industry; and
5 Experimental drugs developed outside the mainstream pharmaceutical industry.

Legal doping and impartial advice in the triangle of death and injury

Let us consider the average professsional footballers (i.e. soccer players), rugby players or handball players. They will be on contract with a specific club and will usually play when, but only when, the coach says so. Their main income will be from the club, and although they will be earning well, they will not be able to build up savings that will allow them to walk away from the game before late in their career, if ever.[5] Their medical adviser will be a doctor employed by the club.[6] They will thus have the least personal control over their situation and their adviser of any professional sportsperson, according to the distinctions drawn above. Many other sportspersons on national teams receiving personal sponsorship from the national sports organisation will be in an essentially similar situation.

In this case we have a triangle with the employer, the sportsperson and the sports doctor at each corner (see Figure 3.4.1), although the employer's influence on the sportsperson is often mediated through the team coach or manager.

Within this triangle it is worth considering to what degree the sports doctor acts or can act as the agent of the sportsperson or to what degree he or she acts or will have to act as (at least partially) the agent of the employer. There are numerous examples of players who have been given dangerous treatments for injuries, or told to play despite injury, in the interest of the team winning, without being told what the real risk were. This indicates that at least some sports doctors do act as agents for their employers, even when this is of detriment to their patients.[7]

If the sports doctor is rational, and unencumbered by adherence to the traditional ethical standards of the medical profession or the newer ethical standards of sports medicine, it is also easy to see that this is the decision he or her must rationally make. A sports doctor who knows on which side his bread is buttered will also know that stable employment often requires that one does not act in ways that are too contrary to the interests of the principal. The

sportsperson could of course go elsewhere to get a second opinion, but he or she would often be forced to follow the club doctor's advice even if it was problematic.

This means that even if doping became legal and sports doctors could therefore legitimately advise sportspersons about doping methods, their effects and their side effects, we should not expect sports doctors to provide impartial advice if they, and the sportspersons they advise, are in the position outlined above.

If the sportsperson is living off prize money and employing his or her own advisers the situation will be different. In that case the advisers will have no interest in offering partial advice, and may even have a positive interest in giving impartial advice.[8] Truly independent sportspersons will therefore be able to get impartial advice if doping became legal, but this would not be the case for most professional sportspersons.

Remaining competitive in an era of legal doping

Let us imagine that the ban on doping has been lifted and I am a sportsperson who is being given the option of using a new experimental drug developed by the best sports pharmacologists the nation can afford. I am told that it can probably boost my performance significantly but that its side-effects are not known, since it is just out of the laboratory. It does, however, not seem to be particularly harmful to the rats and mice it has been tested on.

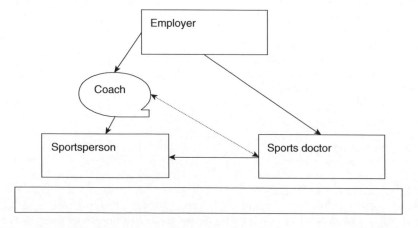

Figure 3.4.1. The relation between sportspersons and other relevant parties.

Because I am known to be a person of good judgement I am also told that I can decide whether or not the existence of this drug should be made public, and whether it should be provided to other sportspersons who want it.

What should I do? If I want to gain and maintain a competitive advantage, and it is probably safe to assume that I do given the huge amounts of training I am and have been putting in, it will in many circumstances be rational for me to ask that the existence of the drug be kept secret. As long as the drug is a secret my competitors will not have access to it and I can keep my advantage. I may realise that this will not last forever – someone is sure to find out at some point (although the risks of that must decrease if there are no doping controls) – but that is irrelevant to the rationality of my decisions as long as I get a reasonable spell of exclusive use.[9]

If I thought that there was a high risk of side-effects, it would change the rationality of my decision, since knowledge about side-effects and how to deal with them could be generated much faster if more people took the drug; but then a high risk of side-effects would make my decision to take the drug in the first place of questionable rationality.[10]

If we formalise the situation, we can see that it is a classic game-theoretical problem, where the option to 'take and hide' dominates the other options under reasonable assumptions about effects and side-effects; and furthermore that if we reject that option, 'reject and hide' becomes the dominant option. It is thus only if the pay-off matrix is changed that it becomes

rational to choose to take the doping substance openly. If a sportsperson was driven by a motive of general benevolence, or adhered to a strictly utilitarian calculus, 'reject and hide' would again be the dominant option in a condition of imperfect compliance (i.e. if not everyone is generally benevolent) or if 'trembling hand' considerations apply so that some might take the drug (e.g. because of weakness of will), and it would only be in ideal theory that 'reject and tell' would become dominant, since no one would desert from the common optimum to seek their individual optimum.

We can therefore conclude that in a situation where the ban on doping is dropped, the positive 'publicity' consequences are unlikely to occur in any situation where the drug itself, or the doping effect of the drug, can be kept secret by those who first discover or use it. We should therefore expect to see open use of well-known drugs with well-known doping effects, but hidden use of other doping methods.

If doping effects varied between athletes, for instance according to some genetic factor, we might expect the game-theoretical calculations to become more complicated. And so they are, but not hugely so. There is only one situation in which differential effect can make 'take and tell' the rational option, and that is if the sportsperson has a high degree of certainty that he or she will be at the top end of the differential effectiveness scale. Although this situation is unlikely to occur, it will make 'take and tell' slightly more likely than it would otherwise be, but it would conversely also make the two 'hide' options slightly more prevalent, since the

Table 3.4.1. Game theoretical analysis of the openness of legitimate doping

Option	Take and hide	Take and tell	Reject and hide	Reject and tell
Consequences for the sportsperson	Competitive advantage, but larger risk of untreatable side-effects	Competitive status quo, with lower risk of untreatable side-effects	Competitive status quo, no side-effects	Competitive disadvantage, no side-effects
Consequences for other sportspersons	Competitive disadvantage, no side-effects	Competitive status quo, with lower risk of untreatable side-effects	Competitive status quo, no side-effects	Competitive advantage, with lower risk of untreatable side-effects

Note: This analysis is under the assumption that if the drug becomes known a significant number of competitors will take it sportsperson knowing that he or she was at the lower end of the differential effectiveness would have a stronger incentive to hide the knowledge about the substance.

If I was employed by a club or on a national team in a situation as described above it is probably highly unlikely that I would be given the choice. From the employer's point of view the 'take and hide' option is even more dominant because it is unlikely that the full costs of any side-effects will fall on the employer. Few handball clubs for instance compensate, or have to compensate, their retired players for the damaged joints resulting from an often too early return to competitive sport after the first knee injury.

Bring back the good doctor?

Two possibilities might be suggested to avoid the negative conclusions reached above concerning the positive effects of legal doping. We could impose, or perhaps more accurately re-impose, obligations on sports doctors to act as exclusive agents for the individual sportsperson. Or we could impose obligations on both sportspersons and sports doctors to be fully open concerning their doping practices. The latter of these options, if enforced with suitable punishments for non-compliance constitute an adjustment to the pay-offs in our game, imposing a penalty for the 'hide' option. The first of these options would essentially amount to reaffirming the traditional obligation of the medical doctor not to act against the interests of his or her patient as it is for instance expressed in a large number of oaths and declarations. The World Medical Association's International Code of Medical Ethics states that:

A PHYSICIAN SHALL not permit motives of profit to influence the free and independent exercise of professional judgement on behalf of patients.

A PHYSICIAN SHALL in all types of medical practice, be dedicated to providing competent medical service in full technical and moral independence, with compassion and respect for human dignity.

A PHYSICIAN SHALL deal honestly with patients and colleagues, and strive to expose

those physicians deficient in character or competence, or who engage in fraud or deception ...

A PHYSICIAN SHALL owe his patients complete loyalty and all the resources of his science. Whenever an examination or treatment is beyond the physician's capacity he should summon another physician who has the necessary ability.[11]

And The Code of Ethics of Sports Medicine Australia holds that members shall:

- Uphold the mission of Sports Medicine Australia.
- Respect human life and well being ...
- *Provide an objective and confidential service to the best of his/her ability – with the sports person's best interests in mind.*
- Show prudence and balanced judgements when dealing with any situation that may confront them, whilst upholding the mission of Sports Medicine Australia.
- Never deny attention to any sports person on the basis of their culture, ethnicity, religion, political beliefs, sex, sexual orientation or the nature of their injury or condition.
- Inform and advise the sports person about the nature of their injury or condition and its possible consequences, the probable cause and available treatments or programs with the likely benefits and risks of each ...
- Make available, any knowledge acquired through further study or other avenues, for the benefit of all.[12]

If we could successfully enforce such an obligation the sportsperson would at least be offered impartial advice, and would thus be in a better position to make informed decisions concerning doping. We would not, however, have ensured any better reporting of doping use, effects and side-effects.

The second option would require us to impose a new obligation, but would probably be more effective if it could be enforced. It would make it possible to collect complete information about doping use, effects and side-effects and make this information available to all sportspersons and sports doctors. As long as there is some advantage in hidden doping we can, however, only expect compliance with a reporting obligation if there are ways of catching and punishing the cheats (i.e. those who do not report as they ought to). To ensure compliance with a reporting obligation we will therefore need doping control, bringing us back to square one.

There is also another problem with these two suggestions. Neither of them are available to most of the philosophers who advocate an end to the doping ban, if they want to avoid inconsistency.

Most of the philosophers who argue against the ban on doping do so from premises that are either strongly conventionalist or strongly libertarian, or in many cases a mix of these.

One prominent type of conventionalist argument is that the ethics of a sport is what the players of the sport say it is, either in their verbal statements or in their actions on the playing field. It is thus only if the players want a ban on doping, and do not regularly engage in doping, that such a ban is justified. It cannot be imposed because of some abstract notion of the ethics (or essence) of the sport held by, for instance, the sport's governing body. The governing body is almost never composed of those who are currently active in the sport and thus lacks the legitimacy to impose rules on those who are active, according to the conventionalist argument. But it is rather obvious that an exactly parallel argument can be made with regard to sports doctors. The ethics of sports doctoring is what sports doctors say it is etc. If sports doctors in a particular sport therefore regularly put the interest of the team, or the interests of their employer above the interests of the individual player who is their patient, that is how it should be, and they should not be forced to change just because outsiders have other views concerning this ethical issue.[13]

The libertarian line of argument is also, as most libertarian arguments, rather simple.[14] Unless it can be shown that some action I want to take is directly harmful to others – and both libertarians and liberals often operate with rather narrow conceptions of what constitutes a harm – it is unethical to prevent me from performing the action if I want to, even if it is harmful to myself. If I want to take doping that is my decision, unless it can be shown that my action is directly harmful to others. A subsidiary line of argument points out that doping control in itself constitutes an infringement of liberty.

This may seem to give us a reason to require doctors to be impartial since partial advice may harm the recipient. But it would not give us a reason to impose this obligation on doctors who do not hold themselves out to be impartial. If my patients know that I am not their agent, and ask for my advice anyway, I do not harm them by giving them partial advice.[15] *Volenti non fit injuria*. That they may be somewhat coerced by another agent to use me as an adviser is not my problem.

And the libertarian argument even more strongly undermines any reason to require openness about doping. If no one is harmed by doping in the current situation where doping is illegal, and accordingly rather secretive, it is very hard to see how they could be damaged if someone kept his or her doping secret in a context where doping was legitimate. If secret doping does not constitute cheating now, it could not constitute cheating if doping was legalised.

Safe drugs for doping?

A further issue is whether legalisation of doping will lead to drugs for doping being tested more thoroughly than they are currently before they are used by sportspersons. Will the pharmaceutical industry have an interest in developing and testing doping substances, and will sportspersons have an interest in waiting to use the substances until they can be marketed under current regulatory standards for drugs or nutritional supplements?

Whether the pharmaceutical industry will have an interest in developing and testing completely new doping substances almost exclusively depends on the size of the market, and thereby probably on (1) whether these substances can also be successfully marketed to non-elite sportspersons, or (2) whether they have non-doping uses. If doping became legitimate we would probably see firms studying and promoting the doping effects of drugs they had developed for other purposes, but it is unclear whether a drug whose sole use was for doping could ever economically repay the very large investment necessary to develop it so that it could be registered according to current regulatory standards. The only exception being drugs that would be of benefit to both elite and non-elite sportspersons across a range of sports, for instance drugs that speed up recovery after injury. It is therefore likely that many promising (or tempting) doping substances will not be registered as pharmaceutical specialties or nutritional supplements, and furthermore that it will become evident to inventors or producers of these substances very early on in the development process that it does not make economic sense to perform the necessary testing, because it will be impossible ever to recoup the investment. This does, however, not mean that the substances cannot be sold as pure chemicals and used by sportspersons, just that they will be untested and that the producers cannot refer to their possible doping effects in any way. A regulator might well find this an unsafe and unsatisfactory state of affairs and try to ban the sale of such substances if there is evidence of misuse (i.e. any use by human beings). It is therefore likely that a range of doping substances will still be illegal to sell, even if the practice of doping itself becomes legal.

But now our libertarian interlocutor will be eager to put forward an objection that goes to the second part of our question above, and which is almost identical to the original objection concerning the prohibition of doping in sport. It is fairly obvious that elite sportspersons may have an interest in using a doping substance long before it has reached the high standard of evidence concerning safety and efficacy that is necessary to have it formally registered as a drug, especially if this means that their competitors are less likely to use it (e.g. because of lack of knowledge about its effects, or lack of access). If the sportsperson thinks that the risk is worth taking in order to increase the chances of a good performance, what would the justification be for intervening? Would an intervention not be pure paternalism? Yes, an intervention would be pure paternalism, but it might be the only way to ensure safe doping procedures.

We have therefore again come up against an impasse in the argument. We can only have the good effects of doping under medical control if we continue to restrict the actions of sportspersons and sports doctors. The restrictions will be different than the restrictions we have now when doping is illegal, but they will still not allow the sportsperson to take any doping substance he wants to take in the way he or she wants to take them. Only open doping can be

allowed, and this would require the continuation of doping control to detect those who cheat by hiding their doping use.

Conclusion

In this paper I have shown that we have no reason to believe that the legalisation of doping will lead to a situation where open doping under medical control will become the norm. This means that one of the alleged positive effects of legalising doping is unlikely to occur.

This does not show that doping should not be legalised, but just that we should not expect the world of sports to become a much better place if it is, or doping a much safer practice.

Notes

1. I use the slightly artificial term 'sportsperson', not primarily because it is gender-neutral, but because it is neutral between different sports. It does not, as the term 'athlete', have connotations of athletics and/or individual competition. Lifting the ban on doping would presumably also make it legitimate for firms producing doping substances to market these for their doping effects under similar rules to the marketing of other pharmacologically active substances.
2. I include those sports where the right to compete in a given tournament is decided according to a transparent merit system, such as tennis and golf (apart from the existence of wild cards), in the group of sports where a sportsperson can have full personal control over the decision to play.
3. The choice and the employment issues can obviously be disentangled, but since they very often go together I do not think that it is necessary to introduce a further distinction here.
4. This group also include those drugs that are no longer in clinical use, like most anabolic steroids. Our medical knowledge about such drugs varies enormously depending mainly on the time span during which they were in clinical use.
5. Note that the average Premier League or Serie A player is not the average professional player in economic terms. Income in the lower leagues is much less than in the top leagues. Whereas the average wage for an English Premier League player was £676,000 in 2005, it was less than £50,000 in the old fourth division (now 'League Two'). See '£676,000: The average salary of a Premiership footballer in 2006', *The Independent* (London), 11 April 2006, available at http://sport.independent.

co.uk/football/news/article357006.ece, accessed 23 November 2006.

6. They may also receive health advice from the club's physiotherapist, masseur, sports psychologist, nutritionist and so on, but to simplify I will here only consider the doctor.

7. The same phenomenon is well documented for coaches who are also supposed to have the best interests of the sportspersons they coach as their main concern. Whereas we may not think that coaches in professional sports should always prioritise the interests of the individual sportsperson, even when that interest is an interest in life and limb, it is generally believed that coaches of young sportspersons should prioritise the health interests of their charges, but even with regard to young athletes there are many examples of coaches prioritising other interests.

8. Unless the sportspersons become so rich, famous and self-important that advisers just tell them what they want to hear.

9. That is, for instance, also the reason that certain business secrets (and drinks recipes e.g. for Coca-Cola and Drambuie) are kept as proprietary information and not patented, which would make them public.

10. I am here assuming that we can simplify the problem and consider only the involved sportspersons. This is probably a reasonable assumption in most cases, but we can imagine situations where the general elation if a certain record is broken or a certain achievement is achieved will be so great that it could make the 'take and tell' option the option preferred in a utilitarian calculus because it increases the chance that the record will be broken, and many people made happy.

11. World Medical Association International Code of Medical Ethics.

12. Sports Medicine Australia Code of Ethics.

13. This kind of conventionalist argument occurs in many discussions about whether something (X) is a practice that doctors should be involved in (e.g. plastic surgery or abortion). Opponents say that X is outside medicine, but proponents counter that medicine is what doctors (and perhaps society) makes it.

14. In the doping debate it is often difficult to distinguish libertarians from liberals since the arguments against the ban on doping mainly concern a right to be free from restrictions, an area where liberal and libertarian arguments concur.

15. This is simply a version of the well-known doctor/schmoktor argument. There may be special ethical rules for doctors, but if I am a schmoktor and everyone knows that, there is no reason why I should be bound by the rules for doctors.

References

Coakley, Jay J. 1994. *Sport in Society: Issues and Controversies.* New York: McGraw-Hill.

Kayser, B., A. Mauron and A. Miah. 2005. Viewpoint: Legalisation of performance-enhancing drugs. *The Lancet* 366 (1): S21.

Sports Medicine Australia. Code of Ethics. Available at http://www.sma.org.au/about/ethics.asp, accessed 23 November 2006.

Spriggs, M. 2005. Hypoxic air machines: Performance enhancement through effective training – or cheating? *Journal of Medical Ethics* 31: 112–13.

Tamburrini, C.M. 2000. *The 'Hand of God'? Essays in the Philosophy of Sports.* Göteborg: Acta Universitatis Gothoburgensis.

———. 2006. Are doping sanctions justified? A moral relativistic view. *Sport in Society* 9 (2): 199–211.

Tännsjö, T. 2005. Hypoxic air machines – commentary. *Journal of Medical Ethics* 31: 113.

World Medical Association. International Code of Medical Ethics. Adopted by the 3rd General Assembly of the World Medical Association, London, England, October 1949, and amended by the 22nd World Medical Assembly, Sydney, Australia, August 1968 and the 35th World Medical Assembly, Venice, Italy, October 1983.

Ethical aspects of controlling genetic doping

Christian Munthe

Introduction

The continued successful development of the science and technology of genetics, combined with the evaluative and motivational forces at work in elite sports, makes it increasingly likely that, in the not too distant future, gene technology will be used for the purpose of enhancing the various performance capacities of elite athletes.[1] In response to this prospect, the international elite sports movement has recently decided on a strong commitment to fight such uses of gene technology – so-called gene doping. In a statement from a conference on genetic enhancement of athletic performance arranged by the World Anti-doping Agency (WADA) in 2002, it was said that: 'WADA is committed to confronting the possible misuse of gene transfer technology in sport. The same kinds of people who cheat in sport today will probably try to find ways to misuse genetics tomorrow'[2] and that, therefore,

> There are evident risks that genetic transfer technologies might be used in a manner that would be contrary to the spirit of sport or potentially dangerous to the health of athletes. Akin to doping in the present generation, genetic transfer technology that is non-therapeutic and merely performance-enhancing should be prohibited.[3]

In consequence, the updated 2003 version of the Anti-Doping Code of the Olympic Movement now includes among its listed 'prohibited methods' the item 'gene doping'. This, in turn, is defined as the 'non-therapeutic use of genes, genetic elements and/or cells that have the capacity to enhance athletic performance.'[4] Obviously, if this commitment to the fight against gene doping is to have any force, it must also include the aim of developing control programmes for the detection of gene doping in athletes. This issue was also addressed at the above-mentioned WADA conference and it was stated that:

> The scientific community has recognized the need for the continued development and refinement of methods that will permit the detection of the misuse of genetic transfer technologies in sport. The conference noted there are a number of approaches that currently exist, or are in development, that will permit such detection.[5]

And, furthermore, that: 'The present focus of WADA's research grants toward the study of the detection methods for the misuse of oxygen carrying agents and growth factors should be extended to include the detection of genetic transfer technologies and their effects.'[6] As a consequence of this, in recent communications, WADA has announced the availability of funds for the research on and development of detection methods that may be used in control programmes for gene doping.[7]

In this chapter, I will outline and, to some extent, address the ethical implications of this development. The reason for highlighting this aspect is that the methods for detecting gene doping will necessarily have to include procedures of genetic testing, i.e., the detection of genetic sequences within athletes. Without doubt, it is such procedures that are alluded to when, in the quotation above, WADA talked about 'a number of approaches that currently exist, or are in development, that will permit such detection [of gene doping]'. However, since the practice of genetic testing within medicine and health care has come to actualize a number of hard ethical issues, this means that the international sports movement are seriously contemplating the use of ethically controversial medical procedures on perfectly healthy people. Thus, it is a matter of urgency to consider to what extent this ethical controversy can be predicted to extend also to such uses, and what implications this will have for the question of what ethical requirements must be met by a control programme for gene doping, in order for it to be a defensible practice. Procedures and programmes for doping control have until now been treated mainly as an internal affair of the sports community (controversies having to do mainly with the reliability of tests and the handling of conflicts between anti-doping regulation and the legislation of individual countries). In contrast, the newly adopted stance on gene doping necessitates the adoption of a broader perspective, where general considerations of medical ethics (and regulations based on that) are taken heavily into account when designing the envisioned handling of gene doping. Otherwise, not only will the activity of gene doping control be morally unjustified, it will be unjustified for the very same reason used when advocating that gene doping should be banned – namely, that it constitutes a serious misuse of medical technology.

I will start in the next section by outlining the various forms of genetic interventions that might be considered to fall under the new ban, to what extent it is realistic to believe these forms are detectable and what is required of a control programme to secure such detection to a sufficient degree. The conclusion is that the kind of gene doping that may be reasonable to target both from the perspective of general anti-doping ideology and that of practicality is the so-called somatic genetic modification of athletes. Moreover, it is argued that the envisioned possibilities of detecting this form of gene doping presented by WADA and the Olympic Movement are overly optimistic and simplified. Reliable control programmes will have to include quite extensive procedures of repeated sample taking and genetic mapping of athletes.

In the third section, I will proceed by giving a brief overview of the ethical issues of genetic testing arising in the context of health care. In connection to that, I will also present some standard views (and arguments supporting these) present within medical ethics as to what requirements must be met by genetic testing programmes in the health care setting in order for these to be morally acceptable. Some important similarities and differences between the case of genetic testing for disease (or predisposition for disease) and the case of such testing being undertaken with the purpose of detecting gene doping in the elite sports context will be noted.

Finally, I will sum up my conclusions regarding the extent to which the ethical issues of genetic testing in the health care setting are relevant for gene doping control programmes and what this implies regarding moral requirements that have to be met. It is argued that while some of the problems of genetic testing for disease seem to be much less troublesome when considering the detection of gene doping, others are instead becoming significantly more serious. I conclude that considerations from medical ethics seem to imply that control programmes for gene doping will have to be much more complicated and expensive than the more traditional anti-doping procedures. Moreover, ethical considerations speak strongly in favour of the claim that some degree of reliability in such control programmes will have to be sacrificed if they are to be ethically defensible.

Genetic interventions: prospects of detection

In order to correctly assess the prospects of detecting gene doping, it is necessary to begin by considering what kind of genetic interventions may be taken to be covered by the newly adopted ban. Unfortunately, however, already at this basic level, the understanding within the international elite sports community of what genetic interventions may amount to and, in fact, how genes function seems to be seriously lacking. For if we reconsider the Olympic Movement's definition of gene doping in the quotation above – the 'non-therapeutic use of genes, genetic elements and/or cells that have the capacity to enhance athletic performance' – and take it literally, it would seem to ban all athletic activity. This is due to the elementary fact that genes, genetic elements and cells are natural entities present in all living organisms and governing their functions whatever these are – hence also the performance of any athlete. However, to be a bit more charitable, what the definition is supposed to say is obviously that it is the use of *artificially modified* genes, genetic elements or cells that are prohibited. In effect, a reliable control programme for gene doping must be able to detect not only genes etc., but also the presence of artificially modified elements of this kind. The importance of including the requirement of artificiality here is that the ban is surely not intended to stop athletes from competing because they happen to have been subject to natural mutations (i.e. changes in their genetic make-up caused by something else than human intervention, such as radiation, toxic exposure or viral infection). In conclusion, therefore, any method for detecting gene doping must be able to distinguish between atheletes who have an enhanced capacity for performance due to (1) their natural genetic make-up; (2) a genetic make-up changed by natural causes; and (3) a genetic make-up modified through human intervention.[8]

As a direct consequence of this, the implied optimism in the quotation above talking about existing methods that permit the detection of gene doping is hardly warranted. These methods all amount to the same thing, namely producing information about the genetic make-up of an individual through some sort of genetic testing procedure. In the case when one knows that a genetic modification of such an individual has been attempted (as in the case of research on gene therapy), such methods may be used for investigating whether or not the modification attempt has been successful. One simply examines whether or not the desired end result is present within the genetic make-up. However, this method lacks any capacity to distinguish between different reasons for the presence of any given genetic variant, should this be unknown. In elite sports, we may plausibly expect most top athletes to be equipped with a genetic make-up that, in comparison to the average person, may be labelled as performance-enhancing (this is what explains their initial talent for sports). Therefore, to discover such genetic variants will be quite far from discovering any gene doping. In order to do that, the methods must be able not only to discover genetic variants with performance-enhancing functions, they must also be able to separate the above mentioned cases (1) and (2) from (3) – where only (3) would indicate a case of gene doping.

Bearing these complications in mind, let us now take a look at the chief possibilities of genetic intervention that may hope to count as artificial modification of the kind that is (or, rather, should be) covered by the gene doping ban.[9]

The first family of interventions is the use of genetic testing for selection purposes. Testing procedures of this kind are already a reality and are applied in health care for a variety of purposes and in different stages of human development, from gametes to grown-ups. The testing itself reveals genetic information about individuals – in this case, information of relevance for athletic performance capacities – and this information can, in turn, be used as a basis for selective decisions regarding single individuals or within groups, such as who is to be given the opportunity to develop his or her capacity for athletic achievement. The most obvious example of this would be the selection among promising and seemingly talented junior athletes as to who among these would be further supported by sports organizations, sponsors, etc. However, the selection may also take place before birth, pregnancy or even conception – thereby constituting a preselection of foetuses, embryos or gametes with elevated genetic potentials to give rise to an individual with enhanced capacities for athletic performance.[10]

It seems quite clear that none of these interventions could ever be detected. A genetic test may, of course, reveal that an individual is a carrier of a genetic trait that enhances athletic performance capacities. However, this says absolutely nothing about whether or not he or she has been the subject of a genetically informed selection or preselection procedure. At the same time, however, this may not be such a big worry, since it seems quite plausible to argue that such interventions should not be counted as gene doping anyway (although that is not made clear by the newly adopted ban). For, in spite of the fact that these kind of interventions may be very powerful indeed in producing individuals with elevated athletic performance capacities, they do not involve any modification of the initial genetic make-up of any of these individuals. They merely amount to choosing among them on the basis of knowledge about this make-up.

The second family of interventions consists of using methods of so-called germ-line gene therapy to produce inheritable changes of the genome built into the initial genetic make-up of individuals. Although applied to various types of animals and plants, such modifications have not yet been attempted on human beings[11] and are also, at the present stage, viewed as ethically very controversial. However, with time, it is not unreasonable to expect such methods will be developed and refined in the context of medical research on genetic disease. And, once they are, there seems to be no further technical or scientific barrier impeding their application for the purpose of producing individuals with increased genetic capacities for athletic performance.

Also in this case, the prospects of detecting genetic interventions seem to be rather slim. Again, it is, of course, quite possible to use genetic testing to detect the presence within an individual of genetic variants that increase athletic performance capacities. But, as before, this will in itself not reveal anything about the reason for the presence of such genetic variants. Since the result of a germ-line genetic modification will be built into the individual's initial genetic make-up, a genetic test will be unable to tell us whether an individual has this genetic make-up due to natural causes or some kind of germ-line genetic intervention. To complicate things even further, since this kind of genetic modification is inheritable, the individual that carries a genetic variant that has been introduced through such modification may not have been subject to such a procedure him- or herself – not even at the gamete stage. He or she may simply have inherited it from his or her parents (who, in turn, have been genetically modified or inherited the genetic variant from their parents who have been modified, etc.).[12] Again, however, although this is a bit more controversial than in the case of genetically informed selection, there appear to be quite strong reasons to claim that these kinds of interventions should not be counted as gene doping at all. To be valid, an artificial procedure must have been applied and this procedure has introduced a genetic variant that would otherwise not have been present. In this sense, we are dealing with artificially modified genes, genetic elements, etc. However, it is much harder to claim that this modification has been made on any specific individual and that this individual, therefore, has had his or her athletic performance capacities enhanced. Rather, what has been achieved is the construction of one specific individual with one specific genetic make-up rather than another individual who would have had another genetic make-up.[13] Or, at least, what has been achieved is the construction of an individual including his or her initial genetic make-up. In any case, it would seem impossible to speak about any modification of this individual's initial genetic make-up having taken place.

This brings us to the third and last family of interventions, so-called somatic genetic modification. In this case we are dealing with modifications that clearly change an individual's initial genetic make-up and, moreover, modifications that affect only specific parts of the human body (although these may be parts that, in turn, have a widespread influence on this individual's physical capabilities – such as bone marrow cells governing the production of components of the blood). In this case, the present stage of development can be called very experimental but much less of science fiction than in the case of germ-line genetic modification procedures. As in the case with germ-line gene therapy, we may safely expect that when we have reliable procedures for somatic genetic gene therapy, some people will be very prepared indeed to use these for somatic gene doping purposes. Somatic genetic modification may be achieved either through direct modification of the genome of the cells of an individual or through transplantation of 'foreign' cells that may or may not have been subject to genetic modification.[14] Moreover, and more important in the present context, the modifications may be introduced either in their 'natural' place in the body (modified muscle cells within the muscles, modified blood cells in the blood, etc.) or as 'depots' of modified or 'foreign' cells producing natural bodily substances that enhance athletic performance capacities. These depots can then, in turn, be 'hidden' in suitable places within the body – such as deep inside any of the great muscles of the buttocks (musculus gluteus maximus).[15]

Although the possibility of this last strategy of hidden depots creates serious complications, in contrast to the aforementioned types of genetic intervention, detection of somatic genetic modifications seems to be a definite feasibility from a purely technical point of view. Again, of course, mere detection of a genetic variant with the potential of enhancing athletic performance capacities will not do. However, in the case of somatic modifications there is something to compare with, namely those parts of the individual's body that have not been genetically modified. The most straightforward strategy here would seem to be to take cell samples from those body parts most likely to be tampered with and compare the genetic make-up of these with other parts of the body. In order to know the original genetic make-up of the individual, this procedure presupposes that the complete genome has been scanned quite early on (preferably in childhood or early adolescence when the use of somatic gene doping is still quite unlikely). If this has been done and if a genetic aberration is found that is also in favour of the individual's chances of athletic achievement, it may be concluded that a case of gene doping has been detected.[16] However, the risk of missing those cells that have undergone modification would seem to be quite high and if we add the possibility of the hidden depot strategy, it would seem that even minor chances of detection would have to involve very extensive sample taking indeed. Not only would tissue samples have to be taken from a whole collection of different body parts, the hidden depot strategy would force very many samples to be taken from each such part in order to secure a reasonable chance of detecting hidden depots of genetically modified cells. Moreover, since a modification could occur at any time, reliable detection chances would seem to presuppose that this procedure be repeated quite often.

Now, sometime in the future it may become possible to increase the reliability of detection while actually reducing the amount of sample-taking. This could be achieved when genetic knowledge has developed so far as to permit predictions for any genetic variant (or, rather, genetic make-up) what bodily substances it will and will not produce. On this basis, it would in theory be possible to say whether or not the presence of a particular bodily substance is consistent with the genetic make-up of a person. Should this possibility become feasible, there would no longer be a need for actual sampling of the genetically modified cells – it would suffice to measure the presence of the substances produced by these cells and discover if this measure is inconsistent with the individual's initial genetic make-up.[17] However, apart from the sample-taking that would still have to be performed in order to detect the bodily substances to be compared to the individual's genome, this strategy would presuppose very detailed analysis of the individual's complete genetic make-up that may be expected to reveal a lot of things about him or her that has nothing to do with doping or athletic performance capacity. Although this information would be produced also by the initial genome scan presupposed in the more basic method involving much more sample-taking described above, in that case the information would to a large extent merely be latent and possible to decipher only when genetic research had made the advances presupposed in this latter sketch of a detection method. It should be observed, however, that also a complete genome scan done on the basis of present genetic knowledge would produce quite large quantities of information of no relevance to sport but of clear relevance to the individual in question, such as information on genetic predispositions for various diseases and corresponding hereditary risks to the offspring of the athlete.

The ethics of genetic testing: a crash course

Let me now move on to give a brief overview of the main ethical issues arising in the area of genetic testing in the health care setting.[18] In passing, I will also make some comments on the applicability of these issues to the case of genetic testing for the purpose of detecting gene doping.

Risks and problems involved in sample-taking

First, we have issues regarding the safety of and possible problems with the taking of bodily samples necessary for any genetic analysis. In the health care context, this issue arises mostly in the areas of prenatal and pre-implantation genetic diagnosis, where the sample-taking involves advanced invasive procedures penetrating the uterus of a pregnant woman or the inner cell mass of an early embryo and thereby presenting peculiar risks of, for example, miscarriage. Otherwise, however, the sample-taking needed for genetic testing (i.e., that performed on people) is no more risky or burdensome than the taking of a regular blood sample. In some cases, it may actually cause even less inconvenience, since our DNA may be analysed many times from cells, the collection of which do not require penetration of the skin. For this reason, risks in and possible problems with sample-taking have not been much of an issue in the ethical discussion of genetic testing on people.

However, in light of what has been outlined in the preceding section, it would seem that genetic testing for the purpose of detecting gene doping is a radically different case. Due to the apparent need for quite extensive and repeated sample-taking, health risks due to the repeated application of biopsy procedures to various parts of the body have to be taken quite seriously. The same goes, of course, for the direct and rather obvious inconvenience of the athlete who has to be subjected to such procedures. Any programme for controlling gene doping would therefore have to consider the risks and problems created by the sample-taking alone as an ethically highly relevant factor that needs to balanced against the reasons for enforcing and upholding the ban on gene doping.

Reliability of results

This brings us immediately to the next issue, since a key element of any successful control programme for gene doping is the reliability of applied detection methods. The issue of reliability is also a key issue in the ethics of genetic testing in the health care context, since reduced reliability always brings risks of missing either the presence of disease or risk thereof (so-called false negatives) or its non-presence (so-called false positives). While it may be seen as a serious flaw in itself that patients are given false information, what is much worse, this in turn brings serious risks of important decisions being based on such faulty information – in the worst case with fatal results.

In the context of detecting gene doping, such drastic scenarios do not seem very relevant. However, the reliability of applied detection methods is still an issue from an ethical point of view in at least three ways. Moreover, these ways seem to pull in slightly different directions as to what they imply regarding desirable features of a gene doping control programme.

First, since the aim of the programme is to provide information that will be used in decisions about the application of various anti-doping sanctions, basic considerations of judicial security require that applied testing procedures have a very high reliability in the sense of not missing the non-presence of artificially modified genes (i.e., of avoiding false positives). Second, since the aim of the control programme is to fight the use of gene doping as efficiently as possible, applied testing procedures need to have a very high reliability in the sense of avoiding false negatives, that is, of not missing the presence of artificially modified genes that enhance athletic performance capacities. However, since this last requirement would seem to imply the need to include testing also when the result of the test does not unequivocally indicate the presence of such genes (but only makes it a bit likely), there is a conflict between this second requirement regarding the efficiency in the fight against gene doping and the first requirement regarding the judicial security of athletes.[19] Third, due to the possible strategies of gene doping mentioned above, high reliability in the sense of avoiding false negatives would seem to require quite extensive procedures of sample-taking. However, this, as we have already seen, may lead to conflicts with considerations regarding the medical safety and other problems for the athletes.

In all, this situation highlights the fact that the decision regarding what tests to actually include in a control programme for gene doping has to be made on the basis of a delicate balance of ethically highly relevant considerations regarding legitimate claims on behalf of athletes and the value of a successful prevention of gene doping. This balance may seem comparable to the balance between the value of avoiding false negatives and that of avoiding false positives in the health care context. However, while in health care the concern for avoiding false positives only has to do with the importance of avoiding negative effects on patients effected by the false belief that they are afflicted by disease (such as fear, anxiety and the application of unnecessary medical procedures), in the sports context we also have to add the legitimate interest of athletes not to be subjected to anti-doping sanctions in the absence of adequate proofs of guilt. Moreover, while in the health care case the importance of avoiding false negatives has to do with the rather serious possibility of people contracting diseases or missing possible treatment options, in the sports context what is risked is merely that a number of athletes may get away with cheating.

Risks of misunderstanding

A central element in ethical discussions of genetic testing is the concern for the patient's ability to understand the information produced by such a test. This, in turn, has to do with three different factors. First, when used in the health care context, the general value of genetic testing is that it may provide information about the presence or non-presence of some particular disease (or risk thereof) that is more precise and accurate than the information that may be obtained by other means. This is of value since such information may be used by the patient to improve his or her decision-making regarding the application of medical procedures or various health-related 'life-style choices'. Second, the information regarding the nature of a detected disease and the pros and cons of available medical procedures that may be used for counteracting this disease may be highly complex and ambiguous and, therefore, hard to comprehend even for a medical specialist. Third, in most cases, the information provided by a genetic test will be ambiguous, since it will only say something about the likelihood of contracting this or that disease. Moreover, when the heredity of

the trait tested for is complex (or, as it is sometimes called, polygenetic), this information regarding likelihood will be very complicated and difficult to interpret. In all, then, although a genetic test may in theory provide information that helps the patient to make better-informed decisions, in practice, the complexity of the information may in fact make more confusion than clarification. In effect, the patient's ability to predict the consequences of different choices may actually be impaired rather than strengthened by a genetic test. These problems are further accentuated by the fact that these patients are often afflicted by emotional stress, anxiety, guilt feelings towards relatives and similar states that further impair their capacity both to adequately comprehend the information provided by a test and to relate this information to a clear conception of what they want to achieve in the choices that are actualized by this information.

Now, in the gene doping context, the situation may seem to be radically different. Here, the purpose and value of genetic tests are not to help guide the decision making of athletes, but to detect the illegitimate use of genetic modification. In the course of this, it may be discovered that an athlete carries a genetic trait that enhances athletic performance capacities (be it present due to natural causes or due to some form of gene doping). This, however, does not seem to actualize any important decisions on the part of the athlete on a par with, for example, the choice between medical procedures aimed at preventing a grave disease. At worst, a misunderstanding of the test result may make the athlete overconfident regarding his or her inborn talent for sports. Of course, the test may instead reveal that the athlete in question lacks such traits and this may actualize the question of whether or not he or she should continue a career in elite sports. In this case, a misunderstanding may cause the athlete to needlessly disrupt his or her career due to exaggerated interpretations of the implications of the test result, or, conversely, to hopelessly continue the struggle to reach the top due to lack of understanding of the significance of genetic traits for athletic performance. Again, however, none of these worst-case scenarios seem even remotely comparable to the kind of choices and possible negative effects of misunderstandings of test results that are actualized in the health care context. For this reason, then, the risk that the athlete does not fully comprehend the information provided by a genetic test undertaken in the context of a programme for controlling gene doping may appear to provide no grounds for ethically relevant concern. This, however, is a premature conclusion that rests on a grave simplification of the nature of genetic information.

Additional information

While the information sought by a gene doping control programme is not in itself relevant for any important decisions on behalf of the athlete, the information provided by a genetic test made in order to detect gene doping may always produce additional information that is relevant for this. This is true also of genetic testing in the health care context. However, while in that context it merely adds to the ethical concerns that are already present regarding possible misunderstandings, in the sports context it radically changes the situation regarding such concerns.

Already today, it is well known that some genetic traits that may enhance athletic performance capacities also bring peculiar health risks. Testing for such traits will therefore produce information of direct relevance to health. Moreover, even if this is not the case, genetic traits that may enhance athletic performance capacities are almost always peculiar variants (or mutations) of genes that in other variants may cause impairment or disease. This means that if an athlete is aware of the presence of hereditary pathological traits in his or her family, and the gene doping test produces information regarding the non-presence of such a trait, the above-mentioned peculiar guilt feelings towards those relatives that carry the trait may be actualized.

These aspects may seem serious enough. However, if we consider what was said in the preceding section regarding the need for complete genome scans and extensive sample-taking in order to secure the reliability of applied detection methods, the seriousness of the problems of this kind actualized by a control programme for gene doping seems to expand exponentially. For if such measures are applied, it is unavoidable that they will produce vast amounts of genetic information about athletes of direct relevance to their health. This includes information about causes of pathologies from which the athlete suffers, elevated vulnerability in the face of various environmental exposures (such as toxic substances, drugs, and particular types of food) and, most important, elevated risks of contracting various diseases. Already today, quite a lot is known about genetic factors connected to such phenomena. However, as research in genetics and medicine proceeds further, we may safely expect that in the future this body of knowledge will expand considerably.

The consequence of all this seems to be that the likelihood of misunderstandings of genetic information produced by a control programme for gene doping that may have serious consequences increases drastically. Such a programme will inevitably make athletes vulnerable to more or less the same risks of misunderstanding as in the health care context. Moreover, in the sports context, this risk actually seems to be greater, since the athlete subjected to a gene doping test is not prepared to receive health-related information in the same way as a patient in the health care setting who undergoes a genetic test because of initial health-related worries. Besides being serious as such, these facts also add to the above mentioned tension between the concern of efficiency of control programmes for gene doping and the concern of not harming athletes.

Third party interests

One peculiar family of issues in ethical debates about genetic testing is related to the fact that the information produced by such tests is of considerable interest not only to the person being tested, but also to various third parties. The most obvious of these are the relatives of the tested person. If a test reveals the presence of a health-related genetic trait in an individual, this immediately implies that the relatives of this individual have elevated risks of carrying the same trait. The question then arises whether or not these relatives can be said to have a legitimate claim to the information in question and, if so, how one should handle the not very uncommon phenomenon of people who do not wish their relatives to be informed about the result after having been subjected to a genetic test. On the one hand, informing the relatives in such cases may be seen as a serious invasion of the privacy of the patient through the compromising of the integrity of patient records. On the other, the very fact that the patient is given the information from the genetic test means that he or she receives genetic information about his or her relatives without their prior consent. Moreover, if the relatives are informed, it may turn out that they do not want this information and consider this act an invasion of their privacy. However, whether or not they actually will react in that way is impossible to know beforehand. In practice, many clinics where genetic testing is performed try to handle this problem by handing it over to the patient. However, this increases the risk of the patient not informing relatives who for good reasons would have preferred to be informed. Moreover, if the patient does choose to inform relatives, the risk of serious misunderstandings increases, since the patient is not an expert on the subject. Finally, this strategy in no way makes the aforementioned ethical problems disappear – it merely shifts the burden of responsibility from health care to the patient – and it may plausibly be argued that health care is still responsible for the possible unethical results of this shift.

Besides relatives, there are also a number of other parties who have an interest in the information produced by genetic tests. The most obvious of these are insurance companies providing life and health-insurance policies. First, if these companies are allowed to demand genetic tests, they can adapt the insurance premiums to reflect the actual risks of the individual insurance-holders in a more adequate way. This obviously brings the risk that those who are most in need of insurance cannot have it, since it will be too expensive or since the companies will refuse them insurance altogether. Second, if insurance-holders are allowed to have genetic tests without revealing the results of these, they may use this information for a peculiar form of insurance scams. Knowing that they have a high risk of contracting some disease in the future they may buy a life or health insurance policy with a very high return without having to pay the high premium that would reflect their actual risk. This, in turn, forces insurance companies to raise premiums for all insurance-holders in order to avoid bankrupcy. If some companies are allowed to demand such information and some are not, the result will then be that the latter companies will eventually lose those customers who know themselves to be at low risk for contracting genetic diseases to the former companies, which in turn will leave the latter companies in an impossible situation, where also those who have high risks of contracting genetic diseases will lose their insurance coverage. If, instead, these companies are allowed to demand such information, the result will be the same: those who run high risks will be left without insurance coverage due to high premiums or refusal of insurance altogether. This has been put forward as a reason for an obligation of those who have genetic tests that indicate elevated risks of disease to reveal this information to insurance companies. However, again, this will mean that many of these people will be left without insurance altogether. True, they may avoid this risk by abstaining from having genetic tests. However, since such tests may be very beneficial to them in terms of health, this may be seen as too high a price to require them to pay.

At the moment the situation regarding regulations that affect this problem is varying across the world and seems also to be very dynamic. This regards not least the possibility of individuals who are unable to obtain private insurance to cover their losses by seeking help from systems of publicly financed health insurance. There is a rapid development in the West where such systems are being gradually deconstructed to the benefit of privately financed insurance and this, of course, sharpens the seriousness of the issues mentioned above.[20] Moreover, the case of insurance companies will most likely soon be complemented by the interest of employers to avoid an unhealthy workforce – especially so if employers (as is often the case) are responsible for paying the insurance premiums of employees in a predominantly private system of health insurance.

From the point of view of programmes for controlling gene doping, this complex of problems is actualized mainly due to the phenomenon of additional information. Since the gene doping tests will unavoidably produce health-related information about athletes, the latter will be exposed to the various risks arising out of the interest in this information from various third parties. Moreover, sports officials will therefore have to consider the peculiar issue of whether or not the results of tests should be revealed to such third parties when requested.

In the case of tests done within health care, the normal procedure is that the tested individual is the owner of the information produced by the test. Therefore, if he or she agrees to the right of, for example, an insurance company to inspect his or her medical records, health care has no right to refuse. But records of doping tests are usually surrounded by much more secrecy and it is therefore far from clear how these should be handled in similar situations.

Informed consent

One important conclusion reached within health care on the basis of all the aspects mentioned above is that an ethically acceptable practice of genetic testing presupposes that tested individuals have given their informed consent. Basically, this involves four separate things. First, the individual is ascribed an absolute right to refuse testing. Second, he or she is ascribed a similar right to abandon an initiated testing procedure at any stage. For example, the individual may take the test, but refuse to be informed about the results or about some particular part of these results. Third, this right can be exercised without any adverse consequences besides the possible loss of benefits that would have resulted from the testing itself. That is, refusal of testing or abandonment of an initiated testing procedure must in no way affect the access to other benefits, such as health care and social support. Fourth, the individual has a right to be provided with accurate, comprehensible and sufficiently substantial information about their rights and the various risks and possible benefits of testing in order for the individual to be able to make a rational decision as to whether or not to undergo it. The underlying rationale for the informed consent model is that it must be up to the affected individual to assess and evaluate whether or not the various risks of a particular genetic testing procedure are worth taking in light of its possible benefits. After all, it is this individual and no one else who will have to live with the result of accepting or refusing an offer to undergo a test.

In light of what has been said above about the extent to which atheletes undergoing genetic testing in a doping control setting will be exposed to the prospects and dangers facing people who undergo genetic testing in a health care context, the rationale of the informed consent model seems to be at least as applicable to the former group as it is to the latter. However, at the same time, the setting of doping control within an elite sports context makes the full application of informed consent impossible. For, in this setting, if someone refuses to participate in the programme, the rule that access to other benefits must not be affected by such a decision will not be in effect. On the contrary, athletes who refuse to take the required tests in a doping control programme will normally be punished by temporary or permanent expulsion from competition.

It may be argued that this breach of the basic requirements of informed consent is not that serious. After all, athletes are not in the situation of a patient who depends on health care for upholding a minimally decent quality of life. To be true, an elite athlete often makes a living from his or her athletic achievements, however, in most cases, could surely just as well make a living from something else instead. Of course, choosing another profession may mean some loss of benefits, however, the seriousness of this loss comes no way near that of the loss affecting a patient in health care who is deprived of access to further care. Nevertheless, even though it may in the just indicated way be possible to make a case for the acceptability of such a practice, it is no doubt that a control programme for gene doping will mean that people are pressured into undergoing medical procedures associated with a rather large number of risk scenarios.

However, even if this is accepted, there remain the other requirements of informed consent. First, there is no reason why, in the anti-doping context, atheletes should be deprived of the right to decide for themselves, on the basis of accurate and relevant information, whether or not to participate in a doping control programme. Of course, should they come to the decision not to participate, this will mean giving up their athletic career, but then at least they have made this decision themselves on the basis of information that provides a picture of risks and possible benefits that is accurate and relevant. Furthermore, regarding genetic testing in a doping control context in particular, there remain very good reasons indeed for giving tested athletes the opportunity of deciding for themselves what in the results of the tests they are to be informed about (not counting, of course, the detection or non-detection of gene doping). Again, this presupposes access to accurate and relevant information in light of which people may make rational decisions about such matters.

Genetic counselling

What has just been said implies that a minimal requirement that must be met by any gene doping control programme in order for it to be ethically defensible is that it provides a set-up for informing athletes about the purpose and set-up of the programme, as well as the various risks and possible benefits associated with participation or non-participation. This, however, involves a whole body of further ethical issues. For it is a long-standing lesson from the field of genetic testing in health care that providing such information in a way that actually promotes rational decision-making is not an easy task. The collected experience on this has provided the foundation for what is nowadays usually referred to as genetic counselling, i.e., the peculiar art of informing people about genetic matters and procedures, and taking care of them in an appropriate way in connection to this, in order to actually promote their chances of making rational decisions about things related to such information.

I will not go into the various difficulties involved in genetic counselling, but merely point to the fact demonstrated above that the possible implications of taking or not taking a genetic test may be highly complex and involve a number of other hard choices. Issues about risky medical treatments, family relations or whether or not to have children, as well as such things as the ability to get a job or being able to purchase health insurance, are all relevant when facing the choice of whether or not to take a genetic test. As we have seen above, despite the initial appearance that gene doping tests would not involve such matters, in fact, they would have to if they are going to be minimally efficient.

The lesson learned within genetic counselling is primarily that this activity requires quite a lot of time and resources. A tentative conclusion would therefore seem to be that if gene doping control programmes are to be ethically justified, they will at least have to be much more time-consuming and expensive than envisaged in the minds of those sports officials supporting the ban on gene doping.

What is good enough to offer?

This takes us to the final of those ethical issues arising in the field of genetic testing in health care on which I will comment. For, on the basis of all those other issues that have been described above, it is always an open question whether a certain genetic test should be offered or not. Furthermore, the decision to offer such a test is open to moral criticism if the test can be shown not to be 'good enough'. As a general possibility regarding all medical procedures, assessing whether or not a genetic test is good enough, of course, includes balancing its risks and possible benefits. However, as we have seen above, the possible risks associated with genetic tests go far beyond the possibility of direct and simple physical injury. For this reason, in many cases, health care may decide not to offer genetic tests that are from a narrow medical perspective not very dangerous. This is due to the large number of secondary risks associated with the phenomena of misunderstanding and additional information, as well as the problems involved of providing appropriate genetic counselling.

These decisions are taken despite the fact that the tests may also provide some medical benefits. However, in the case of gene doping control programmes, the benefits of the tests are not even medical. They are about upholding and enforcing a rule within the peculiar field of elite sports. On this basis, it does not seem unreasonable to conclude that normal medical ethical reasoning would not approve of the use of several genetic tests in this area, although these may be approved in a health care setting. Or, at least, such reasoning would require much more limitations and safeguards than would be required in a health care context.

Conclusion

It may, of course, be questioned why the international elite sports community should worry about standards and values adopted and developed in the health care context. After all, elite sports is a world of its own and in many ways it may seem to celebrate values and virtues quite opposed to that of medicine and care. However, when the sports community starts to incorporate and advocate the use of medical procedures, it may be argued that considerations of medical ethics become paramount. To this may be added that one powerful reason put forward in official anti-doping statements, including those concerning gene doping, refer to doping procedures as a misuse of health care resources. If the sports community embarks on control programmes for gene doping without taking into serious consideration those aspects related in this chapter, it may quite reasonably be claimed that such programmes would be at least as much of a misuse of health care resources as would gene doping itself.

Summarizing what has been concluded above, the most important lesson seems to be that considerations of medical ethics make a strong case for the claim that a maximally efficient control programme for gene doping is impossible to justify from an ethical point of view. First, there seem to be powerful reasons supporting the suggestion that at least some of the reliability of such a programme would have to be sacrificed. Second, equally powerful arguments support the requirement that an ethically defensible programme of this sort would need to include procedures for genetic counselling and informed consent that will require quite a lot of time, manpower and, therefore, money. Some of the aspects necessitating such steps may be avoided, but then the reliability of the programme would be significantly affected for the worse. On top of that, sports officials will have to consider appropriate policies regarding the handling of genetic information resulting from such a programme, for example, in relation to the interest of insurance companies.

If the international sports community continues to follow the route relating to gene doping on which it has embarked, it is of considerable importance that the discussion of the ethical implications is given a high priority. If not, not only will this run contary to values that are condoned by the rest of society, as well as this community itself, but the programmes designed to protect the dignity of the institution of elite sports will run evident risks of causing serious harm to many athletes as well as their relatives.

Acknowledgements

The work on this chapter has been undertaken within the research project 'Genetic Counselling and Presymptomatic Genetic Testing: Goals and Ethics for Clinical Practice, Caring and Education'. I am grateful to the Swedish Ethics in Health Care Programme for the generous funding of this project. The first draft of the chapter was presented at the conference 'Gene Technology in Elite Sports', May 22–23 2003, Stockholm. I am grateful to the organizers of this conference for inviting me and, in particular, to the participants for comments and questions that have made several substantial improvements to the chapter.

Notes

1. In a recent overview by leading experts in the field (Pérusse *et al.*, 2003), it is reported that the number of genes identified to have some type of relevance to physical performance has increased from 29 in 2000 to 106 in 2002 – and this in spite of the fact that there are still large portions of the human genome left unaccounted for. Various ways in which such knowledge may be used for the enhancement of athletic performance capacities and reasons for why these will quite likely be used when technically feasible are described in Munthe (2000, 2002).
2. WADA statement available at: http://www.wada-ama.org/en/t3.asp?p=29627&x=1&a=58573 (16 June 2003).
3. Ibid.
4. 'Olympic Movement Anti-doping Code, Appendix A: Prohibited Classes of Substances and Prohibited Methods 2003', available at http://multimedia.olympic.org/pdf/en_report_542.pdf (accessed June 16, 2003).
5. See note 2.
6. Ibid.
7. Available at: http://www.wada-ama.org/en/t3.asp?p=31748, and http://www.wada-ama.org/en/t3.asp?p=31750 (accessed 16 June 2003).
8. A further problem, of course, is to draw the line between therapeutic and non-therapeutic modifications. However, this problem is less of a technical nature, but rather has to do with the problem of distinguishing clearly between normality and pathology on the conceptual level.

9. I am here building heavily on Munthe (2000), and, to some extent, also Munthe (2002).

10. See Munthe (1999a), for more about such possibilities, as well as the ethical issues arising due to these.

11. Actually, one such attempt has been reported. However, this attempt did not involve changes of that part of the DNA residing within the nucleus of our cells, but rather the so-called mitochondrial DNA, which resides in the plasma of the cell, outside of the nucleus, and governs some basic functions of the energy supply and transport of the cell (see Barritt *et al.*, 2001). Changes to this form of DNA will not be inheritable in the simple way as other germ-line genetic changes, but only if the carrier of the modified DNA is a woman (since the heritability of mitochondrial DNA is strictly maternal). Moreover, the attempt to modify this type of DNA in the germ-line that has been reported was not done in order to achieve any special result regarding the features of the resulting child, but only to facilitate the successful procreation of couples burdened by very peculiar types of fertility problems. Nevertheless, however, it is in the report regarding the ongoing mapping of genetic traits relevant to athletic performance.

12. In conversation with various geneticists, I have been presented with the suggestion that genetic sequences inserted through gene therapy may be 'marked' in some way (such as a small part of 'empty' DNA of the type used for the so-called DNA-fingerprinting used in forensic medicine). Such marking may, it has then been proposed, be made obligatory through various regulations (such as rules for genetic research and for the patenting of genetic sequences) and subsequently used for distinguishing genetic variants which are present due to human intervention from those that are not. However, this suggestion presupposes that those who make use of gene therapy for enhancing athletic capacities will actually adhere to the requirements of such regulations – something that may be seriously doubted if such uses of gene therapy are covered by the ban on gene doping.

13. See Munthe (1999b) for a more in-depth argument to this effect.

14. To be more precise, cells that are neither part of this individual's initial cellular make-up, nor products of the regeneration of this make-up.

15. Edvard Smith, Professor of Molecular Genetic Medicine at the Karolinska Institute, made me aware of this important possibility. Professor Smith presented this idea at a Swedish conference on the use of genetic technology in sports – 'Sport, hälsa och genteknik' – held in Stockholm, 3 October 2002.

16. There are, it must be admitted, also the theoretical possibilities of the individual being a so-called genetic mosaic (i.e., carrying different genetic make-ups in different cells) and that this condition has been missed by the initial genome scan (which is not unlikely), or having been the subject of a local natural genetic mutation since the intial genome scan took place. However, the first of these conditions is extremely rare and, although natural mutations are not uncommon, the likelihood of any of these phenomena to be combined with a distinct enhancement of athletic performance capacities is so unlikely that it may reasonably be claimed to be virtually non-existent.

17. Not that the picture needs any further complications, but it must be mentioned that this latter method may be counteracted if it becomes possible to turn the modified genes 'on' and 'off' at will, i.e., to intentionally and precisely regulate whether or not they produce any bodily substances that may be compared to the initial genetic make-up. In that case, athletes could have their modified genes 'turned off' up to the point of competition, eat or inject something (which may in itself be a completely innocent thing to consume) that turns them 'on' just before competition, and then again use the intake of something else to turn the modified genes 'off' as soon as the competition is finished.

18. For a standard presentation of these issues, see, for example, 'Genetic Testing and Screening' in the *Encyclopedia of Bioethics*.

19. In particular, this concerns traits of relevance to athletic performance capacity, the heredity of which is more complex than classic monogenetic heredity.

20. See Radetzki *et al.* (2003) for more on this.

References

Barritt, J.A., Brenner, C.A., Malter, H.E. and Cohen, J. (2001) 'Mitochondria in Human Offspring Derived from Ooplasmic Transplantation', *Human Reproduction*, 16(3): 513–16.

Encyclopedia of Bioethics (1995) 'Genetic Testing and Screening', revised edition, vol. 2, London: Simon & Schuster and Prentice Hall International.

International Olympic Committee (IOC), Official website of public documents, URL: http://multimedia.olympic.org

Munthe, C. (1999a) *Pure Selection: The Ethics of Preimplantation Genetic Diagnosis and Choosing Children without Abortion*. Göteborg: Acta Universitatis Gothoburgensis.

Munthe, C. (1999b) 'Genetic Treatment and Preselection: Ethical Similarities and Differences', in

A. Nordgren (ed.) *Gene Therapy and Ethics*. Uppsala: Acta Universitatis Upsaliensis.

Munthe, C. (2000) 'Selected Champions: Making Winners in the Age of Genetic Technology', in C.M. Tamburrini and T. Tännsjö (eds) *Values in Sport: Elitism, Nationalism, Gender Equality and the Scientific Manufacture of Winners*. London: E & FN Spon.

Munthe, C. (2002) 'Prospects and Tensions in the Meeting of Bioethics and the Philosophy of Sports: Reply to Miah', in A. Miah, and S.B. Eassom (eds) *Sport Technology: History, Philosophy, Policy*. Amsterdam: JAI/Elsevier Science.

Pérusse, L., Rankinen, T., Rauramaa, R., Rivera, M.A., Wolfarth, B. and Bouchard, C. (2003) 'The Human Gene Map for Performance and Health-related Fitness Phenotypes: The 2002 Update', *Medicine and Science in Sports and Exercise*, 35(8): 1248–64.

Radetzki, M., Radetzki, M. and Juth, N. (2003) *Genes and Insurance*. Cambridge: Cambridge University Press.

World Anti Doping Agency (WADA) (2002) Official website, URL: Http://www.wada-ama.org.

Bionic athletes

Michael J. Sandel

One aspect of our humanity that might be threatened by enhancement and genetic engineering is our capacity to act freely, for ourselves, by our own efforts, and to consider ourselves responsible—worthy of praise or blame—for the things we do and for the way we are. It is one thing to hit seventy home runs as a result of disciplined training and effort, and something else, something less, to hit them with the help of steroids or genetically enhanced muscles. Of course the roles of effort and enhancement will be a matter of degree. But as the role of the enhancement increases, our admiration for the achievement fades. Or rather, our admiration for the achievement shifts from the player to his pharmacist.

The athletic ideal: effort versus gift

This suggests that our moral response to enhancement is a response to the diminished agency of the person whose achievement is enhanced. The more the athlete relies on drugs or genetic fixes, the less his performance represents his achievement. At the extreme, we might imagine a robotic, bionic athlete who, thanks to implanted computer chips that perfect the angle and timing of his swing, hits every pitch in the strike zone for a home run. The bionic athlete would not be an agent at all; "his" achievements would be those of his inventor. According to this view, enhancement threatens our humanity by eroding human agency. Its ultimate expression is a wholly mechanistic understanding of human action at odds with human freedom and moral responsibility.

Though there is much to be said for this account, I do not think that the main problem with enhancement and genetic engineering is that they undermine effort and erode human agency.[1] The deeper danger is that they represent a kind of hyper-agency, a Promethean aspiration to remake nature, including human nature, to serve our purposes and satisfy our desires. The problem is not the drift to mechanism but the drive to mastery. And what the drive to mastery misses, and may even destroy, is an appreciation of the gifted character of human powers and achievements.

To acknowledge the giftedness of life is to recognize that our talents and powers are not wholly our own doing, nor even fully ours, despite the efforts we expend to develop and to exercise them. It is also to recognize that not everything in the world is open to any use we may desire or devise. An appreciation of the giftedness of life constrains the Promethean

Michael J. Sandel 'Bionic Athletes', from *The Case Against Perfection: Ethics in the Age of Genetic Engineering*, © 2007 Michael J. Sandel. Reprinted by permission of The Belknap Press of Harvard University Press.

project and conduces to a certain humility. It is, in part, a religious sensibility. But its resonance reaches beyond religion.

It is difficult to account for what we admire about human activity and achievement without drawing on some version of this idea. Consider two types of athletic achievement: We admire baseball players like Pete Rose, who are not blessed with great natural gifts but who manage, through effort and striving, grit and determination, to excel in their sport. But we also admire players like Joe DiMaggio, whose excellence consists in the grace and effortlessness with which they display their natural gifts. Now suppose we learn that both of those players took performance-enhancing drugs. Whose use of drugs do we find more deeply disillusioning? Which aspect of the athletic ideal—effort or gift—is more deeply offended?

Some might say effort; the problem with drugs is that they provide a shortcut, a way to win without striving. But striving is not the point of sports; excellence is. And excellence consists at least partly in the display of natural talents and gifts that are no doing of the athlete who possesses them. This is an uncomfortable fact for democratic societies. We want to believe that success, in sports and in life, is something we earn, not something we inherit. Natural gifts, and the admiration they inspire, embarrass the meritocratic faith; they cast doubt on the conviction that praise and rewards flow from effort alone. In the face of this embarrassment, we inflate the moral significance of effort and striving, and depreciate giftedness. This distortion can be seen, for example, in television coverage of the Olympics, which focuses less on the feats the athletes perform than on heart-rending stories of the hardships they have overcome, the obstacles they have surmounted, and the struggles they have waged to triumph over an injury, or a difficult upbringing, or political turmoil in their native land.

If effort were the highest athletic ideal, then the sin of enhancement would be the evasion of training and hard work. But effort isn't everything. No one believes that a mediocre basketball player who works and trains even harder than Michael Jordan deserves greater acclaim or a bigger contract. The real problem with genetically altered athletes is that they corrupt athletic competition as a human activity that honors the cultivation and display of natural talents.

From this standpoint, enhancement can be seen as the ultimate expression of the ethic of effort and willfulness, a kind of high-tech striving. The ethic of willfulness and the biotechnological powers it now enlists are both arrayed against the claims of giftedness.

Performance enhancement: high tech and low tech

The line between cultivating natural gifts and corrupting them with artifice may not always be clear. In the beginning, runners ran barefoot. The person who donned the first pair of running shoes may have been accused of tainting the race. The accusation would have been unjust; provided everyone has access to them, running shoes highlight rather than obscure the excellence the race is meant to display. The same cannot be said of all devices athletes employ to improve their performance. When it was discovered that Rosie Ruiz won the 1980 Boston Marathon by slipping away from the pack and riding the subway for part of the race, her prize was withdrawn. The hard cases lie somewhere between running shoes and the subway.

Innovations in equipment are a kind of enhancement, open always to the question of whether they perfect or obscure the skills essential to the game. But bodily enhancement seems to raise the hardest questions. Defenders of enhancement argue that drugs and genetic interventions are no different from other ways athletes alter their bodies to improve their performance, such as with special diets, vitamins, energy bars, over-the-counter supplements, rigorous training regimes, even surgery. Tiger Woods had eyesight so poor he couldn't read the large E on the eye chart. In 1999 he underwent Lasik eye surgery to improve his vision, and he won his next five tournaments.[2]

The remedial nature of the eye surgery makes it easy to accept. But what if Woods had normal vision and wanted to improve it? Or suppose, as seems to be the case, that the laser treatment gave him better eyesight than the average golfer. Would that make the surgery an illegitimate enhancement?

The answer depends on whether improving the eyesight of golfers is more likely to perfect or to distort the talents and skills that golf at its best is meant to test. The defenders of enhancement are right to this extent: The legitimacy of vision enhancement for golfers does not depend on the means they employ—whether surgery, contact lenses, eye exercises, or copious amounts of carrot juice. If enhancement is troubling because it distorts and overrides natural gifts, the problem is not unique to drugs and genetic alterations; similar objections can also be raised against types of enhancement we commonly accept, such as training and diet.

When, in 1954, Roger Bannister became the first person to break the four-minute mile, his training consisted of a run with friends during his lunch break at the hospital where he worked as a medical student.[3] By the standards of today's training routines, Bannister might as well have been running barefoot. Hoping to improve the performance of American marathon runners, the Nike corporation now sponsors a high-tech training experiment in a hermetically sealed "altitude house" in Portland, Oregon. Molecular filters remove enough oxygen from the house to simulate the thin air found at altitudes of 12,000 to 17,000 feet. Five promising runners have been recruited to live in the house for four to five years, to test the "live high, train low" theory of endurance training. By sleeping at the altitude of the Himalayas, the runners boost their production of oxygen-carrying red blood cells, a key factor in endurance. By working out at sea level—they run more than 100 miles a week—they are able to push their muscles to the maximum. The house is also equipped with devices that monitor the athletes' heart rates, red blood cell counts, oxygen consumption, hormone levels, and brain waves, allowing them to set the time and intensity of their training according to physiological indicators.[4]

The International Olympic Committee is trying to decide whether to ban artificial altitude training. It already prohibits other means by which athletes boost stamina by increasing their concentration of red blood cells, including blood transfusions and injections of erythropoietin (EPO), a hormone produced by the kidneys that stimulates red blood cell production. A synthetic version of EPO, developed to help dialysis patients, has become a popular if illicit performance enhancer for distance runners, cyclists, and cross-country skiers. The IOC instituted testing for EPO use at the Sydney games in 2000, but a new form of EPO gene therapy may prove more difficult to detect than the synthetic version. Scientists working with baboons have found a way to insert a new copy of the gene that produces EPO. Before long, genetically modified runners and cyclists may be able to generate higher-than-normal levels of their own natural EPO for an entire season or longer.[5]

Here is the ethical conundrum: If EPO injections and genetic modifications are objectionable, why isn't Nike's "altitude house" also objectionable? The effect on performance is the same—increasing aerobic endurance by boosting the blood's capacity to carry oxygen to the muscles. It hardly seems nobler to thicken the blood by sleeping in a sealed room with thin air than by injecting hormones or altering one's genes. In 2006 the ethics panel of the World Anti-Doping Agency followed this logic in concluding that the use of low-oxygen chambers and tents (artificial "hypoxic devices") violates "the spirit of sport." This determination brought protests from cyclists, runners, and companies that sell the devices.[6]

If some forms of training are questionable routes to enhanced performance, so are some dietary practices. Over the past thirty years, the size of football players in the NFL has dramatically increased. The average weight of an offensive lineman in the 1972 Super Bowl was an already ample 248 pounds. By 2002 the average Super Bowl lineman weighed 304 pounds, and the Dallas Cowboys boasted the NFL's first 400-pound player, tackle Aaron Gibson, officially listed at 422 pounds. Steroid use no doubt accounted for some of the weight gain among players, especially in the 1970s and 1980s. But steroids were banned in 1990 and the weight increase continued, largely through food intake of gargantuan proportions by linemen eager to make the roster. As Selena Roberts wrote in the *New York Times*, "For some players under intense pressure to add pounds, the science of size comes down to a cocktail of unregulated supplements and a bag of cheeseburgers."[7]

There is nothing high-tech about a mountain of Big Macs. And yet encouraging athletes to use mega-calorie diets to turn themselves into 400-pound human shields and battering rams is as ethically questionable as encouraging them to bulk up through the use of steroids, human growth hormone, or genetic alterations. Whatever the means, the push for supersized players is degrading to the game and to the dignity of those who transform their bodies to meet its demands. A retired NFL Hall of Fame lineman laments that the overgrown linemen of today, too big to run sweeps and screens, are capable only of high impact "belly-bumping": "That's all they're doing out there. They are not as athletic, not as quick. They don't use their feet."[8] Enhancing performance by mainlining cheeseburgers does not cultivate athletic excellence but overrides it in favor of a bone-crushing spectacle.

The most familiar argument for banning drugs like steroids is that they endanger athletes' health. But safety is not the only reason to restrict performance-enhancing drugs and technologies. Even enhancements that are safe and accessible to all can threaten the integrity of the game. It is true that, if the rules permitted all manner of drugs, supplements, equipment, and training methods, their use would not constitute cheating. But cheating is not the only way a sport can be corrupted. Honoring the integrity of a sport means more than playing by the rules, or enforcing them. It means writing the rules in a way that honors the excellences central to the game and rewards the skills of those who play it best.

The essence of the game

Some ways of playing the game, and preparing for it, run the risk of transforming it into something else—something less like a sport and more like a spectacle. A game in which genetically altered sluggers routinely hit home runs might be amusing for a time, but it would lack the human drama and complexity of baseball, in which even the greatest hitters fail more often than they succeed. (Even the fun of watching the annual home-run hitting contest staged by Major League Baseball, a fairly innocent spectacle, presupposes some acquaintance with the real thing—a game in which home runs, far from routine, figure as heroic moments in a larger drama.)

The difference between a sport and a spectacle is the difference between real basketball and "trampoline basketball," in which players can launch themselves high above the basket and dunk the ball; it is the difference between real wrestling and the version staged by the World Wrestling Federation (WWF), in which wrestlers attack their opponents with folding chairs. Spectacles, by isolating and exaggerating through artifice an attention-grabbing feature of a sport, depreciate the natural talents and gifts that the greatest players display. In a game that allowed basketball players to use a trampoline, Michael Jordan's athleticism would no longer loom as large.

Of course, not all innovations in training and equipment corrupt the game. Some, like baseball gloves and graphite tennis rackets, improve it. How can we distinguish changes that improve from those that corrupt? No simple principle can resolve the question once and for all. The answer depends on the nature of the sport, and on whether the new technology highlights or obscures the talents and skills that distinguish the best players. Running shoes improved foot races by reducing the risk that runners would be hampered by contingencies unrelated to the race (like stepping barefoot on a sharp pebble); shoes made the race a truer test of the best runner. Allowing marathon runners to ride the subway to the finish line, or wrestlers to fight with folding chairs, makes a mockery of the skills that marathons and wrestling matches are meant to test.

Arguments about the ethics of enhancement are always, at least in part, arguments about the telos, or point, of the sport in question, and the virtues relevant to the game. This is as true in controversial cases as in obvious ones. Consider coaching. In *Chariots of Fire*, a movie set in 1920s England, authorities at the University of Cambridge chastised one of their star athletes for employing a running coach.[9] Doing so, they argued, violated the spirit of amateur athletics, which included, they thought, training wholly on one's own, or with one's peers. The runner believed that the point of college sports was to develop one's athletic talents as fully as possible, and that the coach would help, not taint, the pursuit of this good. Whether the coach was a legitimate means of performance enhancement depends on which view of the purpose of college sports and their attendant virtues was correct.

Debates about performance enhancement, arise in music as well as sports, and take a similar form. Some classical musicians who suffer from stage fright take beta-blockers to calm their nerves before performing. The drugs, designed to treat cardiac disorders, help nervous musicians by reducing the effect of adrenaline, lowering the heart rate, and enabling them to play unimpeded by quivering hands.[10] Opponents of this practice consider drug-becalmed performance a kind of cheating and argue that part of being a musician is learning to conquer fear the natural way. Defenders of beta-blockers argue that the drugs do not make anyone a better violinist or pianist but simply remove an impediment so that performers can display their true musical gifts. Underlying the debate is a disagreement over the qualities that constitute musical excellence: Is equanimity before a packed house a virtue intrinsic to a great musical performance, or is it merely incidental?

Sometimes mechanical enhancements can be more corrupting than pharmacological ones. Recently, concert halls and opera houses have begun to install sound amplification systems.[11] Music lovers complain that putting mics on the musicians will sully the sound and degrade the art. Great opera singing is not only about hitting the right notes, they argue, but also about projecting the natural human voice to the back of the hall. For classically trained vocalists, projecting one's voice is not simply a matter of cranking up the volume; it is part of the art. The operatic star Marilyn Horne calls sound enhancement the "kiss of death for good singing."[12]

Anthony Tommasini, classical music critic for the *New York Times*, describes how sound amplification transformed, and in some ways degraded, the Broadway musical: "In its thrilling early decades the Broadway musical was a bracingly literate genre in which clever words were mixed in ingenious ways with snappy, snazzy, or wistfully tuneful music. In its essence, though, it was a word-driven art form.... But when amplification took hold on Broadway, audiences inevitably grew less alert, more passive. It began changing every element of the musical, from the lyrics (which grew less subtle and intricate), to the subject matter and musical styles (the bigger, the plusher, the schlockier, the better)." As musicals became "less literate and more obvious," singers with voices of "operatic dimensions became marginalized," and the genre devolved into melodramatic spectacles like *Phantom of the Opera* and *Miss Saigon*. As the musical has adapted to amplification, "the art form has diminished, or at least become something different.[13]

Fearing that opera may suffer a similar fate, Tommasini wishes that traditional, unamplified opera could be preserved, as an option, alongside the electronically enhanced version. This suggestion recalls proposals for parallel sports competitions for the enhanced and the unenhanced. One such proposal was offered by an enhancement enthusiast writing in *Wired*, a technology magazine: "Create one league for the genetically engineered home-run hitter and another for the human-scale slugger. One event for the sprinter pumped up on growth hormones and another for the free-range slowpoke," The writer was convinced that the bulked-up leagues would draw higher television ratings than their all-natural counterparts.[14]

Whether amplified and traditional opera, or bulked-up and "free-range" sports leagues, could coexist for long is difficult to say. In art as in sports, technologically enhanced versions of a practice seldom leave old ways undisturbed; norms change, audiences become rehabituated, and spectacle exerts a certain allure, even as it deprives us of unadulterated access to human talents and gifts.

Assessing the rules of athletic competition for their fit with the excellences essential to the sport will strike some as unduly judgmental, reminiscent of the arch, aristocratic sensibility of the Cambridge dons in *Chariots of Fire*. But it is difficult to make sense of what we admire about sports without making some judgment about the point of the game and its relevant virtues.

Consider the alternative. Some people deny that sports have a point. They reject the idea that the rules of a game should fit the telos of the sport, and honor the talents displayed by those who play it well. According to this view, the rules of any game are wholly arbitrary, justified only by the entertainment they provide and the number of spectators they attract. The clearest statement of this view appears, of all places, in a U.S. Supreme Court opinion by Justice Antonin Scalia. The case involved a professional golfer who, unable to walk without pain due to a congenital leg disease, sued under the Americans with Disabilities Act for the right to use a golf cart in professional tournaments. The Supreme Court held in his favor, reasoning that walking the course was not an essential aspect of golf. Scalia dissented, arguing that it is impossible to distinguish essential from incidental features of a game: "To say that something is 'essential' is ordinarily to say that it is necessary to the achievement of a certain object. But since it is the very nature of a game to have no object except amusement (that is what distinguishes games from productive activity), it is quite impossible to say that any of a game's arbitrary rules is 'essential.'" Since the rules of golf "are (as in all games) entirely arbitrary," Scalia argued, there is no basis for critically assessing the rules laid down by the association that governs the game.[15]

But Scalia's view of sports is far-fetched. It would strike any sports fan as odd. If people really believed that the rules of their favorite sport were arbitrary rather than designed to call forth and celebrate certain talents and virtues worth admiring, they would find it difficult to care about the outcome of the game.[16] Sport would fade into spectacle, a source of amusement rather than a subject of appreciation. Safety considerations aside, there would be no reason to restrict performance-enhancing drugs and genetic alterations—no reason, at least, tied to the integrity of the game rather than the size of the crowd.

Notes

1. For this reason, I do not agree with the main thrust of the analysis of performance enhancement presented in *Beyond Therapy: Biotechnology and the Pursuit of Happiness*, A Report of the President's Council on Bioethics (Washington, DC: 2003), pp. 123–156, at *http:// www.bioethics.gov/reports/ beyondtherapy/index. html*.

2. Hank Gola, "Fore! Look Out for Lasik," *Daily News*, May 28, 2002, p. 67.

3. See Malcolm Gladwell, "Drugstore Athlete," *New Yorker*, September 10, 2001, p. 52, and Neal Bascomb, *The Perfect Mile* (London: Collins Willow, 2004).

4. See Andrew Tilin, "The Post-Human Race," *Wired*, August 2002, pp. 82–89, 130–131, and Andrew Kramer, "Looking High and Low for Winners," *Boston Globe*, June 8, 2003.

5. See Matt Seaton and David Adam, "If This Year's Tour de France Is 100% Clean, Then That Will Certainly Be a First," *Guardian*, July 3, 2003, p. 4, and Gladwell, "Drugstore Athlete."

6. Gina Kolata, "Live at Altitude? Sure. Sleep There? Not So Sure," New York Times, July 26, 2006, p. C12; Christa Case, "Athlete Tent Gives Druglike Boost. Should It Be Legal?" *Christian Science Monitor*, May 12, 2006; I am grateful to Thomas H. Murray, chairman of the ethics panel of the World Anti-Doping Agency, for providing me a copy of the panel's memo, "WADA Note on Artificially Induced Hypoxic Conditions," May 24, 2006.

7. Selena Roberts, "In the NFL, Wretched Excess Is the Way to Make the Roster," *New York Times*, August 1, 2002, pp. A21, A23.

8. Ibid., p. A23.

9. I am indebted to Leon Kass for suggesting the *Chariots of Fire* example.

10. See Blair Tindall, "Better Playing through Chemistry," *New York Times*, October 17, 2004.

11. Anthony Tommasini, "Pipe Down! We Can Hardly Hear You," *New York Times*, January 1, 2006, pp. AR1, AR25.

12. Ibid., p. AR25.

13. Ibid.

14. G. Pascal Zachary, "Steroids for Everyone!" *Wired*, April 2004.

15. *PGA Tour, Inc., v. Casey Martin*, 532 U.S. 661 (2001.) Justice Scalia dissenting, at 699–701.

16. Hans Ulrich Gumbrecht makes a similar point when he describes athletic excellence as an expression of beauty worthy of praise. See Gumbrecht, *In Praise of Athletic Beauty* (Cambridge, MA: Harvard University Press, 2006). Tony LaRussa, one of baseball's greatest managers, applies the category of beauty to plays that capture the subtle essence of the game: "Beautiful. Just beautiful baseball." Quoted in Buzz Bissinger, *Three Nights in August* (Boston: Houghton Mifflin, 2005), pp. 2, 216–217, 253.

Whose Prometheus?

Transhumanism, biotechnology and the moral topography of sports medicine

Mike McNamee

Introduction

The rise of sports medicine to the apex of sports science is something that I believe has not been commented upon. There are hierarchies within hierarchies. Sports medicine sits over sports science which sits in panoramic ascendancy over what I take to be the humanities of sport: history, literature, philosophy and theology. I wish, against that hegemony, to challenge some of the more self-aggrandising possibilities of sports medicine. Its most recent incarnation is the image of 'genetically modified athletes'.[1] Recognising limits is not, however, a prominent feature of modern medicine. Indeed it is sometimes extremely unclear where medicine ends and other social practices such as social care, welfare or education begin.[2] If, however, this conceptual inflation spreads horizontally it effects a process widely referred to as the medicalisation of everyday life. It is not the sheer spread of medicine that concerns me here, but rather its vertical ambition in transforming our very nature as humans.

In a recent book, the American conservative bioethicist Leon Kass has written, somewhat polemically, that 'human nature itself lies on the operating table, ready for alteration, for eugenic and neuropsychic "enhancement", for wholesale design. In leading laboratories, academic and industrial, new creators are confidently amassing their powers, while on the street their evangelists are zealously prophesying a posthuman future' (Kass 2002, 4). It is against this evangelising and self-promoting backdrop that I wish to problematise the unfettered application of science and technology to the sphere of sports medicine. To do this I wish first to note elements of science derived from the English philosopher, politician and polymath Sir Francis Bacon from the sixteenth and seventeenth centuries, which survive and in some sense shape the hubris of modern biomedical science. Secondly, I wish to challenge the assumptions of transhumanism, an ideology which seeks to complete the merely 'half-baked' project of human nature (Boström 2004). In response, I sketch out two interpretations of the myth of Promethus in Hesiod and Aeschylus which can help us see aright the moral limits of sports medicine. I conclude with a banal reminder: we are mortal beings. Our vulnerability to disease and death, far from something we can overcome or eliminate, represents natural limits both for morality and medicine generally and sports medicine in particular.

Baconian science, biomedical technology and the perfection of the body

Though the ancient Greeks and, more generally, artists throughout history have had a deep and significant aesthetic respect for the perfection of human form, the obsession with physical perfectionism arises as a moral imperative, as sociologists of the body[3] have noted, with the increasing pervasiveness of modern technology. In the writings of Bacon, and also of Descartes, the impulse of experimental philosophy (conjoining the rational and the empirical) finds new expression in medical science. The allusion to the Baconian ideal itself belongs to Hans Jonas, whose railing against the hubris of medical technology prefigured much work in the fields of medical ethics and medical theology. Jonas wrote, as early as 1974, regarding the potential pitfalls of 'biological engineering'. Slightly, less rhetorically than Kass, he wrote that:

> The biological control of man, especially genetic control, raises ethically questions of a wholly new kind for which neither previous praxis nor previous thought has prepared us. Since no less than the nature and image of man are at issue, prudence itself becomes our first ethical duty, and hypothetical reasoning our first responsibility.
>
> (Jonas 1974, 141)

It will be clear that the presence of Greek myths, which raise in our imagination the proper limits of the human, cast a shadow of doubt on the uniqueness of the controlling aspects of modern biology or genetics. And despite offering two contrasting lenses with which to view biotechnology, my own preference is marked by a precautionary stance. Moreover, I will claim in the final section that there is no need for the generation of a new ethics; rather that the moral sources for such evaluations as the proper ends of medicine and sports medicine themselves go back at least as far as Plato.

What is of particular interest, though, in the foundational drive for medical technologies in particular is one that fits with a very traditional conception of medicine as a healing art or as in the relief of suffering. The telos of such technology and its initial, moral, motivation is captured by Borgmann:

> The main goal of these programs seems to be the domination of nature. But we must be more precise. The desire to dominate does not just spring from a lust of power, from sheer human imperialism. It is from the start connected with the aim of liberating humanity from disease, hunger and toil, and of enriching life with learning, art and athletics.
>
> (Borgmann 1984, 36)

The relief of suffering is, of course one noble end associated with medicine traditionally conceived (Porter 2002; Cassell 2004; Edwards and McNamee 2006). But that is not the object of my concern, nor typically those of sports medics associated with elite sports. The idea is captured brilliantly in Gerald McKenny's excellent book on bioethics, technology and the body, *To Relieve the Human Condition* (1997). It is as if the fulfilment of science's quest for domination of nature was itself to culminate in overcoming *human* nature. Now, of course, the denial or denigration of human nature is not new: early behaviouristic psychology often included a claim that human nature was no more than a myth or a hangover from a pre-scientific age, and this ideology was given further impetus in the sociobiological movements of the 1980s. Nevertheless, modern science takes the body as an object in nature, capable of precise observation and minute description. The uses of science extend not merely to intervening in, but also to re-envisioning, the body. The rise of medical technology, however, opens entire new vistas for medicine as a social practice.

Technology in medicine and sports

It is easy to think of technology as a modern social practice and to assume a particular kind of technology (such as computer technology) to represent a paradigmatic example. Nye (2006) ties technology to tool-making but reminds us of the narratives in which our appreciation of those tools are rested. For example,

> In Herman Melville's *Moby Dick*, Queequeg, a South Sea harpooner visiting Nantucket, was offered a wheelbarrow to move his belongings from an inn to the dock. But he did not understand how it worked, and so, after putting

215

all his gear into the wheel barrow he lifted it on to his shoulders. Most travellers have done something that looked equally silly to the natives, for we are all unfamiliar with some local technologies. This is another way of saying that we do not know the many routines and small narratives that underlie everyday life in other societies.

(Nye 2006, 6)

This commonplace example is a reminder of the importance of locating our views of technology historically but also brings to mind a less manipulative conception than the kind which those opposed to radical biotechnologies conjure up as counter-examples. The term 'technology' has a venerable past. It derives from the conjoining of two Greek words *techne* and *logos*. *techne* refers to the kind of skill (practical knowledge) involved in making things, while by *logos* is meant a form of reasoning aimed at understanding the nature or form of things. Although we think of the term as a modern one, it was in fact first coined by Aristotle (Mitcham 1979) – but his meaning for it was the technical skills of rhetoric; literally the *techne* of *logos* (Kass 2002).

It is not uncommon, however, in everyday talk to slide the concept of science together with the concept of technology. Indeed, in the UK at least, sports scientists very often conflate their activities with what should properly be called sports technology.[4] Today philosophers of science clearly distinguish theory generation (science) and its application (technology), though the distinction is rather lost in the natural scientific study of sport. We could imagine then, that the domains of medical and sports technology might simply be taken to include the theoretical knowledge, practical knowledge and the instruments and products that bring about the ends of medicine or sports respectively. If this were acceptable, then their salient characteristic would be a 'means-end' structure. Technology might be thought of as the means utilised to pursue chosen ends. It would appear to follow, then, that technology is, in a sense, neutral. It is neither good nor bad *in itself*. Rather, its normativity is typically governed by the uses to which it is put. An example of this conceptualisation is found in the recent literature on philosophy of technology: 'Technology in its most robust sense ... involves the *invention*,

development, and cognitive deployment of tools and other artifacts, brought to bear on raw materials ... with a view to the resolution of perceived problems ... which, together, allow [society] to continue to function and flourish' (Hickman 2001, 12). An equally sympathetic account is to be found in the UN Convention on Biological Diversity where biotechnology is defined thus: 'Biotechnology means any technological application that uses biological systems, living organisms, or derivatives thereof, to make or modify products or processes for specific use' (Article 2, Use of Terms).

Less authoritatively, and even more broadly, biotechnology can also be commonsensically defined thus: 'Biotechnology is the manipulation of organisms to do practical things and to provide useful products'.[5] While such global definitions are useful as a starting point, it is important to note that they fail to distinguish ethically important characteristics of different forms of practice that fall under the headings 'technology' or 'biotechnology'.

By contrast, then, a stronger line of criticism is found especially in continental European writers who have made problematic the assumption that technology is itself a neutral means to chosen (good or bad) ends. Mitcham (1995) gives an account of this history of technological scepticism in medicine (Kapp 1877; Dessauer 1927; Ortega y Gasset 1939; Heidegger 1977) and also notes more fundamental criticisms of technology as ideology where technology, far from being the handmaiden of man, comes full circle to be its master (Marcuse 1964; Habermas 1968; Foucault 1988). Although not as radical in her writings as these latter philosophers, Lee (2003) helpfully marks the following distinction in the application of science in the form of technology whose goals are: (1) explanation; (2) prediction; and (3) control.

It is the last of these aims that I want to pick up on in relation to any ethical evaluation of technologies. Nye, a historian of technology, arrives (far too swiftly for my liking) at a softer conclusion about the relations between technology and human kind. He writes: 'Stonehenge suggests the truth of Walter Benjamin's example that "technology is not the mastery of nature but of the relations between nature and man"' (Nye 2006, 7). Nevertheless, we find more classical sources that are to be interpreted less generously. Francis Bacon (1561–1626) is well known for his remarks on the development of scientific and technological methods whose aim would be 'to relieve man's estate' (i.e. of suffering/vulnerability), and likewise René Descartes (1596–1650) had wanted 'to use this knowledge … for all the purposes for which it is appropriate, and thus make ourselves, as it were, the lords and masters of nature'. Of course, as C.S. Lewis (1943) pointed out in his essay, 'The abolition of man', every time we hear the phrase 'mastery of nature' we ought to be alerted to the fact that it is some particular group that is doing the mastering for its own reasons and in the light of its own version of the good, rather than the good of humanity (whatever that might look like).

Again, Lee distinguishes the types of control: (1) *weak*: avoid the occurrence; and (2) *strong*: prevent occurrence. And the facets comprising weak or strong control technological control of nature (or for my present concerns 'human nature') range from theoretical knowledge, through practical knowledge and skills, to instruments and products. Notwithstanding these cautionary considerations, I will consider biotechnology and sports technology respectively to refer to those technologies deployed to meet the ends or goals of sports medicine or sports respectively. What forms, more specifically, might this technology take? The most obvious uses by sports scientists and sports medics might be instrumentation such as hypoxic chambers (to assist the fastest recovery times for soft tissue and bone injuries[6]); gas analysers (to measure anaerobic contributions to exercise); and isokinetic strength testers or 'bod-pods' (to assess body density). Finally, the scourge of sports, many would say, fall into the category of 'technological products'. Most obvious here might be anabolic steroids or other doping supplements such as EPO or human growth hormone. Nevertheless, it is important to note that these products are often designed with medical therapies in mind. It is their use in the elite sports population that is problematic, not the nature of the products themselves.

What I want to do now is to step back a little from a discussion of the enhancement mantra that governs elite sports and some sections of what is called sports medicine and consider a broader and, to my mind, more problematic application of biotechnology to enhance human nature. It is an ideology that falls under the label 'transhumanism' (TH).[7] Rather than a unified entity, TH is a broad and heterogeneous group of thinkers who give technology a grander, Promethean, aim.

What (good) is transhumanism?

A range of views fall under the label of TH.[8] The most extreme is a view according to which TH is a project to overcome the inherent limitations of human nature. Examples of these limits, which most of us take for granted as part of the human condition, are appearance, life span and vulnerability to ageing, disease and so on. There is, however, a more extreme version of TH that sees the role of technology as one to vastly enhance both the person and his/her environment by exploiting a range of technologies including genetic engineering, cybernetics, computation and nanotechnology.

Recruitment of these various types of technology, it is hoped, will produce selves who are intelligent, immortal etc. but who are not members of the species *homo sapiens*. Their species type will be either be ambiguous, e.g. if they are cyborgs (part human, part machine). If they turn out to be wholly machines, they will lack any common genetic features with human beings. Extreme TH strongly supports such developments. Less extreme TH is satisfied to augment human nature with technology where possible and where desired by the individual.

At present TH seems to command support mostly in North America, though there are some adherents from Europe (see the website of the World Transhumanism Association). On one level it can be seen as an extension of neoliberal or libertarian thought transferred into biomedical contexts. This is because the main driver appears to be the valorisation of autonomy as expressed in the economic choices of individuals. If certain technological developments enable greater defences against senescence, or if they can significantly enhance my powers of thought, speed and movement, then TH argues that anyone (as competent consumers) should be allowed to obtain them – if they can afford them, of course. Sandberg attempts to give an ethical underpinning to this essentially

217

political programme. He argues that we must consider 'morphological freedom as a right' (Sandberg 2001).

Before TH is considered to be the product of outlandish free-thinkers who have enjoyed too much certain medico-technological products themselves, we must consider that it embodies two aims that are widely thought to be valued in the West. These are: (a) The use of technology to improve the lot of humans. Work in public health, e.g. construction of sewage systems, fluoride additives to water supplies to prevent dental decay and so on, is all work to facilitate this noble end that is shared with the entire medical enterprise, (b) The other widely shared value is that of increased autonomy such that the individual has greater scope in governing his own life-plan.

Moreover, proponents of TH say it presents an opportunity to plan the future development of human beings, the species *homo sapiens*. Instead of this being left to the evolutionary process and its exploitation of random mutations, TH presents a hitherto unavailable option, tailoring the development of human beings to an ideal blueprint. Typically educational, social and political reformers have been unable to carry forward their project with the kind of control and efficiency (it is said) that biologically driven technologies can.

Against transhumanism

One can ascribe to Ellul a certain prescience: without knowledge of ideologies such as TH, he pointed out in 1965 that the development of technology will lead to a 'new dismembering and a complete reconstitution of the human being so that he can at least become the objective (and also the total object) of techniques' (Ellul 1965, 431). One possible consequence that can be read into the grander claims of some TH proponents is that, in effect, TH will lead to the existence of two distinct types of being, the human and the posthuman. The former are most likely to be viewed as some kind of underclass.

It is worth pursuing this argument a little. It is said that 'we' have a 'self-understanding' as human beings. This includes, for example, our essential vulnerability to disease, ageing and

death. Parens (1995), in reversing the title of Nussbaum's celebrated book *The Fragility of Goodness*, captured this idea memorably when speaking of the 'goodness of fragility'. Suppose, however, that the strong TH project is realised. We are no longer so vulnerable, immortality is a real prospect. This will result in a change in our 'self-understanding'. This will have a normative element to it; most radically it may take the form of a change in what we view as a good life. Hitherto such a life this would have been assumed to be finite, but now this might change.

Habermas's (2003) objection can be interpreted more or less strongly. The strongest one is that *any* change in self-understanding is a morally bad thing. But this move is not a defensible one. Consider the changes in self-understanding that have occurred over the centuries: the advent of Christianity or Islam; the intellectual revolutions that preceded Copernicus; and Darwin. It does not follow necessarily that any particular change in self-understanding logically entails moral decline. There are many who would advocate that this constitutes not decline but rather moral progress.

There are, to my mind, more telling and less abstract arguments that can be marshalled effectively against TH. These concern, in the first place, a simple argument against inequality. The second relates to the unarticulated ends of TH. What is its telos? What do we enhance and why? Let us consider, albeit briefly, the first consideration.

Rather than considering two species of humanity, we might (perhaps crudely) consider the two categories of economics: the rich and the poor. The former can afford to make use of TH while the latter will not be able to. Given the commercialisation of elite sports, one can see both the attractions (for some) and the dangers here. Mere mortals – the unenhanced poor – will get no more than a glimpse of the transhuman in competitive elite sports contexts. There is, then, something of a double-binding character to this consumerism. The poor, at once removed from the possibility of choosing augmentation, end up paying for it by pay-per-view. The weak thus pay the strong for the pleasure of their envy. By contrast, one might see less corrosive aspects of this economically driven argument. Far from being worried about it, it might be said, TH is an irrelevance, since so few will be able to make use of the technological developments even if they ever manifest themselves.

Still further, critics point out that TH rests upon some conception of the good. As seen, for one group of TH advocates, the good is expansion of personal choice. But some critics object to what they see as consumerism of this kind. They suggest that the good cannot be equated with that which people choose. With regard to the other kind of TH proponents, those who see TH as an opportunity to enhance the general quality of life for humans, critics point out that this again presupposes some conception of the good, of what kind of traits are best to engineer into humans (disease-resistance, high intelligence etc.), and they disagree about precisely what 'objective goods' to try to select for installation into humans/posthumans. A further and stronger, though more abstract, objection is voiced by Habermas. This is that interfering with the process of human conception, and by implication human constitution, deprives humans of the 'naturalness which so far has been a part of the taken-for-granted background of our self-understanding as a species' and that 'Getting used to having human life at the biotechnologically enabled disposal of our contingent preferences cannot help but change our normative self-understanding' (Habermas 2003, 72). And will those TH agents (athletes and non-athletes alike), genetically and technologically modified to their autonomous heart's content, never escape from being the objects of never-ending resentment?[9]

We have seen, then, that there are a variety of arguments for and against transhumanism. It will be clear that I am not in favour of the radical or the less extreme versions. It seems clear to me at least that the project is an undesirable utopianism. We have enough problems with the human nature we struggle with, let alone another nature that we neither control nor understand anywhere near as fully. At TH's heart, it seems to me, is a view of technology at the mercy of scientists generally (or in the case of athletic powers, sports 'medics'), which is simply a case of Prometheanism. This charge is often labelled against genetic and other technologists without proper explanation. And it strikes me that the charge is not properly understood.

In order to move beyond mere slogans or name-calling, then, I shall offer two contrasting lenses through which these claims may be viewed by returning to the roots of the Promethean myth itself.

Whose Prometheus: Hesiod or Aeschylus?

In order to understand the charge of Prometheanism one might begin by asking 'What is the myth of Prometheus?' I think the better question is 'whose myth of Prometheus should we concern ourselves with?' I take my cue from Conacher's (1980) account and also from Kerenyi's (1963). though I do not attempt fully to do justice to their accounts here.[10] I merely use them for my own purpose of providing lenses to view the unrestrained enhancement ideology of TH which, it seems to me, can find an easy footing in the unreflective pools of sports medicine and sports sciences more generally.

First, let us say that there is no single Greek account of Prometheus's deeds. There are at least two sources and even among these sources there are variations. The two sources, in chronology, are Hesiod and Aeschylus. In Hesiod there are two accounts: *Theogony* and *Works and Days*. And the only full text from Aeschylus is *Prometheus Bound*, though we know it to be part of a trilogy (with *Prometheus Unbound* and *Prometheus the Firebringer*).

Theogony is Hesiod's account of the beginning of the world. The Titans (giants) challenged Zeus and the Olympian Gods for the supremacy of the world. *Works and Days* is said to be a similar account, but one that celebrates the ideas that labour is the universal lot of mankind but that those willing so to do can get by. This is important to appreciate in order to evaluate the act for which Prometheus became (in) famous. Prometheus, acting against his fellow Titans, sided with Zeus and his cunning aided Zeus's victory over the Olympian Gods. In consequence he was honoured by Zeus and seems to have some kind of dual nature: both God and mortal. Sometimes the two are simplistically dichotomised: Zeus as power, Prometheus as cunning reason or intellect (Conacher 1980).

219

Prometheus is said to have stolen fire and to have cheated the gods out of their proper share of a sacrifice. Which came first is not always clear as there are different interpretations. But both acts, according to Kerenyi, evidence the claim that Prometheus is of deficient character. He writes:

> Prometheus, founder of the sacrifice, was a cheat and a thief: those traits are at the bottom of all the stories that deal with him. The meaning of his strange sacrifice in which the gods were cheated out of the tasty morsels is simply this: that the sacrifice offered up by men is a sacrifice of foolhardy thieves, stealers of the divinity round about them – for the world of nature that surrounds them is divine – whose temerity brings immeasurable and unforeseen misfortune upon them.
>
> (Kerenyi 1980, xxii)

A little amplification is in order. Both Prometheus (often translated as 'foresight') and his somewhat bungling brother Epimetheus (sometimes translated as 'aftersight') set out on Zeus's orders to fashion creatures to populate the earth. Lacking wisdom (or 'foresight') Epimetheus fails to consider what qualities are necessary as he goes about making the 'animal kingdom'. Prometheus fashions mortals in the vision of the gods. Epimetheus, having used all his gifts from Zeus, has failed to clothe them and Prometheus watches pitifully as they shiver in the cold nights. It is here that, rebelling against Zeus's authority, Prometheus sides with mankind, and steals fire – hidden in a fennel stalk. The mortals are thus warmed.

In order to appease and honour Zeus, Prometheus reveals his disrespectful cunning. He offers him an ox. In one half he hides the bones with a rich layering of fat which appears on the surface to be the greater and more desirable share. Under the entrails of the animal he hides in the other skin all the good meat. Zeus, apparently understanding the deception as part of the unchanging fate of mankind, accepts the lesser share.

By way of punishing Prometheus and all mortals, Zeus withheld fire from mortals.[11] The hubris of Prometheus in particular, though, is captured by his punishment: he is to be chained to a tree on Mount Caucasus where an eagle will eat at his liver all day only for it to be replenished

over night for the cycle of suffering and humiliation to continue the next day, and so on.

In Aeschylus we get a different interpretation of events, one that is at once more sympathetic to Prometheus. First, a more optimistic conception of 'human initiative' (Conacher 1980, 13). A further aspect of this is the fact that hope is hidden from men in Hesiod ('fortunately', it is said in Hesiod, or rather 'for their sakes') whereas in Aeschylus it is one of the gifts from Prometheus. As Conacher puts it:

> To put the point in the broadest possible terms, the Hesiodic Prometheus, by his deceptions and frustrations of Zeus in his relations with man, is presented (however 'artificially') as the indirect cause of all man's woes; the Aeschylean Prometheus, on the other hand, by his interventions on behalf of man, is presented as the saviour of mankind, without whom man would have ceased to exist and with whose help he progresses from mere subsistence to a state of civilization.
>
> (Conacher 1980, 13)

Aeschylus does this by suppressing the sacrifice deception and transforms the fire-stealing act as one of daring rather than hubris. For without the deception there is no occasion for the withholding of fire, which is the consequent punishment. For fire is seen not merely as the warmth that forestalls the chill of the night but – more importantly – as the precondition of craft, trade, even civilization. But what has all this got to do with tranhsumanism generally, and sports medicine more specifically?

A moral topography for sports medicine

In the rise of psychiatry, much was made of the scientism that bedevilled the then emerging profession. Disputes raged as to whether there could be such a thing as mental illness (akin to physical illness) or whether this constituted the imposition of normative patterns of thought and action by state powers. The more pharmacologically inclined argued that mental illness did indeed exist but that its basis was chemical, not political. Others took it to be a case of the medicalisation of everyday life. In all of this Thomas Szasz was (and still remains) a trenchant critic. Like Kass, Szasz has been charged with providing powerful polemic more than patient argument. Notwithstanding this, he once crafted the memorable, remark that 'Formerly, when religion was strong and science weak, men mistook magic for medicine; now, when science is strong and religion weak, men mistake medicine for magic' (Szasz 1973, 115).

This juxtaposition of religion, magic and science is a troublesome one for the public no less than for gullible and overcommitted athletes who appear to lack any kind of moral framework within which to evaluate their Herculean efforts. The main concern which TH raises for sports is the following, rather general, concern: 'How are we to evaluate the enhancement agenda?' It is clear that there are strong advocates such as Miah who want to extend autonomous choice by athletes in ways that may easily open the door for unprincipled biomedical and sports scientists. Equally clearly there will be traditionalists, myself included, who find the unfettered use of technology to augment human nature utterly repellent.

One way forward is to establish better spaces of dialogue between opposing camps in order to establish what Taylor (1991) calls 'moral topography'. I take this to be a loose application of what he had in mind in his articulation of the moral sources of modern identity. Moral topography in sports medicine might be about drawing out the conceptual relief and the natural and artificial aspects of the work of scientists therein. I use moral topography as a metaphor for teasing out what I take to be the 'traditional' (natural?) work of medicine in the relief of suffering and the more recent (and artificial) goal of performance enhancement or the augmentation of natural abilities as opposed to the traditional therapeutic role of medicine. This may help develop critical but informed attitudes to, for example, the new genetic technologies which are likely to invade elite sports over the next decade and which threaten to make arcane the worries over steroids, EPO or human growth hormone.

But in contrast to Miah (2004), and to Jonas (1974) and Kass (2002) before him, the new biology and biotechnology or indeed the new genetics need not require us to rethink a new ethics *abinitio*. The sources for the evaluation of medical and sports technology were revealed long ago in the ancient Greek writings of Plato. The historian of medicine Edelstein (1967) notes the ancient Greek philosopher's task of undermining the glorification of the body. And building upon his insight McKenny (1997) noted Plato's observations, considering the education of the 'Guardians' so that medicine may serve rather than hinder or dominate our moral projects. In this vein we too should ask: How much attention should we devote to our bodies in the effort to optimise our capacities? How much control should we allow physicians to exercise over our bodies? What ends should determine what counts as a sufficiently healthy body? What limits should we observe in our efforts to improve our bodily performance and remove causes of suffering?

Elite sportsmen and women, their coaches, sports national governing bodies and even sports promoters and institutions such as the IOC, the IAAF and FIFA, all have an interest in surpassing limits. Athletes are deemed to have failed if they do not 'peak' at big events, breaking their own personal best times, heights or distances. World records must tumble at every event, it seems. At this macro-level, enhanced performances are wrapped up in celebratory spectacles primarily to sell media and marketing packages. And the circus rolls on to the next event, the next town. This denial of the necessity of limits in nature by some, the desire to remove or delay their onset in the shape of disease or burnout-syndromes and to control these human-limiting factors by the unfettered use of biotechnology is something that should concern us all in sports. I submit that philosophers of both sport and medicine begin to press such questions home in the public spaces of the media as well as the gymnasium and the university so that sports do not become the vanguard of Hesiod's Promethean project.[12]

Notes

1. The best known advocate for which is Andy Miah 2004.
2. For an example of such conceptual inflation see Brülde 2001.
3. See for example Shilling 2005.
4. The conflation of terms goes worse than this. In my view a significant portion of what is called

221

'sports medicine' is not medicine at all, but more commonly sports science or sports technology. See Edwards and McNamee 2006.

5. See http://en.wikipedia.org/wiki/Biotechnology, accessed 6 June 2006.

6. For a debate on the pros and cons of hypoxic chambers as (il)licit uses of sports medicine see Spriggs 2005 and the collected responses by Fricker 2005, Tamburrini 2005 and Tännsjö 2005 which were published recently in the *Journal of Medical Ethics*.

7. For a fuller account of the nature(s) of TH see McNamee and Edwards 2006.

8. The clearest expositor is Nick Boström, See his 'Transhumanist values' (2005b). See also Boström 2005a, and contrast with the outline of one of the movement's founding fathers Max More (More 1996; 2005). For a more detailed summary of the purported features of TH see McNamee and Edwards 2005.

9. As Rollin 2003 remarked of those who in the future might develop, and retain the secrets of, extreme longevity.

10. A short summary of the two accounts, though with no comparison or contrast, can be found in Price and Kearns 2004, 453.

11. There is some ambiguity as to whether mortals had fire before. Conacher (1980, 12) is in no doubt that Prometheus stole it back for them, which entails their prior possession of it. I set to one side here Hesiod's misogynistic account of the first punishment intended for Prometheus, where Zeus has Hephaestus fashion woman from fire (namely Pandora) whose jar (and not 'box' as is commonly thought) contains all the portents for the suffering of mankind.

12. I am grateful to Fritz-Gregor Herrman for his insight and guidance regarding the myths of Prometheus. I am especially grateful to my colleague Steve Edwards, with whom I have collaborated closely on issues regarding both transhumanism – especially in the light of 'slippery slope' arguments – (McNamee and Edwards 2006) and also regarding the conceptual relations between medicine and sports medicine (Edwards and McNamee 2006). This essay is an offshoot from those discussions and conferences which was previously presented at a conference in Prague and which was published in an earlier form in Slovenian (McNamee 2005) and has been significantly revised.

References

Bacon, F. Jardine, L. and Silverthorne, M. (eds) (2000) *Novum Organon* Cambridge University Press, Cambridge.

Borgmann, A. (1984) *Technology and the Character of Everyday Life* University of Chicago Press, Chicago.

Boström, N. (2004) Human genetic enhancements: A transhumanist perspective. *The Journal of Value Inquiry* 37:4, pp. 493–506.

Boström, N. (2005a) The fable of the dragon tyrant. *Journal of Medical Ethics* 31, pp. 231–237.

Boström, N. (2005b) Transhumanist values. – available at http://www.nickBoström.com/ethics/values.html, accessed 19 May 2005.

Brülde, B. (2001) The goals of medicine: towards a unified theory. *Health Care Analysis* 9, pp. 1–13.

Cassell, E. (2004) *The Nature of Suffering* 2nd edn, Oxford University Press, Oxford.

Conacher, D. J. (1980) *Aeschylus' Prometheus Bound* University of Toronto Press, Toronto.

Desauer, F. (1927) *Philosophie der Technik* Verlag, Bonn.

Descartes, R. Desmond, M. Clarke (ed) (2003) *Discourse on method and related writings* Penguin, London.

Edelstein, L. Temkin, O. and Temkin, L. (eds) (1967) *Ancient Medicine* Johns Hopkins University Press, Baltimore, MD.

Edwards, S. D. and McNamee, M. J. (2006) Why sports medicine is not medicine. *Health Care Analysis* 2006:14, pp. 103–109.

Ellul, J. Wilkinson, J. (ed) (1965) *The Technological Society* Cape, London.

Foucault, M. Martin, L. H., Gutman, H. and Hutton, P. H. (eds) (1988) *Technologies of the Self* University of Massachusetts Press, Amherst, MA.

Fricker, P. (2005) Hypoxic air machines: Commentary. *Journal of Medical Ethics* 31, p. 115.

Gasset, J. Ortega Y. (1941) Man the technician. *Towards a philosophy of history* Norton, New York.

Habermas, J. (1968) *Knowledge and Human Interests* Polity, Cambridge – (repr. 1986).

Habermas, J. (2003) *The Future of Human Nature* Polity, Cambridge.

Heidegger, M. Lovitt, W. (ed) (1977) *The Question Concerning Technology and Other Essays* Harper Row, San Francisco, CA.

Hickman, L. A. (2001) *Philosophical Tools for Technological Culture: Putting Pragmatism to Work* Indiana University Press, Bloomington, IN.

Jonas, H. (1974) *Philosophical Essays: From Ancient Creed to Technological Man* University of Chicago Press, Chicago.

Kass, L. (2002) *Life, Liberty and the Defense of Dignity* Encounter Books, San Francisco, CA.

Kapp, F. (1877) *Grundlinien einer Philosophie der Technik* Westermann, Braunschweig.

Kerenyi, C. (1963) *Prometheus* Princeton University Press, Princeton, NJ.

Lee, K. (2003) *Philosophy and Revolutions in Genetics* Palgrave, London.

Lewis, C. S. (1943) *The Abolition of Man* Oxford University Press, Oxford.

McKenny, G. P. (1997) *To Relieve the Human Condition* SUNY Press, Brockport, NY.

McNamee, M. J. (2005) Transhumanizem in moralna topografija sportne medicine ['transhumanism and the moral topography of sports medicine', in Slovenian]. *Borec* 57, pp. 626–629.

McNamee, M. J. and Edwards, S. D. (2006) Transhumanism, medical technology, and slippery slopes. *Journal of Medical Ethics* 32, pp. 513–518.

Marcuse, H. (1964) *One Dimensional Man* Beacon Press, Boston, MA.

Miah, A. (2004) *Genetically Modified Athletes* Routledge, London.

Mitcham, C. Bugliarello, G. and Doner, D. B. (eds) (1979) Philosophy and the history of technology. *The History and Philosophy of Technology* University of Illinois Press, London.

Mitcham, C. Reich, W. T. (ed) (1995) Philosophy and technology. *Encyclopedia of Bioethics* pp. 2477–2484. Simon and Schuster, London.

More, M. (1996) Transhumanism: Towards a futurist philosophy. – available at http://www.maxmore.com/transhum.htm, accessed 20 July 2005.

More, M. (2005) – Available at http://www.mactonnies.com/trans.html, accessed 13 July 2005.

Nye, D. E. (2006) *Technology Matters* MIT Press, London.

Parens, E. (1995) The goodness of fragility: On the prospects of genetic technologies aimed at the enhancement of human capacities. *Kennedy Institute of Ethics Journal* 5:2, pp. 131–143.

Porter, R. (2002) *Blood and guts: A short history of medicine* Penguin, London.

Price, S. and Kearns, E. (2004) *Oxford Dictionary of Classical Myth and Religion* Oxford University Press, Oxford.

Rollin, B. Baillie, H. W. and Casey, T. K. (eds) (2003) Telos, value and genetic engineering. *Is Human Nature Obsolete?* pp. 317–326. MIT Press, Cambridge, MA.

Sandberg, A. (2001) Morphological freedom – why we not just want it but need it. Paper presented to TransVision 2001 conference Berlin – available at http://www.nada.kth.se/~asa/Texts/MorphologicalFreedom.htm, accessed 5 Oct. 2005.

Shilling, C. (2005) *The Body in Culture, Technology and Society* Sage, London.

Spriggs, M. (2005) Hypoxic air machines: Performance enhancement through effective training – or cheating?. *Journal of Medical Ethics* 31, pp. 112–113.

Szasz, T. (1973) *The Second Sin* Routledge, London.

Tamburrini, C. (2005) Hypoxic air machines: Commentary. *Journal of Medical Ethics* 31, p. 114.

Tännsjö, T. (2005) Hypoxic air machines: Commentary. *Journal of Medical Ethics* 31, pp. 112–113.

Taylor, C. (1991) *Sources of the Self* Cambridge University Press, Cambridge.

United Nations convention on biological diversity (1992) – Available at http://en.wikipedia.org/wiki/Convention_on_Biological_Diversity, accessed 10 June 2006.

World Transhumanist Association – Available at http://www.transhumanism.org/index.php/WTA/index/, accessed 7 April 2006.

Cultures of equality and difference

Dis/ability, gender and race

Introduction

Mike McNamee

The general aim of Part 4 is to connect, to a certain degree, descriptive and normative ethics aspects of sports scholarship. There is, by and large, little by the way of fruitful collaboration between philosophers and social scientists on ethical issues in sports. Philosophers are apt to invent or give caricatures of facts and contexts in order to develop the theses they wish to. They are apt to say, 'consider for the purposes of argument …' or 'suppose that X or Y is the case'. Sociologists and others such as sports administrators or policy makers often complain about philosophers for the neglect of actual contexts or the latest empirical findings regarding this or that issue under consideration. Notwithstanding this, philosophers have scarcely been shy of criticizing social scientists who have ventured on empirical enquiries with insufficient attention to conceptual nuances and, perhaps more often these days, of failing to offer normative critiques of the practices they (more or less critically) describe.

In contrast to this warfare of words and interdisciplinary dissonance, each of the contributors to this Part discusses relevant models, policies or practices with varying degrees of focus on the descriptive or the normative. And the contexts for the essays relate to three complex and contested subjects that modulate difference and equality in sports: ability and disability, gender, and race.

Ivo van Hilvoorde and Laurens Landeweerd tackle a theme that spans both disability and abled body sport. In 'Disability or Extraordinary Talent' they address the conceptualisation and ethical significance of classification, performance and our attitudes towards performers normally thought to be disabled. They begin by problematising the naturalistic model of health as species-typical functioning which forms the bedrock of the medical model of disability. Here disabled persons are deviations from normality (statistically derived) and thus disabled sportspersons are those exhibiting disability who also play sport. They contrast this model with a social one where disability is thought to be a relational quality between the individual and their environment. Under this conception, any and all persons may be disabled or enabled in particular circumstances. They note that much of the ethical discussion around disability sports and sportspersons has been historically dominated by the former, and the accompanying discourses have focused on issues of inclusive access and participation.

Their essay takes two novel case studies to challenge the dominant understanding: Francesco Lentini (a circus performer born with three legs) and Oscar Pistorius (the 400 metre runner often referred to as the man with no legs). Through careful analysis[1] of the abilities of both individuals along with their specially configured embodiment (one the product of natural deviation the other through artificial prosthetic technology) they problematise our received ideas of ability, abnormality and super-ability.

They connect their social model of disability to the relational characteristics of the individual, the test and the abilities in order to match the test to the participants in meaningful competitive ways while achieving fairness among competitors.

One of the areas of sports studies that has experienced exponential growth in recent years is a sub-field of Disability Studies. As with all fields of study in their formative years much attention is paid by all scholars therein, and not just philosophers, to the conceptual landscape. Subtle nuances often bring with them complex political stances. There is surprisingly little philosophical attention to central concepts such as 'ability', 'disability' or 'therapy', among others. Elite disability sport forms the backdrop to Michael Gard and Hayley Fitzgerald's 'Tackling *Murderball*' which discusses the modes of media representations of elite athletes in wheelchair rugby in the film *Murderball* and the subsequent debates it spawned. One important aspect of this essay is to ask and answer the question 'What can disabled bodies do?' The wheelchair version of this invasion game (where one team invades the territory of another while maintaining possession of the ball in order to score a 'try' (i.e. goal) at the end of a line representing the end zone of the opposition's territory), is substantially modified to suit its wheelchair-bound athletes. Like its abled-bodied and historically male counterparts (American football, basketball, rugby), it is a game that necessarily engenders considerable collision and contact ('hits'). These 'hits' form the basis of important self-representations (strong, skillful, hard, etc.) and are exaggerated in the film which opens with a gladiator-like conflict between players. The narrative also highlights the performative sexuality of wheelchair-bound athletes inbetween the sports action.

The athletes themselves seem to go out of their way to disassociate themselves from other disability sports such as the Special Olympics, which caters also for those with cognitive difficulties. Their ethos is characterised by discourse that is, according to Gard and Fitzgerald (2008) 'hyper aggressive' and celebrates a much criticised disposition of footballers and rugby players worldwide. They pursue their goals with the intensity of a zealot: to outsiders it appears to be a case of deviant exaggeration. The extent to which *Murderball* accurately portrays the aggressive and masculinist ethos of elite wheelchair rugby is left open by the authors, who instead invite the readers' reflection on the stereotyped constructions of conceptions of ability and sexuality that are enacted in the emerging disability sports cultures.

The notion of equality in relation to gender is addressed in Torbjörn Tännsjö's 'Against Sexual Discrimination in Sports'. Tännsjö argues that sports represent a 'remarkable exception' to the norm of non-sex-based discrimination. Tännsjö argues that three widely used arguments to sustain separate sex sports participation are inadequate. First, he argues that they are not analogous to widely supported weight-based classifications, since they are based on average comparisons between men and women which elide different capabilities that are not sexual in genesis. Indeed, some women will be much better than most men in certain activities (e.g. ultra distance running). Secondly, the presence of exaggerated male aggression ought not be used as a reason to exclude participation on sex grounds since, he argues, we should modify rules to exclude this possibility occurring in the first case. Thirdly, he rejects the argument that women will be discouraged from sports if there are mixed-sex contests. Tännsjö also rejects the claim that sex classification sustains female-only sports that have unique value in virtue of their exclusively female participation. Fourthly, he problematises three variants of gender verification tests that might establish whether a person should compete with men or with women, and proposes three criteria that might guide policy-making in moderating sports towards sexual inclusion.

Much of what Tännsjö has to say resonates with Angela Schneider's 'On the Definition of "Woman" in the Sport Context'. She argues that both idealistic philosophies of 'sport' and 'women' lie behind much of the organisation and structuring (both playing and officiating) of sports activities. She argues that the notion that it would be 'bad' (i.e. deleterious to their health) has historically acted as a paternalistic prevention against women's participation in sports. It expressed in some cases a benevolent attitude by medical men who took themselves to know precisely what was, and was not, in women's best interests regarding sports participation. She notes how this position was based on poor science and worse ethics: that it disrespected women's right to choose. She also notes how this exclusion was based partly upon an unethical desire to retain all (or the vast majority) of funding for male sports to the detriment of women's sport. There are medical and moral considerations for women's and girls' sports that are noteworthy though. She draws attention to the 'female athlete triad' (a combination of disordered eating, amenorrhea and osteoporosis) that has arisen in elite women's sports and also social body-type pressures to conform to harmful stereotypes of ultra-slimness in certain judged sports such as gymnastics. She observes how these problems are exacerbated in girls' sports in addition to the long-standing fight against traditional stereotypes of the ideal woman.

Unlike Tännsjö, Schneider considers the extent to which advocates of an exclusionary – 'separate but different' – path to the development of girl's and women's sport might be a good thing. It might allow the development of female norms that oppose 'viewing sport as a battleground on which one conquers one's foes' (2000: 19). It might also allow for the public celebration and development of capacities that run counter to this masculinised conception of sport (drawn out by Gard and Fitzgerald in disability sports) such as empathising, nurturing and sympathising. Importantly, given the recent high-profile case regarding the gender verification of the World Athletics female 800 metre champion Caster Semenya, Schneider lays out three possibilities: (i) test all contestants; (ii) randomly test some contestants; and (iii) test targeted contestants. She notes that it is problematic to merely hand over the task to medical experts since gender (a social category) is not to be conflated with sex (a biological category). She argues that dispute regarding cases ought to combine social and biological markers of identity. Finally, following Tong (1995), she articulates a more gender-sensitive methodology that provides a better framework for thinking about issues in women's sports that is both politicised and justice-driven. Following this suggestion she concludes by challenging some of the ideas proposed by Tännsjö and stating that there is still a space for some sex-divided sports.

The last two essays of this Part focus on ethical issues relating to race and ethnicity, an area little discussed in the ethics of sports, or in the philosophy of sport more generally.

Carwyn Jones and Scott Fleming's 'I'd Rather Wear a Turban than a Rose' is a critical commentary on the phenomenon of crowd chanting at sports which often takes on a morally problematic character. In their essay they discuss racialised chanting intended to insult the opposition and their supporters. Jones and Fleming focus on a chant heard at an international rugby match (although it is clear that this is a token of more widespread abuse that has been heard at a wide variety of sports in Europe, from Formula 1 motor racing to football (soccer)) between England and Wales which is the subject of intense partisanship that often borders on xenophobia. They discuss criteria of the concept of 'offensiveness' and conclude that it is not absolutely clear whether objective grounds can be found for justifying the offensiveness of certain chants often heard in sports stadia. Nevertheless, the chant which gives the essay its title is, they argue, offensive *qua* racist. They discuss how the two objects of the chant, the turban and the rose, are themselves important carriers of cultural and national identity for Sikh men and English rugby supporters respectively. The chant entails an intended derogation of English supporters by first denigrating Sikh's identity and them implying that 'even' being a member of this ethnic group is preferable to being an English supporter. Both groups are thus the object of a racist slur.

There is much shared terrain between this essay and Mike McNamee's 'Racism, Racist Acts and Courageous Role Models'. Each agree that 'race' and 'racism' are social constructs whose biological basis has been discredited, and both reject simple binary classifications of persons as either racist or not racist as conceptually crude (even though such classifications may at times be politically useful). He sets out a moral register that can more felicitously capture the range and depth of racism as a vice. To do this he distinguishes racist acts from racist agents. Understood in this way, to label a person a 'racist' entails that the reprehensible attitude expressed towards another in virtue of their (perceived) racial identity, is not simply a one-off act but the product of a complex and interrelated pattern of thoughts, feelings and acts that inferiorise or express antipathy towards racialised others. Moreover, allowing for degrees of racist actions, he argues that we can develop appropriate levels of opprobrium according to the degree to which the behavior is racist. Fully and properly to label someone racist is an utterance not to be issued lightly.

Having established this kind of moral economy of racism, he goes on to ask how one responds virtuously to racism. To do so he discusses the case of two Zimbabwean cricketers, Andrew Flowers (white) and Henry Olonga (black) who joined in public protest at their Prime Minister's racist policies against the white minority in their country who had been run off their land with more or less the acquiescence of the state's forces. They did so in the midst of a cricketing tour of England, thus ensuring high-profile exposure and at considerable personal cost. Subsequently, a warrant for arrest on grounds of treason was made against Olonga and both were forced to flee their native country in fear of their lives. Courage in sport is often cited in examples where a football (soccer) goalkeeper dives at the feet of the oncoming striker to prevent a goal, or when a tennis player goes for a big service at set point down. But these strategic decisions pale into insignificance when we consider the courage of Flowers' and Alonga's public anti-racist stand.

Note

1. They refer to biomechanical analyses, although conceptual analyses of Oscar's gait and whether it is proper running has also been discussed (Edwards, 2008).

References

Edwards, S. D. (2008) 'Should Oscar Pistorius Be Excluded from the 2008 Olympic Games?' *Sport, Ethics and Philosophy*, 2: 112–26.

Gard, M. and Fitzgerald, H. (2008) 'Tackling *Murderball*: Masculinity, Disability and the Big Screen', *Sport, Ethics and Philosophy*, 2: 126–41.

Schneider, A. (2000) 'On the Definition of "Woman"', in *Values in Sport*, T. Tännsjö and C. Tamburrini (eds), London: Routledge.

Tong, R. (1995) 'What's Distinctive about Feminist Bioethics?', in F. Baylis, J. Downie, B. Freedman, B. Hoffmaster and S. Sherwin (eds), *Health Care Ethics in Canada*, Thomas Nelson: Toronto.

Disability or extraordinary talent

Francesco Lentini (three legs) versus Oscar Pistorius (no legs)

Ivo van Hilvoorde and Laurens Landeweerd

Introduction

The highly talented and the disabled person seem, at first sight, to be living in completely different worlds. Gifted persons will be celebrated because of their culturally valued talents and may enjoy a lifetime of social advantages as a result. But instead of being praised for their deviation, a disabled person may need to adapt to a world that is primarily built around standards of normality and even experience a lifetime characterised by stigmatising and discrimination. Therefore, there seems to be a sharp contrast between the athlete as a cultural hero and icon and the disabled person that needs extra attention or care; the one incorporating the peak of normality, human functioning at its best, the other often representing the opposite. The concepts of 'talent' and 'handicap', however, bear certain family resemblances. Both concepts of dis-ability and super-ability are based upon deviations from standards of normality.

Disabilities are seen as a dysfunctional deviations from normality. The division between the dysfunctional and the healthy is often built from a bio-statistical notion of normal functioning. Though a dysfunction can also be the result of an accident, these deviations are in many cases the result of genetic inheritance and mutations. In the literature there is an extended discussion on how to distinguish between impairment, disability and handicap, a classical categorisation (cf. Sherill 2004a; Ustun 2004). The semantic jungle that followed from this discussion still obstructs clear debates on disability rights and public duties. We will try to avoid touching upon this jungle by merely using the term disability as a generic term.

Athletes with a disability are classified within the following disability categories (cf. Tweedy 2002; IPC 2006; Kioumourtzoglou and Politis 2004; Klenck and Gebke 2007; DePauw and Gavron 2005):

- Wheelchair athletes;
- Athletes with cerebral palsy;
- Amputees;
- Athletes with total or partial loss of sight;
- Athletes with intellectual disability and learning difficulties; and
- 'Les autres' disabilities (a complex 'all the rest category')

Both the concept of 'sport' and 'disability' have their own specific distinctions and internal differentiations, such that a combination of both gives rise to all sorts of complexities and new issues, in particular regarding definition and fairness. The distinction between different disabilities listed above is only relevant for disability sports. There is no medical categorisation of disabilities that fits smoothly and logically into the context of sport. What is considered a disability in 'regular life' may even become an advantage in the context of elite sports. In basketball, extreme height is considered to be an advantage rather than a disability, while possibly posing a disability, albeit slight, in daily life. A huge sumo wrestler may have problems travelling on a bus, but at the same time be celebrated as a Japanese sport hero. A genetic mutation that corresponds to extreme muscle growth can be classified in one case as a high-risk potential for disablement and in another as a precondition of being exceptionally talented. It appears that in many ways the scales on which one ranks human traits are not value-neutral, or are at least established from a very specific (albeit hidden) perspective. This poses the question whether one can neutrally or objectively define what should count as a disability (or impairment), what as a trait within a normal variance and what as a super-ability.

Several authors have shed light on the philosophical dimensions of classification, categorisation, merit and justice related to disability sports (cf. Bowen 2002; Wheeler 2004; Pickering 2005; Jones and Howe 2005). Categorisation and classification are ongoing processes and discussions need to be continued, not least because our views on disabilities change and evolve, as does the technology to compensate for certain disabilities. From an egalitarian perspective one can strive for the neutralisation of luck and reward specific talents (cf. Bailey 2007). On the other hand, specific distinctions between (severity of) disabilities can be drawn in such a way that extreme efforts are awarded in order to compensate for a lack of talent. Categorisations within disability sports appear to be the site of an 'ongoing struggle' to find the right balance between a good competition based on differences in talent on the one hand and the demonstration of excellence within a group with relevant similar skills on the other. We will try to show that this tension eventually also bears relevance for the distinction between elite sports and disability sports.

Defining disability: normative or neutral

The concept of disease and disability was heavily debated in the 1970s and 1980s by Christopher Boorse (1975, 1976, 1977) and H. Tristam Engelhardt and S.F. Spicker (1974). Boorse looked upon the difference between health and diseases as a natural given, basing his stance on a statistically derived definition of normal and abnormal function. Health was therefore defined as 'the ability to perform all typical physiological functions with at least typical efficiency level' (Boorse 1977, 542). Correspondingly, disease is any state that interferes with this normal functioning. In Boorse's words:

> An organism is healthy at any moment in proportion as it is not diseased; and a disease is a type of internal state of the organism which (i) interferes with the performance of some natural function—i.e., some species-typical contribution to survival and reproduction—characteristic of the organism's age; and (ii) is not simply in the nature of the species, i.e., is either atypical of the species or, if typical, mainly due to environmental causes.
>
> (Boorse 1976, 62)

This means that Boorse's account of the concepts of health and disease is heavily dependent on an objective image of 'nature', 'natural' or 'normal functioning'. Among others, Tristam Engelhardt criticises this naturalist approach to the conceptualisation of diseases. In his opinion, one cannot analyse concepts of health and disease solely on the basis of the biological nature of the organism and its functioning. The social context needs to be taken into account as well. In this normative approach diseases are normative constructions with a specific socio-cultural background, rather than natural givens within a bio-statistical framework. In the words of Toulmin, supporting Engelhardt's view,

> The nature of health is, at one and the same time, a matter for empirical discovery and a matter of evaluative decision. We refine our sense of how the human body ought to work, and ought to be helped to work, in the course of and in the light of our empirical studies of how it does in fact work.
>
> (Toulmin 1975, 51)

So, according to the normativists, what counts as a disability and what not is as much dependent on socio-cultural values and decisions as on medical standards. Essentially, within this perspective, the latter are even to be seen as a subcategory of the former. The discussion between the bio-statistical and the normative or contextual definition of diseases and disabilities has continued up to now. As has been put forward by Moser (2006, 374), 'Being disabled is not something one is by definition, but something one becomes in relation to specific environments. Disability is enacted and ordered in situated and quite specific ways.' People can become disabled by the environment or by specific (lack of) technologies. A person with an average intellectual ability may 'become' disabled in an environment with just highly gifted people. An elite athlete who chooses not to use performance-enhancing substances may become disabled in a context in which the use of doping is 'normalised'. In these cases (and in many similar cases) one can argue that one is free to choose the 'right' environment in which specific qualities can be shown and compared to 'relevant others'. The person that one wants to be cannot be detached from the financial rewards that are attached to specific practices, as well as the status and meanings that are intrinsically related to the community of superior athletic performances. The valuation of human performances cannot be effected irrespective of a social-cultural hierarchy, ranking specific talents and making differences between highly valued talents (e.g. the ability to throw a ball in a basket) and less valued talents (e.g. running on prostheses).

New technologies such as prostheses apparently help to turn disabled people into 'normal' subjects. This may explain the urgent wish of Oscar Pistorius, an athlete who usually competes in races for disabled athletes, to become part of the 'normal Olympic Games'. What may be considered 'normalisation' in the context of daily life is at least ambivalent in the context of elite sport. Running on prostheses may be defined as crucial for the specific talent that is tested in a competition against 'relevant others': athletes who have the ability to show a similar talent. The wish of a disabled person to become part of 'normal' elite sport may be framed as a way of 'inclusion' or 'integration', but this at the same time reproduces new inequalities and asymmetries between performances of abled and dis-abled bodied.

If one is to enhance the traits needed to function optimally in society, one takes that society as a universal standard against which the functioning of people is measured, while one could also say that within a just society people should not be made to follow the dictations of a larger ideal. When one defines what counts as a disability in a normative rather than a descriptive fashion the notion of a disability also becomes political. In contemporary (Western) democracies, each citizen is presupposed to be self-reliant within a competitive capitalist environment. Therefore, society is set up to deal primarily with an idealised version of the 'average person' (Taylor and Mykitiuk 2001, 1). Anything that falls below this picture of the ideal citizen is treated as abnormal. In many respects, however, the ideal of the elite sportsman has all the characteristics of abnormality as well. But in contrast to the disabled, the elite sportsman is not considered a political and medical burden. So on the one hand society invests quite willingly in the 'abnormal' super-abilities of the elite sportsman, while on the other it does this only reluctantly, and from a ethics of inclusion, with respect to the disabled. In the case of disabilities, one wants to eradicate abnormalities by equalising on the basis of 'sameness' (Taylor and Mykitiuk 2001, 1), while in the case of super-abilities we support abnormalities. This 'selective investment in the abnormal' and the admiration for the 'genetically superior' could be seen as a token of a society that cannot meet up with the criteria for justice (cf. Tännsjö 2000). On the other hand, sport is a competitive practice, whose internal logic consists of the display of an unequal distribution of abilities. These internal goods are considered worth striving for, for their own sake (cf. MacIntyre 1985; Brown 1990; McNamee 1995). Sport consists of an internal logic that may conflict with more societal ideals (for example concerning justice or equality). These internal goods cannot be brought in agreement with the ideal, for example, to create as many sport categories as possible with the aim of producing as many sport stars as possible. It may be that everyone has certain abilities and disabilities; we cannot however freely choose the practice in which our own specific abilities are admired by people around the world.

Rawls and a just distribution of disabilities

In the 1970s, Rawls, among others, gave rise to a revival of liberal political philosophy. Next to his general influence on political and ethical philosophy, Rawls also had an extensive influence on bioethics and sport ethics. Rawls's most important contribution to juridical and political philosophy was his publication in 1971 of *A Theory of Justice*. In *A Theory of Justice*, John Rawls set out to find a more rational basis for the contractualist tradition in political and ethical theory. He tried to find general principles of justice that would function as basic rules for justice in society. These principles would, as is typical for contractualism, be supported by a social agreement. However, Rawls combined this with a stronger notion of justice which he derived from Kantian philosophy, and with the utilitarian notion of costs and benefit calculus to find the best overall balance for individual and collective well-being or happiness. Rational agreement was to be the basis of this philosophical system. For Rawls, principles of justice

> are the principles that free and rational persons concerned to further their own interests would accept in an initial position of equality as defining the fundamental terms of their association. These principles are to regulate all further agreements; they specify the kinds of social cooperation that can be entered into and the forms of government that can be established.
>
> (Rawls 1971, 11)

So, in Rawlsian philosophy, the basic principles of justice should balance individual liberty with an equal distribution of liberty. This should be combined with a provision of the greatest benefit for the least advantaged. People should come to this agreement through rational reflection, unaware of their specific individual place, talents or background in society. This is what Rawls called 'original position'. Rawls's conception of an 'original position' forms the rationale behind these basic principles of justice. It stems from the contractarian tradition in political theory. The original position was usually posed as the beginning position from which the social contract was formulated, from within a 'state of nature'. In Rawls's work, this construction of an original position should be regarded as a hypothetical position rather than a true historical occurrence. It functions as a maxim rule; it is the basic position one should take to come to the principles for a just society. In Rawls's original position, one is supposed to wear a 'veil of ignorance'. With this construction, Rawls tried to find a tool that can balance freedom or liberty and equality and leave out any prejudices stemming from one's class or one's ethnic, linguistic, religious or cultural background.

In Rawls's vision, those who are at the same level of talent and ability, and have the same willingness to use them, should have the same prospects of success regardless of their initial place in the social system. Social class, gender or any other contingency should have no influence on the liberty individuals are to enjoy in the pursuance of his or her goals in life. Moreover, social and economic inequalities should be distributed in such a way that they can reasonably be expected to be advantageous to all those who are the worst off in the first place. Rawls aimed at a distributive justice to compensate for the differences in fortune that we come across. Justice is seen as being independent of luck and favouring more equal distribution.

This position, although dominant in our current theoretical framework of justice, is on a par with the notions of both talent and disability. Our world is primarily designed for the average human being. People with a disability cannot partake in it as fully as they should according to the principles of distributive justice. By redesigning the world around us, however, we can make this world more accessible for the disabled. The question remains what obstacles can and should be taken away in order for the disabled to become part of other spheres of life. Making a building accessible is not the same thing as trying to become (a successful) part of one of the most competitive practices on earth. Following Rawls, we should adjust the person rather than the environment. Therefore, a defence of plurality is often not the outcome of a Rawlsian approach to justice. Our dominant understanding of elite sport cannot be brought in agreement with the right to become an elite athlete, similar to the right for example to receive good education. It may be difficult to justify the difference in admiration for the elite athlete and the disabled athlete just based upon such concepts as 'talent' or 'effort'. Some talents are more valued in a society than others in spite of a (changing) terminology, one that sometimes even seems to suggest that being disabled is the norm for each human being.

Adaptation of terminology

The inclusion of people with disabilities within regular sport and physical education has become daily practice in many countries (cf. Doll-Tepper *et al.* 2001; Vanlandewijck and Chappel 1996; Block and Obrusnikova 2007). The aims of participation and inclusion have also influenced debates about terminology and disability sports. This issue of terminology and language is important when it comes to matters of categorisation, and also with regard to the distinction between elite sport and disability sport. How does this categorisation, between sport for the 'normal' and sport for the disabled, in itself contribute to our understanding of what is and what should be considered 'ab-normal'? What equalities and what inequalities are considered justified in our society and in what way does the internal logic of sports challenges the understanding of justice in relation to matters of inclusion and exclusion? In order to be able to deal with these questions we will have to go back to some of the debates on terminology and classification.

In 1980, the World Health Organisation introduced the International Classification of Impairments, Disabilities and Handicaps (ICIDH). It was followed by years of dispute about the medical and social model of disabilities. This dispute finally resulted in the presentation of the International Classification of Functioning, Disability and Health (ICF) in 2001. Within this new model, disability is not regarded a characteristic (that is present all the time) but a state that may be present in certain environments or resulting from specific interactions with other people (cf. Ustun 2004). Following this new terminological proposal all people possess a multitude of abilities and disabilities. Sherill (2004b, 9) optimistically writes about this change of terminology: 'The worldwide trend is on appreciating, embracing and celebrating individual differences as opposed to glorifying the norm, the normal, and normalisation as was done in the 1900s.' Since everyone has disabilities and abilities, there is no need

to make a rigid distinction between abled and dis-abled bodies. 'Being disabled is the norm for humanity' (Ustun 2004, 1). In this sense, the Paralympics is understood as 'parallel Olympics', not special nor separate or inferior. The change of terminology can not hide the huge difference in status attached to winning a medal as an able-bodied or a disabled athlete. This difference very clearly explains the ultimate wish for a disabled athlete to become part of the competition for elite athletes. With two cases we ask if certain limits to normalisation and inclusion may conflict with 'a distribution of resources'. Having three legs or no legs does not, in and of itself, necessarily entail being disabled. In relation to sport it does however raise questions regarding which inequalities are 'relevant inequalities' based upon the internal logic of sport. It also presents us with an example of the reproduction of normality through sports. Although sport and the circus have very similar historical roots, elite sport in the twentieth century has differentiated from the early 'freak shows'. Nowadays it celebrates the ultimate, but at the same time normalised, two-legged human abilities and performances. Even in elite sport 'more' is not necessarily 'better', as can be illustrated by the story of Franceso Lentini, the 'three-legged football player'.

Lentini: super- or dis-abled?

Francesco Lentini (1889–1966) was born in Sicily in Italy with three legs, and a rudimentary foot growing on one of his legs. As a child he was brought to a home for disabled children. Initially, Lentini experienced his impairment as a disability (mainly because his third leg was six inches shorter than the two other legs). After being brought into this home of disabled children (with children who were deaf, blind or mute) he found out for himself that he was not disabled at all. Lentini writes about his childhood 'transformation':

> I could appreciate the fact that I was possessed of all my faculties and senses. I could hear, talk, understand, appreciate and enjoy the beauties of life. I could read and they couldn't. I could talk to my friends, but some of them couldn't because they were dumb. I could hear and enjoy beautiful music, while some of them

235

couldn't because they were deaf. I had my mental faculties and began to look forward to my education, and some of them couldn't because they were idiots.

(Nickell 2005, 131–2)

Lentini learned to use his 'disability' as an advantage. He entered the circus in the USA as a young child. One of his acts was playing soccer on a stage, which explains his show name: the 'Three-Legged Football Player'. How fair it would have been if Lentini would have entered a regular soccer competition is purely hypothetical, since he was only acting in the circus, and his third leg would have given him a disadvantage over his opponents rather than an advantage. More interesting in this respect would be the case of swimming.

Lentini talks about this advantage:

No, my limb does not bother me in the least. I can get about just as well and with the same ease as any normal person—walk, run, jump; ride a bicycle, horse; ice and roller skate; and drive my own car. I can swim—one advantage I have over the other fellow when I swim is that I use the extra limb as a rudder.[1]

There is a clear difference between a performance in the circus and elite sport, and between the performances of able (two-legged) and disabled (three-legged) athletes. This difference can however not be inferred from a definition of 'the normal'. Modern elite sport celebrates abnormalities in many shapes and appearances, varying from extreme-sized sumo wrestlers to extremely undersized gymnasts. What is considered a sport performance or a circus performance has to be primarily understood from the historical and cultural context. Yet comparing them does raise some interesting issues regarding the definition of being disabled, the 'boundaries of normality' and the manner in which modern, competitive sports may challenge some of the accepted categories and definitions. Having three legs may become a disability in a world where two legs presents the dominant norm, similar to Lentini's observation: 'If you lived in a world where everyone had one arm, how would you cope with two?'

In the case of Lentini, uniqueness is not a reason for admiration, just because of the deviation from the standard (as is the case in elite sport). Admiration and heroism is afforded on the basis of a multitude of factors including training, discipline, showing and mastering certain skills. Differences between elite sport as a global entertainment industry and the circus are related to conceptual differences between 'admiration' and 'amazement'. One can be amazed by looking at 'physical abnormalities', but this amazement may turn into admiration when an 'extraordinary feature' is mastered and turns out to be an extraordinary sport talent.

Without the prospect for the kind of heroism that is attached to modern elite sport, large deviations from the standards of being 'normal' may still end up in a circus. It is interesting to see that, although many acts in the circus are the result of years of hard and vigorous training, these performances are still very much associated with the historical roots of the freak show, or any other public place for the 'unlucky mutants' exposing or trading upon their abnormalities. Elite sport and the circus have similar roots, based upon the celebration of extraordinary talent. European countries share a similar history in the knowledge and popularisation of physical culture, thanks to the circuses, the acrobats, the pioneering bodybuilders and other body artists who travelled through Europe. In the late eighteenth century, people already watched strongmen and other athletes performing at fairs, festivals and in all kinds of theatres. Long before the idea of training and building muscle mass became a 'normalised' kind of behaviour, people saw extraordinarily strong men (and children) primarily as 'miracles of nature'. Until around 1850, it is hard to draw clear distinctions between sport, acrobatics and circus-like activities.

Thanks to the globalisation of modern sport, many 'mutants' are nowadays cheered for their achievements. They set a norm for human performance and virtuosity to be strived for also by elite athletes in disability sports. The classical distinction between elite sports and the disabled athlete is blurring, as well as the distinction between the athlete as hero, excelling on the basis of what counts as 'normal', and a (former) 'patient combating his limitations', falling outside this normal variance. In this respect, modern disability sports have made much progress in terms of admiration and respect. Nowadays, some so-called 'disabled' performances sometimes even come close to those of elite athletes. It raises the question of what counts as normal in order to become part of the competition for able-bodied athletes. How much of a disablement can and should be compensated for in order to be (re)defined as a 'normal athlete'?

Oscar Pistorius: super- or dis-abled?

South African Oscar Pistorius is known as 'the fastest man on no legs'. He runs with artificial limbs and is world record holder in the 100, 200 and 400 metres. He runs that fast thanks partly to his carbon-fibre legs. He can even compete with elite athletes on 'natural legs'. In fact, he did so in July 2007, when he ran a 400-metre race at the British Grand Prix. His participation in a regular competition is, however, surrounded by controversy. His artificial limbs (also called 'cheetahs') may give him extra advantages which, as some argue, makes the running competition unfair.

Pistorius is not the first disabled person competing in an able-bodied event. In most historical cases there was no reason for concern about the justification of the participation of disabled athletes. In the 1904 St Louis Olympics, George Eyser won three gold medals in gymnastics while competing on a wooden leg. Neroli Fairhall, a paraplegic, competed in archery in the 1984 Olympics, and in 2000 blind runner Marla Runyan raced against able-bodied runners in the 1,500 metres athletics competition. Ajibola Adeoye (Nigeria) is an arm amputee who holds the Paralympic record in the men's 100 metres (10.72 seconds). If his time would allow it, there is little reason why he couldn't compete in the regular Olympics. The loss of one of his arms does affect his ability to run, but not in such a way that it causes concern about the fairness of the competition. These examples illustrate that unless their disadvantage is a certain disability people can still compete in regular competition. In these cases, no use is made of any prosthetic that influences the athletic performance, at least not in such a way that it raises concern about the fairness of the competition.

The case of Pistorius is rather special, because his disability may, with the help of his prostheses, turn out to be an unfair advantage. This is why the IAAF amended its competition rules in 2007, banning the use of 'any technical device that incorporates springs, wheels or any other element that provides a user with an advantage over another athlete not using such a device' (IAAF Rule 144.2). IAAF spokesman Nick Davies commented after the British Grand Prix, 'We all wish him [Pistorius] well. The point here is what's going to happen in ten years? What happens if it continues to evolve?' In November 2007 the IAAF asked the Institute of Biomechanics and Orthopaedics (German Sport University, Cologne) for an independent biomechanical and physiological study. Early in 2008 the results were presented. Some of the main results, as presented on the IAAF site[2] were that:

- running with prosthetics needs less additional energy (up to 25 per cent) than running with natural limbs;
- the amount of energy return of the prosthetic blade has never been reported for a human muscle-driven ankle joint in sprint running;
- the returned energy from the prosthetic blade is close to three times higher than with the human ankle joint in maximum sprinting.

Based on these findings, the study concluded that an athlete running with prosthetic blades has a clear mechanical advantage (more than 30 per cent) when compared to 'someone' not using the blades. According to Pistorius, however, other experts contradicted these findings. Not all of the relevant variables were taken into consideration. Pistorius and his coach responded to some of these arguments by claiming that his prosthetics confront him with other disadvantages, such as rain (which reduces his traction), crosswinds (which can blow the device sideways), and that some of his energy is more easily dispensed at the start of the race than the energy of other runners. The discussion and main arguments in this case were primarily focused on the empirical question of what is considered an athletic advantage. This debate cannot, however, be detached from the more conceptual question on the definition of running, and what could still be considered a norm for (human) running. The main question preceding any empirical research is of course: with whom is Pistorius compared, and based upon what arguments? Compared to the world record holder, any runner may be defined as 'disadvantaged'.

The fact that running with prosthetics needs less additional energy (up to 25 per cent) than running with natural limbs is in itself insufficient to keep Pistorius from competing in the Olympics. Based on the same arguments, sport authorities could have forbidden the introduction of klapskates in speed skating or even the Fosbury flop in high jumping (cf. van Hilvoorde *et al.* 2007). There seems to be a fear that running on prosthetics might become faster than 'normal' running. It may conflict with our understanding of elite sport. Does it show the conservatism of sport and the public that wants to hold on to the familiar distinction between elite sport and disability sport?

Enhancement and 'boosting' in disabled sport

In discussing the ethical issues that Paralympic sports are confronted with, Wheeler (2004) states that most ethical issues may be classified as 'boosting'. Well-known in disability sports are physiological, pharmacological and intellectual boosting. In the context of this paper the discussion on technical boosting is of great relevance. Similar to sport in general, there is an ongoing discussion on unfairness as a result of inequalities in (financing) new technology. Differences in the availability of new products (wheelchairs that are made of lighter material for example) and increasing inequalities between developing and industrialised countries highly affect the fairness of disability sports worldwide. Wheeler also mentions 'osseointegrated prostheses', a new technology that improves (enhances) the integration of the prostheses with the human part of the leg. This is a positive development for people who are hindered by their current prostheses, but it also creates new inequalities in the context of elite disabled sport.

Special concern is also raised by the issue of 'classification boosting', which is unique to disability sports. Instances have been described where athletes misrepresent their functional abilities during the process of classification (Wheeler 2004, 4). The matter of defining dysfunctions is both complex and contentious, being susceptible to deceptive manipulation and fraud. Think for example of the misrepresentation or misclassification of persons with

average or above average intellectual abilities as intellectually disabled. Not much is known about this phenomenon, but it raises reasons for concern about the (future) credibility of disability sports—not least because there do not seem to be easy measures to prevent this type of athletic fraud. The 'pre-game process' of classification influences possible outcomes of a contest to a considerable degree. Wheeler's pledge for a code of ethics for disability sport could be a first step, but needs to be followed by measures of administrators to formalise observational criteria and investigate possibilities of manipulation.

At the same time it raises the question of how objective the presentation of functional abilities can be. Every boundary that is drawn between certain types of disability creates some injustice (cf. Jones and Howe 2005). In every category there are the 'lucky' and 'unlucky' ones. In one category one could qualify as highly talented (Pistorius in the Paralympics for example), in the other just as an average athlete (Pistorius in the regular Olympics). This injustice is in many ways similar to the kind of injustice that is intrinsic to sport in general (cf. Loland 2002). Sport intrinsically differentiates between (in some respect arbitrary) differences in genetic makeup. Dysfunctions need to be recognised as similar/dissimilar and, to an acceptable degree, responsible for the outcome of the sport. Athletic competitions are ideally set up in such a way that obvious differences in biological makeup do not determine the outcome at forehand. On the other hand, some people will always be naturally faster or stronger in ways that no training regimen can correct for.

While recognising that Paralympics do not imply inferior performances, based upon a static and absolute distinction between able and disabled bodies, one can expect that these games are increasingly confronted with discussions about classification, credibility and also about unfair methods of 'enhancement'. The optimist could say that the increase in sport-ethical concerns in the Paralympics (whether because of fraud or illegal enhancement) is a good sign, because it shows that the Paralympics are taken more and more seriously by both competitors and the audience. The more status is attached to winning medals, the more attention there is for possible fraud (such as classification boosting). This might, however, appear to be too optimistic. The struggle, for example, within professional cycling as a result of doping scandals is grounded in the fear of losing credibility within a sport that already enjoys a worldwide popularity. Disability sports start with a lack of popularity (and credibility) and have, in this sense, not much to lose. The Paralympics are not considered to be 'truly' interesting by the larger portion of the general public since disabled sportsmen (defined as an impaired deviance of normality) are not the best athletes in the world from the perspective of 'normal sports'. In this respect, the urgent wish of Pistorius to compete within the 2008 Olympic Games paradoxically underlines the differences and reproduces the current order and hierarchy between able and disabled bodies. It would be as if Pistorius, being the best disabled runner, is promoted from an inferior division to the premier league of international sport. For most disabled athletes there is no reason (and no possibility) to aim for this kind of ranking and 'promotion'. Pistorius's 'promotion' may even contribute to a loss of credibility and appreciation of the performances of disability athletes.

Some argue that athletic enhancement by means of an increase in the quality of prosthetics is similar to the use of doping. In terms of enhancement there is, however, more at stake within disability sport, more than just trying to become the best athlete within a specific category. Disability sports are about showing performances within categories of similar disabilities, without making those disabilities the central element of athletic prowess. Elite sport is about excellence within the boundaries of 'self-chosen' limitations; disability sports originated from limitations through fate. Elite sport symbolises the athlete as hero; it reproduces elitist ideals about the body ('athletic' and 'beautiful'), about good sportsmanship and national pride. For many people in disability sport, the athlete is still a 'patient combating their limitations', instead of an elite athlete with specific talents or virtuosity.

It is, however, a different matter if disabled elite athletes may in some cases be eligible to compete with able athletes. Arguments against the inclusion of three legs or prosthetic limbs may be focused too much and selectively on visible differences between athletes. Take for example Floyd Landis, who injured his hip in 2003 and received a hip prosthesis in 2006.

Why is Floyd Landis's hip not regarded as an advantage or an ('artificial hip') enhancement, while his usage of testosterone was? What's the difference between the internal prosthesis of Landis and the external ones of Pistorius? The advantages of a prosthesis in this case bear upon the relevant inequalities of the sport. Some actually claim this is also the case for running competitions between Ethiopians and Caucasians, and that therefore they should compete in separate categories. The question is whether Pistorius is playing the same game as his opponents. We argue that he is not because he is showing another and extra skill, namely handling his prosthesis in an extremely talented way. Prostheses may have a considerable influence on the outcome of the game. This, however is not an argument in itself that this competition should be excluded from the regular Olympic Games.

Conclusion

Problems with classification and categorisation in sport for the disabled confront us with the intrinsic inequalities and unfairness of any competitive practice that depends upon the classification of people based upon both equalities and ('relevant') inequalities. A three legged swimmer or a sprinter with prostheses who might become faster than the elite sprinters can be excluded from regular competition, not because of their inferiority but instead because a disability may appear to be a superior advantage. It is easy to point at the conservative elements within traditional sport, in order to explain the exclusion of Pistorius from the Olympic Games. There is, however, more at stake, from the perspective of the internal goods of the sport. In sport there is no purely rational logic in the definition of rules, neither in classification nor categorisations, in order to make the competition as 'fair' as possible. Rules are always a combination and compromise of tradition and a sport-ethical ideal of 'equality' (the 'level playing field'). People with three legs would allow for a separate competition when the third leg has a considerate influence on the outcome of the game.

When discussing relations and remarkable differences in admiration between elite sport and disability sport, the traditional sport world is confronted with matters of inclusion and a fair distribution of resources and rewards for the achievements of all athletes. As we have seen in the case of Rawls's philosophy of justice, however, these mechanisms of inclusion and fair distribution are often based upon a very narrow image of the average person, therefore again excluding the possibility of a pluralistic society. Sport is a social practice with an internal logic that does not always conform to these general principles of justice, specifically as we have come to embrace them now. It therefore proves to be a good case for further analyses of the distinction society draws between normal and disabled, between natural and dysfunctional.

Sports are a well-defined form of cultivation of specific abnormalities, and what is traditionally understood as professional sportsmanship has socio-cultural roots in history. Abnormality is the common denominator for both. The direction of excellence can be framed socio-culturally, and from that perspective, there is not that much of a difference between Paralympics and Olympics. The genetically fortunate and unfortunate share the exceptional position on the scale of normality. And sometimes they meet, at the circus or in a sports arena. Many biological exceptions are the result of certain genetic mutations that may result in either a talent or disability. Depending on the time and context in which a 'mutant' is being nurtured, one could either end up in a freak show, at the circus or in a modern sport arena.

Notes

1. See http://www.sideshowworld.com/blowoff-RFlentini.html, accessed 10 March 2008.
2. Available at http://www.iaaf.org/news/Kind¼512/newsId¼42896.html, accessed 10 March 2008.

References

Bailey, R. 2007. Talent development and the luck problem. *Sport, Ethics and Philosophy* 1 (3): 367–77.

Block, M.E. and I. Obrusnikova. 2007. Inclusion in physical education: A review of the literature from 1995–2005. *Adapted Physical Activity Quarterly* 24: 103–24.

Boorse, C. 1975. On the distinction between disease and illness. *Philosophy and Public Affairs* 5: 49–68.

——. 1976. What a theory of mental health should be. *Journal for the Theory of Social Behaviour* 6 (1).

——. 1977. Health as a theoretical concept. *Philosophy of Science* 44.

Bowen, J. 2002. The Americans With Disabilities Act and its application to sport. *Journal of The Philosophy of Sport* XXIX: 66–74.

Brown, W.M. 1990. Practices and prudence. *Journal of the Philosophy of Sport* XVII: 71–84.

Buchanan, A.B., D.W. Brock, N. Daniels and D. Wikler. 2000. *From Chance to Choice.* Cambridge: Cambridge University Press.

Depauw, K.P. and S.J. Gavron. 2005. *Disability Sport,* 2nd edn. Champaign, IL: Human Kinetics.

Doll-Tepper, G., M. Kroner and W. Sonnenschein. 2001. *New Horizons in Sport for Athletes with a Disability.* Aachen: Meyer & Meyer Sport.

Engelhardt, H.T. and S.F. Spicker, eds. 1974. *Evaluation and Explanation in the Biomedical Sciences.* Dordrecht: Netherlands: Reidel Publishing Company.

IPC (2006) *Athletics Classification Handbook.*

Jones, C. and P.D. Howe. 2005. The conceptual boundaries of sport for the disabled: Classification and athletic performance. *Journal of the Philosophy of Sport* 32: 133–46.

Kioumourtzoglou, E. and K. Politis, eds. 2004. *Paralympic Games from 1960 to 2004.* Athens: Organising Committee for the Olympic Games.

Klenck, C. and K. Gebke. 2007. Practical management: Common medical problems in disabled athletes. *Clinical Journal of Sport Medicine* 19 (1): 55–60.

Lindstrom, L.L. 1992. Integration of sport for athletes with disabilities into sport programmes for able-bodied athletes. *Palaestra* 8 (3): 25–59.

Loland, S. 2002. *Fair Play in Sport: A Moral Norm System.* London and New York: Routledge.

Macintyre, A. 1985. *After Virtue.* London: Duckworth.

McNamee, M. 1995. Sporting practices, institutions, and virtues: A critique and a restatement. *Journal of the Philosophy of Sport* XXII: 61–82.

Moser, I. 2006. Disability and the promises of technology: Technology, subjectivity and embodiment within an order of the normal. *Information, Communication and Society* 9 (3): 373–95.

Nickell, J. 2005. *Secrets of the Sideshows.* Lexington, KY: University Press of Kentucky.

Pickering, Francis L. 2005. Competitive sports, disability, and problems of justice in sports. *Journal of the Philosophy of Sport* 32: 127–32.

Rawls, J. 1971. *A Theory of Justice.* Oxford: Oxford University Press.

Sherill, C. 2004a. *Adapted Physical Activity, Recreation, and Sport. Crossdisciplinary and Lifespan,* 6th edn. New York: McGraw-Hill.

——. 2004b. The changing terminology of "ability" and "disability" in the sport context. *In Paralympic Games from 1960 to 2004,* edited by

E. Kioumourtzoglou and K. Politis. Athens: Organising Committee for the Olympic Games.

Tännsjö, T. 2000. Is our admiration for sports heroes fascistoid? In *Values in Sport: Elitism, Nationalism, Gender Equality, and the Scientific Manufacture of Winners*, edited by T. Tännsjö and C.M. Tamburrini. London and New York: E&FN Spon/Routledge.

Taylor, K. and R. Mykitiuk. 2001. Genetics, normalcy and disability. *ISUMA: Canadian Journal of Policy Research/Revue canadienne de recherche surles politiques* 2 (3): 65–71.

Toulmin, S. 1975. Concepts of function and mechanism in medicine and medical science. In *Evaluation and Explanation in the Biomedical Sciences*, edited by H.T. Engelhardt and S.F. Spicker. Dordrecht: Netherlands: Reidel Publishing Company.

Tweedy, S.M. 2002. Taxonomic theory and the ICF: Foundation for the Unified Disability Athletics Classification. *Adapted Physical Activity Quarterly* 19: 221–37.

Ustun, T.B. 2004. Celebrate individual differences. The ICF model of disability. In *Paralympic Games from 1960 to 2004*, edited by E. Kioumourtzoglou and K. Politis. Athens: Organising Committee for the Olympic Games.

van Hilvoorde, I., R. Vos and G. de Wert. 2007. Flopping, klapping and gene doping: Dichotomies between 'natural' and 'artificial' in elite sport. *Social Studies of Science* 37 (2): 173–200.

Vanlandewijck, Y.C. and R. Chappel. 1996. Integration and classification issues in competitive sport for athletes with disabilities. *Sport Science Review* 5: 65–88.

Wheeler, G.D. 2004. Ethical aspects in sports participation. In *Paralympic Games from 1960 to 2004*, edited by E. Kioumourtzoglou and K. Politis. Athens: Organising Committee for the Olympic Games.

Tackling *Murderball*

Masculinity, disability and the big screen

Michael Gard and Hayley Fitzgerald

Introduction: *Murderball* and wheelchair rugby

The sport of wheelchair rugby (sometimes called 'quad rugby') is the subject of Henry Alex Rubin and Adam Shapiro's 2005 documentary *Murderball*. The film tells the story of the apparently intense rivalry over a number of years between the Canadian and United States men's national teams. In part, the story is told through the lives and personalities of some of the game's leading players and coaches. Although we use the word 'documentary' as shorthand, the film could be interpreted as many other things. For example, the commercial-release DVD of the film includes a range of extra material, including an episode of *The Larry King Show* in which the host interviews the players mostly prominently featured in *Murderball*, takes live phone-in questions from viewers and generally promotes the (then) upcoming cinematic release of the film. Throughout the interview both King and the players talk about the value of *Murderball* in advertising the sport of wheelchair rugby and, in fact, canvass the idea of wheelchair rugby becoming a big-money, high-profile sport. So, although we use the word 'documentary', it is clear that some of *Murderball*'s proponents also see it as a piece of commercial sports promotion. In addition, both the film itself and the Larry King interview explicitly deal with a series of ethical and political questions. For example, how should disabled people be represented? What do non-disabled people know about disabled people? To what extent are non-disabled people's fears of disabled bodies a product of their wilful ignorance or the victim mentality of disabled people? And perhaps even more controversially, how should disabled people (particularly those who have recently acquired a disability) deal with their disability and what role might sport play in their 'empowerment'. The on-screen participants in *Murderball* all offer answers to these questions and, at least for this reason, the film deserves thoughtful consideration.

At the same time, the on-screen narrative of *Murderball* appears to be highly contrived (even choreographed) such that there are at least arguments against describing it as a documentary at all. In short, we argue that *Murderball* is a groundbreaking film and in some (if not all) respects a daring and complex piece of social activism. With these preliminary points in mind, in this paper we offer a thematic

Michael Gard and Hayley Fitzgerald 'Tackling *Murderball*: Masculinity, Disability and the Big Screen', from *Sport, Ethics and Philosophy*, Vol. 2, Issue 2, pp. 126–141, © 2008 Michael Gard and Hayley Fitzgerald. Reprinted by permission of Taylor & Francis.

critique of *Murderball*. We do so in the knowledge that a mean-spirited 'trashing' of the film is possible but that this is an approach we firmly reject. We hold some of the explicit and implicit arguments made in *Murderball* 'up to the light' and consider their origins, efficacy and implications. We examine some of the questions and issues raised by *Murderball* and attempt to analyse the techniques used to address them. Furthermore, we are aware that *Murderball* has aroused lively discussion in the print and electronic media. Our purpose, therefore, is to make a scholarly contribution to this discussion and, in particular, to consider the implications of this film for physical education (PE) contexts. We want to make a connection with PE because we believe *Murderball* has the potential to raise important questions about the relationship between disability, PE and sport. Before moving to our critique of *Murderball* we examine the broader literature focusing on sport, media and disability. First, we discuss participation in sport by disabled people and highlight the tensions that can arise when dominant understandings of sport and disability attempt to coexist. We then focus on media and disability and briefly explore the different ways in which disability has been represented in films. Next, we identify the methodological approach we used to develop our critique of the film. Finally, we present our critique of *Murderball* under three thematic headings. The first of these, 'What can disabled bodies do?', centres on the film's use of representations of the players' lifestyles and a hypermasculine physicality and sexuality. Within our second theme, 'This is not the Special Olympics', we describe the way the sport of wheelchair rugby and its athletes are actively and explicitly distanced from people with intellectual disabilities and the sports they play. *Murderball* leaves us in little doubt that its stars see this form of disability sport as superior to the sports we might see at events like the Special Olympics. Our last theme, 'Hot and disabled', shows how the film's makers seem (from our point of view) to prosecute an agenda that sees wheelchair rugby as a viable, media friendly, big-money sport. A specific model of sport has been chosen in *Murderball*, a model that uses music, the manipulation of video footage and a set of narrative set pieces to produce not just a sport, but a media sport. Taken together, we conclude that these three themes offer us new intellectual

challenges for thinking about such issues as the PE experiences of young disabled people and their progression in disability sport. That is, we do not presume to know how young disabled people will respond to or 'read' *Murderball*. Rather, we argue that *Murderball* moves disability issues into new intellectual terrain, thus increasing the ways in which people who work with young people and sport might need to take account of disability.

Physical education, sport and disability

Historically, the development of sport and PE for disabled people has been influenced by medical understandings of disability (Sherrill and DePauw 1997). Medicalisation is particularly evident in the United States and United Kingdom, where rehabilitation centres and therapeutic recreation programmes attempt to use sport as a means of remedying or adjusting patients to the 'limitations' of their disability. Internationally, legislation and policy developments in recent years have explicitly sought to address issues relating to inclusion generally within education. Within PE this has led to the development of numerous resources and guidelines and the publication of a number of syllabuses that address, to differing degrees, issues of inclusion (DfEE/QCA 1999; Ministry of Education 1999; Downs 1995). The purported goal of these developments is to contribute to more positive and inclusive PE and sporting experiences for students, including those who happen to be disabled. Articulating precisely what 'inclusive' PE looks like, however, has been problematic and is a source of confusion and debate among physical educators (Vickerman 2002). Recent research in this era of apparent inclusion suggests that the realities of disabled students' broader school experiences remain complex and reflect practices that reinforce oppression, while at the same time supporting conditions that can enable disabled students to be agents of change (Davis and Watson 2002). In addition to using PE and sport for rehabilitative and educative means, disability sport has also emerged as an avenue for disabled people to engage in competitive pursuits.

Pathways have been developed that enable disability sports to be played from recreational to competitive levels. Some disability sports, such as wheelchair rugby, wheelchair basketball, seated volleyball and table cricket, are adaptations of what could be considered 'mainstream sports' played by non-disabled people. Other disability sports such as goalball and boccia have been developed with specific impairment groups in mind.[1] The need for adaptation or the creation of new sports signal as least some level of tension between sport and disability (DePauw 1997).

To clarify this point, a significant dimension of competitive sport is its concern with developing, refining and performing athletic techniques while adhering to rules (Coakley 2007). Typically, and especially (but not only) for boys and men, this practice is associated with aggression, competition and masculinity (Connell 1995; Light and Kirk 2000; Wellard 2002). In contrast, disability often signifies deficiency and impaired bodies are frequently viewed in negative ways. In this context, non-conforming disabled bodies are commonly perceived as 'spoilt' (Goffman 1968) and 'flawed' (Hevey 1992). The tension, then, arises when disabled bodies are expected to conform to the accepted and normalised practices dominating PE and sports discourse (Barton 1993). Even though adapted and disability sports serve to provide an alternative means of participation, the same kind of status or recognition as their non-disabled counterparts has not yet been achieved by its best proponents (Barton 1993; Fitzgerald 2005).

Some significant developments have taken place and are undoubtedly intended to promote the value of disability sport. These include closer alignment of the Paralympics to the Olympics, the organisation of disability sport world championships and an increasing commitment by mainstream sporting organisations to player development pathways for disabled people. One of the purposes of these developments seems to be to legitimise what Siedentop (2002) describes as the 'elite development goal'. According to Siedentop, a central feature of the elite development goal concerns the need for members of the sporting practice to work towards established standards of excellence. The development of player pathways within disability sport would seem to signal the possibilities that elite disability sport will achieve greater recognition. Yet the standards of excellence aspired to in relation to the elite development goal remain predominantly

aligned to normalised understandings of ability and sporting performance.

With this as a background, we now turn to the ways in which the tensions between sport and disability have been interpreted and negotiated in popular media.

Media, disability and sport

It has long been recognised that the media are a key arena in which society's attitudes and values are shaped and reinforced. There is no reason to see this as any less true for disability (Norden 1994; Swain *et al.* 2005). According to Darke (1998, 181), 'images matter; for the disabled, images of themselves are especially important as they are presumed by virtually all critics and audiences to be essentially self-evident in the truths they reveal about impairment, the "human condition" and, as such, disability'. A critical question to ask here is: What images and discourses of disability dominate the mass media? Mitchell and Snyder (2006) suggest tragic news stories highlight accidents that result in disability and then focus on how individuals learn to manage, regain normal life or miraculously recover. Similarly, it has been argued that telethon events and other charity promotion organisers seek to secure public donations by portraying disabled people as needy and pitiful. Furthermore, the printed media have been accused of misrepresenting imagery of disability (Swain *et al.* 2005) and in particular coverage of disability sport has been marginalised (Thomas and Smith 2003). In relation to these 'deficit' understandings of disability it has been suggested that 'With so little exposure to contrary messages, this reinforces a straightforward "hypodermic syringe" model in which the "naturalness" of disability is seen to be confirmed to the media' (Barnes *et al.* 1999, 197).

Issues relating to disability and disabled characters have featured in many films (Norden 1994). For example, Hayes and Black (2003) contend that understandings of disability often emphasise a discourse of pity and this is articulated through storylines and characters that encourage audiences to associate disability with (1) confinement, (2) hope for rehabilitation, (3) denial of rehabilitation and (4) reconciliation of confinement. Confinement is concerned with spatial, physical or social forms of restriction and limits participation in social life. *Elephant Man* (1980) illustrates this with the main character initially restricted to a dark cellar and later isolated in hospital. Storylines focusing on rehabilitation and denial of rehabilitation highlight hope, often with the support of other non-disabled people, for overcoming disability. Lenny, in *Of Mice and Men* (1992), dreams of raising rabbits with his friend George. In this way the film depicts aspirations that will lead to a normal life. Nevertheless, this film and others also reinforce a view that rehabilitation may not always be achieved—Lenny kills the farmer's wife and is subsequently killed himself. Some films emphasise a reconciliation of confinement and in this way re-articulate confinement in a manner that transforms this from intolerable to an accepted benevolence. Lenny is killed by a friend so that he does not have to experience punishment and ridicule from others within his community. Within these different understandings of disability, disabled characters are regularly depicted at different ends of a continuum—either 'villains' (violent, evil and repulsive) or 'saints' (courageous, innocent and thankful) (Norden 1994). As a consequence of these kinds of representations, disabled people are often positioned as 'other' and 'isolated' in a similar manner to experiences encountered in wider society.

A number of film storylines have focused, in differing ways, on sport and disability including: *The Other Side of the Mountain* (1975), *Ice Castles* (1979) and *Million Dollar Baby* (2004). *Ice Castles* tells the story of an 'up and coming' ice skater who becomes visually impaired. Following a period of depression, she begins to skate again and gains competitive success. Although the film conveys an important message that if you become disabled you can still do sport, it also has heroic undertones that emphasise the incredible feat of the visually impaired skater. Dahl (1993, 141) describes the film as featuring 'two dimensional characters who "learn to cope" and "live happily ever after"'. In contrast, *Million Dollar Baby* is the story of a female professional boxer who, following a world championship fight, becomes a quadriplegic. After acquiring a disability the boxer loses the will to live and her trainer supports her request to end her life. In the USA the film evoked considerable criticism with

Duncan (2007) describing it as 'bleak and depressing'. Disability activists were particularly critical of the film and outspoken about the way in which euthanasia was presented (Haller 2006). According to Boyle *et al.* (2006) *Million Dollar Baby* perpetuates 'able-centric' notions of normality and reinforces negative perceptions of disability—such that it is better to die than live with a disability.

In the selective context of this paper's discussion of *Murderball*, two general points emerge from this brief account of popular media and disability. First, there is the obvious conclusion that popular media encourage their consumers to see disabled bodies as grotesquely 'other' and therefore objects of pity. Secondly, because its assumed consumers are non-disabled people, the popular media offer a tragic/heroic account of disabled lives and the subjectivities of disabled people. While readers may have their own views about whether this is a fair or helpful state of affairs, what these representations consistently leave out is much sense that a disabled life can be, in many respects, just like a non-disabled life. In popular media disabled lives are very rarely playfully enjoyable (as opposed to heroically triumphant), sexually active or curious, hip or in tune with modern fashions and cultural trends. They are, instead, a ghetto.

Constructing a thematic critique

We want to stress that the 'research' we present below is not, in any straightforward sense, empirical. Two points can be made by way of initial justification for this claim. First, our intention was not to offer a definitive analysis of what *Murderball* is 'really' about or what its effects in the world might be. Secondly, we attempted to connect with, and develop upon, existing conversations about disability. For example, we are aware that *Murderball*'s release occasioned a great deal of spirited online debate. This debate centred on whether or not *Murderball* was good for disabled people and, as a result, was played out through quite predictable ideological positions. That is, *Murderball* was either seen as a bit of high-spirited fun which offered disabled people another way of being in the world or, on the other hand, as crude, sexist and out of touch with the realities of the majority of disabled people who will never be elite athletes.

By contrast, we sought to bring a range of academic perspectives to bear on *Murderball*. However, we wanted to work through the film in a comparatively systematic way but to do so without the pressure of being sure that we had 'captured' its apparent essence.

Both authors viewed the film separately and then met informally to discuss their impressions of it. We then independently compiled and later compared lists of questions and issues that we felt the film was trying to answer or address. Through discussion, we settled on a shortlist of specific questions/issues that we agreed were central to the composition of the film. We then watched the film again (and the extra material contained on the commercial-release DVD) and wrote our separate reflections about how these questions and issues are dealt with. Once again, we brought these reflections together with a view to doing two things. First, we wanted to decide whether we still felt our short-list of questions/issues needed to be collapsed or expanded. Secondly, we looked for similarities and differences in the techniques that the two of us perceived operating in the film to answer or at least address these questions and issues. For example, we agreed that the film's makers appeared to want to educate viewers and to address misconceptions about disabled bodies. So when we re-watched the film we did so with an eye on this issue. As indicated above, however, we did not do this in order to simply describe the issue and to report on the film's content. Rather, we analysed what we took to be the film's explicit arguments, what we call its discursive techniques: what did we understand to be the film's explicit intentions and how does it try to communicate these intentions? What discursive techniques appear (to us) to have been used and which were ignored? For example, we would argue that the film's makers chose to construct disabled bodies as not so different from non-disabled bodies and, in fact, to draw on fairly mainstream ideas about heterosexual masculinity to do so. That is, *Murderball* tells its audience that disabled male bodies can be beautiful, muscular and sexually active. Is this a 'good' use of the educative potential of documentary film? For this paper we mostly suspended judgement on this kind of question and, instead, discuss the potential consequences of the choices that appear (to us) to have been made in the making of *Murderball*.

In short, our analysis begins by engaging with *Murderball* on what we might provisionally call 'its own terms'. We are, of course, aware that such a claim invites the criticism of essentialism. We take for granted the possibility that our analysis totally misrepresents the actual intentions of the film's makers. More to the point, we accept the possibility that no single coherent statement of intention could capture the disparate agendas and aspirations of the many people who, no doubt, participated in the film's construction. Our use of the phrase 'its own terms' indicates our focus on what we took to be the film's most important content. We treated the film, as it were, like an interviewee; we listened and then tried to interpret what it said. Whether our interpretations are justified is for others to judge. On the other hand, however, we also wanted to emphasise that we were not concerned with what the film might have said or should have said. We focused on what the film actually said. We wanted to engage in dialogue with the film, not lecture to it.

Finally, having arrived at a determinate list of questions/issues and a summary of our discussions about them, we watched the film together to test our tentative conclusions. We bore in mind questions such as whether we had missed anything important or whether we had made too much of particular question or issue, or been too harsh in our reactions to them. In the following section we offer a summary of our analysis.

Tackling *Murderball*

Three major themes emerged from our critical analysis of *Murderball*. They are (1) What can disabled bodies do? (2) 'This is not the Special Olympics' and (3) 'Hot' and disabled.

(1) What can disabled bodies do?

The narrative of *Murderball* tells a story of the rivalry between the Canadian and USA wheelchair rugby teams. It spans a period from the 2002 World Championships in Göteborg, where the Canadians took first place by upsetting the traditionally dominant USA team, to the 2004 Athens Paralympics in which Canada again defeated the USA but were themselves beaten by New Zealand for the gold medal. Wheelchair rugby is a game played between two squads of players. The aim of the game, played on a standard basketball court, is for teams (a maximum of four players are allowed on court at any one time) to advance the ball downfield by either passing it among themselves or by players rolling with the ball in their possession. A point is scored when a player wheels over their scoring line at the end of the court with the ball in their possession.

The purpose and techniques of the game are significant because it is not actually clear why the sport should be called wheelchair rugby at all. Wheelchair rugby has many dissimilarities to mainstream rugby; forward passes are allowed in wheelchair rugby, players must bounce or pass the ball once every ten seconds, a round ball instead of an oval ball is used and there is only one way of scoring points. Wheelchair rugby and mainstream rugby are far less similar than the disability sport and mainstream versions of other sports such as tennis, volleyball, basketball, track and field or cricket, and it is at least debatable whether many first-time viewers would actually recognise wheelchair rugby as a form of rugby. In fact, the two sports arguably share only two significant similarities: both games involve passing a ball (a feature of many other sports) and points are scored when a ball carrier crosses a line at one end of the field.[2]

Although the naming of the sport preceded the making of *Murderball*, our argument here is that the choice of the name wheelchair rugby suggests an obvious desire to be linked with mainstream rugby and other heavy contact sports. Early in the film we see the New Zealand team doing a wheelchair 'Haka', the Maori ceremonial dance made famous by the New Zealand men's rugby team. Likewise, *Murderball* spends much of its time linking its main characters to a series of sporting and, in particular, masculine sporting stereotypes. Indeed, whatever else might be said about *Murderball*, it is, first and foremost, a story about the performance of masculinity. And as a generation of scholarship has shown, rugby and other forms of football such as American football are sports that in many Western countries signify 'normal', hegemonic and heterosexual masculinity. In short, *Murderball* is a film about a sport that has already tried to draw on the masculine cachet of

mainstream men's rugby and contact sport. Specifically, the film appears to imagine a non-disabled audience asking 'How is it possible for disabled people to play a rough game like rugby?' Having posed the question, *Murderball* constructs an answer. Unlike the disabled men interviewed in a Sparkes and Brett's study (2002), the wheelchair rugby players in *Murderball* emphasise, in a positive way, how the similarities between the sports they played prior to acquiring their disability attracted them to wheelchair rugby. The action of the film constantly reiterates the physical toughness of the players and, moreover, the way the players relish the sport's alleged brutality. One of the USA players featured in the film, Bob Lujano, gleefully announces that basic aim of the sport is to 'kill the man with the ball'. During the Larry King interview Lujano says 'I'm a huge football fan, Dallas Cowboys fan, so I definitely love the physical contact'. Andy Cohn, another USA player, emphasises his desire to play physical contact sport: 'It's not that I wanted to play despite all the contact, I wanted to play because of all the contact. I played high school football. As soon as I saw you could totally hit someone as hard as you can ... I'd found the perfect sport for me.'

It would be perhaps churlish to note that nobody actually 'hits' anybody in wheelchair rugby, at least not in the games featured in *Murderball*. What is emphasised is the collisions between wheelchairs. The opening sequences of the film have Marty, a member of the USA team's 'pit crew', describing the wheelchairs used. The wheelchairs themselves are a mass of roughly welded metal, the wheel hubs resemble barbarian warrior shields, while the overall effect is the stylised ultra-violent grunge of the Australian film *Mad Max*. Marty sees the resemblance as well, calling the wheelchair a 'gladiator, battling machine, a *Mad Max* wheelchair that can stand knocking the living daylights out of each other'. Wheelchair collisions, which sometimes result in the chair and player toppling on their side, accompanied by heavy death-metal guitars, are a mainstay of the movie's action.

The jock-ish masculinity that we see as a central discursive ingredient in *Murderball* is most obviously prosecuted through the personality of the USA player Mark Zupan. Zupan appears to have become the public face of wheelchair rugby and his macho attitudes, goatee beard, large tattoos and bodily muscularity are proudly and repeatedly displayed in the film. For example, the film presents Zupan visiting a spinal injury rehabilitation centre and promoting wheelchair rugby to patients. During this scene Mark takes a 'question and answer' session:

STAFF MEMBER:	Do you wear helmets?
ZUPAN:	No Mam.
STAFF MEMBER:	And why not?
ZUPAN:	You don't to do it, wearing helmets, elbow pads, shin pads, a helmet or whatever. but that may just be a macho man thing.

What is interesting here is the self-conscious use of 'macho' masculinity. It is as though it were not enough for the film to leave viewers with a strong sense of the macho behaviours of the players. Rather, the film wants you to know that the players see themselves as macho men. Early in the film the featured players talk about their aggressive rejection of condescending comments while drinking in pubs or doing the shopping. Zupan recalls daring another man to hit him and promising to hit him back. All this is accompanied with a regular stream of swearing.

In attempting to show what disabled bodies can do, *Murderball* does not simply present the central figures doing remarkable things like play a heavy contact sport; this is not just a story about 'supercrips'. For example, large sections of the film are spent showing that these disabled men are capable of doing 'normal' everyday things like driving, cooking, having sex and being a father to their children. In the case of sex, the film tells the viewer that lots of people, particularly young women, are curious about the sexual functioning of disabled men and, therefore, seek to answer this curiosity. All the central characters in the film are presented as keen to articulate their sexual abilities. Here Andy Cohn proudly reflects upon his first sexual encounter after acquiring his disability: 'My first full-on sex after being in a wheelchair was a very great moment in my life. Just knowing that I could still, not just the physical act but the, you know, you could still go out, meet a girl and get lucky.'

Another player describes his use of 'modified doggy style' while Zupan claims that 'when you're in a chair you usually like to eat pussy'.

The part of the film that explicitly deals with the players' heterosexual functioning appears early in the film when the personalities of the main characters are being established. But unlike other aspects of the film's narrative (such as the physicality of wheelchair rugby or the intensity of the rivalry between the Canadian and USA teams), the sexual functioning of these disabled bodies appears in a short, clearly self-contained section, almost like a commercial break. It is as if the film makers decided that this topic needed to be dealt with and, once dealt with, the film could move on. We think this raises an obvious question: why is it there? After all, there is no particularly obvious reason why *Murderball* needed to spend time 'educating' its audience about the sexual capacities and predilections of its male stars.

It is possible that this section is included simply to titillate and attract viewers. Sex sells, after all. And yet we would argue that it is precisely because *Murderball* is a film about sport, with its historic and symbolic relationship to heterosexual masculinity (Connell 1995; Light and Kirk 2000; Wellard 2002) that a connection to sexuality can be made in the minds of the film's makers. While to us this section seems a gratuitous and somewhat clumsy insertion, it makes more sense if the intention of the film is to establish its characters as 'real sporting men'. That is, addressing the question of heterosexual functioning makes symbolic sense alongside the claim that these men are tough, cool, masculine men. Our claim would be, then, that given the film's intended mainstream audience, the claim that these men are 'normal', 'typical' sporting jocks was understood (consciously or unconsciously) as less convincing if there was suspicion that they were either gay or sexually impotent. Although one of the USA players, Scott Hogsett, mentions that sexual function depends on the kind of injury sustained, all the stars of *Murderball* claim to be sexually active. The one exception is Bob Lujano, about whose sexual life we learn nothing.

In short, rather than saying nothing about the sexual lives of these men (a perfectly reasonable choice, given that it is predominantly a film about sport), *Murderball*'s makers included a short, sharp statement that links wheelchair rugby players to symbols of hegemonic, straight, non-disabled masculinity—sports-loving, physically tough and 'horny'.

(2) 'This is not the Special Olympics'

Perhaps a more surprising aspect of *Murderball* is its assertive repudiation of other areas of disability sport. For its participants, wheelchair rugby is presented as an extremely competitive sport requiring the same aggressive outlook and physical excellence of nondisabled elite sport performers. However, as with the displays of heterosexual masculinity discussed in the previous section, there is a sense of 'protesting too much' in that the film appears to have consciously chosen to prove its bona fide nature through exaggeration.

For example, *Murderball* offers viewers a window into a world of almost apocalyptic competitive intensity. Team huddles involve red-faced, screaming team chants while coaches 'candidly' claim 'we're going to kick the shit out of them'.

Although non-disabled elite sports cultures are diverse, the modern discourse of coaches and players in the heavy body-contact sports (such as rugby and American football) tends, at least when communicating with the media, to obscure or downplay inherent violence. Instead, talk of 'process', 'accountability', 'controlled aggression', 'discipline' and 'minimising errors' dominates. In this respect, the hyper-aggressive banter in *Murderball* is a kind of throwback; there is virtually no mention of tactical subtlety throughout the entire film. At the end, viewers are none the wiser about how a game of wheelchair rugby is won or about how the Canadian and USA teams differ in their styles of play. All we are told is that they hate each other.

For example, the film makes much of the fact that Joe Soares, the Canadian coach, is an American and ex-USA star player who defected to Canada in order to prolong his career. A number of times during the film Joe is accused by USA players of 'betraying his country'. Of Soares, Zupan says: 'If Joe was on the side of the road on fire I wouldn't piss on him to put it out'. When Joe comes face to face with ex-teammates they trade obscenities in an almost pantomime demonstration of mutual antipathy. In the two of the medal presentations captured in the film, losing players cry inconsolably while winners sing national anthems at the top of their voices, seeming almost to take pleasure in taunting their defeated opposition.

For his part, Soares is portrayed as a brooding, intense and manically competitive individual who is determined to take revenge on the USA for trying to finish his sporting career. In a television story about the lead up to the Athens Paralympics, a sports reporter says that 'Joe's one of the most competitive men I've ever been around'. Soares's family life and, in particular, his relationship with his 'nerdy' violin-playing son is framed as a test of whether he can curtail his competitive sporting nature and be a 'good father'. The resolution of this subplot, in which Soares and his son are finally able to communicate their affection for each other, is achieved only once Soares's sporting intensity is portrayed as an all-consuming threat to his health (during the film he suffers a heart attack) and family life. In our view, these displays of hatred are included in order to distance wheelchair rugby from other disability sports. That is, they are designed to distance the sport from the participatory 'feel-good' ethos of other disability sport and position it closer to the competitive seriousness of elite mainstream sport. For example, the USA coach comments that 'there is a perception that everyone can play this game' and then goes on to describe how the final 12 players in the USA squad are ruthlessly culled from a much larger field of participants. This distancing finds full voice in the film's climax, the build-up to the Athens Paralympics. In a collage of short sections of footage accompanied by the obligatory heavy metal music, fans are shown with national emblems tattooed on their face; the Olympic flame burns; lycra-clad athletes carry a USA flag in victory, while others celebrate deliriously. The message is clear: this is real sport. There is no 'feel-good' here. This is about winning. In a hotel room prior to the Paralympics, Hogsett and Zupan drive the no-feel-good point home. Hogsett is talking about his wedding day where a relative came to him and said that she had heard he was going to the Special Olympics:

HOGSETT: And all of a sudden I went from being the man at the wedding, to a fucking retard. And it was the worst feeling. The Special Olympics are something that happens once a year and it's for people who are mentally challenged. What they do in the Special Olympics is very honourable. It's amazing what

	they can do. But this is something that's totally different.
ZUPAN (WITH IRONY)	It's a little different. We're not going for this feel good 'please, pat me on the back. Thank you. Thank you for participating.' No, no, no, no.
HOGSETT:	We're not going for a hug. We're going for a fucking gold medal.

Whatever else we might think about this section of dialogue, we can say that a choice has been made to include it. Therefore, we might justifiably ask why this kind of distancing work seemed necessary or desirable to the film's makers. Once again, *Murderball* seems in a timewarp, back to the 1970s catch-cry 'winning isn't the main thing, it's the only thing'.

Today, it is almost impossible to imagine non-disabled elite athletes talking openly and publicly about disabled athletes in this way and escaping public censure. In fact, the archetypal modern non-disabled sports star works hard to cultivate a more wholesome image that will be attractive to sponsors. This is not to pass particular moral judgement on Hogsett and Zupan. Rather, it is to simply note that *Murderball* seems to be saying that entry to the club of 'real sport' means, in part, defining itself by reference to what it is not. In the previous section, we saw how *Murderball* explicitly links wheelchair rugby to the conventions of heterosexual sexuality and aggressive, male dominated mainstream sports.

(3) 'Hot' and disabled

The final theme that we discuss follows closely on from the previous theme. However, while we have just discussed the way *Murderball* attempts to assert its sporting credentials, in this section we see how the film tries to position wheelchair rugby as an exciting, media-friendly sport with the potential to attract greater media exposure, fans and sponsors. This point is made explicitly and repeatedly during the *Larry King Show* interview. At the beginning of the show, King invites his audience to stay watching by presenting the players as 'must watch' stars and athletes. King announces: 'Tonight! They're handsome, sexy, world class athletes and they're quadriplegics in wheelchairs.' Later, discussion turns to the potential and future possibilities for wheelchair rugby:

KING:	Does the sport, does it draw people Scott?
HOGSETT:	Yeah, especially with this movie out it's going to get bigger. Next year we're really excited for it.
KING:	Where are you playing, what sort of gyms?
HOGSETT:	We'll play in high schools, we'll play arenas, we'll play in community centres.
KING:	Do you think you'll play one day at Madison Square Gardens?
HOGSETT:	We'd like that.
ZUPAN:	That's the biggest stage.
KING:	I know the people there. Why wouldn't they be interested in this? Especially, they could put on a two-day tournament.
ZUPAN:	What we've been talking about is incorporating it into the X-Games.

Murderball says to its viewers: 'With the right marketing, disabled people can be sports megastars too.' This point is implicitly reiterated by emphasising the media build-up prior to the Athens Paralympics. A video collage shows TV anchors talking to cameras, television crews going about their business and a series of press conferences. The message is that this sport is 'hot' and people really are excited about it. In one of these press conferences Zupan answers a question about wheelchair rugby: 'It used to be called "Murderball", but you can't really market "Murderball" to corporate sponsors.'

Murderball swings between framing wheelchair rugby in a WWF-style hypertheatricality—heavy metal music, lighting effects, rapid-fire editing and fast camera zooming—and, in the final section of the film, presenting it as a poignant and serious sporting contest: the final moments of the Athens match between USA and Canada unfolds in agonising slow-motion, string accompaniment and, later, the defeated and distraught USA players are greeted post-match by tearful friends and family.

Our argument here is that *Murderball* is much more than a conventional piece of film-making that strives for roughly equal measures of human pathos and sporting spectacle; it is not simply that the film's makers wanted to make it entertaining for a mainstream audience. There are, after all, many ways to make a film entertaining.

Rather, *Murderball* employs an eclectic set of tools to chart a discursive course towards (to paraphrase Kuhn) 'normal sport'. Sex, masculinity, hyper-aggressive competition and media stardom come together to construct a disabled athlete who claims both elements of elite sport's macho past and a popular-culture future for disability sport. This is interesting for many reasons but particularly because there is also a clear agenda within the film to connect with other disabled people. Zupan's outreach work in hospital spinal units makes it clear that *Murderball* sees itself as reaching up—to sporting stardom—and down—to other disabled people. This raises a tension to which, in conclusion, we now turn.

Pleasure, disability and physical education

There is a moment in *Murderball* during Zupan's visit to the spinal injury clinic where he meets Keith, a young man recently injured in a motorcycle accident. Keith is clearly excited by what he hears about wheelchair rugby and sees on the video that Zupan plays. He is captivated by the metallic wheelchair Zupan has brought with him and pleads with his nurse to let him try running into something in the chair. Eventually she reluctantly relents and, using Zupan's chair, Keith gently bumps, to and fro, into Zupan who is now in a standard wheelchair. There is no music, just the soft bumping sound of metal on metal. The scene ends.

It is as if we have just witnessed an awakening moment. Keith's tiny collisions are miniaturised version of the fierce wheelchair impacts that litter the action of *Murderball*. Although the film's makers may not put it this way, they seem to be saying that disabled boys and men have the same drives and impulses as other boys and men. We are not inclined, here, to buy into an implied biological determinism about masculinity, but *Murderball* is a plea for more fully embodied physical experiences for disabled boys and men. In this respect, the film is simply part of a long established movement to push through one more sporting barrier while, at the same time, pushing through one more sociocultural barrier—legitimate access to a macho, sporting, hyper-heterosexual masculinity that is celebrated in the wider culture. It is difficult to

see how *Murderball* could be criticised for this, just as it is difficult to see how (putting to one side the thorny question of legal liability) physical educators could deny these kinds of desires, pleasures and identities to young disabled people. There will, one day, be female 'murderballers' too and physical educators have to begin to think about how the desires of students who want to 'get more physical' will be managed and supported.

In exactly the same way, there may be some viewers of *Murderball* and readers of this article who are concerned about the 'corrupting' influence of corporatised sport on disability sport. The stars of *Murderball* make it clear that they will have no patience for those who are queasy at the sight of disabled athletes behaving badly or, indeed, ultracompetitively. They say 'not all disabled people will want to be like us, but those who do, come along for the ride!' In this sense, they pre-empt those who might wonder about how young disabled people, who will never have the capacity to be assertive, aggressive elite athletes, will 'read' *Murderball*. The answer is that they will read it in the same way non-disabled young people 'read' non-disabled athletes: in a variety of ways and without the sky falling in. Once again, what *Murderball* does is unveil a set of desires which both are legitimate but potentially unsettling to some viewers simply because they are being felt by disabled bodies. But desires are always scary to somebody and physical educators are now faced with potentially new answers to questions about disabled identities and what disabled young people want.

In the end, the question for us is not whether *Murderball* is an accurate or positive symbol for all disabled young people; of course it is not and could never be. As we tried to stress in the methodology section above, we did not see a fair-minded critique of *Murderball* harping on about the female or gay or old athletes or black athletes not being depicted. These depictions are for another day. The question that we would raise about *Murderball* is the way it both tries to build certain bridges but, in the process, seems intent on destroying others. The victims of *Murderball* are those that are explicitly marginalised in the film, particularly intellectually disabled people. *Murderball* argues that in order for some disabled people to be lifted up, others have to be pushed down. It does this over and over again by selectively using non-disabled stereotypes—about masculinity, sport, and sexuality—that the film's stars can measure up to. In the world of *Murderball* the film, sexual incapacitation, being a 'retard' and being a happy and gracious loser are the ways you let the side down.

We should not forget that *Murderball* is, among other things, a commentary on, even a parody of, non-disabled mainstream sports culture. And yet, drawing on our thematic critique, in order to establish wheelchair rugby's sporting legitimacy, certain dominant ideas about sport are not so much rehearsed in *Murderball* as amplified. This leaves physical educators with a new set of questions about the hierarchies that might exist between different forms of disability and the formation of new disabled sporting cultures. *Murderball* wants to tell us that certain forms of disability sport are more legitimate than others. This should prompt us to think about the application of Siedentop's 'elite development goal': who is it for and why?

Notes

1. For further information about these disability sports see http://www.paralympic.org
2. Though in rugby the ball must be grounded on or over the line.

References

Barnes, Colin, Geof Mercer and Tom Shakespeare. 1999. *Exploring Disability A Sociological Introduction*. Cambridge: Polity Press.

Barton, Len. 1993. Disability, empowerment and physical education. In *Equality, Education and Physical Education*, edited by J. Evans. London: Falmer Press: 43–54.

Boyle, Ellexis, Brad Millington and Patricia Vertinsky. 2006. Representing the female pugilist: Narratives of race, gender, and disability in *Million Dollar Baby*. *Sociology of Sport Journal* 23: 99–116.

Coakley, Jay J. 2007. *Sport in Society: Issues and Controversies*. London: McGraw-Hill Higher Education.

Connell, Robert, W. 1995. *Masculinities*. Sydney: Allen & Unwin.

Dahl, Marilyn. 1993. The role of the media in promoting images of disability – disability as metaphor.

The evil crip. *Canadian Journal of Communication* 18 (1), available at http://www.cjc-online.ca/viewarticle.php?id¼4141, accessed 15 March 2006.

Darke, Paul. 1988. Understanding cinematic representations of disability. In *The Disability Reader: Social Science Perspectives*, edited by T. Shakespeare. London: Cassell: 181–200.

Davis, John and Nick Watson. 2002. Countering stereotypes of disability: Disabled children and resistance. In *Embodying Disability Theory, Disability/Postmodernity*, edited by M. Corker and T. Shakespeare. London: Continuum: 159–74.

Depauw, Karen P. 1997. The (in)visability of disAbility: Cultural contexts and 'sporting bodies'. *Quest* 49 (4), 416–30.

DfEE/QCA (Department for Education and Employment/Qualifications and Curriculum Authority). 1999. *Physical Education: The National Curriculum for England*. London: HMSO.

Downs, Peter. 1995. *An Introduction to Inclusion Practice*. Canberra: Australian Sports Commission.

Duncan, Barbara. 2007. Disability in the US media—notes on 2006, available at http://www.disabilityworld.org/01_07/media.shtml, accessed 12 Feb. 2008.

Evans, John and Brian Davies. 2002. Theoretical background. In *The Sociology of Sport and Physical Education*, edited by A. Laker. London: Routledge/Falmer: 15–35.

Fitzgerald, Hayley. 2005. Still feeling like a spare piece of luggage? Embodied experiences of (dis)ability in physical education and school sport. *Physical Education & Sport Pedagogy* 10 (1), 71–89.

Goffman, Erving. 1968. *Stigma*. Harmondsworth: Pelican.

Haller, Beth. 2006. Thoughts on *Million Dollar Baby*. *Journal of Research in Special Educational Needs* 6(2), 112–14.

Harding, Marie M. and Brent Harding. 2004. The 'Supercrip' in sport media: Wheelchair athletes discuss hegemony's disabled hero. *Sociology of Sport Outline* 7 (1), available at http://physed.otago.ac.nz/sosol/v7i1/v7i1_1.html, accessed 27 July 2006.

Hayes, Michael T. and Rhonda S. Black. 2003. Troubling signs: Disability, Hollywood movies and the construction of a discourse of pity. *Disability Studies Quarterly* 23 (2), 114–32.

Hevey, David. 1992. *The Creatures That Time Forgot: Photography and Disability Imagery*. London: Routledge.

Light, Richard and David Kirk. 2000. High school rugby, the body and the reproduction of 'hegemonic' masculinity. *Sport, Education and Society* 5 (2), 163–76.

Mitchell, David and Sharon Snyder. 2006. Narrative prosthesis and the materiality of metaphor. In *The*

Disability Studies Reader, edited by L.J. Davis. London: Routledge: 205–27.

Ministry Of Education. 1999. *Health and Physical Education in New Zealand Curriculum*. Wellington: Learning Media.

Norden, Martin F. 1994. *The Cinema of Isolation*. New Brunswick, NJ: Rutgers University Press.

Pointon, Anne, ed. 1997. *Framed Interrogating Disability in the Media*. London: British Film Institute.

Priestley, Mark. 1999. Discourse and identity: disabled children in mainstream high schools. In *Disability Discourse*, edited by M. Corker and S. French. Buckingham: Open University Press: 92–102.

Shakespeare, Tom. 1994. Cultural representation of disabled people: Dustbins for disavowal? *Disability and Society* 9 (3), 283–99.

Sherrill, Claudine and Karen P. Depauw. 1997. Adapted physical activity and education. In *The History of Exercise and Sport Science*, edited by J.D. Massengale and Richard A. Swanson. Champaign, IL: Human Kinetics.

Siedentop, Daryl. 2002. Junior sport and the evaluation of sport cultures. *Journal of Teaching in Physical Education* 21: 392–401.

Smart, Julie F. 2001. *Disability, Society, and the Individual*. Gaithersburg, MD: Aspen Publishers.

Sparkes, Andrew C. and Brett Smith. 2002. Sport, spinal core injury, embodied masculinities, and the dilemmas of narrative identity. *Men and Masculinities* 4 (3): 258–85.

Sport England. 2001. *Disability Survey 2000 Young People with a Disability and Sport, Headline Findings*. London: Sport England.

Swain, John, Sally French, Colin Barnes and Carol Thomas. 2005. *Disabling Barriers–Enabling Environments*. London: Sage.

Thomas, Nigel and Andrew Smith. 2003. Pre-occupied with able-bodiedness? An analysis of the British media coverage of the 2000 Paralympic games *Adapted Physical Activity Quarterly* 20 (2): 166–81.

Vickerman, Philip. 2002. Perspectives on the training of physical education teachers for the inclusion of children with special educational needs – Is there an official line view? *The Bulletin of Physical Education* 38 (2): 79–98.

Wellard, Ian. 2002. Men, sport, body performance and the maintenance of exclusive masculinity. *Leisure Studies* 21 (3 & 4): 235–47.

4.4

Against sexual discrimination in sports

Torbjörn Tännsjö

Introduction

Sexual discrimination is a widespread and recalcitrant phenomenon. However, in Western societies, explicit sexual discrimination, when exposed, is seldom defended straightforwardly. There is one remarkable exception to this, however. Within sports sexual discrimination is taken for granted. It is assumed that, in many sports contexts, it is appropriate to discriminate (distinguish) between women and men and to have men competing exclusively with men, and women competing exclusively with women.[1] Even by radical feminists this kind of sexual discrimination has rarely been questioned. This is strange. If sexual discrimination is objectionable in most other areas of our lives, why should it be acceptable within sports?

The thesis of this chapter is that it is not. Even within sports, sexual discrimination is morally objectionable. No sexual discrimination should take place within sports. At least, the International Olympic Committee (IOC) and the leading national sports organisations should give it up.

The reasons for giving up sexual discrimination within sports, and for allowing individuals of both sexes to compete with each other, is simple. In sports it is crucial that the best person wins. Then sexual differences are simply irrelevant. If a female athlete can perform better than a male athlete, this female athlete should be allowed to compete with, and beat, the male athlete. If she cannot beat a certain male athlete, so be it. If the competition was fair, she should be able to face the fact that he was more talented. It is really as simple as that. Sexual discrimination within sports does not have any better rationale than sexual discrimination in any other fields of our lives.

However, arguments against giving up sexual discrimination within sports are not hard to come by, and in this chapter I will focus on such arguments. My thrust here is that, in various different ways, these arguments against abolition of sexual discrimination within sports are flawed. However, I will not restrict my argumentation to a discussion of arguments for sexual discrimination. One important argument against sexual discrimination, apart from the general observation that, from the point of view of sports itself it is irrelevant, will also be developed.

These are the main arguments *for* sexual discrimination within sports – some of them, no doubt, striking an indistinguishable (yet false) chord of special concern for women:

- Sexual discrimination within sports is no different from the use of, say, different

Torbjörn Tännsjö 'Against Sexual Discrimination in Sports', from *Values in Sport*, T. Tännsjö and C. Tamburrini eds, © 2000 Torbjörn Tännsjö. Reprinted by permission of Routledge.

weight classes in certain sports, intended to make the result less predictable. We use sexual discrimination because we seek, to use Warren Fraleigh's term, 'the sweet tension of uncertainty of outcome'.

- If women and men compete, and women defeat men, then this will cause violent responses from men. So we had better retain the discrimination.
- If we give up sexual discrimination in sports, then probably all women will find (because on average they perform poorly in comparison with men) that they are always defeated by some men. This will be discouraging for women in general and for female athletes in particular.
- Female sports are different from male sports. They represent a unique value, and if we gave up discrimination this unique value would be foregone. A similar argument can be devised with reference to male sports, of course.

I will discuss these arguments in order. After having done so I will give my positive argument in defence of giving up sexual discrimination, which is that the rationale behind sexual discrimination is simply too good. If we consistently hold on to it, we are led to all sorts of discrimination which, upon closer examination, we do not want to accept. So a kind of reductio ad absurdum leads us to the conclusion that sexual discrimination within sports should be given up.

I conclude the chapter by summing up the main tenets of my argument and by proposing, constructively, that sport as a phenomenon should not be conceived of as static. A development of various different sports takes place, and has to take place. We should consciously mould the phenomenon of sports in a certain desirable direction. We should mould sports in a direction of more moderation. If we do, then we will be able to abolish sexual discrimination altogether within sports, thereby gaining a great deal from the point of view of gender equality and fairness, without having to pay any price at all for this timely reform.

If sexual discrimination within sports is abolished, this will not only be an advance from the point of view of feminism and the women's rights movement, I conclude, but from the point of view of sport itself. For the abolishment of sexual discrimination may render natural a development of sport in a direction which is, even if we put the matter of sexual discrimination to one side, of the utmost importance for sport itself, conceived of broadly as a cultural phenomenon. It may well be the case that, unless some sports develop in a direction where women and men *can* compete safely on equal terms, then there will be no future for these sports at all – or so I will argue, at any rate.

Sexual discrimination as no different to the use of weight classes?

When I have proposed that sexual discrimination within sports should be abolished, I have sometimes met the objection that sexual discrimination in some sports is no different to the use of weight classes in, say, boxing. We have such weight classes in order to ascertain that the outcome of a competition is not too easily predictable. This (evasive) argumentative strategy is completely misplaced, however. I have no objection to weight classes in boxing and some other sports. As a matter of fact, I think we should develop this kind of system even within other sports. There should be weight classes even in running, and heightclasses in basketball, and so forth. Such classes are constructed with reference to crucial characteristics of the individual athlete, characteristics with relevance for the capacity to perform well in the sport in question, and they are created in the interest of making the outcome of the competitions less predictable. It is crucial that the classes are constructed on the grounds of characteristics actually exhibited by the people who get sorted with reference to the characteristics in question, and that these characteristics are of *immediate* relevance to the capacity to perform well within the sport in question.

Sexual discrimination is different: it takes place on the ground that, *on average*, women perform less well than men in certain sports. This is objectionable. First of all, this putative fact, that women perform less well than men, is hard to ascertain beyond reasonable doubt. Perhaps this is a mere statistical accident. Perhaps it is due to socially constructed gender differences rather than biological sexual differences and, hence, could be abolished. And even if the statistical correlation is due to biological sexual differences (more below about sexual differences, and how to define them), and even if it has a law-like character, it is still only a *statistical* difference. It is only indirectly, then, that sex is relevant to the outcome of a fair competition. It is relevant in the sense that it predisposes, statistically, for more or less of a certain characteristic, crucial to performing well in a certain sport. But then, if we should discriminate at all, we should discriminate in terms of this characteristic itself and not in terms of sex.

This means that some women, who are not (statistically speaking) 'typical', perform better than many (most) men do. They do so because to a considerable degree they possess the characteristics that are crucial to winning, and possess more of these characteristics than do most men. Consequently, there are some rare women who perform better than most men in the sport in question.

It is 'discrimination', then, not only in a factual sense (in the way the term is used in this chapter), when a competent woman, who can and wants to defeat a certain man, is prohibited from doing so, on the ground that women in general do not perform as well as men in general. But it is also 'discrimination' in a *moral* sense, and such discrimination is morally reprehensible.

So while there is nothing objectionable in having weight classes in boxing (a sport in which weight is of direct relevance to winning), it *is* objectionable to have sexual classes (sex is only indirectly and statistically relevant to winning in boxing).

If boxing should be allowed at all, it should be allowed in a form where individuals of both sexes can compete safely with each other. To render this possible we would have to retain weight classes, of course. We may also have to make some other improvements of this noble art of self-defence, but I will not elaborate on this point in the present context. However, I conjecture that, unless boxing can be performed in a manner where men and women can compete safely against each other, there will (and should) not be any such thing as boxing in the future.

Sexual discrimination because of male aggressiveness?

What I have just said connects with a second argument against abolishing sexual discrimination within sports. Not only boxing, but also many other sports, are aggressive and involve a considerable amount of physical contact and encounter between competing athletes. Now, if women and men are allowed to compete against each other, and if some women defeat some men, then this would trigger violent responses from these men, or so the argument goes. In order to protect women against such outbursts of male aggressiveness, we had better let women and men compete apart from each other.

Is this a good argument? I admit that there is something to it, and it points at a real danger. However, it would be wrong to surrender to the argument, for there is another way of responding to the phenomenon of male aggressiveness against women. I am thinking here of the possibility of rendering impossible the aggressive response. This could be done if the rules of the game in question were changed. Aggressive assault on competitors could be punished much more severely than it is in many sports currently. One physical assault could mean a red card – and the aggressive male competitor would be out.

The rules of the game could be modified in other ways as well, so that the assault would be made more difficult to perform in the first place. Then there would be little need for punishment. And the sports could be modified, to render aggressiveness within the sports, even within the limits that are permitted, less rewarding and also never decisive.

Take tennis as an example. In modern tennis, the service is of enormous importance: an efficient service presupposes a lot of physical strength from the server. At the same time, an effective service tends to render the sport rather boring: it kills the game by taking the elegance out of it. An obvious solution to this problem would be to introduce a rule saying that a service is not successful unless the receiver has successfully returned it. Until it has been successfully returned, the server is granted a new opportunity. This would certainly reintroduce certain desirable qualities in tennis, and at the same time such a change in the rules of the game would mean better possibilities for women to compete successfully with men. Men would not defeat women merely by virtue of their superior strength and aggressiveness.

Were all this to be accomplished, I think we could make great strides in the general aim for sexual equality in society. *Some* women can defeat *most* men who perform any sport. Because of sexual prejudices, this is a hard lesson for a man to learn. It is hard even for me, a middle-aged man who regularly goes jogging, to be defeated now and then by a female jogger. As a matter of fact, I hate the defeat, and I go to considerable lengths to avoid it – but I sometimes fail. When I do, I get angry. I am enlightened enough to realise, however, when I do get defeated by a female jogger, that this teaches me a lesson. It is good for my mental development to be defeated by female runners: it teaches me to control my anger and it shows me something about the relation between the sexes. Some sexual stereotypes and (my) prejudices get exposed in the most efficient manner.

If this is correct, then we have good reasons not to surrender to this male aggressiveness argument regarding sexual discrimination within sports. We should allow women to defeat men in sports, and we should render it impossible for men physically to punish the women who do defeat them.

If we do so, in the long run certain sexual prejudices will hopefully wither.

Women will be discouraged?

The response to the argument relating to male aggressiveness may be considered overly optimistic. It is true that in most sports there are some women who can beat most men, but it is also true that in many sports some men can beat all women. So, even if it is a good thing from the point of view of sexual equality when a woman beats a man, is it not a bad thing, from the same point of view, when the best women in certain sports find that they cannot compete with the best men? Wouldn't this fact be disappointing for these women?

Well, I suppose this depends on whether (due to sexual differences) it is *impossible* for these women to defeat the best man, or whether there is something that can be done about this fact (the problem lies not in the sexual differences themselves but in socially constructed gender differences, which could be abolished). If there is something that can be done about it, if the problem is socially constructed gender differences rather than sexual differences, then

these women may view the fact that they get defeated as a challenge. And they may take it as their mission to abolish the gender bias within sports.

This is basically the case in many other fields of society. There are men within certain sciences and arts, such as mathematics and musical composition, who perform better than all women (there is no female Gödel or Bach, for example). Should this be disappointing for women? I think not. I think rather it should be considered a real challenge, for we do not believe that it is because of their biological sex that no women solved logical problems like Gödel or composed like Bach. Typically, the lack of outstanding female logicians and composers is due to socially constructed gender differences, not to biological sexual differences as such.

There are reasons why women do not perform as well as some men do in these fields, of course, and these reasons, which are to do with gender rather than sexual differences, should come under close scrutiny. Such obstacles, when identified and publicly recognised, should come under severe attack. Schneider has correctly observed that these obstacles are the outcome of a deeply entrenched ideal, according to which, from inception, 'the ancient and modern Olympic Games, and the ideal Olympic athlete, applied specifically and exclusively to men'. This is how she describes this ideal:

> From Pausanias' references to dropping women from the side of a cliff if they even observed the ancient Olympic Games, to de Coubertin's ideal that the goals that were to be achieved by the athletes through participation in the Olympic Games were not appropriate for women (de Coubertin 1912), one can easily see that the place of women in sport has been, for the most part, foreign at best. It is this basic idea, the idea that sport (or sometimes even physical activity), particularly high-level competitive sport, is somehow incompatible with what women are, or what they should be, that must dominate any discussion of the unique issues for women in sport. Philosophies of ideal sport, and ideal women, lie behind discussions of permitting women to compete, of choosing the types of sport in which women can compete, in developing judging standards for adjudicated (as opposed to refereed) sports – contrast gymnastics and basketball – in attitudes to aggression, and

competition, and indeed to the very existence of women's sport as a separate entity at all.

[Chapter 4.5, p. 264]

I believe that, if such obstacles are eliminated, if new weight and length classes are introduced in many sports, if the rules are changed so as to render it impossible for aggressive athletes to punish their competitors, and if severe punishments are introduced for violations of the rules, then women can actually compete successfully and safely with men in many sports. In fact, they do so today in some sports, such as some shooting events, all the equestrian sports, parachuting, and so forth, and the list of these sports is growing all the time – and is likely to continue to get longer in the future.

But what if this belief is not borne out by realities? What if there are some sports where the elite is made up of men exclusively – would this be disappointing to women?

Yes, of course it would. But, for all that, this seems to me to be a kind of disappointment that should be acceptable as a natural part of life. Sexual distinctions are genetic in origin, and so are racial distinctions. After all, there may be all kinds of genetic distinctions of importance for how on average people of various different kinds perform in sports, and one of these is race. Perhaps black Africans perform better on average than Caucasians in some sports. This is disappointing to white people, of course, but is no reason to introduce racial discrimination within sports. But if this is not a reason to introduce racial discrimination in sports, then we should not retain sexual discrimination either.

To elaborate this point, allow me to return to the comparison with the sciences and the arts and take my own subject, philosophy, as an example. Women are poorly represented, not only among logicians and composers, but also within the philosophical world in general. Most people believe that the reason for this is to do with gender rather than with sex, and this is what I happen to believe. It is because women have been met with the wrong expectations, when they have taken up philosophy, it is because they have not been given proper credit for their achievements, and so forth, that they have had difficulties in performing well within philosophy. However, what if it turned out that, even after this kind of gender bias had been successfully abolished, women were still poorly represented within (a certain field of, say) philosophy, would this be disappointing for women?

Perhaps it would be (to some women), but then I think it should be possible for them to live with this kind of disappointment. It would be absurd, for this reason, to have sexual discrimination within philosophy and to have female positions and special journals for women in these fields of philosophy – specially designed for them because they do not perform well enough to hold standard positions or to publish in ordinary journals within (these fields of) philosophy.

Maybe it would not be at all disappointing to (other) women, however, if it turned out that a kind of philosophy exists that is just poorly suited to the female brain or heart. Another reaction from women (and many men) upon finding this out could be the following. If this philosophy is essentially without appeal to one of the sexes, if it does not fit women, then this indicates not that there is anything wrong with women but that there is something wrong with this kind of philosophy.

We could adopt the same stance towards the more plausible putative fact that there are some sports that simply suit (on average) men better than women; that is, we could say of these sports, 'So much worse for them!'

One of my colleagues, who likes to go to further extremes than I do,[2] has objected to my argument in the following way. If we should abolish sexual discrimination within sports, he asks, why not abolish species discrimination as well? Why not have men competing with animals? Why not have Carl Lewis running over 100m against a hunting leopard?

Well, the reason not to arrange such competitions is not only (or mainly) that it would be a difficult task to arrange them, or that such competitions are hardly likely to be rewarding to animals. Perhaps the difficulties could be overcome and perhaps some animals would take some pleasure in competing with men. The main reason for not arranging such competitions is that *no* man can beat *any* (healthy) hunting leopard. This is not merely a matter of a statistical generalisation. If there were a system similar to weight classes for running, then people and hunting leopards would have to compete in different classes.

However, if the differences between men and hunting leopards were merely statistical, so that some men could beat some hunting leopards, then I am not sure that competitions between men and beasts would seem so outlandish; after all, they used to have such competitions during antiquity. It is a delicate question for the animal liberation movement, of course, whether they should promote (because of an interest in abolishing species discrimination) such competitions or oppose them (because they may fear that the animals would not take pleasure in them).

To return to the human case. It is hard to assess finally how important the statistical genetic differences are between human beings within sports. And the assessment should not be made in any simplistic manner, where gender gets conflated with sex, nor should it be taken for granted that sport is a static phenomenon. The sports evolve, to some extent in a natural way, and to some extent as the result of our active and intentional intervention. If we do not like the fact that statistical genetic differences, such as sexual or racial differences, are decisive within sports, there is a lot we can do about it.

This leads to the next argument.

Female sports represent a unique value

It may seem that female sports are different from male sports, and so they represent a unique value. To give up sexual discrimination would therefore be like giving up valuable existing sports. It would be like giving up soccer or baseball, or basketball or hurdles in running.

How should we assess this argument? The answer to it is that, largely speaking, it is false and, to the extent that there is a grain of truth in it, this grain of truth does not warrant the conclusion that we should retain sexual discrimination in sports. Rather, it does warrant the conclusion that many aspects of sports need to be reformed, so that 'female' qualities are added to them or, even, so that 'female' qualities are exchanged for 'male' ones.

Let me first comment on the major aspect of this objection – the mere falsity of it. In many ways, female sports are no different from male sports.

Angela Schneider has eloquently elaborated on the falsity of the objection. To a considerable

and frightening extent, in many sports the male is simply the ideal. The good athlete is the hunter, the warrior, the man. And the conception of the masculine warrior is a narrow and simplistic one. In most athletic sports, Achilles could easily beat Ulysses. The cunning of the latter counts for nothing, whereas the superior strength of the former is decisive. This is also true when women take up these sports, and this is why women have to compete against each other and not against men. To put it drastically, therefore, I think it is fair to say that, in many sports, women compete against each other in masculinity, narrowly conceived. It is hard to find any special feminine qualities in *such* competitions.

What is the appropriate reaction to this obvious but little-publicised fact? Of course, this is hard to say. Some may find it unobjectionable. For my own part, I have to admit that I don't: I find the fact simply degrading, to both women and men. I also find that, if some women do want to compete in masculinity, why should they restrict themselves to a competition against each other? Why not compete also with men? After all, the best among them are capable of defeating most men even in masculinity. So why not do so?

I suppose that when Schneider describes how, in many sports, the male is the ideal, she intends this as a criticism. However, her criticism does not strike me as thorough enough. She seems to believe that the fact she describes in so many words is due mainly to gender aspects of sports, i.e. to aspects relating not with biological sex but to socially constructed roles and expectations. However, it is not far-fetched to believe that, even if we *were* to do away with all kinds of gender bias within sports, in many sports a genuine sexual bias would remain. Statistically, men *are* better than women in many existing sports. I will return to this fact below and to the question of what to do about it.

However, there may still be a grain of truth in the saying that women's sports in some aspects have unique qualities. I think, then, of qualities that are less to do with mere physical strength and more to do with inventiveness, sensibility, cooperation, strategy, playfulness, wit, and so forth. There may be more room for these qualities in women's competitions. And, to the extent that this is true, I think we are dealing with genuine and unique (female) qualities. However, there exists an obvious and better way of retaining these qualities than to retain sexual discrimination within sports. These qualities should be introduced in *all* sorts of sport, and they should not only be added to existing qualities but, in many cases, be exchanged for existing qualities.

It may be fruitful to speak of these unique qualities, which I suspect are more frequent in women's sport than in men's sport, as qualities of – to use Sigmund Loland's term – 'moderation'. Moderation in terms of what, though? Here I would like to be a bit more specific, in terms of gender, than Loland is himself. The object of the moderation, that which ought to be moderated, is arrogant outbursts of (male) aggressiveness and (mere) strength. These phenomena need not go away altogether, to be sure, but simplistic expressions of them should be countered. They should be moderated in the direction of values such as inventiveness, sensitivity, cooperation, playfulness and wit.

I think we are facing a happy coincidence here. Moderation is of great and growing importance within sports, not only as a means of rendering possible the abolition of sexual discrimination, but also as a means of saving sports as such, as a cultural phenomenon, from the most obvious threat to its continued existence (genetic engineering).

The observation that moderation and sexual equality should go together is in accordance with a suggestion put forward in Jane English's much-discussed article, 'Sex Equality in Sports', even though (eventually) English reaches the conclusion that sexual discrimination within sports is necessary. She suggests that we develop a variety of sports in which an array of physical types can expect to excel:

> We tend to think of the possible sports as a somewhat fixed group of those currently available. Yet even basketball and football are of very recent invention. Since women have been virtually excluded from all sports until the last century, it is appropriate that some sports using women's specific traits are not developing, such as synchronised swimming.
>
> (English 1995: 287)

A similar view has been put forward by Iris Marion Young, with reference to Mary E. Duquin. Young describes Duquin's position eloquently as follows:

> Androgyny in sport means for her the incorporation of virtues typically associated with women into the symbols and practices of sport – such as expressiveness and grace – along with a corresponding decline in the present overly aggressive and instrumentalist aspects of sport which are typically associated with masculinity.
>
> (Young 1995: 266)

Sports without moderation means competition in aspects such as mere strength. The problem with this is not that there is no public interest in competitions in strength; I think there is too *much* interest in such competitions. The problem with our fascination with strength is that it has a 'fascistoid' value basis. A further problem, of importance in the present context, is that mere strength, or the disposition for it, is a very simple and congenital quality, so mere strength is what we could call a *non*-moral virtue: either you have it or you don't. Moreover, there is every reason to believe that, not only is the disposition for strength congenital, but it has a rather simple *genetic explanation*. If this conjecture is borne out by realities, this means trouble for sports. For, certainly, once we can identify the genes for strength, which are really genes for winning in many existing sports, then it becomes possible genetically, not only to pre-select the winners, something that may seem frightening as such, but to *design* them. And, considering the enormous amounts of money and prestige that are invested in winning in sport, once the genetic design of winners becomes possible, it will take place. However, if we do design the winners genetically, then the public interest in sports competitions is likely to wither, or so I believe.

Genetic engineering, once it becomes possible, will be just as inevitable in sports as doping – unless we can render its application to sports impossible. And a way of rendering the genetic design of winners impossible is to change sports and to allow *moral* virtues to become crucial, for there are hardly any genes for inventiveness, sensitivity, cooperation, playfulness and wit in sports. All these virtues are true moral virtues: they can be learned (through training, to follow Aristotle) and, since there is a use for them outside the sports arenas as well, there is a point in learning them. To a considerable extent it is fair to say that these moral virtues, in contradistinction to the non-moral ones in sports, are typically 'female' (in the sense that there exist more of them in female sports than in male sports). So, at the same time, when we introduce more moderation into sports, in order to save sports from going extinct, we abolish the rationale behind sexual discrimination in sports, and we deepen the inherent value of sports as a cultural phenomenon.

All this means that, when we admire the winners of reformed (moderated) sports, our fascination for the winners will no longer bear a similarity to fascism, which is certainly an additional gain to be made.

Once we have reformed sports, by introducing more moderation into existing branches, and by adding new games to (and subtracting old ones from) the IOC list, we may safely give up sexual discrimination within sports and allow men and women to compete against each other on equal terms.

A reductio ad absurdum of sexual discrimination

We have seen that the standard arguments in defence of sexual discrimination within sports are weak. Let me just add one more positive argument in defence of abolishing sexual discrimination; an argument that is a reductio ad absurdum of the rationale behind sexual discrimination.

What are we to test for, when we test whether a certain athlete qualifies as female or male? Three options are open to us. We could test for genitalia, for gender, or for chromosomal constitution.

There are obvious difficulties with all three options. However, we need to stick to some of them, otherwise we will not be able to guard ourselves against athletes who want to cheat – against athletes who are really men, but prefer to compete with women under the false pretext that they *are* women. Moreover, if we have a system of sexual discrimination, and do not perform tests, there is a positive risk that women who excel in sports are being mistakenly suspected of really being men rather than women. These excellent women need the chance to reject, once and for all, these kinds of rumours and false allegations, and only efficient tests can accomplish this task.

There are many problems connected with testing for genitalia. First of all, the criterion is vague. We are operating here with a continuum. After all, even if rare, there are examples of hermaphroditism. Second, it is not clear that the test for genitalia is a valid one. In what sense are genitalia relevant? In what sports *could* genitalia be relevant? I blush when I seek an answer to that question. Finally, genitalia can easily be manipulated with: such tests are bound to be inefficient when it comes to people who (in an attempt to cheat) are prepared to undergo surgery.

The problems associated with testing for gender are even more obvious. First of all, this criterion is extremely vague. Perhaps the test should be the subjective sexual identification of the person in question, but this identification may be indeterminate. Furthermore, it may change over time. And then, once again, it is difficult to see any validity of such a test. In what sense does gender matter within sports? Finally, like a test for the appropriate genitalia, a test for appropriate gender would be only too easily fiddled with.

What, then, about chromosomal tests? These tests are what we rely on today, and I suppose that, if we want to retain a system of sexual discrimination within sports, then chromosomal tests are what we have to rely on even in the future. The problem with chromosomal tests is not that they are vague or that they are easily manipulated with. They rate high on measurements of specificity and sensitivity, if conducted in a meticulous way. They are also fairly easily conducted, they are not very invasive and, from the point of personal integrity, they are certainly less intrusive than tests for the appropriate genitalia.

Are chromosomal tests valid? Well, if we want to find variables that, statistically speaking, correlate with sports performances, chromosomal tests may well be valid in some sports. I have argued that we should not discriminate on these grounds but, for the sake of the argument (for the sake of our reductio ad absurdum) let us assume that we should. Then a problem with our sex chromosomes is that, even if most people conform to a typical male constitution (they have the genotype XY) or a typical female constitution (they have the genotype XX), not everyone does. There are individuals with only one X chromosome (they have the genotype X0; that is, they suffer from what has been called Turner's syndrome), and there are individuals with two X chromosomes and one Y chromosome (they have the genotype XXY; that is, they suffer from what has been called Klinefelter's syndrome). Even these aberrations are of interest here. For it is natural to believe that, statistically speaking, people (women?) suffering from Turner's syndrome perform, in many sports, less efficiently than do 'ordinary' women, and it is also likely that, statistically speaking, people (men?) suffering from Klinefelter's syndrome perform less efficiently than do 'ordinary' men in many sports. There may also be sports where some of these groups have, statistically speaking, a slight advantage. This may have been true of a well-known Polish sprinter, Ewa Klobukowska, who turned out to have the chromosomal pattern XXY. This person may well have had an advantage in certain sports over most people with the XX chromosomal pattern because of her extra Y chromosome (she held the world record for the women's 100m).

All this means that, if we want to be consistent, and if we want to be true to the rationale behind sexual discrimination, we should go a step further and even introduce new discrimination categories (people suffering from Turner's syndrome and Klinefelter's syndrome, and people exhibiting other aberrations such as XYY, to mention just three examples). And, as was alluded to above, we may even have to introduce other kinds of genetic discrimination, such as racial discrimination, within sports, for different human races may on average perform more or less efficiently in certain sports.

However, this may strike most of us as downright absurd. But if it does, it means that we must give up the premise that led us to this conclusion. We must give up the very rationale behind the idea of sexual discrimination within sports. We must drop the assumption we adopted for the sake of the argument – that it is appropriate to discriminate on grounds of genetic characteristics that, statistically speaking, favour or disfavour certain kinds of individuals in a certain sport.

We could add an even simpler argument to this. If we have sexual discrimination in sports, then (in order to avoid cheating and fraud) we need to have tests for sex. We have seen that these tests need to be chromosomal tests. However, it runs counter to a highly plausible idea of genetic integrity that information about a person's genetic constitution should ever be forced upon him or her. We have a right *not* to know our genetic makeup, if we do not *want* to know it. Compulsory chromosomal tests for athletes violate this right.[3]

Conclusion

I have argued that, if we reform sports in the direction indicated by Sigmund Loland, and introduce more moderation into all kinds of sports, then we may safely give up sexual discrimination within sports. This is something that the IOC and the national sports organisations should do. And even if moderation in sports will prove to be utopian, I think we should give up sexual discrimination. But then the appropriate reaction from women may be to turn their backs on those kinds of elitist sports where males (on average and for simple genetic reasons) have the upper hand.

Certainly, this abolition of sexual discrimination is consistent with there remaining a possibility for those who like to arrange sports competitions for one sex exclusively, just as there exists a possibility for arranging special sports competitions for certain races, political beliefs or sexual orientations. However, in more official settings there should exist a strict ban on *all* such sorts of (from the point of view of sports itself) irrelevant discriminations. It should be incumbent upon the sports organisations themselves to make sure that such a ban becomes a reality. And it should also be a condition of obtaining public funding that a sport organisation does not discriminate between women and men.

The reform of sports indicated here does not guarantee that there are no branches where, statistically speaking, men will perform better than women (just as there may exist sports where, say, black people perform better than Caucasians), but this does not warrant that we retain a system of sexual discrimination, nor that we introduce racial discrimination within sports. We should all be perfectly capable of living with the truth that such differences exist – and freely allow them to surface in sports competitions. Yes, there are also likely to exist examples of sports where the order is reversed. This is certainly true of some equestrian sports, such as dressage. There has been only one male Olympic winner in dressage since 1968 but surely this is no reason to reintroduce sexual discrimination in dressage.

What should the reform of sports look like in more detail? I will leave this as an open question. The examples I have given (additional weight and height classes, the abolition of the winning service in tennis, and so forth), are mere speculations on my part. To develop this line of thought takes a kind of expertise that I do not possess. And the method of reform must of course be piecemeal rather than utopian. The various different sports events should be put under scrutiny, one at a time. However, the direction of change should be the same all over the field of sports events. Three desiderata of moderation should be met, when interventions in the development of sports take place:

- Non-moral virtues (such as strength) should be given a less important role, and moral virtues (such as playfulness, inventiveness, sensitivity, cooperation and wit) a more important role, within sports.
- Sports should be developed in a direction that renders our admiration for the winners of sports competitions more decent.
- Sports should develop in a direction that makes it possible to abolish without any cost all kinds of sexual discrimination within sport.

If, and only if, these desiderata of moderation are met, sports will be able to thrive and flourish in the future and continue to add to the quality of our lives.

If these desiderata are (arrogantly) rejected, then, in a world where genetic engineering is quickly becoming a reality, the future prospects for athletics are bleak.

Arrogance and continued sexual discrimination will mean the marginalisation of athletics, or so I suggest here. In particular, unless women are given an equal chance to compete with, and defeat, males within elitist sports, they have a good reason to turn their backs on elitist sports. And unless sports are made immune to the threat posed by genetic engineering, they will be looked upon with little interest by the general public, and will lose their role as important cultural phenomena.

Notes

1. I use the word 'discrimination' in a neutral, purely descriptive sense. Sexual discrimination takes place whenever men and women are treated differently, no matter whether or not this difference in treatment is warranted.
2. Hans Mathlein, Stockholm University.
3. I defend the right in this strong form – which forbids insurance companies and employers to ask for information about the genotype of people or to use such information for any purposes whatever – in my book *Coercive Care* (Tännsjö 1999).

References

Coubertin, P. de (1912) 'Women in the Olympic Games', *Olympic Review*.

English, J. (1995) 'Sex Equality in Sports', first printed in *Philosophy and Public Affairs* 7 (1978), reprinted in *Philosophic Inquiry in Sport*, 2nd edition, Champaign, IL: Human Kinetics, pp. 284–288.

Tännsjö, T. (1999) *Coercive Care: The Ethics of Choice in Health and Medicine*, London and New York: Routledge.

Young, I.M. (1995) 'The Exclusion of Women From Sport: Conceptual and Existential Dimensions', first published in *Philosophy in Context* (1979) 9: 44–53, reprinted in *Philosophic Inquiry in Sport*, 2nd edition (1995), ed. W.J. Morgan and K. Meier, Champaign, IL: Human Kinetic Publishers, pp. 262–266.

On the definition of 'woman' in the sport context

Angela J. Schneider

Any discussion of the status of women in the sport context would benefit greatly from examining the underlying premises regarding the definition of 'woman' within (and outside) that context. Even on the surface level it becomes readily apparent to even the less-informed reader that the story to be told of women's participation in sport in general is the story of two ideals in apparent conflict. For example, from inception, the ancient and modern Olympic Games, and the ideal of the Olympic athlete, applied specifically and exclusively to men. From Pausanias' references to dropping women from the side of a cliff if they even observed the ancient Olympic Games, to de Coubertin's ideal that the goals that were to be achieved by the athletes through participation in the Olympic Games were not appropriate for women (de Coubertin 1912), one can easily see that the place of women in sport has been, for the most part, foreign at best. It is this basic idea, the idea that sport (or sometimes even physical activity), particularly high-level competitive sport, is somehow incompatible with what women are, or what they should be, that must dominate any discussion of the unique issues for women in sport. Philosophies of ideal sport, and ideal women, lie behind discussions of permitting women to compete, of choosing the types of sport in which women can compete, in developing judging standards for adjudicated (as opposed to refereed) sports – contrast gymnastics and basketball – in attitudes to aggression, and competition, and indeed to the very existence of women's sport as a separate entity at all.

Before examining some of these issues in detail, it is worth making a point and a distinction at the outset. The point is that many of the issues, even moral issues, that arise in sport, arise equally for men and women. At the personal level, the decision whether or not to cheat, or what attitude you will take to your opponents or the unearned win, are moral problems any athlete must face. At the institutional level, decisions about rules prohibiting drug use, or equipment limitations designed to improve participant safety, should apply equally to women as to men. As such, those concerns common to the realm of sport, important as they are, are more appropriately discussed elsewhere.[1] This chapter is devoted to the issues that arise because it is women, by virtue of the definition of who they are, who are the athletes. Thus the discussion that follows below will be focused on gender and sport, and the inter-relationships between them.

Angela J. Schneider 'On the Definition of "Woman" in the Sport Context', from *Values in Sport*, T. Tännsjö and C. Tamburrini eds, © 2000 Angela Schneider. Reprinted by permission of Routledge.

The philosophy of 'woman' versus the ideal athlete

Ideal woman

The battles that represent the basis for contentious issues for women in sport will be fought over conceptions of women – their bodies and their minds. The traditional ideals of woman during the ancient Olympic Games and the revival of the modern Olympic Games (up to and including some current ideals) are intimately tied to a particular view of woman's body. Some of these characteristics are soft, graceful, weak and beautiful. The desirable qualities for a woman in the time of the ancient Olympics can generally be summarised as beauty, chastity, modesty, obedience, inconspicuous behaviour, and being a good wife and a good mother (Lefkowitz and Fant 1985). Of course, these characteristics are tied to the roles of wife, mother and daughter. They are not similar to those of the traditional ideal of man, as hard, powerful, strong and rational, which are tied to the roles of leader, warrior and father. But, more importantly, if we examine the underlying characteristics of the traditional ideal athlete, we can plainly see that the ideal man and the ideal athlete are very similar, particularly in the role of warrior.[2] Conversely, we can plainly see that during the times of the ancient Olympic Games (and during the rebirth in the modern Olympic Games) the ideal woman and the traditional ideal athlete are almost opposites, so much so that women were hardly ever mentioned in conjunction with sport.

In contrast to these infrequent and casual references to women's sport, accounts of men's sport and athletics abound in ancient Greek literature. Homer vividly describes events from chariot racing to boxing. Pausanias furnishes a detailed account of the Olympic Games, and Herodotus, Thucydides and other Greek authors refer to the Olympic Games and athletic festivals such as the Pythian, Isthmian and Nemean Games (Spears 1988: 367).

There were also some exceptional counter-examples from ancient Greece – in the writings of Plato, for example – even though it is not well-known that girls competed in athletic festivals in ancient Greece. Plato, at the peak of his writing, argued that women should be accorded the right to soar to the highest ranks he could conceive of in human excellence – the philosopher ruler; and be equally educated in the gymnasium by exercising naked with the men (Bluestone 1987). Other exceptional counter-examples from ancient Greece that stress physicality and a warrior nature for woman are the archetypes of Artemis, Atalanta and the Amazons, who all rejected the traditional role for women (Creedon 1994).[3]

Of course, book V of Plato's *Republic* is not nearly so well cited by feminist critics as Aristotle's 'On the Generation of Animals' and 'Politics', and quite rightly so, because of the extremely negative philosophy of woman put forward by Aristotle. However, the fundamental issue in this entire discussion is who gets to choose which images of woman are permitted, desired or pursued in life and in sport. The primary question behind the role for women in sport is inextricably linked to the question of power and autonomy. At the institutional level, if it is the case that men decide, for example, the sports that women are permitted to attempt; the standards of physical perfection that are to be met in adjudicated sports; or the levels of funding accorded to women's as opposed to men's sport, then women have a legitimate grievance that they are not being treated with due respect. Just as it is the responsibility of each male to decide for himself, his conception of the type of body and, indeed, the type of life he wishes to pursue, moral or otherwise, it is the responsibility and right of each woman to deal with the challenges female athletes must deal with.

Paternalism and autonomy

The *Oxford Dictionary of Philosophy* defines paternalism as 'government as by a benign parent'. Paternalism is not necessarily sexist, although it often has been in sport and sport medicine (it could be called maternalism in a case where it was another woman making the decision on behalf of the individual, or perhaps parentalism), and it is often well-meaning. It occurs when one person makes a decision on behalf of (or speaks for) another, in what he or she takes to be the latter person's best interest. In the case of children, this is of course a necessary part of the parenting process until the child becomes an adult. Paternalism is also morally acceptable in cases where the person concerned is unable, for good reason, to speak or make decisions for himself or herself. It becomes morally troubling when it occurs on behalf of competent adults.

The concept of autonomy in ethical decision-making is very important. Autonomy is defined as the 'capacity for self-government'; furthermore, 'agents are autonomous if their actions are truly their own'. The crucial point here is that an essential part of being human is having the right and the capacity to make the choices and decisions that most affect oneself. Each competent human adult has the right to choose to pursue the projects and endeavours that he or she most cares about. That right is naturally limited by the rights of others to pursue their own desires and interests, but what the concept of autonomy takes for granted is that no one is entitled to speak on another's behalf, without that person's permission.

Sport paternalism and women's participation

Is there any reason why women should not participate in sports that men have traditionally played? It is instructive to look at what could possibly count as a morally acceptable answer. If there were a sport practised by men that was physiologically impossible for women, it would count as a reason for women not participating. But there is no such sport. To qualify, the sport would probably have to centrally involve male genitalia – funnily enough, we have no institutionally sanctioned sports of this type.

A second possibility would be if there were a sport, played by men, that no women in the world actually wanted to play. It is logically possible that such a sport might be invented, that not one woman anywhere would want to play, but then the reason the women would not be playing would be that they had *chosen* not to play, not that someone else had decided that they should not. Morally unacceptable answers for prohibiting women from playing sport would include: 'It would be bad for women to participate', or 'There is not enough money to allow women to participate'. Each of these two responses requires independent examination.

'It would be bad for women to participate' is the standard line that has been used throughout the history of sport. The exact nature of the harm that would befall women changes. It could be that it 'defeminises' (which might mean that it would make some women less attractive in the eyes of some men – either physically or mentally), or that it would be harmful for women, that they (or sometimes their not-yet-conceived children) would suffer some physiological damage. (For a good discussion of these points, see Cahn 1994.) There are two points to be made here. The first is practical. Assertions that strenuous physical exertion harms women, but not men, are simply not true. But it is the second point that is more important – women have the right, just as men do, to decide what risks of harm they will run. Subject to the normal limitations on every person's freedom, it is immorally paternalistic to decide, on behalf of another competent adult, what personal risks he or she can choose to accept.

The argument that 'There is not enough money to allow women to participate' can be more difficult to answer. It cannot be morally required to do the impossible, however 'There is not enough money' often masks an inequitable distribution of the resources that are available. If there is money available for anyone to participate in sport, then that money must be available on an equitable basis for both women and men. Men's sport is not intrinsically more important or more worthwhile than women's sport, and therefore has no automatic right to majority funding.

Specific challenges to women athletes

In the discussion that follows, some of the challenges faced by women athletes will be examined from a philosophical point of view. Some challenges are a result of the institutional climate for women in sport (e.g. biased, resistant and 'chilly'), and will thus require policy and practice changes in sport. Others – physical, mental and indeed, spiritual – occur at a personal level.

From a physical perspective these challenges may include, but are not limited to, body composition and development issues related to the health and wellbeing of the athlete. Three issues in particular – disordered eating, amenorrhoea and osteoporosis – are called the 'female athlete triad'. Some of these problems are a direct result of the demands of a particular woman's participation in her sport. *Citius, altius, fortius* – pushing the human limits, male or female, has its effects. For example, many elite-level sports present high risks of injuries and, generally speaking, elite-level training produces fit, but not necessarily healthy, athletes. The results of those pressures can be, and are in many cases, different for men and women, but the choice whether or not to train and compete is parallel. However, there is a special class of cases where the sport (such as gymnastics) is essentially judged (Suits 1988) – here the physical requirements and resulting risks are directly caused by decisions about what counts as excellent sport. The judging criteria for these sports should be tailored so as to minimise the health risks they impose on the athletes.

This is particularly a problem for women's events, as women athletes have a much higher prevalence of disordered eating than men. Women athletes have, at various times, faced different ideals (Creedon 1994; Hargreaves 1995), but the greatest tension is the initial tension – between the traditional ideal athlete and the traditional ideal woman. This modern tension is readily identified in the brief history of women's competitive body building and the conflicting judging practices. Further, if it is true that most women in the general population have eating problems as well (Szekely 1988; Bordo 1990; Sherwin 1992: 189), based on the problem of unattainable ideals (in North America, for example, the two ideals have been the Barbie doll and the super-waif model), then this problem is cultural, and medical control may not be the best, and certainly not the only, way of addressing the issue.

Amenorrhoea and pregnancy are unique to women athletes and raise issues that are tied to the implications that all women have faced when reproductive aspects of their lives have been designated as illness; and the tension between the two conflicting traditional ideals of woman and athlete. An essential part of the traditional ideal woman is fertility, because it is necessary for child-bearing. Fertility and child-bearing are not only not essential to the ideal athlete, they are antithetical to the role of athlete as warrior; for example, the Amazons. In many ways the Amazons were viewed as

monstrosities because they rejected the essential biological role of woman as primary.

It is also the case, historically, that some medical authorities have created for women a series of double binds, situations where options are reduced for oppressed groups to a very few, all of them exposing these groups to penalty, censure or deprivation (Frye 1983: 2; Sherwin 1992: 179), through the decision to view menstruation, pregnancy, menopause, body size and some feminine behaviour as diseases (Lander 1988; Broverman *et al.* 1981). For the female athlete the situation becomes even more complicated because she can be classified as even more abnormal when reproductive changes become evaluated in the context of the traditional male sports arena. For example, if the normal healthy woman is standardly, from a medical perspective, an unhealthy adult, because the ideal healthy adult is based on being male (Broverman *et al.* 1981), then it follows that the female athlete starts out an unhealthy adult because she is a woman. But, further, if the female athlete shows signs of becoming masculine, such masculinisation is thought of as further abnormality because it is not normal for a woman to have masculine characteristics. Following this kind of medical classification, when a woman bleeds, she is ill ('Woman … is generally ailing at least one week out of four … woman is not only an invalid, but a wounded one'; Lander 1988: 48), and if she does not bleed (due to amenorrhoea, menopause, pregnancy) she is ill, because it is not normal for her to be unable to conceive, thus making successful use of her biological organs (Sherwin 1992; Lander 1988; Zita 1988). Pregnancy, then, theoretically constituting a state of health for the traditional ideal woman, should not be treated as a disease requiring a significant amount of specialised treatment. However, women, and women athletes in particular, are not encouraged to think of themselves, or their lifestyles throughout pregnancy, as healthy. Serious charges of irresponsibility can occur when the relationship between women athletes and their foetuses is characterised as adversarial. (Some countries – Canada, USA and Australia – have begun to imprison women for endangering their foetuses; see Sherwin 1992: 107.) Most pregnant women athletes who are falsely charged with harming their foetuses face, at the very least, moral pressure that is based on the view that being pregnant and participating in sport is a socially unacceptable behaviour. However, in some cases, genuine harm to the foetus may occur with participation in sport (oxygen deprivation, for example). But, rather than licensing interference with a female athlete's reproductive freedom, that denies her interest in the health of her foetus and her role as an active independent moral agent, our focus should be on education.

The classification of these reproductive aspects of women's lives as illnesses can, and have, led to wide-scale paternalistic medical management of women under the claims of beneficence (Sherwin 1992: 180). In sport, these so-called illnesses have been part of the basis for excluding women. This does not mean that serious complications requiring medical interventions cannot occur with any aspect of a female athlete's reproductive life or life-cycle changes and ageing. (For example, that older women athletes have experienced pain during their menopause has always been a fact. Sport physicians and coaches, predominantly male, simply had to learn to take their female Master's-level athletes seriously before they could recognise that this pain was all over women's bodies, not just in their heads.) There will be particular cases where the label of 'illness' or 'disease' is appropriate, provided that ascription does not then lead to harming women athletes from a sport policy perspective (for example, banning them from participation in sport rather than educating them about coping with their illness and participating in sport).

The female athlete must also face challenges regarding the mental requirements of sport competition, aggression and violence. Male athletes also face these challenges, but it is considered 'normal' for men and 'abnormal' for women to engage in violence. Traditionally it has also been predominantly men who have committed sexual abuses against women (and minors) in sport. (Some researchers suggest that this predominance may be linked to the socially and legally accepted high levels of violence in some sports; Kirby and Brackenridge 1997.) The control over, and moral responsibility for, violence, abuse, harassment and discrimination, in sport and surrounding sport, lies mainly in the hands of those in the sport community, and it is a concern for both men and women. Some women, weary of not having their voices heard

on these issues (and for a host of other reasons), advocate completely separate sport for women as opposed to any integration at all.

One argument against integration is that women have to accept the current selection of sports, primarily designed for and practised by men, with an established culture with rewarding and recognising values (such as viewing sport as a battleground on which one conquers one's foes) that most women do not hold; whereas separation might allow women the freedom to create sport based on the values they choose (Lenskyj 1984). Capacities that are viewed as unique to women – sharing, giving, nurturing, sympathising, empathising and, above all, connecting as opposed to dividing – are stressed in this argument. Nevertheless, some would urge women to pay the high price of integration, so that they can have the same opportunities, occupations, rights and privileges that men have had in sport. This drive for women's sameness with men has sometimes denied women's qualities and how these qualities might contribute in a very positive manner to sport. The argument is that, if women emphasise their differences from men, viewing these as biologically produced and/or culturally shaped differences, they will trap themselves into ghettos, while men will carry on as before.

If we think that women athletes either act as men, if they accept the male ideal, or must be separate and generate their own ideal, the sport experience is highly gender-specific. But, the two views of sport – sport as competition (agon), test against others to overcome; or as connected co-questers searching and striving for excellence – may well be logically independent of the gender of the athlete.

However, the greatest tension arises for women if we have an 'agonistic' view of sport and women are found to be inherently ('essentially') caring and connected to others (Noddings 1984). In such a model of sport, women may be required to disconnect from their embodied experience. This could be the case for some form of alienation. Most athletes (male and female) probably find themselves torn between conflicting views of sport because pushing oneself to one's limits challenges even the strongest sense of self, and because in their moments of agony and joy they tend to experience themselves as both radically alone (because no one else can really understand what they feel) and fundamentally united to their team-mates, their competitors, particularly when this experience happens during a major competition.

The logic of gender verification

Entirely separate sport, and even just separate women's events, inevitably leads to the question of the logic of gender verification. If we are to have separate sport, or sporting events for women only, logically it must be possible to exclude any men who may wish, for whatever reason, to compete. This means that there must be a rule of eligibility that excludes men. (Conversely, if we have such a rule for excluding men, should we, for consistency, have such a rule excluding women from men's events even if the women believed they would inevitably lose, but wanted to take part anyway?) This in turn requires that we have a test of gender and/ or sex, that can be applied fairly to any potential participant. There are at least three methods of applying any such test: the first would be to test all contestants; the second, random contestants; the third, targeted individuals.

Before looking any more at testing, we must first deal with the response that we do not need to test because a man would never wish to compete in a women's event. 'Never' is a very strong word. It is not beyond the realm of imagination that a money-hungry promoter might decide that it was a great publicity stunt to enter men in a women's event. A male may even, with good intentions, choose to enter a women's event (such as synchronised swimming) as a form of protest against gender discrimination. Without a test to decide just who is eligible, we could be forced to accept, in women's events, participants who were quite obviously and unashamedly male, but who merely professed to be female.

There is a great deal of debate about how sex roles and gender are established (Tavris, Hubbard and Lowe, Schreiber, Blau and Ferber, and Lindsey). Mercier, in her gender verification report (1993), takes the position that sex is one's biological characteristics, and gender is one's socially learned characteristics. The standard practice in the Olympic Games is to have medical experts verify gender. But, by delegating gender verification to medical experts, the sport community (and society in general) has given great power to medical experts on an issue

that is in great dispute by researchers. Gender may not be merely a medical question, though it involves medical questions. Dialogues on gender, and gender in sport, have serious social, political and legal dimensions, making the medical story only part of the story.

Berit Skirstad gave several examples to illustrate the conceptual and moral issues that litter gender verification. Here is another. In 1976 a new player, Renée Clarke, appeared on the US women's tennis circuit, who 'soundly thrashed' the defending champion in the women's division. She was subsequently shown to be Renée Richards, who had recently undergone a sex-change operation and who had previously been a male elite-level tennis player (Birrell and Cole 1994: 207–237). The US Women's Tennis Federation wanted to exclude, as unfair competition, a player who was genetically male, but was reconstructed physiologically and now (presumably) psychologically female. The United States Tennis Association, the Women's Tennis Association and the United States Open Committee therefore introduced the requirement that players take a chromosomal test called the Barr test (Birrell and Cole 1994: 207). Richards refused, and went to court to demand the right to participate in women's events. In court she was deemed to be female on the basis of the medical evidence produced by the surgeons and medical professionals who had overseen his transformation from male to female. In the media this story played as an example of a courageous individual fighting for personal rights against an intransigent and uncaring 'system' (Birrell and Cole 1994). There are other ways of viewing the story, however.

What makes a woman a woman? Is it chromosomes, genitalia, a way of life or set of roles, or a medical record? It is not clear why medical evidence of surgery and psychology should outweigh chromosomal evidence. In fact it is not clear why any one criterion should be taken as categorically overriding any other.

How to approach issues for women in sport

In the field of bioethics, Rosemarie Tong (1995) has suggested that there are three standard elements of a methodology that can be used to deal with concerns for women. I believe this methodology may also be very useful for issues regarding women in sport. The first element suggested involves asking what was originally referred to as 'the woman question' and is now called by some researchers 'the gender-biased question' (Tuttle 1986: 349). This question challenges the supposed objectivity of scientific research findings regarding the nature of woman and the objectivity of the professions (such as sport medicine) based on that research (Dreifus 1977; Corea 1985; Okruhlik 1995; Schiebinger 1989, 1993). Underpinning this question is the suggestion that many of the 'facts' about female 'nature' actually result from values founded on biased social constructions.[4] The precepts and practices of sport can be, and are, misshaped by gender bias.[5] This gender bias works almost unconsciously and occurs when decision-makers, physicians and coaches in sport treat all athletes, all human bodies, as if they were all male athletes and male bodies. They would then view athletes, or their bodies, as dysfunctional if they failed to function like male bodies, or expressed little or no curiosity or interest in the problems unique to women. There are issues in sport that are, for the most part, unique to women (for example, the female athlete triad – eating disorders, amenorrhoea and osteoporosis; and gender verification, reproductive control and pregnancy, sexual harassment, etc.). There are issues unique to men. There are issues unique to certain sports. There are common issues for participants across regions, sports and particular quadrennial cycles. Physicians, coaches and sport organisers need to be aware enough of sex/gender similarities and differences to deal with these issues.

The second suggested part of this methodology is that of consciousness-raising, which requires that women be seriously invited to contribute their personal experiences into sport, so that it has wider meaning for all women. It is postulated that women who share sexual stereotyping or harassment stories in sport, for example, often come to realise that their feeling of having been treated as a girl, rather than a woman, or treated as a man, are not unique to them but common to most women. Such women, if given the opportunity, routinely gain the courage and confidence to challenge those who presume to know what is best for them, as they become increasingly convinced that it is

not they, but (in this case) the sport 'system', that is crazy. The purpose of this consciousness-raising is to achieve fundamental changes by connecting the personal experiences of women to developments in sport. Consciousness-raising suggests that women, sharing among themselves, will become empowered and able to take on some of the responsibility of changing the sport world.

The last part of Tong's methodology is based on at least three philosophical moral theorists: Aristotle's *Nicomachean Ethics* (1976: book 8), Rawls' *A Theory of Justice* (1971) and Mill's *Utilitarianism* and *On Liberty* (1972). She suggests it is an attempt to gain a Rawlsian reflective equilibrium between principles, rules, ideals, values and virtues on the one hand, and actual cases in which moral decisions must be made on the other.[6] It is also proposed that Aristotelian practical reasoning assumes that moral choices are made, for the most part, between several moral agents, rather than isolated within one individual. Finally, Mill's views on the importance of listening, as well as speaking, in the course of a moral dialogue is stressed. Tong's claim that the practice of ethics requires communication, corroboration and collaboration, and that we are not alone when we grapple with applying ethics, is true and can be utilised in the realm of sport.

Such a methodology may assist us in discovering mutually agreeable ways to weaken patterns of male domination and female subordination in the realm of sport. As suggested, this type of discussion requires adopting a particular stance and raising a particular set of questions. The answers to these questions must be dealt with and understood within the context of women's experiences in sport. If we truly seek understanding of these issues, we must understand the perspective, and thus the social, psychological and political predispositions, that we ourselves bring to the discussion. For example, differences in race, gender, education, social/political position, nationality, religion and sexuality are going to bring different perspectives and contexts to the questions of gender, ethics and sport. This fact does not mean that we cannot reach some agreement on important issues, but it does mean that we must be willing to listen, and give due respect, to differing perspectives in our search for justice. This search for justice also requires an understanding of where the power to make changes lies, and the willingness of those who hold it, to share that power. So far the predominant male power-brokers in sport have not demonstrated this willingness.

If we apply this methodology to the questions surrounding gender verification in sport – by taking the three steps of asking 'the woman or gender-biased question'; raising consciousness by connecting the personal experiences of women to developments on gender verification in sport and sport medicine; and using practical reasoning that attempts to gain a reflective equilibrium and accepts our limited ability to explain and justify our decisions, while simultaneously insisting that we try harder to find the appropriate ways – women themselves will (and should) be the guardians and decision-makers concerning women's sport.

Some women argue that any gender or sex test is demeaning (especially visual confirmation of the 'correct' genitalia) and discriminates against women athletes if it is not also applied to men. Clearly the use of any test, given the complexity of human sex and gender, may lead to anomalies and surprises. Yet many women wish to have sporting competition that excludes men. The best result we can achieve will be one that arises through discussion, debate and consensus and it will be the fairest we can reach. A coherent understanding of the causes of women's subordination to men in sport, coupled with a refined programme of action designed to eliminate the systems and attitudes that oppress or neglect women in sport, must guide this complex approach. A detailed analysis of the distribution of power in each case can identify a particular factor as the primary cause of women's subordinate status in sport, which, for the most part, has traditionally been based on biology. Researchers can, and should, attempt to ascertain the actual status of women in sport and determine how far that condition deviates from what justice prescribes.

The current sport conditions may be made more objective by providing more facts, as opposed to myths or stereotypes, about women athletes, thus alleviating or even eliminating the past and ongoing injustices. The knowledge required to create good, just and rational sport practice can be acquired; it is a matter of discovering and acknowledging all of the true facts.

Everyone's knowledge about sport, sport science, and the health and wellbeing of all athletes, including women athletes, is limited. If we wish to understand a broader experience in sport than just the dominant male one, we must talk to, and take seriously, as many athletes as possible. Women athletes are now beginning to be credited with being able to see things about the reality of sport that men do not typically see (Messner and Sabo 1990). The dominant position in any set of social relations – the general position of men *vis-à-vis* women in sport – tends to produce distorted visions of the real regularities and underlying causal tendencies in social relations. Men experience their power over women in sport as normal – even beneficial – and this is not women's experience. Women see systems of male domination and female subordination in sport as abnormal and harmful.

Political, social and psychological position are not irrelevant. These criteria contribute significantly to the way in which we see the fundamental facts about the athlete's body and mind. Women in sport may possibly find truth and justice, but right now they are nebulous and, unfortunately for women athletes, it may still be some time before they emerge. Right now, however, not all reasonable people necessarily see the same thing when the facts about women and sport stare them in the face.

A postscript to Tännsjö's radical proposal

Imagine a world where men and women are treated equally. Imagine a world where boys and girls are brought up together, where they learn the same things, participate in the same activities, and where they are taught to share the same hopes and aspirations. Imagine that in this world all forms of human excellence are encouraged, valued and rewarded. Imagine that in this world there is not a huge disparity in wealth and power between those who excel at a given activity and those who merely strive to do their best. Imagine also that in this world many activities are valued, that activities that exhibit grace or dexterity are as cherished as those that display speed and power. In such a world as this I would be the first person to stand side by side with Torbjörn Tännsjö to celebrate sport that did not distinguish on sex or gender lines, but merely on the basis of ability.

In a system like this people would be able to develop at their own pace and to their own level. In this system young boys would not get discouraged as they watched their pre-adolescent female peers systematically beat them in academic achievement or the full range of sport. Nor would they get discouraged knowing that in certain activities – in particular those that value cooperation over competition, or grace over power, or extreme endurance – they would never do as well as their female counterparts. They would know that, in certain highly circumscribed areas, those that rely on strength and power, they will have their turn.

Nor, of course, would girls and women get discouraged. In this society, because all forms of excellence are equally valued, and because there are as many ways that women are likely to excel as men, and because the rewards for excellence are not targeted towards a small set of predominantly male activities, women as well as men would be motivated to strive for the common good.

Tännsjö's vision [in Chapter 4.4] – of sport transformed – fits into a long line of utopian visions of societies transformed. If we lived in Plato's Republic, where philosophers were kings, there would be no reason to segregate men's and women's sport. (Plato himself included the revolutionary proposals that not only should women be guardians – for there are no relevant differences between women and men in the business of being guardians – but also that women should go through precisely the same sort of training as men, with the men, including naked gymnastic exercises. If we lived in a utopia like Plato's *Republic* we might be able to have Tännsjö's vision of sport. But unfortunately we do not.

We could imagine another society, one rather closer to our own. In this society there are great disparities of income and power. Some activities are cherished, valued and rewarded. Let us imagine that those cherished and rewarded activities include the bearing and rearing of children. Let us also imagine that some sports are valued. Those who achieve the pinnacles of excellence in these sports are treated and rewarded as heroes or, rather, treated and rewarded as heroines. Let us imagine that the popular sports, the sports that attracted the big audiences, the sports in which athletes could command huge fees in endorsements, were extreme long-distance swimming, ultra-marathons (or triathlons) and synchronised swimming. (It happens to be the case that in extreme endurance sports – events over about twenty-four hours in length, women currently hold the world records.) Imagine how boys and men would feel knowing that in this society the activities that are rewarded all happen to be dominated by women. How would they feel, knowing that they could never hope to compete at the highest levels in the sports that dominate their culture and that bring huge personal rewards? What would they do?

In this society, men might say: 'Look at us – we can do some things really well; we can fight, for instance. Look at us,' they would say, 'when we hit each other as hard as we can, we can get up and do it some more. Please give us some money so that we can go and practise our sports, the activities we are good at.' Would the women who administer and control sports in this imaginary community mind if sport were desegregated? Probably not, but why would they? The sports that everyone cares about would still be dominated by women. Women would still make all the money and enjoy all the glory and prestige.

The proposal contained in Tännsjö's chapter is dangerous, because it masquerades as a genuine proposal for changing sport as it is currently practised, whereas it is really a utopian fantasy, first of a society – and then of sport – transformed. If the world were a radically different place, then yes, the vision of sport where discrimination is based on ability not on gender (or weight or size, for that matter) would be good.

But let us look at the world in which we live. In our world sport plays a whole variety of functions and is played for a great variety of reasons, at a wide range of levels. Let us look first at sport for young children. Their sport exists primarily to give them an opportunity to experience the joy of physical play. Sport for children is about creating opportunities for pleasure. There is no reason to segregate sport for young children. Boys and girls can play perfectly well alongside each other. There are some worries about the ways in which boys are socialised to play competitive games and girls tend to be socialised to play cooperative ones. But, if we leave those aside, the fact that young girls tend to be bigger and stronger than boys the same age tends to be countered by boys' greater desire to play, and their unfounded (and unbounded) self-confidence. Boys and girls ought to be able to play together to the best of their ability, and the experience ought to be enjoyable and challenging for both.

In adolescence things start to change. By this time our acceptance of gender roles is rather more fixed (probably more fixed than it will become in later life as we become more comfortable with who we are as individuals). Girls may start to be self-conscious around boys. Boys may feel that they have to be aggressive and 'masculine' in order to attract the attention of girls. At this age girls, who until now have been self-confident and have generally been beating boys at the full range of academic pursuits (including mathematics), begin to defer to boys in the classroom. What is sport for at this age? I would argue that its primary function is still to allow young people to experience the joy of physical activity and competition. Should we segregate sport at this age? If this is the means of encouraging young people to continue to play and enjoy sport – then yes.

Let us skip a few years and look simply at elite sport. Should it be segregated? In some sports, no. There are some sports where women and men can compete equally against each other, and here there is no good reason to continue to segregate. (In fact, one sport that attempted to desegregate – shooting – rapidly reversed their policy when they found out that women were winning medals.) But in many of the other sports that go to make up the professional leagues, or the Olympic Games, women at present would systematically lose at the highest levels of competition. That probably would not matter if there were as many sports we really cared about where women tend to excel as there were sports where men tend to excel. But there are not. If we desegregate sport we eliminate women from sporting competition at most Olympic events. Would this be a good thing?

Even at the very highest levels, sport is about something more than merely being the fastest, or the strongest, or jumping the highest. Sports are complex social institutions that partially shape and define our images of who we are and what is possible for human beings. Given the sports that currently dominate our attention (and why we value these sports rather than others is an interesting inquiry), it would not help our view of either women or men only to see images of men in elite athletic competition. Seeing, and valuing, strong athletic women provides not only an example to younger women of the range of the possible for women, but it also changes our social views of what is appropriate and good for women to do. This *is* a good thing.

In a society where men's interests and strengths dominate cultural attention through the media, in a society where our social institutions are structured and controlled by men, and in a sport culture where male-dominated sports are the best-funded, most powerful and most-watched, excluding women from elite sport (on whatever grounds) would have the morally disastrous consequences of further restricting the realm of what is possible for women. Tännsjö looks at one little argument based on the pursuit of excellence, in one small context – that of sport functioning at the highest possible level – and he concludes that there is no place for discrimination on the basis of sex. In a world that was fair, and where there was no systematic discrimination on the basis of sex, he would be right. But we do not live in that world. We live in a world where women are systematically denied positions of power and public attention. We live in a world where men's efforts are systematically praised and rewarded. We live in a world where the aptitudes and achievements of women tend to go largely unrecognised and unheralded. In our world, excluding women from the publicity that comes from the highest levels of sporting achievement would merely serve to reinforce women's systemic subservience to men.

I assume that that is not Tännsjö's intention. I assume that, perhaps like in Plato's *Republic*, he wishes that women could play their full roles in all aspects of human life and endeavour. I assume that Tännsjö's vision of philosophical purity momentarily clouded his perception and knowledge of the world in which we actually live. Other things being equal, I'm sure the picture he paints would be good. But other things are *not* equal.

Notes

1. See Schneider (1992, 1993), and Schneider and Butcher (1994, 1997).
2. For a current personal account of the relationship between masculinity and sport in North America, see Messner and Sabo (1994).
3. However, Coubertin apparently never saw women as having central roles in Olympism. He preferred them as spectators and medal-bearers for presentation to the victors.
4. See Ehrenreich and English (1989) and Fausto-Sterling (1985) for this critique of medicine.
5. See Tong (1995) and Sherwin (1992) for this discussion in the profession of medicine.
6. Tong has suggested this for the area of bioethics (1995: 27).

References

Birrell, S. and Cole, C.L. (eds) (1994) *Women, Sport and Culture*, Champaign, IL: Human Kinetics, pp. 207–237.

Bluestone, N. (1987) *Women and the Ideal Society: Plato's Republic and Modern Myths of Gender*, Amherst, MA: University of Massachusetts Press.

Broverman, I., Broverman, D., Clarkson, F., Rosenkrantz, P. and Vogel, S. (1981) 'Sex Role Stereotypes and Clinical Judgments of Mental Health', in *Women and Mental Health*, ed. E. Howell and M. Bayes, New York: Basic Books.

Bordo, S. (1990) 'Reading the Slender Body', in *Body/Politics: Women and the Discourses of Science*, ed. M. Jacobus, E. Fox Keller and S. Shuttleworth, New York: Routledge, pp. 83–112.

Cahn, S. (1994) *Coming on Strong: Gender and Sexuality in Twentieth-Century Women's Sport*, New York: The Free Press.

Corea, G. (1985) *The Hidden Malpractice: How American Medicine Mistreats Women*, revised edition, New York: Harper Colophon Books.

Creedon, P. (ed.) (1994) *Women, Media and Sport*, California: Sage Publications.

Coubertin, P. de (1912) 'Women in the Olympic Games', *Olympic Review*.

Dreifus, C. (ed.) (1977) *Seizing Our Bodies: The Politics of Women's Health*, New York: Vintage/Random House.

Ehrenreich, B. and English, D. (1989) *For Her Own Good: 150 Years of the Experts' Advice to Women*, Garden City, NY: Anchor Books.

Fausto-Sterling, A. (1985) *Myths of Gender: Biological Theories About Women and Men*, New York: Basic Books.

Frye, M. (1983) *The Politics of Reality: Essays in Feminist Theory*, Freedom, CA: Crossing Press.

Hargreaves, J. (1995) 'A Historical Look at the Changing Symbolic Meanings of the Female Body in Western Sport', in *Sport as Symbol, Symbols in Sport*, ed. F. van der Merwe, ISHPES Studies/Germany: Academia Verlag, vol. 4, pp. 249–259.

Kirby, S. and Brackenridge, C. (1997) 'Coming to Terms: Sexual Abuse in Sport', unpublished manuscript.

Lander, L. (1988) *Images of Bleeding: Menstruation as Ideology*, New York: Orlando Press.

Lefkowitz, M. and Fant, M. (1985) *Women's Life in Greece and Rome: A Source Book in Translation*, Baltimore, MD: The Johns Hopkins University Press.

Lenskyj, H. (1984) *Sport Integration or Separation*, Ottawa: Fitness and Amateur Sport.

Messner, M. and Sabo, D. (eds) (1990) *Sport, Men and the Gender Order: Critical Feminist Perspectives*, Champaign, IL: Human Kinetics.

—— (1994) *Sex, Violence and Power in Sports: Rethinking Masculinity*, Freedom, CA: Crossing Press.

Noddings, N. (1984) *Caring: A Feminine Approach to Ethics and Moral Education*, Berkeley: University of California Press.

Okruhlik, K. (1995) 'Gender and the Biological Sciences', *Canadian Journal of Philosophy* 20: 21–42.

Schiebinger, L. (1989) *The Mind Has No Sex? Women in the Origins of Modern Science*, Cambridge, MA: Harvard University Press.

—— (1993) *Nature's Body: Gender in the Making of Modern Science*, Boston: Beacon Press.

Schneider, A.J. (1992) 'Harm, Athletes' Rights and Doping Control', in *First International Symposium for Olympic Research*, ed. R.K. Barney and K.V. Meier, London, ON: University of Western Ontario, Centre for Olympic Studies, pp. 164–172.

—— (1993) 'Doping in Sport and the Perversion Argument', in *The Relevance of the Philosophy of Sport*, ed. G. Gebauer, Berlin, Germany: Academia Verlag, pp. 117–128.

Schneider, A. J. and Butcher, R. B. (1994) 'Why Olympic Athletes Should Avoid the Use and Seek the Elimination of Performance-Enhancing Substances and Practices in the Olympic Games', *Journal of the Philosophy of Sport* 20, 21: 64–81.

—— (1997) 'Fair Play as Respect for the Game', *Journal of the Philosophy of Sport* 24: 1–22.

Sherwin, S. (1992) *No Longer Patient: Feminist Ethics and Health Care*, Philadelphia: Temple University Press.

Spears, B. (1988) 'Tryphosa, Melpomene, Nadia, and Joan: The IOC and Women's Sport', in *The Olympic Games in Transition*, ed. J. Segrave and D. Chu, Champaign, IL: Human Kinetics Publishers, pp. 365–374.

Suits, B. (1988) 'Tricky Triad: Games, Play and Sport', *Journal of Philosophy of Sport* 13: 1–9.

Szekely, E. (1988) *Never Too Thin*, Toronto: The Women's Press.

Tong, R. (1995) 'What's Distinctive About Feminist Bioethics?' ed. F. Baylis, J. Downie, B. Freedman, B. Hoffmaster, S.

Tuttle, L. (1986) *Encyclopaedia of Feminism*, Essex: Longman.

Zita, J. (1988) 'The Premenstrual Syndrome: Dis-Easing the Female Cycle', *Hypatia* 3(1): 77–99.

I'd rather wear a turban than a rose

A case study of the ethics of chanting

Carwyn Jones and Scott Fleming

Introduction

At the end of the 2005 Six Nations men's rugby union (hereafter 'rugby') tournament, Wales had won every game and were crowned champions. This had not been achieved by Wales since the golden era of the 1970s. The Welsh nation celebrated enthusiastically, and the success was commodified brazenly and consumed avidly. The first step was taken when England, the 'old enemy', were defeated in a close game at the Millennium Stadium in Cardiff on 5 February. The match was fairly unspectacular in comparison to the matches and performances that followed. Both sets of supporters cheered their teams enthusiastically and sang songs that have been long associated with supporting their respective nations.[1]

Importantly, though, in an episode more characteristic of British association football (hereafter 'football') fandom,[2] large sections of the Welsh crowd were heard clearly to respond to the English supporters' renditions of *Swing Low Sweet Chariot* with their own ditty. To the tune of *She'll Be Coming Round the Mountain*, the lyrics to the first verse were: 'You can stick your f***ing chariot up your a**e.' These were already well known to many English and Welsh rugby supporters alike. In contrast, the lyrics of the second verse, 'I'd rather wear a turban than a rose,' were less familiar—at least to us in this particular context. This second verse seemed intuitively problematic and potentially offensive.

In this paper we explore the moral status of the specific chant: 'I'd rather wear a turban than a rose.' Specifically, we examine: whether the chant is offensive; whether the chant is racist; the extent to which the chanters can be labelled racists; and what, if any, might be the appropriate response(s) to the chant?

Is the chant offensive?

In the discussion that follows, we situate our analysis within a conceptual framework mapped out by a recent public debate between Robin Barrow (2005, 2006) and Graham Haydon (2006). In it they address the key themes of 'offence' and 'respect', and provide a valuable backdrop to a consideration of the chant that is the focus of our attention here.

Upon hearing the chant in the stadium, it is likely that different people would have reacted differently. Some may have thought the chant amusing, harmless and inoffensive; others may have found the chant in bad taste and offensive.

Carwyn Jones and Scott Fleming 'I'd Rather Wear a Turban Than a Rose: A Case Study of the Ethics of Chanting', from *Race Ethnicity and Education*, Vol. 10, Issue 4, pp. 401–414, © 2007 Carwyn Jones and Scott Fleming. Reprinted by permission of Taylor & Francis.

What is the appropriate response? Barrow (2005) argues that in the current climate, people take offence too readily and are encouraged to do so. Too often, he argues, any type of personal slight, joke, insult or comment is taken as grounds for not only being offended, but also for taking some form of action (perhaps legal) in light of the perceived slight. It is true that different people may be variously sensitive, or predisposed, to taking offence. Sensitivity to offence, it could be said, is relative to each individual's character or personality. It could be argued that those spectators who were offended by the chant are simply too sensitive.

To discuss offensiveness in this subjective or individualistic way is problematic and provides no critical or educational leverage. The term 'offensive', when referring to a particular act, is used to pick out features of the act that are offensive rather than features of a subject who may or may not be taking offence.[3] To equate 'offensive' with whatever causes anyone to feel offended is, to paraphrase Barrow (2005, p. 267), mindless. From a moral perspective, then, the extent to which the chant is racist, offensive or both cannot simply be read from the level of offence taken. The moral status of the chant is not an empirical matter to be ascertained by a show of hands.[4] The fact that someone may actually take offence, in this case *vis-à-vis* the chant, is not in itself sufficient grounds to take prohibitive or retributive action. Taking offence and subsequent action must be connected strongly to sound moral reasons.

Barrow (2005) argues that from an ethical point of view, it is crucial to distinguish between actions that are meant to offend, actions that actually offend and actions that are likely to cause offence. Each may be evaluated differently from a moral point of view. The first two reflect the broadly non-consequentialist/consequentialist division in ethics (Parry, 1998): intention is the target of evaluation for the former and consequences the focus for the latter. From a non-consequentialist perspective our evaluation of the chanters would depend upon whether as a matter of fact they intended offence. From a consequentialist point of view our evaluation would depend upon whether as a matter of fact anyone was offended (or more were offended than not). This does not help us in our discussion, however, because we are back to a kind of empirical assessment of whether people were subjectively offended and whether people subjectively intended offence. The perplexing and unsatisfactory result is that from a consequentialist perspective we are not sure how to calculate the net offence taken; and from a non-consequentialist perspective those who intended offence are culpable, and those who did not are not culpable, even though they engaged in precisely the same activity. Actions that are likely to cause offence are, for Barrow (2005), more problematic and raise more questions about what, in fact, are actions likely to cause offence.

Our moral evaluations, however, are not simply restricted to matters of intention and consequences in this way. Parry (1998) reminds us of the moral significance of recklessness. If we act in a way that might cause offence then we might rightly invite moral condemnation, mitigation notwithstanding. We will return to discuss the appropriate moral evaluation of chanters later in the paper, but the foregoing discussion reinforces the need to move towards establishing, so far as is possible, an objective account of offensive in this case.

Before we can determine whether the chant in question is 'objectively' offensive, some conceptual ground-clearing is required. The first important distinction to draw is between the concepts of offended and offensive. The former, as has been discussed above, refers to a particular stance taken by a particular person in light of events or circumstances that may have perturbed them. Feeling offended is usually characterized by an emotional experience of indignation, anger or somesuch. One can be offended by another's bad manners, rudeness or crass sense of humour. It is reasonably clear that the chant mentioned above is intended to cause some emotional response in its target. It sits neatly within a tradition (possibly historically more usually connected with men's association football) where supporters attempt to rile their opposites through communal singing and chanting. The aim is to offend the opposing team's players and fans, and the funnier or nastier the better. In English football, songs about the Munich plane crash and songs about the Hillsborough disaster have been traded between fans of Manchester United and Liverpool with equal venom (see Redhead, 1987). There is no doubt that this chant in particular and chanting in general generates offence in at least some of the intended target.

Whether the chant was objectively offensive is a different matter. It is both possible and desirable to stipulate the possibility of something (the chant) being objectively offensive. Making the case for the possibility of 'objectively' offensive is similar to making the case for the possibility of morally wrong. If the possibility is not accepted then further discussion is futile and the concept 'offensive' 'has no purchase; it is simply the emotivist shriek of distaste' (Barrow, 2005, p. 269). Barrow does not equate objectively offensive with morally wrong without remainder, but his argument suggests a strong link. Acts of murder, cruelty, unfairness, injustice or discrimination are described as inherently offensive and deserving of offence to morally sensitive witnesses. He concludes that 'something that is objectively offensive would have to be rationally defensible to all as reprehensible' (2005, p. 268). Haydon (2006), however, is reluctant to define objectively offensive in this way. For Haydon, the notion of inherent offensiveness makes reference 'to sensibilities that have been appropriately educated or, at least, not thoroughly miseducated' (p. 23). Sensitivity to inherently offensive acts, particularly those that involve the use of language rather than, say, physical violence, is predicated on the development of capacities, including conceptual capacities, that frame the act. Some form of moral knowledge, education and grasp of principles, virtue or somesuch is necessary to recognize the inherently offensive. We end up with a chicken and egg situation: are there *a priori* offensive acts, or are acts offensive in light of a certain moral theory or moral agency? This question touches on the central debates in ethics and cannot be adequately dealt with here. Notwithstanding this difficult issue, racism, we argue, registers as 'inherently' offensive (if we accept the possibility of inherently offensive) on most ethical scales.

Barrow (2005) would, we presume, agree that racism is inherently offensive, but it does not follow that the particular chant in question is offensive. In fact Barrow challenges 'the common assumption that such things as jokes or unflattering generalizations about ethnic or gender groupings are inherently offensive' (p. 273). The inherent offensiveness or otherwise of this chant depends, therefore, on a contextual evaluation of whether it counts as a particular instantiation of racism.

Is the chant racist?

Racist chants from spectators at association football games have been documented extensively (e.g., Fleming & Tomlinson, 1996; Garland & Rowe, 1996; Back *et al.*, 2001a, 2001b; King, 2004). Indeed, during the mid-1990s the tune *She'll Be Coming Round the Mountain* was appropriated by football fans in the UK with the lyrics: 'I'd rather be a Paki than a Scouse.'[5] Back *et al.* (2001a; see also 1998) report that this was heard frequently during the 1995/96 season during Millwall games when the opponents were from Merseyside, and also at Manchester City in games against Liverpool. They observed that the chant was a 'racialized expression … generically mobilized against fans from Merseyside with the intention of offending the Scouse regional identity and its associated perceived racial preferences' (p. 55). Before conducting a contextually informed semiotic analysis of the chant, they also noted the theoretical and practical problems posed by the chant for an understanding of racism in football: 'Is *I'd rather be a Paki* a racist chant? If it is a racist chant why is it principally directed at white supporters?' (p. 56).

Determining whether or not 'I'd rather wear a turban than a rose' is an instantiation of racism is not straightforward. In order to evaluate the extent to which the chant ought to be thought racist, it is necessary first to identify what characteristics it might possess that would constitute the necessary and sufficient conditions for reaching such a conclusion. This is no easy matter as the concept of racism has been the source of considerable debate. It is premised on the flawed assumption of the existence of 'races' (see, *inter alia*, Miles, 1989, 1993; Cole, 1996), and the ascription of unchanging characteristics to them.[6] However as Cole (1996) notes, even though the concept of 'race' has no scientific utility, it still has currency as a social construct. That is to say, discourses are predicated upon its existence. In particular, characteristics (whether essentially positive or negative) become the basis of stereotypes and are likely to be both distorted and based on false universalism. Indeed, while some stereotypes may appear to be benign, the logic that underpins them is more pernicious and ultimately leads to many more negative assumptions, attitudes and behaviours that often become embedded in commonsense (mis)understandings—especially in sport. Moreover, 'race' was never solely a biological division of the species. It was also the basis of structural and symbolic differentiation, creating inequity, exclusion, oppression and exploitation (Mason, 1994).

Given this rather shaky ontological basis for racism, conceptual clarity about its operational definition is also problematic. In their careful synthesis and critique of the theoretical and political discourses surrounding race relations, Solomos and Back (1994) argue against unitary or simplistic definitions of racism, and for rigorous contextualization of racist discourses (inevitably, therefore, acknowledging other social relations—for instance gender, sexuality and so on). Elsewhere and drawing on the work of Miles (1989), Back (1996) summarizes an account of racisms[7] as:

> an ideology that defines social collectivities in terms of 'natural' and immutable biological differences. These are invested with negative connotations of cultural difference and inferiority, whereby the presence of other 'races' can be correlated with the economic and social health of either a specific region or the nation as a whole.
>
> (p. 9)

More specifically, and moving towards a set of criteria against which to evaluate the focus of our concern, the chant, racist discourse is described by Van Dijk (2004) as:

> a form of discriminatory social practice that manifests itself in text, talk and communication. Together with other (non verbal) discriminatory practices, racist discourse contributes to the reproduction of racism as a form of ethnic or racial domination.
>
> (p. 351)

It can, he argues, take two particular forms: directed at ethnically different others; and about ethnically different others.

Let us begin, therefore, by interrogating these lyrics, for there are (at least) three key themes embedded within them. First, as a carrier of cultural identity, the turban is a head covering worn by many Sikh men. Made of cloth wrapped around the head, it has been an integral part of the Sikh tradition since the time of Guru Nanak Dev (1469–1639 CE). It gives Sikhs an easily recognizable identity (Sikh Coalition, 2006) and

has also led Sikhs into various religious, cultural and political struggles—not least concerning the law of the land.[8] In short, it is not mere cultural paraphernalia.[9]

Second, the rose refers to the red emblem worn on the shirts of the England rugby team.[10] Introduced in 1871 when England first played against Scotland, more recently it has become the battleground in a dispute over trade marks and intellectual property rights. In a legal ruling, the red rose was judged to be emblematic of England or the England team in the same way that the thistle is of Scotland, the shamrock is of Ireland and the ('Prince of Wales') feathers are of Wales (BBC News, 2002). Both the turban and the rose are, in their different ways, important carriers of identity. We argue, though, that while the former has profound religious and cultural significance, the latter (notwithstanding its historical derivation) is merely a 'badge'. That is to say, they are qualitatively different.

Third, there is the expression of preference for the turban ahead of the rose. The message here is an important one. The rivalry between England and Wales on the international rugby field is intense, and has been fuelled by representations of the other in both the print and broadcast media. Spectators at the games themselves are generally well-behaved and good-humoured, although when England has been defeated by Wales in recent times the reaction has been an extreme display of identity and pride. As with the football chant, for the insult to work there needs to be 'an implicit ideal or normative structure of collective identity' (Back et al., 2001a, p. 56).

In the chant 'I'd rather wear a turban than a rose,' the normative structure involves three main elements: carriers of ethnic identity and national pride—the turban and the rose; hierarchical re-ordering of racialized identities—Welsh ahead of (superior to) Sikhs ahead of (superior to) English; and the 'playfulness' of parody—where the bite of an insult is softened and the likelihood of hostile reaction to it lessened. In summary, therefore, if the chant is a form of discriminatory social practice (which it is) that manifests itself in communication (which it does) and is directed at ethnically different others (which it is), we may conclude (after Van Dijk, 2004) that it carries manifestations of racism.

Finally, there is a further point about the chants. The vocabulary of 'I'd rather be a Paki than a Scouse' is recognized to be racist when uttered by white persons. The term 'Paki' is not merely an abbreviation of 'Pakistani'. It is a racialized category often used pejoratively to convey contempt. When spoken or in this case chanted by a group of predominantly white persons, it is properly thought to be a form of racist language. The vocabulary of 'I'd rather wear a turban than a rose' is not value-laden negatively in the same way—the words themselves are not racist. However, notwithstanding this distinction about the way in which the discourses are presented, the elements of the normative structure of each chant are the same. Both hierarchically re-order South Asian (or British Asian) racialized identities ahead of (and superior to) those of the object of the insult.

The disposition(s) of the chanters

Having established that the chant itself is racist, what may we conclude logically about the chanters? There are some who would assert that those persons who engage in racist behaviour are themselves racists. Yet this interpretation does not accommodate satisfactorily the possibility of unwitting racism (e.g., Macpherson, 1999; Back *et al.*, 2001a). This theme is pursued by Long and McNamee (2004) in their exploration of the moral scales of racism. They argue convincingly that instantiations of racist behaviour are profoundly context-sensitive and conclude that it is possible for racist actions or attitudes to be a product of ignorance; hence they may be unintentional. What follows logically from this is that the response to racist behaviour should differentiate properly between that which is unwitting (and hence ethically excusable) and that which is deliberate (and hence ethically inexcusable)—not as a crude binary, but 'in subtle gradations, and/or subtle inflections activated by particular contexts' (p. 412).

Long and McNamee (2004, p. 408) pose the following questions in an attempt to differentiate with greater sensitivity than is often the case: Can racist beliefs be held, or racist acts performed, by persons we ought not to label racists? Is it helpful to articulate an underlying scale of racism-ness? When does racist thought, feeling or action genuinely form a part of one's character as racist?

In answering these questions it is possible to ascribe differential blameworthiness. A 'one size fits all' approach to sanction is both unreasonable and impractical; different degrees of severity require commensurate moral opprobrium.

Let us consider three particular examples that illuminate the need for this more nuanced understanding of those who engage in racist behaviours. Former England footballer John Barnes (1999, pp. 69–70) recounts one episode:

> I first encountered the worst strain of nationalism, unadulterated racism, on that 1984 tour to South America. ... Sitting at the back of our scheduled fight [*sic*] were four National Front sympathisers, occasionally shouting abuse down the aisle in the direction of England's three black players – myself, Viv Anderson and Mark Chamberlain. They kept saying, 'England won only 1–0 because a nigger's goal doesn't count.'... The NF guys also heckled Ted Croker, the Football Association secretary, saying, 'You fucking wanker, you prefer Sambos to us.'... When the plane landed in Santiago, the four NF guys joined some others already there and unfurled a banner for the TV cameras. It read: 'NF – Send Them Back'.

Although it does not involve a chant *per se*, these behaviours were enacted in a public forum. If characteristic of a particular racist disposition it does not require a great leap of the imagination to see how this attitude would find expression as a chant at a football stadium. For instance, King (2004, p. 19) describes the experience of a black player in the 1980s 'playing at Leeds for Portsmouth where you had people shouting for ninety minutes "shoot that nigger", "kill that nigger".' Together, this set of premeditated behaviours, likely to be typical of the malevolent characters of the persons involved, is unambiguously and unashamedly racist. It is at the ethically inexcusable extreme of Long and McNamee's (2004) typology.

The second example is the now notorious episode (in the UK) of football pundit Ron Atkinson's on-air criticism of Marcel Desailly. In April 2004 Atkinson had been providing expert analysis of Chelsea's 3–1 Champions League semi-final defeat to AS Monaco, and was evidently frustrated and dismayed at the performance of the Chelsea team. In what he thought was a private conversation but was actually being broadcast Atkinson is reported to have commented: 'He [Desailly] is what is known in some schools as a f***ing lazy thick ni**er' (quoted in Fleming, 2005, p. 20). Atkinson was condemned immediately, yet maintained with apparent sincerity that he was not being racist. He provided various bits of (spurious) evidence to substantiate his claim, and some black former players defended him publicly. This outburst includes some of the same vile invective as in the example above but is qualitatively different. Atkinson's behaviour was not uniquely aberrant, but it was far from typical. In Long and McNamee's (2004) terms he may be ethically negligent, guilty of misperception/misrecognition and incapable of change—but is more ethically excusable.

The third example has already been problematized persuasively by Ben Carrington (1998, pp. 106–110) and deals with the intersections of popular culture, media and sport. It concerns the popular television magazine show *Fantasy Football*. In it, sketches by presenters Frank Skinner and David Baddiel included one about the black former Nottingham Forest footballer Jason Lee which became the butt of a long-running 'joke'. Carrington (1998, p. 108)

David Baddiel 'blackened up' (evoking the barely-coded racist imagery of the minstrel shows), with a pineapple on his head, out of which Jason Lee's dreadlocks were growing – the 'joke' being that Jason Lee's dreads resembled a fruit on top of his head.

The 'joke' gathered momentum, and entered the public consciousness in ways unconnected to football, ultimately to become a form of ridicule for other black persons with a hairstyle similar to Lee. To decode the dispositions of Skinner and Baddiel in this example requires yet another lens for interpretation. In Long and McNamee's terms they may be ethically immature, having engaged in behaviour that is unintentionally racist in a way that is out of character for them.

These latter two examples illustrate the complexity of understanding the extent to which the persons involved ought to be thought racist. In each there are characteristics that Long and McNamee (2004) associate with being ethically excusable, but there are also other characteristics that are not. Whether Skinner and Baddiel are more or less ethically excusable than

Atkinson is debatable. However, all three are more excusable (or less inexcusable) than the members of the National Front described in the first example.

To return to the 'I'd rather wear a turban than a rose' chant, let us suppose that the general attitude of the group of predominantly white but otherwise largely heterogeneous Welsh supporters was to engage in terrace 'banter' with English supporters, and in doing so to assert some superiority over a set of ethnically different others. While we have argued that the chant itself is racist, to condemn all of the chanters as racists is troublesome, and to do so in a way that would not differentiate between the different possible dispositions among the chanters is even more so.

For instance, young children joining in with the chanting may be completely ignorant of the racist elements of the chant directed at the English—they may not even comprehend that the chant is intended to offend anyone. There may also be others who join in the chant cognisant of the aim of the chant, namely to insult the English supporters, but, through ignorance, are not fully aware of its racist undertones. Neither of these first two groups may be aware of the indirect racist sentiment being directed at the second group of ethnically different others—the Sikh community (and perhaps, by implication and association, South Asian communities more generally). The primary intention of the chant is focused on the English and not an insult directed at Sikhs. There may be others still who are fully aware that the chant is predicated, through a shared appreciation of the normative structure, on the implicit understanding that Sikhs assumed to be 'inferior'.

This brush may, of course, be too broad, but these distinctions and the moral blame attached to each highlight the importance of understanding the dispositions of those who act in a racist way.

Appropriate reactions to the chant

Having argued that the chant is racist and that the chanters can be placed on a scale of moral blameworthiness, we now turn to the question of appropriate response. What ought a morally sensitive and mature character do in this situation?

If what we have argued above is accepted, the chant should prick the moral sensibilities of such a character (they should be offended by it). Following Blum (1994), a feature of a well-formed moral character is perception, or a degree of moral sensitivity. The offensiveness of the chant ought minimally to be noticed. In other words, the chant should register on the moral radar. Perhaps, then, some further level of cognitive understanding of the moral status of the chant, its demeaning intention and racist connotations might also be expected. Finally, some sort of emotional response to it, anger or taking offence, might be expected.

There may have been (at least) two different constituencies offended by the chant. First, there are the unintended targets of the chant—Sikhs (and perhaps South Asian or British Asian persons more generally). Their offence is both understandable and justifiable, for we have demonstrated that the chant is objectively racist. Second, there are the intended targets of the chant—the English. We argue, though, that any offence that they experience ought not to have been a response to the anti-English sentiment in the chant itself. Rather, their offence ought to be to the anti-Sikh racism implicit within the chant.

Barrow (2005) argues that it is often a sign of moral weakness to take offence, and he believes that people take offence too readily and too easily. In fact Barrow argues further that in some cases taking offence is a necessarily self-regarding stance: 'By definition, if you take offence at some joke, you are being humourless, self important and arrogant' (Barrow, 2005, p. 273). In the latter two examples examined above, and in particular the one about Jason Lee, accusations were made about 'overreacting' and taking things 'too seriously'. However, there are times when taking offence is the right thing to do. Haydon (2006) argues that if we think of taking offence in an Aristotelian sense, then the disposition to feel offended should manifest itself at the right time, for the right reason and to the right extent. If an act is inherently offensive, therefore, being offended is not only justified but praiseworthy.

Does the inherent offensiveness of the chant constitute grounds for action? Barrow's (2005) objection to taking action motivated by offence is to do with the self-regarding nature of the behaviour. He explains:

> Taking offence, when it means treating one's personal hurt as grounds for punitive response, involves a refusal to show tolerance, to allow freedom or to play fair – for why should you be allowed to say what you want, when others are denied the right by you?
>
> (p. 274)

Freedom of speech is a universally vaunted right, but faces epistemological and ethical difficulties in the current postmodern climate. Nevertheless, Barrow points out that claiming or advocating this right entails that others have the right to say things that are offensive. It is a logical consequence of the claim that one is entitled to voice one's opinion that others are entitled to do likewise, regardless of the message. To take action against those who have caused offence is to show a distinct lack of tolerance—or as Barrow puts it, a lack of 'putting up with things that you don't want to put up with' (p. 274). We have argued, however, that this particular chant is racist and racist chanting, all other things being equal, ought not to be tolerated. Contrary to Barrow's reservations, therefore, we firmly believe that some action ought to be taken in this and other similar cases.

The final point, therefore, relates to the nature of the action to be taken. We have argued that the chanters themselves may be deficient in different ways. Any intervention or action should aim at developing or rectifying the deficiency in knowledge, sensitivity, perception or courage. Those in the crowd with the requisite moral sensitivity, however, need not necessarily take direct action there and then by registering their offence. Davis (1994) has argued in relation to an analogous example that a failure to register disapproval directly, or a failure to try and stop the chanting there and then, is morally defensible. 'Failure to act neither collapses into approval, nor entails a flippant attitude towards the indiscretion witnessed' (Davis, 1994, p. 156). It is not hypocrisy to be tuned in to the moral transgression, yet not deal with it directly. It is a feature of human character that our moral strengths may lie in different directions. A nurse and a soldier may attend to a particular moral outrage in different ways. The soldier might courageously intervene to stop harm or suffering, whereas the nurse might compassionately try to relieve suffering. In this present example an attempt at intervention might be risky and might not make any difference anyway. The context of the situation and the highly charged emotional atmosphere might negate space for reflection on the chanters' behalf.

Any intervention ought to aim at changing the behaviour by promoting respect for Sikhs and English people alike. Haydon (2006, p. 31) argues: 'Offensive remarks about others are disrespectful to those others even when they do not hear the remarks.' Cultivating respectful attitudes and nurturing a respectful disposition is crucial, and an appropriate moral response to the chanting should be calculated with this in mind. Responsibility for developing respect is a shared responsibility. Different people, agencies and institutions may have different qualities of character and different opportunities that they are able to marshal for the purpose. The coach of the Welsh rugby team, the stadium managers, the players themselves, the parents of children, the stewards and the police, for example, may have different moral and possibly legal obligations, and different opportunities both to stop the chanting and to nurture respect. For us this might mean drawing attention to the issues in classes and in conversations with students and colleagues, writing to the Welsh Rugby Union to draw its attention to the matter, writing to the local press or publishing an academic paper.

Concluding comments

Chanting at international rugby matches is an audible and visible manifestation and celebration of national identity and ethnic pride. However, it is only a short step from these behaviours to their much more sinister and pernicious cousins, xenophobia and racism. Part of the danger of failing to mark this distinction carefully is an unquestioning acceptance of racism, especially among the ethically ignorant or ethically immature. When discourses are also shrouded in the veil of terrace banter, they can become even more difficult to detect accurately and act on accordingly.

In this paper we have argued that there is a four-part consideration and response to the chant 'I'd rather wear a turban than a rose.' First, the chant ought to be considered inherently offensive if it can be demonstrated to be objectively racist. It is quite possible for behaviour to be

offensive but not racist (e.g., bad manners), but not for behaviour to be racist yet not offensive. Racism breaches ethical frameworks and moral principles.

Second, even though the chant contains no racist language *per se*, it is racist. Within a normative structure embracing symbolic carriers of national identity and ethnic pride, it hierarchically orders racialized identities (albeit within the 'playfulness' of terrace banter) and is directed at ethnically different others.

Third, having established that the chant is both offensive and racist, we argue that those who chant it should not be considered as an undifferentiated group with a single racist disposition. Instead, we note the importance of recognizing the gradations between the ethically excusable (e.g., unwittingly racist through ignorance) and the ethically inexcusable (e.g., deliberately racist and evil), which should have different levels of moral blame attached to them.

Finally, there is a set of responses that are appropriate when encountering a chant of this kind. Each person has 'individual capital' to exercise, and as Davis (1994) notes, there are different morally consistent approaches. Within a social climate of shared responsibility for moral education (especially of those who are ethically immature), there is a duty for a person to do whatever is within their individual means to raise awareness of this manifestation of racism (and others), and to cultivate and nurture a respectful and tolerant disposition among others. More specifically, persons encountering chanting of this kind may register their disapproval with match stewards, on-duty police officers, the national governing body, the local press and political representatives, and engage with other fora for educational debate.

More strategically, as part of the overall educational process, the Personal and Social Education curriculum in schools might embrace this illustration of morally inadequate behaviour to tackle the particular focus of racist and offensive behaviour, and to address themes and issues concerned with respect and tolerance more widely. Inculcating children with a sensitivity to racism in all its guises, knowledge of its moral inadequacy and a willingness to confront it are worthy educational goals. Educating young people in this way may also help to challenge some parents who would sing the chant to reflect on the racist nature of their conduct—at the next rugby match in particular, and their attitudes to 'race' and ethnicity more generally.

Notes

1. The Welsh fans sing a mixture of hymns (*Bread of Heaven* and *Calon Lân* among the most popular) and songs (such as Tom Jones' hit single *Delilah* and Max Boyce's *Hymns and Arias*). The English supporters, for their part, sing *Swing Low, Sweet Chariot*, an African-American spiritual song/hymn that was appropriated during the 1988 season and has been sung regularly ever since.
2. For those familiar with the nature of chanting at British men's football encounters, there was a predictable mixture of good humour, irony and insult. For an outsider's perspective on this, see Reilly (2006).
3. For an extended discussion of our intended distinction between subjective and objective, see McFee (2006, chapter 5).
4. A quick straw poll of an undergraduate class of over 100 sport students showed that opinion about the chant was divided. The students thought that the chant was either harmless fun or offensive in roughly equal measures. Essentially, from a moral perspective, the extent to which the chant is either racist, offensive or both, cannot be read from these prevailing views.
5. 'Scouse' is the dialect and accent of the people of Liverpool in the north west of England. Liverpudlians are sometimes referred to as 'Scousers'.
6. Back (1996) notes quite properly that the critique of the legitimacy of the concept of 'race' was a characteristic of early writers (e.g., Banton, 1970). In connection with sport, however, it remains an important part of the discourse that surrounds the differentiated nature of sporting successes (e.g., Hoberman, 1997; Entine, 2000; Cashmore, 2001; Fleming, 2001).
7. Back (1996) argues that racism is defined according to social and historical context, and hence that there is not one monolithic racism, but many racisms.
8. For example, in 1969 Sikh bus drivers and conductors in Wolverhampton won the right to wear turbans at work after a long dispute (*BBC News*, 2006). Later, in 1973, legislation was introduced that required those riding motorcycles or motorized scooters on public highways to wear a protective 'crash helmet'. Members of the Sikh community resisted this paternalism and were held to be guilty of a minor offence. The law was relaxed in 1976 through the Motor-Cycle Crash Helmets (Religious Exemption) Act, after significant campaigning by members of the Sikh community (including the imprisonment for a week of community leader Gyani Sunder Singh Sagar for not paying his fines).
9. The 2001 census revealed that the Sikh community in Britain is relatively small, numbering only 336,000 or 0.6% of the total population (Office for National Statistics, 2001).
10. The historical derivation of the appropriation of the red rose by the England rugby establishment is uncertain, though Smith (2006), writing on the website of the Museum of Rugby at Twickenham, notes three possibilities: first, the royal English rose is red and white, but because many monarchs after the War of the Roses were descended from the House of Lancaster, it was the red rose which came to symbolize England; second, Elizabeth I presented a coat of arms to Rugby School and allowed the adoption of her own (red) rose on the school's crest—and the white kit worn by England later was taken from the kit used at Rugby School; and third, the subcommittee who selected the first England side included two representatives of clubs in Lancashire, and it is possible that they also chose the England kit (incorporating the red rose).

References

Back, L. (1996) *New ethnicities and urban culture* UCL Press, London.

Back, L., Crabbe, T. and Solomos, J. Brown, A. (ed) (1998) Racism in football: patterns of continuity and change. *Fanatics – power, identity and fandom in football* pp. 71–87. Routledge, London.

Back, L., Crabbe, T. and Solomos, J. (2001a) *The changing face of football* Berg, Oxford.

Back, L., Crabbe, T. and Solomos, J. Carrington, B. and McDonald, I. (eds) (2001b) 'Lions and black skins': race, nation and local patriotism in football. *Race, sport and British society* pp. 83–102. Routledge, London.

Banton, M. Zubaida, S. (ed) (1970) The concept of racism. *Race and racialism* pp. 17–34. Tavistock, London.

Barnes, J. (1999) *John Barnes: Autobiography* Headline, London.

Barrow, R. (2005) On the duty of not taking offence. *Journal of Moral Education* **34**:(3), pp. 265–275. [informaworld].

Barrow, R. (2006) Offence and respect: some brief comments. *Journal of Moral Education* **35**:(1), pp. 33–36. [informaworld].

BBC News (March 2002) *Thorny issue over rugby's rose* — Available online at: http://news.bbc.co.uk/1/hi/england/1895184.stm (accessed 31 July 2006).

BBC News (April 2006) *1969: Sikh busmen win turban fight* — Available online at: http://news.bbc.co.uk/onthisday/hi/dates/stories/april/9/newsid_2523000/2523691.stm (accessed 31 July 2006).

Blum, L. (1994) *'I'm not a racist, but ...': The moral quandary of race* Cornell University Press, Ithaca, NY.

Carrington, B. Brown, A. (ed) (1998) Football's coming home: but whose home? And do we want it? Nation, football and the politics of exclusion. *Fanatics – power, identity and fandom in football* pp. 101–123. Routledge, London.

Cashmore, E. (2001) *Making sense of sports* (4th edn), Routledge, London.

Cole, M. Merkel, U. and Tokarski, W. (eds) (1996) 'Race', racism and nomenclature: a conceptual analysis. *Racism and xenophobia in European football* pp. 11–22. Meyer & Meyer Verlag, Aachen.

Davis, P. (1994) Collective responsibility and the subjective standpoint. *Cogito* **8**:(2), pp. 155–158.

Entine, J. (2000) *Taboo* Public Affairs, New York

Fleming, S. Carrington, B. and McDonald, I. (eds) (2001) Racial science and black and South Asian physicality. *Race, sport and British society* pp. 105–120. Routledge, London.

Fleming, S. Hogenová, A. and Moskalová, J. (eds) (2005) Racialised media discourses: the case of big(ot) Ron. *Pohyb ve výchové, umnía sportu Movement in education, sport and art* pp. 17–30. Univezita Karlova Praze, Prague.

Fleming, S. and Tomlinson, A. Merkel, U. and Tokarski, W. (eds) (1996) Football, racism and xenophobia in England (I): Europe and the old England. *Racism and xenophobia in European football* pp. 79–100. Meyer & Meyer Verlag, Aachen.

Garland, J. and Rowe, M. Merkel, U. and Tokarski, W. (eds) (1996) Football, racism and xenophobia in England (II): Challenging racism and xenophobia. *Racism and xenophobia in European football* pp. 101–128. Meyer & Meyer Verlag, Aachen.

Haydon, G. (2006) On the duty of educating respect: a response to Robin Barrow. *Journal of Moral Education* **35**:(1), pp. 19–32. [informaworld].

Hoberman, J. (1997) *Darwin's athletes* Houghton Mifflin, New York.

King, C. (2004) *Offside racism: playing the white man* Berg, Oxford.

Long, J. A. and McNamee, M. J. (2004) On the moral economy of racism and racist rationalizations in sport. *International Review of the Sociology of Sport* **39**:(4), pp. 405–420.

Macpherson, W. (1999) *The Stephen Lawrence enquiry* Commission for Racial Equality, London.

Mason, D. (1994) On the dangers of disconnecting race and racism. *Sociology* **28**:(4), pp. 845–858.

McFee, G. (2006) *Sport, rules and values: philosophical investigations into the nature of sport* Routledge, London.

Miles, R. (1989) *Racism* Routledge, London.

Miles, R. (1993) *Racism after 'race relations'* Routledge, London.

Office for National Statistics (2001) *Census, 2001* ONS, London — Available online at: www.statistics.gov.uk/cci/nugget.asp?id=293 (accessed 31 July 2006).

Parry, S. J. McNamee, M. and Parry, S. J. (eds) (1998) Violence and aggression in contemporary sport. *Ethics and sport* pp. 205–224. Routledge, London.

Redhead, S. (1987) *Sing when you're winning* Pluto, London.

Reilly, R. (2006) The sweet songs of soccer. *Sports Illustrated* p. 78.

Sikh Coalition (2006) *The Sikh theology* — Available online at: www.sikhcoalition.org/sikhism11.asp (accessed 31 July 2006).

Smith, J. (2006) *Rugby football union and the red rose* — Available online at: www.sportnetwork.net/main/s245/st74325.htm?fromrss=1 (accessed 31 July 2006).

Solomos, J. and Back, L. (1994) Conceptualising racisms: social theory, politics and research. *Sociology* **28**:(1), pp. 143–161.

Van Dijk, T. A. and Cashmore, E. (eds) (2004) Racist discourse. *Encyclopedia of race and ethnic studies* pp. 351–355. Routledge, London.

Racism, racist acts and courageous role models

Mike McNamee

Racism and responsibility

Having argued the case for the possibility of ethical development in and through sports, I now want to argue further what this development does and does not consist in. One obvious challenge to such a claim is the sheer ubiquity of vicious behaviours in sports. Social scientific research abounds that shows how sports can be a vehicle for child abuse, misogyny, sexism and of course racism. To my knowledge, however, despite the voluminous literature on racism and sport, there has been no attempt to give an aretaic account of it: that is to say, of racism as a vice. This chapter attempts to articulate a clearer picture of the repugnance of racism as it manifests itself in sport and to develop a virtue-ethical perspective by considering racism as a vice. In particular, I explore questions of responsibility and culpability for both committed and less-entrenched racism in sports.

I argue against the binary understanding of persons as either racist/not racist which brings with it an undifferentiated moral response. Thus understood, the almost universal acceptance that racism is wrong somewhat ironically brings its own problems. It is sometimes suggested by anti-racist scholars that there is an unwillingness to acknowledge certain practices, within and outside sport, as racist because that might require us to recognise, at least potentially, the racism within ourselves. More importantly, for my purposes at least, the homogeneity of moral opprobrium attached to racist attitudes, policies or utterances effectively carries disproportionate sanctions and thereby threatens to jeopardise more considered, and perhaps more productive, ethical responses to it. I explore here the desirability of imagining a scale of severity rather than the more common but analytically crude binary categories of racist/ non racist. In an attempt to do justice to the complexities of the debate I offer what I hope is a more nuanced appreciation of racism, taking account of context, intentionality and the centrality of the trait to the identity of the person alleged to be racist. To do this I consider the case of a high-profile football commentator and former manager, Ron Atkinson, whose racist remarks lost him his job in 2004. In arguing for an ethically salient distinction between a racist act and a racist character I offer a clearer conceptual schema for evaluating beliefs and behaviour in this highly charged arena. I conclude the chapter with one of the finest examples of role modelling by sportspersons, the Zimbabwean cricketers Andrew Flower and Henry Olonga, who were prepared to forego their participation in the Cricket World Cup of 2003 in order to declare objectionable the racism of their own nation's political policies.

Mike McNamee 'Racism, Racist Acts, and Courageous Role Models', from *Sport Virtues and Vices: Morality Plays*, © 2008 Mike McNamee. Reprinted by permission of Routledge.

Understanding racism

Among social scientific scholars the concept of 'race' is a discredited biological concept. Hence in sociological writings 'race' commonly appears within inverted commas, and is taken to refer to the antipathy that people experience because of their appearance/inheritance, which arises from other people's designation of them as 'others'. But this discredit has a longer history than might be assumed. The invidious tendency to consider racial characteristics as scientifically endorsed rather than as the product of a merely convenient biological classification as Darwin had intended (Appiah, 1996) often goes unnoticed even in modern times. Yet Ralph Waldo Emerson had challenged and discredited the convenient race classification well over a century ago:

> An ingenious anatomist has written a book to prove that races are imperishable, but nations are pliant constructions, easily changed or destroyed. But this writer did not found his assumed races on any necessary law, disclosing their idea or metaphysical necessity; nor did he on the other hand count with precision the existing races and settle the true bounds; a point of nicety, and the popular test of his theory. The individuals at the extremes of divergence in one race of men are as unlike as the wolf to the lapdog. Yet each variety shades down imperceptibly into the next, and you cannot draw the line where one race begins or ends. Hence every writer makes a different count. Blumenbach reckons five races; Humboldt three; and Mr Pickering, who lately in our Exploring Expedition thinks he saw all kinds of men that can be on the planet, makes eleven.
> (cited in Appiah, 1996: 68–9)

The emergence of genetic discoveries threw into the dustbin of scientific anachronism the idea of there existing separate races in nature. Nevertheless, despite its redundancy the continuing significance of racism as a social process and lived experienced still resonates today and shows no ready signs of giving way. Wieviorka (1995) draws on Guillaumin's (1972: 63) explanation that 'imaginary and real races play the same role in the social processes and are therefore identical as regards their social function'. As a falsehood or product of bad science Massara (2007: 498–9) argues that race is ontologically false. Although, in opposition to the ideas put forward here, he neatly captures their stance: 'race cannot tell us anything about who we really are as individuals – it does not function, that is as a causal explanation of behaviour – however strategically necessary in the short term the concept may prove for political resistance'. The use of the concept of 'racism' has been extended to a consideration of the treatment of ethnic groups and a range of signifiers that may or may not include skin colour (e.g. Miles, 1989). Whether or not it can legitimately be applied to the treatment of religious groups is a matter of some dispute in the literature (Hall, 1992; Modood, 1997; Solomos and Back, 1996).

In other writings the term 'racism' has been re-labelled to as the 'new racism' or 'cultural racism' (e.g. Back, 1996; Barker, 1981; Gilroy, 1987; Parekh, 1995). The terminology is designed to indicate a more defensive mode of racism that seeks (allegedly) more to preserve a given way of life against the incursions of those labelled 'outsiders' rather than a direct assault on those so labelled. This can raise uncomfortable issues around the difference between asserting one's identity as a statement of difference, and racism. Paradoxically, as Solomos and Back (1996: 27) put it, this line of argument 'can produce a racist effect while denying that this effect is the result of racism'.

Some writers, such as Connolly (2000), suggest it is not just direct actions, but all those beliefs, behaviours, practices and processes that contribute either directly or indirectly to the racialisation of certain groups that can be designated as racist. Connolly also notes that this is seen to arise because of the way in which the signification of certain groups comes to 'shape the development of future social relations, institutions and processes' (2000: 503). Similarly, in a passage where it is easy to draw parallels with sport, Macpherson (1999: 17) noted:

> Unwitting racism can arise because of lack of understanding, ignorance or mistaken beliefs. It can arise from well intentioned but patronising words or actions. It can arise from unfamiliarity with the behaviour or cultural traditions of people or families from minority ethnic communities. It can arise from racist stereotyping of black people as potential criminals or troublemakers. Often this arises out of uncritical self-understanding born out of an inflexible police ethos of the 'traditional' way of doing things.

Furthermore such attitudes can thrive in a tightly knit community, so that there can be a collective failure to detect and to outlaw this breed of racism.

In keeping with these anti-racist positions, it is necessary to hold on to the ideas of 'race' and 'racism' despite their having no genuine ontology because they function wrongly to privilege or derogate social groups. Within the broad framework that this represents, the basis for prejudice and discrimination is multidimensional, embracing culture, ethnicity and nationality.

D'Souza (1995: 27) presents an account of racism as 'an ideology of intellectual or moral superiority based upon the biological characteristics of race'. This hierarchical portrayal of superior and inferior races is obviously central to white supremacists, but offers an incomplete definition of racism. This can be seen particularly clearly in the sporting arena where the apparent and widespread celebration of black sporting prowess has failed to eradicate racism.

More subtle variations of racism play along the borders of ethnocentrism. It is not always clear where to draw the line when what is perceived as benign ethnocentrism may be perceived as more exclusionary and properly deserving of the label racism. In an effort to counteract protestations of innocence it has been suggested that an action should be deemed to be racist if it is perceived as such by the person subjected to that action (see, for example, the report of the inquiry into the police investigation into the murder of the British African-Caribbean schoolboy, Stephen Lawrence: Macpherson, 1999). This position effectively embodies a relativistic argument (typical of some social constructivists) that reflects an inadequate way of conceptualizing the phenomenon of racism. If it is desirable to argue that people may be being racist even when they protest their innocence (as I do), then it is necessary to argue that people may not be being racist when others believe they are. Racism, to corrupt a well-known phrase, cannot therefore merely be 'in the eye of the beholder'.

Other writers have sought to dismantle conceptions of what they see as falsely unified accounts of racism, drawing attention to its variegated nature, its different forms and levels. Carrington and McDonald (2001), for example, illustrate dimensions of racism in cricket that extend beyond the immediate form of crude racial abuse. They see two further levels evidenced through racial stereotyping of cultural essentialisms that discriminate against black and Asian people, and racial exclusion based on a conception of white Englishness that creates a form of institutional racism serving to limit access to socially valued opportunities. Others have stressed the importance of analysing racism within the triplex of concepts: 'race', 'class' and 'nation' (e.g. Balibar and Wallerstein, 1991).

Wellman attempts to demonstrate that racism is not simply reducible to the concepts of 'bigotry' or 'prejudice', instead he sees racism as 'culturally acceptable beliefs that defend social advantages that are based on race' (Wellman, 1993: 4). I have considerable sympathy with the proposition that we all have embedded racial constructions affecting the way we think and behave towards each other, and that most, if not all, of us in the West at least, operate within social structures that favour certain ethnic groups. Indeed, it is important that people recognise this before they become too free in their criticism of others.

Without gainsaying the possibility of institutional racism, or the defence of social advantage, there is an important distinction to be noted between sometimes behaving in a way that reflects thinking grounded in racially prejudicial thought and being 'a committed racist'. Note this distinction is not backsliding. Nor is it intended to exculpate those whose racism is simply not as strong as others'. The distinction is clearly put in Aristotle's *Nichomachean Ethics* between an act and a character (see Williams, 1980: 1901). It is important to uphold in order to not treat as equals those who behave in a racist manner unknowingly and those who do so characteristically and reflectively as part of a chosen way of life.

To examine whether one might exhibit racist behaviour without properly being a racist, consider a paradigmatic case of racist language. In his discussion of the use of the word 'nigger' in the context of the legacy of white supremacy, Blum (2002: 19) notes that its use by certain young blacks as a term of affection and bonding is a context-bound use that has confused many whites, and is objected to by many, especially older, blacks. This leads to the point that our evaluations of racism, though not relativistic, are deeply context-sensitive (cf. Wellman, 1993).

To treat them otherwise is not (socio)logical. True, there are actions that require little understanding of context to be appreciated, but some knowledge of context is always necessary to evaluate social action.

In order to appreciate the intentionality of racism we need to appreciate historically the shifting attitudes towards racism. Nonetheless, as Blum (2002: 18) argues:

> In general, people beyond a certain age should recognise what is racist; their moral responsibility for perpetrating racism when they do not recognise it is analogous to the fault of citizens who cause injury through negligence rather than direct intent. They could be reasonably expected to recognise or anticipate the moral damage. Except for people with extraordinarily sheltered lives and upbringings, ignorance of racism does not absolve one from responsibility, although, everything else being equal, intentionally demeaning a racial group is morally more blameworthy than unintentionally doing so.

To some the possibility of racist actions or attitudes being 'innocent' or 'ignorant' is politically indefensible. Nevertheless, it *is* logically possible. And if we find those to whom it might apply, however unlikely, our position is that we should not treat it in the same way as fully conscious or premeditated racism. In estimating the potential grounds for latitude the following questions might be useful:

1 Can racist beliefs be held, or racist acts be performed, by persons we *ought* not to label 'racists'?
2 Is it helpful to articulate an underlying scale of racism?
3 When does racist thought, feeling or action genuinely form a part of one's character *as* racist?

There are those who will reject (1) the logical possibility, and/or (2) the normative justification that such questions attempt to create a space for. I believe, however, that the preservation of these possibilities is both logically possible and morally desirable.

If sociological understandings of action are always to be context-sensitive, then our moral responses should be the same. Children raised in a racist family who merely mouth racist sentiments are, however, less culpable than their elders. If it is true that our moral responses to racism should be sensitive to these features, perhaps we can extend that list. Consider the level of entrenchment of racist beliefs. Some, who though prejudiced (and thus deserving of moral opprobrium), when challenged might concede that their views are based on ignorance or prejudice born of reprehensible socialisation. To what extent ought we to treat such a person *in the same way* as an otherwise intelligent white supremacist? In such a case might it not be better to think of them as 'ethically disabled' (Jacobs, 2001) and therefore not fully responsible for their agency? The level of awareness of one's racism appears to be an important contextual feature to be taken into account in the moral register of racism presented below.

The level of premeditation or reflective awareness should also be considered. Contrast the deliberate use of racist language to antagonise an opponent (e.g. 'sledging' in cricket or 'trash talking' in basketball) with an abusive racial remark blurted out in the heat of the moment. It might be appropriate to ask to what extent the racist remark is characteristic of the person's other conduct or 'merely a lapse'. This is not an apology for the equivalent of racist Freudian slips. Yet if we acknowledge that, for the sake of argument, anyone over 50 years old (in Britain or the USA at least) was brought up in a society that harboured deep and widespread racist prejudices, then it is reasonable to suspect that their early socialisation contained at least some pernicious social and moral views based improperly on racialised characteristics.

While modern moral theories in some sense mirror the rationalist idea of universal reason – and hence universal moral registers (impartiality, universality, prescriptivity) – virtue-theoretical evaluations of moral character and agency, as we have seen, pay significant attention to the forces of habituation in the learning of our im/moral responses as patterns of thought, feeling and action. Of course the questions remain open as to what we should do with our knowledge of such habituation in and outside sport; how it is that people come to hold racist views, feel racist emotions and act in racist ways. We need to consider this properly in our evaluation of persons, but not to use it as a ready excuse for racists proper, whose acts and attitudes are not merely 'disabled' but self-consciously vicious. Of the latter, the more vicious end of the racist register, there are others for whom such abuse is not out of character in time of stress, but reveals their 'true' character.

Such non-benign contextual features require moral responses to racism to be classified in a more subtle manner than the in/out, yes/no binary divide of racist/not-racist. We need a vocabulary that qualitatively discriminates appropriately and does so in an ethically self-conscious way. The philosophical task as I see it is to set out the moral scales of racism from innocence, ignorance and ambivalence on to outright bigotry, and show why this more conceptually and morally nuanced vocabulary is important. Only after this is done can we consider the extent to which racist actions or utterances genuinely form part of the character of the person labelled 'racist'.

Articulating the moral repugnance of racism

To help resolve these questions I draw heavily on the work of Lawrence Blum (2002). Blum draws upon the widely used distinctions of personal, social and institutional racism, and we concur with his suggestion that merely to consider racism individualistically (Allport, 1987) or socially (Ture and Hamilton, 1992) is to replace one partial definition with another. However, we focus here on the individual while being aware that, in its ontology, racism can never in reality be separated from other levels. Blum (2002: 9–10) writes:

> We do better to accept the plurality of items that can be racist (beliefs, institutions, systems, attitudes, acts and so on), without thinking that one of these needs to be the foundation of all the others. Personal, social and institutional racism are each morally problematic, in at least partially distinct ways.

His starting point is a categorisation of racial discrimination/differentiation derived from his assertion that all forms of racism relate to two general themes or paradigms: *inferiorisation* and *antipathy*. Blum's inferiorising racism is expressed in attitudes and actions that variously show disrespect, contempt, derision, derogation or are demeaning. While an inferiorising racist generally thinks that the racial other is inferior, sometimes people believe their own

group to be inferior. In sport we have witnessed interesting reversals in this process. For example, the previous common presumption of the inferiority of black athletes has been inverted in many events. The populist position has become one that asserts that black athletes are 'naturally' better equipped to run the 100 metres and other power-based activities involved in, for example, American football. But even on its own terms this prejudice is limited since one cannot ignore how many more Olympic and World Championship medals are won over 800 and 1500 metres by Sudanese and Moroccan athletes, nor the complete dominance of Kenyan long-distance runners on the track. The implication is that black athletes have an unfair advantage so there is no point in 'our' valiant men and women trying to compete. In the 1990s there was even discussion of limiting athletes from African nations on the televised American running circuit.

In Blum's construction, inferiorising and antipathy racists are distinct because the former do not necessarily hate the target of their beliefs. It is quite possible for them to have a paternalistic concern for people they regard as their inferiors. So not every race-hater is supremacist, nor is every supremacist a race-hater. Moreover, antipathy might be based on feelings of inferiority as well as superiority. Blum argues that 'racial prejudice' is illustrative of the antipathy theme. Although the linguistic root suggests a prejudging of something precipitously, racial prejudice, he suggests, is a generalised antipathy towards another racial group, or members thereof, merely in virtue of that membership. He draws upon Allport's (1987) definition that prejudice is antipathy based on erroneous generalisation, but argues in addition that all antipathy to a racial group must be considered prejudicial since the variegated nature of the group would deny the validity of grounds for antipathy to the entire group based on race-founded suppositions. The notion of racial prejudice, as we have noted, can cut across the conscious/unconscious division. One may have prejudices towards others and be unaware of it. Much racism falls into the category of racist views without the people holding them necessarily identifying self-consciously with those views. A reasonable anti-racist expectation in those circumstances is that, when made aware of the damaging consequences of such prejudice, those who do not on reflection subscribe to racist values ought to seek to instigate change in themselves. Blum (2002: 13) modifies Allport's definition:

> [P]rejudice is a kind of antipathy, toward a race-defined group and would by my definition appear to count as a form of 'racism'. Indeed racial prejudice is often called 'racism'. But, 'prejudice' often implies dislike or antipathy, but not necessarily hatred or strong antipathy. … Because prejudice is, in general, a less malevolent attitude than hatred and intense hostility, it is less morally evil. It is not clear whether we should call weaker forms of racial prejudice 'racism'. These forms should, in any case, evoke opprobrium in their own right.

Thus, someone who might typically be considered as racist may yet have grounds for less than total moral condemnation. There are a few cases where a lack of moral agency (e.g. the very young, the severely intellectually challenged) may to a certain extent yield cases where there cannot be ascription of responsibility. There are also clear-cut cases of vicious racists whose attitudes may be the result of inferiorising or antipathy or both. While the former may be racial supremacists in less corrosive ways, still heavy moral opprobrium attaches to them while antipathy-based racists appear to be *ceteris paribus* the group to be most morally reviled. There is a rather grey area, then, involving those who hold racist views, beliefs or attitudes, or who commit racist acts on a non-regular basis, that we need to consider more fully. If vice is typically the opposite of virtue, what grounds are there for thinking that a certain person exhibits the vice of racism? Which beliefs mould it? What language evidences this? Which acts typify it?

Racism and a vice

While the dominant moral theories of utilitarianism and deontology are diametrically opposed to each other in the direction of their moral schemes, they are similar in form. Just as deontological concerns direct our moral salience to universal rights and duties that we 'know' to be true before we act (don't harm people, don't disrespect them, allow free speech and movement to all, etc.), utilitarianism pushes us to maximise good outcomes while at the same time treating all persons as equal in our calculations. As guides to the moral life, deontology, or duty-based ethics, is thought of as an ethics of the 'right action', whereas utilitarianism is a teleological theory of the 'good living'.[1] It may at first be difficult to see how utilitarianism can make sense of the idea of racial wrongs. One of the foundational premises of utilitarianism is that everyone must be treated as equals so racism is ruled out *ab initio*. Beyond arguing that maximising the good entails the calculation of pleasures/utility of all relevant persons, utilitarianism offers little in the way of theoretical resources to understand the wrongness of racism, though its consistent application (the impartial treatment of all, considered equally, in order to maximize happiness in the world) might help significantly to remove racism.

Deontology fares better. Sharing the principle of impartial treatment of all persons, and the universalisation of rights and duties, it illuminates proper guides to conduct in its foundational ideas such as equal treatment, respect and autonomy among others. Nevertheless, deontology with its resolute focus on moral *reasons* is commonly held to be inadequate in terms of moral psychology. It holds, in the classic form of moral cognitivism from Kant and Plato, that merely by knowing the right thing to do one will act in accordance with the dictates of moral reason; moral reasoning and moral action are one. Such a theory holds no space for either weakness of will or for inconsistencies of thought and action. I attempt, in some small way, to defend Kant against this pernicious characterisation by considering some remarks within his theory of virtue as opposed to his overall moral philosophy of duties. Virtue ethics is more hospitable to social and psychological factors, attempting to take seriously the agency of embedded and embodied agents in the particularity of time and place.

To think of someone as a racist is a particular way of conceiving someone as possessed of a vicious character. A racist character is not typically revealed in a one-time activation, but through a complex and interrelated pattern of thoughts, feelings and acts relating to inferiorising and/or antipathy racism over time. The particular configuration of this patterning will be person-specific and derivative of the usual catalogue of social indexicals: age, embodiment, class, gender, intelligence, sexual orientation, wealth and so on. It may range, as we have seen, from unacceptable paternalism to wicked subjugation and violence. Equally, contrast the disaffected youth for whom overtly racist political parties become a source of self-esteem with the controlling mind of the organisation; or with the international sportsmen who were apologists for apartheid sport. All are racists, but surely of different depth and intensity. Racists are not a 'natural kind'; they do not form a homogeneous class. What can be said more generally though, is that to ascribe the condemnatory title 'racist' to a person, like any other aspect of their character, it should be one that typically informs their modes of being in the world in relatively consistent ways that they understand to be part of their identity:

> A racist *person* is not merely someone who commits one racist act or acts on a racist motive on a small number of occasions. Motives and attitudes such as bigotry, antipathy, and contempt must be embedded in the person's psychological makeup as traits of character. In this sense being a racist is like being hateful, dishonest, or cruel, in implying an ingrained pattern of thought and feeling as well as action.
>
> (Blum, 2002: 14–15)

Rather than a binary thing, perhaps it is better to think of racism in subtle gradations, and/or subtle inflections activated by particular contexts. This is why the question 'When is a racist a racist?' is unhelpful. There may be cases when one act is sufficiently malevolent, but more typically there will not be. Blum argues that holding one racist view, or making one racist remark, or telling one racist joke ought not necessarily induce the label racist:

> The beliefs themselves were genuinely racist, but belief in them had not been deeply enough rooted in her psychological makeup to make her 'a racist'. She must be *genuinely committed* to and invested in racist beliefs in order to be a racist.
>
> (Blum, 2002: 21; emphasis added)

Of course, everything hangs on what is meant by the elliptical phrase 'genuinely committed' here. The committed racist in his or her actions is ethically inexcusable. No one would seriously dispute that (except, presumably, a racist).

However, defining a person as 'racist' may not require so strict a condition as 'genuine commitment'; reserving the term only for 'genuinely committed' racists may be to 'throw the baby out with the bathwater':

> Calling the belief in question, or the believing of it, racist, emotionally overloads a discussion of the validity or worthiness of the belief and leads us to think that because a view may have undesirable racial implications, it should be dismissed prior to discussion.
>
> (Blum, 2002: 22)

The point is well made, but fails to accord fully with some of the more subtle ways in which racist attitudes move from embryo to actuality. We need to attend to the processes of racialisation that are present in contextualised evaluations of those we consider more or less racists. These are captured well by Connolly (2000: 503) who, following Miles, notes:

> The signification of certain groups is not only grounded in the specific social relations that exist, but will also come to inform and shape the development of future social relations, institutions and processes. As such … all those beliefs, behaviours practices and processes that contribute, either directly or indirectly, to the racialisation of certain groups can be designated as racist … [I]t is not just overt racist attitudes and discriminatory and exclusionary practices that constitute racism, but all of the more subtle ideas and processes, however indirect and unintentional, that tend to maintain and reproduce the racialisation.

There can be no sharp distinctions here that will be conceptually felicitous, though those more politically inclined may say that the price of greater subtlety is simply not worth paying given the scope of the problem. A register of race as a vice would need to pay attention at least to the factors outlined in Figure 4.7.1.

What no typology can achieve is a complex grasp of the relationality of agency, context and structure. Nor should it aim to. In articulating this register I am merely trying in a preliminary way to draw attention to the degrees of viciousness that are often unhelpfully lumped together under the label 'racist'. Yet the moral economy of racism must be more differentiated than this. By contrast, I am suggesting that there exist degrees of culpability that allow us to

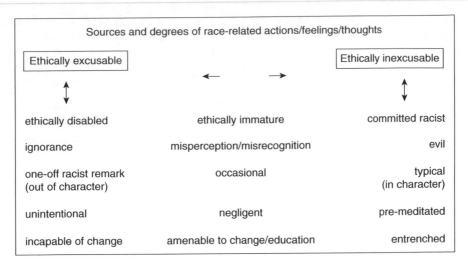

Figure 4.7.1. A racist register.

differentiate the viciousness of different kinds of characters labelled racist. Consider the following example:

Cricketers and baseball players commonly rail against the decisions of umpires. In a recent study of cricketers in the north of England, Long *et al.* (1997) report that one of the Asian batters in the study protested that he had been the victim of a bad decision by an umpire, protesting: 'I was never "out". He gave me out because I'm Asian … and he did that for three others.' The perception of racist behaviour makes it a racial issue, but does not mean that any racism has necessarily been committed. That is to say, a perception of racism by an apparently maltreated other is neither a necessary nor sufficient condition of its existence. In this case, the umpire may indeed have been racist, but he may also have been an incompetent umpire judging them incorrectly out (or struck out in baseball). Or he may not be racist in anyway shape or form and the batter is merely using the racist slur to bring pressure to bear on the umpire for future decisions or to mask their own incompetence. There is also the possibility that the umpire is indeed a repugnant racist but feels bound in this situation by the ethos and laws of cricket to make impartial decisions.

Just as the belief that one is the subject of racist sentiments does not automatically mean that another is a racist, so another's denial that they are being racist is insufficient to deny the truth of the assertion. The remark or behaviour does not stand alone. Consider a circumstance in which a player or official has told a racist joke, used racial abuse or made a decision on the basis of some racial presumption. Interpretation of the significance of that might vary depending upon whether the perpetrator: says sorry (then or later) or shakes hands with a 'Well played mate' at the end of the game; insists it was 'just in the heat of the moment'; does so in a team founded on the principles of cultural pluralism; or elsewhere engages in actions to counter racism. Even then there are other contextual layers that those involved will use to arrive at their interpretation of meaning. It was clear that the black players in Long *et al.* (2000) viewed and responded to incidents in a differentiated manner depending upon the context. Quite properly, it seems to me, they attached varying degrees of moral opprobrium to those whom they perceived had acted in the 'heat of the moment incidents' to those whose behaviours displayed a clearer pattern of consistency.

If virtues and vices are enduring traits of character, it should mean that the idea of a one-off racist would be an oxymoron. To be a racist it must be part of one's character; one's relatively settled dispositions to think, feel and act in regular and interrelated ways. As I have said above, this makes judging whether a person is a racist, in the light of the register above, a more complex matter than some allow.

In their discussion of identity and agency, Rorty and Wong (1997: 20) attempt to explore the questions one might ask in order to judge whether a given trait is central to one's character. Their questions have salience for a more nuanced understanding of racism as a vice. They list seven ways in which a trait may be central in virtue of:

■ the degree of its objective ramification, the extent to which other traits (that is dispositions to beliefs, desires, habits, attitudes and actions) are dependent on it;

■ the degree of its contextual or regional ramification, that is, the extent to which a trait is exemplified across distinctive spheres (e.g. public and private domains, work and leisure) and across different types of relationships (as they are differentiated by gender, status, class, age, etc.);

■ the degree for which it is difficult for a person to change the trait (which is often a function of its temporal persistence);

■ the degree of its social ramification, the extent to which the trait affects the way the person is categorized and treated by others;

■ the extent to which it is dominant in situations that require coping with stress or conflict;

■ the extent to which it is dominant when it conflicts with other traits (e.g. when generosity conflicts with vengefulness); and

■ the degree to which it is appropriated as important in that the person regards herself as radically changed if the trait is lost or strongly modified. Such appropriations may, but need not be, explicitly articulated; they can be sporadic or contextualized; a person can appropriate a trait without succeeding in acting from it habitually. Sometimes what matters to a person's identity is that she centrally strives to strengthen and exercise a trait. Important traits are often also the focus of self-evaluation and self-esteem.

It is useful to illustrate the power of these questions in the context of a real example from sports. In 2004 the veteran English football manager, commentator and pundit, Ron Atkinson, resigned from his job immediately upon hearing that remarks he had made about the lacklustre performance of Chelsea's French defender Marcel Desailly in the European Champions League had in fact not been completely "off-air" but had been broadcast to several international audiences. Big Ron (as he was affectionately referred to) remarked: 'He's what is known in some schools as a fucking lazy thick nigger.' Naturally, and properly, the media frenzy that followed was immediate and severe. But where ought we to place Atkinson on the racist register above?

At first sight it appears to be a one-off racist remark that was not premeditated. But does this make him merely ethically disabled? His immediate resignation shows some level of remorse and recognition of the wrong committed. Much will hang on whether the remark was the product of an entrenched disposition or whether it was "out of character" so to speak. This is where things get philosophically interesting. To go further down this road we need to ask some conceptual questions about the centrality of the disposition to this attitude/remark and some empirical ones about his biography. Rorty and Wong's questions become particularly helpful here and I want to situate them in the Atkinson case along with the remarks of other media commentators from within and outside of sport.

Atkinson's remarks seem to be without objective ramification. That is to say, the racist trait does not appear to form a central part of his identity. After his resignation and the widespread condemnation of his comments, Atkinson made several protestations about his career being one that had been supportive of players of colour. During the 1970s, as a manager Atkinson had helped to develop several British African-Caribbean players not only to top division football but also the point where they represented their national team: England. This is one reason why so many people were shocked. Atkinson remarked himself: 'What I said is racist, I understand that, but I'm not a racist.' Moreover, he insisted in an interview with the editor of *New Nation* (a leading newspaper of the black community): 'I've offended nobody more than me at the moment. Christ almighty it's cost me roughly a million quid. I've done my penance.' Beyond the blasphemy that some might take offence at, one must ask whether Atkinson has the conceptual wherewithal to distinguish between penance and sanction. It's clear he has lost out financially and that, to his credit, he did not wait to be sacked. What is there to be said of the contextual ramification of the trait? Is Big Ron a racist in private but not in public (or at least not normally in public)? Critics have suggested that this is not the first such slip he has made. I shall discuss them further below. The point seems ambiguous but resonates with the idea of the social ramification of the trait. Clearly Atkinson's capital has fallen through the floor with nearly all sports fans and the wider public. He has not been associated with racist remarks and they hitherto formed no part of his social standing – unlike those whose standing, say, in a white supremacist movement is predicated on their racist credentials, Atkinson's certainly is not. Moreover, in his interview, Atkinson inadvertently displayed all of his non-politically correct credentials in his casual acceptance of the historical use of derisory language (queer, nigger etc.). One thing in Atkinson's defence is the clear idea that his remark is at odds with his promotion of black players within the football teams he has managed. Whether this is equity or expediency (it might be argued, though I think unfairly, that the black players were simply the only ones of any quality he could afford or attract) is open to question though certain black players who played for him appear to give support to his testimony. He has succeeded in his career without the trait; he does not depend on it for his success or self-esteem. It seems clear that the trait of racism is not central to his identity. Though the opprobrium that flew his way was well deserved, and though his utterance was utterly repugnant, it seems fair to conclude that despite his racist act(s) he himself is not possessed of a committed racist character.

Ron's racism, sports reporting and other courageous role models

Some media colleagues offered levels of support for Atkinson's person though not his remarks. A fellow football TV pundit, the septuagenarian[2] Jimmy Hill, offered the quasi defence that the remarks were no more than 'fun' between footballers. Hill, a former anchor man of the most popular British football programme of the last 30 or so years is reported to have said the following on the web site for Football Against Racism in Europe (2004):

> In that context, you wouldn't think that words like 'n****r' were particularly insulting: it would be funny. Without meaning to insult any black men, it's us having fun. What about people who make jokes about my long chin? I mean, n****r is black – so we have jokes where we call them n****rs because they're black. Why should that be any more of an offence than someone calling me chinny?

Now Hill is well known in the UK to have a pronounced chin but to equate his facial characteristic with the use of a word so historically loaded with disrespect and the fundamental denial of human rights, coupled with abusive derogation of Desailly's character, seems not so much bizarre but the product of a limited intellect. Despite Hill's being in his seventies, and Atkinson in his sixties, it seems clear that both person's characters have been forged in racist times and neither has been able to break free of those limiting shackles.

On the basis that racial groups have been historically subjected to destructive forms of prejudice, stigma, exclusion and discrimination, Blum (2002: 96) notes that 'a somewhat greater wrongfulness attaches to racial differentiations than to others. Race *is* an especially invidious category, both uniquely inferiorising and uniquely divisive'. In a similar vein, Muhammad Ali taunted Joe Frazier before their first fight for the Heavyweight Championship of the World. This was in response to Frazier's refusal to call Ali by his adopted Islamic name and, instead, by his former name Cassius Clay. Ali had called Frazier an 'Uncle Tom' meaning to demean Frazier whom he mocked as a gorilla; an unthinking beast, a person of colour insufficiently intelligent or articulate enough to challenge the hegemonic racial order, one happy (and with complicity) to preserve the racially based social hierarchies. Moreover, in the one-sided and bitter fight that followed, Ali berated Frazier 'what's my name? … what's my name?' repeatedly whilst brutally beating him. In 2001 Ali offered an apology in the *New York Times* but Frazier, though appearing to accept it, later remarked that the apology had been made to the paper rather than him. In Atkinson's case, the instant apology might incline us to move Atkinson to the centre of the register in

Figure 4.7.1, but if subsequent events confirm that this is representative of an underlying trait we would return him to the right of the register.

If Hill's remarks are those of denial, how much better are the inflammatory remarks of the columnist Darcus Howe?:

> Football managers tend to be dictatorial brutes. They treat their charges with a paternal brutality that would have any father hauled up in court for child abuse. These men, almost all of them white, behave in a way that would not be tolerated in any other area of modern society. They infect the players with the brutishness they dispense. As a consequence, women and blacks – perceived as the weaker sections of society – are deemed the lowest of the low. Gang sex and racial barracking are the stock-in-trade of players. The game has become a sewer containing all sorts of filth not permitted elsewhere.
>
> Atkinson is up to his neck in it. He pleaded a lapse in an otherwise unblemished career, which included signing several black players when he was manager of West Bromwich Albion. Yet Atkinson once alluded to a Cameroonian player's mother who, he claimed, lived up a tree in Africa. He boasted about how he had made Cyrille Regis, one of the blacks he signed while at West Brom, travel to away games at the back of the bus, as blacks were once forced to travel in the American South. Ian Wright, the Arsenal and England player, once asked a players' representative to warn Atkinson about his racial jibes.
>
> (Howe, 2004)

It appears then that, given the truth of the claims above, Atkinson was no one-off racist. The trait had surfaced elsewhere in public but was clearly at odds with others in his character. But having made his point, Howe then descends into a diatribe of disrespect that robs him of the moral high ground. He continued:

> So steeped is football in racist muck that nobody thought Atkinson's behaviour exceptional. Even black people accepted it. He demanded from them, and got, gratitude for letting darkies into the game. Hence several black players were at the front of the queue saying that, though his remarks on Desailly were wrong, he is no racist.
>
> Then what is he? A leader in the vanguard of anti-racism? All I have to say to Atkinson is: 'Get thee hence.' In case he doesn't know what that means, I'll translate into dressing-room jargon: 'Fuck off.'
>
> (Howe, 2004)

But if we are to understand racism in sport in the round, it is appropriate to ask what kind of response is ethically called for to such situations; what is the virtuous response to racist sports journalism or reporting? At first sight it appears that Howe's diatribe has some provenance from no lesser figure than Aristotle, who argued that anger was the virtuous response to injustice. As we read on though, we find that it is not simply the angry response that is just:

> [A]nyone can be angry – that is easy – or give or spend money; but to do this to the right person, to the right extent, at the right time, with the right motive, and in the right way, *that* is not for everyone, nor is it easy; wherefore goodness is both rare and laudable and noble.
>
> (*NE* II Bk. 9; 1109a25–30)

And later, in a slightly different context, Aristotle notes: 'It is not easy to determine both how and with whom and on what provocation and how long one should be angry ...' (*NE* II Bk. 9; 1109b14–16).

Of course there is some irony in quoting Aristotle here. For like other great philosophers he too was a hostage to the times. He had a conception of aristocratic nobility that appeared to influence heavily his conception of the good life for 'man'. Slaves and women were distinctly second class.

The idea of racism in sports has a long history. Though shorter, there is also a history of defiance against racial barriers, which perhaps achieved its epitome when in front of the Aryan supremacist Adolf Hitler, Jesse Owens won his Olympic sprint title in 1936 in Berlin. More recently, and against the racially segregated and vengeful backlash against white imperial rule in Zimbabwe, one black and one white cricketer stood together in defiance of the widespread racially motivated violent repatriation of land, and unlawful acquisition of property under the acquiescence (and some would say active support of) President Mugabe. On the eve of the Cricket World Cup, to be hosted by Zimbabwe for the first time, Andrew Flower and Henry Olonga, two of their leading players, wore black arm bands during a World Cup match to protest at their nation's racist policies. Not since the 'black power' protest of Tommy Smith and his fellow American athlete John Carlos in the Mexico Olympics had sportsmen or women put their head above the parapet to enter the political arena. Flower and Olonga jointly made the following pronouncement to the media:

It is a great honour for us to take the field today to play for Zimbabwe in the World Cup.

We feel privileged and proud to have been able to represent our country.

We are, however, deeply distressed about what is taking place in Zimbabwe in the midst of the World Cup and do not feel that we can take the field without indicating our feelings in a dignified manner and in keeping with the spirit of cricket.

We cannot in good conscience take to the field and ignore the fact that millions of our compatriots are starving, unemployed and oppressed.

We are aware that hundreds of thousands of Zimbabweans may even die in the coming months through a combination of starvation, poverty and Aids.

We are aware that many people have been unjustly imprisoned and tortured simply for expressing their opinions about what is happening in the country.

We have heard a torrent of racist hate speech directed at minority groups.

We are aware that thousands of Zimbabweans are routinely denied their right to freedom of expression.

We are aware that people have been murdered, raped, beaten and had their homes destroyed because of their beliefs and that many of those responsible have not been prosecuted.

We are also aware that many patriotic Zimbabweans oppose us even playing in the World Cup because of what is happening.

It is impossible to ignore what is happening in Zimbabwe. Although we are just professional cricketers, we do have a conscience and feelings.

We believe that if we remain silent that will be taken as a sign that either we do not care or we condone what is happening in Zimbabwe.

We believe that it is important to stand up for what is right.

We have struggled to think of an action that would be appropriate and that would not demean the game we love so much.

We have decided that we should act alone without other members of the team being involved because our decision is deeply personal and we did not want to use our senior status to unfairly influence more junior members of the squad.

We would like to stress that we greatly respect the ICC (International Cricket Council) and are grateful for all the hard work it has done in bringing the World Cup to Zimbabwe.

In all the circumstances we have decided that we will each wear a black armband for the duration of the World Cup.

In doing so we are mourning the death of democracy in our beloved Zimbabwe.

In doing so we are making a silent plea to those responsible to stop the abuse of human rights in Zimbabwe.

In doing so we pray that our small action may help to restore sanity and dignity to our nation.

Andrew Flower, Henry Olonga
(http://news.bbc.co.uk/sport3/
cwc2003/hi/newsid_2740000/
newsid_2744700/2744795.stm;
accessed 10.4.06)

It seems to me this is as moving and powerful an example of a virtuous response to racism in society through the equally powerful medium of commercialised sports. Their act was courageous. They knew in publicly articulating the racism of the ruling regime they not merely ended their international sporting careers but would in all likelihood face retribution from the governmental security forces, not known for their polite treatment of political dissenters. And it did. The proclamation led to a warrant for the arrest of Olonga on the grounds of treason and the pair were forced into hiding and then to move from the country. Finally, their statement expresses the anger and indignation that is apt in response to injustice even if others will merely see it as a small corrective of the vicious historical white domination of that continent. It also shows how sport, far from standing outside of the ordinary business of living, can seek to act as a powerful agent for social change.

On a final note, I am conscious that the examples mentioned here are both males and I certainly do not wish to give the impression, perhaps suggested by Rorty (1980) that courage as bravery needs detoxifying. Rather these examples of courage show its fortitudinal aspect and not merely its risk-engendering aspects. Some examples to counter this tendency would include Julie Krone who, in 2004, won the Wilma Rudolph Courage Award recognising her 18-year career as a top-flight female jockey fighting both injury and prejudice alike. Equally, Hassiba Boulmerka had to overcome considerable sexist prejudice and threats against her performing in immodest Western athletics clothing in order to represent her country and eventually win the 1991 1500m gold medal at the World Championships (see Morgan, 1998). It is a sad fact indeed, then, that the less noble role models who so often attract the media's attention, such as Mike Tyson and Michael Vick, regrettably endure as racially stereotyped role models. Whether this is indicative of some unacknowledged racism in sports journalism is itself a moot point.

Conclusion

Research on racism in sport has tended to adopt an on/off conceptualisation of racism: either that person is a racist or they are not; that it was a racist incident or it was not. Such certitude is enviable, but does scant justice to a complex phenomenon. I recognise the problem with facilitating the nuanced appreciation of racism set out here, with its degrees of severity. Nonetheless, an appreciation of the register suggests the need for more subtly differentiated anti-racism campaigns and targeted actions in the playing, administering and reporting of sport. Of course, there is the danger that it may give succour to those not inclined to act to counter racism if they can justify inaction on the basis that there are others who are worse than they are. It might, however, be counter-productive to alienate potential allies in campaigns against racism in sport by berating them for what they consider to be minor indiscretions. In presenting this register of racism I have tried to open up a space for an appreciation of the significance of context, the possibility of a dynamic process of alignment on racial issues and the moral opprobrium that ought differentially to attach according to these factors.

Notes

1. Perhaps the best-known advocate for the former is Warren Fraleigh's (1984) *Right Action in Sport*, while the utilitarian case is less popular, Claudio Tamburrini's (2000) *The Hand of God* is the best example of a sustained defence of a utilitarian position in sports ethics.

2. Why, it might be asked, have I indicated the age of Hill? As will become clear, the reference to Hill's age is entirely relevant to the formation of racist attitudes masked as benign humour.

References

Appiah, K. A. (1996) 'Race, culture, identity', in K. A. Appiah and A. Guttman *Color Conscious*, Princeton, NJ: Princeton University Press.

Allport, G. (1987) *The Nature of Prejudice*, Reading, MA: Addison-Wesley.

Aristotle (1980) *Nichomachean Ethics*, Oxford: Oxford University Press (trans. W. D. Ross; updated J. O. Urmson and J. L. Ackrill).

Back, L. (1996) *New Ethnicities and Urban Culture*, London: UCL Press.

Balibar, E. and Wallerstein, I. (1991) *Race, Nation, Class: Ambiguous Identities*, London: Verso.

Barker, M. (1981) *The New Racism*, London: Junction Books.

Blum, L. (2002) *'I'm Not a Racist, But ...' The Moral Quandary of Race*, Ithaca, NY: Cornell University Press.

Carrington, B. and McDonald, I. (2001) 'Whose game is it anyway? Racism in local league cricket', in B. Carrington and I. McDonald (eds) *Race, Sport and British Society*, London: Routledge, pp. 50–69.

Connolly, P. (2000) 'Racism and young girls' peer group relations: the experiences of South Asian girls', *Sociology*, 34: 499–519.

D'Souza, D. (1995) *The End of Racism*, New York: Free Press.

Football Against Racism in Europe (2004) 'Hill backs Big Ron', Online. Available at: http://www.farenet.org/news_article.asp?intNewsID=204 (accessed 12 September 2007).

Fraleigh, W. P. (1984) *Right Actions in Sport*, Champaign; IL: Human Kinetics.

Jacobs, J. (2001) *Choosing Character: Responsibility for Virtue and Vice*, New York: Cornell University Press.

Jacobs, J. (2001) *Choosing Character: Responsibility for Virtue and Vice*, New York: Cornell University Press.

Gilroy, P. (1987) *There Ain't No Black in the Union Jack*, London: Hutchinson.

Guillaumin, C. (1972) *L'Ideologie raciste: Genèse et langage actuel*, The Hague: Mouton.

Hall, S. (1992) 'New ethnicities', in J. Donald and A. Rattansi (eds) *'Race', Culture and Difference*, London: Sage, pp. 252–9.

Howe, D. (2004) 'It was not a lapse: Atkinson was up to his neck in football's endemic racism', *New Statesman*, 3 May, Online. Available at: http://www. newstatesman.com/200405030005 (accessed 12 September 2007).

Long, J., Nesti, M., Carrington, B. and Gilson, N. (1997) *Crossing the Boundary: A Study of the Nature and Extent of Racism in Local League Cricket*, Leeds: Leeds Metropolitan University.

Macpherson, Sir William, of Cluny (1999) 'Report of the Stephen Lawrence Inquiry' (Cm 4262–I, 1999), London: Stationery Office, Online. Available at: http://www.archive.official-documents.co.uk/document/cm42/4262/4262.htm (accessed 1 April 2004).

Massara, A. (2007) 'Stain removal: on race and ethics', *Philosophy and Social Criticism*, 33: 429–528.

Miles, R. (1989) *Racism*, London: Routledge.

Modood, T. (1997) '"Difference", cultural racism and anti-racism', in P. Werbner and T. Modood (eds) *Debating Cultural Hybridity*, London: Zed Books, pp. 154–72.

Morgan, W. J. (1998) 'Multinational sport and literary practices and their communities: the moral salience of cultural narratives', in M. McNamee and J. Parry (eds) *Ethics and Sport*, London: Routledge, pp. 184–204.

Parekh, B. (1995) 'The concept of national identity', *New Community*, 21: 255–68.

Rorty, A. O. (1980) *Explaining Emotion*, Berkeley: University of California Press.

Rorty, A. O. and Wong, D. (1997) 'Aspects of identity and agency', in A. O. Rorty and D. Wong (eds) *Identity, Character and Morality*, Cambridge; MA: MIT Press, pp. 19–36.

Solomos, J. and Back, L. (1996) *Racism and Society*, Basingstoke: Macmillan.

Tamburrini, C. (2000) *The Hand of God*, Gothenburg: University of Gothenburg Press.

Ture, K. and Hamilton, C. (1992) *Black Power: The Politics of Liberation*, New York: Vintage Books.

Wellman, D. T. (1993) *Portraits of White Racism*, 2nd edn, Cambridge: Cambridge University Press.

Wieviorka, M. (1995) *The Arena of Racism*, London: Sage.

Williams, B. A. O. (1980) 'Justice as a virtue', in A. O. Rorty (ed.) *Essays on Aristotle's Ethics*, Berkeley: University of California, pp. 189–99.

Part 5

Ethical development in and through sports

Rules, virtues and vices

Introduction

Mike McNamee

It has been suggested that the conjoining of sports and ethical considerations is a modern phenomenon that can be traced back to the era of Victorian Britain where sports became codified and regulated in ways that allowed for consistency of structures, meaningful comparisons in performance, the promotion of ideals of manly conduct, and – of course – gambling (Dunning and Sheard, 2005; Eichberg, 1973; Guttman, 2004). While this general position has much to recommend it, it neglects the fact that the gratuitous logic of athletics has infused sports since their creation (Suits, 2005; Morgan, 1994). It also neglects considerations that track back at least to Plato concerning the role of gymnastics and athletics in the good life.

In Part 1 we noted how a distinction could be drawn between the constitutive rules that define the activity and the regulative ones that permitted and prohibited certain forms of conduct. When observers, therefore, say that sports rules are merely technical ones and not moral, it is because they have the template of constitutive rules (the number of players, the duration of the activity, the minimal or maximal perimeters of the playing surface and so on) as their guide. Clearly regulative rules (about how one may or may not contact opponents, that one may not harm them in certain ways, that one must respect one's opponents and the officials, and so on) pertain to important ethical notions. David Carr's essay, entitled, 'What Moral Educational Significance Has Physical Education?' is an apt

choice to begin our considerations of the potential for the ethical development or moral education of players of sports.

Carr notes the logical possibilities that answer his question – sports, games and physical activities – may have negative or positive moral educational potential or they may be morally neutral. Given that no-one can deny the reality of good and bad aspects of sports, he argues that the matter is inconclusive but that there is still value in pursuing his question in order to articulate rival ethical construals of sports. The features of sports playing 'liable for ethical construal' (1998: 122) include well-known features such as co-operation of the will to develop individual excellence, and the duties of contestants to abide by the rules which establish fairness or justice among participants. He offers two cautionary notes: (i) rival ethical traditions will favour (sports)persons of different sorts; and (ii) even where a list of features might be agreed upon (a difficult enough task) they might permit of radically different interpretation: yes, sports may develop courage or tenacity, but that is an undesirable trait in a burglar or a sociopath. Carr also warns that one may not leap to the conclusion that sports are morally educational merely from the fact that sports exhibit morally salutary properties, because it is undeniable that they exhibit repugnant ones also. And, crucially, he adds, whether in fact sports are morally educative will have much to do with the teachers and coaches of the activities

303

whose job it is to initiate children therein, based upon their own powers for serious moral reflection on the ways children are taught, guided, officiated and so on.

Jim Parry takes up similar themes in his 'Sport, Ethos and Education'. He begins his essay with a consideration of how mountain climbers attempting to reach the summit of Everest passed by a fellow climber who eventually died of, it might be said, both physical deterioriation and neglect. How is that an activity appears to have such an ethos lacking in basic attention to the extreme vulnerability of another? He notes how the fostering of a morally praiseworthy ethos is a necessary condition for the cultivation of virtues associated with sports – and which appears to be lacking in the mountaineering example.

Parry builds up a picture of moral education through sports which begins with personal and social dimensions of the role responsibilities of players and their relations to the rules and traditions, which may be in conflict with other corporate values, and is continually negotiated in public spaces. He also notes how both secular and spiritual stories may be told of the development of morally laden laboratories of learning. Parry also addresses the notion of character education generally in the context of liberal humanism as it is found specifically in the context of the Olympic ethos. He then sketches an underlying philosophical anthropology of Olympism which goes beyond the traditional list of personal virtues in sports, to such Olympic ideals as friendship, peace, toleration and mutual understanding.

The tendency in the West to eulogise sports' capacity for ethical development has often been based upon a limited catalogue of the character traits that sports foster. Might it not be the case that there were as many children imbued with spite or envy through sports, than were cultivated to be courageous or co-operative? In moral philosophy generally, Mackinnon (1999) has noted that there has been a tendency to concentrate on explorations of virtues rather than vices. And the same is true of sports ethics. The next essay, Mike McNamee's '*Schadenfreude* in Sport: Envy, Justice and Self-esteem', is also something of a corrective. He first articulates the chequered history of the emotions in moral philosophy and how a negative picture of them has led to a contrast between being rational and emotional (where the latter is thought of as a disparaging remark). The emotions are often thought of as obstacles to good moral reasoning and action. Given the fact that sports are centrally concerned with the display (and only relative control) of the emotions renders them morally suspect. He scrutinises that feeling crystallised in the concept of *schadenfreude* – the pleasure felt at another's misfortune – an experience widely shared in competitive sports.

The popular genesis of *schadenfreude* is simply this: we feel good when our competitors lose. Is this not natural? Two points arise here: first, saying something is natural does not excuse the person who feels it and, second, why do people feel it? McNamee considers two causes: low self-esteem and a commitment to justice. While low self-esteem may erode some of the repugnance of *schadenfreude* he draws attention to the envious aspect it typically entails: our opponent has something we want and we celebrate their fall. When *schadenfreude* is felt at the suffering of another who it appears deserves it (such as the cheat who is caught) is it proper to celebrate? McNamee argues that when *schadenfreude* takes on the quality of a hand rubbing glee while the other suffers, the emotion is morally both culpable and a sign of a deficient character, however natural it may appear.

In the penultimate essay of this Part, Heather Reid addresses the issue of the multiculturality of virtue in her 'Athletic Virtue: Between East and West'. In this essay Reid probes the stereotypical contrast between the aggressive, individualistic and instrumentalist orientation of Western sports and sportspersons with the collectivism, passivity and spirituality of Eastern sports. Her particular lenses are the writings of classical Greek virtue ethics and those of Daoism and Confucianism. She notes the warrior ethos out of which both concepts emerged and were nourished, and which was infused by a certain moral force or 'power in the soul' (2010: 17). Whereas the Greek virtue, *aretē*, is conceived of as excellence of the individual that others should aspire to, the Chinese *de* is more attuned to the metaphor of a magnet that can draw out the goodness in others.

Reid contrasts key values that underwrite Greek athletics and Eastern sports (a label she uses to include martial arts, tai chi, court games and related activities). In comparing and contrasting the Greek *agon* (understood as struggle, which infused all athletic contest and the pursuit of victory) with Chinese *wuwei* (understood as effortlessness – the grace utilised to deflect the power of an opponent and turn it against them) she notes the shared Stoic terrain of seeking only to concern oneself with things that are within one's control. In a way reminiscent of some existential psychology of sport (such as Timothy Gallwey's books of inner tennis, inner skiing and so on (Gallwey, 2009)) she writes:

> Any athlete who has striven to achieve a clear mind by 'not thinking' or to achieve self-control by 'not attacking' but rather letting the play come to him knows the challenge implied by the concept of *wuwei*. In both Eastern and Western traditions, virtue is a hard-won state within which moral action becomes effortless because one always does the right thing
> (2010: 20–1).

Reid also notes how both ancient Greek and Chinese sources both praise the virtue of humility which is as needed now as then. She concludes, however, that it is not so much a list of more or less shared virtues that should be of interest to sports scholars so much as the fact that moral cultures, both East and West, can provide a forum and foundation for ethical agreement.

The final essay in this Part, Graham McFee's 'The Project of a Moral Laboratory; and Particularism', addresses Reid's last point in detail. McFee offers a connection of sport to the moral by unravelling metaphors and principles as they apply in and, importantly are restricted to, local or particular sports. This latter point captures McFee's important reservations about the validity of the claim that sports are a platform from which to develop ethical sensitivities that are not context-bound but rather transfer to all aspects of living.

In sympathy with the foregoing authors, McFee concedes that merely playing sports is inadequate for moral growth, since one may only follow the rules in order to win and avoid penalty, but without subscribing in any purposeful way to the point of regulative rules and norms of sports. He goes on to explore how the metaphors of 'fair play' and a 'level playing field' form background principles for ethically praiseworthy sports participation but also leak into wider living; 'the things ethics gets from sport' (2004: 137) as he puts it. McFee pays particular attention to the particularity of one's learning the demands of ethics, their moral pull so to speak. His is an inductive account: one builds up to the appreciation of principles by the local and particular acts and the perceptions of their salience and aptness. Against the grain of traditional moral educational writings in sport, McFee argues that the demand for transference of ethical behaviour to beyond sports is evidence of a craving for generality of a more profound philosophical kind. He concludes by arguing instead for an appreciation of the occasion-sensitivity of sports ethically educative potential, which gravitates upon its recognition of rule-following in general and justice, in particular.

References

Carr, D. (1998) 'What Moral Significance Has Physical Education? A Question in Need of Disambiguation', in *Ethics and Sport*, M. McNamee and J. Parry (eds), London: Routledge.

Dunning, E. and Sheard, K. (2005) *Barbarians, Gentleman and Players* (2nd edn), London: Routledge.

Eichberg, H. (1973) *Der weg des sports in die industrielle zivilisation*, Baden-Baden: Nomos-Verlagsgesellschaft.

Gallwey, T. History of the inner game http://theinnergame.com/about-2/history-of-the-inner-game/. Accessed 20.11.2009.

Guttman, A. (2004) *From Ritual to Record: The Nature of Modern Sports*, New York: Columbia University Press.

Graham McFee (2004) 'The Project of a Moral Laboratory; and Particularism', in *Sport, Rules and Values*, London: Routledge.

Mackinnon, C. (1999) *Character, Virtue Theories and the Vices*, Toronto: Broadview.

Morgan, W. (1994) *Leftist Theories of Sport*, Chicago: University of Illinois Press.

Reid, H. (2010) 'Athletic Virtue: Between East and West', *Sport Ethics and Philosophy*, 4: 16–26.

Suits, B. (2005) *The Grasshopper: Games, Life and Utopia* (2nd edn), Toronto: Broadview Press.

What moral educational significance has physical education?

A question in need of disambiguation

David Carr

Ethics, sport and physical education

The view that there is some sort of internal (or more than contingent) connection between the practice of sports, games or other physical activities and the development of qualities of moral character or understanding is an ancient and persistent one. It reaches back at least as far as the philosophical writings of Plato (Plato, [Hamilton and Cairns Eds], 1961, Book III, § 2). However, it is also clear from the extensive and expanding literature concerning this topic in the philosophies of sport and education, that there can be different sorts of interest in the possible connection between sport and morality and that questions about the alleged relationship can be raised in a variety of ways. As an educational philosopher of many years service in the training of teachers of physical education I shall here be concerned with only one question about the relationship of sport to morality: whether the teaching of sports and games in schools can be held to have any serious implications – or, at any rate more serious implications than any other curriculum area – for the moral education and development of pupils.

It is more than likely that the vigilant reader will have already registered the note of hesitation in the previous sentence which from the outset betrays a certain difficulty about how we should rightly put the question of the connection between physical education and moral education. This should alert us to the possibility that perhaps a number of rather different questions – implying different claims of varying plausibility on behalf of physical education – are being made here to which it may not be sensible to return one and the same answer. In fact this is very much what I shall be concerned to argue in this chapter. For though it cannot be doubted that physical education has been fortunate to attract the analytical attentions of a legion of extremely able educational philosophers who have greatly contributed in recent times to the clarification of pressing issues concerning the curricular significance of physical activities[1], it is not entirely clear from much of the literature on physical education and morality that certain importantly different questions, issues and claims have been sufficiently distinguished to admit of their proper analysis or assessment.

First, I suspect that one main difficulty to which many discussions of this topic are prone is that although they seem ostensibly to be concerned with the problem of the moral significance or otherwise of physical 'education' – that of what difference the formal teaching of

David Carr 'What Moral Significance Has Physical Education? A Question in Need of Disambiguation', from *Ethics and Sport*, M. McNamee and J. Parry eds, © 1998 David Carr. Reprinted by permission of Routledge.

sports and games might possibly make to the moral development of individuals – they have sometimes taken this question to turn on whether or not we may sensibly speak of 'ethical aspects of sports and games'[2]. In short, at least some discussions would seem to have assumed that any conclusions concerning the moral educational significance or otherwise of physical education must depend crucially on our being able to discern in the nature of physical activities certain properties of demonstrably positive or negative moral value. However, I regard this as a deeply questionable assumption, which is liable to lead to potentially unfortunate consequences for any proper conception of the professional role and responsibilities of the physical educa tion teacher.

Indeed, I should say that it is largely due to this dubious assumption that, so far as I can see, the main arguments on this issue appear to go in one or the other of three following familiar ways:

1 Sports, games and other physical activities exhibit features (of, for example, competition and aggression) which are morally negative; therefore physical education – the teaching of sports and games – can only have negative moral educational value[3].

2 Sports, games and other physical activities exhibit features (of, for example, co-operation and team spirit) which are morally positive; therefore physical education – the teaching of sports and games – can have only positive moral educational value[4].

3 Sports, games and other physical activities cannot be clearly shown to exhibit inherent features of either positive or negative moral significance; therefore such activities are 'hived off' from wider moral concerns and physical education is, to all intents and purposes, neutral from a moral educational point of view[5].

First of all, of course, we should be clear that since these claims constitute an inconsistent set they cannot all be true; what is of greater current interest, however, is whether any of them is true. Most of the intense heat in recent debates would seem to have been generated between supporters of the first and second claims – between those

who are inclined to argue for the positive moral value of sports and games and those who would seem to discern only morally negative features in them. It is also arguable that these differences have been the source of a good deal more heat than light; indeed, some of the debate would seem to have been fuelled by considerations – intense love or hatred of sport, for example – not wholly conducive to the disinterested pursuit of truth. However, if we try for a moment to purge our memories of that school P.E. teacher we either worshipped or detested, it ought to become clear that the nature of any debate between someone who says P.E. is a good thing because it involves co-operation and another who says that it is a bad thing because it involves competition cannot, even if it continues until the cows come home, be other than inconclusive.

In saying this, of course, I am not implying that such debates are a waste of time *because* they are inconclusive; on the contrary, some of the most important of human debates – of which moral controversies provide perhaps the best examples – are inconclusive. My point is rather that because such debates and the arguments which underpin them are inherently inconclusive, they cannot possibly be expected to do the work that those who employ them expect them to do; in short, they cannot be expected to resolve one way or the other the problem of the moral significance of P.E. Moreover, the reason for this is rather ironically that they are themselves moral debates and arguments: that is, arguments not about whether sports or games do in fact exhibit certain features of competition or co-operation, but about the moral value of that co-operation or competition which they discernibly exhibit. But then, in the light of undeniable ethical differences on this question, it can only remain an 'open question' whether or not sports and games are morally valuable – and so this road to the desired justification (or disconfirmation) of the moral educational role of P.E. is once and for all blocked.

Rival ethical construals of sport

I have spoken of moral evaluations of sports and games as both open to question and of their being grounded in objectively discernible qualities or properties of physical activities as such. It is important to appreciate here that a recognition of the essential openness of moral questions is not equal to denying the objective basis of moral reason; on the contrary, such a denial could only issue in the sort of moral subjectivism or non-cognitivism which ultimately undermines the very possibility of moral disagreement. But, if sports and games do actually possess (in some ontologically substantial sense) properties apt for construal as morally significant – and such properties are indeed objectively discernible – what are these properties and how exactly do they give rise to problems of contestability?

In the event, the characteristics of sport and other physical activities which are liable to ethical construal are of different kinds and categories. First, they may be general social ideals like co-operation and corporate pride, or indeed – in a society like ours – the initiative and enterprise often identified with competition. Thus, team games may be regarded as morally valuable either because they serve to promote attitudes of team spirit or because they foster a competitive will to success and personal excellence – or even, with less evident consistency, both. Secondly, the morally significant features might be thought of as duties or obligations to abide by certain rules of conduct devised to ensure the fairness or justice of co-operative or competitive activities. Once again, then, team games are likely to be the focus of attention here – but this time viewed less as social ideals and more as microcosms of the sort of rights and duties based systems of social and moral justice whereby liberal-democratic societies aspire to arbitrate the competing claims of rival social ideals. Here, of course the chief attitude to be cultivated via the teaching of games would be what is ordinarily meant by 'sportsmanship'. Thirdly, however, the features might be thought of more in terms of the qualities of character – or virtues – which are necessary for the successful pursuit of this or that physical activity; for example, rock climbing would appear to require a high degree of courage and running the marathon considerable endurance.

But if these and like characteristics are morally significant and objective properties of sports and other physical activities, wherein lies the problem of their contestability and how does it get in the way of resolving the issue about the moral value of physical education? In fact, problems arise at two main levels. First, of course, there is a problem of the general moral ambiguity of well nigh all the characteristics just indicated. For example, though qualities of co-operativeness or competitiveness – or both – might be required for the successful pursuit of a particular sport, they are clearly susceptible to diverse ethical interpretation. Thus, whilst one person argues that competition is the infernal road to selfish individualism another may prefer to regard it as the primrose path to the responsible exercise of individual initiative – and, likewise, one man's co-operation may be another's herd instinct; in short, notions of co-operation and competition are liable to be accorded rather different ethical status from competing moral perspectives.

But much the same is true of the range of executive virtues or qualities of character generally held to be at least instrumentally necessary for the pursuit of certain nerve-wracking or physically testing activities. For example, it is arguable that far from making someone into a morally better person the qualities of courage or endurance acquired through the pursuit of boxing or mountaineering might simply serve to brutalize or coarsen already calloused sensibilities; for many people it is therefore an open question whether young offenders should be taught boxing or sent on outward bound courses since any 'virtues' of courage and persistence they acquire might simply turn them into more effective thugs or criminals. In general, then, even if there is a clear answer to the question of whether a given sport is or is not competitive, or does or does not assist the development of a given quality of character, one may expect no general agreement concerning the question whether that is or is not a morally bad thing; in the nature of human moral life, any such claim must always be controversial.

However, the second important respect in which any claim that a given sport exhibits this or that morally significant characteristic, must remain open to challenge, reflects the consideration that there has not been overwhelming agreement among those inclined to defend the moral educational value of physical education – from antiquity to the present – concerning which features of physical activities are relevant to moral development. Thus, according to the ancient Greeks (well, at any rate, Plato) and the architects of the public school tradition, the main moral value of physical activities is located in their potential for character development – which meant largely gymnastics and athletics to the former and team games to the latter. According to more recent adherents of post-Kantian liberal conceptions of morality and moral education, however, the moral significance of physical activities is to be sought more in the way they assist participants to observe rules, which are alleged – especially in the context of team games – to model the rights and duties based contracts, conventions and interpersonal negotiations of a liberal-democratic order of social life. But this is just the tip of the iceberg since, of course, these two rather different emphases on what are to count as significant or salient features of moral life represent what have been called 'rival traditions' of moral thought[6] which also appear to be in many respects incompatible. On certain post-Kantian conceptions of moral life, for example, many of the qualities of character regarded by the Greeks as significant virtues would not count as moral qualities at all and certainly no modern teleological conception of ethics (either utilitarian or virtue-theoretical[7]) could make very much sense of the Kantian idea of moral duty for its own sake. So the problem of contestability is a function not just of the ambiguity of moral notions but also of the fact that there are rival philosophical theories of ethics which are disposed to make sense of moral life in different and not obviously compatible ways.

Are sports and games 'hived off'?

These points are related to certain others which are often aired in discussions of this issue – but it is important that they should not be confused with them. For example, the point that any apparent courage displayed in boxing may not qualify from this or that ethical perspective as a genuine virtue should not be confused with a familiar argument about the failure or otherwise of qualities or attitudes acquired in sport to 'transfer' to real life contexts. According to this view, it may be seriously doubted whether the courage needed for a rugby tackle or the sense of obligation that a player acquires in recognizing

the importance for a game of rule-observance, are qualities that he will also bring to bear in the rough and tumble or hurly burly of human moral life; in short, sporting courage or obligation should not be assumed equivalent to moral courage or duty.

However, I am inclined to think that the 'transfer' issue is something of a red herring in the debate about the ethical aspects of sport and that it is a particular mistake to hold that focusing on transfer opens up a route to some sort of empirical resolution of these matters. In the first place, I suspect that the very idea of empirically testing for transfer rests on a crude and ultimately untenable behaviouristic or atomistic theory of human action which is wilfully blind to the complexities of human motivation. Indeed, it may well be doubted that it makes much real sense to ask whether boxing courage readily translates into that which a person may exhibit in coming to terms with a tragic bereavement. Since courage would appear to be what has been called a family resemblance notion[8], which doesn't necessarily indicate any one thing, it seems safest to conclude – from our 'pre-theoretical' understanding of human life – that there is sometimes, but not always, continuity of a trait bearing the same name from one context to another; however, this is very much a matter, as it were, of horses for courses, and it requires each case to be judged on its own particular merits.

But, secondly, it is likely that the so-called problem of transfer matters only in so far as we are prepared to accept other dubious assumptions by which it is doubtless underpinned – the chief of these being that there is anyway some sort of gap to be bridged between sport and 'reality'. The view that there is such a gap and that the concerns of sports and games are essentially self-contained or 'hived off' from the real business of life has been highly influential in recent analytical philosophy of education – especially for the purpose of showing that physical education can have no intrinsic moral educational value (Peters, 1966, Ch. 5). However, this view – which has attracted vehement criticism in recent moral philosophical literature (Midgley, 1974) is worth one or two further comments here.

For, though it is easy to see why the argument for the 'hived off' character of sports and games has found favour among philosophers of liberal education – for whom, if education has predominantly cognitive or intellectual aims, physical education can hardly qualify as educational – it is also worth noting (not without irony) that the same assumptions used to support the case for the self-containedness of games have also been used to underwrite an argument for the moral educational significance of physical education. The essential idea here, of course, is that moral life itself – at least on certain post-Kantian liberal-enlightenment perspectives – exhibits precisely those qualities of rule-governed self-containedness that liberal educationalists have been wont to identify with games. Thus, on this view, one is in the course of playing football or hockey *ipso facto* involved in the observance of rules of precisely the contractual rights and duties based kind which many liberal ethicists have held to be characteristic of morality in general; and given that this is so, why shouldn't games playing therefore be seen as a perfect training ground for moral life?

But surely something has gone rather badly wrong here? Even if we may not regard it as tantamount to a *reductio ad absurdum* of the whole idea of hived-offness that essentially the same argument can be used to demonstrate both the moral significance and insignificance of physical education, it is hardly plausible to regard either games or morality as little more than self-contained systems of rules and the weight of moral philosophical opinion is nowadays very much against these ideas[9]. Indeed, we are likely to misconceive not only sport and morality but also the relationship between them if we persist in tying them exclusively to notions of rule-observance and discontinuity with other human interests and concerns. For example, it seems reasonable to hold that games and other sporting activities are susceptible to moral appraisal and evaluation much to the same extent and in the same manner as any other human activity; thus, we are given to evaluating sporting activities as we would street-trading, bank-robbing or love-making as unfair, deceitful, dishonest or brutal. If, however, we combine the narrow view of morality as the voluntary observance of rules with the idea that sports are self-contained, we are liable to end up placing some deeply questionable, even barbaric, forms of contest – from boxing via bare-knuckle fighting to actual gladiatorial fights to the

death – beyond the reach of serious moral censure or even debate.

Indeed, pro-boxing sentiments – apparently based on some such unholy cocktail of views – may be detected in a common remark to the effect that it is entirely their own affair if two consenting adults, knowing the risks, agree to climb into a ring with the explicit aim of beating the other's brains out[10]. However, it tells forcibly against this *laissez-faire* conception of morality that even in the most liberal of civil and civilized societies such voluntary individual preparedness to enter into such potentially self- and other-destructive bargains is not viewed as being the end of moral matters, and that the State may well feel morally bound to veto some of the free choices of individuals – not only for their own health but for the moral health of society as a whole. Moreover, from this point of view, it would seem only right – even if there is no cut-and-dried moral or legal case for their prohibition – that such activities as so-called blood-sports (into which category some would put – as well as tormenting dumb animals – boxing) should at least continue to be called into question in any would-be civilized society.

Indeed, what also tells reasonably against the view that sports in general are autonomous from or discontinuous with the rest of human life is the fact that what people are inclined to count as legitimate or genuine sports and games – precisely their very notions of 'sportsmanship' – are prone to develop or progress more or less in tandem with what is considered to be morally acceptable or tolerable in wider social terms; from this point of view, sport may be considered one of the many reasonably reliable institutional barometers of the moral climate of society. Thus, just as no contemporary civilized society could countenance or tolerate the teachings of a religious leader who preached a return to human sacrifice, or regard as anything other than morally obscene any purportedly 'scientific' proposal to use the genetically defective for medical experimentation, so it could not tolerate any return to days of gladiatorial combat in which slaves were forced to fight to the death for the sadistic gratification of bloodthirsty crowds. Hence, whatever one's other reservations about competition in football or boxing, it is yet competition between free men rather than slaves, the rules which govern such activities are devised as carefully as possible to legislate against unfair advantages and – although such sports and games may sometimes issue in some loss of blood, broken bones or even death – such calamities are generally regarded as unfortunate accidents or unintentional consequences of sporting engagement rather than as the *raison d'être* of such activity.

Continuity and contestability

But does not the point that nothing can really count as an acceptable sport in a given social context unless it is broadly consistent with the current level of moral understanding or evolution of a given society, amount to the admission that only those sports and games which are widely socially endorsed as morally salutary or beneficial are liable to instruction in contexts of formal institutional schooling? A little thought shows that this could not possibly be the case. For, of course, there are countless occupations, practices and pastimes widely engaged in for profit or pleasure – speculating on the stock-exchange, smoking, drinking alcohol, reading morally questionable literature, even doing medical research or worshipping in church – which are equally commonly viewed as morally dubious or pernicious, despite the fact that they could not reasonably be placed on the index of what is to be prohibited in a tolerably free society. In short, that some sporting practices – for example, gladiatorial contests – are morally ruled out in societies of a reasonably advanced level of moral evolution does not mean that others, such as boxing or Kung-Fu, are automatically ruled in – especially as activities to be taught to young people in contexts of formal schooling.

And, of course, much the same applies to almost every other activity liable to be taught in the context of schooling. Thus, whilst one may regard it as vital in modern post-technological societies to provide young people with some sort of basic scientific education, presumably on the grounds that science has been in many ways a force for human progress, one is also bound to recognize that the cultivation of a certain scientific or technicist mentality has been responsible for the large-scale destruction of the environment as well as other human evils.

Moreover, certain aspects of scientific teaching have been attacked in some parts of the world (albeit mistakenly) because they are alleged to conflict with certain religious beliefs and values. Again, whilst the importance is recognized in some places of introducing children in schools to some kind of religious understanding on the grounds of its potential moral or spiritual benefits, the ethics of such instruction could hardly be more evidently contestable, and many people would be only too ready to insist that religious teaching can never amount to more than indoctrination[11]. Indeed, it is clear that one would not have to look far to find some sort of moral objection to well nigh any subject in the school curriculum – to cookery on the grounds that it did (or did not) encourage meat-eating or to woodwork on the basis that it endorsed deforestation.

Thus, though we can on balance envisage positive human benefits or advantages in making formal public provision for the teaching of certain sorts of subjects or activities to young people which we would not make for others – which may mean ruling in science, religion and physical education and ruling out astrology, witchcraft or pornography – this does not mean that science, religion and physical education are to be regarded as completely within the moral pale or the teaching of them as unexceptionable. The point is, as we have already argued, that it is precisely because sports and games – like science and religion – are continuous with the wider concerns of human life that they cannot avoid moral complexity and that it must therefore remain an open question whether such features of them as competition or co-operation are conducive or otherwise to the promotion of morally desirable traits or qualities of human character.

But, of course, recognizing that the moral value of sports and games is contestable and that there is likely to be little in the way of conclusive agreement concerning the implications for moral good or ill of a given physical activity falls well short of the conclusion that such activities are liable to no morally significant consequences whatsoever – or, yet worse, that physical activities and the teaching of them can only be a morally neutral affair. In fact, this is the way that the argument from self-containment would generally appear to go. From the observation that there cannot be a tight or internal connection between any purported morally significant property of sport – such as competition – and any definite judgement *a propos* its wider moral value, it is concluded that such properties can only inhere in sport in some more restricted constitutive or procedural sense; in short, the 'hived off' nature of sport is read as tantamount to its moral neutrality. But the reason why we cannot be sure whether the moral effects of a sport are morally good or bad is a function of contestability not neutrality – and, of course, sports are not morally neutral.

Indeed, at this point we may bring the general argument of this paper into rather clearer focus. For, on the one hand, I believe that the recognition of the moral contestability of sports and games must effectively demolish any claims to the effect that since sport involves co-operation, which is a morally good thing, the teaching of sports must have positive moral educational value – or, alternatively, that since sport involves competition, which is a morally bad thing, it must have negative educational value. In its positive version, moreover, this argument is often encountered as part of a familiar general package of curricular justification for physical education which I have sometimes referred to as the 'physical education reaches parts which no other subject can reach' view. According to this story, because sport exhibits properties often considered morally salutary, it must be a form of moral education; because it is describable in aesthetic terms, it must be a form of arts education; because it involves reflection (at some level) on movement, it must be a form of scientific education; and so on *ad infinitum*[12]. However, even if we ignore the fact that the claims made by some on behalf of the moral salutariness of sporting properties are hotly contested by others, or that it is acutely short-sighted to observe only the benefits of sports and games and overlook the negative effects they frequently appear to have on both players and spectators, we should suspect that something has gone badly wrong with any argument inclining to such conceptually inflationary conclusions. For we should not normally argue for the educational justification of teaching quadratic equations on the grounds that since it involves encouraging pupils to get calculations right, it must be a form of moral education; or that since it is possible to evaluate equations in aesthetic terms, it must also be justifiable as a form of artistic education. Indeed, we shall shortly return to the curious question of why curricular justifications of physical education so often seem to have gone in this rather Byzantine direction.

On the other hand, however, since most of us can recognize the continuity of sport with moral life – including the respects in which a desire to win at all costs has turned a given runner into a drug-taking cheat, overweening conceit at his talents has made a tennis-player into a bad-tempered and abusive loser, or pride in the local team has been twisted in the mind of a supporter into a kind of mindless and violent tribalism – we should also see that the teaching of games and other physical activities may yet have the highest consequences for the development of a person's moral attitudes and values. But this is all the more reason why the claim that physical activities have moral educational potential, and hence qualify for inclusion in the school curriculum, is liable to be misleading, dangerous or dishonest; for we can readily see that sports and games can be and often are taught and learned in ways that conduce to the promotion of a wide range of morally suspect beliefs, dispositions and attitudes. For example, I have frequently seen school departmental statements of aims of physical education in which the positive moral educational significance of physical activities was strongly asserted – but in contexts where it was also not obvious that the teachers responsible for formulating these aims had ever experienced a moment of serious moral reflection in their lives.

A surfeit of questions

By now, then, it should be fairly clear that the time-honoured question of the moral-educational significance of physical education stands in serious need of disambiguation. In the first place, for example, the question could be construed as directly equivalent to that of whether physical education – the teaching of hockey or gymnastics – is itself a form of moral education. The only coherent response I think we can return here – like that we should give to any similar question about mathematics, home economics or any other subject – is that it isn't; the fact that any school subject is likely to involve learning to do things correctly or working co-operatively with others does not qualify it as a form of moral education, although it may well be a place where moral education can happen. Moreover, it would not seem that physical activities are in any way indispensable for the practice of moral education, so that a person might come to lack certain moral qualities by virtue of never having experienced physical education; indeed, I am inclined to the plausible enough view that other school subjects such as literature and history are probably far better vehicles of moral education than, say, games or metalwork.

In the second place, however, the question might be read as asking whether physical activities have any moral educational significance. This, of course, is ambiguous in its turn. On the one hand, it might be asking whether a game of hockey – viewed abstractly, as it were, as a set of formally prescribed rules and procedures – has any inherent moral significance; once again, it would appear difficult to respond to this – in so far as it makes sense – other than negatively. On the other hand, however, it might well amount to an enquiry concerning whether a game of hockey or the regular playing of it can have significant implications for the cultivation of moral attitudes or the development of moral character; and, of course, we have already conceded that it can from the argument for the continuity of sport with life – though what is here true of hockey is also trivially true of any human activity whatsoever.

But, finally, a question about the moral educational significance of physical education might be raising the rather different issue of whether the teacher of physical education may be rightly regarded as a moral educator. To this question one may return a tentatively affirmative answer; the teacher of physical education does indeed qualify as an agent of moral education, but solely by virtue of being a teacher rather than an expert on physical activities. In short, it is nothing peculiar to the nature of physical activities as such which gives the physical educationalist any moral educational authority he might have; it is rather his occupation of a particular professional role *vis-à-vis* young people and his willingness to recognize as part of that role a particular responsibility to encourage them in the development of positive values and right conduct.

Put in this way, of course, it is clear that it will not quite do to say that a teacher of physical activities is a moral educator in so far as he is a teacher – for there are clearly teachers of such and other activities who have no particular responsibility for the moral formation of those in their charge; thus, just as a piano teacher may be hired for no other purpose than to give the child the benefit of expert instruction in a range of practical skills, so the coach of gymnastics or athletics may have no remit other than high-level instruction in a repertoire of physical skills. Moreover, we know full well that many coaches and trainers are extremely successful in this despite the fact – perhaps even because of the fact – that the only value they communicate to their pupils is that of a ruthless will to succeed at whatever cost to themselves or their nearest and dearest.

So it may well be more correct to put the point of the moral role of some teachers of physical activities by saying that they are moral educationalists only in so far as they are willing or able to locate what they are primarily employed to teach in a context of wider concerns about how to live and what to value in life. In short, the teacher of sports and games makes sense as a teacher of moral understanding only in so far as he takes his teaching seriously as one aspect of the much wider business of education, for indeed – as a familiar story goes[13] – it is the fundamental concern of education as opposed to training (which is the province of the gymnastics or piano coach) to open up the minds of young people to precisely the kind of critical appreciation of basic human values and aspirations which is the hallmark of moral understanding. On this view, then, the teaching of any subject or activity whatsoever is moral teaching precisely in so far as it is educational – and coaching or training is essentially what is left over when the all-important human concern with the promotion and acquisition of values and virtues is subtracted from the narrower and more routine business of transmitting theoretical knowledge or practical skills.

Thus, it is only after considerable qualification and disambiguation – acknowledging certain crucial educational-philosophical distinctions – that we may give some limited assent to the idea that physical education is a matter of moral educational significance. However, it is crucial to appreciate here that this assent is no more than that which we might also give to a question of whether mathematics or home

economics has any moral educational significance; in short, there is no very compelling reason for regarding physical education *per se* as in
some more privileged position than any other
curriculum area *vis-à-vis* the educationally vital
business of communicating a critical sense of
what is right and wrong and fostering dispositions to do what is right on the part of pupils. In
short, the moral of this paper is that such moral
educational significance as we are honestly able
to recognize in relation to the teaching of
sports, games and other physical activities in no
wise suffices to justify the place of these activities in the school curriculum – despite what
many philosophers of physical education would
appear to have thought. On the other hand, however, it does provide a strong argument for the
professional education of teachers – aiming to
teach physical activities (or, indeed, anything
else) in formal contexts of education – in the
all-important implications of their teaching for
the promotion of moral sensitivity and the cultivation of positive human values on the part of
young people.

By way of conclusion it is perhaps worth asking briefly why there has been down the years a
marked inclination on the part of some to associate physical education with moral education?
Actually, I suspect that a full exploration of this
question would be likely to uncover a number
of quite different reasons – none of which, individually considered, is very compelling; Plato,
for example, merely uses physical education to
patch a hole in a leaking theory of moral motivation which is no more watertight after the
repair than before (Plato, 1961, Book III, § 2).
However, it also seems that more recent versions of the story about the privileged moral
significance of physical education have been
entirely and artificially constructed in response
to a problem about the justification of physical
activities engendered by certain contemporary
theories of education of a liberal-rationalist
flavour. For if – as has been widely taught in
recent times[14] – the heart of a child's education
lies in the development of his understanding of
certain rationally or theoretically conceived
forms of knowledge, what then becomes of the
educational status of physical education?

In the light of this deeply confused question
theorists of physical education have in large
numbers been tempted to route the educational
justification of physical activities through

forms of knowledge which are legitimated on
liberal educational theories[15]. Ironically, the
connection between games and morality has
seemed all the more tempting here because liberal theories of moral education are themselves
inclined to regard the rules of morality on the
lines of something very like the rules of a game –
though we also see liberals employing the idea
of games as self-contained systems of rules to
support the view that the purposes and goals of
sports and games are 'hived-off' from the main
moral concerns of human life. In any event,
I consider all these arguments – whether they
follow from profound mistakes in the liberal-
rational theories to which they are offered as
a response, from gross misreadings of those
theories, or from general failures to distinguish
the various ways in which different human
physical activities are enmeshed in the larger
web of human affairs and concerns – to be both
unnecessary and confused. Interesting as these
confusions are, however, they must be topics
for other occasions.

Notes

1. The literature is too extensive to rehearse in detail
   here; but by way of an introduction to some of the
   important disputes in this area see, Mike McNamee
   (1992) 'Physical education and the development
   of personhood', *Physical Educational Review*,
   Volume 15, No. 1; and (a reply to this paper)
   Derek Meakin (1994) 'The emotions, morality
   and physical education', *Physical Education Review*,
   Volume 17, No. 2.
2. Indeed, this expression is taken directly from a
   well-known early discussion of this topic. See,
   David Aspin (1975) 'Ethical aspects of sports and
   games, and physical education', *Proceedings of the
   Philosophy of Education Society of Great Britain*,
   Volume 9.
3. In particular, see Charles Bailey (1975) 'Games,
   winning and education', *Cambridge Journal of
   Education*, Volume 5, No. 1.
4. Any number of apologists for physical education
   have taken this line. See, for example, Derek
   Meakin (1981) 'Physical education: an agency of
   moral education?' *Journal of Philosophy of
   Education*, Volume 15, No. 2; and also (1982)
   'Moral values and physical education', *Physical
   Education Review*, Volume 5, No. 1.
5. Perhaps the most celebrated contemporary source
   of this view is to be found in Peters, R. S. (1966)
   Ethics and Education, London: Allen and Unwin,
   Chapter 5. However, Peters does there sometimes

speak – not with complete consistency – of sports and games being utilized as vehicles of moral education.

6. For the main source of this view see, MacIntyre, A. C. (1981) *After Virtue*, Notre Dame: Notre Dame Press.

7. For a short discussion of this distinction, as well as some of the other ethical views referred to here, see my two-part paper 'The primacy of the virtues in ethical theory: Part I', *Cogito*, Volume 9, No. 3 (1995); and 'The primacy of the virtues in ethical theory Part II', *Cogito*, Volume 10, No. 1 (1996).

8. For the source of this idea, of course, see L. Wittgenstein (1953) *Philosophical Investigations*, Oxford: Blackwell.

9. In particular, the essentially liberal philosophical idea that morality might be understood as a system of rules and principles for the negotiation of conflicts of individual self-interest has been roundly criticized by a number of important contemporary philosophers, standing in a broadly neo-Aristotelian communitarian tradition, of whom Alasdair MacIntyre (1981) *op. cit.*, is a good example.

10. For important recent discussions of this issue see, Radford, C. (1988) 'Utilitarianism and the noble art', *Philosophy*, Volume 63; and Davies, P. (1995) 'Ethical issues in boxing', *Journal of the Philosophy of Sport*, Volume XX–XXI.

11. On this and other questions about religious education, however, see my (1994) 'Knowledge and truth in religious education', *Journal of Philosophy of Education*, Volume 28, No. 2.

12. For a particularly extravagant statement of this view see Arnold, P. J. (1979) *Meaning in Movement, Sport and Physical Education*, London: Heinemann.

13. For example, see once more, Peters *op. cit.*, especially Part I.

14. For a classic statement of this view see, Hirst, P. H. (1974) 'Liberal education and the nature of knowledge', in his *Knowledge and the Curriculum*, London: Routledge & Kegan Paul.

15. So far as I am aware, the first educational philosopher to have approached the problem of the justification of physical education in this way appears to have been Carlisle, R. (1969) 'The concept of physical education I', *Proceedings of the Philosophy of Education Society of Great Britain*, Volume 3.

Bibliography

Arnold, P.J. (1979) *Meaning in Movement, Sport and Physical Education*, London: Heinemann.

Aspin, D. (1975) 'Ethical aspects of sports and games, and physical education', *Proceedings of the Philosophy of Education Society of Great Britain*, Vol. 9.

Bailey, C. (1975) 'Games, winning and education', *Cambridge Journal of Education*, Vol. 5, No. 1.

Carlisle, R. (1969) 'The concept of physical education I', *Proceedings of the Philosophy of Education Society of Great Britain*, Vol. 3.

Carr, D. (1994) 'Knowledge and truth in religious education', *Journal of the Philosophy of Education*, Vol. 28, No. 2.

Carr, D. (1995) 'The primacy of the virtues in ethical theory: Part I', *Cogito*, Vol. 9, No. 3.

Carr, D. (1996) 'The primacy of the virtues in ethical theory: Part II', *Cogito*, Vol. 10, No. 1.

Davies, P. (1995), 'Ethical issues in boxing', *Journal of the Philosophy of Sport*, Vol. XX–XXI.

Hirst, P. H. (1974), *Knowledge and the Curriculum*, London: Routledge & Kegan Paul.

MacIntyre, A.C. (1981), *After Virtue*, Notre Dame: Notre Dame Press.

McNamee, M. (1992), 'Physical education and the development of personhood', *Physical Education Review*, Vol. 15, No. 1.

Meakin, D. (1981) 'Physical education: an agency of moral education?', *Journal of Philosophy of Education*, Vol. 15, No. 2.

Meakin, D. (1982) 'Moral values and physical education', *Physical Education Review*, Vol. 5, No. 1.

Meakin, D. (1994) 'The emotions, morality and physical education', *Physical Education Review*, Vol. 17, No. 2.

Midgley, M. (1974) 'The Game Game', *Philosophy*, Vol. 49.

Peters, R.S. (1966) *Ethics and Education*, London: Allen and Unwin.

Plato, *Republic*, in: E. Hamilton and H. Cairns (Eds) (1961) *Plato: The Collected Dialogues*, Princeton: Princeton University Press, Book III, Section 2.

Radford, C. (1988) 'Utilitarianism and the noble art', *Philosophy*, Vol. 63.

Wittgenstein, L. (1953) *Philosophical Investigations*, Oxford: Blackwell.

Sport, ethos and education

Jim Parry

The Sunday Times, 24 September 2006: **Investigation.**

Left to die at the top of the world.
The British climber David Sharp suffered a slow, painful death on Everest in May. As he lay dying, 40 climbers passed him by. Did their lust for the summit override their humanity? Peter Gillman investigates.

A few days before Christmas last year, David Sharp sent an e-mail to a climbing friend in Kathmandu, saying; "I'm (stupidly) contemplating a final (final) attempt on Everest." The friend, the New Zealander Jamie McGuinness, had been on Everest with Sharp when he failed in an attempt in 2003. Sharp had failed again in 2004, vowing not to return. Yet McGuinness was not surprised that Sharp was intent on a third try: "David knew he could do it, but he still had to prove it." Another climbing friend, Richard Dougan, says that where Everest was concerned, "David had stars in his eyes."

For Sharp to consider a third attempt says much about both the lure of the world's highest peak and a streak of stubbornness in Sharp himself, particularly as frostbite had cost him several toes in 2003. In May, Sharp, 34, paid a far higher price. He almost certainly reached the summit. But during his descent he died of cold, exhaustion and lack of oxygen in the scant shelter of a rock alcove on the crest of the mountain's northeast ridge.

There have been numerous deaths on Everest – almost 200 at the last count – but this was a spectacularly public one. Some 40 climbers, bidding to reach the summit via the north side of Everest that day, all passed Sharp during their ascent and descent, stepping within a few feet of his prostrate but still sentient body. It was a desolate place to die, ravaged by wind and cold, overlooking the slopes of Everest's monumental northwest flank. The manner of his death was equally disturbing. Climbers describe how his hands and arms were deformed by frostbite how, when he was hauled to his feet, he was unable to stand; and how he was finally left to die alone.

Sharp's death led to anguished debate in the climbing world and the international press. Mountaineers of the stature of Sir Edmund Hillary have weighed in, complaining of the "horrifying" attitudes it revealed. The 40 or so climbers involved stand accused of putting their own summit ambitions ahead of saving Sharp's life. Such is the draw of Everest that the climbers involved are drawn from nations across the world, including Australia, New Zealand, Lebanon, Turkey and the US. Interviews with many of them, however, present a more complex picture than the accusations allow.

From one interested party, meanwhile, there has been only pained silence. That is David's family – his parents, both in their sixties, and his younger brother, Paul – who have recoiled from the media furore as they contend with their grief. From the accounts of friends, David emerges as a personable young man, close to his parents. He relished new challenges and, crucially, he was a loner who backed his own judgments.

There are contradictions too: a trained scientist renowned for his analytical thinking who, despite himself, was lured back time and again to Everest. So is this a parable of climbers passing by on the other side? What do the climbers have to say for themselves? To those questions may be added a third: was Sharp so blinded by the stars in his eyes that he took a risk too far?

The story that Peter Gillman begins to tell was one that many found shocking, not least because there was amongst many climbers a view that there was a settled ethos in their community. Spirituality and ethics come together perhaps most strongly in the idea of ethos. Ethos can be summed up as the distinctive character, spirit and attitudes of a group or community. As such it is something about the distinctive values and meaning of that community, but also the actual practice of those values. It is thus summed up not just in concepts but also in how people behave to each other, including the tone of communication. The ethos is discovered in relationship; in attention given, or not given, to the other, in concern for key values and purposes in practice, and so on.

For the climbers the ethos was one that was worked out within and around an environment of risk shared by all. At its centre was the belief that, however good any climber might be, he or she might at any time depend upon other climbers to survive. From that awareness of physical vulnerability, danger and need came the core principle that one always helped another climber in need. Ethicists as different as McIntyre (1999) and Levinas (1998) both agree on this point, that concern for the other arises from an awareness of vulnerability. Hence, for Levinas ethics begins with the face of the other, that which sums up the limitations, and ultimately the mortality of the other.

Such was the strength of this ethos for the climbing community that figures such as Edmund Hillary immediately condemned what they saw as its erosion in the Sharp case. Two things seemed to threaten this ethos. The first was the quest for excellence and achievement. Why was Sharp so determined to make it by himself and with limited resources? The irony

was that Sharp had more than enough money on him to have paid for a Sherpa to accompany him. The people who walked past did not even do so 'on the other side'. They had to unclip themselves from the safety line to get round Sharp. These included Mark Inglis, a remarkable New Zealand climber with two artificial legs. Inglis had himself suffered in climbing accidents and seems to have been driven in his desire to overcome his handicap.

The second challenge to the ethos was from the commercial operation. Everest increasingly represents significant financial opportunities, with companies providing Sherpa support, and even fixed safety lines most of the way up. The argument runs that this focuses the concern of the company on the profits, and purely the care of their clients, ignoring the wider ethos of inclusive care for fellow climbers. The Sharp case is complex, and many of the factual details are disputed. It is argued by some that the company who had climbers on Everest that day knew of the Sharp situation and had the capacity to effect a rescue, but did not.

Much analysis has followed this case, including the view that at such extreme heights exhaustion and lack of oxygen make it very difficult to think through ethical challenges. However, it is precisely the point of an ethos that, it enables ethical response at a very basic level. In this case the inclusive concern would come first, provided that there were the resources to effect a rescue.

In relation to education ethos becomes central. Any corporate activity expresses value, tells us something about what that group or community find important. In the case of education, ethos will be connected to the core purpose of learning and the conditions that enable that learning, including mutual respect, a safe environment for mutual critique, and the practice of academic freedom. Education, however, can provide an ethos that has a much wider focus, and this chapter will explore first how the ethos of sport itself can be central to the education process and experience, and then will suggest that Olympism provides an ethos that connects to broader values, such as fairness, justice and peace. It will then focus on how such an ethos can be sustained and how this involves an ongoing development of meaning. In one sense this will move from the commitment to an ethos to the contract or compact that can articulate that ethos and sustain it. Finally, in relation to education, it will examine the ethos and spirituality of the learning organisation.

Moral education, sport and games

Jones (2005, 140–142) argues against the Kohlbergian cognitive development theory of moral education, on the grounds that it is primarily a theory of moral understanding, not of moral action. Instead, he suggests, the education of moral character is not essentially about the cognitive resolution of moral argument, but about the development of those moral dispositions or virtues that enable a person to act morally and to become a good person.

Jones's critique coheres with one view of the morally educative potential of sports and games:

> Games are laboratories for value experiments. Students are put in the position of having to act, time and time again, sometimes in haste, under pressure or provocation, either to prevent something or to achieve something, under a structure of rules. The settled dispositions which it is claimed emerge from such a crucible of value-related behaviour are those which were consciously cultivated through games in the public schools in the last century.
>
> (Parry 1986, 144–145)

A good moral education, therefore, would involve the cultivation of an ethos or a 'moral atmosphere' (Jones 2005, 145) that presents and nurtures examples of good behaviour. Sport ought to be seen as 'a moral practice for the cultivation of habits of virtue as well as habits of skill' (2005, 146). Sports and games are a form of 'moral association' (Carr 2003, 266), and successful engagement in them is a matter of learning how to cultivate those dispositions appropriate to the context, and how to behave within it.[1]

However, we are confronted with the obvious fact that competitive games are contests, which raises the possibility that their primary function is to establish superiority over others, and that this feature presents the temptation to cheat or behave badly in order to secure victory. Whence derives the 'moral push' towards virtue?

Part of Fraleigh's answer (1984, 41ff) is that there are certain prerequisites for a good sport contest:

- First, there is a presupposition of equality of opportunity to contest (equality under the rules), without which the game could not be demonstrated unless all other variables are strictly controlled.
- Second, no contest could exist without the opponent, which would seem to require at least the minimum respect due to a facilitator – to one whose own level of performance is a major contributor to the very possibilities for excellence open to oneself in that category of endeavour chosen by both.
- Third, although it is clearly possible to break the rules, to do so alters the conditions of the contest, so that a range of abilities not specified by the rules comes into play. A good contest will maintain the framework, that secures the integrity of the contest, and this requires rules adherence and fair play.

In addition, there are other necessary features of a sports contest. So:

- Fourth, there is a knowledge of relative abilities, which is a necessary outcome. This might be construed as permitting a form of braggadocio, but Reddiford (1982, 115) reminds us that 'you win some, you lose some' and so to make the game the occasion for 'marking up superiorities and inferiorities' is a short-term and self defeating attitude. We play to produce an outcome favourable to ourselves, but we should not allow the actual outcome to be of persisting importance. Humility and generosity are at least as likely an accompaniment to a demonstration of one's relative abilities as overweening pride and conceit.
- Fifth, I would add that in games there is a simple right and wrong, easily enforceable by a clearly identified authority. At the same time, there is some possibility of differing interpretation and judgment. In playing games, students learn how to follow explicit rules, how to bend

318

them and evade them, and how to operate within a system of penalties and consequences, both official and unofficial.

▪ Sixth, I would suggest that this application, interpretation and appreciation of rules returns us to the idea of ethos, which we shall now explore further.

Part of Fraleigh's case is that the internal values of sport itself, as exhibited by its rules, impose upon us certain ethical requirements for its successful practice. But this is only part of the story, since these rules are interpreted and applied from within a context of the more broadly understood values of a community which supports the practice. (Later we will look at the philosophy of Olympism as an example of a proposed set of such community values, which provides an account of sport at its best, together with an ethics and politics within which sport can flourish and to which it can contribute.)

The ethos of sport

Take the example of any team game, to begin with. There is an immediacy about this playing experience which focuses on several aspects of activity in relation to others. First, there is a build-up of trust within in any team, which is mediated by the physical experience. Not only do the team members have to be clear about roles and rely on each other fulfilling those roles, but they also have to rely on the physical presence and support of their team-mates, since their own physical well-being (and even safety) depends upon the role and function of their team-mates. This suggests the kind of responsibility which team members owe to and feel for each other. In this sense, responsibility begins to emerge from the physical awareness of the other and the needs and concerns of the other in the context of risk.

Second, responsibility goes beyond the team. At one level the ethos of concern for all who are playing the game is embodied in the rules. Such rules look to a system of justice and respect. At another level, though, there is a sense of interdependence between teams. Although there may be intense rivalry, the wellbeing of the individual depends upon members of all teams playing fair, and respecting the rules and ethos of

the activity. Hence, there is a major outcry whenever a player is injured by an intentional and career-threatening foul such as an elbow to the face. The responses to such outrages stress the common perspective of the professional sportsperson.

Third, all teams play in the context of a much wider community that includes both the fans in the ground and a wider audience reached by media who themselves project certain values. At this point the ethos of the sport might be in conflict with the values and concerns of media or related sponsors.

Fourth, sport beyond media communications becomes 'public property', not least as part of the identity of the local community, and partly through general interest that will from time to time examine and analyse the behaviour of the teams and individuals.

The ethos of sport, then, is:

▪ based on experienced interdependence, at team level or beyond;
▪ inclusive, moving out from the experience on the field to the wider community of supporters and stakeholders;
▪ always being tested, either by problems on the field or by potential value conflicts with related groups.

It could be argued that the idea of ethos is not in itself fixed or settled, but that it provides the basis of embodied values that are and always must be tested. In other words the testing is critical, to sustaining the ethos. Indeed, it might further be argued that such critical testing is in itself a part of any ethos. An ethos that is not open to interpretation, or dispute is one that embodies some form of exclusion.

Looked at in another way this begins to show the different ways in which spirituality and ethics relate. At one level ethics grows out of spirituality. Holistic awareness of the other leads to an awareness of the needs of the other, a sense of interdependence and with that a sense of shared responsibility (Robinson 2007). Hence, an irreducible moral concern grows from spirituality.

At another level, the development of life meaning is being constantly tested by a variety of things, from conflicting values to set ethical principles. The story of the Abraham's challenge of God in Genesis 18:25 illustrates this.

God has determined that he will destroy Sodom. Abraham challenges God as to how he could kill the 'righteous with the wicked', Abraham is challenging God based on a simple view of justice, or perhaps even on the basis of what he saw as God's inclusive spirituality. Fasching and Dechant (2001) suggest that this story illustrates a Jewish tradition of 'audacious' challenge, and how such challenge was a core part of spirituality.

So the ethos of the sport can embody core and settled dispositions, but it also takes place within the laboratory 'for value experiments' where individuals and the team as a whole have to continuously respond to challenges under great pressure.[2] The more the ethos is challenged through practice, the more it is articulated and clarified:

> [P]articular practices like sport can offer arenas where ethical discourse can flourish and where a morally and psychologically binding consensus, based on both tradition and the more or less tacit knowledge of how to play the game, can come under the scrutiny of all practitioners. Moreover, we believe that the morality of particular sporting games is being presented, challenged and negotiated, not always in articulate forms, but in terms of embodied interaction throughout sports performances.
> (Loland and McNamee 2003, 75)

Character education

The virtues are what constitute the so-called 'character', in the sense of a particular identity and the capacity to relate. How then are the virtues developed? Aristotle suggests that they have to be developed in practice, through habituation. This is not about mindless conditioning. On the contrary it involves getting used to, and practising, *phronesis*. This means that it enables the person to take responsibility for performing moral actions. As Burnyeat (1980) puts it, this is the sort of person 'who does virtuous things in full knowledge of what he is doing, choosing to do them for their own sake.'

As McIntyre (1981) notes, the virtues, such as justice and courage, are embodied as internal goods in a community of practice.[3] So it is through these practices that we learn just what the meaning of justice or courage is in the particular, and begin to embody it ourselves, simply in the doing. We can contrast that with didactic teaching that simply sets out rules or principles, known only in their generality. However, acquiring virtues through practice does not mean that we have, to ignore the written articulation of meaning – on the contrary, as McIntyre argues, there is a need for stories and other discourses that can communicate meaning in the tradition of the community, and also for broad statements of value. Nor does it mean that we must reject reflection upon moral matters – on the contrary, it is the dialectic of 'testing' between practice and thoughtfulness that produces wisdom in virtue.

It must not be forgotten, however, that none of this is simply about getting across values accepted by the community, but about the individual developing a personal and practical understanding of those values and the capacity to respond to others in the light of them. The development of virtues looks to a settled character that can reflect on internal goods, and this takes place not just within the practice, but also through continued reflection and debate within the community. Moreover, such debate will not end simply where the community ends. If sport is an outward-facing community it will embody in its practices values and virtues that are more universal, and which resonate (or not) with wider communities.

Indeed, sport may contribute insights about values (such as equality, fairness, justice, respect for others) beyond sport itself. Hence, there is much talk of the example given by sportspersons to wider society and especially to young children. Important in the development of such awareness is inter-textual dialogue – dialogue that takes into account different views of the good. Van der Ven (1998) suggests that this is critical to moral development, not least because it causes one to look again more closely at one's own values and beliefs, and their coherence.

Modelling of the virtues is clearly an important part of learning in and through practice (and this should cause us to reflect upon the virtues-in-role of the PE teacher and the sports coach). However, such learning is not simply about discrete actions but rather about actions in relationship. It is the relationality of the practice that actually enables the development of virtues. Players and clubs develop relationships that build up an inclusive attitude. Players relate to each other in ways that develop trust and thus faith in each other, and in the club. Players feel valued through the response of the club. As such relationships build up, so the affective as well as cognitive awareness of moral and spiritual meaning is developed (Robinson 2001), and the person is empowered through developing their role and responsibility and the underlying meaning that they give to and find within their activity.

The Olympic ethos

Pierre de Coubertin, the founder of the modern Olympic Games, was very conscious of the way in which sport connected with wider society, and he developed the idea and practice of Olympism as a means of connecting with and actively influencing social development, especially through education. He argued for the revival of the Olympic Games as a means to the popularisation of his ideal of holistic education centred on ethical sport and active physical education for all.

We can briefly note two key Fundamental Principles from the Olympic Charter (International Olympic Committee 2006).

Fundamental Principle 2 states:

> Olympism is a philosophy of life, exalting and combining in a balanced whole the qualities of body, will and mind. Blending sport with culture and education, Olympism seeks to create a way of life based on the joy found in effort, the educational value of good example and respect for universal fundamental ethical principles.

Fundamental Principle 6 states:

> The goal of the Olympic Movement is to contribute to building a peaceful and better world by educating youth through sport practised without discrimination of any kind and in the Olympic spirit, which requires mutual understanding with a spirit of friendship, solidarity and fair play.

J.A. Samaranche (1995, 3), former President of the International Olympic Committee, has suggested that, a modern Olympism can be described in six 'basic elements':

- tolerance;
- generosity;
- solidarity;
- friendship;
- non-discrimination;
- respect for others.

I have suggested elsewhere (Parry 2006, 191) that this echoes the basis of Olympism in liberal humanism, stressing as it does the values of equality, justice, fairness, respect for persons and excellence. Underlying such values and principles there is a holistic philosophical anthropology of sport, first sketched by Coubertin. He speaks (1966/1894) of the human not as a simple dualism of body and soul, but as a more complicated mix of body, mind and character, with character seen as formed primarily by the body:

> [T]here are not two parts to a man – body and soul; there are three – body, mind and character; character is not formed by the mind, but primarily by the body. The men of antiquity knew this, and we are painfully relearning it.

And later (1918):

> I prefer to harness a foursome and to distinguish not only body and soul, ... but muscles, intelligence, character and conscience.

Although this is not an entirely perspicuous account of the elements of personhood, it is important in showing his concern for the whole person, the relation between sport and moral education, and the role of properly designed physical activity in character development. Coubertin often made the point that Olympism seeks to promote moral sport and moral education through sport. Referring to the UK school reforms of 1840, he says:

> In these reforms physical games and sports hold, we may say, the most prominent place: the muscles are made to do the work of a moral educator. It is the application to modern requirements of one of the most characteristic principles of Greek civilisation: to make the muscles the chief factor in the work of moral education.
>
> (Coubertin 1896, 11)

Sport, then, not only provides a context of equality and fairness within which the individual

321

can strive for excellence, but also forms a community within which friendships are developed and sustained and through which a wider vision of peace is articulated and pursued. The idea of pursuing peace through the Olympic Movement is partly about bringing together different nationalities and transcending different national concerns in collaborative endeavour. At one level this involves a concerted effort by the Olympic Movement to bring nations together and to influence future generations through education.

Reid (2006) begins to focus this international framework into peace-making through sport in the community. She connects three elements to this peace-making in practice that sport provides. First, 'we must deliberately set aside a time and place' for sport. This is both a sanctuary and a truce, in which differences are put to one side and the focus of the activity is for that time shared. In spiritual terms this is an experience which enables the participants to transcend the particular in disputes and differences. Reid (2006, 208) suggests that the ancient Greeks associated a strong inclusive idea, with this coming together of difference, through the concept of *xenia*, or hospitality to the stranger. The practice of *ekecheiria*, a truce enabling safe travel to the Games, extends this hospitality to the enemy.

The second element is the establishing of equality and fair play. No matter what the differences, coming together in sport demands equality before the rules, or law, the Greek concept of *isonomia*. I would add to Reid that the experience of that equality is another part of the lived ethos of sport, and that the different contestants come together to share that meaning. It is thus both a lived experience of shared meaning, reinforced by the sporting rituals, and a lived experience of being perceived of as equal value. Hence, once more, the meaning operates cognitively, affectively and somatically. The true power of this lived experience comes when, as Reid suggests, sport can show aggression and even anger, expressed within a context of equality. As Robinson notes (2001), when equal respect is offered in the context of difference and emotion, this further develops awareness and acceptance of the other. Hence, in the relationships developed through sport, a level of empathy and commitment to the other can begin to emerge.

Reid's final element extends from this. The ethos of Olympism enables an evaluation of the other based on their personal qualities and how these relate to the situation. This develops respect for the other in the context of a shared community. At one level it focuses on personal and positive difference. At another level it enables the person to operate in the shared community which is different from his or her own. This can raise great challenges in terms of spiritual and moral development. In itself, it enables a transcendence of the community. However, this does not simply involve going beyond the community, it involves espousing values that either are in a very different context or may have points of direct difference from the home community. This sets up a real 'intertextual dialogue' between different communities and thus the possibility of critique of the home or other community, which nonetheless respects differences globally. Handled properly this sets up the development of forms of internationalism or even cosmopolitanism, the possibility of a world community, which is aware of and appreciates differences.

Cosmopolitanism is about being aware of difference and being at ease with it. However, this does not mean that we must accept difference that is unjust, and the Olympic Movement has in the past challenged such behaviour. When the International Olympic Committee took action to withdraw the recognition of the South African Olympic Committee on 15 May 1970 (see Mbaye 1995, 116–117), it was not simply because the IOC disagreed with its government's politics. IOC President Avery Brundage's letter (reproduced in Mbaye 1995, 279) makes clear his view that the IOC could not penalise a National Olympic Committee simply because it disagreed with some policy or another of its government, otherwise 'we will not have any left.' Rather, it was because, in the case of the South African government, its policies produced an apartheid sport which was unjust sport – the laws and local rules of the apartheid system were racially discriminatory, making it impossible for different sectors of the community to compete fairly, and thus violating Article 1 of the Olympic Charter (Mbaye 1995, 115.)

All of this reinforces the ethic, espoused by Coubertin, that although winning is important it is taking part in fair and ethical sport that is critical.

This ethos fits well into the stages of spiritual development suggested by Fowler (1996). His first two stages involve a genetic faith that is determined by the family. The next two are determined by the community. Stage 5 then has the individual taking responsibility for his or her own faith in relation to the communities of which he or she is a part. He or she is still part of a community but understands its limitations, and is also part of and appreciates other communities.

Two central ideas begin to sum up the virtues that Olympism strives for, *kalos k'agathos* and *areté*. Nissiotis (1984, 64) sees the Olympic ideal as a means of educating 'the whole man as a conscious citizen of the world'. He defines this ideal as:

> that exemplary principle which expresses the deeper essence of sport as an authentic educative process through a continuous struggle to create healthy and virtuous man in the highest possible way (*kalos k'agathos*) in the image of the Olympic winner and athlete.

Areté is the idea of excellence, with the Olympian striving to better him or herself. If the focus of education is on the development of transcendence beyond one's home community, then *areté* looks at another aspect of transcendence, beyond physical and intellectual limits. Hence, Nissiotis (1984, 66) writes,

> The Olympic idea is thus a permanent, invitation to all sportsmen to transcend ... their own physical and intellectual limits ... for the sake of a continuously higher achievement in the physical, ethical and intellectual struggle of a human being towards perfection.

Of course, perfection cannot be achieved, and in falling short one becomes clearer about one's limitations. However, only through that striving can one be aware of and accept limits, and move beyond the self.

The underlying philosophical anthropology of Olympism may be summed up as:

- striving towards excellence and achievement;
- through effort in competitive sporting activity;
- under conditions of mutual respect, fairness, justice and equality;

- with a view to creating lasting personal human relationships of friendship;
- with international relations of peace, toleration, and understanding;
- and cultural alliances with the arts (Parry 2006, 199).

The Olympic ethos thus provides a real focus for wider education. With the core ideas of fair play, the value of competition, the nature of a good contest (including equality before the law and equality of opportunity), the very activity of sport, in education provides a focus for the presentation of and reflection on values. This can be part of any school's approach to sport education. The pedagogy would focus on the ethical practice of sport, and there would also be opportunities for reflecting on its ethos and values, and how this allows us to connect with other groups.

Too often, sport or other activity at school is seen as meaningless beyond, its simple activity. However, where a group, in school or higher education, is taken to outdoor activity weeks (for example), it is possible to begin the process of reflecting on the interdependence required for success and how this shapes core values of that community. Here we could see ethics and spirituality come together, focusing on meaning at cognitive, affective and somatic levels. There might also be a greater focus on Olympism per se. This can include:

- youth work, such as Young Olympians Clubs;
- involvement of Olympians as role models;
- special space and time, such as Olympic museums and heritage sites, and Olympic Day celebrations;
- arts-related events.

Education

There are, however, two issues that need to be noted with respect to education, spirituality and ethos.

First, no ethos can be set for all time and, as noted above, there has to be a continual reflection on and debate about the meaning and tone of the ethos. The very idea of generic spirituality is built around a learning or journey model which seeks to articulate meaning and to reflect on practice, both for the individual and the group. Hence, attention then has to be paid to what Hawkins (1991) refers to as the spiritual dimension of the learning organisation.

Hawkins argues that beyond the level of operations and strategy the developing organisation needs to attend to questions of underlying identity and purpose. At this level there is the development of 'integrative awareness' which ensures that there is transparency and participation such that all involved recognise shared life meaning and begin to accept mutual responsibility and interdependence. This may be the function of good planning, which allows wide participation in reflection on purpose aims and objectives. It may also enable the learning process to occur in any organisation. One example of this is the provision of whistle-blowing and anti-bullying procedures which enable transparency such that conflict can be dealt with constructively (Armstrong *et al.* 2006).

However this also raises the second issue, which questions how the ethos at the centre of sport might relate to the ethos of the wider learning organisation, for example the school or higher education institution. Should there be an effort to make them the same or, given the multicultural context of sport and the Olympic ideal, should the two be in dialogue? Should there be a stress on discourse which is not just within the sport, but also with the other institutions that sport partner's. One way of setting this question is to ask how ethical principle and ethical practice can cohere in sports practice in an educational situation? At this point, let us remind ourselves of a thought of Coubertin's (1966/1894):

> character is not formed by the mind, but primarily by the body. The men of antiquity knew this, and we are painfully relearning it.

And let us recall the idea of games and sports as laboratories for value experiments, in which participants are forced to react to opportunity and circumstance in the pursuit of some goal in a rule-structured environment. The idea here is that sport, properly conducted, might be capable of developing character, the virtues and moral behaviour, especially if we set out consciously to do so in pursuit of some rationale, or ideal, such as Olympism.

In discussing such a possibility (Parry 1988, 117) I have argued that we should:

> seek to develop an account of culture and human experience which gives due weight to those forms of athletic, outdoor, sporting, aesthetic activities which focus on bodily performance, and which are generally grouped under the heading of physical education. Such an account, combining claims about human capacities and excellences with claims about the importance of a range of cultural forms, would seek to develop arguments which could justify the place of PE on the curriculum.

The suggestion here is that PE activities should be seen as 'practices' which act as a context for the development of human excellences and 'virtues', and the cultivation of those qualities of character which dispose one to act virtuously.

In an oft-quoted passage, MacIntyre (1981, 194) describes a 'practice' as:

> Any coherent; and complex socially established co-operative human activity through which goods internal to that form of activity are realised in the course of trying to achieve those standards of excellence, and human conceptions of the ends and goods involved are systematically extended.

Carr (1987, 173) has applied the insights of MacIntyre to education:

> 'What is an educational practice?' The answer I have tried to provide is one which is firmly grounded in those developments in post-analytic philosophy which seek to re-establish the classical concept of 'practice' in the modern world.

Hirst, too, has picked up the theme:

> It is those practices that can constitute a flourishing life that I now consider fundamental to education.
>
> (1993, 6)

and he goes on to suggest that a curriculum should be organised in terms of 'significant practices'. However, just *which* practices constitute a flourishing life, or just which practices are to be deemed significant, remains opaque in his account. Above, I have tried to sketch out some considerations in favour of sport, under the umbrella of Olympism, as a significant practice.

Practices, then, promote those human excellences and values that constitute a flourishing life. But, more than that, practices are the very *sites of development* of those dispositions and virtues, for it is *within* practices that opportunities arise for (e.g.) moral education, including the nurturing and development of the virtues discussed in the last chapter. It is by *participating* in a practice (and by practising its skills and procedures) that one begins to understand its standards and excellences, and the virtues required for successful participation.

As Piers Benn puts it (1998, 167–168):

> we do not become virtuous ... by learning rules ... We gain virtue, and hence learn to make right decisions, by cultivating certain dispositions ...
>
> ... we can see the importance of the education of character – the acquisition of these firm dispositions ... this does not come naturally but must be taught.
>
> ... there is some similarity between acquiring virtue and acquiring skills such as the mastery of a musical instrument; both require practice before the appropriate habits are acquired. You get the dispositions by first of all acting as if you had them – you train yourself to do the right things, and gradually you gain a standing disposition to do them.

The suggestion here is that the practice of sport, informed by the philosophical anthropology and ethos of Olympism, offers a context and a route for us to achieve a number of important aims relating to moral education:

- to further our traditional concern for the whole person whilst working at the levels both of activity and of ideas (because the practical work can be seen as a kind of laboratory for value experiments);
- to show coherence between approaches to practical and theoretical work (because the physical activity is designed as an example and exemplar of the ideas in practice);
- to explore in later years ideas implicit in work in earlier years (because the practical work encapsulating the values and ideas can be taught well before the children are

old enough to grasp the full intellectual content of the ideas).

I would wish to commend to teachers and coaches the values of Olympism, not just not just as historical anachronisms or moralising dogmas, nor as inert ideas to be passed on unthinkingly to students and athletes, but as living ideas which have the power to remake our notions of sport in education, seeing sport not as mere physical activity but as the purposeful physical activity of an educated and ethical individual, infused by an ethical ethos, and aiming at the cultivation of virtuous dispositions.

Notes

1. McFee (2004, chapter 8, and especially p.140) further explores the notion of sport as a 'moral laboratory'.
2. So, an ethos account – following the spirit of the rules – 'can do justice to features of rule-following or rule-breaking not capture by a simple statement of the rules.' (For this, and a detailed discussion of ethos accounts, see McFee 2004, 56ff.)
3. For a concise discussion of internal and external goods, see Loland and McNamee (2000, 73).

References

Armstrong, J., Dixon, R. and Robinson, S. (2006) *The Decision Makers: Ethics in Engineering*. London: Telford.

Benn, P. (1998) *Ethics*, London: UCL Press.

Burnyeat, M. (1980) 'Aristotle on Learning to be Good', in A.O. Rorty (ed.), *Essays on Aristotle's Ethics*, Berkely, CA: University of California Press, pp. 69–92.

Carr, D. (2003) 'Character and Moral Choice in the Cultivation of Virtue', *Philosophy*, 78, 219–232.

Carr, W. (1987) 'What is an Educational Practice?', *Journal of Philosophy of Education*, 21(2): 163–175.

de Coubertin, P. (1966/1894) 'Athletics in the Modern World and the Olympic Games', in Carl-Diem-Institut (ed.), *The Olympic Idea: Pierre de Coubertin – Discourses and Essays*, Stuttgart: Olympischer Sportverlag, pp. 7–10.

de Coubertin, P. (1966/1896) 'The Olympic Games of 1896', in Carl-Diem-Institut (ed.), *The Olympic Idea: Pierre de Coubertin – Discourses and Essays*, Stuttgart: Olympisher Sportverlag, pp. 10–14.

de Coubertin, P. (1966/1918) 'Olympic Letters III', in Carl-Diem-Institut (ed.), *The Olympic Idea:*

Pierre de Coubertin – Discourses and Essays, Stuttgart: Olympicher Sportverlag, p. 54.

Fraleigh, W. (1984) *Right Actions in Sport*, Champaign, IL: Human Kinetics.

Fowler, J. (1996) *Faithful Change*. Nashville, TN: Abingdon.

Fasching, D. and Deschant, D. (2001) *Comparative Religious Ethics*, Oxford: Blackwell.

Hawkins, P. (1991) 'The Spiritual Dimension of the Learning Organisation', *Management, Education and Development*, 22(3): 172–187.

Hirst, P.H (1993) 'Education, Knowledge and Practices', in Robin Barrow and P. White (eds), *Beyond Liberal Education: Essays in Honor of Paul H. Hirst*, Lonton: Routledge.

International Olymphic Committee (2006) *The Olympic Charter*, Lausanne: IOC.

Jones, C. (2005) 'Character, Virtue and Physical Education', *European Physical Education Review*, 11(2): 139–151.

Levinas, E. (1998) *Entre Nous: On Thinking-of the-Other*. New York: Columbia University Press.

Loland, S. and McNamee, M. (2000) 'Fair Play and the Ethos of Sport: An Eclectic Philosophical Framework', *Journal of the Philosophy of Sport*, 28: 63–80.

McFee, G. (2004) *Sport, Rules and Values*, London: Routledge.

McIntyre, A. (1981) *After Virtue*, London: Duckworth.

McIntyre, A. (1999) *Dependent Rational Animals*, London: Duckworth.

Mbaye, K. (1995) *The IOC and South Africa*, Lausanne; IOC.

Nissiotis, N. (1984) 'Olympism and Today's Reality', *Proceedings of the International Olympic Academy*, 24: 57–74.

Parry, J. (1986) 'Values in Physical Education'. in P. Tomlinson and M. Quinton (eds), *Values across the Curriculum*, Brighton: Falmer Press, pp. 134–157.

Parry, J. (1988) 'Olympism at the Beginning and End of the Twentieth Century', *Proceedings of the International Olympic Academy*, 28: 81–94.

Parry, J. (2006) 'Sport and Olympism: Universals and Muticulturalism', *Journal of the Philosophy of Sport*, 33: 188–204.

Reddiford, G. (1982) 'Playing to Win', *Physical Education Review*, 5(2): 107–115.

Reid, H. (2006) 'Olympic Sport and its Lessons for Peace', *Journal of the Philosophy of Sport*, 33: 205–214.

Robinson, S. (2001) *Agape, Moral Meaning and Pastoral Counselling*, Cardiff: Aureus.

Robinson, S. (2007) *Spirituality, Ethics and Care*, London: Jessica Kingsley.

Samaranche, J.A. (1995) 'Olympic Ethics', *Olympic Review*, 25(1): 3.

Van der Ven, J. (1998) *Formation of the Moral Self*, Grand Rapids, MJ: Eerdmans.

Schadenfreude in sports

Envy, justice and self-esteem

Mike McNamee

Introduction

Sports administrators, media commentators and policy makers have tended to focus on the big ethical issues such as child abuse, doping and violence in their pronouncements upon the moral health and ailments of sports. Yet it is often the smaller acts of kindness and unkindness that are better indications of the moral health of sporting practices. The aim of this chapter is to scrutinise the feeling crystallised in the concept of *schadenfreude* – the pleasure felt at another's misfortune – and argue that one's feeling it is both a culpable and, at the very least, undesirable aspect of the ethico-emotional ecologies of sport.

In order to attempt to show that *schadenfreude* is a morally objectionable emotion in sport as elsewhere, and one that can be curbed, I first offer some conceptual remarks about emotions generally and their differential treatment in philosophical discussions. Second, I argue that the rationality of the emotions is crucial to our self-understanding as persons in general and sportspersons in particular, attempting to live good lives and play good sport. I situate this point within an understanding drawn from both Aristotle and Kant. Third, I argue for its undesirability in the character of the one who feels the emotion (the *schadenfroh*)

and their relations to those who suffer. I offer a critique of the argument for the ethical excusability of *schadenfreude* in Portmann (2000) and argue that he fails to defend his position coherently. Specifically, I show how his defence of the emotion's genesis in low self-esteem and a commitment to justice is not compelling and suggest that one's feeling *schadenfreude* is itself evidence of poor sporting character and sporting culture.

Ir/rationality and the emotions: Kant and Aristotle

When an actor at an audition says to his or her fellow actor 'break a leg', it is ordinarily understood that the saying is one of encouragement. When some sporting competitors utter the same remark, I fear, it is often tinged with a less metaphorical desire. When we see the delight on the face of a contestant whose competitor falls at the last hurdle, fails their final jump, or injures themselves in the warm-up, some of us at least are troubled by this. Ought we to be? *Schadenfreude*, the joy or pleasure felt at another's harm, is something sportspersons and coaches undeniably feel. Is it felt for reasons good or ill, one may ask? Whichever is the case, we ought first to ask, more generally, what it means to say that one feels an emotion and to consider why it is worthwhile paying philosophical attention to the emotions. I want first to observe what Bernard Williams wrote more than a quarter of a century ago, and which has applied to much recent sports ethics talk:

> Recent moral philosophy in Britain has not had much to say about the emotions. Its descriptions of the moral agent, its analyses of moral choice and moral judgement, have made free use of such notions as attitude, principle and policy, but have found no essential place for the agent's emotions, except perhaps for recognising them in one of their traditional roles as possible motives for backsliding, and thus potentially destructive of moral rationality and consistency.
>
> (Williams, 1973: 207)

The thought that emotions are themselves irrational has a long and varied history spanning folk psychology and a number of academic disciplines. Emotions appear to have a dual nature; on the one hand they refer to bodily sensations and on the other to expressions of judgement. In philosophy, no less than in certain scientific writings, a peculiarly pejorative and simplified picture of emotions emerged only to be dismissed. And this disposition is no new one. Plato talks in the *Republic* (1974: 440a) of 'reason and its civil war with desire'. He also writes in the *Phaedrus* (1962: 246a8) of the Soul being a composite power, a pair of winged horses and a charioteer. Reason, our ruling part, is the charioteer of course, and while one of the horses is of good and honourable stock, the other is not and 'makes our chariot wayward and difficult to drive' (1962: 246a 8).

This picture of rationality both controlling and prosecuting the emotions remained dominant in philosophy and religion into modernity, where Kant gave it particular prominence. This picture demands correction if we are to understand engagement with sports in a manner that is more than one of mortal machines. As part of an evaluation of the moral emotions Wollheim referred to Kant's position as being a 'singularly bleached moral psychology' (1993). Kant is traditionally attributed with denying the rationality of the emotions and therefore derogating their value, both of which are said to be conceived of as obstacles to rational moral action (Williams, 1973). More recently, however, scholars have been at pains both to look for similarities in the ethical writings of Aristotle and Kant (Engstrom and Whiting, 1998) and to give a more generous evaluation of Kant, particularly in relation to his writings in the *Metaphysical Principles of Virtue* and *Anthropology from a Pragmatic Point of View* (Baron, 1995; Sherman, 1997).[1]

The widespread, though less favourable, Kantian interpretation is summarised by Montada (1993: 295) thus: (1) that emotions are transitory and capricious; (2) that conduct issuing from emotions is therefore unreliable and unprincipled, even irrational; (3) that the moral perception of right and wrong entails abstraction from our emotions; (4) that emotions are passively experienced and we are not responsible for them; and (5) being attached to particular persons and not universal principles, they are partial and therefore not belonging to the moral realm.

I will comment below partly in defence of Kant's position. I draw out some counterpoints to Montada's characterisation in respect of the relations between passivity and responsibility in our emotional experiences they often held to be part of the Kantian position. Depicting the difficulties that attend to the passivity of, and responsibility for, emotional experiences may help us to understand better the ethical import of emotions generally, but specifically here in relation to human suffering or misfortune, and the experience of *schadenfreude*.

Baldly put, Montada asserts that under a Kantian description we experience emotions passively and that, therefore, we are not responsible for them. This position, though not wholly wrong, lacks precision. Specifically, it is based on an inaccurate reading of Kant since it fails to recognise that, as a response to Hume and others, Kant distinguished between affects or emotions on the one hand, and passions, on the other in his *Metaphysical Principles of Virtue*. A point about nomenclature is necessary here. Kant refers both to '*Affekt*' and '*Leidenschaften*' In the Mary Gregor translation '*Affekt*' is affect whereas in the Ellington translation it is referred to as 'emotion'.[2] Thus if we use the term emotion – in some recognisably modern sense – we may both (1) obscure the distinction;

or worse (2) take his more negative stance to *passions* and apply it inappropriately to what we call emotions. In the Gregor translation Kant says:

> *Affects* and *passions* are essentially different from each other. Affects belong to *feeling* insofar as, preceding reflection, it makes this impossible or more difficult. Hence an affect is called *precipitate* or *rash* (*animus praeceps*), and reason says, through the concept of virtue, that one should *get hold of* oneself. [...] Accordingly a propensity to an affect (e.g., *anger*) does not enter into kinship with vice so readily as does a passion. A *passion* is a sensible desire that has become a lasting inclination (e.g., *hatred*, as opposed to anger). The calm with which one gives oneself up to it permits reflection and allows the mind to form principles upon it and so, if inclination lights upon something contrary to the law, to brood upon it, to get it rooted deeply, and so to take up what is evil (as something premeditated) into its maxim. And the evil is then *properly* evil, that is, a true *vice*.
>
> (Kant, 1991: 208)

To give a fairer reading to Kant, especially in respect of our emotional responses to human suffering or misfortune we must bear this distinction in mind. One important aspect of this distinction for Kant's understanding the emotions (in this case elicited by the suffering of others) is that in passions a 'lasting inclination' is formed and that this entails choice and judgement, which in turn carry the agent's experience into the realm of responsibility. I shall comment further on this point in the section on the culpability of *schadenfreude* below. A second point pertains to the passivity of the experience and is brought out nicely by Baron when commenting on a section from *Anthropology from a Pragmatic Point of View*:

> Kant's distinction between sensitivity and sentimentality is further evidence that in his view we play a significant role as agents in determining how we respond affectively. 'Sensitivity is a *power* and *strength* by which we grant or refuse permission for the state of pleasure or displeasure to enter our mind, so that it implies a choice.' By contrast 'sentimentality is a weakness by which we can be affected, even against our will, by sympathy for another's plight' (Kant, 1974: 236). Clearly, then, we are not always passive with respect to our emotions

and feelings: sensitivity does not involve such passivity.

> (Baron, 1995: 196)

Sherman too offers a useful summary of Kant's point here: that his intention is to 'repudiate sentimentalism, not sentiment' (1997: 153). So, let us first allow that Montada's position is Kantian, rather than Kant's. Second, and more substantively, despite Baron's protest at the lack of agency ascribed to Kantian emotion, our passivity in the experience of sentimentality entails a lack of responsibility. But, with Kant's distinction above in mind, we should say that the point refers to emotions as affects (i.e. sentimentality) – rather than passions (i.e. sensitivity). And this is important in his consideration of the cultivation of sympathy as a moral duty. One point that Baron takes from all this, and one that I am in *sympathy* with (if you will excuse the pun) is that we should not use feelings and emotions as objects to excuse our moral responsibility. And this, I contend, is often what happens when people say that the experience of an emotion such as *schadenfreude* is felt by someone in relation to a suffering other. But the experience of emotions such as *schadenfreude* need not be considered like what might be termed 'immediate natural responses' such as a knee-jerk or anxiety at the onset of a sharp toothache.

Consider a sports physician who refuses pain relief to the athlete on the grounds that they do not believe the level of pain reported is either accurate or authentic. On reflection the physician wonders whether their mistrust and hostility to the patient is, for the purposes of example, driven by their guilt-ridden recollection of giving a questionably high dose of pain killer to an ageing athlete who played on in ignorance of the damage being done to him, and was forced subsequently to retire. In such cases colleagues might claim that the physician's judgement was 'clouded by emotion.' Thinking carefully through such scenarios requires a consideration of the relations between cognition and the relevant emotions at play.

All cognitive theorists of emotion have argued that simply characterising emotions as subjective feelings – as biological theorists do – ignores two important aspects: first, that emotions entail judgements and second that they are to a considerable degree influenced by space and time. One important part of this strategy is to argue that feelings and modes that are not in some way suffused with some cognition are not emotions proper (G. Taylor, 1985), and the very fact of our making linguistic choices signifies this. Early analyses of emotions, inspired by Wittgenstein's anti-essentialism in conceptual analysis, conceived of emotions-talk as illustrating the family resemblances idea: there is neither an essence nor unifying set of properties to them. Some are voluntary, some involuntary, some passive yet others are active. Likewise, their intensity, though typically greater than felt moods, can vary too; compare a punch in anger in the playground, to the studied resentment of a colleague's unmerited promotion where one may stew for days, weeks, even years in one's own acidic feelings, memories and thoughts. Those familiar with British soccer may recall the Manchester United player Roy Keane in his recent autobiography revealing that he harboured resentment for an opposing Norwegian player (Alfe Haaland) for a full year before exacting revenge in a violent, career-threatening tackle. Even allowing for their biological bases, we must agree with Rorty (1988: 1) that 'the emotions do not form a natural kind'. Sometimes the emotions are felt in anticipation of action; at other times they succeed it. Sometimes they are directly motivational, at other times they are not. Moreover, certain emotions such as panic are experienced as self-referring while other emotions such as humiliation or shame have a very significant interpersonal role in preserving boundaries of conduct by reinforcing norms of the acceptable and unacceptable. Emotions such as guilt, remorse, regret and shame all have a negative power that we typically seek to avoid or to work off.

The emotions can be allowed a much more positive role in our identification of what matters to us in both fleeting and more considered ways. While it is easy to recall instances when emotions have got in the way of good judgement, or indeed been obstacles to right action, we can also think of examples where our emotionally driven responses of, say, compassion or mercy are salient. To conceive of the emotions more generously opens a conceptual space in which we can consider more broadly the roles they play in our lives beyond exculpation and the denial of responsibility. To elicit the ethical import of the emotion of *schadenfreude*

(or any of its close cousins in the emotional field – envy, spite, resentment, to name a few[3]) we must accept that the feeling is imbued with a judgement or an interpretation of their situation.

Aristotle's writings are typically taken to afford a more generous interpretation of the emotions in the good life than Kant's, though as I hoped to illustrate above, perhaps too much has been made of the contrast. Aristotelian commentators note how the emotions record and convey our values in a manner that is constitutive of ethically defensible and desirable living (Sherman, 1989). Of course they can only perform these functions when attuned habitually to (wise) judgement. His account of emotions is not, however, encumbered, by the top-down Kantian approach where the absolute value of the moral law and the autonomous will 'shape and regulate the emotions' (Sherman, 1997: 157). Precisely what form the judgement takes is highly disputed in the literature on the philosophy of emotions. Few cognitive theorists would deny that the desires, motivations and feelings we experience involve a sense of our situation. The strongest account of the cognitive element is found in what Griffiths (1997) labels the 'propositional attitude school'.[4] Griffiths argues that in its strongest form, in Solomon's early writings, the emotion simply is a judgement about ourselves and the world. Other accounts (e.g. Roberts (1988) and Armon-Jones (1991)) have shied away from the propositional reductionism that can be attributed to Solomon and others. What is at issue among them is the extent to which language captures the construal. Charles Taylor's writings might be criticised for having emphasised the linguistic dimension of emotional experience whereas Roberts' (1988) and Armon-Jones' (1991) accounts lean towards less propositional elements of emotion and view them under the aspect of some kind of 'construal' of events. Nevertheless, it is sufficient for my purposes here to note that in both cases language and the construal are internally related to the experienced emotion.[5]

What I shall do now is to interrogate the specific emotion of *schadenfreude* and to consider the extent to which the occurrence of the emotion in a sportsperson might make it a reason for us to think of them as lacking virtue or exhibiting vice.

Emotions, good sportspersons and good sporting lives

So, far from being blind passions, as Hume would have it, or wayward steeds as Plato preferred, I have tried to show how our emotions can shape our moral responses. We feel guilt properly at transgressions, remorse at serious violations, and shame at our inability to match well-founded social expectations. These negative emotions can act as powerful sensitisers to the worth of respective courses of action just as they can give evidence of our sensitivities, or lack of them in consequence. Whether sportspersons do experience these emotions is of course not guaranteed, however strong the social expectations for them might be. Thus, for example, many people could not understand the Argentine footballer Diego Maradona's *post facto* rationalisations of his cheating in the 1986 football World Cup quarter-final when he deceived the officials into thinking that he had headed the ball past the English goalkeeper, though in fact he had illegally punched it. His now infamous remark – that it was the 'Hand of God' – was later retracted and explained by him with reference to the more obvious motive that he was seeking a competitive advantage by a strategy that he had used successfully before. What is central to his reaction is the lack of regret (let alone remorse) expressed for his actions. (At least Ron Atkinson had publicly expressed his deep chagrin in the wake of his racist remarks.) So it is not merely, then, that we hold sportspersons responsible for their emotions and emotional outbursts, but a fortiori that we properly hold them culpable at times for their failure to experience and signal them too.

It is in this vein that Nancy Sherman writes of seeing through the emotions:

> We can think of them [emotions] as modes of attention enabling us to notice what is morally salient, important, or urgent in ourselves and our surroundings. They help us to track the morally relevant "news". ... In addition to their role as modes of attention, emotion plays a role in communicating information to others. They are modes of responding. Putting the two together, emotions become modes both for receiving information and signalling it.

> Through the emotions we both track and convey what we care about.
>
> (Sherman, 1989: 40)

In making a strong evaluation, we are articulating the import to which the feeling aspect of emotion relates. And in doing so, we display our own moral sensitivities and insensitivities. Our emotions typically carry information to our reflections. Frequently, after a sporting encounter, and occasionally in the midst of one, we may ask ourselves, 'Why did I do and feel this and not that?', 'To what extent am I a worse or better person for feeling this and not that?' In this vein, consider the example of a recent international cricket match between Sri Lanka and England that descended into a bitter farce when members from both teams deceived and harassed each other and the umpires to such an extent that the debacle sparked a near crisis in a game renowned for its civility. After all, in how many sports does the opposing team welcome the opposing batter(s) to the crease by clapping them? In this scenario, what were thought of as hitherto unreflective professional sportsmen began asking themselves how their actions may be seen to tarnish the game irreparably. Without recourse to convenient exculpations such as the pressure of the event, the heat of the moment and so on, players came to think of themselves as having diminished a noble tradition. The players from both sides began to speak of (and therein to reconceptualise) themselves as 'custodians' of the game whose conduct and character had failed to appropriately reflect that role. The inner dialogue that prompts such questioning frequently follows our pre-reflective responses to situations that are typical of our emotional life. It was a direct consequence of the regret and even the shame many of them felt and acknowledged publicly in respect of their actions. The game emerged stronger in response to their public self-purging. Envy, like resentment and spite, can simmer. I do not want, therefore, to make too much mileage out of the episodic nature of many emotions. In a fuller discussion of the emotions in sport, and their ethical significance, there would need to be room for the full array of associated concepts such as the ranges of cognitive components and their significance. The sources of retaliatory acts of violence, for example, have a quite different aetiology than

331

the premeditated ones that are cultivated in the locker room and practised with more or less conscientiousness on the playing field. What is important to note, however, is that our habituation into certain modes of emotionally laden attributions and responses is central to our self-development as characters of a given kind.

Thus far I have argued against the naive irrational feeling model of emotion. I have also suggested how the cognitive element of emotion renders intelligible our evaluations of good lives. It is worth developing this idea a little while connecting it more closely to the idea of virtuous and vicious character. What is required now is to interrogate the specific emotion of *schadenfreude* and to consider the extent to which the emotion is good or bad and whether the person who experiences it is necessarily to that extent a person of good or bad character.

What is *schadenfreude*?

The idea of taking pleasure in another's misfortune is one that probably translates across the world without remainder. Precisely why it is that, in modern times, only the Germans have a word for it (or as is quite often the case in German, two words joined together) is something imponderable.[6] Quite literally the word means 'harmjoy'. Before analysing the concept of *schadenfreude* and evaluating its normative status, it is worth illuminating some comical observations beyond the paradigmatic Germanic sense. Terry Lane has defined *schadenfreude* as the sensation experienced when you see two Mercedes Benz collide, but that may reflect a preference for Australian-made cars more than his misplaced egalitarianism. Philip Howard, parodying Oscar Wilde's famous remark about homosexuality, describes it as the sentiment that dares not speak its name (in English). In a similar vein, Clive James admits to feeling *schadenfreude* when he sees his rival's books in the remainders bin. Is there something distinct about the source of the feeling, which effectively designates two emotions, not one? There is something more than the comic at play in James', albeit witty, construal. One of my fellow competitors is suffering in contrast to me. What this emotion resonates with is me and my self-esteem. What seems to lie behind the first

example might at least be the murky construal that the Mercedes drivers in some way deserved their comeuppance by virtue of their wealth.

Is there a morally righteous and morally repugnant conception of *schadenfreude*? Imagine a basketball player who has consistently fouled his way through a game, and done it so slyly that his actions have gone unnoticed and unpunished by the officials. In the last second of a tied match, he drives for the basket, misjudges his approach, trips over your foot, and tears his ankle ligaments without making the shot. You smile wryly to yourself. Are you really any the worse for your reaction? Are you thereby a sportsperson of deficient character? Part of a reasoned evaluation of this type of scenario must always be particularised; it must always take account of the relations between the sufferer and the judger. Another part of our response or evaluation should concern the normative codes that structure their relations. Is the *schadenfroh* deserving of the harm? Of course, again, for these questions to make sense, we must reject the anti-cognitivist picture of the emotions. For to appreciate their sense and value is already to be committed to the cognitive dimension of emotions and thereby their rationality.

We need to be able to distinguish when what seems to be *schadenfreude* is an emotional corollary of justice – if indeed this is the case – and when it is really envy or resentment in disguise. It is clearly not born of a sense of justice when the emotion becomes active and turns into a malicious glee. In some cases of course, the experience of the emotion is not spontaneous or episodic. On the contrary, we cultivate it; sometimes cherish it; it curdles over time, and if not attended to, depletes our moral resources. This is why I have sketched the non-episodic account of *schadenfreude* in the example above. We can only attend to this task of recognition and (re)appropriation if, as Neu (2002) notes, we are able to discriminate among the sources of our emotions and thereby to understand and evaluate ourselves more judiciously. The experience of *schadenfreude* is clearly not born of a sense of justice when the emotion becomes active and turns into a malicious glee. This is the point made specifically by Kant about the experience passion being turned into a lasting inclination. Indeed he writes specifically of *schadenfreude* (translated as 'malice' in both the Ellington and Gregor editions) in this regard:

Malice, which is directly contrary to sympathy, is also not foreign to human nature; when it goes as far promoting evil or wickedness itself, then as a special kind of malice it reveals a hatred of mankind, and appears in all its horrors.

(Kant cited in Ellington, 1994: 124–5)

This malicious glee is not, according to Portmann, *schadenfreude* proper despite the widespread understanding of it under such a description. What the matter hangs on, so to speak, is the idea of whether the harm is deserved or undeserved, and whether indeed one can take an attitude of detached impartiality towards the suffering wrongdoer.

If we wish to appraise the character of the one who feels *schadenfreude*, we need to determine the extent to which, when judging the pleasure felt at another's misfortune, they are active or passive in the generation of the emotion. Now, to intend that another be harmed is part of an active strategy – Portmann argues that the pleasure, which is consequent upon this, is not *schadenfreude* proper but rather a malicious glee. Portmann argues that *schadenfreude* proper requires the re-drawing of the emotion away from that particular misconception. As part of his recognition of the passivity of *schadenfreude*, he goes on to suggest an analogy between sympathy and *schadenfreude* – both come uninvited or not at all. Just as manufactured sympathy is not sympathy proper, so in experiencing *schadenfreude*, we experience a pleasure *that* they are harmed without a prior desire for them to be harmed. When set against our earlier account of emotions being necessarily partly constituted by a cognitive element (a construal), this looks odd. What sort of construal is going on then? *Schadenfreude* surely does not visit us uninvited as a guest might. Portmann (2000: 27–8), in his defence, says:

> In speaking of the passivity of *Schadenfreude* I do not mean to imply that we are victims of our emotions in the sense that emotions seem to toss us about like ships in a storm. I do not claim that either malicious glee is beyond our control; indeed because we are not purely passive in the fact of feelings and emotions, our efforts to manage our emotions sometimes succeed. Alternatively, we can rationalise our enjoyment of the suffering of another; we can tell ourselves that we take pleasure in the fact that another suffers (as opposed to pleasure in

the actual suffering) and that this pleasure results from the love of justice. Such mental dodges attest to the rationality of *Schadenfreude*, as well as to our responsibility for it.

The passivity of all emotions was, perhaps too swiftly, attributed to the Kantian picture of emotion and their non-existence in morally autonomous persons. And Portmann is surely right not to give in to that particular temptation in his defence of *schadenfreude*. But the key to his position is his use of the word 'rationalisation'. For that is exactly what, I will argue below, his position is. That an ethically defensible (praiseworthy?) sense of *schadenfreude* exists, where one can love a sinner while hating the sin and take pleasure in justice being served is precisely that: a rationalisation. Can we hate the foul but love the fouler? Love the cheat but hate the cheating? I will argue that this, in the context of stratified and hierarchically structured activities such as sports, is no more than a rationalisation and that its genesis is typically envy and not a love of justice or low self-esteem, as Portmann argues. But that is to move ahead of the game. Let us next consider the genesis *of schadenfreude*.

The genesis of *schadenfreude*

Articulating the genesis of *schadenfreude*, precisely why the *schadenfroh* feels pleasure at another's misfortune, should open the door to an evaluation of the ethical status of the emotion and the character of the *schadenfroh*. I take the categories from Portmann. He argues that *schadenfreude* may be born of: (1) low self-esteem; (2) loyalty and commitments to justice; (3) the comical; and (4) malice. I shall be concerned here only with the first and second categories. While Portmann maintains that the first three are still liable to be appraised in the guilt and blame we apportion to the *schadenfroh*, the latter is always to be condemned. My position, which I merely assert at this point, is that the third and fourth categories are not philosophically interesting, since the third is not a paradigmatic sense of the concept,[7] because it relates properly to instances of embarrassment rather than harm, while the fourth is obviously despicable and therefore uncontentious.

Let us consider, then, the idea that low self-esteem might give birth to feelings of *schadenfreude* that are ethically excusable. Early on in Christine Mackinnon's consideration of the cultivation of the self in virtue theory, she remarks that 'everybody is faced with the task of constructing a self, but not everybody starts with the same equipment' (1999: 37). Is it the case for those who feel *schadenfreude* that they necessarily think so little of themselves?

Francis Bacon captured something like the point nicely when he said that a recognition of others' sufferings can redeem our own.[8] This seems to be the case with our basketball player. He was on the wrong end of his opponent's cheating, made to look bad because of it, and feels relieved that the game has not been lost by virtue of his inability to master his cheating opponent. Of course, the precise identity of the other sufferer and their relation to us is a crucial variable. This is what generates remarks such as Clive James's above: it is *his* competitor's book in the remainder bin. Portmann argues that self-esteem enhances our sense that we are leading good lives. More specifically, he asserts: 'Self-esteem does not blind us to interpersonal differences; rather, it prevents us from concluding that the superiority of one person signifies the worthlessness or inherent defect in another' (2000: 33).

It seems clear to me here that he is talking about self-respect, which is not exclusive – the possession of self-respect by one does not entail its exclusion in another. Where, however, our sense of our own worth in relation to others is set in a competitive structure (going for the head coach position, achieving a promotion from one division to the next, breaking the record), it seems that self-esteem is characteristically exclusive.[9] My having won entails your loss, and vice versa. The objects of envy are typically positional goods. This is precisely the theme of a remark attributed to Gore Vidal that 'whenever a friend succeeds a little something in me dies'. Now the distinction is crucial for Portmann, since the *schadenfreude* born of low self-esteem is of a deficient sense of self; it is a weakness of character. He takes this to entail its ethical excusability. He takes his cue here from Rawls' (1972: 534–40) remarks on envy and, in quoting Rawls approvingly, conflates self-esteem with self-respect:[10] 'When envy is a reaction to the loss of self-respect in circumstances

where it would be unreasonable to expect someone to feel differently, I shall say it is excusable' (Portmann, 2000: 34).

Now where resentment is felt as an affront to one's dignity – and here we can say he has shifted to self-respect again – the feeling of anger may be justified. He says it reflects a healthy self-esteem, but here he is trading again on self-respect. While self-respect has a categorical status (one either has it or not), self-esteem derives and is measured from our evaluations of ourselves in social structures according to a good or range of goods or abilities.[11] He concludes: 'To the extent that a feeling of inferiority seems to invite celebration of other's woes, condemning a *Schadenfroh* person is a bit like blaming him or her for dissatisfaction with an unjust social framework' (Portmann, 2000: 35).

Now it is clear that if we feel pleasure when someone has, for example, strongly humiliated another (where the limit case is torture), then Rawls' exculpation might be reasonable. Other cases of celebration of loss by others in sport are worthy of consideration. Consider someone who is a not a regular player in the starting line-up, but is a solid and reliable substitute 'quarterback' (in American Football) or 'stand-off' (the equivalent in Rugby Union), whose fitness levels and tactical and technical abilities are not developed to the elite level of his starting team-mate. When the starting player is stretchered from the field of play, the substitute rejoices inwardly at his chance to shine and to show his talents. Where this feeling is not directly driven by the player's negative attitude towards the starting 'quarterback' or 'stand-off', I think we ought to be careful not to excuse the pleasure he experiences. On the one hand, what should rankle with us is not merely the lack of empathy and sympathy with a team-mate but the egoistic quality of his celebration, which is dependent upon a team-mate's suffering. Nevertheless, the relationship between his joy and the harm of the star player is not one of cause and effect but rather mere correlation. So the concept of *schadenfreude* does not apply properly here even if we think of the substitute's inward celebration as disrespectful or callous. It is not clear to me that sports are unique in this matter. I see no reason why one would not find considerable evidence for this emotion in a whole range of competitively structured practices from work to politics. We might, however, think that paradigm cases of *schadenfreude* were those in which persons were pitted against each other in some antagonistic way. What may be slightly unusual in this example is the fact that the type of emotion can perhaps as easily be felt in relation to those with whom I share goals and aspirations. I do not want to make too much of this, however, since it is perfectly possible that competition and the exclusivity of goods on offer (especially the positional ones, such as status, ranking, hierarchy and power) might as easily obtain in other practices of an inherently competitive kind. I shall return to this issue below with a slightly more difficult example from a recent Ryder Cup contest.

Part of why I think *schadenfreude* is problematic is because of the envy that often accompanies the emotion. Both Solomon (2000) and Herzog (2000) get much closer to the relationship between envy and *schadenfreude* than Portmann. Everyone seems to agree that envy is a 'loser's emotion' resulting from a failure accurately to assess one's self-worth. We might conclude that *schadenfreude* harms no one but the *schadenfrohe* themselves. Let them stew in their bitter juices, we might think. Harm them nonetheless it does by generating false pictures of their relations with those who facilitate what it is they are committed to – sporting excellence. In developing our attitudes to these emotions dependent on self-evaluation, we might also consider the pathologically 'humble' who ritually deprecate themselves and seek to defer to and emulate others. Of course, we might then see envy as emulation gone bad. For emulation is, on the face of it, a good thing, and in virtue theory in particular, it is the wise person (in Aristotle, the *phronimos*) whom we seek to model our choices and character upon. In envy, however, our admiration goes awry; the negativity overtakes what benefits could be had from emulation. If we are to believe the Catholic tradition, then envy first leads to sadness, then to gossip, then to *schadenfreude*, then to hatred (Solomon, 2000). If indeed this is so, then although the lack of self-esteem that can give birth to *schadenfreude* may not be as vicious as resentment, or spite or malicious glee, it is nevertheless something we should be on our toes to avoid and/or acknowledge on our path to making ourselves better (sports) persons.

In respect of the slide between emotions of lesser and more corrosive power, Herzog picks out the comic dimension sometimes associated with *schadenfreude* that is morally unobjectionable. I have asserted above that this emotion is better conceptualised in terms of the concept of embarrassment because of the relative seriousness or significance that attaches to each. Herzog shows how our comical responses to embarrassment can slide into the deeper, nastier emotion, which can find root in envy at the same time as being productive of it:

> The heart that's heavy seeing other men more worthy in anything is the motive for a certain kind of *Schadenfreude*. Not the snicker that greets the pompous speaker who rises to the lectern with resolute gravity, oblivious to the lobster bisque splattered across his tie; so much doesn't require any antecedent envy. But suppose you had previously noted your dismay that he cut a more imposing figure in public than you, that the thought rankled, and that now you rejoice in seeing the fates bring him low precisely because his humiliation makes him less of a threat to your self-esteem.
>
> (Herzog, 2000: 148)

So it is often the case, and is by no means ethically excusable, that the *schadenfreude* born of low esteem masks a more or less bitter envy, not because one has been robbed of one's self-respect, but rather because one has suffered a blow to one's self-esteem that one simply cannot handle.

In this vein, Dr Johnson remarks that envy, not selfishness, is the mother of all malevolence:

> Most of the misery which the defamation of blameless actions, or the obstruction of honest endeavours brings upon the world, is inflicted by men that propose no advantage to themselves but the satisfaction of poisoning the banquet which they cannot taste, and blasting the harvest which they have no right to reap.
>
> (Cited in Herzog, 2000: 149)

Moreover, when we think of envy, it is important to consider who is envied and what are its characteristic objects (from material goods, to appearances and talents). Like *schadenfreude*, envy is felt paradigmatically, but not exclusively, in relation to those in whom we have antagonistic relations. Consider the jealousy that drives so many of the characters of *The Iliad* against both friend and foe alike as they seek to claim that most competitive of goods, honour, from the gods. What often drives envy is not so much the desire to be the greatest; that is too limited a preserve to be psychologically credible. Rather, what motivates a sportsperson's emotional set more frequently is the desire to be seen to be (even a little bit) better than one's nearest rival. Two qualities of this desire for status strike me as important in an attempt to better understand what is going on when *schadenfreude* is felt, either in terms of opponents or indeed of team-mates occupying the starting line-up. First, it is the narcissism of minor differences, in Freud's term, that seems to drive the emotion. Second, the joy felt at our antagonist's harm is therefore driven by our familiarity with them. Or, as Hume puts it, 'tis not the great disproportion betwixt ourself and one another, which produces it, but on the contrary, our proximity' (cited in Herzog, 2000: 155).

There is a further, related point that is worthy of notice. Ought we to think of the celebration of a loss by one team, or indeed a vital mistake by our opponent, as being born necessarily of *schadenfreude*? The much discussed response of the American Ryder Cup team of 1999 who ran across the eighteenth green before the hole had been finished is paradigmatic of this category. Were they celebrating their European opponent's failed putt or their own win? It seems to me, although the matter is open to subsequent empirical refutation, that in the heat of the moment, the relief and joy expressed in their actions was symptomatic of mere catharsis and not inherently the rejoicing at their opponent's suffering. If my reading of this is correct, then it would be improper to think of their actions under the description of *schadenfreude*. It was of course still highly undesirable; the best that one can say is that it evidenced a lack of respect – and against the grain of what is undeniably among the nobler sports. This is not to say that in all such cases, the celebration of such an incident could not be classified as *schadenfreude*. If they were genuinely rejoicing the miserable failing of their opposition, and the celebration of their victory was secondary in importance, then it is clear that the description of *schadenfreude* would be properly applied – and our responses to it should alter accordingly.

I see no reason to suppose that any particular sports culture is more given to *schadenfreude* than another. What strikes me as noteworthy, if you will pardon the pun, is that in the sport where direct harm is intentionally and legally inflicted, boxing, *schadenfreude* is almost conspicuous by its absence among the boxers themselves. It might be argued more generally that spectators or followers of clubs, teams, and individual sports stars revel in opponents' harms rather more so than the players themselves. Where the clubs have intense geographical and cultural rivalries, it seems that this is perfectly plausible, though no less regrettable. For my own part, this might well be explained by a deficient sense of self, where spectators appear to believe that their self-worth is vicariously tendered by their identification with a successful other (be it team, club or player). Further exploration of this issue is, however, beyond the scope of the present discussion.

That we can reflect on the antecedents to our emotions is one clue as to how we may think about working upon our emotions and perceptions of others and selves, in order to go about educating ourselves in that respect.[12] They do not *all* visit us as uninvited guests might. Moreover, correct perceptions of others and selves are surely part of what we call a good life. And I want to emphasise that it is only a virtue-theoretical position that attempts to take this feature of our experience seriously. For to act well is not merely to do so for the right reasons, to the right extent, at the right time, and so on, but also to feel these reasons and responses while so construing and responding. And this, I fear, is simply ignored, not merely in much of the flourishing sports ethics literature but also in the sociology of sport.[13] Having rejected Portman's first defence of *schadenfreude*, I will consider his second, rather stronger account for excusability: a loyalty to justice. If he is right that the feeling of *schadenfreude* may be justified as a function of justice then it might be seen as a virtuous rather than a vicious emotional response.

The sense that most of us may feel both familiar and warranted is in the *schadenfreude* felt by those who believe that another has violated an expectation or obligation and suffers in relation to their transgression. (How many times have you heard in post-match conferences: 'They got their just desserts!'; or 'I am glad they got their comeuppance', or, in both anticipation and desire, 'What goes around comes around'? Portmann writes:

> There is an important difference between enjoying *that* someone suffers and enjoying actual suffering. The former case must be held apart from *Schadenfreude*, for the attendant pleasure is not properly in seeing someone suffer but in the hope that someone will learn a valuable lesson in having suffered. Thus we take pleasure not in the suffering of another, but in the hope that he or she will correct a mistake.
>
> (Portmann, 2000: 48)

The pleasure felt at seeing justice done, he argues, must not be confused with a pleasure that a given person is actually suffering themselves. But it seems to me that 'pleasure' is not the right concept here. To take pleasure in suffering is too active, too destructive of human sympathy to be evidence of a love of justice. Now lest it be suggested that I am promoting a picture of sport devoid of intense commitment, let me make it clear that I do not approve of a sporting ethics of indifference. To the contrary, anger is an entirely appropriate emotional response to injustice.

How it is registered, how accounted for and how exacted – these are further questions. I am merely arguing that pleasure felt at another's suffering is itself not desirable, even when the suffering is experienced by a wrongdoer. I think the more appropriate model may be a legal one. What one seeks through the courts is often described as 'satisfaction'. I want my transgressor to be adjudged wrong in public and admonished. A more appropriate emotional response, then, will be a less hedonistic or egoistic one; not cold, impartial, empathy-lacking justice, and certainly not an active, hand-rubbing glee. It strikes me that the proper emotional response to justice being served, and subsequent harm befalling the wrongdoer is captured by the concept of 'satisfaction'. Such is the feeling that ought to characterise our basketball player's emotional response. This concept denotes emotional neutrality and a certain passivity that is entirely absent in the positive and corrosive *schadenfreude*.

Of course this distinction regarding our rejoicing in the seeing of justice done begs wider questions about the role of human suffering in our lives. The position here is in debt to St Augustine in *Summa Theologiae*: Love the sinner, hate the sin is the exhortation. But Portmann's gloss seems unreal. 'We take pleasure in hoping they will correct the mistake' (2000: 156), he says. Well this *may* be the emotion felt by the zealous reformer, but the attitude of the *schadenfroh* seems not of this kind. 'You're bad but look how good in contrast I am', seems closer to the mark. What is missing here is any reference to sympathy – note, *not* empathy – with the sufferer. Of course, the resenting sportsperson may well, like Keane above, have empathy with his opponent, as he writhes on the floor in agony; it is precisely that empathy that fuels his enjoyment.

Schadenfreude and sporting sympathy

I have tried to show that Portmann's defences for *schadenfreude* are unacceptable. In the first instance, his conflation of self-respect and self-esteem undercuts his defence of the emotion. Second, the idea that low self-esteem and a commitment to justice might drive an excusable pleasure at another's suffering is at odds with any basic notion of human sympathy that will be at the core of all moralities I (perhaps too boldly) assert.

In summary, it seems more felicitous to link *schadenfreude* with a lack of spirit – an othering[14] of my opponent or competitor, or a failure to connect with their humanity as opposed to a deficiency in one's self-esteem. It is clear that our attitudes towards *schadenfreude* will alter accordingly with the severity of the suffering and the greatness of their deficiencies in conduct and character. What seems clear, however, is that the 'trick' of loving the sinner but hating the sin is a perception that will not find a home in the capriciousness of human character (however much we might want to cheer with the angels). Better that we recognise the nature of the occurrence and reflect on our own motivations in relation to the sufferer before we revel too much in the baseness of others and, by contrast, our own righteousness. In sports practice communities, no less than in social science research, we do well to observe Owen Flanagan's principle of minimal psychological realism. 'Make sure when constructing a moral theory

337

or proposing a moral ideal that the character, decision-processing, and behavior are possible, or are perceived to be possible, for creatures like us' (Flanagan, 1991: 32).

This dictum could be seen to work both for and against the position I have set out above. It is natural that our responses to competitors' sufferings will not be driven by feelings so impartial that their losses strike us as heavily as our own. To an extent this is obviously true. Of course, one cannot hope to develop in sportspersons so detached a consideration of human interests, a point made more frequently these days against modern moralities of both utilitarian and deontological persuasion. But the active pleasure at another's misfortune goes beyond the asymmetry of self and other. *Schadenfreude* passes beyond the excusable and into both the realms of culpable and responsible emotion. Worse, where it is cultivated or merely utilised to enhance and celebrate our own esteem and achievements, *pace* Gore Vidal, a little something in us dies too.

Notes

1. I shall attempt a more balanced account of Kant's stance towards the emotions in his own virtue theory here, in contrast to the more one-sided account I gave in the original publication of this essay (McNamee, 2003b) and an earlier article on the emotion of guilt as a response to injury infliction (McNamee, 2002).
2. This is the case of the 1991 translation of the *Metaphysics of Morals*. In a footnote (91n, p. 292) to this very point, however, she notes that in the earlier 1974 translation 'affect' had been preferred to the earlier translation as 'agitation' where as 'passions' were previously labelled 'obsessions'.
3. The point may be put more generally that the emotions come in clusters (Baier, 1990: 4–5). Not surprisingly, Rorty (1988) had earlier put that observation to effect in the context of virtue theory: the virtues, she says, hunt in packs. It seems only a short leap to imagine that the vices too rarely work alone. To support this point, I shall attempt to show below that it is not justice which triggers *schadenfreude,* but envy.
4. Griffiths takes Anthony Kenny's 1963 work *Act, Emotion, Will* to be seminal here. It has found its strongest expression in the work of Robert Solomon but also is a cornerstone of Charles Taylor's theory of human agency and personhood and is central to his celebrated distinction between strong and weak evaluation.

5. It might seem reasonable to suggest that the extent to which this is the case is a hostage to the heterogeneity of emotions. Typically one might think that this propositional element may be more developed according to the complexity and/or nuance of the emotion at hand. When one feels uneasy in the dark one might say one is afraid but unable to articulate the object of the fear. Or think of long-term injured athletes who go through moods of depression without some precisely foeused object as their source.
6. Philip Howard identifies *schadenfreude* as one of the black holes in English. One commentator (R. C. Trench, etymologist and author of *English Past and Present* and On *the Study of Words*) celebrates this gap, saying:

   > What a fearful thing it is that any language should have a word expressive of the pleasure which men feel at the calamities of others; for the existence of the word bears testimony to the existence of tht thing. And yet in more than one, such a word is found: in the Greek *epikairekakia,* in the German, *Schadenfreude.*
   > (Retrieved at http://www.users.bigpond. com/burnside/black_holes.htm)

7. It could be argued that the comic is only a token of a wider class that might issue *Schadenfreude* vis-à-vis the trivial or insignificantly harmful.
8. As cited in Portmann (2000: 33).
9. It will probably be clear that I take my lead here from Nozick (1974: 239–46). As he puts it:

   > People generally judge themselves by how they fall along the most important dimensions in which they *differ* from others. People do not gain self-esteem from their common human capacities by comparing themselves to animals who lack them. (I'm pretty good; I have an opposable thumb and can speak some language) ... self-esteem is based on *differentiating characteristics:* that's why it's called *self* esteem.
   > (1974: 243, emphasis thus)

10. In the introductory section of 'Envy and equality', Rawls (1 972: 604) writes:

    > We are now ready to examine the likelihood of excusable general envy in a well-ordered society. [...] Now I assume that the main psychological root of the liability to envy is a lack of self-confidende in our own worth combined with a sense of impotence. [...] This hypothesis implies that the least favoured tend to be more envious of the better situation of the more favoured the less secure their self-respect and the greater their feeling that they cannot improve their prospects.

Here, then, we see the further conflation of related concepts, since self-confidence is not a synonym either for self-respect or self-esteem. Interestingly, in the index to Rawls's magnum opus, under 'self-esteem', it actually says, 'see self-respect'.

11. I am indebted to David Sachs' (1981) paper where a more subtle version of the relations between self-respect and self-esteem can be found.

12. The phrase 'education of the emotions' sounds odd here despite its common currency. Do we not better speak of education in and through the emotions?

13. Among the sociological theories of sport, figurational explanations of sport violence centre upon the emotions, but even there surprisingly little, beyond noting the obvious emotions of anger, excitement, and frustration, is to be found. See, for example, Dunning (1999), for a collection of essays by one of the founding fathers (*sic*) of that school of thought.

14. *Othering* is a term of art invented by feminists, I believe, to capture the manner in which non-heterosexuals are pejoratively defined as non-normal as part of a subconscious psychological process of preparing them for maltreatment or at least inequitable treatment.

References

Armon-Jones, C. (1991) *Varieties of Affect*, Toronto: University of Toronto Press.

Baier, A. C. (1990) 'What emotions are about', *Philosophical Perspectives*, 4: 1–29.

Baron, M. (1995) *Kantian Ethics Almost Without Apology*, London: Cornell University Press.

Dunning, E. (1999) *Sport Matters*, London: Routledge.

Ellington, J. W. (1994) *Immanuel Kant: Ethical Philosophy*, Cambridge: Hackett Publishing Company.

Engstrom, S. and Whiting, J. (1998) *Aristotle, Kant and the Stoics*, Cambridge: Cambridge University Press.

Flanagan, O. (1991) *Varieties of Moral Personality: Ethics and Psychological Realism*, London: Harvard University Press.

Griffiths, P. (1997) *What Emotions Really Are: The Problem of Psychological Categories*, Chicago: University of Chicago Press.

Herzog, D. (2000) 'Envy', in R. C. Solomon (ed.) *Wicked Pleasures*, Oxford: Rowman and Littlefield, pp. 141–60.

Kant, I. (1974) *Anthropology from a Pragmatic Point of View*, The Hague: Nijhoff (trans. M. Gregor).

Kant, I. (1991) *The Metaphysics of Morals*, Cambridge: Cambridge University Press (trans. M. Gregor).

Kenny. A. J. (1963) *Act, Emotion, Will*, London: Routledge.

Mackinnon, C. (1999) *Character, Virtue Theories and the Vices,* Toronto: Broadview.

McNamee, M. J. (2002) 'Hubris, humility and humiliation: vice and virtue in sporting communities', *Journal of the Philosophy of Sport*, 29(1): 38–53.

McNamee, M. J. (2003) 'Is guilt a proper emotional response to the causing of an unintentional injury?', *European Journal of Sport Science*, 2(1): 1–10.

Montada, L. (1993) 'Understanding oughts by assessing moral reasoning or moral emotions', in G. G. Noam and T. Wren (eds) *The Moral Self*, London: MIT Press, pp. 292–309.

Nozick, R. (1974) *Anarchy, State, Utopia*, Oxford: Blackwell.

Nue, J. (2002) *A Tear Is an Intellectual Thing: The Meaning of Emotion*, Oxford: Oxford University Press.

Plato (1962) *Phaedrus*, London: Penguin.

Plato (1974) *Republic*, 2nd edn, London: Penguin (trans. D. Lee).

Portmann, J. (2000) *When Bad Things Happen to Other People*, London: Routledge.

Rawls, J. (1972) *A Theory of Justice*, Oxford: Clarendon Press.

Roberts, R. C. (1988) 'What an emotion is: a sketch', *The Philosophical Review*, XCVII: 183–209.

Rorty, A. O. (1988) *Mind in Action: Essays in the Philosophy of Mind*, Boston: Beacon Press.

Sachs, D. (1981) 'How to distinguish self-respect from self-esteem', *Philosophy and Public Affairs*, 10: 346–60.

Sherman, N. (1989) *The Fabric of Character*, Oxford: Clarendon Press.

Sherman, N. (1997) *Making a Necessity of Virtue*, Oxford: Clarendon Press.

Solomon, R. C. (2000) 'Introduction', in R. C. Solomon (ed.) *Wicked Pleasures*, Oxford: Rowman and Littlefield, pp. 1–17.

Taylor, G. (1985) *Pride, Shame, Guilt*, Oxford: Clarendon Press.

Williams, B. A. O. (1973) *Problems of the Self*, Cambridge: Cambridge University Press.

Wollheim, R. (1993) *The Mind and its Depths*, Boston: Harvard University Press.

5.5

Athletic virtue
Between East and West

Heather L. Reid

Introduction

Some of my deepest thinking about the comparison between Eastern and Western philosophy of sport was inspired by a lazy student's answer on an essay test. Our textbook had distinguished Eastern from Western-style sports according to their underlying philosophies: Eastern sports were associated with passivity, collectivism and spirituality while Western sports were characterised by aggression, individualism and instrumentalism. The student, who, as usual, hadn't read the book, nevertheless presented a strong argument for the opposite case. He contrasted (what he saw as) the violent, individualistic and self-serving nature of Eastern martial arts such as karate with the Western preference for team sports, such as football, that emphasise cooperation, team spirit and community representation. His answer made me wonder whether the differences between Eastern and Western sports were less fundamental than their stereotypical representations would suggest. And this question made me wonder whether the differences between Eastern and Western philosophy were likewise less profound than commonly thought – especially as they apply to sport. After all, both Daoism and Confucianism focus on virtue, while Classical Greek virtue ethics underpin

the 'Western' conception of sport.[1] Could it be that the virtue potentially cultivated by the practice of all sports is valued in Eastern and Western traditions alike?

This essay is a comparison of classical Greek and Chinese ideas about virtue applied to the practice of sport, where 'sport' is understood to include Olympic-style athletic games as well as martial arts, dance and related activities such as t'ai chi and chi gong. I will begin with well-known contrasts between Eastern and Western traditions, specifically the issues of struggle versus effortlessness, external rewards versus internal harmony and individualism versus collectivism. The comparisons will result in a breaking down of contrasts which affirms common ground without homogenising out important distinctions. We will find not only that Eastern and Western philosophical traditions have much in common that is relevant to sport, but also that they contain important differences, which might be instructive to both sides as we deal with the challenges of globalisation.

De vs aretē

The first question to be examined is whether the concept of virtue is itself compatible between

Heather L. Reid 'Athletic Virtue: Between East and West' from *Sport, Ethics and Philosophy*, Vol. 4, Issue 1, pp. 16–26, © Taylor & Francis 2010. Reprinted by permission of Taylor & Francis.

the traditions. Do the Confucian and Daoist conceptions of *de*, already quite distinct from one another, bear any resemblance to the Classical Greek conception of *aretē* The historical connection between *aretē* and athletics was derived partly from aristocratic values such as *kalokagathia* (being both beautiful and good) and *aristeia* (a drive to be the best and outdo all others).[2] These ideals grew out of an intensely competitive culture in which authority was routinely challenged (witness Achilles's defiance of King Agamemnon in Homer's *Iliad*), and where lucrative prizes were awarded to those who proved their competitive worth. Confucianism and Daoism emerge from an equally warlike age in China, but rather than associating *de* with challenges to authority, they advocate introspection, non-contention and sometimes social withdrawal. To the extent that *de* is associated with sports and physical movement, it is in reference to personal development or gentlemanly manners while engaged in traditional activities such as archery, chariot racing and court games.

Despite this contrast, however, both *de* and *aretē* turn out to be similar kinds of things. They are both understood as a kind of power in the soul; what the Greeks called *dynamis* and sinologist Arthur Waley translated as 'moral force'.[3] In both traditions, this soul-power is connected with the body: for the Chinese because they made no strict distinction between body and soul, and for the Greeks because bodily movement (*kinēsis*) was a product of the soul and therefore a means both to cultivate and to demonstrate the health of one's soul.[4] Plato, who was himself a competitive wrestler, accordingly makes extensive physical training part of his educational programmes for *aretē*, and indeed athletic activities were a common part of young Hellenic men's lives.[5] In Kongzi's milieu, by contrast, the task was not to challenge leaders' authority, but rather to convince them to act virtuously for the good of the community as a whole. Whereas Greek *aretē* is conceived as a means of overthrowing others, Chinese *de* seems to function more like a magnet that naturally draws others in, obviating the need for force. In response to a question on how to govern people Kongzi says:

> What need is there for executions? If you desire goodness, then the common people will be good. The Virtue of a gentleman is like the wind, and the Virtue of a petty person is like the grass – when the wind moves over the grass, the grass is sure to bend.
>
> (*Analects* 12.19)[6]

This contrast between competitive and magnetic models of virtue derives more from cultural context than from deep conceptual differences. It seems fair to say that Eastern and Western traditions alike expect virtue to wield both competitive advantage and inspirational power. What is Plato's depiction of Socrates, if not an attempt to inspire others toward *aretē* And why did the Chinese assign civil service jobs on the basis of competitive examination if they didn't think virtue could be tested and contested? Likewise, the differences between particular virtues identified as parts of *de* and *aretē* are grounded primarily in cultural rather than conceptual differences.[7] In both traditions virtue is ultimately unified, with the parts working together to make up the whole.[8] In neither Greek nor Chinese philosophy is virtue inherited from ancestors or transferred from teachers to students. Nor does either tradition think that virtue is specific to a particular culture, race or ethnicity. Philosophers on both sides of the world conceived of virtue as a perfection of universal human traits – what the Confucian philosopher Mengzi (Mencius) called 'sprouts', as natural as the four limbs, which are developed through activities requiring discipline and effort.[9] But even if *de* and *aretē* are both forms of psychic power cultivated through training, it does not follow that the desired states of virtue resemble one another, much less that athletics might be a means toward those ends.

Struggle (*agon*) vs effortlessness (*wuwei*)

For starters, let us compare the Hellenic view of life as essentially struggle (*agon*) with the Chinese view of life as essentially peaceful and harmonious. In the former context, virtue is associated with power and courage, while the latter context emphasises yielding and acceptance. The Chinese idea of *wuwei*, 'non-action' or 'effortlessness', is valued in both Confucian and Daoist traditions, even though they disagree about its exact meaning. Laozi often expresses the ideal specifically as non-contention: 'Only do not contend, and you will not go wrong' (*Daodejing*, chapter 8, trans. Addiss and Lombardo). But it would be rash to conclude that Laozi's non-contention entails avoidance of athletic games. After all, he associates non-contention with victory.[10] More likely his point is akin to the Stoic mantra of not desiring what one cannot control. As Epictetus says, 'you are invincible if you never enter a contest in which victory is not under your control' (Epictetus, *Handbook* 19) Both Stoics and Daoists would define victory not in terms of the contest outcome itself, but rather according to factors under their control. In so far as we use sport to learn about ourselves – our potential, our limitations, our relationships with others and the natural world – we may compete without contending and cultivate virtue as a result.

Wuwei also manifests itself in competition through the familiar martial arts tactic of using opponents' aggression against them. The Daoist lesson is one of strength in yielding. 'The accomplished person is not aggressive,' says Laozi (*Daodejing* 68, trans. Addiss and Lombardo). 'The most fruitful outcome/Does not depend on force/but succeeds without arrogance/Without hostility/Without pride/Without resistance/Without violence' (ibid. 30) Likewise, the courage (*andreia*) constituent of Hellenic *aretē* is not mere boldness; it is always coupled with self-control or *sophrosyne*. The important thing in *agon* is to act in accordance with wisdom; in fact Plato describes virtue partly in terms of the spirited part of the soul being able to follow reason's lead (*Republic* 430b, 442c). Socrates's historic *retreat* in the battle of Delium can be seen as an example of *wuwei* virtue that saved many lives and so enabled the Athenians to fight another day.[11] Socrates also displays virtuous non-action in response to the immoral government command that he bring Leon of Salamis to trial; the philosopher simply went home (Plato, *Apology* 34b–f). It turns out that yielding and non-action may be as important for Western *agon* as they are for Eastern harmony.

But what is most familiar to athletes about the concept of *wuwei* is that achieving effortlessness is anything but effortless. Usain Bolt's 100-metre world record in the Beijing Olympics was the picture of effortlessness, but only the most naive would believe that this state of excellence was achieved without effort. It takes a lot of work to arrive in the place where one can act in complete harmony with nature. We may compare the cultivation of *wuwei* to the acquisition of language: it is learned with difficulty at first but eventually fluency is achieved, and for some even poetic eloquence at last becomes effortless. By his own account, it took Kongzi 70 years to achieve the state where his 'heart's desire' was congruent with propriety.[12]

For Laozi, the endeavour faces backwards towards one's original state of virtue – a kind of de-civilisation process that runs counter to conventional ideas of effort and achievement but presents its own challenge nonetheless. Any athlete who has striven to achieve a clear mind by 'not thinking' or to achieve self-control by 'not attacking' but rather letting the play come to him knows the challenge implied by the concept of *wuwei*. In both Eastern and Western traditions, virtue is a hard-won state within which moral action becomes effortless because one always desires the right thing. In Platonic ethics, this phenomenon is dubbed the denial of *akrasia* or weakness of will. As Zhu Xi remarks in commenting on *Analects* 14.4, 'when [the Good person] sees what is right to do, he simply must do it'. (Zhu Xi quoted in Slingerland 2003, 113). Although athletics can hardly claim to teach the kind of moral effortlessness associated with *de* and *aretē*, it does teach us that patient training can bring us to a state in which the right athletic actions become second nature.

External rewards vs internal harmony

Perhaps the intended purposes of *de* and *aretē* are different. At first glance it might seem that Hellenic *aretē* derives its worth from concrete, external rewards such as victory in war, physical beauty, even holiness – traits that translated into practical benefits for and from one's family and city. Indeed the Greek preoccupation with the aesthetics of the athletic body is rarely replicated in Chinese art or poetry, and the practical military benefit of athletic training seems more or less disconnected from Eastern discussions about virtue. Far from associating *de* with practical benefits, both Daoism and Confucianism constantly warn against the desire for praise or profit. Says Laozi, 'The worst calamity is the desire to acquire' (*Daodejing* 46, trans. Ivanhoe).

Kongzi actually distinguishes the virtuous person from the non-virtuous by explaining that the former 'understands rightness' while the latter 'understands profit' (*Analects* 4.16, trans. Slingerland). He adds that good people feel at home in goodness whereas others pursue virtue only in the hopes of profiting from it (ibid., 4.2). *De* seems to be an end in itself, whereas *aretē* is understood as a means to external rewards.

But again this distinction breaks down under scrutiny. As far back as Homer, the suggestion is made that good athletes are not always good soldiers (*Iliad*, 23.741–52). Gymnasium culture in Greece had a military function, but athletic festivals were primarily religious in nature and the *aretē* associated with athletics was valued first and foremost for its intrinsic worth.[13] Indeed it was a sign of value and dignity to engage in activities for their own sake (music and philosophy included); the mythical Prometheus's gift of divinity made such activities possible, thereby distinguishing human beings from other animals who act only as a means to survival. Although famous Greek athletes were well compensated (as are, for example, modern artists) it does not follow automatically that external reward is what motivated them.[14] Kongzi's and Laozi's chastisements against fame and acquisitiveness are less an exhortation to poverty than a warning about misplaced motivations. In that sense they reflect Socrates's shaming of the Athenians for their 'eagerness to possess as much wealth, reputation, and honours as possible' rather than virtue. He explains that virtue does not come from wealth, but that wealth and 'every other good for mankind' comes from virtue (Plato, *Apology* 29de). The primacy of virtue over such external concerns as wealth and fame is common to both Eastern and Western traditions.

Of course the reality in ancient Greece and most of the modern world (East and West) is that athletic success can lead to increased wealth and social prestige, and as a result it is often undertaken in hopes of those rewards. Similar desires no doubt motivated many of Kongzi's followers; today pilgrims actually pray and sacrifice to him at temples, hoping for success in their exams and lucrative careers. The philosophical point is that the best (and statistically more likely) benefits of athletic activities are intrinsic – specifically the cultivation of virtue or character. And, as the Stoic Epictetus explains,

pursuing virtue may bring fame and fortune in its wake, but those who pursue fame and fortune we will never achieve virtue (*Handbook* 1). Says Kongzi: 'Do not worry that you are not recognised by others; worry rather that you yourself lack ability' (*Analects* 14.30, trans. Slingerland). Mengzi adds that 'gentlemen are ashamed to have their reputation exceed what they genuinely are' (Mencius 4B18). And Laozi points out that the virtuous person acts without expectation of reward.[15] In both traditions, virtue turns out to be inward-looking. The harmonious flow of blood (*xue*) and energy (*qi*) valued in the East resembles the harmonious function of Plato's tripartite soul.[16] And the Hellenes' aesthetic appreciation of the muscular athletic body derives from their belief that such physical beauty expresses a harmonious and beautiful soul.[17] Both *de* and *aretē* are internal qualities that can be cultivated through physical movement: whether Confucian ritual (*li*),[18] Daoist martial arts,[19] or Hellenic gymnastics. In both Eastern and Western traditions, however, the desire for external reward interferes with the cultivation of virtue.

Individualism vs collectivism

One reason external concerns interfere with virtue in Eastern philosophy is the famed collectivism of that tradition. Says Mengzi, 'if righteousness is put behind and profit is put ahead, one will not be satisfied without grasping from others' (Mencius 1A1). Daoism too, despite its occasional advocacy of social withdrawal, associates virtue with benevolence. 'Sages do not accumulate,' says Laozi. 'The more they do for others, the more they have; the more they give to others the more they possess' (Laozi 81 trans. P. Ivanhoe). Echoing Buddhist metaphysics, Zhuangzi goes so far as to eliminate distinctions between oneself and the world: 'Heaven and earth were born when I was born,' he says; 'the ten thousand things and I among them are but one thing' (Zhuangzi, quoted in Waley 1939, 9). It is said that, in general, Easterners defer to group interests while Westerners affirm the primacy of the individual. The observation has even been offered as an explanation for the relative absence of sport in Asian history: activities that select and exalt a single winner while causing those defeated to 'lose face' in public seem antithetical to the community orientation of the East. At the 2008 Beijing Olympics, Western journalists expressed surprise at Chinese athletes who had the temerity to show individual joy at their victories. But are such displays evidence that modern Chinese have lost touch with their collectivist heritage? And are Western athletes as individualistic as charged?

To be sure, there is an important contrast between the loose collection of independent city states we now call ancient Greece, and the relatively stable and structured empires of ancient China. The Hellenic model of open competition in athletics, drama, rhetoric, even philosophy, has no ancient counterpart in the East. However, the function of athletics in the ancient West was to bring diverse states together and inspire cooperation, most notably in the case of the Persian Wars.[20] Furthermore, the success of individual athletes brought glory to their families and their city states, inspiring a sense of representation and service that overshadowed individual interests. Indeed Western sports have retained this communitarian function, not least by focusing on teamwork even in 'individual sports' such as athletics, cycling or gymnastics. American gymnast Kerri Strugg was lauded for vaulting on an injured leg to help her team win gold at the 1996 Olympic Games. Meanwhile the honour of representing one's club, school, city, state or country remains a prime motivator for modern athletes – Eastern and Western. We can say that participation in sports helps athletes to appreciate the political tension between individual and community – whichever side of that equation their cultural heritage favours.

Enlightened athletes rightly celebrate their individual achievement, but they should also exhibit the humility that comes from knowing that there is no such thing as *purely* individual achievement. For the ancient Greeks, this humility is reflected in the posture and expression of athletic statues. For modern athletes it is expressed in kind gestures towards their opponents and the symbolic sharing of victory with their country, team and sponsors. Again, the experience of sport ought to foster humility, not least because athletes must constantly deal with failure. And humility is foundational to both *de* and *aretē*. Says Laozi; 'Because *Dao* never considers itself great, it is able to perfect

its greatness' (*Daodejing* 34, trans. P. Ivanhoe). Likewise Socrates's wisdom derives from an awareness of his ignorance (Plato, *Apology* 21d); indeed the Greek term *philosophia* indicates the love of wisdom in contrast to the presumed possession of it. 'To know that one does not know is best,' concurs Laozi. 'Not to know but to believe that one knows is a disease. Only by seeing this disease as a disease can one be free of it' (*Daodejing* 71, trans. P. Ivanhoe). One of the greatest gifts that athletics can give is an opportunity to understand our individual imperfections and to appreciate the brevity of our moments of excellence – excellence that depends upon and should be shared with our communities. The truth is that human experience requires both individual and collectivist perspectives and sport can help us to improve our awareness of both.

Conclusion

So what are the virtues common to *de* and *aretē* cultivated by athletics? The answer is not a list of particular terms such as courage, benevolence and honesty. Just as different languages carve up the world differently by assigning names to different pieces of it, the important thing is to understand the whole rather than aligning its various parts. Let us focus on what is common to Eastern and Western conceptions of virtue. First, virtue is an excellence of the natural person available to anyone who pursues it. Second, this excellence is cultivated by training, which may involve effort and struggle, but in its maturity virtue approaches effortlessness by achieving harmony between oneself and one's world. Third, although virtue is associated with external wealth and honours, the pursuit of the latter must be guarded against because it interferes with the attainment of the former. Fourth, virtue involves both individual achievement and community engagement, thus reflecting the natural state of humanity.

Participation in athletic activities – recreationally or competitively, individually or as part of a team – has the potential to cultivate these virtuous qualities as long as it achieves the following. First, the chance to participate must be open to everyone and the rules of the sport must reflect the principle of equal opportunity – this reflects concern with the cultivation of virtue.

Second, the emphasis should be on process rather than results; both athletic and moral effortlessness come only as the result of patient training. Third, learning and personal development should always take precedence over prizes and honours in the enlightened practice of sport. Fourth, the athlete should experience both individual and collective responsibility, combining the exuberance appropriate to hard-won achievement with the humility appropriate to a realistic understanding of human interdependence. None of these considerations requires us to change sport itself, or even to downplay cultural distinctions. Rather they ask us to appreciate and emphasise those aspects of sport that provide a common foundation for ethical agreement among cultures. *Wushu* (Chinese martial arts) should not become more like boxing any more than Laozi should be more like Plato – or even more like Kongzi, for that matter. The goal is not to homogenise sport or philosophy or even conceptions of virtue. The point is to recognise that the enlightened practice of sport has the potential to cultivate aspects of virtue common to East and West, and these common values may provide a foundation for ethical interaction in this rapidly shrinking world.

Notes

1. I place 'Western' in quotes because I regard it as controversial that ancient Hellenic philosophy is characteristically Western rather than Eastern. Like the location of Hellas itself, I think it is best represented as 'between East and West'. For a full account of this thesis see Evangeliou (2006).
2. Homer, *Iliad* 6.208 and 11.784.
3. For more on the nature of *dynamis* and its connection to *aretē*, see Plato, *Republic* 477bc and 430b. Waley (1989, 33) says that *de* 'is a force or power closely akin to what we call character and contrasted with *li*, physical force'.
4. For the connection between *kinesis* and *psyche*, see Plato *Phaedrus* 245c 246a; *Laws* X, 894c; *Sophist* 254d; and Aristotle *De Anima* 413a–b, 432a–433b.
5. Plato, *Republic* 410b–412a. Plato explains that physical training is used in combination with music and poetry to balance and harmonise the rational and spirited parts of the soul. In particular, gymnastics arouses the spirited part of the soul and keeps a philosopher from becoming too weak and soft. In *Phaedrus* 246a–257a, he offers an illuminating illustration of this ideal with his

analogy of a charioteer who coaxes the best performance from his team by balancing noble and wicked horses, which represent the rational and appetitive parts of the soul. For an analysis see Reid 2007.
6. See also *Analects* 12.17: 'To "govern" [*zheng*] means to be "correct" [*zheng*]. If you set an example by being correct yourself, who will dare to be incorrect?'
7. For example, the cardinal Platonic virtues are: *eusébeia* (respect), *andreia* (courage), *sophrosyne* (self-discipline), *dikiaosyne*, (justice) and *sophia* (wisdom); Aristotle has a much longer list. In Confucius we find *ren* (humanity, benevolence), *xiao* (filial piety), *yi* (righteousness), *li* (ritual, propriety) and *chih* (wisdom).
8. For Plato's unity of the virtues see Penner (1992). For Confucius, see *Analects* 17.8: 'Loving Goodness without balancing it with a love for learning will result in the vice of foolishness. Loving wisdom without balancing it with a love for learning will result in the vice of deviance. Loving trustworthiness without balancing it with a love for learning will result in the vice of harmful rigidity. Loving uprightness without balancing it with a love for learning will result in the vice of intolerance. Loving courage without balancing it with a love for learning will result in the vice of unruliness. Loving resoluteness without balancing it with a love for learning will result in the vice of wilfulness.'
9. 'From this we can see that if one is without the heart of compassion, one is not a human. If one is without the heart of disdain, one is not a human. If one is without the heart of deference, one is not a human. If one is not without the heart of approval and disapproval, one is not a human. The heart of compassion is the sprout of benevolence. The heart of disdain is the sprout of righteousness. The heart of deference is the sprout of propriety. The heart of approval and disapproval is the sprout of wisdom. People having these four sprouts is like having four limbs. To have these four sprouts is to say of oneself that one is unable to be virtuous is to steal from oneself. To say that one's ruler is unable to be virtuous is to steal from one's ruler. In general, having these four sprouts within oneself, if one knows to fill them all out, it will be like a fire starting up, a spring breaking through! If one can merely fill them out, they will be sufficient to care for all within the Four Seas. If one merely fails to fill them out, they will be insufficient to serve one's parents' (Mencius 2A6).
10. 'The Way does not contend but is good at victory; does not speak but is good at responding; does not call but things come of their own accord' (Laozi, 73, trans. P. Ivanhoe).

11. A historical event recounted at *Symposium* 221ab.

12. Kongzi, *Analects* 2.4. The Master said: 'At 15 I set my mind upon learning; at 30, I took my place in society; at 40, I became free of doubts; at 50, I understood Heaven's Mandate (*ming*); at 60, my ear was attuned; and at 70, I could follow my heart's desire without overstepping the bounds of propriety.'

13. Indeed, Plato has Socrates compare as 'counterparts' proper engagement in philosophic argument with proper participation in physical training at *Republic* 539d. His point here is that those who use argument for the 'sport' of defeating others rather than the higher goal of finding truth and leading a virtuous life, are akin to those who practice athletics for *philonikia*, the love of victory, rather than the pursuit of personal excellence or *aretē*. Plato feels that the former are not worthy of the name 'philosopher' – are the latter worthy of the name Olympian?

14. Prizes are inherent in the very idea of athletics, which shares its etymological root with the word for prize: *athlon*. But prizes can take forms other than the monetary and social benefits derided by the philosophers. In any case, participation in prize games is compatible with the intrinsic motivations advocated in both traditions.

15. 'To produce without possessing;/To act with no expectation of reward;/To lead without lording over;/Such is enigmatic Virtue!' (Laozi 51, trans. P. Ivanhoe).

16. For the Eastern idea of internal harmony, see Inoue 1999, 165. For Plato's theory of the tripartite soul, see *Republic*, especially book IV.

17. In fact, those fat Buddha bellies may do the same thing. Westerners tend to associate thought with the brain, while the ancient Chinese located thought in the middle of a body, associating it with the 'heart-mind' and sensations experienced in the belly. See Waley 1939, 44.

18. See Brownell 1995, 125: 'They make use of a principle recognized by Confucius fifteen hundred years before Bourdieu: when structured body movements are assigned symbolic and moral significance, and are repeated often enough, they generate a moral orientation toward the world that is habitual because the body as a mnemonic device serves to reinforce it.'

19. Daoist martial artists use movement to cultivate *qi*, the 'floodlike energy' Zhuangzi takes to be

source of virtue: 'Zhaungzi' in Ivanhoe and Van Norden 2001, 365.

20. For more on the political function of the ancient Olympic Games, see Reid 2006.

References

Aristotle. 1984. *Complete works, vol. 2*, ed. Jonathan Barnes. Princeton, NJ: Princeton University Press.

Brownell, Susan. 1995. *Training the body for China*. Chicago, IL: University of Chicago Press.

Epictetus. 1983. *The handbook*, trans. Nicholas P. White. Indianapolis, IN: Hackett.

Evangeliou, Christos. 2006. *Hellenic philosophy: Origin and character*. Burlington, VT: Ashgate.

Homer. 1990. *The Iliad*, trans. Robert Fagles. New York: Penguin. 1990.

Inoue, Akio. 1999. Critique of modern Olympism: A voice from the East. In *Sports – the East and the West*, edited by G. Pfister and L. Yueye. Sant Agustin, Germany: Academia Verlag: 163–7.

Ivanhoe, P. and B. Van Norden, eds. 2001. *Readings in classical Chinese philosophy*, 2nd edn. Indianapolis, IN: Hackett.

Lao-Tsu. 2003. *Tao de Ching*, trans. S. Addiss and S. Lombardo. Indianapolis, IN: Hackett.

Laozi. 2001. 'Daodejing', trans. P. Ivanhoe. In *Readings in classical Chinese philosophy*, 2nd edn, edited by P. Ivanhoe and B. Van Norden. Indianapolis, IN: Hackett.

Mencius. 2001. 'Mengzi', trans. B. Van Norden. In *Readings in classical Chinese philosophy*, 2nd edn., edited by P. Ivanhoe and B. Van Norden. Indianapolis, IN: Hackett.

Penner, Terry. 1992. The unity of virtue. In *Essays on the philosophy of Socrates*, edited by H. Benson. New York: Oxford University Press: 162–84.

Plato. 1997. *Complete works*, ed. John Cooper. Indianapolis, IN: Hackett.

Reid, Heather L. 2006. Olympic sport and its lessons for peace. *Journal of the Philosophy of Sport* 33 (2): 205–13.

——. 2007. Sport and moral education in Plato's *Republic*. *Journal of the Philosophy of Sport* 34 (2): 160–75.

Slingerland, Edward, (Trans. 2003). *Confucius: The Analects*. Indianapolis, IN: Hackett.

Waley, Arthur. 1939. *Three ways of thought in ancient China*. Stanford, CA: Stanford University Press.

The project of a moral laboratory; and particularism

Graham McFee

The moral imperative sometimes (and, I would claim, rightly) located within sport is often not a *direct* consequence of the rules or laws of particular sports: this fact is recognized when appeal is made, not to those rules themselves, but to the *spirit* of the rules, or to considerations of fair play, or some such. [...] the acquiring of principles is prior to, and the basis for, (appropriate) learning of rules. As Dworkin (1978: 115) puts it, the principles provide a 'gravitational force' operative within the rule. Discussion there put due weight on the moral metaphors of justice – 'level playing field', 'fair play' and such like – in their use in the specifics of sport. This chapter will say a little more – still sketchily – concerning two of the most important moral notions here, notions used to ground *moral metaphors* in general use: *fair play* and *level playing-field*. Doing so will offer a stronger version of our connection of sport to the moral.

There is a weaker and a stronger thesis here. By the weaker, the kinds of moral engagement required of rule-following – understood in our particularist fashion – indicate a moral imperative for sport sufficient to justify a weak version of the *moral laboratory*: rule-observance takes place in sport when rule-observance as such is, at bottom, a moral injunction on those engaged in the relevant activities. The constraints here were met simply when appeal to underlying principles was seen as *moral* appeal to *moral* principles: the moral dimension integral to sport was visible when the principles guiding the discretionary judgements of umpires or referees were recognized as moral principles.

But by the stronger thesis, deployed here, the *content* of sporting rules also has a moral dimension, visible in the moral use of sporting metaphors: in particular, *fair play* and *level playing-field*. Then learning to deploy the principles, and the moral metaphors they support, might offer a picture of the value of sport. For, in learning the exact application of these key metaphors, by learning how to make sense of these ideas *as they apply in particular sports*, one is at the same time learning the general moral principles. Positively, these notions indicate two major constraints on justice: namely, the ideas of equal treatment and of equality of initial condition. But, negatively, *all* sports cannot realistically be treated in such justice-related terms: those notions will be central to the mastery of only *some* sports at *some* levels. Hence, they will be learned in learning 'how to go on' rule-followingly – and to abide by the principles (in Dworkin's sense) – only in those sports. Or so I shall urge. So this reading of the moral imperative of sport will support ascription to the moral laboratory of only some sport on some occasions.

However, both readings of the moral imperative idea share a problem: how to relate the general (the rule) to the particular (the action learnt or performed) – since '[t]he general cannot take the place of the particular'. Or, more perspicuously, how the general notions of *morality* can grow from the particular events (and notions) of *sport*.

[…] value of sport must be importantly different from that ascribed to, say, soap operas – which, while informative as a 'cultural lens' (Beckles 1995: 1) for society, are of no redeeming value intrinsically. The argument is in four main parts:

- First, it presents an abstract account of what would be needed for a *moral* picture of the intrinsic value of sport (compare McFee 2000c). One virtue of this procedure is that – once again – there is a formal argument to be considered: here, the student can attempt to deploy arguments in favour of each premise (or against them), reconsider the *logic* of the argument (and how, if at all, it might be augmented), and consider what should follow from the argument. (Formalizations make these processes easier for the [relative] beginner.)
- Second, the argument elaborates a picture of moral judgement and moral reasoning (a particularist or contextualist one) on which to defend an account of sport such as that sketched above.
- Third, it develops that account as it applies within sport, showing moral issues made *concrete* by sporting situations.
- Fourth, and finally, it asks what might be said of the value of (any) sport not justified in this way. Certainly the earlier explanations could not apply to any such sport. Central here (once again) is the contrast between intrinsic and extrinsic justifications of sport – or intrinsic and extrinsic attributions of the *value* of sport.

The argument concludes both that extrinsic justifications leave a 'sport-shaped hole' in one's theory – an accusation that might be levelled against much sociology of sport (especially the sociology of sporting consumption) and that an account of the intrinsic value of sport is sustainable.

Sport's moral dimension?

A moral imperative within sport might be identified in many ways. But, if our aim here is to explore the stronger thesis identified above, we must make sense of sport as intrinsically valuable. How? Part of the motivation of the Olympic Games – in the rhetoric of Pierre de Coubertin at least – turned on just such *moral* possibilities of sport: that participation in sport was (potentially) morally educative. So this might offer a model. For example, de Coubertin (2000: 537) writes that:

> wise and peaceful internationalism will make …
> [its] way into the new stadium. There … [it]
> will glorify the honour and selflessness that will
> enable athletics to carry out its task of moral
> betterment and social peace …

This idea of sport as morally educative had, of course, a developed history, to which de Coubertin appealed, in the athleticist rhetoric of the English public schools – with two fundamental theses emphasizing the (supposed) moral benefits of participation in sport. As expressed by Peter McIntosh (1979: 27): '[t]he first was that competitive sport … had an ethical basis, and the second was that training in moral behaviour on the playing field was transferable to the world beyond'.

If correct, such a position has the *potential* to justify a quite widespread concern with sport, for it claims to identify a valued characteristic intrinsic to sport. I am drawn to such a *general* idea of sport as having some such morally educative potential – indeed, I do not see how else some general (intrinsic) value might be ascribed to sport.

But is such moral justification for sport needed? Does its place (its social role) as a leisure activity not provide all the justification that is required? This is no justification at all, because it is no intrinsic justification. If one wants to justify *sport*, that justification must rely on features of sport, as such – hence on intrinsic features – rather than on features which, while explaining concern (say, 'I do it for the money'), fail to explain that concern in terms of sport's features: features *extrinsic* to sport could be in place for something entirely without merit – as one might regard soap operas as entirely without merit and yet not deny their importance viewed as commodities. Moreover, those who regard sport as 'our most sophisticated and sensitive cultural lens' (Beckles 1995: 1) use sport to investigate society – as this lens metaphor makes plain. Although both legitimate and rewarding, this is not the only interest that one might have in, say, cricket (Beckles's example), or in sport more generally.

This discussion identifies *a sport-shaped hole* in those social theories which take sport as, say, opiate of the masses, prison of measured time, force in the civilizing process.... The sociology of sports consumption can tell us everything about sport *except* what makes it sport – for the terms of the (sociological) discussion apply as well to activities other than sport as they do to sporting activities.

Suppose we characterize sport in Britain as John Hargreaves (1986: 209) does, as 'implicated in the achievement, maintenance and development of bourgeois hegemony in British society during the last century and a half' (Sugden and Bairner 1993: 133).

Then we use terms in respect of sporting events which also have application outside of sport. Or, again, Paul Willis (1973), writing about women's place in sport, simply applies insights which – were they sound – would apply equally to women's place in the world of work (from where in fact, Willis developed them). Broadly sociological concerns of this sort are extrinsic to sport: they can (at best) explain human motivations in these general ways. But none of these remarks bears on the *distinctive* nature or role of sports (or games). To see this, we need only recognize that a related but non-game ritual activity (a) might be *mistaken* for sport, and (b) would be explained in this way as adequately as sport was.[1] So this mode of explanation is extrinsic to sport itself: the features it mentions are not features essential to sport. For we have seen the best that can be made of a 'purpose within the game': and that was *intrinsic*. Thus, if we compare these kinds of explanation with an (imaginary) theory which had an intrinsic connection to the world of sport, we could see clearly what the expression 'sport-shaped hole in one's theory amounts to here (compare 'art-shaped hole' [McFee 1992: 294–7]).

Yet the first athleticist thesis – that competitive sport had an ethical basis – seems just false: sport neither necessarily promotes ethical performance on the field nor necessarily teaches ethical principles. Even those formalists who take merely playing sport according to the rules to be ethically approvable behaviour should admit that the rules must be actualized in practice. Yet the behaviour must depend on the rules, not simply conform to them. And no rule uniquely circumscribes the behaviour it requires or prohibits, as we acknowledged: rather, any rule's application to behaviour involves an exercise of judgement, of a kind a referee or umpire might make. Practical sense must be made of these (formal) rules. For any activity, appeal to rules *alone* cannot be sufficient. There remains a gap between sporting activity and the moral (McFee 2000b: 173–4): merely participating in sport might or might not actualize the rules in a morally-relevant way. But one need not (indeed, if I am right, cannot) claim that sport, *always* has this impact: rather, it might in certain cases. Even *that* connection of sport to the moral sphere is sufficient to warrant taking sport seriously.

But how might, this educational potential for sport be argued for? In reply, I will present a research agenda of mine – motivating both the general agenda and its specific premises.

Explanations and qualifications

It is worth entering three notes of caution and a fourth in explanation.

First, my reference to *the moral* must be understood as to the *sphere of* morality, rather than simply to what is (morally) good. Nevertheless, such a connection to the sphere of morality could only be sustained if, at least *some* of the time, the outcome was right-thinking or right-action. For we only recognize concerns as moral – rather than, say, prudential[2] – by exploring obligations, and the like, investigating how they are (appropriately) explained; and finding morally-relevant explanations must, in some cases, mark-out at least right-thinking. Still, there is no suggestion here that *all* connections with sport will *always* have a *positive* moral impact.

Second, morality has a complex relation to questions of human harm – better, to explaining some of the ways humans can *be* harmed (see Parry [1998] for some connection to sport). Here, I simply put that issue to one side, accepting Konrad Lorenz's view that human sports aim 'to ascertain which ... [team] ... is the stronger, *without hurting the weaker*' (Lorenz 1966: 94; orginal emphasis). For this locates *our* issue – although we might still want to highlight the degree of ear-biting and cheek-breaking in the sporting world that is thereby put aside!

Third, potentials are not always achieved: suppose some IOC members are scoundrels, self-serving and corrupt (Jennings 1996: 301–4). We should not conclude that the Olympic Ideal therefore does not exist – although we might wonder about its realizability! Here, the *execution* of the project is flawed, not the project itself. So the view explored here accepts a morally educative potential for sport, even if that is neither inevitable, in ways de Coubertin seems to have thought, nor to be understood as generalizing quite as sometimes hoped (or idealized).

In this context, corruption in sport's practice intersects with our concerns; here, exemplified via the Olympic movement. Suppose that the process of selection of a host city for the Games has been corrupt, at least in the last few years – with Salt Lake City a clear example (Jennings and Sambrook 2000: 19–48). Still, did this really disadvantage the athletes/competitors? If it did not, perhaps the values of the sporting event itself were not (much) compromised. Salt Lake City might offer facilities at least as good as those of its rivals. Then, no damage was done to the sport itself – the damage was to the context, not to the competition! This sort of corruption is regrettable (and, ideally, should be eliminated). But it does not tarnish the Olympic *values* as such, merely their implementation in practice.

The other extreme might be exemplified by the boxing finals in Seoul: if even half of what Andrew Jennings (1996: 79–92; Jennings and Sambrook 2000: 205–8, 212–16) describes is correct, these events involved unfair judging. Here the corruption operates in the sporting practices themselves. Again, the corruption is to be regretted (and, ideally, eliminated) but now the task is more pressing: any virtues that accrue to *sporting* contests cannot accrue to these – they are *not sporting* (in the other sense of the word) because not fair. (This case is of

systematic and deliberate lack of fairness, not merely occasional error.)

The issue of drug-taking might be somewhat intermediate. In part, and like the initial case, Olympic rhetoric does not match practice: former IOC President Samaranch says that, 'The message is very clear. This is a new fight against doping' (quoted Sullivan 2000: 55), but proscribed drugs are taken at the Olympics. An Olympic movement genuinely committed to the elimination of such activities would not act as this one has (Jennings 1996: 232–49, 298–9; Jennings and Sambrook 2000: 290–306): but, again, that is corrupt practice only. But (like our other case) there is an unfairness here too: some athletes will be punished for drug-taking while, for others, the documents necessary to identify their 'B' samples will have been shredded in error – in Seoul 1988 (Jennings 1996: 241–3) and, perhaps, Atlanta 1996 (Mackay 1996: 2)! If these athletes *were* guilty (and, after all, their 'A' samples were ruled positive), they 'got away with it'. Here too, though, the IOC should be more vigilant, and perhaps differently motivated.[3]

Whatever their detail, such cases indicate different obligations which (one might think) have not been met. But every case suggests something *remediable* by a more scrupulous Committee, more consistent in the understanding and application of its own rules, and more attentive to the demands of natural justice.

The fourth element returns us to our starting point in connecting sport to the moral sphere. The rhetoric of sport is replete with metaphors employed in general ethical discussion – our examples: the idea of fair play and of a level playing field. These reflect ethical concerns *within* sport. And de Coubertin's amateurism (whatever its faults in theory or practice) was fuelled by concerns with sport done 'for its own sake', and with fairness: with behaving fairly (appropriately, justly) towards others ... here, in the sporting context.

Yet what exactly do these two metaphors – 'fair play' and 'level playing field' – offer to sports practice: what precisely do they suggest or proscribe? Also, what does some root metaphor tell us about moral situations more generally – what would it be to require fair play or a level playing field in one's business dealings, say, or one's interactions with others?

Our initial concerns are with the sporting case. So let us briefly consider each of these examples:

- *Fair play*: not fairness, notice, which might relate to the starting point of the contest (and is picked up in the other metaphor) but with the manner of the contest, having implications for how to interpret the rules as they relate to the manner of playing. For example, if there is no rule specifically against taking a knife into the rugby scrum, but there are rules about what it *is* permissible to take onto the field, then other questions are raised. Here, a principle on which to base, say, refereeing decisions is more helpful than a list of what is permitted, since it offers help with as-yet unconfronted cases.
- *Level playing field*: we roughly understand the root metaphor, and the reason for it: that neither side should be unfairly advantaged initially – this is also the basis for, say, the practice of changing ends at half-time: that inbuilt advantage be equalized.

So, as suggested, the primary concern of each is with considerations of justice: with getting one's just deserts (on the day!).

At the level of *principles* here, one thinks first of equality, and of fair treatment. But I am drawn to the idea that, in practice, *fairness* (in this sense) is a 'trouser-concept' (Austin 1962: 70) – that *unfair* 'wears the trousers'. That is, we do not really decide that such-and-such is fair; rather, we conclude that it is *not unfair*. That is to say, the *content* of fairness in a particular sporting context is wholly given by what is proscribed, explicitly or implicitly. Then arguments will always turn on whether or not such-and-such is unfair, in relation to the specific rules of *this* sport, or some more general context of principles or *ethoi*. As with *complete* (Baker and Hacker 1980: 79–81; we arrive at what is fair by contrast. So really no sharp account of *fair play* is possible. Rather, what is not unfair is thereby acknowledged as fair. And even when we formulate the issue differently – that is, we ask, 'Is doing such-and-such *fair*?' – that question is given content by the idea of the unfairness of behaving differently.

The relevant comparison (Austin 1962: 62–77) is with the term 'real': we know what

the *real* colour of her hair is only by recognizing (and contrasting) the ways its colour might not be *real*: say, by being dyed, by being in such-and-such light, by now reflecting the ravages of age. Any of these applies differently from, say, the real colour of a curtain or the real shape of a cat. All in all, no neat account can be offered here: the matter is contextual.

We can sketch some broad contours: (a) the rules determine what is and what is not unfair, by articulating the kinds of (un)fairness involved; (b) this relation to the rules (and to rule-following) precludes there being a full-stop here, since there is no set of behaviours *absolutely* ruled out;[4] no sense of *all* here (c) the principles we can extract from the cases we confront, or which, we learn in learning the sport, allow us to make sense of – and perhaps adjudicate on – future cases.

So, when we ask if such-and-such is fair, we are really asking whether it is not unfair (see above). But this is another way to recognize that a definition of fair play, accurate for all past occasions, could never be useful here.[5] And neither would a parallel account of fairness.

A good example here: the regulations for 'permitted' drugs – are they fair? What is needed is equal treatment, in a respect where – at present – that treatment is not equal. For instance, those competitors who abide by a sports federation's regulations, when (say) the Olympic ones are more lax, will effectively be penalized – this occurred for Valium and Librium in the modern pentathlon at the 1976 Olympic Games: the drugs (agreed to be advantageous in the shooting phase of the discipline) were used by *some* competitors and, since they were permitted by Olympic regulations (at the time), such competitors gained an advantage over those who stuck to the regulations of the International Modern Pentathlon Union, which had banned the use of these drugs (Wallechinsky 1988: 368). Equally abiding by the more stringent rules of FIFA (the International Soccer Federation) for the use of ephedrine (a common component of medication for colds) would at one time have disadvantaged players in the NBA, where this substance was not forbidden (Tamburrini 2000: 36). So the various athletes were not starting on equal terms. Still, at least we see fairness if all the competitors from a particular sport are constrained in the *same* way during a particular competition.

We have seen how the various sports should be regarded as underpinned by various principles (especially those concerning fairness, in both the ways discussed above). But what inequalities do not contradict these principles, and the concern with fairness they embody?

Real equality is not to be expected: this point is made eloquently in an advertisement, featuring John McEnroe as a commentator, of an 'endless' tennis match between Pete Sampras and Andre Agassi, because both are evenly matched. One point continues for months, McEnroe grows a beard ... and finally the point is a let: it must be replayed! Here, you might think: they were *too* equal. We go by: 'May the best man win' – that is, there is deemed to be a *better man*, on the day.

Rather, *equality of opportunity* is taken as meaning that certain specific 'advantages' have been ruled out (in principle): for example, certain kinds of performance-enhancing drugs (and, if we cannot make some analysis stick, there is no reason for, nor principle behind, such an exclusion). Why, therefore, are they excluded? Without answering this difficult question, consider two specific issues:

1. 'Natural inequalities' – consider, as an analogy, a mathematics test: I find myself up against Isaac Newton – neither of us is advantaged, beyond Newton's natural advantage. Isn't this just like, for instance, boxers of different weights being separated? How *far* should we take this idea? What about limiting matches between basketball teams of different (average) heights? Or, perhaps, basketball teams of different skills?
2. Inequalities of resource – you have the fine shoes, and I do not: or the fine training regime, or the funding to not have to work full time, or the funding to not have to work ... etc. etc. – lots of (different?) issues.

So even the *detail* of these metaphors is not clear. Still their motivations is: and that is enough – we cannot expect any fuller account. Any answer would need to be contextualized. Of course, many issues concerning the nature of fairness are not explored here, although some are helpfully discussed in Loland (2002: 71–6 especially). But these remarks should be seen as offering helpful hints and reminders for particular discussions, were we to consider them.

Finally, throughout this chapter, the focus is on *competitive sports*. But what about non-competitive sports (including my own favourite, sub-aqua)? Given my starting point in this chapter and the fact that they are not in the Olympics, they can be ignored. Further, they do not provide opportunities for fair play or the requirement for a level playing field – although they may well offer other moral opportunities, not considered here. So such sports can be excluded from this consideration, as being unsuitable.

In summary, these two metaphors – of fair play and level playing field – are (among) the things ethics gets from sport: I suggest that *a* value in sport resides precisely here – the metaphors or slogans available in sporting contexts, and sport provides concrete instantiations of relevant principles. Moreover, this possibility offers some detail to *an* account of sport's value.

The argument

In summary, and presented hypothetically, the argument is this:

1. *If* sport is valuable, of its nature or intrinsically;
2. *If* such value has some connection to the moral (as it must, for Olympism);
3. *If* moral judgements are essentially *particular*;
4. *If* sport can present the particularization of (moral?) cases; and
5. *If* such cases concretize moral metaphors, such as 'fair play', 'level playing field'; then
6. Sport might function as a moral laboratory.

In explaining *how* sport might function in the moral sphere, I offer both *reason* to think that it does and a *basis* for investigation.

Now, any argument may be contested only either by contesting the premises or by disputing that the conclusion follows from those premises – that is, by disputing the logic. Those who find this conclusion uncongenial, or even those who think it wrong, must show what is amiss with the argument that leads to that conclusion, in one of these ways.

As to the logic of the argument – that the conclusion follows from those premises – it is easy to see how that conclusion depends on those premises. Even if the argument is not formally valid, it should be accepted as compelling. Making the formulation impeccable would make it both a lot longer and considerably more complex. But surely this argument is sufficiently transparent at present, as we can see if we make the assumptions that the premises articulate.

From the identification, in the first premise, of a *value* for sport, we recognize that value as moral (second premise) and then characterize moral value as particular (third premise). Once these premises are granted, it follows that sport *has* a moral value of a particularized kind (like other moral value). Now premises four and five contribute the idea that this (particularized) value might be exemplified in sporting situations, and hence might be learned from them. And this suggests how sport might function as a site of moral exploration, investigation and education. So granting the truth of the premises *does* (at first blush) guarantee the conclusion's truth; or, at least, give us reason to adopt it.

However, before saying something in explanation – and in justification – of each premise in turn, notice that finding my argument flawed is not equivalent to finding my conclusion flawed: that other arguments might yet be offered. But in that situation one has no *reason* to accept my conclusion – as one would have if the argument were sound; further, I would not be considering *this* argument if another were obvious.

Investigation of the premises

We now turn to the question of whether the truth of the premises should indeed be granted. Here I urge simply that we have reason to adopt each. Indeed, in part, this is a research agenda precisely because the truth of each premise requires investigation. Were the conditional importance of the argument granted, such investigation becomes justified.

Let us, therefore, consider each premise, reminding ourselves what it contributes to the argument, and asking if it seems plausible.

The first two premises: sport as morally valuable

The first premise picks out a condition to be met if sport deserves the importance I, and others, claim attaches to it. Moreover, were this premise denied, some other starting point for the value of sport must be offered: but if, as I have urged, such a justification must be an *intrinsic* one, it will come to roughly this one. For value attaching to the interpersonal is typically moral, at least in the most generous sense. That is what the second premise asserts, in taking the value at issue to be a *moral* value. Since central moral principles concern fairness (and therefore justice), if the potential value of sport is moral value, considering sport here is indeed considering a sense of justice as inculcated. [...] Although the truth of these premises is not *demonstrated*, I have done enough to make them more plausible than their respective denials.

Premise three: moral judgement as essentially particular

My main point here will be served if it is granted that we learn moral concepts in particular cases: learn what lying is, and what is wrong with it, by considering cases of lying, in the real world or in fictions; and that even if we are sometimes presented with general abstract rules ('thou shalt not kill'), we must make sense of them in concrete contexts, applying them to the situations in which we find ourselves.

Yet how does one *learn* moral concepts, learn to *use* them and to *understand* them? The insight of particularism is that, in learning morality, one does not learn a set of principles (only?), much less a set of rules – rather, one learns to make moral judgements; and one learns that first in specific contexts (Dancy 1993: 56–7). Since any such learning must take place in *some* particular situation, one might hope for learning-situations, *not* ones of maximum risk to life, limb, sanity or world peace.

The cases here give us an initial reason to adopt this particularist conception of moral judgement: give it the balance of probabilities. Two misconceptions might seem to speak against it: first the view of morality as a system of *rules* – we have highlighted the mistakes here, namely that the application of rules cannot itself be a matter of rules. So something other than rules is required. Second, the assumption of a tension between particularism and moral principles; but, as we will see, particularism is only opposed to *substantive* moral principles, not to moral principles *as such*. For such substantive moral principles are of precisely the kind claimed to apply clear in one situation, because applying in another. On the contrary, for particularists, 'no set of [substantive] principles will succeed in generating answers to questions about what to do in particular cases' (Dancy 1993: 56).

Our discussion of 'thou shalt not kill' highlighted the difficulties here. The insight is 'that the moral relevance of a property in a new case cannot be predicted from its relevance elsewhere' (Dancy 1993: 57). Here 'predicted' is the key term: for, of course, we will agree – once the plan of action is decided upon – that this case *instantiates* the principle. But we could not know this before the fact.

Suppose such a particularized character is granted for sporting value. But, then, how is that value to be learned, or explored?

Premises four and five: particularization through cases exemplifying sporting situations

Premises four and five together sketch our solution. Crucial here is the central moral role of *justice*. Dworkin (1985: 219) rightly calls 'the practice of worrying about what justice really is ... the single most important social practice we have' (my order). And that is just what, is happening here. To begin with premise five, the metaphors of fair play and level playing field give only the abstract form of, say, the complaint against unfairness, or the requirement for equal consideration: sporting situations make these considerations concrete (in line with the particularism of premise three).

Sporting contests always admit the possibility of someone not participating fairly (that is, contravening the fair play condition) or of participation from a position of unfair initial disadvantage (that is, contravening the level playing field condition) – this seems built in to the possibility of competitive activity. So a framework for any practice worthy of the name

'sport' may support these two metaphors. That the contextualizations here are indeed moral is suggested both by the prevalence of the sporting metaphors in moral contexts and by reflection on the (typical) experience of learning sporting principles. This usually happens in *appropriate* teaching of the sporting activity: what one learns is not – and could not be – just a formulation of the principle (a principle-formulation) but how to *behave* in accordance with the principle: for instance, how to manifest fair play (which is, of course, no guarantee that one will then actually play fairly). In effect, then, principles are taught when rules are properly taught – where the term 'properly' makes just that point! In teaching the rules of a game (for example, cricket), a teacher sensitive to the principles might inculcate those principles too. As we recognized, we at least *know* how to teach such principles, even if we cannot *say* how. For we learnt them in this way. Thus the model is of abstract principles learned from (and in) concrete instances in sport, then applied to concrete moral situations. Taken together, these warrant my commitment to the moral possibilities of sport.

The argument's conclusion: the moral laboratory

Sport, then, has the possibility of providing us with just such concrete cases where we can behave fairly (or justly) – examples of fair play – and also cases where inappropriate initial advantage can be taken (cases where there *isn't* a level playing field): hence, sport offers people a chance to operate with these concepts, and to act on them; to use them in discussion and to have others offer them. It also offers opportunities to confront others *not* acting on them – and, even, to fail to act on them oneself. In this way, one can explore the contours of morally-relevant possibilities. This is what I mean in speaking of sport as a *moral laboratory*.[6]

Moreover, sport has – typically – at least two main advantages as a learning site over encountering moral problems in one's life more generally. Both relate to the essential nature of sport. First, sport typically has a set of *codified* rules: in this way, the rules (and the manner both of implementing and of changing them) are more straightforward than (other?) moral rules – which is not to say, of course, that their implementation is straightforward: judgement is still required. Second, the consequences of *failing* to behave in line with the rules (etc.) are typically much less severe: no-one ends up dead or maimed, for example – even if this does happen sometimes. So sport offers the possibility of learning judgement with less (than usual) consequences, less risked.

Suppose these ideas are accepted: do they achieve what is required? The original de Coubertin position, drawn from athleticism, urged both the moral character of sport and the transferability of that morality to the rest of one's life. Our particularist account of morality might accord *a* place within sporting situations for (the possibility of) moral choice – not the kind of *essential* moral education de Coubertin believed in, but more plausible for that. So we have a limited defence of this thesis.

Yet its very particularism might seem to undermine the usefulness of such a conclusion: for in the moral laboratory crucially I learn *sport-morality*, rather than something which automatically generalizes. Yet Olympism's justification lay in the possibility of a quite *general* good – one not circumscribed by sport. But, as we shall see, our particularism is not a kind of 'no-transfer' thesis. For, if in learning moral judgement one learns 'how to go on', one is *automatically* learning notions which might, in principle, have application elsewhere; and, since every later application will typically be *different* (from a particularist perspective), learning the concepts at all amounts to the first steps in learning to apply them *outside* familiar cases.

Particularism and moral judgement

It is worth saying a little more about a particularist account of moral judgement, and the connection of particularism both to morality (on the one hand), and to the generality of rules and principles in Dworkm's sense (on the other).

Then, the general thesis of *particularism* has two aspects: first, the particularity of moral judgement, noted above, where 'the moral relevance of a property in a new case

cannot be predicted from its relevance elsewhere' (Dancy 1993: 57).

As we recognized, particularism is opposed to *substantial* moral principles, not to moral principles *as such*. The point is just that we could not know this principle (in its application *here*) before the fact. More recently, Dancy (2000: 132) has made the point explicit in terms of two principles:

- That what is a reason in one situation may alter or lose its polarity in another;
- The way in which the reasons here presently combine with each other is not necessarily determinable in any simply additive way.

So that one cannot infer from the fact that such-and-such was a reason for so-and-so judgement in *this* case that it will be in *that* case.

A second, related aspect of particularism is that general rules (exemplified by, say, the Ten Commandments) cannot be efficacious, since there is room for a decision or choice as to what behaviour the rule prescribes or proscribes in this situation. Here, Martha Nussbaum (1990: 38) rightly highlights the priority of 'particular perception … over fixed rules'. Even general abstract rules ('thou shalt not kill') must be made sense of in concrete contexts, applying them to the situations in which we find ourselves.

This can be difficult. A young soldier who thinks that, say, this general rule against killing might be rendered inapplicable by, for instance, his duty to his country in a just war or an order from his commanding officer, might revise that conclusion, faced with a real, live enemy soldier. Equally, he might not! Clearly, one would have liked (and hoped) to resolve such a question before one was in front of the enemy's bayonet. How might moral judgements be learned with less risked?

One cannot simply appeal to one's rule ('thou shalt not kill'): for what does that rule amount to in *this* situation? Knowing the rule alone does not look promising here: that is just a *formalization*, to be applied (where possible) in the new situations faced. Is killing still as *absolutely* prohibited in this new context? Or was the prohibition never *that* absolute? The rule alone cannot decide. Equally, further rules will not help – on pain of the regress. And this was part of our earlier rejection of formalism. As we put

355

it before, the insight of particularism is that, in learning morality, one does not learn a set of principles (only?), much less a set of rules – rather, one learns to make moral judgements; and one learns that first in specific contexts.

The particularism here stresses the specificity of questions and answers; differing little in upshot to the previous contextualist ideas. Dancy (1993: 64) offers a version of this sort of particularist picture:

> our account of the person on whom we can rely to make sound moral judgements is not very long. Such a person is someone who gets it right case by case. To be so consistently successful, we need a broad range of sensitivities, so that no relevant feature escapes us, and we do not mistake its relevance either. But that is all there is to say on the matter. To have the relevant sensitivities just is to be able to get things right case by case. The only remaining question is how we get into this enviable state. And the answer is that for us it is probably too late .... moral education is the key; for those who are past educating, there is no real remedy.

The counter-thought might be that this view lacks a prior appeal to moral psychology. For me, the absence of a moral psychology is a virtue of the position: 'In the beginning was the deed'.

Nor should we see particularism as closing the book on all generality. After all, what is the point of consideration of what others ought to do *here* and *now*? The issue is raised in an amusing way by Allan Gibbard (2002: 52), in terms of the 'Jack and Jill' nursery rhyme:

> Jack and Jill need water ... but the hill is slippery. I say that Jack ought not to go up the hill, but you disagree. What's the issue between us? ... It's not an issue of what to do in your case or in mine, but somehow in Jack's, in Jack's shoes.

Still, the issue is not simply one of the here and now. If it were, there would be no point in any speculation as to what he *should* have done, by us – or even by Jack: 'Why ... should Jack rethink his decision, when the moving finger has writ and he can't unbreak his crown?' (Gibbard 2002: 52). Gibbard's answer seems the right one for Jack; and, in that way, explains both that present reflection bears on future

cases but that it does not do so by creating an immutable ride:

> Jack reconsiders after the fact because he will face such choices again; he is engaged in a kind of rehearsal for future choices. ... Jack's exact circumstances include everything about him, and our question is what to do if one is he – and thus like him in every respect in which we differ.
>
> (Gibbard 2002: 52–3)

But we will never be in precisely that situation: nor could we be – we are not Jack. Yet neither can Jack himself, at least if he has the capacity to remember (and perhaps profit from) his past. So the argument suggests that what is learned from thinking about Jack's case, and his decisions, may be brought to bear on our (rather different) cases, and our decisions. But, since the cases are different, what is learned will need to be *applied* in this new situation. That cannot simply amount to the mechanical application of a rule. Or, perhaps better, if we think of it as *the application of a rule*, that will be because we recognize that all rules require such application – that it is never purely mechanical.

This particularist conception of moral judgement is both a specific thesis in philosophy and highly contentious. Still, the cases here make it attractive. So this position is at least arguable. Here, Nussbaum offers considerations against generality, commenting on 'the need for fine-tuned *concreteness* in ethical attention and judgement' (Nussbaum 1990: 38), and sketching key elements of 'the priority of the particular' (Nussbaum 1990: 37). Three aspects making problematic any general account, 'fixed in advance of the particular case' (Nussbaum 1990: 38), are:

- New and unexpected features;
- The context-embeddedness of relevant features;
- Ethical relevance of particular persons and relationships.

The first two are familiar from our discussion of particularity in relation to rules. Moreover, the second, and perhaps the third, are characteristics of my general account of understanding while recongnizing the first is part of its motivation. For why is greater generality either desirable or attainable? Indeed, the priority of argumentative strategies wherein we look (or hope) for persons in exactly similar circumstances is disputed, as in our hypothetical case above (from Gibbard). Of course, in one sense, it is trivially true that *if* I am in exactly the same circumstances as another person, and like them in all the other ways, I *should* act as that person should have – this is trivialized by taking 'exactly the same circumstances' in this powerful fashion. In reality, the difficulty lies in what might be relevantly similar here. To reuse an example (see McFee 2000a: 125), the Meryl Streep character in the film *Sophie's Choice* (1982) has to choose which of her two children will be adopted by a Nazi family (and therefore be likely to survive), which child goes to the concentration camp and likely death. In the film, the choice Sophie makes is *explicable* – we see the predicament of a Jewish woman and her children, during the Second World War, in Hitler's Europe, and so on. We recognize the pressures that require her to choose in this ghastly situation. Yet is Sophie's actual choice *inevitable*? Might we have chosen differently? That question has a point only for someone in a relevantly similar situation. But which are the *relevant* similarities? What is the weight of the woman's being, say, Jewish, given that Hitler's Europe was horrible for gypsies also? What is the weight of its being the *mother* who faces the terrible choice rather than, for instance, (two different cases) the father or an aunt? (And so on, for various aspects of the case.) There are no clear answers here – we might understand what 'caused' *this* woman in *this* situation to make *this* choice; but have we a basis for moving beyond such specificities? Suppose that, discussing the film, I say, 'In her position, I would have done the same.' This is plausibly true, as long as I am being honest, and so on. Yet, at best, this is made true by the way the explanation is constructed: were I roughly in her position, and yet chose differently, that would show that I was not in her *precise* position. Surely we have reason to suppose that *her* choice is necessarily specific: there is no hope of producing a 'law' that could then be used in *other* cases – for example, in *my* case. But that must make us give up the longing for a wholly general principle. And this will support the particularism which, I have urged, is central to my conception of the moral laboratory.

Thinking about the moral laboratory

An overriding concern of the *moral laboratory*[7] is with fairness: rules in sport are sometimes changed to facilitate just performance (fair play). For example, the introduction of the idea of a professional foul into soccer: that is, a foul which would be penalized sufficiently to equalize the situation. And this is regularly offered as an explanation of proposed rule changes.

Of course, this is a silly method, given the need for judgement in the application of *all* rules (that is, the impossibility of sealing off all possible [mis-] interpretations). The arguments show us that the hope for definiteness here – sealing off all possibilities – is vain. One cannot expect any rule change to necessarily succeed in imposing fairness, no matter how well drafted. However carefully one builds-in details of this situation only, other 'readings' of it – and hence other ways of treating it – are always possible: indeed, this is a quite general thesis from the philosophy of language, the thesis of occasion-sensitivity.

So the hope for rules which in and of themselves 'improve' fairness in a particular sport is vain – if we cannot find such exceptionless rules elsewhere, we should not expect them for sport. Yet, nevertheless, this does represent one rationale! The proposed rule change would indeed be justified to the extent that it really enhanced fairness or fair play. To that degree, this aspiration is consonant with, and exemplifies, the moral character of sport. That it fails in *practice* might just be taken to reinforce that point.

This chapter began from the interpenetration of moral notions with our lives – the moral metaphors from sport recognize that these notions (also?) have a role in sport. But, as noted, those ideas are either *not* metaphorical or are *less* metaphorical in the sporting context – there really can be fair playing and the levelness of actual playing fields! Seeing how these ideas interact with the rules and principles (and spirit) of sport can show us how such notions might *apply* – and hence, perhaps, how they might be applied more generally. So the moral laboratory is only teaching morality in sport (if it is), but that itself might have the possibility to achieve more: that is, to teach one to be a better human – perhaps, in learning to take *fragments* of one's life seriously, one learns to take life seriously.

357

This parallel also makes plain a limitation of the moral laboratory, a problem for the practice, not the theory. Just as someone might be a master of pure mathematics but unable to manage elementary applied maths (say, unable quickly to check one's change after buying a round of drinks), so a master of the moral concepts in the sporting context might be unable to apply them outside the laboratory. There is no theoretical safeguard here, no guarantee that generalizability won't be thwarted (*pace* de Coubertin) – although eternal vigilance might work against this being a regular occurrence; and valuing sport partly as a moral laboratory might make such vigilance easier to organize!

As moral laboratory, sport is not a site for *trying out* morality: rather, it concerns learning to play within rules … to circumscribe one's conduct within explicit rules: later, such 'rules' will not (typically) be (so) explicit. So having learned *principles* will be more important.

Its possibilities as a moral laboratory are *intrinsic* to sport – they derive from its being rule-governed, involving human interactions where both fairness and harm are possible, and where the risk is not too great (perhaps there are other characteristics too). But this possibility is not *unique* to sport – although it is hard to think of plausible candidates.

Problem: the moral nature of sport?

But is sport as I have described it? If it is not, this project is misconceived.

Certainly, not all uncontentious sport *conforms* to this description – a fact not *that* important, if most sport did. It might seem, then, that one must determine whether or not the *majority* of sports are like this. But it also seems inappropriate to be counting heads here, to determine what *most* sports do (in theory and in practice). Even if there are exceptions, sports not fitting the model sketched above, that model would still be useful if it offered us insight into *some* sports. Yet it does seem important to plot the scope and limits of any such model. For clearly, not all sport operates by emphasizing fairness and suchlike (the rules of basketball [as interpreted] require players to foul) – a horrible possibility here is the morally harmful side of sport. That is, the *moral* force in some sports might be

towards *immoral* action. For if the connection is just to moral *issues*, then first there is no guarantee that contact, with sport will be *positively* educative in respect of morality *and* second it is not clear that sport is *always* committed to the educative matters; or, better, that *all* sport is.

Of course, the connection to rule-breaking activity might still be seen under the aspect of rule-related activity – and, as such, enjoys the moral commitment to the rules in their constitutive understanding. But this is a much weaker requirement than the more explicit concerns with justice, fairness and the like which have grounded this chapter.

It is difficult to move on from here in the abstract: some concrete cases are needed. Yet sport operates for many purposes, and at many levels of performance and spectatorship. Which should be selected? Having begun the chapter from de Coubertin (and in line with my interests), the examples, come from high-level performance: namely, from Olympic sport. But the substance of these points could be restructured for other cases. (For example, with playground activities where considerations of fair play had *no* place, one can readily imagine disputes about the sport status of the activity.)

One way forward from these recognitions – especially for Olympism – would be the road of exclusion. Only some sports are appropriate to the moral laboratory, which is not to deny the interest of others, but just to deny them *this* interest. Take this to supply *appropriate* sports (for Olympism) as a basis for including/excluding 'candidate' Olympic events, given the need to reduce the size of the Games.

Let us briefly consider some candidates, to show *some* of the relevant considerations:

- Boxing – the essential violence of the sport, the essential damage to others, precludes it from sensible consideration for the moral laboratory. Whatever the redeeming social values of, say, fighting for the Holy Family,[8] little of *moral* worth is to be found in boxing itself, even in its amateur incarnation (that is, before we turn to biting chunks from the opponent's ear). Were I wrong, advocates of boxing would show that it has *indeed* a place in the moral laboratory – that is, conduct the argument in my terms, so that (at worst) I am wrong only about empirical details.

- Synchronized swimming – this activity does not conduce to inappropriate moral values (as one might urge for boxing) so much as have no bearing on morality one way or another. Again, were this clear, its place could then be argued against. If a retort emphasizes its competitive nature, our counterblast should stress the difficulty of integrating such competitiveness into essentially aesthetic activities. (And then we should also look hard at gymnastic vaulting, for instance.)

  Of course, its (weaker) connection to morality, though the moral imperative of the 'contract' to deploy constitutive rules, might be enough here. That would grant that sport *as such* had some place in our moral laboratory. Still, one would still contrast this case (and similar ones) with sports where the stronger connection to justice and fairness was apparent.

- Basketball – basketball was initially a non-contact sport under one of its original thirteen rules,[9] 'shouldering, holding, pushing, tripping or striking an opponent was not allowed'. Equally, these rules are now interpreted so as to require of players foul play (rule-breaking in precisely this aspect). For instance, as Wilkes (1994: 96) notes, 'Though basketball is sometimes referred to as a noncontact sport, it is far from that – aggressive play with bodily contact is the rule rather than the exception.'

Moreover, such behaviour is expected by both coaches and referees. So that there is certainly a conflict here between the spirit of one rule and the interpretation of others.

The issue for basketball is *not* just that of players seeing what they can get away with – what the referee will not notice, for example; or will not penalize. So the situation differs from that in some other sports.

Specific penalties for rule-breaking *within* the rules of the game do not exclude the player from the game permanently, do not result in automatic advantage to the other side in terms of the score (although giving a high probability of the other side scoring). An initial rationale for such rules was to equalize a situation where a player makes *accidental* contact with another (say, through over-enthusiasm), and where this would advantage his team. Moreover, the fixing of some permitted *number* of such infringements (and the associated penalties) is explained by the thought that accidents and over-enthusiasm do not strike in the same place an infinite amount of times: more than a few occurrences and it looks deliberate.

More important for us, the proscribed behaviours are now seen as what a player *ought* to do in certain circumstances – further: the idea of 'drawing the foul' means that this is part of the game not only for those who perform this behaviour, but equally for their opponents. This activity is *within* the ethos of basketball – the distinction between the spirit and the letter of the rules (or between principles and rules) seems to break down. This is *not* the suggestion that cheats are not playing the game at all, because they are not abiding by its constitutive rules. Here, though, rules of the game *regulate* this way of behaving.

While showing nothing in and of themselves, these points sketch good reason to suppose that participation in such a sport (basketball is not alone here) could not possibly be morally educative through the inculcating of moral principles. Here we see some practical possibilities of our investigations. With no place in the moral laboratory, such activities need have none in the Olympics (for instance).

These three cases illustrate one aspect of pursuing the idea of a moral laboratory where it leads, as well as a (potential) normativity to such an idea, one which might be applied elsewhere – say, in schools or in leisure centres – although I have not suggested how! We should now turn to other cases, as well as interrogating the premises of the argument that generates such conclusions.

Outcomes

As noted earlier, this whole argument is a research agenda. If, in offering concrete realizations, sport can function as a moral laboratory for the (particular) engagement with moral concerns, it has the potential for *a* kind of moral educativeness not so far removed from de Coubertin's dream (Of course, this is at best only one aspect, of sport: I am *not* urging that it is the most important.)

Nothing here sustains de Coubertin's optimism about sport: the moral laboratory may

359

teach *immorality*, or some people learn nothing from it – there is no *guarantee* of learning; and also no guarantee, even for those who have picked up the moral dimension of sport, that there will be any transfer to the rest of their behaviour. These are reasons for pessimism about the Olympic Ideal. But they also indicate potentials or possibilities of sport, ways in which sport might help us to transcend our petty concerns with self, and so on; and thus might serve the grand purposes de Coubertin envisaged.

Notes

1. The explanation does not have to be good in either case (although often it is very good): my point is that each would be equally good; and for the same reasons.
2. Obeying rules for, say, fear of punishment (hence, prudentially) is not recognizing that one ought (morally) to act in that way: compare Nagel (1986: 132–3).
3. Jennings (1996: 237) quotes from the *Olympic Review* (1981: 158): 'the Olympic Games in Moscow had been the most "pure". Proof of this is the fact that not one case of doping was registered'. Although later withdrawn, this comment (attributed to Prince de Merode) indicates a certain attitude to evidence: there was no drug taking because none was found! This is just what sponsors want to hear!
4. It might seem that one cannot, say, bring a machine gun onto the rugby field: that this is *absolutely* precluded. But we can imagine cases where the object is not classified as a machine gun (but as, say, a peculiar kind of watch), where the prohibition focuses most strongly on what players (rather than referees) bring onto the pitch. And now the prohibition can begin to look like a border-line case – certainly no longer *absolute*!
5. Conversations with Sigmund Loland over the years certainly influenced my thinking, as did his arguments (Loland 1998). However, I cannot subscribe to the project of Loland (2002): this attempt to produce norms is also based on unsustainable assumptions about determinacy (witness, for instance, its taxonomic intentions). The intention to deal with *all* cases through norms is problematic, if there is no *all*: when not exceptionless, these norms still function generally, with application to all cases, even if they 'have the character of guidelines' (Loland 2002: 33) – that will be fine if thought of as a codified (non-contextual) guidance for coaches; a bit like, 'Honesty is the best policy' in a corrupt world.

6. Perhaps, as Jones and McNamee (2003: 42) suggest, this idea was first formulated in Parry (1988): I certainly *thought* I had come to it independently; and our uses of it differ.
7. After I had been working with this idea for some time, I read Nussbaum (2001: 238), in which she writes that '[n]arrative play . . . provides the child with a "potential space" in which to explore life's possibilities'. My thought was to see sport offering something similar, but (a) for adults, and (b) in the limited sphere of (some) moral possibilities – at least on the stronger reading of what is available for my moral laboratory.
8. See Sugden (1996), where this is the title of Chapter Three. My point here could be exemplified by seeing how – having described boxing's political economy in general terms, and engaged in careful ethnographies – its last chapter is a discussion of boxing and society, concluding with an analysis of boxing in relation to inequality and poverty: as we are told, 'The boxing subculture grows when poverty stands in the shadow of affluence' (Sugden 1996: 195). This comment – arguably, *profound* – concerns what boxing can 'tell us' about the global social order: boxing is here our 'sensitive cultural lens' (Beckles 1995: 1 [quoted earlier]).
9. As recorded in Ebert and Cheatum (1977: 4), to instantiate the principle 'no tackling or other rough conduct'. A more modern commentator expressly discusses this idea in terms of personal fouls, rather than the prohibition against contact: see Wilkes (1994: 96):

> A *personal foul* results when contact is made with an opponent while the ball is alive.
>
> In general, the personal foul is charged to any player who causes bodily contact . . . [with an opponent].
>
> (Wilkes 1994: 97)

References

Austin, J. L. (1962) *Sense and Sensibilia*, Oxford: Oxford University Press.

Baker, G. P. and Hacker, P. M. S. (1980) *Wittgenstein: Understanding and Meaning – An Analytical Commentary on the Philosophical Investigations*, Oxford: Blackwell.

Beckles, H. McD. (1995) 'Introduction', in Beckles, H. McD. and Stoddart, B. (eds) *Liberation Cricket: West Indies Cricket Culture*. Manchester: Manchester University Press.

Dancy, J. (1993) *Moral Reasons*, Oxford: Blackwell.

—— (2000) 'The particularist's progress', in Brad Hooker and Margaret Little (eds) *Moral Particularism*, Oxford: Clarendon Press.

de Coubertin, P. (2000) *Olympism: Selected Writings*, Lausanne: International Olympic Committee.

Dworkin, R. (1978) *Taking Rights Seriously*, Cambridge, MA: Harvard University Press.

—— (1985) *A Matter of Principle*, Cambridge, MA: Harvard University Press.

Ebert, F. H. and Cheatum, B. A. (1977) *Basketball*, second edn, Philadelphia, PA: W. B. Saunders Co.

Gibbard, A. (2002) 'The reasons of a living being', *Proceedings and Addresses of the American Philosophical Association*, 76: 2: 49–60.

Hargreaves, J. (1986) *Sport, Power and Culture*, Cambridge: Polity.

Jennings, A. (1996) *The New Lords of the Rings*, London: Simon and Schuster.

Jennings, A. and Sambrook, C. (2000) *The Great Olympic Swindle: When the World Wanted its Games Back*, London: Simon and Schuster.

Jones, C. and McNamee, M. (2003) 'Moral development and sport: Character and cognitive developmenlalism contrasted', in J. Boxill (ed.) *Sports Ethics: An Anthology*. Oxford: Blackwell.

Loland, S. (1998) 'Fair play: Historical anachronism or topical ideal?', in M. J. McNamee and S. J. Parry (eds), *Ethics and Sport*. London: Routledge.

—— (2002) *Fair Play in Sport: A Moral Norm System*, London: Routledge.

Lorenz, K. (1966) *On Aggression*, London: Methuen.

McFee, G. (1992) *Understanding Dance*, London: Routledge.

—— (2000a) *Free Will*, Teddington: Acumen.

—— (2000b) 'Spoiling: An indirect reflection of sport's moral imperative?', in T. Tännsjö and C. Tamburrini (eds) *Values in Sport*, London: Routledge.

—— (2000c) 'Sport: A moral laboratory?', in M. McNamee *et al.* (eds) *Just Leisure: Policy, Ethics and Professionalism*, Eastbourne: Leisure Studies Association.

McIntosh, P. (1979) *Fair Play*, London: Heinemann.

Mackay, D. (1996) 'Olympic cheats go unnamed', *The Observer*, Sunday 17 November: 2.

Nagel, T. (1986) *The View from Nowhere*. Oxford: Oxford University Press.

Nussbaum, M. (1990) *Love's Knowledge: Essays on Philosophy and Literature*, Oxford: Oxford University Press.

Nussbaum, M. (2001) *Upheavals of Thought: The Intelligence of Emotions*, Cambridge: Cambridge University Press.

Parry, J. [S. J.] (1988) 'Physical education, justification and the National Curriculum', *Physical Education Review*, 11: 2: 106–18.

Sugden, J. and Bairner, A. (1993) *Sport, Sectarianism and Society in a Divided Ireland*, Leicester: Leicester University Press.

Sullivan, R. [with S. Song] (2000) 'Are drugs winning the Games?', *Time*, 156, 11: 54–6.

Tamburrini, C. (2000) *The 'Hand of God': Essays in the Philosophy of Sport*, Göteborg, Sweden: Acta Universitatis Gothobergensis.

Wallechinsky, D. (1988) *The Complete Book of the Olympics*, Harmondsworth: Allen Lane.

Wilkes, G. (1994) *Basketball*, sixth edn, Madison, WI: Brown & Benchmark.

Willis, P. (1973) 'Women in sport in ideology', in J. E. Hargreaves (ed.) *Sport, Culture and Ideology*, London: Routledge & Kegan Paul.

Part 6

Commercialism, corruption and exploitation in sports

Introduction

Mike McNamee

One common answer to the question 'What's gone wrong with sports?' revolves around the idea that they have been exploited by the forces of commercialism by being turned into commodities to sell in the market place. The response comes in many variants and is the subject of critical sociological enquiries.[1] To some extent their nature and variety became less dramatic and tense as the Berlin wall came down and accessions were made in the East over two decades to market-oriented economic and political structures. Nevertheless, being sociological, these critiques often turn on empirical descriptions of sports that are instantiated in this culture or that, within differing geo-cultural and political contexts, and so on. Often, though not always, philosophers of sport have objected that these characterisations of sports – and the various ills that bedevilled them – neglected what many philosophers, following Suits, thought to be the core concept of sports.

In a modern classic, Christopher Lasch attempts to uncover the social and economic aetiology of the state of modern sports in American society. One should not commit the genetic fallacy by thinking that his critique, 'The Degradation of Sport', is a hostage to its genesis in American capitalism. Rather, he points out (prophetically, it must be said, since the original essay was published in 1976[2]) a litany of ills that have corrupted sports. Lasch takes his cue from Huizinga and draws attention to play-generated aspects of sports,

such as freedom and the striving after the ends of sports in all their glorious pointlessness. Whereas Huizinga derided the infusion of seriousness into the world of play, Lasch turns the idea on its head and argues that the corruption of sports lies in not taking their pointless, gratuitous, logic seriously enough. A considerable portion of his critique rests upon the recognition of internal ends to sports (the commitment to the pre-lusory goal, pursued by lusory means, for its own sake: in Suits's terms) enshrined in the rules. He notes how sport has always been subjected to external ends or purposes whether commercial, educational, militaristic or patriotic. It is the commercial exploitation of sport that attracts his attention and ire. But his critique is not naive. He recognises (as did Skillen in Part 1) that play and display are both elements of modern spectator sports. Nevertheless, he rejects the processes whereby spectators are cut off, in various ways from a commitment to sports. He decries the fact that their engagement is one of 'vegetative passivity' (1979: 185) consuming the commodified, over-organised and profane rituals that play once celebrated. Perhaps ironically, then, he writes that 'Ceremony requires witnesses, enthusiastic spectators conversant with the rules of the performance and its underlying meaning' (1979: 190). Lasch gestures towards an ethics of spectatorship that is committed or educated such that it can appreciate the standards of excellence that the activity demands and reproduces in its best moments. And any amateur psychologist can confirm the 'audience effect' where the mere presence of others can lift players to their best performances. But the reason why 'every' player prefers to play at home rather than at an away venue, is not necessarily because they can draw upon and perform to an educated audience. More important is the fact that they can play with the support of the home crowd, who will respectively cheer and abuse in equal measure the heroes (the home team) and villains (the away team). In generalising here, it is worth mentioning the heterogeneous structures of sports competitions. True, in some competitions, such as the oldest knockout competition (the Football Association Cup in the UK), the winner of a one-off contest secures victory. Others, however, are settled over the course of a season. Others still, notably in the USA, but not exclusively there, prefer a format of extended competition that enables teams to enter into an end of season play-off system. These points are discussed in detail by Morgan, in the subsequent chapter. For the moment it is important simply to note that Lasch recognises that catering to a mass market of uneducated spectators requires re-organising or re-structuring sports toward the end of mass-consumption-driven profit. Along with Huizinga, he observes how the 'sacred' ritual of play turns profane.

Yet Lasch does not give in to the romantic refrain that if we could only return to amateur days all would be well with sports. He argues that the cure might be worse than the disease: sports ought not to be structured 'solely for the edification of the players' (1979: 192). In tying together players and spectators he writes 'By entering imaginatively into their world, we experience in heightened form the pain of defeat and the triumph of persistence in the face of adversity' (1979: 193). For Lasch the relationship is, when it is at its best, a symbiotic one. His conclusion is that the degradation of sports, contra Huizinga, consists not in their being taken too seriously, but rather in their trivialisation. He proceeds to locate that trivialisation in the expulsion of spontaneity and disorder from organised work-driven culture, a distaste for the non-productive or idle forms of pleasurable activity, the excessive win-at-all-costs culture of corporate capitalism, and the disconnection of the traditional ties of place and space between audience and players.

Bill Morgan's essay 'The Moral Case Against Contemporary American Sports' takes up the cudgel laid down by Lasch, updating and refining the original analysis in specifically moral terms. He wastes no words on characterising the modern malaise in his introductory paragraph:

> to say that American sports are in a sorry moral condition today is to say, among other things that a thorough going narcissism permeates their ranks, a narcissism whose self-serving ways leave little, if any, room for consideration of the welfare of others in sports or for the larger good of these practices themselves.
>
> (2006: 29)

From here Morgan goes on to argue that commercialisation is the cause of the denigration of athletic excellence traditionally conceived. Following Dixon (1999) he notes the rise of the end of season play-off system, so attractive to mass-revenue-producing television audiences, is itself a usurpation of the normatively superior season-long method of determining athletic superiority. Here a team that merely scrapes into the lucrative end of season play-off may well win the title that should properly be reserved for the winners of the season-long campaign. The truncated play-off system is vulnerable to luck, poor officiating and atypical good/bad performances that are normally ironed out over the course of a season. Another case where the logic of athletic excellence is undermined is in the use of lead runners who take fellow athletes through portions of a race at a pre-agreed pace, so as to transform a race where all compete to win and complete the distance into a pre-staged routine that is designed to afford the favourites the best possible circumstances in which to produce record-breaking times. Here then, traditionally constituted individual excellence – where the athletes must concentrate hard on their own internal rhythm, keep a close eye on all competitors or develop strategy and tactics in the thick of things, is usurped by the logic of pre-planned and sensationalised spectacle.

Morgan cites other factors that undermine modern sport, such as endorsement contracts that dwarf already inflated salaries, the hyper-valorisation of individual excellence in team events, sensationalist media reporting, anti-educational specialisation media-driven intercollegiate sports, and the fostering of a climate where moral criticism is seen as acting in bad taste. Elite sports, driven by the spirit of commercialisation, have been morally anaesthetised.

To this legion of criticism Walsh and Giulianotti add a new dimension. Their critique casts a broader net to capture the range of pathological conditions of elite sport that has become in their words 'hyper-commodified'. In their 'Moral Philosophy Out on the Track' four such commodity-driven pathologies are outlined; (i) where the motivations of players have been corroded to the extent that their focus is no longer on internal goals; (ii) where other athletes and sports themselves are seen only as a means to external ends; (iii) where distributive injustice of rewards arises; and (iv) where the long term welfare of the activity is undermined. They argue that 'commodification is morally undesirable when it gives rise to any of these pathologies' (2006: 120).

Walsh and Giulianotti do not object to commodification per se, but wish to see it regulated, and argue, following Kant's well-known distinction between things that may be the bearers of dignity while others have a price; that certain social goods ought not be bought and sold. They argue that just as it is widely accepted that the selling of children is morally objectionable and thus properly subjected (in economic terms) to a blocked exchange, while other market transactions ought to be regulated by the state. Thus for certain sporting occasions so significant (for example) in the life of a nation, it would be wrong to treat them as exclusive goods accessed only by a sufficiently wealthy consumer group. There will be other cases where a state or private parties may only exhort the corporate forces of sport to moral improvement (such as the location of workforces in exploitative conditions).

In terms of political economy, they point to the prospect of alternative models of ownership of sports franchises in Europe and North America. Additionally, they ask if states' powers can be exercised to regulate public utilities, why not consider such organs to regulate sport for the greater good too? Might not sports governing bodies be developed under a public service model of governance rather than a private-equity model? The latter is a direct response to a growing phenomenon of club/franchise buyouts by wealthy businessmen who have no attachment or loyalty to their latest acquisition except as a fecund investment opportunity. They also go on to make suggestions for more active spectatorship, even to the point of shared ownership and social models of fans contributing to a club or franchise's social responsibilities as a corporate entity.

The wide-ranging ethical improvements suggested by Walsh and Giulianotti are underwritten by models of organisation and identity that are drawn from economic and political writings. By contrast, the final two essays of this Part are drawn from the exploitation of sports labour in general and with respect to children in particular.

As if to remind readers that it is not only under the conditions of capitalism that sports and sportspersons are exploited, Giselher Spitzer's essay, 'Sport and the Systematic Infliction of Pain' focuses on the former state-socialist German Democratic Republic (DDR) where athletes were the object of systematic state sponsored doping. From the 1950s to the late 1980s an elite sport structure was developed to showcase the superiority of Communistic life through athletic victories on the world stage. In absolute terms, the DDR achieved a rank of third place in the Olympic medal table, only behind the vastly more populous USSR and USA. In terms of Olympic medals per capita, the DDR was easily the most successful. The price paid, however, for such state-organised, medically controlled, and politically motivated success was high indeed. Sports were organised along military lines, producing (ironically enough) an elitist system of athletes who were effectively servants of the state from the cradle to the grave. Spitzer describes how children were forced to join training centres on the basis of early talent identification programmes, through to adulthood with a high degree of social or economic incentives. Their enlistment was characterised by a coercive offer. Adult athletes became, in effect, highly paid civil servants.

Considered as a captive population, East German athletes were, as a rule, exposed to mandatory or compulsory doping. Based on documentary archives gathered after the fall of the Berlin wall, and the reunification of Germany, Spitzer argues that relatively few were aware of the doping they underwent and, moreover, '*every* selected athlete was doped – it was impossible to refuse' (2005: 110). He also documents the collusion of the medical fraternity with the political elite and security services to plan, provide and monitor doping-enhanced training and performances. In addition, he notes how knowledge of scientifically monitored side effects was withheld from athletes. Spitzer goes on to describe case studies where athletes were subjected to pain – not merely that which arises from elite sport as a necessary by-product – but as part of a systematic process of talent development. This occurred in the use of painful practices to produce absolute discipline among athletes; the refusal to recognise and treat pain and injury except by chosen medical personnel at times convenient to the regime; and the enforcement of participation in competitions irrespective of their ill or injured condition.

Spitzer's analysis might be something of a corrective to the earlier essays of this Part if the reader were to conclude that there were systems of political and economic organisation that were thought exclusively to be corruptive. In the final essay of this Part, children become the focus of 'Sharp Practice' as observed by Paulo David. Success in any sphere of life demands both commitment and sacrifice in addition to talent. There is a thin dividing line between the development of training for the achievement of sporting potential and the abuse or exploitation of children in the name of the same goal. David draws on international policies from health, sport and even human rights frameworks to illustrate how training regimes are already recognised as problematic and offers a useful typology for unethical practices from physical abuse to emotional neglect. The term 'child abuse' is typically understood within contexts of paedophilia. Nevertheless, David offers argument and evidence that might legitimately force us to reframe some sports regimes as a form of child abuse. Beyond the harms visited on children by excessive physical, psychological and emotional demands of training and performance, a further feature he sets out is the idea of a lost childhood. The opportunity cost of athletic achievement is often irreversible. While it is true that each time slice is valuable, certain carefree or developmental activities one engages in as a child cannot feasibly be entertained by an adult. The liberties one enjoys there are not captured later in life. Moreover, if so many hours per day are spent training,

children necessarily incur closures on other options in their lives. To this point, David adds in conclusion an often overlooked feature of elite sports children's lifestyle: the right to rest, to be free of work-like pressures, to recover and be refreshed whether in sleep or relaxation. These latter essays are not deeply philosophical in content or approach. They tend toward what was earlier called 'descriptive ethics'. Their inclusion is certainly warranted, however, since they offer rich details, in the form of athletes' experiences in their own voices, as well as nuanced descriptions of organisational and policy contexts, that offer a rich basis for substantive ethical discourse on the varieties of exploitation in sports.

Notes

1. See, among many examples, Jarvie and Maguire (1994), Sugden and Tomlinson (1999), and Tomlinson and Whannel (1984) on Olympic sport in particular.
2. Although the original essay was published in the *New York Review* in 1976, references here are to the version of the essay as printed in Lasch's *Culture of Narcissism* 1979.

References

Dixon, N. (1999) 'On Winning and Athletic Superiority', *Journal of the Philosophy of Sport*, XXVI: 10–26.

Jarvie, G. and Maguire, J. (1994) *Sport and Leisure in Social Thought*, London: Routledge.

Lasch, C. (1979) 'The Degradation of Sport', in *The Culture of Narcissism: American Life in an Age of Diminishing Expectations*, New York: Norton.

Morgan, W. (2006) 'The Moral Case against Contemporary American Sports', in *Why Sports Morally Matter*, London: Routledge.

Spitzer, G. (2005) 'Sport and the Systematic Infliction of Pain: A Case Study of State-Sponsored Mandatory Doping in East Germany', in *Pain and Injury in Sport: Social and Ethical Analysis*, S. Loland *et al.* (eds), London: Routledge.

Sugden, J. and Tomlinson, A. (1999) *Great Balls of Fire*, Edinburgh: Mainstream Publishers.

Tomlinson, A. and Whannel, G. (1984) *Five Ring Circus*, Sydney: Pluto Press.

Walsh, A. and Giulianotti, R. (2006) 'Moral Philosophy Out on the Track: What Might be Done?, in *Ethics, Money and Sport: This Sporting Mammon*, London: Routledge.

The degradation of sport

Christopher Lasch

The spirit of play versus the rage for national uplift

Among the activities through which men seek release from everyday life, games offer in many ways the purest form of escape, Like sex, drugs, and drink, they obliterate awareness of everyday reality, but they do this not by dimming awareness but by raising it to a new intensity of concentration. Moreover, they have no side effects, hangovers, or emotional complications. Games simultaneously satisfy the need for free fantasy and the search for gratuitous difficulty; they combine childlike exuberance with deliberately created complications. By establishing conditions of equality among the players, according to Roger Caillois, games attempt to substitute ideal conditions for "the normal confusion of everyday life." They re-create the freedom, the remembered perfection of childhood, and mark it off from ordinary life with artificial boundaries, within which the only constraints are the rules to which the players freely submit. Games enlist skill and intelligence, the utmost concentration of purpose, on behalf of activities utterly useless, which make no contribution to the struggle of man against nature, to the wealth or comfort of the community, or to its physical survival.

The uselessness of games makes them offensive to social reformers, improvers of public morals, or functionalist critics of society like Veblen, who saw in the futility of upper-class sports anachronistic survivals of militarism and prowess. Yet the "futility" of play, and nothing else, explains its appeal—its artificiality, the arbitrary obstacles it sets up for no other purpose than to challenge the players to surmount them, the absence of any utilitarian or uplifting object. Games quickly lose their charm when forced into the service of education, character development, or social improvement.

Today the official view of the beneficial, wholesome effects of sport, which has replaced the various utilitarian ideologies of the past, stresses their contribution to health, fitness, and hence to the national well-being, considered as the sum of the nation's "human resources." The "socialist" version of this ideology hardly differs from the capitalist version promulgated, for example, by John F. Kennedy in his tiresome pronouncements on physical fitness. Attempting to justify the creation of his President's Council on Youth Fitness (headed by the Oklahoma football coach, Bud Wilkinson), Kennedy cited the consistent decline of strength and fitness as measured by standard tests. "Our growing softness, our increasing lack of physical

Christopher Lasch 'The Degradation of Sport', from *The New York Review of Books*, Vol. 24, Issue 7, © Christopher Lasch 1977. Reprinted by permission of Nell Lasch.

fitness, is a menace to our security." This attack on "softness" goes hand in hand with a condemnation of spectatorship.

Socialist pronouncements sound depressingly similar. The Cuban government announced in 1967 that sport should be considered part of the "inseparable element of education, culture, health, defense, happiness and the development of people and a new society." In 1925, the central committee of the Soviet Communist party declared that sport should be consciously used "as a means of rallying the broad masses of workers and peasants around the various Party Soviet and Trade Union organizations through which the masses of workers and peasants are to be drawn into social and political activity." Fortunately, people of all nations intuitively tend to resist such exhortations. They know that games remain gloriously pointless and that watching an exciting athletic contest, moreover, can be emotionally almost as exhausting as participation itself—hardly the "passive" experience it is made out to be by the guardians of public health and virtue.

Huizinga on *Homo Ludens*

Modern industry having reduced most jobs to a routine, games take on added meaning in our society. Men seek in play the difficulties and demands—both intellectual and physical—they no longer find in work. It is not perhaps monotony and routine in themselves that take the enjoyment out of work, for any job worth doing entails a certain amount of drudgery, but the peculiar conditions that prevail in large bureaucratic organizations and increasingly in the modern factory as well. When work loses its tangible, palpable quality, loses the character of the transformation of matter by human ingenuity, it becomes wholly abstract and interpersonal. The intense subjectivity of modern work, exemplified even more clearly in the office than in the factory, causes men and women to doubt the reality of the external world and to imprison themselves, in a shell of protective irony. Work now retains so few traces of play, and the daily routine affords so few opportunities to escape from the ironic self-consciousness that has itself assumed the qualities of a routine, that people seek abandon in play with more than

the usual intensity. "At a time when *image* is one of the most frequently used words in American speech and writing," Joseph Epstein notes in a recent essay on sports, "one does not too often come upon the real thing."

The history of culture, as Huizinga showed in his classic study of play, *Homo Ludens*, appears from one perspective to consist of the gradual eradication of the play element from all cultural forms—from religion, from the law, from warfare, above all from productive labor. The rationalization of these activities leaves little room for the spirit of arbitrary invention or the disposition to leave things to chance. Risk, daring, and uncertainty—important components of play—have no place in industry or in activities infiltrated by industrial standards, which seek precisely to predict and control the future and to eliminate risk. Games accordingly have assumed an importance unprecedented even in ancient Greece, where so much of social life revolved around contests. Sports, which satisfy also the starved need for physical exertion—for a renewal of the sense of the physical basis of life—have become an enthusiasm not just of the masses but of those who set themselves up as a cultural elite.

The rise of spectator sports to their present importance coincides historically with the rise of mass production, which intensifies the needs sport satisfies while creating the technical and promotional capacity to market athletic contests to a vast audience. But according to a common criticism of modern sport, these same developments have destroyed the value of athletics. Commercialization has turned play into work, subordinated the athlete's pleasure to the spectator's, and reduced the spectator himself to a state of vegetative passivity—the very antithesis of the health and vigor sport ideally promotes. The mania for winning has encouraged an exaggerated emphasis on the competitive side of sport, to the exclusion of the more modest but more satisfying experiences of cooperation and competence. The cult of victory, proclaimed by such football coaches as Vince Lombardi and George Allen, has made savages of the players and rabid chauvinists of their followers. The violence and partisanship of modern sports lead some critics to insist that athletics impart militaristic values to the young, irrationally inculcate local and national pride in the spectator, and serve as one of the strongest bastions of male chauvinism.

Huizinga himself, who anticipated some of these arguments but stated them far more persuasively, argued that modern games and sports had been ruined by a "fatal shift toward over-seriousness." At the same time, he maintained that play had lost its element of ritual, had become "profane," and consequently had ceased to have any "organic connection whatever with the structure of society." The masses now crave "trivial recreation and crude sensationalism" and throw themselves into these pursuits with an intensity far beyond their intrinsic merit. Instead of playing with the freedom and intensity of children, they play with the "blend of adolescence and barbarity" that Huizinga calls puerilism, investing games with patriotic and martial fervor while treating serious pursuits like games. "A far-reaching contamination of play and serious activity has taken place," according to Huizinga. "The two spheres are getting mixed. In the activities of an outwardly serious nature hides an element of play. Recognized play, on the other hand, is no longer able to maintain its true play-character as a result of being taken too seriously and being technically over-organised. The indispensable qualities of detachment, artlessness, and gladness are thus lost."

The critique of sport

An analysis of the critique of modern sport, in its vulgar form as well as Huizinga's more refined version, brings to light a number of common misconceptions about modern society and clarifies some of the central issues of this study, especially the nature of spectacle and the difference between spectacle and other kinds of performance, ritual, and contest. A large amount of writing on sports has accumulated in recent years, and the sociology of sport has even entrenched itself as a minor branch of social science. Much of this commentary has no higher purpose than to promote athletics or to exploit the journalistic market they have created, but some of it aspires to social criticism. Those who have formulated the now familiar indictment of organized sport include the sociologist Harry Edwards; psychologist and former tennis player Dorcas Susan Butt, who thinks sport should promote competence instead of competition; disillusioned professional athletes like Dave Meggyesy and Chip Oliver; and radical critics of culture and society, notably Paul Hoch and Jack Scott.

A discussion of their work helps to isolate what is historically specific to the present cultural malaise. The critics of sport, in their eagerness to uncover evidence of corruption and decline, attack intrinsic elements of athletics, elements essential to their appeal in all periods and places, on the erroneous assumption that spectatorship, violence, and competition reflect conditions peculiar to modern times. On the other hand, they overlook the distinctive contribution of contemporary society to the degradation of sport and therefore misconceive the nature of that degradation. They concentrate on issues, such as "over-seriousness," which are fundamental to an understanding of sport, indeed to the very definition of play, but peripheral or irrelevant to their historical development and contemporary transformation.

Take the common complaint that modern sports are "spectator-oriented rather than participant-oriented." Spectators, in this view, are irrelevant to the success of the game. What a naïve theory of human motivation this implies! The attainment of certain skills unavoidably gives rise to an urge to show them off. At a higher level of mastery, the performer no longer wishes merely to display his virtuosity—for the true connoisseur can easily distinguish between the performer who plays to the crowd and the superior artist who matches himself against the full rigor of his art itself—but to ratify a supremely difficult accomplishment; to give pleasure; to forge a bond between himself and his audience, which consists in their shared appreciation of a ritual executed flawlessly, with deep feeling and a sense of style and proportion.[1]

In all games, particularly in athletic contests, display and representation constitute a central element—a reminder of the former connections between play, ritual, and drama. The players not only compete; they enact a familiar ceremony that reaffirms common values. Ceremony requires witnesses: enthusiastic spectators conversant with the rules of the performance and its underlying meaning. Far from destroying the value of sports, the attendance of spectators makes them complete. Indeed one of the virtues of contemporary sports lies in their resistance to the erosion of standards and their capacity to appeal to a knowledgeable audience. Norman Podhoretz has argued that the sports public remains more discriminating than the public for the arts and that "excellence is relatively uncontroversial as a judgment of performance." More important, everyone agrees on the standards against which excellence should be measured. The public for sports still consists largely of men who took part in sports during boyhood and thus acquired a sense of the game and a capacity to distinguish among many levels of excellence.

The same can hardly be said for the audience for artistic performance, even though amateur musicians, dancers, actors, and painters may still comprise a small nucleus of the audience. Constant experimentation in the arts has created so much confusion about standards that the only surviving measure of excellence is novelty and shock value, which in a jaded time often resides in a work's sheer ugliness and banality. In sport, on the other hand, novelty and rapid shifts of fashion play a small part in games' appeal to a discriminating audience.

Yet even here, the contamination of standards has already begun. Faced with rising costs, owners seek to increase attendance at sporting events by installing exploding scoreboards, broadcasting recorded cavalry charges, giving away helmets and bats, and surrounding the spectator with cheerleaders, usherettes, and ball girls. Television has enlarged the audience for sports while lowering the level of its understanding; at least this is the operating assumption of sports commentators, who direct at the audience an interminable stream of tutelage in the basics of the game, and of the promoters who reshape one game after another to conform to the tastes of an audience supposedly incapable of grasping their finer points. The American League's adoption of the designated-hitter rule, which relieves pitchers of the need to bat and diminishes the importance of managerial strategy, provides an especially blatant example of the dilution of sports by the requirements of mass promotion. Another is the "Devil-Take-the-Hindmost Mile," a track event invented by the San Francisco *Examiner*, in which the last runner in the early stages of the race has to drop out—a rule that encourages an early scramble to avoid disqualification but lowers the general quality of the event. When the

television networks discovered surfing, they insisted that events be held according to a pre-arranged schedule, without regard to weather conditions. One surfer complained, "Television is destroying our sport. The TV producers are turning a sport and an art form into a circus." The same practices produce the same effects on other sports, forcing baseball players, for example, to play World Series games on freezing October evenings. The substitution of artificial surfaces for grass in tennis, which has slowed the pace of the game, placed a premium on reliability and patience, and reduced the element of tactical brilliance and overpowering speed, commends itself to television producers because it makes tennis an all-weather game and even permits it to be played indoors, in sanctuaries of sport like Caesar's Palace in Las Vegas. Television has rearranged the athletic calendar and thus deprived sports of their familiar connection with the seasons, diminishing their power of allusiveness and recall.

As spectators become less knowledgeable about the games they watch, they become sensation-minded and bloodthirsty. The rise of violence in ice hockey, far beyond the point where it plays any functional part in the game, coincided with the expansion of professional hockey into cities without any traditional attachment to the sport—cities in which weather conditions, indeed, had always precluded any such tradition of local play. But the significance of such changes is not that sports ought to be organized, as a number of recent critics imagine, solely for the edification of the players and that corruption sets in when sports begin to be played to spectators for a profit. No one denies the desirability of participation in sports—not because it builds strong bodies but because it brings joy and delight. It is by watching those who have mastered a sport, however, that we derive standards against which to measure ourselves. By entering imaginatively into their world, we experience in heightened form the pain of defeat and the triumph of persistence in the face of adversity. An athletic performance, like other performances, calls up a rich train of associations and fantasies, shaping unconscious perceptions of life. Spectatorship is no more "passive" than daydreaming, provided the performance is of such quality that it elicits an emotional response.

It is a mistake to suppose that organized athletics ever serve the interests of the players alone or that professionalization inevitably corrupts all who take part in it. In glorifying amateurism, equating spectatorship with passivity, and deploring competition, recent criticism of sport echoes the fake radicalism of the counterculture, from which so much of it derives. It shows its contempt for excellence by proposing to break down the "elitist" distinction between players and spectators. It proposes to replace competitive professional sports, which notwithstanding their shortcomings uphold standards of competence and bravery that might otherwise become extinct, with a bland regimen of cooperative diversions in which everyone can join regardless of age or ability—"new sports for the noncompetitive," having "no object, really," according to a typical effusion, except to bring "people together to enjoy each other." In its eagerness to remove from athletics the element that has always underlain their imaginative appeal, the staged rivalry of superior ability, this "radicalism" proposes merely to complete the degradation already begun by the very society the cultural radicals profess to criticize and subvert. Vaguely uneasy about the emotional response evoked by competitive sports, the critics of "passive" spectatorship wish to enlist sport in the service of healthy physical exercise, subduing or eliminating the element of fantasy, make-believe, and playacting that has always been associated with games. The demand for greater participation, like the distrust of competition, seems to originate in a fear that unconscious impulses and fantasies will overwhelm us if we allow them expression.[2]

The trivialization of athletics

What corrupts an athletic performance, as it does any other performance, is not professionalism or competition but a breakdown of the conventions surrounding the game. It is at this point that ritual, drama, and sports all degenerate into spectacle. Huizinga's analysis of the secularization of sport helps to clarify this point. In the degree to which athletic events lose the element of ritual and public festivity, according to Huizinga, they deteriorate into "trivial recreation and crude sensationalism." Even Huizinga misunderstands the cause of this development, however. It hardly lies in the "fatal shift towards over-seriousness." Huizinga himself, when he is writing about the theory of play rather than the collapse of "genuine play" in our own time, understands very well that play at its best is always serious; indeed that the essence of play lies in taking seriously activities that have no purpose, serve no utilitarian ends. He reminds us that "the majority of Greek contests were fought out in deadly earnest" and discusses under the category of play duels in which contestants fight to the death, water sports in which the object is to drown your opponent, and tournaments the training and preparation for which consume the athletes' entire existence.

The degradation of sport, then, consists not in its being taken too seriously but in its trivialization. Games derive their power from the investment of seemingly trivial activity with serious intent. By submitting without reservation to the rules and conventions of the game, the players (and the spectators too) cooperate in creating an illusion of reality. In this way the game becomes a representation of life, and play takes on the character of play-acting as well. In our time, games—sports in particular—are rapidly losing the quality of illusion. Uneasy in the presence of fantasy and illusion, our age seems to have resolved on the destruction of the harmless substitute gratifications that formerly provided charm and consolation. In the case of sports, the attack on illusion comes from players, promoters, and spectators alike. The players, eager to present themselves as entertainers (partly in order to justify their inflated salaries), deny the seriousness of sport. Promoters urge fans to become rabid partisans, even in sports formerly ruled by decorum, such as tennis. Television creates a new audience at home and makes "live" spectators into participants who mug for the camera and try to attract its attention by waving banners commenting on the action not on the field but in the press box. Sometimes fans interject themselves into the game more aggressively, by dashing onto the field or tearing up the stadium after an important victory.

The rising violence of crowds, routinely blamed on the violence of modern sports and the habit of taking them too seriously, arises, on the contrary, out of a failure to take them seriously enough—to abide by the conventions that should bind spectators as well as players. After the exciting match between Vilas and Connors, in the 1977 finals of the U.S. Open at

Forest Hills, an unruly crowd spilled onto the court immediately after the last point and thus broke the hours of tension that should have been broken by the traditional handshake between the players themselves—incidentally allowing Connors to escape from the stadium without acknowledging his rival's victory or taking part in the closing ceremonies. Repeated transgressions of this kind undermine the illusion games create. To break the rules is to break the spell. The merging of players and spectators, here as in the theater, prevents the suspension of disbelief and thus destroys the representational value of organized athletics.

Imperialism and the cult of the strenuous life

The recent history of sports is the history of their steady submission to the demands of everyday reality. The nineteenth-century bourgeoisie suppressed popular sports and festivals as part of their campaign to establish the reign of sobriety. Fairs and football, bull-baiting, cockfighting and boxing offended middle-class reformers because of their cruelty and because they blocked up public thoroughfares, disrupted the daily routine of business, distracted the people from their work, encouraged habits of idleness, extravagance, and insubordination, and gave rise to licentiousness and debauchery. In the name of rational enjoyment and the spirit of improvement, these reformers exhorted the laboring man to forsake his riotous public sports and wakes and to stay at his hearth, in the respectable comfort of the domestic circle. When exhortation failed, they resorted to political action. In early nineteenth-century England, they were opposed by a conservative coalition that crossed class lines, the commoners having been joined in the defense of their "immemorial" enjoyments by traditionalists among the gentry, especially the provincial gentry not yet infected with evangelical piety, sentimental humanitarianism, and the dogma of enterprise. "What would be the Consequence," they asked, "if all such Diversions were entirely banished? The common People seeing themselves cut off from all Hope of this enjoyment, would become dull and spiritless … : And not only so, but thro' the absolute Necessity of diverting themselves at

Times, they would addict themselves rather to less warrantable Pleasures."

In the United States, the campaign against popular amusements, closely associated with the crusade against liquor and the movement for more strict observance of the Sabbath, took on the character of an ethnic as well as a class conflict. The working class, largely immigrant and Catholic, struggled, often in uneasy alliance with the "sporting element" and with "fashionable society," to defend its drink and its gambling against the assault of middle-class respectability. In mid-nineteenth-century New York, for example, the Whig party identified itself with enterprise, improvement, sobriety, piety, thrift, "steady habits," "book-learning," and strict observance of the Sabbath; while the Democrats, at once the party of rural reaction and the party of the immigrant masses, appealed among other constituencies to the sporting set—in Lee Benson's characterization, to lovers of "hard liquor, fast women and horses, and strong, racy language." The passage of blue laws, which rendered many popular amusements illegal and drove them underground, testifies to the political failure of the alliance between sport and fashion. Middle-class reformers enjoyed the advantage not merely of superior access to political power but of a burning sense of moral purpose. The spirit of early bourgeois society was deeply antithetical to play. Not only did games contribute nothing to capital accumulation, not only did they encourage gambling and reckless expenditure, but they contained an important element of pretense, illusion, mimicry, and make-believe. The bourgeois distrust of games reflected a deeper distrust of fancy, of histrionics, of elaborate dress and costume. Veblen, whose satire against middle-class society incorporated many of its own values, including its hatred of useless and unproductive play, condemned upper-class sports on the grounds of their "futility"; nor did he miss the connection between sport and histrionic display: "It is noticeable, for instance, that even very mild-mannered and matter-of-fact men who go out shooting are apt to carry an excess of arms and accoutrements in order to impress upon their own imagination the seriousness of their undertaking. These huntsmen are also prone to a histrionic, prancing gate and to an elaborate exaggeration of the motions, whether of stealth or of onslaught, involved in their deeds of exploit."

Veblen's satire against the "leisure class" miscarried; in America, where leisure found its only justification in the capacity to renew mind and body for work, the upper class refused to become a leisure class at all. Fearful of being displaced by the rising robber barons, it mastered the art of mass politics, asserted its control over the emerging industrial corporations, and embraced the ideal of the "strenuous life." Sports played an important part in this moral rehabilitation of the ruling class. Having suppressed or driven to the margins of society many of the recreations of the people, the *haute bourgeoisie* proceeded to adapt the games of its class enemies to its own purposes. In the private schools that prepared its sons for the responsibilities of business and empire, sports were placed at the service of character building. The new ideology of imperialism, both in England and in the United States, glorified the playing field as the source of qualities essential to national greatness and martial success. Far from cultivating sport as a form of display and splendid futility, the new national bourgeoisie—which at the end of the century replaced the local elites of an earlier day—celebrated precisely their capacity to instill the "will to win."[3]

At a time when popular preachers of success were defining the work ethic to stress the element of competition, athletic competition took on new importance as a preparation for the battle of life. In a never-ending stream of books turned out to satisfy the rising demand for sports fiction, popular authors upheld Frank Merriwell and other athletes as models for American youth. The young man on the make, formerly advised to go into business at an early age and to master it from top to bottom, now learned the secret of success on the playing field, in fierce but friendly competition with his peers. Proponents of the new strenuousness insisted that athletics trained the courage and manliness that would promote not only individual success but upper-class ascendancy. "In most countries," according to Theodore Roosevelt, "the 'Bourgeoisie'—the moral, respectable, commercial, middle class—is looked upon with a certain contempt which is justified by their timidity and unwarlikeness. But the minute a middle class produces men like Hawkins and Frobisher on the seas, or men such as the average Union soldier in the civil war, it acquires

the hearty respect of others which it merits." Roosevelt believed that sports would help to produce such leaders; at the same time he warned his sons not to regard football, boxing, riding, shooting, walking, and rowing as "the end to which *all* your energies must be devoted, or even the major portion of your energies."

Athletic competition also laid the foundations of national greatness, according to ideologues of the new imperialism. Walter Camp, whose tactical innovations at Yale brought into being the modern game of football, argued during World War I that the "grand do-or-die spirit that holds the attack on the one yard line was what made Chateau-Thierry." General Douglas MacArthur echoed these platitudes in World War II: "Upon the fields of friendly strife are sown the seeds which, on other days, on other fields, will bear the seeds of victory." By this time, however, the cult of the strenuous life was as obsolete as the explicit racism that once informed imperialist ideology. MacArthur himself was an anachronism in his flamboyance and his reactionary faith in clean living and high thinking. As American imperialism allied itself with more liberal values, the cult of "manly arts" survived as an important theme only in the ideology of the far right. In the sixties, reactionary ideologues extolled athletics as "a fortress that has held the wall against radical elements," in the words of the head football coach at Washington State University; or as Spiro Agnew put it, "one of the few bits of glue that holds society together." Max Rafferty, California superintendent of schools, defended the view that "a coach's job was to make men out of wet-behind-the-ears boys" and tried to reassure himself that "the love of clean, competitive sports is too deeply imbedded in the American matrix, too much a part of the warp and woof of our free people, ever to surrender to the burning-eyed, bearded draft-card-burners who hate and envy the athlete because he is something they can never be—a *man*."

Corporate loyalty and competition

Left-wing critics of sport have made such statements the focus of their attack—another sample of the way in which cultural radicalism, posing as a revolutionary threat to the status quo, in reality confines its criticism to values already obsolescent and to patterns of American capitalism that have long ago been superseded. Left-wing criticism of sport provides one of the most vivid examples of the essentially conformist character of the "cultural revolution" with which it identifies itself. According to Paul Hoch, Jack Scott, Dave Meggyesy, and other cultural radicals, sport is a "mirror reflection" of society that indoctrinates the young with the dominant values. In America, organized athletics teach militarism, authoritarianism, racism, and sexism, thereby perpetuating the "false consciousness" of the masses. Sports serve as an "opiate" of the people, diverting the masses from their real problems with a "dream world" of glamour and excitement. They promote sexual rivalry among males—with "vestal virgins" leading the cheers from the sidelines—and thus prevent the proletariat from achieving revolutionary solidarity in the face of its oppressors. Competitive athletics force the "pleasure oriented id" to submit to "the hegemony of the repressed ego" in order to shore up the nuclear family—the basic form of authoritarianism—and to divert sexual energy into the service of the work ethic. For all these reasons, organized competition should give way to "intramural sports aimed at making everyone a player." If everyone "had fulfilling, creative jobs, they wouldn't need to look for the pseudo satisfactions of being fans."

This indictment, offensive in the first place in its assumption that cultural radicals understand the needs and interests of the masses better than the masses themselves, also offends every principle of social analysis. It confuses socialization with indoctrination and takes the most reactionary pronouncements at face value, as if athletes automatically imbibed the right-wing opinions of some of their mentors and spokesmen. Sport does play a role in socialization, but the lessons it teaches are not necessarily the ones that coaches and teachers of physical education seek to impart. The mirror theory of sport, like all reductionist interpretations of culture, makes no allowance for the autonomy of cultural traditions. In sport, these traditions come down from one generation of players to another, and although athletics do reflect social values, they can never be completely assimilated to those values. Indeed they resist assimilation more effectively than many other activities, since games learned in youth exert their own

demands and inspire loyalty to the game itself, rather than to the programs ideologues seek to impose on them.

In any case, the reactionary values allegedly perpetuated by sport no longer reflect the dominant needs of American capitalism at all. If a society of consumers has no need of the Protestant work ethic, neither does it need the support of an ideology of racism, manliness, and martial valor. Racism once provided ideological support for colonialism and for backward labor systems based on slavery or peonage. These forms of exploitation rested on the direct, unconcealed appropriation of surplus value by the master class, which justified its domination on the grounds that the lower orders, disqualified for self-government by virtue of racial inferiority or lowly birth, needed and benefited from their masters' protection. Racism and paternalism were two sides of the same coin, the "white man's burden."

Capitalism has gradually substituted the free market for direct forms of domination. Within advanced countries, it has converted the serf or slave into a free worker. It has also revolutionized colonial relations. Instead of imposing military rule on their colonies, industrial nations now govern through client states, ostensibly sovereign, which keep order in their stead. Such changes have made both racism and the ideology of martial conquest, appropriate to an earlier age of empire building, increasingly anachronistic.

In the United States, the transition from Theodore Roosevelt's jingoism to Woodrow Wilson's liberal neocolonialism already spelled the obsolescence of the older ideology of Anglo-Saxon supremacy. The collapse of "scientific" racism in the twenties and thirties, the integration of the armed forces in the Korean War, and the attack on racial segregation in the fifties and sixties marked a deep-seated ideological shift, rooted in changing modes of exploitation. Of course the relation between material life and ideology is never simple, least of all in the case of an ideology as irrational as racism. In any case, de facto racism continues to flourish without a racial ideology. Indeed it is precisely the collapse of de jure racism in the South and the discovery of de facto racism in the North, sheltering under the ideology of tolerance, that distinguishes the most recent phase of the race problem in the United States.

The ideology of white supremacy, however, no longer appears to serve any important social function.

"Martial machismo," as Paul Hoch calls it, is equally irrelevant to an age of technological warfare. The military ethic, moreover, required the athlete or soldier to submit to a common discipline, to sacrifice himself for the good of a higher cause; and it thus suffers the general erosion of organizational allegiance in a society where men and women perceive the organization as an enemy, even the organizations in which they work. In sport as in business, group loyalties no longer temper competition. Individuals seek to exploit the organization to their own advantage and to advance their interests not merely against rival organizations but against their own teammates. The team player, like the organization man, has become an anachronism. The contention that sport fosters an unhealthy spirit of competition needs to be refined. Insofar as sport measures individual achievement against abstract standards of excellence, encourages cooperation among teammates, and enforces rules of fair play, it gives expression to the competitive urge but also helps to discipline it. The crisis of athletic competition today derives not from the persistence of a martial ethic, the cult of victory, or the obsession with achievement (which some critics still see as the "dominant sports creed"), but from the collapse of conventions that formerly restrained rivalry even as they glorified it.

George Allen's dictum—"winning isn't the most important thing, it's the only thing"—represents a last-ditch defense of team spirit in the face of its deterioration. Such pronouncements, usually cited as evidence of an exaggerated stress on competition, may help to keep it within bounds. The intrusion of the market into every corner of the sporting scene, however, re-creates all the antagonisms characteristic of late capitalist society. With the free-agent draft, the escalation of athletic salaries, and the instantaneous stardom conferred by the media on athletic success, competition among rival organizations has degenerated into a free for-all. It is no wonder that criticism of competition has emerged as the principal theme in the rising criticism of sport. People today associate rivalry with boundless aggression and find it difficult to conceive of competition that does not lead directly to thoughts of murder. Kohut writes of one of his patients: "Even as a child he had become afraid of emotionally cathected competitiveness for fear of the underlying (near delusional) fantasies of exerting absolute, sadistic power." Herbert Hendin says of the students he analyzed and interviewed at Columbia that "they could conceive of no competition that did not result in someone's annihilation."

The prevalence of such fears helps to explain why Americans have become uneasy about rivalry unless it is accompanied by the disclaimer that winning and losing don't matter or that games are unimportant anyway. The identification of competition with the wish to annihilate opponents inspires Dorcas Butt's accusation that competitive sports have made us a nation of militarists, fascists, and predatory egoists; have encouraged "poor sportsmanship" in all social relations; and have extinguished cooperation and compassion. It inspires Paul Hoch's plaintive cry: "Why bother scoring or winning the game at all? Wouldn't it be enough just to enjoy it?" In all likelihood, the same misgivings lie behind Jack Scott's desire to find a proper "balance" between competition and cooperation. "Competitive sport is in trouble," Scott says, "when the balance is tipped toward competition." An athlete should strive for accomplishment, according to Scott, but not "at the expense of himself or others." These words express a belief that excellence usually *is* achieved at the expense of others, that competition tends to become murderous unless balanced by cooperation, and that athletic rivalry, if it gets out of hand, gives expression to the inner rage contemporary man desperately seeks to stifle.

Bureaucracy and "teamwork"

The prevalent mode of social interaction today is antagonistic cooperation (as David Riesman called it in *The Lonely Crowd*), in which a cult of teamwork conceals the struggle for survival within bureaucratic organizations. In sport, the rivalry among teams, now drained of its capacity to call up local or regional loyalties, reduces itself (like the rivalry among business corporations) to a struggle for shares of the market. The professional athlete does not care whether his team wins or loses (since losers share in the pot), as long as it stays in business.

The professionalization of sport and the extension of professional athletics into the universities, which now serve as a farm system for the major leagues, have undercut the old "school spirit" and have given rise among athletes to a thoroughly businesslike approach to their craft. Athletes now regard the inspirational appeals of old-fashioned coaches with amused cynicism; nor do they readily submit to authoritarian discipline. The proliferation of franchises and the frequency with which they move from one locality to another undermines local loyalties, both among participants and spectators, and discourages attempts to model "team spirit" on patriotism. In a bureaucratic society, all forms of corporate loyalty lose their force, and although athletes still make a point of subordinating their own achievements to those of the team, they do so in order to promote easy relations with their colleagues, not because the team as a corporate entity transcends individual interests. On the contrary, the athlete as a professional entertainer seeks above all to further his own interests and willingly sells his services to the highest bidder. The better athletes become media celebrities and supplement their salaries with endorsements that often exceed the salaries themselves.

All these developments make it difficult to think of the athlete as a local or national hero, as the representative of his class or race, or in any way as the embodiment of some larger corporate unit. Only the recognition that sports have come to serve as a form of entertainment justifies the salaries paid to star athletes and their prominence in the media. As Howard Cosell has candidly acknowledged, sports can no longer be sold to the public as "just sports or as religion. ... Sports aren't life and death. They're entertainment." Even as the television audience demands the presentation of sports as a form of spectacle, however, the widespread resentment of star athletes among followers of sport—a resentment directed against the inflated salaries negotiated by their agents and against their willingness to become hucksters, promoters, and celebrities—indicates the persistence of a need to believe that sport represents

something more than entertainment, something that, though neither life nor death in itself, retains some lingering capacity to dramatize and clarify those experiences.

Sports and the entertainment industry

The secularization of sport, which began as soon as athletics were pressed into the cause of patriotism and character building, became complete only when sport became an object of mass consumption. The first stage in this process was the establishment of big-time athletics in the university and their spread from the Ivy League to the large public and private schools, thence downward into the high schools. The bureaucratization of the business career, which placed unprecedented emphasis on competition and the will to win, stimulated the growth of sports in another way. It made the acquisition of educational credentials essential to a business or professional career and thus created in large numbers a new kind of student, utterly indifferent to higher learning but forced to undergo it for purely economic reasons. Large-scale athletic programs helped colleges to attract such students, in competitive bidding for enrollments, and to entertain them once they enrolled. In the closing years of the nineteenth century, according to Donald Meyer, the development of an "alumni culture" centering on clubs, fraternities, alumni offices, money drives, homecoming ceremonies, and football, grew out of the colleges' need not only to raise money in large amounts but to attract "a clientele for whom the classroom had no real meaning but who were by no means ready to send their sons out into the world at age eighteen." At Notre Dame, as Frederick Rudolph has pointed out, "intercollegiate athletics ... were consciously developed in the 1890s as an agency of student recruitment." As early as 1878, President McCosh of Princeton wrote to an alumnus in Kentucky: "You will confer a great favor on us if you will get ... the college noticed in the Louisville papers. ... We must persevere in our efforts to get students from your region. ... Mr. Brand Ballard has won us great reputation as captain of the football team which has beaten both Harvard and Yale."

In order to accommodate the growing hordes of spectators, the colleges and universities, sometimes aided by local business interests, built lavish athletic facilities—enormous field houses, football stadiums in the pretentious imperial style of the early twentieth century. Growing investment in sports led in turn to a growing need to maintain a winning record: a new concern with system, efficiency, and the elimination of risk. Camp's innovations at Yale emphasized drill, discipline, teamwork. As in industry, the attempt to coordinate the movements of many men created a demand for "scientific management" and for the expansion of managerial personnel. In many sports, trainers, coaches, doctors, and public relations experts soon outnumbered the players. The accumulation of elaborate statistical records arose from management's attempt to reduce winning to a routine, to measure efficient performance. The athletic contest itself, surrounded by a vast apparatus of information and promotion, now appeared almost incidental to the expensive preparation required to stage it.

The rise of a new kind of journalism—the yellow journalism pioneered by Hearst and Pulitzer, which sold sensations instead of reporting news—helped to professionalize amateur athletics, to assimilate sport to promotion, and to make professional athletics into a major industry. Until the twenties, professional sports, where they existed at all, attracted little of the public attention lavished on college football. Even baseball, the oldest and most highly organized of professional sports, suffered from faintly unsavory associations—its appeal to the working class and the sporting crowd, its rural origins. When a Yale alumnus complained to Walter Camp about the overemphasis on football, he could think of no better way of dramatizing the danger than to cite the example of baseball: "The language and scenes which are too often witnessed [in football games] are such as to degrade the college student and bring him down to a par with or even lower than the average professional baseball player."

The World Series scandal of 1919 confirmed baseball's bad reputation, but it also set in motion the reforms of Kenesaw Mountain Landis, the new commissioner brought in by the owners to clean up the game and give it a better public image. Landis's régime, the

success of the eminently respectable and efficient New York Yankees, and the idolization of Babe Ruth soon made professional baseball "America's number-one pastime." Ruth became the first modern athlete to be sold to the public as much for his color, personality, and crowd appeal as for his remarkable abilities. His press agent, Christy Walsh, developer of a syndicate of ghost writers who sold books and articles under the names of sports heroes, arranged barnstorming tours, endorsements, and movie roles and thus helped to make the "Sultan of Swat" a national celebrity.

In the quarter-century following World War II, entrepreneurs extended the techniques of mass promotion first perfected in the marketing of college football and professional baseball to other professional sports, notably hockey, basketball, and football. Television did for these games what mass journalism and radio had done for baseball, elevating them to new heights of popularity and at the same time reducing them to entertainment. In his recent study of sport, Michael Novak notes that television has lowered the quality of sports reporting, freeing announcers from the need to describe the course of play and encouraging them instead to adopt the style of professional entertainers. The invasion of sport by the "entertainment ethic," according to Novak, breaks down the boundaries between the ritual world of play and the sordid reality from which it is designed to provide escape. Broadcasters like Howard Cosell, who embody the "virulent passion for debunking in the land," mistakenly import critical standards more appropriate to political reporting into the coverage of sports. Newspapers report the "business side" of sports on the sports page, instead of confining it to the business section where it belongs. "It is important," Novak argues, "... to keep sports as insulated as we can from business, entertainment, politics, and even gossip. ... The preservation of parts of life not drawn up into politics and work is essential for the human spirit." Especially when politics has become "a brutal, ugly business" and work (not sport) the opiate of the people, athletics alone, in Novak's view, offer a glimpse of the "real thing." They take place in a "world outside of time," which must be sealed off from the surrounding corruption.

379

Leisure as escape

The anguished outcry of the true fan, who brings to sports a proper sense of awe only to find them corrupted from within by the spread of the "entertainment ethic," sheds more light on the degradation of sports than the strictures of left-wing critics, who wish to abolish competition, emphasize the value of sports as health-giving exercise, and promote a more "cooperative" conception of athletics—in other words, to make sports an instrument of personal and social therapy. Novak's analysis, however, minimizes the extent of the problem and misconstrues its cause. In a society dominated by the production and consumption of images, no part of life can long remain immune from the invasion of spectacle. Nor can this invasion be blamed on the spirit of debunking. It arises, in a paradoxical fashion, precisely out of the attempt to set up a separate sphere of leisure uncontaminated by the world of work and politics. Play has always, by its very nature, set itself off from workaday life; yet it retains an organic connection with the life of the community, by virtue of its capacity to dramatize reality and to offer a convincing representation of the community's values. The ancient connections between games, ritual, and public festivity suggest that although games take place within arbitrary boundaries, they are nevertheless rooted in shared traditions to which they give objective expression. Games and athletic contests offer a dramatic commentary on reality rather than an escape from it—a heightened reenactment of communal traditions, not a repudiation of them. It is only when games and sports come to be valued purely as a form of escape that they lose the capacity to provide this escape.

The appearance in history of an escapist conception of "leisure" coincides with the organization of leisure as an extension of commodity production. The same forces that have organized the factory and the office have organized leisure as well, reducing it to an appendage of industry. Accordingly sport has come to be dominated not so much by an undue emphasis on winning as by the desperate urge to avoid defeat. Coaches, not quarterbacks, call the plays, and the managerial apparatus makes every effort to eliminate the risk and uncertainty that contribute so centrally to the ritual and

dramatic success of any contest. When sports can no longer be played with appropriate abandon, they lose the capacity to raise the spirits of players and spectators, to transport them into a higher realm of existence. Prudence, caution, and calculation, so prominent in everyday life but so inimical to the spirit of games, come to shape sports as they shape everything else.

While he deplores the subordination of sport to entertainment, Novak takes for granted the separation of work and leisure that gives rise in the first place to this invasion of play by the standards of the workaday world. He does not see that the degradation of play originates in the degradation of work, which creates both the need and the opportunity for commercialized "recreation." As Huizinga has shown, it is precisely when the play element disappears from law, statecraft, and other cultural forms that men turn to play not to witness a dramatic reenactment of their common life but to find diversion and sensation. At that point, games and sport, far from taking themselves too seriously, as Huizinga mistakenly concluded, become, on the contrary, a "thing of no consequence." As Edgar Wind shows in his analysis of modern art, the trivialization of art was already implicit in the modernist exaltation of art, which assumed that "the experience of art will be more intense if it pulls the spectator away from his ordinary habits and preoccupations." The modernist esthetic guarantees the socially marginal status of art at the same time that it opens art to the invasion of commercialized esthetic fashion—a process that culminates, by a curious but inexorable logic, in the postmodernist demand for the abolition of art and its assimilation to reality.

The development of sport follows the same pattern. The attempt to create a separate realm of pure play, totally isolated from work, gives rise to its opposite—the insistence, in Cosell's words, that "sports are not separate and apart from life, a special 'Wonderland' where everything is pure and sacred and above criticism," but a business subject to the same standards and open to the same scrutiny as any other. The positions represented by Novak and Cosell are symbiotically related and arise out of the same historical development: the emergence of the spectacle as the dominant form of cultural expression. What began as an attempt to invest sport with religious significance, indeed to make it into a surrogate religion in its own right, ends with the demystification of sport, the assimilation of sport to show business.

Notes

1. This does not mean that virtuosity is the principal component of sport. In implying a comparison, here and elsewhere, between athletic and musical performances, I wish to make just the opposite point. A performer who seeks merely to dazzle the audience with feats of technical brilliance plays to the lowest level of understanding, forgoing the risks that come from intense emotional engagement with the material itself. In the most satisfying kind of performance, the performer becomes unconscious of the audience and loses himself in his part. In sport, the moment that matters is what a former basketball player describes as the moment "when all those folks in the stands don't count." The player in question, now a scholar, left big-time sport when he discovered he was expected to have no life outside it, but he retains more insight into the nature of games than Dave Meggyesy, Chip Oliver, and other ex-athletes. Rejecting the simple-minded radicalism according to which "commercialization" has corrupted sports, he says: "Money [in professional sports] has nothing to do with capitalism, owners, or professionalism. It's the moment in some games where it doesn't matter who's watching, all that counts is that instant where how you play determines which team wins and which team loses."

If virtuosity were the essence of sport, we could dispense with basketball and content ourselves with displays of dunking and dribbling. But to say that real artistry consists not of dazzling technique but of teamwork, timing, a sense of the moment, an understanding of the medium, and the capacity to lose oneself in play does not of course mean that games would have the same significance if no one watched them. It means simply that the superior performance has the quality of being unobserved.

2. In any case, the fashionable chatter about the need for greater participation in sports is entirely irrelevant to a discussion of their cultural significance. We might just as well assess the future of American music by counting the number of amateur musicians. In both cases, participation can be an eminently satisfying experience; but in neither case does the level of participation tell us much about the status of the art.

3. The founder of the modern Olympics, Pierre de Coubertin, admired the English and attributed their imperial success to the character-building influence of athletics. "Is Arnoldism applicable in France?" he wondered. Philip Goodhart and Christopher Chataway, in their account of the rise of this new cult of sports, character development, and empire, make it clear that the new view of sports was a middle-class view that unfolded in opposition to both aristocratic and popular traditions. Whereas cricket, boxing, and horse racing had been identified with gambling, the middle class attempted to use sports to promote respectability, patriotism, and manly vigor.

6.3

The moral case against contemporary American sports

William Morgan

I begin this chapter with a sweeping but hardly controversial claim: American sports (i.e., actually existing American sports in most of their various forms) are in dire moral straits today. I shall have a lot to say later about what I mean by *moral* here (i.e., what makes a consideration, point of view, or judgment distinctively moral). For now, however, by moral consideration I mean one that gives pride of place to the good of others with whom we interact and the good of the projects we share and take up together. Morality, in other words, is importantly bound up with the first person plural *we* in a way that it is not with the first person singular *I*. This means, as Bernard Williams nicely puts it, that "simply to pursue what you want ... is not the stuff of morality; if [that] is your only motive ... then you are not within morality, and you do not have ... any ethical life."[1] So, to say that American sports are in sorry moral condition today is to say, among other things, that a thorough going narcissism permeates their ranks, a narcissism whose self-serving ways leave little, if any, room for consideration of the welfare of others in sports or for the larger good of these practices themselves.

Unfortunately, the moral status of present-day sports has sunk so low that merely documenting the extent of their corruption could easily fill an entire book or two or three. I shall, therefore, have to be more selective in making my case, as I want to say something as well about how the present corruption of sports might be undone. That explains why I devote most of my attention to professional and intercollegiate sports in this chapter, have much less to say about Olympic and high-school sports, and have next to nothing to say about adult master sports or youth sports. However, the reason why I chose not to limit my indictment of American sports to professional sports is because of the abysmally low moral expectations we have of them. This is because, as they continue reminding us, they are mainly businesses and, therefore, are usually content to let the market do their bidding for them unless they run up against something (say, trust-busting legislation) that threatens to compromise their market share; only then do they drag out their big guns and try to pass themselves off as respectable moral enterprises. Of course, their public relations approach to moral legitimacy only confirms my point here: professional sports are far too easy targets on which to pin a moral rap.[2]

However, even though any moral indictment of contemporary American sports must span more than the professional realm, starting

William Morgan 'The Moral Case Against Contemporary American Sports', from *Why Sports Morally Matter*, © 2006 William Morgan. Reprinted by permission of Routledge.

with these sports still makes good sense. That is principally because they generally set the tone, morally and otherwise, for what goes on in sports at all other levels. As my opening remarks suggest, that tone is not a morally auspicious one.

The brief against professional sports

Before I proceed, however, I should say that the unfettered role that market forces play in professional sports is not incidental to my moral critique of them here. For this is the main impetus, I argue, behind their excessive individualistic bent. The incursion of the market and the brand of instrumental reason in which it trades, therefore, go a long way toward explaining why in these sports winning trumps fair play; an assertive egoism triumphs over mutual moral respect; an anything-goes-as-long-as-I-don't-get caught attitude prevails over expressions of good will toward others; and a pervasive mistrust poisons most interactions and relations in sports, undercutting any sense of solidarity – of community – within them. To put it bluntly, this is not the kind of ambience that either inspires moral reflection or causes moral sentiments to well up within us. Also, I argue that it infects almost every feature of professional sports, from our interactions with others in sports to our regard for sports themselves. I should also say here that the discussion to follow includes the effects that the market has on both moral and nonmoral features of sports, with emphasis on those nonmoral features that are most complicit in the moral downfall of sports. Of course, this distinction between the moral and nonmoral is one that I will need to sharpen in due course.

The pernicious influence of money is no more apparent than in professional sports. For whatever market-averse motivational pull sports might have had on participants and spectators has been mostly laid low by the market. Basically, this means that in professional sports, just about everybody is (or is encouraged to be) on the take, whether it be to garner a larger contract or to land a lucrative endorsement deal or to secure whatever profitable end to which sports can be fitted. The result is that sports are treated more so as means than ends, as pursuits with a value

to be instrumentally calculated in the same fashion as any other commodity: by the money they fetch. Indeed, the idea that professional sports could be ends in themselves comes off either as wishful thinking or as a willful distortion. This is why professional sports have become more and more like the rest of life rather than offering a welcome departure from it. For in both everyday life and sports these days, an instrumental regard for whatever people do is the rule rather than the exception, as is the concomitant rationalization of the unseemly dealings that are part and parcel of such a self-centered life. So, just as in sports, so too in everyday life: if one does not want to be taken advantage of, one would be well advised to look out for one's own good first and last. All this seems to go on without the slightest moral compunction in or outside sports.

One seldom-remarked result of the market's incursion into professional sports has been a decline in the quality of their play, in athletic excellence, and although excellence is, strictly speaking, a nonmoral quality of sports, it is, as we shall see, freighted with moral meaning. Understanding why this decline has gone largely unnoticed is difficult, as it follows as a matter of course that when winning becomes the primary or only thing because of the external goods it commands, the quality of play is usually the first thing to suffer. True, the fact that one can reap great rewards in select professional sports typically – but not always – does attract both the most talented and the most tenacious players to them. However, when that talent and determination are misdirected, as I am claiming they are in contemporary professional sports, the effect on the game is not the positive one most people suppose. Let me explain.

The decline in athletic excellence that I claim is a byproduct of the greater commercialization of professional sports is evident in the very conception of athletic excellence that informs these elite sports. As Dixon makes clear in his provocative and persuasive essay, "On Winning and Athletic Superiority," at least two rival conceptions of excellence exist in sports. The first holds that the most excellent players and teams are those that perform well under pressure over the entire course of a season. Assuming such excellence is adequately reflected in a team's won-lost record (which, of course, is generally – but not always – the case), this means that

383

those teams with the best record should be regarded as the most excellent teams (i.e., as the champions of that particular sport for that particular season). A second conception of athletic excellence, however, holds that the best players and teams are those that play well when the stakes are the highest, which is in the postseason playoffs.[3] Of course, one cannot get into the playoffs unless one has played reasonably well over the entire season, but teams with less than stellar records are certainly eligible for postseason play and often (as a matter of contingent fact) do make the playoffs. In light of this second conception – but not the first – if they peak at the right time and defeat all comers in the playoffs, they are regarded as the best team, in spite of the fact that they may not (and often *do* not) have the best overall record.

Now, of course, all the most popular professional team sports in the United States – football, basketball, baseball, and hockey – operate under the second conception of athletic excellence, which is why they use a playoff system to determine the best teams. This is certainly an uncontroversial way to gauge athletic excellence, when the winner of the playoffs also happens to have the best won–loss record. And as Dixon duly notes, this is not an uncommon occurrence. Still, that does not change the fact that a playoff system is predicated on the idea that whoever is able, or fortunate enough, to save their best play for last – when everything is on the line – deserves to be called the best. So, we are left with the following question: which conception of athletic excellence deserves our support (i.e., which comes closer to capturing what true athletic excellence is all about)?

Dixon's answer, with which I fully concur, is that the first conception is clearly superior to the second: Assessing how well a player or team has played over the entire course of a season is a far better indicator of athletic excellence than largely limiting such assessment to a truncated playoff system. He offers two arguments to support his claim, both of which I find persuasive. The first is that by judging excellence over an entire season, one is able to give a far more comprehensive, balanced, and nuanced assessment of athletic performance, measuring not just those players and teams that perform well when the stakes are highest but those teams that are able to perform well under pressure

day in and day out by wisely employing their athletic talents and strategic skills.[4] By contrast, the playoff system places far more weight on just one feature of excellent performance: those who perform best when put in do-or-die situations. While this is, no doubt, an important feature of athletic excellence, it is after all only one feature of what goes into an excellent performance in sports.

The second reason why Dixon thinks a comprehensive conception of athletic excellence is superior to a playoff system is that it is less vulnerable to elements that frequently affect the outcome of games but have nothing centrally to do with athletic excellence. Here, we enter more familiar moral territory, as what is at issue in this instance are such factors as refereeing errors, cheating, gamesmanship, and just plain bad luck. If they occur often enough and at propitious times, they can and frequently do play a role in determining who succeeds or fails in sports. Lessening the impact of these extra-athletic features over an entire season (in which they have a tendency to even out over time) is much easier than doing so in a short playoff system in which they may and often do prove decisive.[5]

Now, if Dixon is right about this (and I think he is), he raises the important question: why have all the major professional sports gone to a playoff format? What, precisely, does such a format have going for it that an entire season of excellent play does not? For the reasons just discussed, the answer clearly is not that such a system does a better job of assessing athletic excellence.[6] Nor can it be said that the playoff system is the only true and tested measure for assessing athletic excellence, because, as Dixon points out, professional soccer leagues in Europe and South America have for some time now recognized and awarded teams with the best record over the season as the most excellent teams.

However, a playoff system enjoys one distinct advantage, but it has nothing important to do with athletic excellence and everything to do with money. Playoffs generate more fan interest by giving even relatively poorly performing teams – who would otherwise have long since been eliminated by their season records – a chance to make the playoffs and by requiring superior performing teams (teams with the best overall records), who would otherwise have already been crowned champions, to prove their mettle all over again by submitting to postseason play.

So, there is a perfectly good reason for professional sports to resort to a playoff system, but the trouble is (to reiterate) that the reason is financial rather than athletic. For the allure of playoffs is that they attract large audiences and, in turn, large television revenues that would not be possible under the first, comprehensive conception of athletic success. And here is the rub. By opting for an inferior conception of and way to assess athletic excellence, professional sports are not just sending the depressing message that profits matter more than sporting excellence; after all, most of us knew this anyway. They are sending the far more worrisome message that at least when it comes to such things as athletic excellence, profits come at the expense of excellence, that the pursuit of the former cannot help but serve as an impediment to the latter, that profit and excellence are not only an unwholesome brew but a sulfurous and antiperfectionist one. And this proves my point: by putting dollars above excellence, professional sports have directly contributed to the decline in the quality of their play.

Further evidence of the decline of excellence in professional sports is apparent in the world of professional track and field. It is common knowledge in the track and field circuit, for instance, that world-class runners in hot pursuit of record-breaking performances more often than not stage such feats rather than compete for them. That is, they usually pick their fellow runners, better "rabbits," whose job is to set the pace necessary to run the sought after record time.[7] They then conveniently tuck behind the pace runners at each appointed stage of the race and dramatically break from the pack near the finish, setting up the spectacle of the solitary runner exerting herself or himself with every fiber of her or his being to breast the tape in record time. Now, of course, what we have here is not a footrace in any true sense of the term (i.e., a competition to determine the most excellent, in which the outcome is almost always up for grabs) but a carefully contrived time trial. To be sure, the result is often a superlative athletic performance, and in this sense at least we can say that a performance that has been achieved clearly has raised the level of past athletic accomplishment. However, the con-trived, anticompetitive setting suggests at very least that we call into question its legitimacy. For it is also common knowledge that in such record-breaking quests, the very reason the appointed runners get to pick their "rabbits" is that their agents have cut a deal with the meet director to allow them to do so, to ensure that nobody gets into the race that their runners do not want into it – especially no one who might beat them. This is the Faustian bargain that any meet director of a major track and field event must make to guarantee the presence of star runners. Of course, the reason why meet directors are only too willing to make such odious deals is to bolster the marketability of these events.

Sometimes, however, the decline in quality of play is easier to see. Take NBA basketball as an example. It is hardly a secret that shooting percentages in the league are down, as are assists and other, general nuts-and-bolts basketball skills.[8] The same fate has befallen team play itself and the very idea of what it is. It is surely not what Bradley had in mind when he spoke of five guys playing as one but rather more like five individuals trying their utmost to separate themselves from the rest of the pack by their novel play or by some other eye-catching, marketable touch. In this setting, flair and panache count for a whole lot more than team choreography and feel. Cooperation is indulged only if it abets individual attention getting. Hence the preoccupation with feats of individual virtuosity, such as slam dunking and the decreased importance of team-oriented actions, such as assists and passing. Hence as well the attention lavished on individual stars and the relative obscurity meted out to solid, no-name teams.

In still other cases, the decline in quality of play seems more so a deliberate calculation. This, too, should come as no surprise because, as Sheed notes, market value is set by what draws crowds, and crowds are drawn to sport for reasons other than skillful play.[9] Television is one of the main culprits here, for in its quest to increase audience size for sports, it cannot but help to lower the level of understanding of fans. So, when such games as professional hockey are broadcast to regions of the country where the game has no firm tradition and where the fans lack even a rudimentary understanding of the game, it can hardly dramatize, let alone talk about, the fineries of the game. In order to promote such sports, the game is then reshaped to appeal to what such fans can appreciate. More than a few think this is one of the reasons why professional hockey does not do more to crack down on the violence of its games or on the goons who populate its ranks. In a word, violence sells.

Further, when professional sports expand into such areas to capitalize on television audiences, they dilute their talent pool and, therefore, the level of play. What is more, when television calls the shots, the times and seasons at which sports are played are affected as well: what makes for good television does not always make for good sports. Again, the emphasis is not on quality of play but on the size of the audience; if that means playing football games in cooler temperatures at night, or staging surfing events without regard for weather conditions, or playing World Series games in the cold weather in the fall, so be it.[10]

Finally, when corporations themselves get into the act and stage their own athletic events, quality of play hardly figures in the equation at all. Nike's "Hoop Heroes" basketball series, started in Japan in September of 1996, is a case in point. These games pitted Jordan, Barkley, and other Nike endorsers against 300-pound-plus Japanese sumo wrestlers.[11] The event proved wildly popular, but I think I am on firm ground in saying that its popularity had very little to do with even the basic skills of basketball, let alone its more fine-grained skills.

The emphasis on the star, the individual player, in most professional sports is also no accident but a consequence of the mania for cash and the marketing strategies hatched with that goal in mind that typify sports at this level. Of course, there is nothing worrisome or otherwise loathsome about individual expression itself, for one of the great achievements of modernity was the loosing of the bounds of the self from constraining cosmological schemes (e.g., the chain of being) that slotted individuals into certain realms, shaping and constraining their every move and opportunity. Likewise, the overturning of the reserve clause in professional baseball, which reserved a player's right to play for a specific team for his entire life, was a necessary and good thing. Free agency did not become a bad thing just because it also made many players wealthy beyond their dreams.

Rather, it became a bad thing when it replaced the subjugation of the player to the team owner with the subjugation of the player to the dollar. As Susan Faldi notes, "money decoupled [players] from servitude, but also from the very idea of 'the team,' from any concept of loyalty to anything except perhaps their own agents, their own careers, their own images."[12]

The problem, then, is not individualism, which like most everything else is healthy when dispensed in the right dose; the problem is the kind of hyperindividualism to which markets give rise, wreaking havoc on sports because they turn them into crass exercises of self-promotion and self-assertion. This is why winning a championship in professional sports is nowadays viewed not as an occasion to build collectively on this achievement to attain yet another one but, as Sheed exclaims, as a "bargaining chip" that can be used by individual players "to raise their own price … cooperation is strictly ad hoc. No one wants to get bogged down in it."[13]

This further explains the misplaced allegiances of many professional athletes: why their loyalty is often reserved for the moneychangers of sports (owners, agents, corporations, tax accountants, public relations people, and the like) rather than for sports themselves or their teammates and opponents. Of this hardly distinguished group, professional agents are probably the most visible and perhaps the most transparent in their business dealings. Here, however, transparency is no virtue but simply a mark of the narrow world in which agents operate. For the agent's sole interest in the athletes they represent is, of course, financial, and this financial interest in lining their athletes pockets is predicated on lining their own pockets. This explains superagent David Falk's unabashed declaration to representatives of Reebok on behalf of his client basketball player Allen Iverson, that "Allen Iverson doesn't have to play great. He has to be a great personality on the court."[14] Perhaps I am crediting the forthrightness of such agents as Falk too much here, for when it comes to candor, it is hard to beat Robert Wright's observation, which nicely parses Falk's foregoing words: "Aside from athletic talent, nothing is more helpful in getting [an athlete] a big shoe contract than being an asshole."[15] That such market posturing only exacerbates the narcissistic tendencies of contemporary professional athletes goes without saying, but it is actually much worse than this. For the entire marketing ploy of professional sports agents is to gain for their athletes perks that single them out in no uncertain terms from the rest of the team. For instance, well known agent Scott Boros asked for the following in his negotiations with team ownership for star baseball player Alex Rodriquez: billboard space in the locale in which he plays, first-class airline tickets, offices for Rodriquez's marketing staff, and at spring training a tent in which to sell his memorabilia.[16]

It is little wonder, then, why Michael Jordan and Charles Barkley, both signed by Nike to promote their shoes, balked at wearing their Reebok festooned warm-up suits on the gold medal podium in 1992 and why Jordan was able to get out of this jam (cleverly, he thought; execrably, most everyone else thought) by draping the American flag over the Reebok emblem. Of course, we are not talking about small potatoes here, for when it comes to the financial clout of endorsement deals, the sky is apparently the limit. For instance, in the same Olympic year of 1992, Jordan earned roughly $25 million, of which only $3.8 million was his salary for playing basketball. By 1997, he earned as much as $100 million from endorsement deals spanning some 20 corporations. Though the sums of money cited here are staggering, the real worry is not just that for the right price athletes are willing to forsake their national and political identities – their standing as citizens – for flimsy corporate ones but that they are willing as well to forsake their very practical identities, those identities that underwrite what makes their lives in general (and their sporting lives in particular) meaningful, for a pot of money. This is, to put it mildly, scary stuff. For tethering one's identity to the vagaries of a fickle market is not only asking for trouble, for being sold out at a moment's notice when a better prospect comes along, but asking far too little of oneself (i.e., settling for a monetary calculation of the meaning of one's life). If this does not amount to moral suicide, I do not know what does.

I have already said enough to give the lie to Sheed's sunny consolation that "Fortunately for everyone, the best way ... the player ... can make some money ... is to play the game as well as he can. And that is why the system seems to work despite itself."[17] Sheed is just plain wrong

about this and not just from a narrow technical standpoint. For playing well means not just playing with technical precision or esthetic acclaim but with a moral sense of purpose as well. Of course, this feature of playing well is sorely lacking in modern professional sports and perhaps what is *most* lacking in them. That is why David Remnick was not exaggerating when he declared that in sports at this level, at least "goodness is a bonus, not a requirement." His immediate target was professional basketball player Latrell Spreewell, of coach-choking fame, whose suspect moral character was quickly forgotten when he helped his team, the Knicks, make a rare run at the NBA championship finals. Unfortunately, Remnick's point is easily generalizable to the whole of professional sports, as winning at this level seems to have the same morally anesthetizing effect no matter the sport, the team, or the locale. It is not that losers come in for closer moral scrutiny but only for more callow criticisms of ineffective or seemingly lethargic play. What passes for criticism in both instances, then, has scarcely anything to do with moral concerns.

This would explain the moral obtuseness of professional sports today; why, for example, such highly successful NBA coaches as Pat Riley can get away with fining his players for helping their opponents off the floor without so much as raising an eyebrow.[18] Print and media commentators of sports, who one might have plausibly supposed were supposed to keep tabs on such things, deserve criticism here as well, because they have long given up the mantle of moral criticism in favor of what can best be described as shrill carping: part of what some call the *outrage industry*.[19] Once such commentators found out that there was plenty of money to be made by delivering thoughtless, scandalous, off-the-cuff pronouncements about sports – pronouncements that (for those at least who worked in television) made up for their lack of critical force and then some by the high decibel level at which they were proffered – they gladly gave up the hard work of moral criticism.[20]

Of course, the commentators cannot, as already intimated, shoulder the entire blame, for when it comes to professional sports, it almost seems as if it is in bad taste to venture a moral view at all, to raise even the specter of moral wrongdoing. I am thinking, for instance, of why there appears to be no moral clamor for players to respect the close calls that referees have to make, rather than disputing them without a moment's reflection if such calls go against them or for respecting one's opponents rather than simply manipulating them, or for siding with the game when some policy or rule change is considered for the good of the game, though such might modestly dent the owners' considerable wealth or the players' substantial salaries.[21]

I fear that there is not much prospect of turning around this antipathy to everything moral in professional sports as long as playing well is crudely keyed to winning, which means, among other things, that playing the game well is not only compatible with cheating but obliges one to learn to cheat effectively – without getting caught. It scarcely needs saying that this sort of environment is not conducive to a moral life, to the cultivation of habits of moral reflection and the exercise of moral virtues.

Much of this moral malaise can be chalked up to the absence of a moral community in professional sports, to the mutual distrust of all parties concerned, which is the mark of a morally challenged community. And I do mean mutual distrust: one in which players can, without much effort, see through the aims of greedy owners; spectators and citizens can, again without reflective duress, see through the intentions of money-obsessed players; owners can readily detect players who are solely motivated by money; and – perhaps more important – unknowledgeable, entertainment-driven fans can go to games primarily looking for a good show (free beer, exploding scoreboards, side-shows and, of course, old-fashioned donnybrooks).

To begin at the top (or is it the bottom?) of this morally dysfunctional community: the owners' financial interests in the game color its every feature. It begins with the design of stadiums themselves and includes such breathtaking innovations as extraordinarily long dugouts (e.g., the dugouts in the Houston astrodome, measuring 120 feet in length, built not for the players' comfort but to ensure as many high-priced seats as possible behind each dugout) and luxurious sky boxes to entice business corporations to bring their most prized clients to sporting events without having to bother with the games themselves, because they are so far removed and insulated from the action.

Once the stadium is built, there is the matter of naming rights, which so far has been able to attract a number of premium corporations who are only too willing to shell out whatever it takes to see their corporate name adorn an athletic stadium. The Chicago Bears, out of necessity, took this entrepreneurial step further. Barred by Mayor Daly from putting the name of their newly renovated stadium up for corporate bidding, the Bears (in what many in the business world considered a brilliant coup) instead put the name of their local community affiliation up for sale. Thus, radio and television advertising will from now on refer to the team as the "First Bank" Bears. The fact that all this private profiteering is mostly paid for by public money and that professional sport franchises are routinely afforded antitrust protections and other political privileges usually reserved for public utilities only makes things morally worse.

The erosion of a sense of moral community and the common good extends to the more particular sport community as well. I have already documented that professional athletes' primary concern appears to be furthering their own careers, even if it compromises the good of the sports from which they make their living. That accounts for players' leaving teams and local communities at every chance they get simply to raise their salaries; professional sport franchises do the same, sometimes – despite the formidable logistical difficulties – with greater dispatch (think of the infamous overnight move of the Baltimore Colts to Indianapolis) if the decimal points on the check line up better somewhere else. Even those who stay put are not above blackmailing their current hosts to get a better financial package.

Where does this leave the fans? The short and simple answer is: in a lurch. The longer answer calls to mind Seinfeld's well-known joke that with players and franchises on the constant move, all that is left the spectators to cheer for is laundry.[22] However, even this joke falls flat because, as it turns out, clubs regularly change their team uniforms and logos to boost their merchandising profits. What this really means then is that fans are left out on the cold: the civic functions that sports spectatorship used to serve (mainly class and race mixing) it no longer serves, owing among other things to such crude, cash-raising schemes as professional seat licenses (in which people have to pay for the privilege to purchase tickets, a scheme that some have likened, appropriately, to renting menus in a restaurant) and escalating ticket prices.

Susan Fauldi observes a further fraying of the civic and moral fabric of fandom in her comparison of the fans of the old Cleveland Browns franchise to the fans of its new, present franchise.[23] Paul Brown, the founding coach of the old Browns, cut his teeth in the coaching field at Massillon High School, the football team of which gained national prominence under his tutelage. In the mid-1940s, he sought to forge a tighter relationship with the local community by turning fans into civic boosters. He did mean civic boosters, because the fans (given the times, of course, he was concerned only with the masculine gender) adopted players on the team and served as their surrogate fathers. This approach meant (among other things) spending time with them off the field, helping them if they got into trouble, making sure that they were in good scholastic standing, and occasionally even paying for food and clothing. As one might imagine, the bonding that developed between team and spectators by virtue of the latter's caretaking role was something to behold. What is more, given that America was just coming out from under a devastating depression, one would be hard pressed to overestimate the importance of this mutual bonding of team and community. As Fauldi writes, "For a man to have a hand in the making of a team's fortunes, at a time when the making of everything else was fast slipping out of his grasp, was the root of what it meant to be a 'fan'."[24] Brown was able to carry this paternalistic brand of spectatorship successfully for a time over to the professional Browns when he became their head coach – with the same strong communitarian results. However, in 1961, when Art Modell took over as owner of the Cleveland franchise, the NFL was in the full throes of transforming itself into a highly profitable business. Not long after that, most working-class fans of the earlier era found themselves priced out of the live spectator market, consigned either to watching the games at home alone or with friends or at their local sports bars. Needless to say, this did little to strengthen the bonds between the community and the team. Though those ties remain remarkably strong considering the shoddy treatment that these fans have received, they are less taut than they used to be, meaning that they still bind to a point but lack the moral cohesiveness they formerly had when they verged on the solidarity of friendship.

If one had to offer a *reductio ad absurdum* of the morally dispiriting effects of the wholesale marketing of professional sports, I suppose NASCAR auto racing would be a perfect candidate. The reason why is that the pandering of sports to money here is impossible to miss. To begin with the racing cars themselves, it is exceedingly difficult to find a space on them that is not taken up by some corporate name or logo; the same, by the way, goes for the racers' garb. The appeal to corporate sponsors is crystal clear: they get to display their brand name directly on the cars themselves so that they are constantly in the sight lines of the viewers for hours on end without having to lay out a significant chunk of change on an expensive commercial that runs at most for a few minutes. Of course, this is why different parts of the car fetch different prices. Not surprisingly, the most telegenic parts of the car command the highest prices (e.g., the hood and rear quarter panels of the car go for anywhere from $7 to $17 million). NASCAR drivers are also heavily recruited for television commercials, and they receive intensive media training sessions so that, when interviewed, they can effectively and seamlessly plug their sponsors' products. To make matters worse, corporate sponsors are also given considerable input on a racing team's choice of drivers to ensure that only the most media-friendly and savvy drivers represent that team.[25] This is, I think it is safe to say, professional sport in extremis, where the dominance of the market is so entrenched that one has to pinch oneself repeatedly to remind oneself that it is also a sport.

The brief against intercollegiate sports

Unlike professional sports, college and university sports are freighted with both moral and educational meanings and values. This is why, to reiterate, I have singled them out, along with professional sports, for closer scrutiny. In my analysis, however, I target the moral rather than the educational dimension of intercollegiate sports, because that is my central focus and because the educational shortcomings of these sports have been well documented and widely discussed.[26]

The main difference between intercollegiate and professional sports is the very insistence by the former on this distinction itself, on not running together the aims of these supposed disparate athletic institutions. In fact, it says as much on the first page of the 1997–8 National Collegiate Athletic Association (NCAA) manual, which forthrightly declares that the purpose of sports at this level is "to maintain intercollegiate athletics as an integral part of the educational program and to the athlete as an integral part of the student body and, by doing so, retain a clear line of demarcation between intercollegiate athletics and professional sports."[27] The ethical part of this declaration is itself part of the demarcation effort in so far as it seeks to protect intercollegiate sports from commercial manipulation and exploitation by safeguarding their alleged amateur status, their supposed commitment to the love of athletic struggle rather than the love of money. What we have here then, at least doctrinally, is not only a decidedly ethical model of sports but one that presciently recognizes that one of the main moral evils befouling contemporary sports is their obsession with money. At very least, this should give aid and comfort to moral critics of sports, because they should have no reason to fear that in wielding their critical scalpels they will be regarded as interlopers. For the same reason, they should have no fear that in training their sights on the corrupting influence of money on sports and on subjecting their evidence of wrongdoing to the public, they have somehow deviated from their appointed role and committed some untoward act. After all, moral analysis and talk are built-in features of intercollegiate sports and one of the principal ways in which they represent themselves to the larger public so as not to be lumped together with professional sports.

Unfortunately, the reality of intercollegiate sports, as even the most casual observer of them will be quick to discern, is another matter entirely. For sports at this level are, in fact, almost indistinguishable from professional sports and certainly are driven by the same market imperatives. Indeed, intercollegiate sports is a multimillion dollar enterprise that is financed by large-dollar television contracts, licensing fees for athletic clothing, generous corporate sponsorships, and public financing in the form of bonds that are used, among other things, to build new athletic facilities. This would account for why most Division I athletic programs find it necessary to maintain their own extensive marketing divisions and why they pursue with gusto whatever capital ventures might be available to them: does the refrain *searching for new markets* sound familiar? The very same goes for the NCAA, which, despite its regulatory oversight role, is dependent for most of its funding on the financial success of big-time college football and especially basketball programs. Like professional sport franchises, it sold itself to the highest public bidder when it relocated its headquarters – the lucky (or unlucky) winner was Indianapolis, which offered the NCAA a whopping $50 million public subsidy.

That is not to say, however, that there is no important difference between college and professional sports. Indeed, there is an important difference between them, and it does have something to do with the professed moral aims of the former. However, in this instance the moral difference is of no moment because it merely serves as a cover for an economic difference. And a substantial economic difference at that, for by passing themselves off as amateur, nonprofit, ethically beholden organizations, college athletic departments are obliged neither to pay players for the financial bonanza they reap nor pay taxes on the lucrative television contracts, corporate sponsorships, and licensing deals they sign, which together number in the millions of dollars. What is more, they enable colleges and universities to install the same sort of cartel economic arrangements on which professional sport franchises pride themselves. What we have here, therefore, is moral tomfoolery of the worst sort, one in which greed is given greater scope in intercollegiate sports for ostensibly principled moral reasons.

If there is anything privileged about intercollegiate sports, then, it is their protected economic standing, not their moral standing. So, we have good reason to look with suspicion on their declarations of moral rectitude, as they merely confer legitimacy on all manner of moral mischief. This is, no doubt, why in his widely praised and read book, *Exploitation*, the moral philosopher Alan Wertheimer devoted an entire chapter to the moral chicanery of intercollegiate sports.[28] Further, this is, no doubt, why moral critics of college sports have to tread carefully within their precincts. For the empirical evidence is rather overwhelming that they are more likely to be regarded, on and off campus, as piranhas (under the circumstances, most would welcome the accusation of interloper as a blessing of sorts) and that their public declarations of athletic wrongdoing would be met, again on and off campus, with scorn and ad hominem attacks on their creditability, character, and (not least) mental stability. These are not only inauspicious settings for moral critics to do their work but – especially if the would-be critic is a faculty member – perhaps the most dangerous settings in which to do such work. I do not exclude here either financial or physical peril. So, to pick up intercollegiate sports by the amateur handle is to pick them up by the wrong handle. It is no use, therefore, pretending that they swing free of the market, because it is principally there that they ply their trade and teach their lessons. As was the case with professional sports, the market is no less intrusive here, because it insinuates itself into every nook and cranny of intercollegiate sports. This is no more true than in the practice of intercollegiate sports themselves. For the likelihood that sports will be treated as ends rather than as mere means is no greater here than it was in professional sports. So, once again, athletes are taught the not-so-subtle lesson that it is not only okay to be on the take but that it would be foolish (against their self-interests) not to be so, not to seize every available opportunity to parlay their athletic success into financial success and notoriety. In addition, why should we expect them to behave any differently when everyone else in college sports, from coaches to university presidents, is in it mostly for the money? As Sheed writes of the allure of money in college sports, "That's why the coach is doing it, with his [and her] contract on the side with the shoe company ... And that's why the school is doing it, as it angles to get into the big-bucks tournaments and appear on TV."[29]

Speaking of coaches' shoe contracts (as I soon speak of televised sport tournaments), by the 1990s it was not uncommon for coaches to be paid in the $100,000 range to affix their signatures to such contracts, with successful coaches from high-profile athletic schools commanding four or five times that amount. Shoe companies also lavish college coaches with such perks as stock options and assists, financial and otherwise, and player recruitment.[30] Still other high-profile coaches have been offered executive positions with shoe companies (e.g., John Thompson, former basketball coach at Georgetown, appointed to the board of directors of Nike).[31] Because these lucrative deals are typically publicized by the local media, there is little chance that the players are oblivious to these cozy financial arrangements.

Of course, the NCAA forbids players from seeking their own endorsements, but this only makes matters morally worse because of the massive hypocrisy of such a restrictive policy. After all, if it is okay for coaches to make more than a little money on the side, why not the players? Hence, any invocation of the principle of amateurism in such instances is only likely, and rightly, to arouse moral derision, not moral compliance. For the message conveyed by these kinds of financial transactions, as already noted, is just too clear to be lost on players and, no doubt, instills in them the hardly moral incentive to cash in themselves even if it means breaking rules.

The long arms of the market are further corrosive of college sports because they raise the stakes of winning at the same time that they narrow our understanding and appreciation of the more complex notion of athletic success. It is just not good enough any more to play well – to play to the best of one's ability – if one loses. Despite all the flowery rhetoric to the contrary, players and coaches know that their jobs are on the line no matter how well they perform on or off the field if the board of trustees and college president look askance at their won-loss records. That is why such notions as tenure, so vital to academics who work on the political and moral edges of society, and loyalty, so vital to the maintenance of stable social relations, have no conceptual or practical traction in the sports world. And that is why, no doubt, to add fuel to the already white-hot competitive fire of college sports, the NCAA decided in 1973 to eliminate four-year scholarships in favor of one-year grants that are annually reviewed. In that way, athletes who are not up to the arduous task of playing top-level sports can be quickly dispatched and new, fresh, and more-promising talent can be brought in almost as quickly to right a listing ship. Why, indeed, should colleges and universities be expected to make four-year commitments to their student-athletes when winning rather than the fostering of athletic, moral, or educational excellence is their bottom-line goal?

In this kind of setting, it would take something akin to a miracle for players to come to think of sports as things worthy of pursuit in themselves. So, though amateurism may be the official ideology of college sports, it has next to nothing to do with the practice of these sports. On the contrary, the market reigns supreme here just as it does in professional sports; that is why athletes schooled in the ways of college sports learn pretty much the same lessons as professional athletes. Yet, there is an important difference here and that is that the opportunities afforded to college players are both more limited and more cruelly inflated than for their professional counterparts. Let me explain.

To be on the take at the college level means, above all else, grooming oneself for the professional ranks. The dream of turning professional and earning an extraordinary amount of money is powerful, especially for African-Americans who presently dominate, for example, collegiate football and basketball. However, for many of these athletes, the dream is just a pipedream and a savagely unkind one at that, for their chances of making it to the next level are miniscule. To be exact, as LaFeber notes, "the odds of a 20- to 29-year old African-American playing in the NBA was 135,800 to 1 (and for Hispanics, 33,300,000 to 1)."[32] Despite these formidable odds, few of these athletes are deterred from pursuing their dreams of turning professional and instead use their college careers to prepare themselves for making this transition. There would be something morally uplifting about their diligence, their resolve to chase their dreams no matter the cost, were it not for the fact that a disproportionate number of black college athletes (according to a 1990 survey, some 44 percent) as compared to white athletes (according to the same survey, 16 percent) cling to this dream.[33] There is clearly something quite radically amiss here and, to put it bluntly, it morally stinks. Somehow or other, and I clearly hold athletic officials and institutions at least partially to blame here (not to mention larger

society), black athletes are being encouraged to view sports as their economic salvation, and this only compounds the moral offense of college sports players selling their soul to the highest bidder.

The very same can be said about the so-termed minor, or nonrevenue, college sports. For they, too, are a casualty of the market, as their numbers dwindle in order to stave off the financial drain they exact on the revenue-producing sports. As I mentioned in the introduction, it was a clever ploy on the part of athletic officials (mainly, male athletic directors) to finger women's college sports, and Title IX specifically, for their demise, but that dog won't hunt.[34] Rather, the main culprits are men's basketball and (especially) men's football programs, which are exceedingly expensive to maintain. Of course, they have been able to escape the wrath of nonrevenue sports advocates because of the large pots of money they supposedly contribute to the coffers of the athletic department. In other words, they are the ones – or so it is claimed – that make it possible even to field a program of college sports in the first place, an activity otherwise too costly to support.

However, one of the dirty, large secrets of intercollegiate sports is that most if not all athletic programs lose money. Part of the reason why it remains a secret is attributable to arcane accounting principles. According to Zimbalist, even in the case in which those principles are generally accepted (though they are not, except in one instance, in college sports), they can be used to turn a four-million-dollar profit into a two-million-dollar loss.[35] The other reason why it remains a secret, however, is because of the clever and altogether legal use of these cryptic accounting principles. This requires a little bit of explanation.

If we stand back for a moment, as Zimbalist does in his book, and survey the whole of college sports (in other words, not just Division I A,) we get a better picture of the economic plight of these sports. By Zimbalist's estimates (and this certainly is neither a secret nor a surprise), all the Divisions except I A failed to show a profit. To be more precise, of the 600 plus athletic programs in Divisions II and III, not a single one generated a profit; of the 200 or so Division I AA and AAA programs, again none showed a profit. By contrast, of the 100 or so Division I A programs, a hefty 43 percent reported a surplus.[36]

Now, if we cut the analysis off at this point, it would confirm the idea that close to one-half of the big-time programs are able to operate in the red, and it would also support the plausible inference from this that the reason they are able to turn a profit is because either (or both) their football and basketball teams are bringing in the necessary revenue to pay the bills for everyone else. However, as Zimbalist takes pains to show, any analysis of the economic impact of college sports worth the paper on which it is written must also consider the costs run up by money-making sports, such as football and basketball. Accounting for those costs, however, is easier said than done, owing once again to the clever but quite legal use of largely inscrutable accounting principles. However, it is also difficult to get a fix on their true costs because of a particular accounting technique that, though hardly inscrutable, is just the same very effective in disguising actual costs, something called "related party transactions." For example, athletic departments often charge their scholarship fees to the college's financial aid office, their substantial coaching salaries to the faculty pool, and their debt service on facility construction to the college's general facilities budget.[37] In addition, they frequently assign other big-ticket money items to off-budget accounts, such as the booster's club. However, once we take into account these related costs, as Zimbalist deftly shows, the profits reported by these Division I A athletic schools not only vanish but morph into an average loss of $823,000.[38]

Skeptics, of course, might retort that the reason why these schools run such deficits is that football and basketball profits can go only so far in supporting the increasing costs required to offer a full slate of men's nonrevenue and women's sports. The overall deficits, they might argue further, do not show that football and basketball are not doing their fair economic share, indeed more than their fair share but, on the contrary, that the rest of men's nonrevenue sports and women's sports are not doing their fair share, are not pulling their own economic weight. However, this claim is doubtful. The problem here is yet again – surprise, surprise – an accounting one. For when colleges report their expenses to the NCAA, as Zimbalist points out, they are not required to target those expenses to specific sports. So, for example, facilities maintenance expenses for football stadiums and basketball arenas are routinely charged to the entire program no matter that they are used exclusively by these teams. The same is true of the overhead expenses of the athletic departments, such as administrative salaries, travel, entertainment, advertising, utilities, and the like, which again are assigned to the entire program, even though the lion's share of those expenses is incurred by the football and basketball teams.[39]

When we factor in all the data, then, any notion that college sports operate only partially along market lines (e.g., share the wealth in a manner similar to nonprofits and dissimilar to markets) goes up in smoke. On the contrary, the only thing that distinguishes them from true markets is that they are legally allowed to run their affairs as cartels, which only worsens the moral predicament of college sports, not to mention the bleak economic outlook for African-American college athletes, men's nonrevenue sports, and women's sports. The problem is that there are not any other countervailing regulative forces in the vexed world of intercollegiate sports, on or off campus, to rein in these powerful market forces.[40]

The recent greater involvement of college presidents in athletic matters on their campuses is a case in point. When in 1996 the NCAA was persuaded (by the work of the Knight commission in the early 1990s) to give greater control to college presidents in running athletic programs, many thought this would go a long way toward eliminating abuses at this level. However, college presidents, already overextended and preoccupied with fundraising responsibilities for the general campus, were no match for the athletic juggernaut. In many cases, they proved to be allies, not critics, of the commercialization of college sports, evidently unable to resist the powers that be. As James Duderstadt, former president of the University of Michigan, plainly put it, "When push comes to shove and you put a lot of presidents around the table, they're going to go for the top dollar, whether it's TV negotiations or putting games on at 9 o'clock."[41] Perhaps their reticence to stem the influence of money in college sports is owed to their own complicity in the corporatization of the university itself or to their being star-struck fans themselves or to their toadying to the boards of trustees that they serve or to some combination of these factors. Whatever the reason, the commercialization of college sports grew worse under their watch, enough so to provoke yet another reconvening of the Knight commission in 2000, this time under the tutelage of Hodding Carter, to consider other possible reforms.[42]

It is equally clear that the conferences in which individual schools play and the commissioners who govern these conferences are neither equipped nor inclined to undertake significant reforms of college sports. Truth to tell, they are part of the problem, not the solution. The principal reason why is that conferences have become the main negotiating agents for the television broadcast rights of college games. It was not so very long ago that teams formed themselves into conferences based on athletic prowess and geographical proximity. Since the advent of televised sports, however, and the sculpting of sports into entertainment vehicles for students, alumni, and boosters, money and – as one athletic director crassly but honestly phrased it – "brand image" are the main concerns of conferences.[43] This is why colleges go to great lengths to align themselves with the richest and most powerful athletic conferences. This explains the recent spate of conference jumping by schools as well, in which Miami's and Virginia Tech's (the latter with the lobbying help of the governor) defections from the Big East to the Atlantic Coast Conference (ACC) are perhaps the most notable example. Their protestations to the contrary, cash is the main impelling force here.

The so-termed Big Six, which includes the ACC, the Big 12, the Southeastern Conference (SEC), the Pac-10, the Big 10, and the Big East, should be singled out here, as they attract most of the TV dollars and the teams with the best records from these conferences are guaranteed slots in the football Bowl Championship Series (BCS), thereby assuring them and the conferences they represent a large end-of-the-season pay off. Schools from other lesser conferences have an uphill battle to get into the lucrative football bowl series despite their records. For the BCS puts the accent less on maximizing the highest level of competition and more on advancing the economic fortunes of select schools, especially those with a large

and profligate fan base. It is this built-in disparity that prompted Zimbalist's sardonic remark that "[t]he overall picture of bowl access in Division IA almost makes the income distribution in Haiti look equitable."[44]

So, not only are college sports market vehicles through and through but, especially in their conference getup, retrograde ones at that. Moneymaking and handling is their game, moral reform is not. Since conference commissioners answer to no one in the academic community and are evaluated almost entirely on the size of the television contracts they broker, there is little prospect that things will change for the better anytime soon. It should come as no surprise, then, that the largest moneymaker among the Big Six, the SEC (which took in $81.5 million in 2000), has the worst ethical record. As of 2002, six of the 12 member schools were either on probation or accused of unethical conduct, and since 1990, the SEC has been penalized nine times, far more than any other conference.[45] This is proof enough, I think, that money and college sports is an unseemly and unworkable moral mix.

Of course, I have only in passing mentioned the NCAA, whose main job it is to protect the moral and educational mission of college sports. I have, however, intimated that the NCAA is no moral savior of college sports. On yet closer inspection, however, it is evident that that claim is at best an understatement, as the NCAA is itself complicit in the morally benighted standing of these sports. The reason why is not difficult to discern because, as already mentioned, it depends for most of its revenue on the money generated from the television broadcast of its annual basketball tournament. In 1990, the NCAA signed a huge contract with CBS for $1 billion over seven years to carry the tournament, more than double the annual value of the previous contract, and in 1994 they renegotiated the contract with CBS for $1.75 billion again over seven years. Though that kind of money will not buy you moral integrity, it will buy you plenty of influence over the game. And the NCAA did not disappoint CBS when, in the first half of its 1997 men's final, it allowed an astonishing eight minutes of commercials to 20 minutes of playing time; not even the NBA tolerates commercial interruptions of this length.[46]

To say, then, that the NCAA is primarily a business association and that its main interest is less the moral integrity of the game than the financial returns it generates, is hardly an exaggeration. Of course, that it does not primarily serve the game or the athletes who play it was evident as early as 1953, when the NCAA coined the phrase *student-athlete* not to give voice to the academic commitments of college sports but to help their member schools to fend off legally the workmen's compensation insurance claims filed by injured football players.[47] Further, that the NCAA does not take its regulatory responsibilities for the ethical conduct of these sports seriously is also readily apparent by the resources it devotes to enforcement of its stated principles and rules. As Zimbalist forcefully writes, with around 1,000 schools to regulate, a rulebook that takes up three volumes and 1,268 pages of rules and regulations, and an annual budget in the neighborhood of $283 million, one would think that the NCAA would devote more than $1.5 million to enforcement, would hire more than 15 investigators to check on rule compliance, and would pay them well enough to ensure low turnover in their enforcement staff.[48] However, that paltry sum, woefully inadequate enforcement staff, and poor pay resulting in a large turnover of compliance officers is what the NCAA actually commits to ensure that everything is up and up on the college sports scene.

To make matters worse, even with this pathetic attention to enforcement, the NCAA more often than not finds itself on the wrong side of the ethical divide when it comes to protecting college players from exploitation. For example, when some in congress became distressed with the scandalously low graduation rates of players in high-profile college football and basketball programs (which, as I noted before, is especially egregious given the insurmountable odds that most of these players face in trying to make it to the professional ranks), they introduced the Right to Know Act, which would simply require colleges and universities to publicize the graduation rates of their players. Leading the opposition against the passage of this act was the NCAA, who worked hard (fortunately unsuccessfully) to defeat it. All of this suggests that the NCAA is a regulatory body in name only and that its public moral posture is just a convenient ploy to divert attention from its ruthless economic agenda.

It is thus apparent that college sports are no more suited to a moral life than are professional sports. Indeed, how could they be, when everyone is too busy conjuring up ways to make money off sports or (what comes to the same thing) managing their own careers to give much thought or attention to the moral state of the games that they play or oversee. That is why cheating is as prevalent in college sports as it is in professional sports and why a technical regard has replaced a moral regard for such things as rule breaking and rule bending and the very notion of fair play itself. Those responsible would have us believe that it is aboveboard to break rules when it is to one's advantage and to refrain from doing so when it is not; this attitude reduces fairness to a not-so-fine-grained strategic sense that it is perfectly okay to take advantage of others as long as they are similarly disposed to take advantage of you. And that outlook, in turn, curiously means that what would otherwise be branded as unethical conduct if done in isolation is perfectly ethical if done in concert with others. It would also explain why the observance of even the most elementary moral norms in sports at this level, for example, the refusals of a player to take advantage of, say, an injured player or to accept a tainted victory are often touted or (as the case may be) hyped, as if they were supererogatory acts meriting the highest of moral praise, not to mention publicity. When it comes to the morality of college sports, therefore, the ordinary is made to appear quite extraordinary, and the extraordinary is made to appear as quite technically stupid. The exceptions are those sincere types looking for some moral consolation to justify their involvement in sports and for those less sincere public relations types groping for anything they can find to avert our eyes from the moral mess we call college sports. In other words, there is no reason to worry that fair play and sportsmanship will overtake cheating anytime soon.[49]

Unfortunately (but, of course, not surprisingly), the empirical evidence regarding the moral laxity of intercollegiate sports is rather overwhelming. As Louis Menand reports, college athletes are more likely than their non-athletic peers to regard being very well off financially as an essential or very important goal of life, which would further account for why male athletes at least frequently choose business-related fields for their majors.[50] Now, there is nothing wrong in wanting to make a lot of money – wouldn't we all in the right circumstances? However, there is something morally out of whack with rating this goal as an essential or even very important good, given the values of liberal arts institutions themselves, which place far more emphasis on the moral importance of a reflective life and on the value of public service.[51] It does suggest that there is something about the market trappings of these sports, as I have painstakingly tried to document, that prompts athletes not only to relegate too much importance to money making and not enough to the moral integrity of sports but too often to forsake the latter for the former.

When we couple this inflated importance of earning a lot of money with the further facts that athletes are also more likely than their peers to regard competition as an intrinsic good both on and off the playing field and less likely to assume responsibility for others, we have good cause to be alarmed.[52] Again, there is nothing wrong with competition per se, or at least a certain moral version of competition that is itself based on cooperation, on a consideration of the interests of others, but there is very definitely something morally worrisome about the kind of competition to which most of these athletes have been exposed, the type that places a premium on winning above all else. For when winning becomes this important, athletes and their "superiors" are more apt to cheat to get what they want and to disregard the harm that they do to others in the process, just as colleges are more apt, in Menand's words, "to put money into coaching and [athletic] facilities, and to trade academic promise for athletic talent in admissions."[53] Further, if this were not morally odious enough, a favorite ploy used by students to condone academic cheating – alas, presently on the upswing – is to point to the pervasive dishonesty of the campus athletic program, as if the moral failings of the latter somehow justify the moral failings of the former.[54] Though the students' moral reasoning leaves something to be desired in this instance, the conspicuous moral lapses of college athletic programs provide easy fodder for their sophistry.

The problem here is the same problem that beset professional sports, namely the absence of a moral community. However, unlike professional sports, there is not just a potential moral constituency for college sports but a fairly vocal one if only someone would pay it some mind. I am speaking here, among others, of faculty, alumni, and the general sporting public itself, all of whom are steadfast in their view that college sports are in moral trouble today and have encroached too far into the academic and moral mission of colleges and universities. For example, a 1989 Harris poll showed that 80 percent of Americans surveyed thought college sports have overstepped their proper bounds.[55] A more recent 2003 survey commissioned by the Chronicle of Higher Education reported a similar finding, with close to 70 percent of respondents registering their disapproval of the overemphasis placed on sports in colleges and universities.[56] This same poll showed that of 21 listed goals for higher education institutions, the goal of offering sports for the entertainment of the public ranked dead last by a wide margin. Alumni dissatisfaction with the attention that their colleges and universities shower on sports is also commonplace, no doubt accounting for why the old saw that "athletic success leads to greater alumni giving" does not accord with the evidence (despite unmistakable empirical evidence that enhancement of faculty and student quality does spur greater alumni giving).[57]

To reiterate, then: there is a moral constituency for college sports and one that has not been timorous in expressing its moral discontent with the status quo. What undercuts their moral clout, however, is the inner circle that pretty much rules the roost in college sports today, and the insularity of which largely renders them impervious to the wishes of the larger public. I am referring here to what are euphemistically called the "boosters" of college sports (many would reference them in far less flattering terms), made up of local wealthy businessmen whose ties to the university are typically not academic, meaning that they are for the most part *not* alumni but often find themselves, given their wealth and the influence that follows in its train, sitting on the boards of trustees of these same colleges. Make no mistake about it, however: sports are their bailiwick and what gives them cachet with the proconsuls of the university. In exchange for their generous financial contributions to the athletic department, they are treated as royalty and provided the best seats at athletic events, not to mention highly coveted parking places close to athletic facilities and select audiences with the head football or basketball coach, usually over lunch served in the athletic department. That these seats used to be occupied – before the untrammeled pursuit of cash became the mainstay of sports marketing – by loyal fans who had modest means and could be counted on to cheer for the home team come hell or high water no one seems to notice or care.

The problem is that these so-called boosters are by and large quite content with college sports just as they are and, as one might expect, with their privileged standing within these athletic hierarchies just as they are. Because it is this narrow (both in number and purview) constituency to which university presidents ultimately have to answer (not to mention on whom ultimately have to rely for their all-important fundraising projects), there is not much chance that the larger public's moral misgivings regarding college sports are likely to have any appreciable impact on the way they conduct their affairs. This goes to show that even when a moral community is on hand to register their moral disapproval with what is going on in sports (the same, by the way, goes for politics and practically everything else in contemporary society), markets are not in the least shy about ingratiating themselves with the powers that be to forestall such efforts.

The brief against the rest of the sports world, or at least most of that world

I have already suggested that high-school sports and Olympic sports suffer from the same moral malaise as that of professional and college sports. The only thing preventing me from saying the same about youth sports and masters' sports for adult athletes is, no doubt, the market's thoroughgoing disinterest in their athletic exploits thus far and the lack of data on hand about these sports (itself revealing, as it seems to suggest that if the market chooses not to shine its light on one's athletic engagements, they must not be important enough to

catalogue or document). In any event, I want only to sketch briefly for now the moral travails of high-school and Olympic sports.

As I have already intimated, the coupling of money and sports proves to be just as morally problematic at the high-school level as it has at the college and professional levels. The saga of basketball phenomenon LeBron James is a good illustration of this, as it shows that if your talent is large enough, the director of your high-school athletic program will not hesitate to capitalize on it by playing a national schedule at larger venues to accommodate greater numbers of fans and by signing a television contract to underwrite the costs and bring in a handsome profit to boot. When the money is this good, evidently any suggestion that high-school sports should comport themselves differently than the "big boys" because their aims are not the same is not likely to carry much weight. What is more, it is becoming more commonplace, particularly in such sports as basketball, for high-school seniors to jump directly to the professional leagues, a practice that transforms high-school sports into the same kind of feeder system as the college game, unfortunately with the same predictable and regrettable results.[58] This tapping of precocious high-school athletic talent has of late developed yet a new, more troubling, wrinkle, in the vernacular called "athletic leapfrogging." It involves players skipping their senior year either to play elite college football or professional baseball (for the boys) or professional soccer (for the girls).[59] The same sort of pump priming for athletic talent also goes on outside athletic departments in the schools themselves and in the formulation of educational policy. I have in mind here the increasing reliance on open enrollment policies in schools across the country. The main point of such policies is to make it easier for young gifted athletes to pick and choose the schools for which they want to play. If there is any doubt that the educational standing of these schools figures hardly at all in their decisions, we need only point to athletic powerhouses, such as Dominguez High School in southern California. For it is schools such as these to which talented athletes flock in order to jump-start their athletic careers despite the fact that Dominguez's physical plant is dilapidated, its corridors racked by gang violence, and its basic resources so scant that students greatly

397

outnumber available books.[60] Last, there are the off-season traveling teams and coaches sponsored by the Amateur Athletic Union (AAU), which compete with their school teams and coaches for their loyalty and commitment by, among other things, paying them under the table or by putting them in touch with professional agents.

Perhaps the worse moral offenders at this level, however, are the summer football camps run by prominent university football programs and the summer basketball camps sponsored (and run since the 1980s) by such shoe companies as Nike and Adidas. The purpose of the football camps is to bring in blue-chip prospects (in other words, whom the coaches are eyeing) where they are timed, filmed, and subjected to a battery of drills and tests to gauge their athletic mettle. In effect, these camps serve the same function as that of the combines for professional football teams: the careful evaluation of athletic talent so as to spend their scholarship money wisely. What is morally off-color about these arrangements is that they are used primarily as recruiting devices by major colleges in explicit violation of NCAA policy; worse, such arrangements sometimes operate as coercive devices in the case of athletes who are "on the bubble:" told in no uncertain terms they will not be offered a scholarship unless they go to camp. It should also be said that the other major purpose of these camps is to make money, and lots of it, for the coaching staff, as they attract a large number of lesser athletes as well, those willing to pay hundreds of dollars to hone their modest skills. It is no coincidence, therefore, that colleges stagger their camps to attract the largest pool of athletic prodigies possible, which also means that it is no coincidence that many of these athletes have little choice but to attend as many of these camps as they can afford (charged anywhere from $25 to $425) to showcase their skills. It is there that they learn to talk the talk and walk the walk, becoming street-smart self-promoters on the lookout for whatever favors, financial and otherwise, may come their way. A final moral worry about these summer arrangements is that the high-school coaches who are hired to help to run them are really being hired to bring their best prospects with them, not to mention being paid in large enough sums to cover the costs of bringing them (it is not against NCAA rules for

high-school coaches to pay the camp fees of their own players).[61]

Basketball camps for high-school players sponsored by Nike and other athletic companies are even worse. The idea behind them is to gather the best high-school players from across the country under one roof to show their stuff, with most of the major college coaches in attendance watching their every move. However, the shoe companies' relations with these players begins much earlier than this and is initiated and nurtured by street agents hired by these companies. Their main job is to scour playgrounds frequented by high-school kids, where they look for talented prospects. In addition to evaluating talent, they also play the role of soothsayer, trying to convince such kids that basketball is their future and that they would be well advised to attend schools that endorse the company's athletic products to ensure that future. This would explain why there is a strong correlation between the sneakers that these kids wear and the institutions of higher education for which they end up playing. If such talent scouts happen as well to come across players who possess extraordinary talent, their other, no-less-important job is to establish a relation with these budding stars with the idea of signing them later to a contract endorsing their products. For now, however, those talented kids have to be content with smaller perks, such as free shoes (which are also dispensed to the high-school teams for which they play) and to be emboldened by the promise of greater things to come.[62]

What Nike and others shoe companies get in return for their investment is not insubstantial and includes prominent advertisements for their shoes and athletic apparel, possible future superstar endorsements, and (not least) close relationships with college coaches who have the wherewithal to make those relations pay off in a big way. What the college coaches get in return is no less impressive: a central venue in which to scout the best players (which saves on travel and other expenses), lucrative shoe contracts, and company-based recruitment incentives for athletes to attend their schools. Finally, what the players get is less an honest evaluation of their basketball skills and fortunes than inside knowledge on how to game the system for their own benefit. Of course, no one who is a party to these transactions gets an education in the moral possibilities of sports or a greater appreciation of their internal goods, at least not in any direct or substantive sense. But then again, no one caught up in these affairs seems to have much interest in such moral lessons.

Finally, Olympic sports might be the biggest moral disappointment of all. For what is particularly galling about their mercenary conduct is that these sports were from the "get-go" supposed to be about ethics rather than pocketbooks, to be devoted to such lofty goals as the furtherance of international peace and tolerance than to enriching Olympic officials, sponsors, and participants. That is why the founder of the modern games, Coubertin, and his disciples never tired of promoting the games as a kind of secular religion, devoted in equal measure to athletic excellence and the triumph of a cosmopolitan state of mind, one respectful of different cultures and peoples.

The sad fact, however, is that the Olympics are no longer Olympian, at least from an ethical and political vantage point. For the only secular religion they seem inclined to support and propagate today (public relations campaigns to confuse us aside) is a suspect form of capitalism, which insists on treating and conducting the Games as if they were a string of fast-food restaurants. That explains why they get far more worked up about protecting their brand name and famous interlaced five-ring symbol (which, as Lipsyte ruefully observes, has become just "another sports logo, battling for the public's recognition with the Swoosh and the major league baseball batter's silhouette")[63] than by enacting true reform that would put an end once and for all to the graft and bribery of recent past Games.

If there is blame to be assessed here, it probably should be laid at the feet of past president of the International Olympic Committee (IOC) Juan Samaranch. For it was during his long tenure, beginning in 1980, that the Olympics went on a selling binge lending its name to any firm and product willing to shell out the requisite sum of cash. As a result, the IOC quickly transitioned from a cash strapped, aristocratic top-heavy organization to a cash-loaded, market manager-dominated one, presently presiding over an annual budget of $100 million plus.[64] It is no secret that very little of this money gets down to the grassroots level to develop exemplary sports programs or to disseminate the goals of world peace and respect. What little does trickle down allows the IOC to ponder its ethical dilemmas (mainly, performance-enhancing drugs because they most threaten its corporate image) at five-star hotels in such world-class cities as Paris. Who says doing ethics doesn't pay?

Of course, Olympic athletes are no paragons of virtue either. Most have professional agents at hand, not to mention a retinue of business types and accountants, to cash in immediately on their athletic triumphs. Endorsements, of course, are the major sought-after financial prizes in this regard, and winning a gold medal in the right event can bring in a number of these, not to mention a tidy sum of money. Money is not only a temporary distraction here; it upsets the entire Olympic apple cart, as the key to using sport as the medium to encourage respect for cultural differences is to have athletes bring their culture with them into the international athletic arena. The heavy symbolism of the athletes marching in unison together behind their flags and outfitted in a common national uniform in the opening ceremonies – and the no-less-heavy symbolism in which athletes drop their patriotic pose and in a cosmopolitan gesture mingle with members of all the other countries in the closing ceremony – crucially depend for their significance on the fact that these national and international identities and symbols really mean something to everyone concerned, especially to the participants. However, when athletes change countries to compete in the Olympics (as often as some change their clothes) and when their reason for doing so is based on financial calculations of success and the size of the markets of the countries they represent, these symbols become farcical. Of course, the same criticism holds for the countries that not only gladly accept these itinerant athletes but actively encourage them to jump ship and relax citizenship requirements to make the transition as seamless as possible.

The moral debaucheries of the IOC offering itself and its founding ideals up for sale and of Olympic athletes willingly forsaking their national identity for the right price are one thing (and as I have argued, a very bad thing), but the moral debauchery of the IOC welcoming into its ranks a well-known political thug is quite another thing – and, I want to argue (as if an argument is really needed in this case), a very, very bad thing. I am speaking here of the recent admittance into the IOC of a former Ugandan military commander who was Idi Amin's henchman during his infamous reign of terror. It is incredible, to say the least, that any organization – let alone one supposedly ethical, such as the IOC – could see fit to commit and then, most astonishingly, condone such a thing. But the IOC did indeed do such a thing and had the audacity to try to justify it. As one Olympic spokesman crudely put it, "Do you want to push for human rights around the world? That's Amnesty International. Or do you want African athletes at the Olympic Games?"[65] The appalling ignorance of this incautious declaration (for it is not only the job of the Olympics to promote human rights across the globe but one of its founding ideals to do just that) is matched only by its impudence. It tacitly proclaims that getting as many athletes from as many continents in the world to come to the Olympics (of course, of paramount importance to the furtherance of its financial ambitions) overrides its ethical commitment to do so in a way that promotes world peace rather than setting it back. It implies that there are not enough good and decent people from this part of the world to join the Olympic community without having to recruit and consort with hoodlums. To say this is a new ethical low for the Olympic movement almost sounds like a bad joke were it not for the moral *gravitas* of the situation.

Where does this leave us?

My moral indictment of contemporary sports seems to have landed us in a most unsavory place. For there does not appear to be any form of sport today that has not been sullied in one way or another by the almighty dollar. This has the effect of making my sketch of the Arcadian-like moral ambience of the State of Play seem even more Arcadian and thus plainly unreachable by present standards (in other words, just another in a long line of useless utopian fantasies). My indictment also seems to suggest that what the market has emptied out of sports, precisely those moral qualities I claimed to discover in them in the State of Play, cannot be retrieved because they have been hopelessly compromised. All of which makes it difficult to resist Tannsjo's stunning claim that "if we are to grow as moral agents, we need to cultivate a distaste for our present interest in and admiration for sports."[66]

As one might suspect, however, I regard such misgivings and claims as (though understandable) plainly overstated, as too far removed from the facts to warrant our assent. For though the facts are not especially encouraging, neither are they so damning that we simply have to write off sports as a lost cause. My present assertions to the contrary, however, are just that: mere assertions. So, I will have to make my case, this time with arguments, that sports are not too far gone, that they can be morally rehabilitated by undoing their present marginalization.

I have no illusion, however, that making that case will be easy, will be anything other than a daunting and arduous task. However, as a first step in this direction, I need to provide some larger historical context for my moral critique of present-day sports. I must do so because all I have offered to this point is a synchronic glimpse of sports as they already exist, which – though it may give some tentative clues as to their future development – does not suggest how they have evolved to this point. For this, a diachronic perspective is required, one that situates my present morally disparaging story of contemporary sports into a larger, historically extended story. However, because this taking the longer measure of sports is so vital to making sense of their present moral standing, of how best to interpret that standing,[67] I want first to consider a well-known, if not hegemonic, diachronic historical narrative of sports: one that takes its point of departure from their complicity in the market but that I find unpersuasive and, therefore, reject.

Notes

1. Bernard Williams. *Shame and Necessity*. Berkeley, CA: University of California Press, 1994, p. 77.
2. At the same time, however, it goes without saying that they are too large and influential a target simply to ignore.
3. Nicholas Dixon. "On Winning and Athletic Superiority." In W. J. Morgan, K. Meier,

A. Schneider (eds). *Ethics in Sport.* Urbana, IL: Human Kinetics, 2001, p. 62.

4. Ibid., p. 64.

5. Ibid., p. 65.

6. To the extent that intercollegiate sports likewise rely on an intraleague playoff system, they too are inculpated by Dixon's powerful arguments. However, Dixon offers an important caveat here and one that we need to keep in mind. To the extent that it is impractical if not logistically impossible for teams to play each other regularly over the course of the season, as is the case with the Olympics, World Cup, and (in collegiate sports) national championships, a playoff system is no longer a choice but a necessity. In these special circumstances, then, playoffs are not second best to season records as measures of athletic excellence but the only available method, however imperfect, to assess excellence. This does not, however, lessen the force of Dixon's central arguments, as it still remains the case that overall season records are the most accurate way in which to determine athletic success and that when they are an option they are clearly superior to playoffs. Lastly, collegiate sports are especially guilty of privileging money over excellence when highly talented teams pay relatively lucrative sums to much less talented teams to entice them to play their games in the former's home stadiums. These seldom make for good matchups, but they do enable the host teams both to pad their winning records and to play an extra home game, both of which affect the bottom line. This is a serious problem today because it has become of late a standard practice.

7. I owe this point and the background documentation to Merrell Noden's, "A New Record – By a Mile." *Sports Illustrated*, 91, No. 3 (July 19, 1999), p. 34.

8. See Mike Wise, "As the Stars in the NBA Rise, The League's Level of Play Falls." *New York Times* (February 8, 1998), pp. 1, 18.

9. Wilfred Sheed, "Why Sports Matter." *Wilson Quarterly* (Winter, 1995), p. 22.

10. I am indebted for the points raised in this paragraph to Christopher Lasch's interesting account of sports in his widely celebrated and read book, *The Culture of Narcissism.* New York: Warner Books, 1979, pp. 100–24.

11. On this point, see Walter LaFeber, *Michael Jordan and the New Global Capitalism.* New York: W.W. Norton, 1999, p. 145.

12. Susan Fauldi. "Sold Out: From Team Booster to TV Backdrop: The Demise of the True Fan." *Utne Reader* No. 97 (January–February, 2000), p. 54.

13. Sheed, "Why Sports Matter," p. 21.

14. Wise, "As the Stars in the NBA Rise, The League's Level of Play Falls," p. 18.

15. Robert Wright. "Boycott Nike and Reebok: Not Because They Oppress Asian Sweatshop Workers, But Because They Oppress Black Teenagers." *Slate* (posted May 22, 1997), p. 3.

16. See David Anderson, "Agents and Perks and Harmful Effects." *New York Times* (November 19, 2000), p. 41.

17. Sheed, "Why Sports Matter," p. 65.

18. I owe the point about Pat Riley to George Vescey's article, "Don't Worry: Sportsmanship Won't Be Catching." *New York Times* (February 21, 1999), p. 39.

19. Given my own extensive reliance in this chapter on journalists, especially from the New York Times and other magazines that pride themselves as much on their reporting prowess as on their ability to attract commercial advertising, I must exempt newspapers and magazines such as these and those that emulate them from the present critique.

20. Criminal action that crosses the border of acceptable moral action as well is the notable exception for sports pundits. However, the reportage of such athletic misconduct is almost always dominated by speculations as to the declining market value of the fallen hero, for which so-called public relations and management experts are called on en masse for their counsel.

21. Players, and especially their union representatives, have failed miserably on this score. To cite just one instance: when senator Arlen Specter from Pennsylvania introduced legislation requiring the National Football League to set aside 10 percent of its considerable television revenues for the building and renovating of stadiums, the players and their unions opposed the measure in lockstep with NFL management. Whereas the commissioner of the NFL, Paul Tagliabue, at least tried to offer some justification for his opposition by appealing speciously to the interests of local communities (which in this case was code not for the communities themselves but for the individual owners of sports teams), Gene Upshaw, the executive director of the NFL Players Association, based his opposition to Specter's bill squarely on the negative impact it would have on players' salaries. See Mike Freeman's piece, "Owners of NFL Teams Are Nervously Watching the Estate Tax Bill." *New York Times* (July 30, 2000), p. 26.

22. I lifted this joke from Steve Rushin's essay, "Who Stole the Show?" *Sports Illustrated* 84, No. 22 (June 3, 1996), pp. 26–27.

23. Fauldi, "Sold Out: From Team Booster to TV Backdrop," pp. 53–55.

24. Ibid., p. 53.

25. I gleaned my account of NASCAR from Chris Jenkins's expose "Wanted: Salesman, Must Drive." *USA Today* (July 12–14, 2002), pp. 1A–2A.

26. Two further points: first, this class of sports, in fact, encompasses three subclasses of sports, namely, Divisions I, II, and III. Moreover, Division I has three further subclasses: I A, which includes colleges that have big-time football programs; I AA, which includes colleges with second-tier football programs; and I AAA, which includes colleges with no football programs. Though Division III is actually the largest sub-category of intercollegiate sports, it is politically and economically the weakest in its ability to influence policy and bring in money. Though Division II and III sports are supposed to have athletic missions different from those of Division I (e.g., there are no athletic scholarships awarded to athletes from Division III), the facts suggest that those differences are for the most part nominal. For these reasons, most of my analysis is directed to Division I A sports, because it is clearly the most politically influential and economically powerful subcategory, one that dominates the governing structure of the National Collegiate Athletic Association (hereafter, NCAA), which is the main regulatory agency of intercollegiate sports. The second point is that my effort to highlight the moral side of these sports and not their educational side is problematic to some extent because at times they clearly overlap. That is, the educational justification of sports in liberal arts colleges and universities includes its supposed inculcation of such distinctly moral values as service to and tolerance of others. Where they are clearly intertwined, then, I shall have to talk about both, but where they are not I will, as stated, steer clear of academic matters.

27. On this and other points, see Andrew Zimbalist's path-breaking work, *Unpaid Professionals: Commercialism and Conflict in Big-Time College Sports*. Princeton, NJ: Princeton University Press, 1999. In my estimation, Zimbalist has written the definitive book on college sports, one that anyone interested in the economically convoluted world of college sports would be well advised to read.

28. Alan Wertheimer. *Exploitation*. Princeton, NJ: Princeton University Press, 1999.

29. Sheed, "Why Sports Matter," p. 24.

30. Zimbalist, *Unpaid Professionals*, p. 137.

31. Dan Wetzel, Don Yaeger. *Sole Influence: Basketball, Corporate Greed, and the Corruption of America's Youth*. New York: Warner Books, 2000, p. 25

32. LaFeber, *Michael Jordan and the New Global Capitalism*, p. 92.

33. Zimbalist, *Unpaid Professionals*, p. 11.

34. For a compelling argument why, see Welch Suggs's important essay, "Colleges Make Slight Progress Toward Gender Equity in Sports." *The Chronicle of Higher Education* (July 25, 2003), pp. A30–A32.

35. Zimbalist, *Unpaid Professionals*, p. 153.

36. Ibid., p. 150.

37. Ibid., p. 153.

38. Ibid., p. 150.

39. Ibid., p. 155.

40. To document the ripple effect of top-level, Division I A college sports on other men's and women's sports, all the empirical trends suggest that these latter programs are following in the footsteps of the elite athletic programs. Save a small enclave of schools at the Division III level, which want to deprofessionalize sports by, among other things, restricting the length of seasons, eliminating off-season practices, and abolishing national championships, there is very little discrepancy in outlook and practice among these divisions. Academic underperformance, which used to be the bane only of big-time football and basketball sports, is now a common feature of all college sports and all levels of men's and women's competition. For the first point, see Bill Pennington, "Play to Win, or Just to Play." *New York Times* (May 25, 2003), p. 24; for the second, see James Shulman and William Bowen, "How the Playing Field is Encroaching Upon the Admissions Office," *The Chronicle of Higher Education* (January 26, 2001), p. B8.

41. As quoted in Welch Suggs's article, "Players off the Field," *The Chronicle of Higher Education* (May 24, 2000), p. A61.

42. On this point, see William H. Honan, "Do Big-Money Sports Belong in College?" *New York Times* (January 7, 2001) Section 4A, p. 20.

43. Welch Suggs, "Conference Soap Opera Is Driven by Cash, But Cachet Matters Too," *The Chronicle of Higher Education* (May 30, 2003), p. 37.

44. Zimbalist, *Unpaid Professionals*, p. 106.

45. Mike Freeman, "On College Football." *New York Times* (August 25, 2002), p. 11; Welch Suggs, "Players Off the Field," p. 61.

46. I owe this line of thought and the facts that back it up to Zimbalist, *Unpaid Professionals*, p. 112.

47. Ibid., p. 37.

48. Ibid., pp. 173, 174.

49. For more on this point, see George Vescey, "Don't Worry: Sportsmanship Won't Be Catching.", p. 39. To be fair, I should say that Vescey's focus here is on professional sports. Of course, if my analysis is sound, this is a difference that does not make a difference.

50. Louis Menand. "Sporting Chances: The Cost of College Athletics." *The New Yorker* (January 22, 2001), p. 85.

51. It is not just that liberal arts institutions seem to emphasize values different from their athletic

counterparts but that those values sometimes conflict, and not in trivial ways. For example, the principle of free speech is an important precondition of a reflective life. However, when college athletic entities sign endorsement deals with such shoe companies as Nike, contractually obligating players not to tape over the Nike Swoosh as a gesture of social protest against the wages and working conditions of their workers, they clearly undermine one of the pivotal goals of a college and university education. On this point, see Zimbalist, *Unpaid Professionals*, pp. 50–1.

52. For the first point, see Menand, "Sporting Chances: The Cost of College Athletics," p. 88; for the second, see Zimbalist, *Unpaid Professionals*, p. 51.

53. Ibid., p. 87.

54. Zimbalist, *Unpaid Professionals*, p. 48.

55. Ibid., p. 12.

56. Welch Suggs, "Sports as the University's 'Front Porch'. The Public is Skeptical." *The Chronicle of Higher Education* (May 2, 2003), p. A17.

57. William Honan, "Do Big-Time Sports Belong in College?" p. 21.

58. Jere Longman, "In a Class by Themselves." *New York Times* (May 29, 2003), p. C15.

59. Ibid., p. C15.

60. Alexander Wolff, George Dohrman, "A School for Scandal." 94, No. 9. *Sports Illustrated* (February 26, 2001), pp. 74–84.

61. George Dohrmann, "Sweat Shopping." 94, No. 26. *Sports Illustrated* (June 25, 2001), pp. 61–66.

62. Zimbalist, *Unpaid Professionals*, pp. 138–40,

63. Robert Lipsyte, "The Olympic Moment Isn't What It Used to Be." *New York Times*, p. 29.

64. E. M. Swift, "Made in the USA." *Sports Illustrated* (July 22, 1996), p. 24.

65. Roger Cohen and Jere Longman, "Many Sides of the Olympic Chief." *New York Times* (February 7, 1999), p. 24.

66. Torbjorn Tännsjö. "Is Our Admiration for Sports Heroes Fascistoid?" In W. J. Morgan, K. Meier, A. Schneider (eds). *Ethics in Sport*. Urbana, IL: Human Kinetics, p. 407.

67. It is precisely because so much is at stake in how we are to understand and interpret already existing sports (and therefore of my critique of them) that I do not regard this foray into the historical past as a scholastic exercise in the least.

6.4

Moral philosophy out on the track

What might be done?

Adrian Walsh and Richard Giulianotti

Introduction

Our initial puzzle concerned how we might make sense of the general public disquiet about the influence of money and markets in sport. Do our intuitions that there is something wrong with hyper-commodification have any rational basis to them? Is it possible to explain what is wrong with 'this sporting Mammon' without invoking either the ideals of amateurism or Marxian socialism?

We believe that sports fans are right to be worried about the hyper-commodification of sport, for there is a real danger of many important values in sport being lost. Accordingly, we identified four distinct ways in which the commodification of sport might give rise to undesirable outcomes.

1 *The Motivational Pathology*: the commodification of sport is pathological when it corrodes the attitudes of those who participate in sport so that they no longer pursue sport as a goal in itself.
2 *The Instrumentalist Pathology*: the commodification of sport is pathological when it leads others to regard athletes and sport itself as mere means and not as ends-in-themselves.

3 *The Distributive Pathology*: the commodification of sport is pathological when it gives rise to forms of distributive injustice.
4 *The Pragmatic Pathology*: the commodification of sport is pathological when it undermines the long-term profitability of any sporting activity.

On our account, commodification is morally undesirable when it gives rise to any of these pathologies. Further we suggest that it is the occurrence of these very pathologies that explains much of the unease that the general public have with respect to hyper-commodified sport. In seeking to make sense of the widespread disenchantment of many sports-fans with modern sport, we need to understand the ways in which markets can go wrong. Significantly, our pathologies show how it is possible to object to the undue influence of money, as is the wont of the Amateurist project or the Marxist, without entirely abolishing markets in sport.

The question to which we turn now concerns how, in very general terms, we might prevent such outcomes occurring in sport. What kinds of *sports policies* might we pursue if we wish to avoid these market pathologies arising? As we noted in earlier chapters, our general approach to the problem of commodification is non-abolitionist, in that we support a mixed market economy. Thus we endorse the maintenance of markets as the means of producing and distributing a *great many* social goods so long as such activity is subject to State regulation. At the same time we also maintain that some things should not be bought and sold (for instance, marriage or voting rights) and hence should be placed outside the range of the market.

Applied to sport this means that our policies will fall under one of three general headings. First, there will be some initiatives that will involve *blocked exchange*, that is, the prohibition of market exchanges in a particular good. Just as one might wish to outlaw the selling of children, there will also be some sporting events and objects that should not be bought and sold. Second, some of our suggestions will involve the *regulation* by the State or relevant sporting associations of market exchanges in sporting goods. In such cases, it is not that markets should be prohibited, but rather that the activities of market agents and the outcomes delivered by market processes should be constrained by the State with the aim of realising specific moral and pragmatic ideals. Finally, some of our policy suggestions will involve *moral exhortation*, rather than formal institutional policy. Here the idea is to encourage individuals and groups that operate within the market to take ethical considerations into account when making their decisions. So, to give an example, one might well produce educational material designed to foster a concern amongst elite sports-stars with industrial conditions in which the sports gear they promote is produced and to avoid buying goods from companies that exploit their workers. The aim here would be for clubs, players and associations to buy goods from the least exploitative companies. In this instance, one relies on some form of moral conscience on the part of players, administrators and fans in order to realise the desired social outcomes.

Our strategy then will be to provide a series of suggestions – some of which involve blocked exchange, some of which involve regulation and some of which involve moral exhortation – oriented towards the prevention of the pathologies we have outlined thus far. We begin with the ownership of elite sports teams, and then move to questions of the regulation of market practices, reinvestment in the grass roots and forms of moral edification.

Before exploring these policy suggestions, a few caveats are in order. First, we make no pretence that what we present is a fully developed and thorough blueprint for the ethical reorganisation of sport. Our aim is simply to provide some indication, in broad outline, of the kinds of policies that might be implemented with the aim of preventing commodification being pathological. A genuine blueprint for the avoidance of market pathologies would be a large volume in itself.

Second, we do not wish to give the impression that the moral problems associated with commodification exhaust the ethical concerns to be found in sport. There are many other issues, such as cheating and the use of drugs in sport, which cannot be subsumed solely under the heading of commodification. While it might well be true – and there are good reasons for thinking it so – that money is often causally responsible for such undesirable phenomena, nonetheless they still arise in non-commercial environments. For instance, drug usage to improve sporting performances reached epidemic proportions in many of the Eastern Bloc countries at the height of the Cold War. If we were to provide a blueprint for the 'ethical reorganisation of sport' it would need to deal with many topics over and above those associated with money. Commodification is not the end of the ethical issue.

The organisation, ownership and re-mutualisation of elite sport

Let us begin with the organisation and, in particular, the property arrangements of modern elite sport. We begin with elite sport because it is here that the pathologies of commodification are most evident, since it is top-level sport which is of most value to commercial interests.

Ideally the communities out of which they originally emerged should own sporting associations and sporting clubs. Instead of being run by cliques of investors or multi-national corporations, it would be best if they were owned by and administered through the relevant community groups. We stress this at the outset because many of the pathologies we have discussed are in no small part due to the activities of large commercial organisations. For instance, if we take the tendency to treat sport merely as a commodity, this is certainly more likely to arise when clubs are listed on the stock exchange than when they are not able to be bought and sold. Equally, ownership by such commercial groups will often lead to maximising commercial strategies that take little heed of moral considerations such as justice. All other things being equal, access for less wealthy fans is more likely to be a relevant consideration for a community-based club than it will be for a club owned by a billionaire investor or an investment fund. One way of avoiding such outcomes would be for clubs and associations to be placed on the list of blocked exchanges.

This might appear excessively utopian when one is dealing with elite sport, but we can point to some striking examples of highly successful, community-owned sporting institutions. For example, in the NFL, the Green Bay Packers have a longstanding public tradition founded upon an extremely wide community shareholding, with ceilings placed on the volumes of shares held by any one individual. The club's issue of additional shares in late 1997, to remain competitive in a highly commercial league, was also directed at maintaining this wide community ownership. In soccer, the Barcelona team is effectively a mutual society that is owned by its members – who number over 100,000 – and which is run along democratic lines. Major decision-making powers are held by the General Assembly that represents members. Attempts to commercialise the club by reducing the legislative power of the Assembly have been resisted by supporters' movements, most notably *L'Elefant Blau*.[1]

One possible strategy for preventing the occurrence of our pathologies would be for the private ownership of clubs and leagues to be abolished. This would not mean that markets in elite sport would be entirely abolished or that elite players would not be paid handsomely for their efforts. Indeed, as the example of the Green Bay Packers demonstrates, community ownership does not preclude extensive commercial activity on the part of the clubs and associations. Community owned clubs can licence sporting goods, pay high salaries to athletes, allow their players to engage in commercial endorsements and so on. In making the clubs and associations 'blocked exchanges' we would simply be limiting the range of the market in a way that is intended to prevent the kinds of extreme commercial behaviour that ignores important values and ideals associated with sport. (Here, of course, we assume that such community organisations are, all other things being equal, less likely to be corruptive than large scale capitalist ones.)

Unsurprisingly, we are not the first to make such suggestions. For example, in his book *They Call it a Game* Bernie Parrish offered a similar alternative to the private monopolistic ownership of teams, leagues and players in the United States. Therein he wrote:

> The franchises should be owned by municipal corporations legally tied to the stadium authorities, having public common-stock ownership, with stock being offered to season-ticket holders on the basis of first refusal ... a formula could be worked out to pay the players a percentage of the total income. Then the profits after expenses could be earmarked for the revitalisation of the inner cities – improved wages for police, firemen, teachers and other civil servants; upgrading of city and country hospitals, and care for the aged; to name a few recipients.[2]

Parrish's point here that if municipalities owned clubs, then the revenues could be employed to provide local amenities and facilities is an important one. We see no reason that revenues raised in sport should not be injected back into communities.

Given the current level of private ownership of elite sports teams and events in places like the United States and Europe, any project to foster public ownership would require a massive social change. It would require the remutualisation of sports clubs, a transferring of ownership from private to community groups and as such would meet tremendous opposition from those private interests who currently own and profit from private sports. While it is not unrealistic to believe that those sports teams currently publicly owned can maintain their non-private status, plans for remutualisation are unlikely to succeed in the near future.

If this is true, then any policy prescriptions would need to rely predominantly upon intervention into the activities of the market by both the State and sport's governing authorities.

One minimal strategy would be for the State to appoint independent regulators to oversee specific sports at a national level. There are *analogous precedents* for such appointments. For instance, in the United Kingdom official regulators oversee important public utilities such as gas, electricity and telecommunications, to protect consumer interests in services that are viewed as fundamental needs. The appointment of official regulators for sport would reflect the latter's importance within society.

Sport regulators might also be empowered to investigate and eradicate corrupt practices on and off the fields of play. More broadly, these regulators should safeguard the interests of specific sporting communities that are harmed if abandoned to market forces. For example, sporting regulators might challenge the prices of 'official' merchandise that are often charged by sporting organisations. A prime target here might be the mark-ups on trade-marked replica shirts for sports teams. Sales of replica soccer shirts are worth more than £200 million per annum in the United Kingdom. Alternatively, these sporting regulators might be empowered to monitor the systems employed by governing bodies to distribute tickets for key fixtures.

The role fulfilled by the officials of sport's governing bodies might also be redefined, with greater emphasis placed on public service rather than business interest. In other words, sports officials would ultimately be responsible to their fellow citizens rather than to institutional powerbrokers.

Another possible strategy would be to curtail the role of other private organisations, such as subscription-based media networks, corporate sponsors, and merchandise corporations in the development of sports. While sports clubs may establish partnerships with local businesses at a community level, we should be wary of commercial relationships that would undermine the participatory ethics or symbolism of the sporting institution. Similarly, merchandising and broadcasting organisations should not drive all changes to the organisation and structure of sport. Such changes should come from within the practice of sport itself.

A final institutional strategy would involve both supporters groups and local authorities having a right to be involved in decision-making and administration within privately owned elite sporting clubs. In the United Kingdom, the voice of fans can be heard through the 'Supporter Trusts' that have been established at almost every major soccer club. The Trusts provide each member with a share in the club that it represents, thereby allowing supporters to attend annual general meetings. Trusts also provide a forum for expressing supporter opinions on issues relating to the club and, in the ideal circumstances, they are able to gain a representative seat on the board of directors. Some Trusts have taken over the control of clubs that have suffered very badly in financial terms. Through the participation of fans, the ideals and values of those who regard sport as an end-in-itself are more likely to be part of the decision-making process and in this way pathologies of the market are less likely to arise. Similar points can be made with respect to local authorities. Even if the teams are privately owned, a better system would allow representatives of the local authorities to at least hold a public stake in sports teams.[3]

Interestingly, public input into the development of elite sport is not an entirely novel idea. There are some noteworthy cases in which civic participation has extended into the formation of pressure groups, social movements and providential societies. In the United States, numerous local pressure groups have grown up to challenge extremely expensive stadium-building projects that would be funded by public money. For example, the 'Stadium out of Chinatown' movement in Philadelphia succeeded in blocking construction plans that would have adversely affected residents and the community fabric in one area of the city.[4]

The point is that either through (i) changes to the ownership of elite sporting leagues, clubs and teams or (ii) limiting the prerogatives of ownership, many of the pathologies discussed earlier might be avoided. Ideally clubs would be communally owned. But in the absence of the political will required to bring about such changes, as a second-best option the prerogatives of ownership should be severely curtailed. If the activities of private owners were regulated by the State and relevant sporting authorities, then this might ensure that ideals specific to sport, such as the mutual pursuit of excellence, as well as more general values, such as those pertaining to distributive justice, continue to be part of the landscape of elite sport.

Finally, fans and local authorities could be given a role in the decision-making processes of elite clubs. Through these mechanisms private owners would not, as is currently the case, have *carte blanche* to pursue venal strategies.

The regulation of unjust and counterproductive market practices

Having established the necessity of regulating the commercial activities of private sporting teams, let us now give some attention to the details of such regulation. How might the State and sporting authorities regulate in order to avoid the occurrence of our market pathologies?

To be sure, it must be acknowledged that there are already regulatory practices in place oriented towards limiting the influence of money in sport. For instance, there are a number of measures which were introduced to prevent various forms of corruption in sport, such as the bribing of judges and vote buying by cities competing for the elite events such as the Olympics. For instance, the IOC has introduced some anti-corruption measures to combat vote fixing by cities bidding to host Olympic events.

There are good reasons, however, for going beyond this rather minimal level of regulation. Over and above the prevention of corruption we believe that policies oriented towards both the alleviation of injustice and fostering the long-term health of sport are required. The first of these more extensive policies concerns the method employed to allocate elite players. What we wish to avoid here is the phenomenon of clubs 'buying success' that is injurious to the health of sport. Buying success is 'pragmatically pathological' because it both severely diminishes 'uncertainty of outcome' and often generates forms of distributive injustice, since it is unfair for sporting success to be simply a function of the size of one's bank account. Interestingly, some economists have already speculated that uncertainty of outcome will become increasingly important as the commodification of sport intensifies, for example through vast rises in income from television.[5] This is but an acknowledgement of how a commercial orientation in one area might undermine the commercial viability in another.

In order to prevent the buying of success, associations in team sports might institute salary caps, redistributions of league incomes and a draft system (as indeed the English Rugby Premiership did in recent years). 'Salary caps' involve sports governing bodies introducing financial controls on club rosters. These salary caps would limit the total wage budget at each club, ensuring that there would be no clustering of 'big money' players at any one team. Alternatively one might introduce 'player value caps'. These are more complicated and would function like the 'fantasy league' game that is popular among soccer fans. This system would require a panel of independent arbiters to establish a value for each player in the league; each club would then be required to hold a squad whose total player value did not exceed an agreed universal figure. Another measure to prevent success being bought would involve the pooling of league revenues (such as television monies and income from spectator attendances), and an equitable distribution of these sums among all member clubs.

Draft systems could also be introduced to maintain uncertainty of outcome between clubs. National sporting federations might seek to establish and oversee strong nursery systems for the development of elite players. Such national coaching frameworks would allow the institution of a 'draft system' of player recruitment in team sport. Teams that have been failing to perform might be given first pick of new players. In fact, such a policy is operational in many US sports, notably American football, where a strong college sport system feeds the professional leagues with an annual crop of 'rookies'. Clearly, it would also be more easily implemented in sport systems where the State and sport authorities take an active role in player development. Such a system would require the relevant authorities to exercise substantially greater power than any individual clubs within the sport.

'Buying success' also involves clubs recruiting the best available players, with the aim not only of improving their teams' competitive skills on the pitch, but also to weaken their rivals. The most destructive instance is the stock-piling of excellence which involves recruiting top players who are then simply listed as 'squad members' but have little chance of actually competing in matches. One method of preventing this stock-piling of excellence, would be for associations to restrict the roster sizes of teams to ensure that all players have active roles to play. Each club would be required to field an individual player for a minimum number of competitive games during each season.

A second area where regulation might be required is with respect to the access of fans to sporting events and sporting broadcasts. Let us begin with major sporting events. The hyper-commodification of such events can directly undermine the interests of some of the most dedicated supporters and audiences. In the United Kingdom, for instance, the cost of entry to some sports events has risen by over 800 per cent in the past two decades. Priority access to leading events – such as soccer cup finals, rugby and cricket test matches, and Wimbledon's Centre Court – is increasingly restricted to corporate sponsors. Equally, the most dedicated sports supporters are forced to pay heavily. Sports fans must either pay large amounts of money to maintain their allegiances, reconfigure their identification towards high-profile teams, or give up their support on the grounds of cost.

One response to this problem of access would be for sports governing bodies to set prices for these events at far lower levels than those that currently obtain. Queuing might then be employed to deal with the problems associated with scarcity. It would be a matter of 'first in, first served'. To be sure, this would not solve the problem of scarcity, but would ensure that the allocation of these scarce resources is not solely determined by the relative wealth of those who want them. Another response would be for sporting authorities to ensure also that tickets to the largest events are distributed according to fair criteria. Currently, gaining entry to the world championships or leading finals in most professional sports is best achieved by paying extortionate sums to 'scalper' organisations that have previously acquired large bundles of tickets prior to their sale to the public. Tickets could also be distributed as a priority among the most committed, long-standing supporters of athletes or teams that are involved in these fixtures. For example, if Scotland and Australia were to play each other in rugby's World Cup final, the fans who have attended most fixtures involving either team through to that stage could be given first refusal on tickets. A small

minority of tickets (say 10–20 per cent) might be reserved for individuals who have worked in a voluntary or semi-voluntary role within the host nation, either in regard to the specific tournament or in serving the sport in general. The rationale for such a policy would be that these supporters and dedicated workers within the sport constitute the most deserving recipients of tickets to sporting events. Sport's governing bodies and national governments might also criminalise ticket scalping for profit, as is sometimes currently done, whether this occurs outside the ground or through internet sites.

Another related area of distributive concern involves the siphoning of broadcasts of major events onto pay-TV. In order to safeguard the public provision of elite sport, the State might expand the list of 'crown jewel' sporting events that must be shown on free-to-air television. We noted that European national policies varied on the listing of specific events for free-to-air television, and that in some instances, major political conflicts justifiably arises when pay-TV intrudes upon viewing rights.[6] Of course, there will be crown jewel events in each different country.[7] In Australia, for instance, the list of crown jewel events would include the Melbourne Cup, the Australian Football grand final, the Australian Open tennis competition and the National Rugby League final. Equally, in the United States there are many events, such as the NBA final and the World Series baseball finals that would in all likelihood be included on such a list. The point is that for any particular constituency, there will be a series of important events for which everyone should ideally have access via free-to-air broadcasts.

Some major sports clubs or leagues might well argue in response that they are under intense commercial pressure to sign deals with subscription television stations. However, if sports clubs and leagues introduced some of the measures set out earlier – such as salary caps, and greater equity in the distribution of revenues across clubs – then these pressures would be largely deflated.

A third area where regulation might be enacted is with respect to the activities of sporting agents. In many quarters sport agents have gained some unenviable reputations for their inflation of athlete salaries in some sports. In the short-term, sport authorities should tightly regulate the activities of agents. In the longer-term, it might be preferable for athletes' unions to represent the interests of professional athletes.

Reinvestment in the grass-roots

Our policy suggestions thus far have focused solely on elite sport. But if sport is to remain healthy in all of the relevant respects, the grass-roots must also be healthy and, accordingly, they should also be an important part of any policy initiatives. The grass-roots are not only the breeding grounds for future elite athletes, but of value in their own right for the opportunities they provide for the general public to pursue excellence and enjoy the pleasures of competition. Grass-roots sporting organisations also provide ordinary people with opportunities for participation in decision-making processes in events and social structures that affect them directly.

The first policy suggestion here concerns the reinvestment of resources generated in elite sports into local grass-roots sporting associations. We suggest that a great deal more revenue from elite sporting competitions should be filtered down to grass-roots levels. Currently, the vast majority of revenues from major competitions such as the NFL, the NRL and the English Premiership are distributed among member clubs with little regard to the grass-roots institutions that nurtured and developed the talents of the participating athletes. Equally, the facilities of elite clubs and associations might be opened out of season to local communities at low or no cost to the user. For example, elite sport clubs possess important capital and human resources, such as gymnasia, swimming pools, and often teams of scientists, that would be of major benefit to local communities and which are in any case used only for restricted periods by professional athletes. The move towards the mutualisation of sports clubs would promote the principle that members, supporters and the surrounding community be granted access to elite sporting facilities.

The justification for pursuing such policy initiatives is in one sense pragmatic. If a sport does not reinvest in its grass-roots, and grass-roots participation declines, then in the long run this will be harmful to the elite sport. Indeed it is

from the grass-roots that talented new players emerge and it is through participation in grass-roots sport that many people gain their interest in sport at an elite level. Of course, it is not unknown for an elite sport to flourish and for club level participation to be in decline. Here interest is generated primarily through broadcasts of the elite level competition. But one would have to be concerned about the long-term prospects of any sport in this situation.

But equally there are specifically moral reasons for reinvestment in the grass-roots. Since any sport relies on non-elite competitions for the production of future elite sportsmen and women, it owes the grass-roots a debt. For elite clubs, competitions and sporting corporations not to reinvest in its grass-roots is, in effect, for them to 'free-ride'; to simply take the benefits without contributing to the system that creates those benefits in the first place. Further, playing sport is a good in itself for those who play it. Grass roots competitions are not only valuable for the future champions they produce, but also for the opportunities they provide for people to enjoy the autotelic goods of which we spoke. Therefore it would be a good thing for money to be reinvested in the grass-roots to ensure the continuation of a valuable sphere in which people develop and maintain their fitness, cooperate with team-mates and strive to improve their athletic performances.

A second policy suggestion that might help here involves fostering the participatory element that is a distinctive feature of much grass-roots sport at an organisational level. Through involvement as linesmen, timekeepers, committee members and so on, club supporters engage in an important and immediate form of citizenship. In this there is a marked difference with the depleted social relationships that generally arise within privately owned, profit seeking sports institutions.

Further, it is important to remember that sport is a major cultural activity through which individual people and groups come into contact with one another and develop important social relationships. In team sports part of the frisson of sporting contests – both at an elite and a club level – derives from the social differentiation of players and supporters from those of other teams and the interplay arising from these distinct identities. Such exchanges are notably not founded upon monetary or commodity principles. Of course, such rivalries can sometimes descend into hatred and violence, but such pathologies are the exception rather than the rule. The vast majority involve healthy interactions. In this way, when things go well, sport is capable of facilitating friendly symbolic exchanges between different communities.

Moral education and individual action

So far we have focused on formal institutional responses. But we should not think that this is the only policy route. There are some pernicious elements of commodification of sport that are probably best dealt with outside of state or institutional frameworks through individual action. To bring about change here would require 'moral education' of individuals, rather than State interventions. Indeed this is particularly true of the two pathologies that concern the loss of important participant ideals in sport and the treatment of sport as a *mere* commodity. Actions by the State and sporting institutions can provide a framework in which sport is less likely to be treated as a mere commodity. But so long as money is involved, such institutional action cannot prevent venal attitudes towards sport. If important values, such as for instance the mutual pursuit of excellence, are to survive as operative ideals of those involved in playing elite sport, we will also require individuals to resist the pressures the market places on their value system. To be sure, there are dangers here of 'moralism'. Too often eminent sportspeople and administrators invoke such values only to ignore them in practice, and without accompanying institutional action, moral education is likely to be nothing more than ethical window-dressing. Nonetheless, as part of a broader strategy to avoid the pathologies of hyper-commodification, moral education has an important role to play.

Let us begin here with those responsible for the organisation and administration of sport. Over the past twenty years they have come to be highly influenced by management models that regard sport as a mere commodity. Such managers make decisions solely based on the bottom line. Under this 'market rhetoric' (to use Margaret Jane Radin's evocative phrase),

every human interaction is understood as a market exchange. What might be helpful here are educational discussions that emphasise the importance of non-monetary values in sport and the vulnerability of such values to corrosion by commodification. Administrators need to be reminded constantly that sport is not just a *mere* commodity.

Equally athletes themselves would ideally resist the emergence of venal attitudes. Sport goes best when athletes do not regard sport as a *mere* means to individual wealth. They should maintain their focus on the various non-monetary values – such as the mutual pursuit of excellence – that sport is capable of realising. They should be made aware of the importance of such values and the potential corrosion of them by the commercial world.

Athletes should also be reminded that while self-interest is a legitimate motive in sporting life, it should be leavened by accompanying moral side-constraints. Sportspeople should not act venally and, accordingly, some financial offers they should refuse. For instance, the sportspersons who toured South Africa in the 1980s, in contravention of the Gleneagles Agreement, undermined important movements for social change in the pursuit of quick wealth.[8]

Finally, we should not forget the potential power of sports fans to influence the ways in which sport develops. As both consumers and citizens sports fans make choices which can affect the direction of the development of sport. For instance, sports fans might avoid events, teams or institutions that are driven particularly by corporate greed, financial expansionism or the simple pursuit of large margins. Somewhat ironically, this would be to use market power to prevent particular forms of hyper-commodification.

Summary

What might well strike some readers about these policy suggestions is that a great many of them have been implemented to varying degrees in many sports over the past fifty years. Although some of the suggestions, such as those concerning remutualisation, are rarely enacted, others, such as those relating to the draft system, are quite common. On reflection this should not be all that surprising since community concerns about hyper-commodification, if not expressed using that terminology, run deep. Accordingly, some policies have been enacted to limit the influence of money in sport. But no *systematic* attempt has been made to ensure that money does not undermine the values of sport. Through our identification of the four pathologies we provide the theoretical grounds for a wide-ranging and systematic policy response to hyper-commodification.

It is important here to reiterate the non-abolitionist nature of our policy proposals. In keeping with the general thrust of the book, we have focused on alleviating the particular noxious aspects of commodification within sport, rather than on advocating either the sweeping abolition of all social exchanges that generate surplus value or the immediate termination of all capitalist relations of production.

We do not pretend that our list of possible policies is exhaustive of the measures that are required to deal adequately with the harms associated with the hyper-commodification of sport. Clearly, there will be further measures one might introduce which we have not covered. What we have presented are some important policy ideas that would aid in preventing sport degenerating into a realm of fantastic venality. Nor do we pretend that bringing about such changes would be an easy matter. In order for the kinds of policies we propose to be enacted, it would require considerable resolve on the part of those in charge of sport. Here the power of large commercial interests is not be underestimated. But equally, we do not believe that such changes to sport are impossible. If sport is to survive as a valuable practice that realises important human goods, then these are in fact an urgent necessity and such impediments must be overcome.

Finally, it is important that we note the limits of this inquiry: commodification is not the end of matters of ethics in sport. We should not give the impression that if policies such as ours were enacted then the battle for a more ethically appropriate sport would be won. There are many practices other than those associated with commercialisation that are ethically unsavoury. Here we need think only of issues such as the use of performance-enhancing drugs, cheating and other forms of unsporting behaviour.

These are not directly related to the influence of money, since any sporting competition with highly desired trophies, medals and flags will provide athletes and others with sufficient motivation to act corruptly. Nonetheless, despite all of that, financial incentives undoubtedly increase the temptations for corruption. By diminishing the influence of money in sport, and reawakening in its practitioners a love for goals other than money, then the temptations for corruption will be less appealing. In this way, our policy suggestions are part of a more general project to ensure that sport remains a sphere of life in which the mutual pursuit of excellence, the autotelic goods of participation and the ideals of fair play are realised.

Notes

1. See: www.football-research.org/gof2h/Gof2H-chap12. htm
2. Bernie Parrish, *They Call it a Game*, New York: Dial Press, 1971, p. 290.
3. See Dennis Coates and Brad R. Humphreys, 'The Stadium Gambit and Local Economic Development', *Regulation*, 23(2), 2000, pp. 15–20. In North America, it was estimated that in 2001 the leading 99 clubs in the NFL, MLB, NBA and NHL received public subsidies of US$17.5 billion towards their sporting facilities. See Judith Grant Long, 'Full Count: The Real Cost of Public Funding for Major League Sports Facilities', *Journal of Sports Economics*, 6(2), 2005, pp. 119–143.
4. See: www.fieldofschemes and www.leagueoffans. com
5. Paul M. Downward and Alistair Dawson, *The Economics of Professional Team Sport*, London: Routledge, 2000, pp. 172–173.
6. In the UK, highly valued 'Category A' events currently include Wimbledon, the Scottish and English soccer cup finals, and the European Championships soccer tournament. English cricket's Test matches were demoted to Category B, allowing the subscription channel BSkyB to buy the rights to home fixtures for four years in a highly controversial move.
7. For a discussion of these issues, see David Rowe, 'Watching Brief: Cultural Citizenship and Viewing Rights', *Sport in Society*, 7(3), 2004, pp. 385–402.
8. The 1977 Gleneagles Declaration, signed by all Commonwealth nations, contained a commitment to withholding support for sport-related contact with the apartheid regime in South Africa.

Sport and the systematic infliction of pain

A case study of state-sponsored mandatory doping in East Germany

Giselher Spitzer

Since the fall of the Communist regime in the German Democratic Republic (GDR), a great deal of material has become available which sheds light on the practice of systematic state-sponsored doping in that country. The analysis of archival material and interviews with former athletes has revealed the centrality of doping in sport and the harmful medical side effects of doping (Spitzer 1994a, 1994b, 1994c, 2001c). These data reveal that up to 10,000 male and female athletes were doped, often without their knowledge or consent, while 2 million doses of anabolic steroids were used annually in the preparation of Olympic sports in the GDR.

The use of performance-enhancing drugs not only improved strength and endurance but also had another important effect: it reduced recovery time and thereby made it possible for athletes to train harder, and for longer, than at any time before. The upper limit of time spent on training was increased from about 1,500 to 1,800 hours a year, making it possible for athletes to train for five 45-minute sessions every day, including weekends and holidays.

The Communist Party – or The Socialist Union Party, or SED, to give it its proper name – and the organs of state security integrated doping into the training plans of athletes while techniques of doping were developed in applied sport science. (For an analysis of GDR science as a system and its links with doping and the secret service in East Germany, see Spitzer 1997.) The goal of sport for all was officially declared to be government policy (Spitzer *et al.* 1998), but this policy was in effect underdeveloped while the government devoted huge resources to the use of drugs in developing elite-level sport for political purposes.

Elite sport and doping in the GDR: Some organizational aspects of the background

The main elements of the GDR doping system can be described as follows. From the early 1950s a structure of politically dominated professional sport developed. Within this structure, in return for their unquestioning commitment to the sporting goals of the regime, athletes were offered lifelong employment. This was the nature of the 'social contract' into which athletes were expected to enter. After the 1970s, a system was developed which ensured a flow of athletic 'new blood', through the selection of the top 3 per cent of young athletes. From an analysis of the entire East German youth population, approximately 60,000 children were selected for *enforced* – not voluntary – entry into the 1,800 'training centres'. From those who were admitted to these training centres, almost 10,000 athletes were selected for promotion to the second level. From this selection system, some 2,000 top athletes emerged as, in effect, full-time professional sportspeople, many of whom were to suffer bodily damage as a result of doping.

In reality elite athletes in the GDR were exceptionally well-paid civil servants, soldiers, policemen or officers of the secret state security with a guaranteed career but also, as the other part of the 'social contract', with the obligation not to convey to others information about their day-to-day lives as athletes, including the systematic doping of athletes. Sport was organized on military lines: athletes were expected to follow 'orders' from all those above them in the hierarchy. Athletes were forbidden to have any contact with any persons or organizations not affiliated with the government and, as such, were subject to very rigorous social control. The integration of sport within the political and security system can be illustrated by the fact that the Secret Service, the 'Stasi', needed volunteers or 'unofficial supporters' of the state security system and between 11 and 15 per cent of those involved in sport (coaches, athletes and so on) acted as state security volunteers, with the Socialist Unity Party being the dominant influence in the organization of sport.

There was a massive investment in elite-level sport. More than 4,700 professional trainers were employed in high-level sport, and nearly 1,000 medical doctors and 5,000 administrators were employed in sport – and all this in a country with a total population of just 17 million. All these people were legally employed within sport; in addition, almost 1,500 individuals were active in research or the illegal application of doping substances and techniques (for research on the Stasi volunteers and blood doping, see Spitzer 2002a, 2002b).

This massive investment was made in sport because the Communist Party aimed to beat the West in all things, including sport. The leaders of the GDR set a target of achieving the number three ranking in world sport for East Germany, while the secret internal plans for 1984 and 1988 (now available to scholars, following the collapse of the East German regime) indicate that they later came to see the number one ranking in the world as a realistic target.

Special aspects of GDR doping as a system

The organization of doping in the GDR was highly systematic – about 10,000 athletes were victims of what may be described as *industrial doping*. There were some aspects of the doping system in East Germany which made it quite different from the use of particular performance-enhancing drugs by athletes in most other societies (Spitzer, 2001b, 2001c). In particular: as a rule athletes were exposed to mandatory (or compulsory) doping without their active cooperation; only a few athletes knew about the practice of doping. In addition, *every* selected athlete was doped – it was impossible to refuse.

Compulsory (or mandatory) doping was financed by the state, without *de facto* legal restrictions. The sport associations' central doping guidelines even regulated the dosage for every athlete. The supply of drugs was guaranteed by the state-run Secret Service and the military as well as the Communist Party. Doping was a highly secret, closed system of abuse of children, young people and adults, who were not provided with any real information about what was happening to them (Spitzer 2004a: 416). The President of the East German Sports Federation (DTSB), Manfred Ewald, supervised the work of Dr Manfred Hoeppner of the Sports Medical Service (SMD) and Professor Dr Alfons Lehnert of the secret Research Institute of Leipzig (FKS). These people were responsible for determining the doping guidelines for a four-year period and approving the application of doping policy for the various Sports Federations in the East German Sports Federation on an annual basis for all sports clubs. The acquisition and financing of doping substances took place through the State Secretary's office, the state-run Sports Medical Service and the Elite Sport Commission of the GDR (*Leistungssportkommission der DDR*, LSK). Those responsible for organizing sport in

414

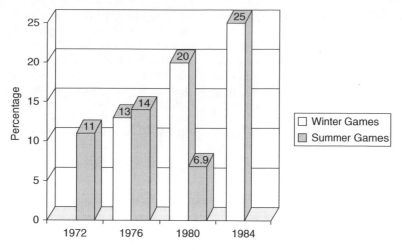

Figure 6.5.1. Active Stasi-volunteers in Olympic teams of the GDR (in per cent) at Winter Games and Summer Games. *Source:* Spitzer 2004c

the Army (*Armeesportvereinigung Vorwaerts*, ASV) and the Security Services (*Sportvereinigung Dynamo*, SVD) were able, through their own pharmacy distribution, to obtain additional doping substances without approval from the Federation (DTSB) or the Sports Medical Service.

Dr Hoeppner of the Sports Medical Service and his co-workers in Berlin directed couriers to transport doping substances and the list of athletes to whom the drugs were to be administered, with applicable dosages, to the sports federations. Occasionally the appropriate federation medical doctor (*Verbandsarzt*) collected the doping substances personally, to distribute them according to the central directive. As a general rule athletes were required to take the 'supporting substances', as the drugs were called, in the presence of the trainer. Injections were administered by the federation's divisional doctor. Athletes received no explanation regarding the purpose, risks or side effects of the drugs used. Occasionally, if this was unavoidable, athletes were told either the truth or a partial truth, though when this happened, they were required to sign a 'confidentiality' paper.

Drugs were frequently administered to young people, even children; in gymnastics, weightlifting and swimming, drug use often began in childhood, from 10 years up. The result was, in many cases, long-term drug abuse.

An assumption of this system was that athletic achievement was of higher value than the athletes' actual or future state of health. Inevitably this policy involved the systematic infliction of long-term suffering and pain on athletes. After the end of an athlete's career the health data in relation to that athlete were falsified – the victims were given no information about damage to their health and future health risks. In some cases those responsible for the doping programme were not able to provide reliable data, for some applications involved experimental substances the side effects, particularly long-term side effects, of which were often not known.

There were, however, some exceptions to this pattern of doping. In football, within the national leagues, doping was forbidden, because of the need to guarantee equality of chances *within* the GDR league. However, national football teams were required to use drugs in order to compete successfully against other nations (Spitzer 2004b). It is not surprising that knowledge about doping in soccer at the national team level filtered down to the club level, where doping was organized and financed, not as part of the state system, but by the club itself. However once again, the victims – the players – were often given no information about the drugs being administered to them, or the possible side effects.

Side effects of doping within the GDR system

An official doping manual indicates that many side effects of doping were well known, but kept secret. Generally doping had, particularly on women, negative side effects on health status (Manual of FKS 1982 in Spitzer 2004c). Although the harmful side effects were known, this did not lead to the cessation of doping. Typical side effects noted in the Manual from 1982 include the following: for men, inhibition of production of sperm as well as *gynaecomastia* (enlargement of the male breast to female profile; for that reason the anti-cancer medicine Tamoxifen was also administered to male athletes) and, for women, 'cycle-anomalies and virilisation when high dosages were used for long periods; these effects are partly irreversible'. These are taken from the written text in the original source (Spitzer, in preparation). Similar data are presented in the official study of the effects of anabolic steroid use on athletes in the long jump and high jump (data provided by W. W. Franke, Heidelberg). Side effects were recorded on the skin, and on organs such as the liver (higher serum-transaminase or cholestase) and the heart, as well as problems such as high blood pressure, and fluid retention in body cells and connective tissue. There is also evidence of psychological damage. Specific side effects on female athletes include the growth of facial and bodily hair, abasement of the sexual hormones and increasing virilization, reduction of the breasts and lowering of the voice. Problems with menstruation and hypertrophy of the clitoris may be followed by polycystic ovary-syndrome. Side effects among male athletes include testicle atrophy, enlargement of the prostate and *gynaecomastia*. There is also evidence that some of these dangerous side effects were passed on to the next generation, for children born to athletes who used drugs appear to have higher risks of developing skin allergies and asthma.

The above list of side effects was associated with anabolic steroid use. However, other, experimental drugs were also used, the side effects of which were not known. Athletes did discuss secretly among themselves some of the side effects which they experienced and, in particular, the possible effects on any children they might have. Psychological and behavioural

disturbances were also noted by the victims: an increase of aggression, libido change, strong mood alterations (for example, mood swings between euphoria and depression) and mental disorder. The enlargement of the male breast caused mental problems for men and, for women, virilization and hirsutism (growth of beard and hair on the body) caused many more problems. Pain, injury and fear about what was happening to their bodies were a part of the sporting life of high-level athletes, as a consequence of the enforced use of performance-enhancing drugs.

Pain in GDR sports: case studies

In this section we will have a glimpse into what was a *terra incognita*, because drug-related pain was not a topic for official investigation in high-level sports in East Germany. In the following case studies, I want to address two key questions:

1 Was there an intention to (ab-)use pain (e.g. to structure and direct training) or was the existence of pain and injury something which was an undesirable, though not a planned, result of participation in sport?

2 What was the function of pain in East German elite sport, within and beyond the use of doping?

The case studies that follow are based on interview data; the interview data from athletes were then checked against information provided by other athletes and also against other data sources such as photographic evidence and medical data.

Case study 1: Pain as a means of producing absolute discipline

The athlete in this case is a female shot-putter, with a weight of about 95 kg and height of 1.72 metres. The treatment of this athlete was described by another athlete who was present and who described what happened:

> It must have been the spring of 1975, when a sportswoman in our *Trainingsgruppe* (a small group of cadre athletes, competing against

each other in the GDR Elite Sport System) did not unconditionally follow our trainer's instructions during the training session. Because of that, our trainer made her do additional training immediately after the regular training session. She had to run another 4000 metres. The reason was, in the coach's words, that she obviously still had some 'reserves' left. She needed even more endurance training, said the coach. Remember: the training partner weighed 95 kg weight and was only 172 cm tall!

For shot putters of both sexes there is hardly any harder training than endurance running, because of the high body-weight of the athletes. After this sportswoman had run 2800 metres, she vomited ... she also interrupted the run against the coach's orders, lay down by the outside of the lane, vomited again and wept, because she was in so much pain from the running and also because she was very ashamed and upset that she vomited in front of the members of the camp. Maybe 100 of the 300 world class athletes of the club were on the ground at that moment.

She wanted to leave the stadium because of the pain and to go into the washroom, to wash herself. However the coach prohibited that, saying that she would have to run three more laps on the track. After that she might take a break. Because of fear of further penalties in the form of being made to do more sprints in future training sessions, she ran with tears and pain the remaining required 1,200 metres.

That day had consequences. We had trained on the same stadium, and had to look on that scene. So the consequence for us was that we were so frightened that we planned, because of that horror, to obey our trainer in future even more unconditionally. The reason for that was to avoid penalties. It was because of fear of the penalties by our coach.

In the above example, the sportswoman describing the situation did not demonstrate her opposition to what the coach was doing and thereby risk losing her job as a well-paid athlete. Solidarity between athletes was rarely seen: year-long selection and socialization into the professional East German sports system made the option of opposition to the infliction of pain in training impossible. The shot putter in the above incident was also a victim of doping and still has the side effects today; the virilizing side effects of anabolic steroids finally become so obvious that eventually she was no longer allowed to take part in public sport-events.

Case study 2: Ignoring athletes' pain

Coaches and doctors may ignore the athletes' pain as a way of imposing discipline, but this may also have results that are the opposite of those intended, as the following case study shows:

In January of 1976 we visited the winter-training camp, in which we had to practise first downhill-ski. So we had only downhill boots, and when we had to do cross-country ski training after that with these hard boots, we all got problems.

The reason for downhill skiing was that the coaches wanted us as athletes to fight against the fear of mountains to develop a better morale, and of course we had to do endurance training in winter also. After a few days almost all of us were bleeding ... from different parts of the feet.

The chief coach had planned for the next day as part of the training programme a journey to Oberwiesenthal, a big winter-ski resort [in Thuringia]. We started with luge-training, but we had to sleigh with the hard ski-boots which had hurt before. The pain in our feet caused by the ski-boots was hard to bear. So we asked our trainer if, instead of the luge-training, endurance-training using running-shoes would be accepted, because we would have less pain. We wanted to avoid the hard and heavy ski boots. The coach did not accept this change of his training programme – the aching feet of our shot put group were no problem for him.

The next morning the bus for the journey ... arrived. Our coach gave an order that we should practise the luge-training as ordered, but in running-shoes. The dangers associated with training for the luge with only light running-shoes on the ice were ignored. However because of the threat of penalties, none of us dared to remind him of the high risk of injury of wearing sport shoes in the downhill luge.

On that day we were all afraid of driving downhill in these dangerous shoes, but our chief trainer demanded to start the race. If we did not do as instructed, it would be a case of 'non-obedience' [like acting against military orders: G. Spitzer]. The consequence would be to get pushed out of the sport club and the school as well as the international college. We would have to pack our things and go home.

But none of us wanted to risk the end of our career. Some of us had been Champions at the last East German Junior competitions, the *Spartakiade* [in 1975; G. Sp.]. So we got on the sleigh, another sportswoman seated in front.

Our chief trainer took a rope and tied his sleigh behind ours. The hill was very uneven, so we hit the ground. Because the two sleighs were connected by the rope, the chief trainer's sleigh went over my right ankle.

At once I had a very strong pain, the ankle swelled up very quickly and turned blue. There were only a few metres to go to the ground station of the hill, which had a rescue-station. However the head coach answered my question, as to whether I should visit a doctor, by saying 'Don't be so snivelling – everything is O.K. with you'. Although my foot was very painful and continued to swell, I had to walk two more hours with the other members of the group.

Back in our hotel, our female club-doctor saw me, not a doctor from the public medical service of the city. She declared that it was only a little sprain which needed no special treatment. The pain became more and more unbearable, so throughout the night the other sportswomen tried to help me with compresses.

My condition worsened during the night, and the doctor allowed me to have an x-ray in the local hospital. It showed a bone had splintered in the ankle, as well as a torn ligament. They advised me to have an operation immediately in the hospital there. The operation in the local hospital was not accepted by our coach and the sports doctor. They wanted the operation to be done in Berlin-Pankow by Professor Kurt Franke. So I had to wait a whole week to be treated at Berlin.

Three operations and 20 months later my sporting career ended, because the doctor could give me no hope that the broken ankle would ever work properly again or be pain-free. He was right, I regret. It was the end of my dream.

The central character in this case study was an elite female athlete who was also the person who observed and described the events in the first case study above. This former high-performance sportswoman now says: 'Nobody should forget that pain, especially in sport, is an alarm-signal of the body, which should not be ignored.' She had herself been given anabolic steroids as a young girl, without her knowledge, by the coach, who was also a woman but one with little concern for the health of her athlete. Pain was a normal part of the working day

in training. The accident and the associated pain were alarm-signals which were disregarded by those in charge of the East German system.

Case study 3: Pain and enforced competition

The next case is based on a letter from a leading gymnast seeking help. It was sent to the Socialist Unity Party in the 1980s, and personally directed to the person with responsibility for Sport in the Central Committee, Egon Krenz. The author was an elite female gymnast; her request for help was ignored. Her letter says nothing about doping, because the use of performance-enhancing drugs in female gymnastics was not revealed until the collapse of the GDR. In her letter to one of the most powerful leaders of the GDR, this young woman sets out her pain and suffering within sport. The letter writer was a leading gymnast for 12 years. She was many times GDR Champion and won medals at the Olympics and European Championships. She wrote in a very open manner to the leading Communist Secretary for Sports (the letter is in *Die Bundesbeauftragte für die Unterlagen des Staatssicherheitsdienstes der ehemaligen Deutschen Demokratischen Republik*):

I have devoted my ... life entirely to the sport; I ... left my parental home eight years ago. All I have done I have done with pleasure, and always with a firm will, to represent our state as a worthy athlete ... I had to stop competing for almost one and a half years because of an injury to my back. During that time I lay in a plaster-bed [bed with gypsum for injured back]. Then, however, unfortunately an old injury to both ankles stopped me from taking part at the World Championships again. Since then I have done gymnastics constantly with a lot of pain, both my feet had to be strapped constantly, but I fulfilled my job as a successful participant at the Olympic Games.

The wear and attrition to the tissue in my feet necessitated operations on [my feet]. My personal experiences about the *Antrainieren* [the quick return to training in high-level sports after a break caused by an injury; G. Spitzer] reminded me that ... after these surgical operations ... it is not possible for me to take part in the World Championships. The continuous backaches have accompanied the problems with the legs and made it impossible to train effectively to come back to medal ranking. A third problem is that the breaks in training have led to weight problems …

(Following this she wrote about problems with weight and weight control and associated problems. She discusses the role of her parents who were excluded from the training process in order to stop their influence, and shows how the coaches and the club cheated – they promised that she could end her career with honour after the next international championship or Olympics, but then did not allow her to retire.)

> Therefore I want to leave elite sports now, with honour, because I did everything and had great results. I personally have wept enough tears through all that pain in all the years … Writing this letter is based on the fact that you met us, the Olympic Winners, at Berlin after the Games and you spoke cordial words to me.

This young woman asked for help. However, she was not allowed to end her career for health reasons. After 12 years of training with increasing and extreme pain, she expressed a desire to retire with honour, but those who controlled the sport system ignored her pain and denied her request. It is important to add that retiring from sport without the permission of those who ran the sport system would have caused major difficulties for the athlete: she would have had no access to a specialist medical service, no sports or training possibilities, no fees or money, no chance to sit exams at high school and no possibility of studying in the GDR. So she asked for permission from the Party in a final attempt to end the pain without losing her existence as a normal citizen. In reply, the letter from Egon Krenz did not answer her question. It simply said that she is a fine athlete and that Krenz hopes she will have good results (a copy of this letter is in the possession of the author). The athlete received no help from anybody in sport. On the contrary, she was given instructions to train for the next competitions: the World Championship and after that the Olympics in 1992. In that desperate situation, it was the opening of the Berlin Wall in November 1989 and the collapse of the GDR regime that saved her. This third sportswoman in our case studies fought against what might be called the functionalization of her body and the enforced acceptance of pain in high-level gymnastics. The data in this case study were confirmed because in 2002 the original sports medicine files became available. In addition, secret medical files indicate that she had been given anabolic steroids, beginning in childhood, and without her knowledge. Training when in pain was accepted by coaches and doctors as well as by the politicians at every level. Pain was seen as a condition for success at the international level. The destruction of the bones and connecting tissues as a result of continuing to train and compete when in pain, as well as the destruction of internal organs by steroids, were recognized as major health problems, but these were kept secret as a means of reaching the goal of international sporting success.

Case study 4: Pain, drop out and defection from East Germany

The captain of the East German gymnastics team in the years between the Mexico and Munich Olympics was told by his coaches to take steroids, though he was not given information about their side effects. He was simply told they would help in training. However, major health problems followed. His muscles developed and he became more powerful, but the steroids reduced his ability to concentrate and, as a consequence, he frequently failed in training to catch the horizontal bar or the parallel bars. As a result, he often fell and was injured and required surgery. (We now know that lapses in concentration may be one of the side effects of anabolic steroids.)

To improve his concentration, the gymnast was given another medication, to be taken shortly before training. This improved his concentration and coordination on the bars, but led to aching in the muscles and joints, tiredness and severe headaches. (It now appears that the gymnast was given Oxytocin, which improves concentration, but is associated with exhaustion and fatigue as side effects.)

The gymnast also required surgery to his foot, legs and shoulders, but the surgery was cancelled in order not to jeopardize his participation in the next world championships. The gymnast was also a member of the army-sport *Vorwaerts* and therefore had the legal status of

419

a soldier. On one occasion, he stopped practising because he was in pain and was afraid of falling, and left the hall. This was interpreted as the refusal of a serving soldier to obey orders.

Manfred Ewald, the President of the gymnastic and sport federation of East Germany and a Central Committee member of the Socialist Unity Party (SED), immediately visited the gymnast. Ewald demanded that the gymnast and national team captain should act 'like a real man and a tough soldier'. The gymnast was suspected of malingering and of refusing to train because of minor aches. The President promised that, if the national team captain would resume training and take part in the coming world championships, then he would afterwards be allowed to retire with honour and would be provided with health care. The 'breach of discipline' would also be forgotten. But if he refused, he would leave sports without *Abtrainierung*. This is the term used to refer to the process of 'detraining', that is the process designed to allow athletes to make a controlled transition from the life of an elite athlete to that of a 'normal' citizen, and would usually involve medical supervision to manage the health risks associated with any long-term sports injuries they had suffered and, of course, the management of the process of coming off drugs and managing the side effects of drugs. This is a highly complex process lasting one or two years, and to end one's career without guided 'detraining' would have meant continued pain and threats to one's health. As a consequence, athletes would not wish to retire without 'detraining'.

For these reasons, the gymnast in this case study returned to training and competition in the short term, but secretly he decided to defect from East Germany and used the occasion of the next world championships to escape from the country. As a result, the East German state and its sport system lost one of its best competitors because he was no longer prepared to suffer the pains associated with enforced training and competition. (This case study is based on five interviews with the former gymnast at Leverkusen, 1998–2000, and on Stasi files which recorded his escape. Defection from East Germany was, of course, a crime and those who were caught trying to defect were liable to imprisonment, so the gymnast was running a considerable risk in defecting.)

These case studies reveal what might be described as the 'dark side' of East German elite sport. The inhumane aspects of the system can be seen clearly. But let us return to a question raised earlier: What was the function of pain in the East German elite sport system, within and beyond doping?

The abuse of pain as a means of maintaining discipline (*Disziplinierungsmittel*)

East German elite sport was based on a military-like structure. Approximately 20 per cent of all elite athletes were actually in the army, or were soldiers of the ministry for state security, or police officers. The other 80 per cent belonged to 'civil' sport clubs, but even here the system was not based on free choice, but on the military concept of 'delegation', which involved assigning soldiers to another service or command; in sport it involved assigning people to a new employment as, in effect, professional athletes. Elite sports people were required to support the regime and, in return, were provided with relatively high incomes and other privileges such as foreign travel and cars.

Under the cloak of coaching, pain was inflicted as a punishment for disobeying instructions and as a means of instilling and maintaining discipline; the similarities to military culture were clear. In the everyday life of sport clubs, the athletes themselves became brutalized and, on occasions, even used aggression, including collective beatings, against other, 'dissident', athletes. Such situations indicate the effectiveness of this system of instilling obedience and discipline in athletes.

Hart sein: being tough and ignoring pain

Interviews and contemporary written sources show that being 'hard' or 'tough' with athletes was seen as a precondition of high performance. Being 'soft', in contrast, was seen as feebleness. Athletes were required to be hard with their own bodies, disregarding their pain in order to fulfil the extreme coaching plans. However, if coaches ignored the pain of the athletes, this could lead to athletes dropping out of sport.

By ignoring pain, injury and illness, coaches could precipitate the end of an athlete's career, so this form of oppressive coaching could be counter-productive.

Drugs and pain as aspects of coaching

The use of anabolic steroids brought a new dimension to the relationship between athletes and coaches in the GDR. Coaches had to learn how their individual athletes reacted to the new doping substances and when and how the individual limits of performance by their athletes were to be reached. In this new process, pain was given a fascinating new function as an aspect of control within the training regime. The use of anabolic steroids dramatically increased the endurance and strength of athletes and reduced the recovery period after intense training. Many athletes were fascinated by these new possibilities of their bodies. But on the other hand there was also a multiplicity of negative changes which they experienced in their everyday lives: muscle cramps, difficulty in relaxing, strong mood changes, manic phases or difficulties in concentration. However, coaches and medical doctors were able to shelter behind the fact that information on these side effects of drugs was not made public and not revealed to the athletes. Thus the athletes did not know the real reasons for either their enhanced performance or the associated pain which they experienced. What they did know was that the more intensive training of which they were now capable was associated both with significantly improved performance and with an increase in pain which was part of their training: such was the life of the elite athlete.

There were two other influences on the coaches and medical doctors in elite sports. First, coaches transformed their own athletic biographical experiences, which for many consisted of the experience of pain as a permanent aspect of the status of the elite athlete, and developed this philosophy in an extreme way.

A second aspect concerned the role of the centralized sport system in setting targets for athletes. The training figures from the science centres indicated that a given level of performance should guarantee a specific haul of medals at championships (and also the income

and continued appointment of the coach or doctor of the sport club). However, this centralized sport system in East Germany had failed to take into account the individuality, the distinctive features, of each individual athlete.

We can find many sources indicating the presence of permanent conflict between central 'scientific' plans and the everyday practical work carried out by coaches with performers on the track. To coaches and doctors, watching the efforts and reactions of athletes in relation to pain was a better measure of athletes' performance than abstract computer-generated plans from East Berlin or Leipzig.

Moreover, the coaches had no trust in general plans because they knew their genesis. The highly complex, secret training plans came from the 'scientific centres' of the national federations and the even more highly secret plans from the doping researchers at Leipzig. But the plans were founded on incorrect premises. The perfect *Norm-Erfüllung* (fulfilling the central orders from Berlin for each individual athlete) was practically impossible. In gymnastics in the 1980s the real performances as compared to the plans were about 40 per cent lower, in soccer 30 per cent and in track and field about 20 per cent.

Because they lacked reliable data, trainers tended to use extreme measures of both training and drugs. This was a crucial element of the success of the East German sport system.

Pain and the role of 'detraining' in the social control of athletes

The continuous abuse of pain as a means of maintaining discipline in training was an aspect of the East German system. But what happened if an athlete was sufficiently mentally strong to resist such pressure? Here the ultimate threat was to terminate the athlete's career without 'detraining', the process designed to manage (relatively) safely the transition from a peak of physical strength and fitness, based on the use of drugs, to a more 'normal' life, and to manage any associated health problems. 'Detraining' was therefore very important for the health of the athletes leaving the cadres of the national teams. But such help was denied to those who were dismissed for political reasons or because they refused to obey instructions.

421

The consequences of withdrawal without 'detraining' were numerous and could result in continued pain and illness. The athlete would be denied the use of sport facilities after retirement. He or she might have to cope with heart and circulatory problems, associated with drug use, without specialist help from others. The withdrawal of the drugs might also be associated with pain as athletes became dependent on the drugs to help them manage the pain of training and competing.

This threat of withdrawing 'detraining' was frequently used to maintain discipline or to compel an athlete to continue competing when he or she wished to retire. In this situation, athletes were likely to choose the lesser evil of continuing the high-level training and competition as a form of self-protection. By making that decision, the athlete ensured that he or she would continue to have access to medical advice and any specialist care which was required, after retirement. The experiences of those who left without help became part of the culture in the sport clubs and therefore reinforced the process of producing discipline on the training grounds.

Ignoring pain as a means of pushing beyond the limits of endurance

Athletes were expected to ignore pain and risk. This was also true for new forms of training or coaching methods. 'Overloading' in training was practised with extremely high weights and to the complete exhaustion of the athletes. There were experiments with a heavy backpack containing a gas cylinder used in hypoxia training. Subterranean bunkers, where there was no daylight, were used in bonding sessions. These sessions produced fear in athletes.

In many sports the objective was to harden athletes against their own experiences of pain. At the army sport organization *Vorwaerts* ('Onwards') athletes were required to take part in repeated sprints wearing a gasmask, which restricted breathing, and amphetamines were administered to athletes in order to enable them to endure excessive training sessions. Athletes who took part in new forms of 'experimental training' did so formally as volunteers, but in reality athletes who had the legal status of soldiers were expected to take part in experiments with untested substances and/or techniques and unknown side effects. A refusal by the soldier-athlete could lead to exclusion from sport, with the consequences noted above.

Relationships within the sport system

What was the pattern of relationships within this system? It is important to understand the hierarchical patterns within the East German sports system, as well as the patterns of communication.

The athlete

His (or her) performance was the focus of the organization. The individual athlete had little power; his or her main source of personal support was the family, from which the athlete was physically removed while at the sport school.

The doctor

Medical doctors wielded considerable power over athletes. The doctor oversaw the administration of appropriate drugs and determined whether an athlete's aches were 'real' or 'imagined' and whether they were pains associated with peak performance or pains which would hinder peak performance.

Data gathered both from archives and interviews indicate that doctors within the sports system were expected to practise in a 'hard-line' manner. Doctors who were more oriented towards the welfare of athletes were removed from the system and relocated into the general medical service.

Analysis of files and interview data covering the last 10 years of the East German system indicates that approximately 10 per cent of the doctors left the sports medical service annually, in most cases for ethical reasons and, in particular, because they did not accept mandatory doping and did not accept the principle of placing athletic performance above the welfare of athletes.

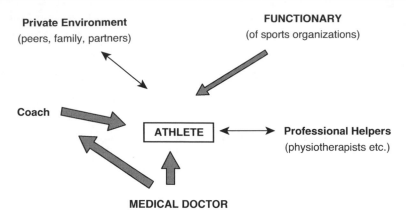

Figure 6.5.2. Relationships within GDR Sport Clubs: the dominance of the doctor and coach.

Note: ↔ = two-channel communication: with equal rights of both parties; → = one-channel communication with direction of hierarchy against individual actors

Source: Following the interpretation (modified) of A. Delow, 'Leistungssport und Ideologie: die Vorbereitung der Olympischen Spiele in einem DDR-Sportclub', *Sozial- und Zeitgeschichte des Sports,* 11 (1997), 2: 62

The coach

The trainer had even more power over the athletes than did the doctors. The trainer had daily contact with athletes and observed them closely, and also had absolute authority in the group of elite athletes. As was the case with doctors, trainers who were considered 'soft' were removed from the system.

If excessive dosages of drugs led to serious health dangers, the trainer still retained his or her position. Trainers responsible for giving excessive doses of drugs continued to be supported by the state security service. For example in Berlin, a female trainer (with the support of the doctor, who was also a woman) gave five times more steroids to female shot putters than were given to the men in the same event. The Stasi was aware of this practice but concealed the side effects and the criminal activity involved.

On a day-to-day basis, it was the trainer in the GDR system who was most closely connected with the athletes. On him or her, juniors, and even older athletes, projected their wishes and needs. So, trainers became in some cases substitute parents, or even sexual partners; in some cases (usually male) trainers became the sexual partners or spouses of athletes 20 or 25 years younger than themselves. In such cases, where close partnerships developed, athletes were to some extent protected within this relationship, but more usually athletes suffered at the hands of their coaches the typical mixture of gratification, doping and infliction of pain.

Summary

Sport in East Germany was a highly complex system. It treated both male and female athletes as objects. The pursuit of sporting performance was the objective of sport scientists, physicians and biologists, even if this meant breaching the law and the conventional understanding of medical ethics.

The masculinization of female athletes through the use of drugs was also an aspect of this system. (Berendonk and Franke have referred to this as 'androgenization' and the virilization of women; see Berendonk 1991). Because of these processes, several female athletes admitted having attempted suicide.

This system was also premised on the view that being 'hard' on athletes was a precondition for athletic success, while 'softness' was seen as weakness. This led to a dominance of a masculine pattern of thought and action which was reinforced through the biological effects of using anabolic androgenic steroids.

423

This system also reflected subjectively and objectively based theories of training. In relation to the latter, athletes who became coaches reproduced with their athletes the experiences they had to go through in their own careers. Objective reasons are to be found in the widespread misconception that only toughness and the overcoming of pain-barriers would lead to maximum performance in the Olympic arena. Pain was therefore to be understood as an indicator of the most effective training. The coach made the decision as to whether the athlete could take no more pain, or whether he or she was just pretending. In summary, one could say that in the East German system, pain was seen as an index of the effectiveness of training.

Seen from this perspective, the body of the athlete was a prison. The body was 'disciplined' as part of a victory-oriented but totalitarian athletic system; within this secret system of sport, there was little transparency and bureaucratic instructions were protected as state secrets.

The case studies in this chapter give a glimpse into pain in East German sport: as a means of producing absolute discipline. But this could also produce opposite, unwanted effects: drop out from sport or escape out of dictatorship. In East Germany, pain, injury and doping were central to the whole system. Causing pain was a method of coaching. Doping generated painful and dangerous side effects. These activities were organized by the state and covered by state security, and athletes were not given accurate information about the health risks to which they were exposed.

To return to the opening question: It is clear that there was an intention to (ab-)use pain to control training programmes. In this regard, pain has to be understood as a component of fundamental significance to the system.

Bibliography

Berendonk, B. (1991) *Dopingdokumente, Von der Forschung zum Betrug*, Berlin Heidelberg: Springer.

Berendonk, B. (1992) *Doping, Von der Forschung zum Betrug*, Reinbek.

Delow, A. (1997) Leistungssport und Ideologie – die Vorbereitung der Olympischen Spiele in einem DDR-Sportclub, *Sozial- und Zeitgeschichte des Sports* 11, 2: 26–56.

Digel, H. and Dickhuth, H.-H. (eds) (2002) *Doping im Sport. Ringvorlesung der Universität Tübingen*, Tübingen: Attempo: 166–91.

Franke, W. W. (1995) 'Funktion und Instrumentalisierung des Sports in der DDR: Pharmakologische Manipulationen (Doping) und die Rolle der Wissenschaft' in Enquete-Kommission (ed.) *Aufarbeitung von Geschichte und Folgen der SED-Diktatur in Deutschland*, Bd. III, 2, Baden-Baden: Nomos: 987–1089.

Hoberman, J. (1994) *Sterbliche Maschinen. Doping und die Unmenschlichkeit des Hochleistungssports*, Aachen, Meyer & Meyer Verlag (Original title *Mortal engines*).

Seppelt, H.-J. and Schück, H. (eds) (1999) *Anklage: Kinderdoping, Das Erbe des DDR-Sports*, Berlin: Transit.

Singler, A. and Treutlein, G. (2000) *Doping im Spitzensport, Sportwissenschaftliche Analysen zur nationalen und internationalen Leistungsentwicklung*, Aachen: Meyer & Meyer Verlag.

Singler, A. and Treutlein, G. (2001) *Doping – Analyse und Prävention*, Aachen: Meyer & Meyer Verlag.

Spitzer, G. (1994a) 'Aktuelle Konzepte zur Zeitgeschichte des Sports unter besonderer Berücksichtigung der aktuellen Diskussion im Bereich der Geschichtswissenschaft', *Sozial- und Zeitgeschichte des Sports*, 8, 3: 56–76.

Spitzer, G. (1994b) 'Eine überflüssige Generation im deutschen Sport? Spitzensportler und Leistungssport unter den Bedingungen der Nachkriegszeit' in G. Spitzer, G. Treutlein and J.M. Delaplace (eds), *Sport und Sportunterricht in Frankreich und Deutschland in zeitgeschichtlicher Perspektive*, Aachen: Meyer & Meyer Verlag: 163–83.

Spitzer, G. (1994c) 'Une génération superflue dans le sport allemand? Sportifs de pointe et sport de compétition dans les circonstances de l'après-guerre' in *Le Sport et L'Education Physique en France et en Allemagne*. Contribution à une approche socio-historique des relations entre les deux pays. Sous la direction de J. M. Delaplace, G. Treutlein et G. Spitzer, Montpellier: 188–212.

Spitzer, G. (1997) 'Die DDR-Leistungssportforschung der achtziger Jahre als Subsystem: Thesen zur interdisziplinären Systemkritik eines historischen Phänomens in differenzierungstheoretischer Perspektive' in N. Gissel, J. Ruehl and H. J. Teichler (eds) *Sport als Wissenschaft*, Hamburg: Czwalina: 151–86.

Spitzer, G. (1999) 'Spätschäden durch Doping bei Sportlern der ehemaligen DDR' in C. Müller-Platz (ed.) *Leistungsmanipulation: eine Gefahr für unsere Sportler. Wissenschaftliche Berichte und Materialien des Bundesinstituts für Sportwissenschaft*, Bd. 12. Cologne: Sport und Buch Strauss: 27–46.

Spitzer, G. (2001a) 'Auswirkungen von Doping bei Frauen. Ethische Grenzen und ihre Missachtung im DDR-Leistungssport', in G. Anders and E. Braun-Laufer (eds), *Grenzen für Mädchen und Frauen im Sport. Wissenschaftliche Berichte und Materialien des Bundesinstituts für Sportwissenschaft*, Bd. 6, Cologne: Sport und Buch Strauss: 83–100.

Spitzer, G. (2001b) 'Doping in the former GDR' in C. Peters, T. Schulz and H. Michna (eds) *Biomedical Side Effects of Doping, Project of the European Union, Bundesinstitut für Sportwissenschaft. Wissenschaftliche Berichte und Materialien*, Bd. 13, Cologne: Sport und Buch Strauss: 115–25.

Spitzer, G. (2001c) 'Doping with Children' in C. Peters, T. Schulz and H. Michna (eds) *Biomedical Side Effects of Doping, Project of the European Union, Bundesinstitut für Sportwissenschaft. Wissenschaftliche Berichte und Materialien*, Bd. 13, Cologne: Sport und Buch Strauss: 127–39.

Spitzer, G. (2001d) 'Remarks to the Hidden System of State-Organized Doping in the German Democratic Republic (G.D.R.)' in J. Buschmann and G. Pfister (eds) *Sport und sozialer Wandel: Proceedings of the ISHPES Congress 1998. Sports and Social Changes. International Society for the History of Physical Education and Sport: ISHPES Studies Vol. 8*, Sankt Augustin: Academia-Verlag: 161–70.

Spitzer, G. (2002a) 'Stasi-Agenten im Olympiatrainer. Der Münchner Terroranschlag von 1972 aus der Sicht des früheren DDR-Ministeriums für Staatssicherheit. Am 5. September jährt sich der Terroranschlag', *Neue Zürcher Zeitung*, 5 September.

Spitzer, G. (2002b) 'Blutdoping als Domäne im Wintersport. Eine Therapie, die in der DDR der Leistungsmanipulation seit 1972 gebräuchlich war', *Neue Zürcher Zeitung*, 16 March.

Spitzer, G. (2004a) 'Doping in der DDR. Ein historischer Überblick zu einer konspirativen Praxis. Genese – Verantwortung – Gefahren. Wissenschaftliche Berichte und Materialien des Bundesinstituts für Sportwissenschaft' (3rd edn), Bd. 3, Cologne: Sport und Buch Strauss.

Spitzer, G. (2004b) *Fussball und Triathlon. Sportentwicklungen in der DDR*, Aachen: Meyer & Meyer Verlag.

Spitzer, G. (2004c) '*Sicherungsvorgang Sport'. Das Ministerium für Staatssicherheit und der DDR-Spitzensport. Projektbericht für den Vorsitzenden des Sportausschusses des Deutschen Bundestages im Rahmen des Forschungsprojektes 'Die Kontrolle von Sport und Sportwissenschaft durch das Ministerium für Staatssicherheit'*, Schorndorf: Hofmann Verlag.

Spitzer, G. (ed.) (2005) *Doping in European Sports* (forthcoming).

Spitzer, G., Teichler, H. J. and Reinartz, K. (eds) (1998) *Schlüsseldokumente zum DDR-Sport, Ein sporthistorischer Überblick in Originalquellen*, Aachen: Meyer & Meyer Verlag.

Sharp practice

Intensive training and child abuse

Paolo David

By nature, competitive sport is a physical activity based on training, sacrifice and effort, with no exception for the youngest practitioners. Success in sports is the result of a complex mixture of qualities, including gift, motivation, family and sport environment, physical and mental capacities. When very young children are involved in *intensive training*, adults are faced with a number of difficulties. A very thin line divides intensive training that allows children to fulfil themselves from that in which they are abused and exploited. It is not easy for adults to assess constantly whether the child's full development is benefiting or not from intensive training.

In extremely demanding competitive sports such as tennis, gymnastics, figure skating, diving, ice hockey, basketball or football, children as young as four years old may have already been pushed by adults to train frequently and some, at around the age of six, may be starting systematic intensive training programmes and competition (Maffuli 1998: 298). At this age, is training two to three hours a day healthy? Too often coaches and parents perceive child athletes as miniature adults and treat them accordingly, forgetting that children are vulnerable and in a state of perpetual physical and psychological evolution.

Both the World Health Organization (WHO) (1998) and the European Commission (2000) have warned that the potential for abuse exists in intensive training regimes and of the importance of guaranteeing the health and protection of young athletes. In 1997, WHO warned that: 'Organization of children's sports activity by adults does have a potential for abuses to occur if those who set the amount of sports participation and the training regimen are inexperienced and use adult models' (WHO 1998).

Unfortunately, many coaches are not sufficiently aware of children's complex physical and psychological developmental needs and the stages they go through (David 1993: 13–16). A survey among 150 British elite coaches showed that an important gap exists between the age at which children actually start intensive training and the coaches' estimates of when they *should* start. In football, gymnastics, swimming and tennis, coaches suggested 14, 10, 12 and 11 years respectively as the age to start intensive training, but the average actual age was, respectively, 11.3, 8.6, 9.2 and 9.5 years (Training of Young Athletes Study (TOYA) 1993: 13).

Although it is obviously necessary for athletes to train a minimum number of hours a week, many top trainers still emphasize the quantity of

---

training rather than focusing on the quality and often base training intensity on that of adults (Bizzini 1993). Scottish cyclist Graeme Obree, world hour record-holder in 1993, admitted focusing mainly on the quality of his training:

> I cannot see the point of training five hours a day; the quality of training is the priority. For me, three or four rides a week of maximum 90 minutes are sufficient. My body doesn't ask for more. When I see the training programmes that are given to kids when they join teams, I am alarmed.
>
> (*L'Equipe Magazine* 1993)

Some top athletes now believe that it is not humanly possible to train more. Frenchman Jean Galfione, for example, Olympic pole-vault champion in Atlanta (1996), thinks that 'people won't be able to train more; we have reached the maximum' (*L'Equipe Magazine* 2000). In a position statement on intensive training, the American Academy of Pediatrics (2000) stated that:

> To be competitive at a high level requires training regimens that could be considered extreme for adults. The ever-increasing requirements for success create a constant pressure for athletes to train longer, harder, more intelligently, and in some cases, at an earlier age. The unending efforts to outdo predecessors and outperform contemporaries are the nature of competitive sports.

Top sports stars are idolized, not only by their fans but by sports institutions and entire nations. Such emulation is natural, but can easily lead to a dangerous escalation of ever-more training in an attempt to beat opponents, with excessive and abusive demands being put on young athletes. For example, Li Hongping, a Chinese trainer who coaches in the United States, was asked about the domination of young Chinese divers in a competition. 'The Chinese and Russians are not more gifted or talented,' he said, 'but they train eight hours a day and we [the Americans] train four' (Litsky 1998).

According to a 1992 Canadian study of 45 retired high-level athletes, one skater had trained 56 hours a week between the ages of 15 and 17 and a swimmer calculated that he had spent 15,800 hours in the water training, which amounts to 22 months of his life at 24 hours a day (Donnelly 1993: 99). When children train this much, it is in the vast majority of cases because they are at best stimulated or at worst forced by adults (especially parents and coaches). 'No child ever thinks of doing 25 hours of practice per week,' said Peter Donnelly, a Canadian sports sociologist at Toronto University (Kleinhenz 2000: 23).

Today, unless a child starts training at a very early age, it is almost impossible to reach the top in many sports, such as gymnastics and figure skating, and increasingly in athletics, diving, tennis, basketball, ice hockey and football. Children do not fully understand the concept of competition before the age of six or seven. But this does not stop some parents from involving their children in a sport as early as three or four years of age, or even planning what sport their child will take up before they are born.

American Dominique Monceanu, gymnastics champion at the 1996 Atlanta Olympics, told *L'Equipe Magazine* (1996), 'When I was a year old, my father suspended me by my feet to a bar fixed to our door to exercise.' And, according to an authorized biography, her parents decided to 'test' her at six months by placing her tiny hands around a clothesline strung across the kitchen to see if she could hang on: 'Remarkably, tiny Dominique firmly gripped the makeshift bar and did not waver. "See," he [the father] said to his wife, "I told you she's going to be a great gymnast"' (Quiner 1997: 5).

The Slovak father of Swiss former number-one tennis player, Martina Hingis, said his daughter started playing tennis at the age of two (Agence France Presse 2001a) and, according to her mother, Jennifer Capriati's father decided before her birth that she would be a tennis player (Baupère 2001). Earl Woods, the father of golf legend Tiger Woods, believes that his son reacted positively to the game when still in his mother's womb, because when 'a golf ball hit the green, it reverberated against the volcanic surface [of the golf course] and produced a thumping sound, similar to a drum' and Tiger 'would suddenly be very still and quiet' (Owen 2001: 60–1).

Sports authorities have rarely questioned the practice of intensive training among very young child athletes, although they are fully aware that it exists and know that it may lead to abuse. After the 1992 Barcelona Olympics, during which 13-year-old Chinese Fu Mingxia became Olympic diving champion, Juan Antonio Samaranch, then president of the International Olympic Committee (IOC), made an ambivalent statement:

> [He] was not in favour of intensive training at such a young age … we [the IOC] believe in the value of models set by champions to develop sports within a country. After the victories of Boris Becker and Steffi Graf [both became champions while they were still adolescents] thousands of tennis courts were built in Germany and millions of Germans began playing the sport. We need to avoid the artificial moulding of champions by all means, but sports is part of education and can become a lifelong discipline.
>
> (Albuy 1993)

Child abuse and sports

In any situation, children are by definition more at risk of abuse than adults, due to their vulnerability and dependence upon others. Competitive sports can create factors that increase the child's vulnerability to abuse (see Table 6.6.1).

Many definitions of child abuse exist, but they vary little. In 1999, WHO defined child abuse or maltreatment as constituting:

> all forms of physical and/or emotional ill-treatment, sexual abuse, neglect or negligent treatment or commercial or other exploitation, resulting in actual or potential harm to the child's health, survival, development or dignity

in the context of a relationship of responsibility, trust or power.

According to the US National Center for Child Abuse and Neglect, maltreatment exists when:

> through purposive acts or marked inattention to the child's basic needs, behaviour of a parent or substitute or other adult caretaker causes foreseeable and avoidable injury or impairment to a child or materially contributes to unreasonable prolongation or worsening of an existing injury or impairment.
>
> (Loe 1998: 472–3)

Abuse and violence against children were long a subject of taboo and only since the 1960s and 1970s have historians started to look closely at the way civilizations treated their children:

> The history of childhood is a nightmare from which we have only recently begun to awaken. The further back in history one goes, the lower the level of child care, and the more likely children are to be killed, abandoned, beaten, terrorized, and sexually abused.
>
> (De Mause 1974: 1)

In the United States, academics began to speak openly about the high occurrence of child abuse in 1962, after the publication of *The battered child syndrome* (Kempe *et al.* 1962). In many other countries, it was only in the last two decades of the twentieth century that child abuse became public knowledge (Gelles and Cornell 1983). For example, in the United Kingdom, a large government-sponsored

Table 6.6.1 Typology of main forms of abuse, neglect and violence in competitive sports

Physical	Sexual	Psychological	Neglect
Excessive intensive training	Verbal comments	Excessive pressure	Failure to provide proper care and attention
Systematic insufficient rest	Physical advances	Verbal violence	Deliberate negligence
Corporal punishment	Abusive touching	Emotional abuse	Imposed isolation
Severe food diets	Forced intercourse and rape		
Peer violence, including 'hazing' or 'ragging'			
Encouragement of 'play hard' or 'play hurt' attitudes			
Imposed usage of doping products			

survey revealed that almost one in six children had experienced 'severe' physical punishment; the vast majority – 91 per cent – had been hit (Nobes and Smith 1997; Nobes *et al.* 1999). A study of Australian primary schoolchildren found that 81 per cent of boys and 74 per cent of girls had been hit by their mother, 76 per cent of boys and 63 of girls by their father (EPOCH Worldwide and Save the Children-Sweden 1999), while, in Switzerland, 11 per cent of children are beaten, of whom 2.5 per cent are beaten with an object (Government of Switzerland 1992). In 1983, research in Canada, the United Kingdom and the United States estimated that domestic violence occurred in between 25 and 28 per cent of marriages and that the children of those families were as much as 15 times more likely also to become victims of the abuse of one or both of their parents (Shupe and Stacy 1983).

For a long time, protection of the privacy of the family sphere did not allow this issue to be adequately addressed by public authorities. Protection from interference has been a traditional justification for not intervening in cases of domestic violence (Kelly and Mullender 2000). Today, it is increasingly accepted that child abuse in its many forms – physical, psychological, sexual, etc. – affects a large number of children in every society and social group (Gelles and Cornell 1983). The UN Committee on the Rights of the Child's monitoring work also clearly confirms this global trend (Hodgkin and Newell 2002: 257–75).

The harmful consequences of child abuse are widely acknowledged – and they are devastating. They include physical injury, gynaecological problems (for girls), headaches, asthma, depression, fear, low self-esteem, poor school performance, inability to trust, guilt, anger, sexual dysfunction, eating and sleeping disorders, fear of intimacy, post-traumatic stress disorder and ultimately suicide (UNICEF 2000: 9; UN Commission on Human Rights 2000; WHO 2002: 69).

In sports, some very specific consequences of abuse and violence against young athletes can be identified, such as obsessive and compulsive behaviours with regard to excessive training; eating disorders relating to diets imposed in certain sports; and self-injurious behaviours regarding the risks of accidents and injury.

As the child athlete's training becomes more intensive, he or she will gradually spend more and more time with adults in sports facilities. Indeed, some children board during the week in training centres where, at the age of ten, they train at least six hours a day. As in a family, the sports environment is a closed world where children usually create strong emotional and dependency bonds with the adults in charge of them; discipline and obedience are also key elements of the relationship (David 1999: 62–4; De Martelaer *et al.* 2000: 6). Nothing suggests that abuse and neglect is more or less frequent in sport halls and training centres than in families, but it is increasingly recognized that young athletes are potentially vulnerable to serious abuses of trust and power, which may lead to severe forms of violence. Especially vulnerable are children who begin intensive training at a very early age and thus spend more time in the care of coaches than with their own parents.

Some experts consider that, in extreme cases, intensive training in itself constitutes a form of child abuse, especially in demanding sports such as gymnastics. For example, in an article published in the *New England Journal of Medicine* in 1996, four leading child health specialists stated that:

> The development of gymnastics champions involves hard training, stringent coaching, and often parental pressure, ostensibly in the best interest of the child. Over-training, injuries, and psychological damage are common consequences. Parents and coaches, in collusion with the young athlete, may seek to experience vicariously the success of the child, a behaviour that could be called 'achievement by proxy' ... Its hallmark is strong parental encouragement of a potentially dangerous endeavour for the purpose of gaining fame and financial reward. We suggest that in its extreme form 'achievement by proxy' may be a sort of child abuse.
>
> (Tofler *et al.* 1996: 281)

The increased awareness of the past 20 years and the multiplication of preventive and protective measures in Western societies regarding domestic and child abuse have not yet sufficiently reached the sports world. Parents and coaches often assume that abuse cannot occur in such a leisure-oriented activity; others believe it is part of an ultra-competitive culture in which sacrifices are essential and inevitable if the athlete is to reach the top. This belief prevails in societies, such as in Eastern Europe, where abuse awareness is low and insufficiently protected by laws that are sometimes weakly enforced. In many countries, too, it is still considered normal that children should be educated and disciplined through physical or psychological intimidation and force. The father of a nine-year-old Romanian elite gymnast explained in a television programme:

> The French, the Americans, they've tried everything. Nothing worked. It doesn't work there. Why? Because this sport [gymnastics] is very hard and children need to be taken care of. Here [in Romania] we push them; this sport is very hard. But with existing laws there [in the West], it would not be possible to do this with the kids. Otherwise we would be working illegally, and this must be an explanation [of the fact that Western gymnasts are not the best]. Look at the hands of my daughter, they are covered with calluses; she has got more than me and I've been working for years with scrap metal ... I am convinced that she will succeed, as long as nothing happens to her health.
>
> (Arte 2001)

Article 24.1 of the Convention on the Rights of the Child requires states to ensure 'the right of the child to the enjoyment of the highest attainable standard of health', but article 19 also obliges them to:

> take all appropriate legislative, administrative, social and educational measures to protect the child from all forms of physical or mental violence, injury or abuse, neglect or negligent treatment, maltreatment or exploitation, including sexual abuse, while in the care of parent(s), legal guardian(s) or any other person who has the care of the child.

The Convention is articulated around the concept of the *inherent dignity of the person* which needs to be respected in all situations.[1] It also recognizes that parents have the main responsibility to bring up, care for and protect their children (articles 5 and 18), but if they fail to do so, responsibility falls to the state.

In situations where children are constantly in the company of their coaches or trainers and where they spend more time with them than with their own parents (or may even live with them), the coach/trainer becomes the main caregiver under article 19 of the Convention and as such is responsible for the protection of the children. Even in less intensive situations, where children train several hours a day, they are considered to be in the care of their coach, who therefore has *de jure* the responsibility to protect the child from all forms of abuse, violence and exploitation. Parents quite often abdicate a substantial part of their responsibilities to a coach when their children train intensively. For young female athletes, a male coach can become a surrogate father, a role model, a source of strength and inspiration. A teenager or college-age athlete may be infatuated with or attracted by their coach (Doherty 1999: 132).

Both public and private sports authorities have a shared responsibility in ensuring that the young athlete's environment is favourable to the enjoyment of their human rights. When discussing the right to health, the UN Committee on Economic, Social and Cultural Rights (2000: para. 42) considered that not only public authorities have responsibilities and obligations in this regard:

> While only States are parties to the Covenant and thus ultimately accountable for compliance with it, members of society – individuals, including health professionals, families, local communities, intergovernmental and non-governmental organizations, civil society organizations, as well as the private business sector – have responsibilities regarding the realization of the right to health

On the basis of article 19 of the Convention, the Committee on the Rights of the Child systematically advocates for 'zero tolerance against violence' (Hammarberg and Newell 2000: 127). Most countries have legislation to protect children from abuse, neglect and violence. Nevertheless, its enforcement greatly depends on the specific grounds that these national laws cover, particularly with regard to mental and emotional violence, and the political will and capacity of governments to enforce them, especially in the private sphere.

Lost childhood

One common characteristic of seriously abused children is that they feel that they had to grow up too soon and that they 'lost' their childhood. Many young athletes involved in precocious intensive training, whose days are spent training, learning and sleeping, do not have the time to enjoy their childhood. This feeling may fuel anger, bitterness and frustration. Although it is far from an objective, quantifiable and scientific criterion, the feeling of 'lost childhood' among young athletes is nevertheless a powerful potential indicator of sport-related abusive trends.

Many former young athletes who underwent intensive training from an early age empathize with this concept. For instance, Olympic figure-skating silver medallist Rosalyn Summers had a nervous depression the year after winning her title. She explained:

> I'd been on ice six hours a day since I was six years old. I turned pro after the Olympics, when I was 20, and I began to wonder: When's my time? When am I going to relax? When am I going to have a boyfriend and go to the movies? I was touring with a professional show, moving from one hotel to another, in bed at eight o'clock and getting up at four to train. I was burnt out, totally burnt out. I wanted to kill myself. I was making a lot of money but I had no life.
>
> (Doherty 1999: 121)

American Dominique Monceanu, who was, at 16, Olympic gymnastics champion in 1996, also felt frustrated: 'I would think: don't you guys know anything besides gymnastics? Can't we go out for ice cream?' (Doherty 1999: 121). During the 1980s, American Chris Evert was one of the world's top tennis players. Now the mother of three boys, she is happy that:

> none of them are tennis players … Once in a while we'll have a junior tournament here [in her tennis club] and I'll see two ten-year-olds play. I'll see the strained look on their faces, and their parents hovering over them. Would I want to do it all over again myself? No way.
>
> (Kleinhenz 2000: 23)

In a study of 46 elite US athletes preparing for the 1998 Olympics Games, more than half said that, if they had a five-year-old child, they would not raise him or her as they had been and would involve the child in activities other than sports (Murphy 1999:115).

Russian Alexei Nemov emerged as the world's best male gymnast during the 2000 Sydney Olympics, winning two gold, one silver and two bronze medals. When he was 14, he joined a full-time training centre in Krugloye, 50 kilometres from Moscow. Just before the 1996 Atlanta Olympics, he admitted:

> You become crazy here. We train three times a day, 30 hours a week. We train up to eight hours a day during intensive preparation phases. I train, I sleep, I train, I sleep. That's my programme. I don't remember the last time I went home. I have never been healthy. My back always hurts. One of my vertebra has moved; I need injections in my hand. I think it is due to working far too much. We do a lot of powerlifting. All gymnasts are like me: destroyed. This must be the price to pay to be at the top.
>
> (Donzé 2000: 21)

Tennis player Mary Pierce was asked whether she felt she had had a happy childhood. 'No, certainly not,' replied Pierce, who has also reported having been abused by her father during her childhood. 'I left school at 13 … Childhood is a time to live a carefree life. This is a stage I have never really known. Or maybe only before I started tennis' (Sainte-Rose 2000: 82).

Despite great advances in addressing child abuse and violence in many countries, these issues are still considered taboo in the sports world. Adults involved in sports tend to be defensive when questioned about the issue, just as parents often are when confronted with domestic violence. Nonetheless, in many countries, especially in the West, attitudes towards child abuse in general have evolved slowly and new laws, policies and programmes have been put in place to protect children.

The right to rest

The Convention also guarantees 'the right of the child to rest' (article 31.1), although this provision is one that countries and adults in charge of children neglect the most. The right to rest is as important as other fundamental rights, such as to nutrition, clothing and housing; not respecting this right can be considered a form of abuse. Children who habitually suffer from insufficient or poor-quality sleep can be made more vulnerable to physical and psychological health problems and to social and

431

learning deficiencies. Two International Labour Organization (ILO) conventions specifically protect children from working at night and stipulate the number of hours of consecutive rest children should have: children under 14 or in full-time education should have 14 hours' rest; those aged 14 to 16, 12 hours; and adolescents aged 16 to 18, at least seven hours (ILO Conventions Nos. 79 and 90). The Committee on the Rights of the Child (1998) expressed its concern in some instances when monitoring children's right to rest, as in Japan, for example, where 'children are exposed to developmental disorders due to the stress of a highly competitive educational system and the consequent lack of time for leisure, physical activities and rest'.

Intensive training and competitive sports are by nature activities that require important physical and psychological efforts. The right to rest is crucial for young athletes who train on a daily basis, sometimes spending more time in sports halls than on school benches. Young competitors often have to get up early to train before school and then train again in the evening; between sports and school they have no time for themselves and not enough time to rest. In 1997, Dr Michel Leglise (1997: 10), at that time chairman of the International Federation of Gymnastics' medical committee, reiterated:

> Another vital point is the need for rest periods and plenty of sleep ... Children need far more sleep than adults; this must be taken into account not only in daily life, by avoiding late training sessions, but also by avoiding early morning qualifying sessions and evening competitions.

Recent research tends to show that, contrary to popular belief, adolescents (aged ten to 17) need as much sleep, if not more, than children under ten (National Research Council and Institute of Medicine 2000). This research recognizes the complex and demanding developmental needs of adolescents, from both an internal (biological) and an external (social, educational, environmental) point of view.

Irrespective of their own interests and perceived obligations, it is crucial for coaches, sports officials and parents to fully acknowledge,

understand and respect the right to rest of young athletes in order to ensure their sound and holistic development. Even adult athletes regularly complain of competition schedules that are too demanding, thus increasing their vulnerability not only to serious injuries but also to taking illegal performance-enhancing products. It is essential, therefore, that sport authorities understand that, for a healthy development, children need sufficient rest periods and that they organize programmes, regulations and policies accordingly.

Note

1. The concept of the dignity of the child is referred to in the Preamble and articles 23, 28, 37, 39 and 40 of the Convention on the Rights of the Child.

References

Albuy, G. (1993) 'Un entretien avec Juan Antonio Samaranch' (A conversation with Juan Antonio Samaranch), *Le Monde*, 21 September.

Agence France Presse (2001) *Karol Hingis, père meurti* (Karol Hingis, wounded father), 6 January.

American Academy of Pediatrics (2000) 'Intensive training and sports specialization in young athletes', *Pediatrics* 106, 1: 154–7.

Arte (2001) *Roumanie, la gymnastique de la rigueur* (Romania: gymnastics of rigour), Equipe TV and PDJ Productions, Strasbourg: Arte.

Baupère, M. (2001) 'Jenny, fille de fer' (Jenny, iron girl), *L'Equipe*, 28 January.

Bizzini, L. (1993) 'Avant-Propos' (Foreword) in David, P. *La protection des droits de l'enfant dans le sport de haute competition* (The protection of children's rights in high-level competitive sports), Geneva: Defence of Children International.

David, P. (1993) *La protection des droits de l'enfant dans le sport de haute competition* (The protection of children's rights in high-level competitive sports), Geneva: Defence for Children International.

David, P. (1999) 'Children's rights and sports. Young athletes and competitive sports: exploit and exploitation', *International Journal of Children's Rights*, 7: 53–81.

De Martelaer, K., De Knop, P., Theeboom, M. and Van Heddegem, L. (2000) 'The UN Convention as a basis for elaborating rights of children in sport', *Journal of Leisurability*, vol. 27, 2: 3–10.

De Mause, L. (1974) 'The evolution of childhood', in De Mause, L. (ed.) *The history of childhood*, Northvale, NJ: Jason Aronson.

Doherty, E.M. (1999) 'Winning isn't everything ... it's the only thing: a critique of teenaged girls participation in sports', *Marquette Sports Law Journal* 10, 1: 127–60.

Donnelly, P. (1993) 'Problems associated with young involvement in high-performance sport', in Cahill, B.R. and Pearl, A.J. (eds) *Intensive participation in children's sports*, American Orthopedic Society for Sports Medicine, Champaign, IL: Human Kinetics Publishers.

Donzé, F. (2000) 'Alexei Nemov, parcours d'une star mondiale de la gym qui a sacrifié sa vie à la compétition' (Alexei Nemov, the path of a world gymnastics star who sacrificed his life to competiton), *Le Temps*, 17 March.

EPOCH Worldwide and Save the Children-Sweden (1999) *Hitting people is wrong – and children are people too.*

European Commission (2000) *Protection of young sportsmen and doping problems: a European answer is required*, statement by Viviane Reding, Member of the European Commission responsible for education and culture, opening ceremony of the ninth European Sports Forum, 26 October.

Gelles, R.J. and Cornell, P.C. (1983) 'International perspective on child abuse', *Child Abuse and Neglect*, vol. 7, 4: 375–86.

Hammarberg, T. and Newell, P. (2000) 'The right not to be hit', *Children's rights, turning principles into practice*, Stockholm: Save the Children-Sweden, UNICEF.

Hodgkin, R. and Newell, P. (2002) *Implementation handbook for the Convention on the Rights of the Child*, 2nd edition, New York: UNICEF.

Kelly, L. and Mullender, A. (2000) 'Complexities and contradictions: living with domestic violence and the UN Convention on the Rights of the Child', *International Journal of Children's Rights*, 8: 229–41.

Kempe, C.H., Silverman, F.N., Steele, B.F., Drögemuller, W. and Silver, H.K. (1962) 'The battered child syndrome', *Journal of the American Medical Association*, 181: 17–24.

Kleinhenz, L. (2000) 'My Dad's cool, but my Mom's a psycho', *The Independent on Sunday*, 25 June.

Leglise, M. (1997) *The protection of young people involved in high-level sport, Limits on young gymnastics' involvement in high level sport*, Strasbourg: Committee for the Development of Sports, Council of Europe.

L'Equipe Magazine (1993) no. 601, 7 August.

L'Equipe Magazine (1996) no. 750, 3 August.

L'Equipe Magazine (2000) no. 935, 1 April.

Litsky, F. (1998) 'She's only 16, but Sorgi is a rising young talent in the diving world', *New York Times*, 26 July.

Loe, S. (1998) 'Legal and epidemiological aspects of child maltreatment', *Journal of Legal Medicine*, no. 471.

Maffuli, N. (1998) 'At what age should a child begin regular continuous exercise at moderate or high intensity?' *British Journal of Sports Medicine*, 32: 298.

Murphy, S. (1999) *The cheers and the tears, a healthy alternative to the dark side of youth sports today*, San Francisco: Jossey-Bass.

National Research Council and Institute of Medicine (2000) *Sleep needs, patterns, and difficulties of adolescents*, Summary of a workshop. Board on Children, Youth and Families, Washington DC: National Academy Press.

Nobes, G. and Smith, M. (1997) 'Physical punishment of children in two-parent families', *Clinical Child Psychology and Psychiatry*, Sage, vol. 2, 2: 271–81.

Nobes, G., Smith, M., Bee, P. and Heveren, A. (1999) 'Physical punishment by mothers and fathers in British homes', *Journal of Interpersonal Violence*, vol. 14, 8: 887–902.

Owen, D. (2001) *The chosen one. Tiger Woods and the dilemma of greatness*, New York: Simon and Schuster.

Quiner, K. (1997) *Dominique Monceanu, a gymnastic sensation*, New Jersey: The Bradford Book Company.

Sainte-Rose, V. (2000) 'Je n'ai jamais été aussi calme' (I have never been so calm), *L'Equipe Magazine*, no. 930, 26 February.

Shupe, A. and Stacy, W. (1983) *The family secret*, Boston: Beacon Press.

Switzerland, Government of (1992) *Enfance maltraitée en Suisse* (Ill-treatment of children in Switzerland), Groupe de travail 'Enfance maltraitée' (ed.), Rapport final présenté au Chef du Département fédéral de l'intérieur, Berne (Final report presented to the Head of the Federal Department of the Interior, Bern).

Tofler, I.R., Stryer, B.K., Micheli, L.J. and Herman, L.R. (1996) 'Physical and emotional problems of elite gymnasts', *New England Journal of Medicine*, vol. 335, no. 4.

TOYA (1993) *Training of young athletes study (TOYA), TOYA and intensive training*, London: The Sports Council.

UN Commission on Human Rights (2000) *Report of the Special Rapporteur on the sale of children, child prostitution and child pornography*, 56th session, E/CN.4/2000/73, Geneva: UN.

UN Committee on Economic, Social and Cultural Rights (2000) *The right to the highest attainable standard of health, article 12 of the International Covenant on Economic, Social and Cultural Rights*, General Comment No. 14, E/C.12/2000/4, Geneva: UN.

UN Committee on the Rights of the Child (1998) *Concluding observations of the Committee on the Rights of the Child: Japan*, 18th session, CRC/C/15/Add.90, Geneva: UN.

UNICEF (UN Children's Fund) (2000) *Domestic violence against women and girls*, Innocenti Digest, no. 6, Florence: UNICEF Innocenti Research Centre.

World Health Organization (1998) 'Sports and children: consensus statement on organized sports for children', FIMS/WHO ad hoc Committee on Sports and Children, in *Bulletin of the World Health Organization*, no. 76(5), Geneva: WHO.

World Health Organization (2002) *World report on violence and health*, Krug, E.G., Dahlberg, L.L., Mercy, J.A., Zwi, A. and Lozano, R. (eds), Geneva: WHO.

Part 7

Ethics and adventurous activity

Introduction

Mike McNamee

Notwithstanding Suits's pioneering work in the philosophy of sports, in the introduction to this volume and in certain essays of Part 1, a case was made that traditional accounts of sport could be viewed as exclusionary or even essentialistic. In the final Part of this volume, a range of outdoor activities are considered in order to extend the often narrow fare of examples that are the subject of essays in sports ethics, and also to highlight connected and insightful analyses of those activities that may shed light on more mainstream discussions.

To ease the reader, who like this author may be something of a prudent player, avoiding excessive risks or deliberately staying well within the sphere of the athletically unspectacular, we begin with John Russell's general consideration of 'The Value of Dangerous Sport'. Russell is not against prudent choices of activities, nor prudence within risky activities. He argues, however, that there is more than mere subjective value in what he calls 'dangerous sports'. Russell's list of 'dangerous sports' includes obvious examples like boxing, downhill skiing, motor racing, rodeo bronco riding and surfing among others. While bodily harm may arise in most sports, its risk is inherently present in these activities, and to a substantial degree so that impairment to some basic human functioning(s) is entailed. Embracing these activities expresses an attitude of self-affirmation, where participants push the very limitations of their being. Arising from this, he argues: 'The opportunities

they provide for flourishing, however, are different than, and often at odds with, those permitted in ordinary life. Hence it is not surprising that certain virtues that are required in this context are not readily transferable to everyday life' (2005: 10). Nevertheless, Russell holds that one clear value is the expansion of available opportunities for human flourishing.

Russell is keen to distance himself from romantic interpretations, despite their attractions, where the value of dangerous activities is understood as a contrast to the everyday, the mundane. And while recognising similarities with romantic militarism, there are important differences too. Encouraging spontaneity and individualism is at odds with militaristic values, but readily present in the playful engagement with dangerous sports. To those who freely and knowingly engage in such pursuits, aware of their potential risks, paternalism is an unwarranted intervention. It represents a wrongful intrusion into the lives of those who flourish precisely because of the immanent danger of the activities they rationally choose, exercising deliberation and creating meaning in their lives in a unifying and self-sustaining way.

In 'Adventure, Climbing Excellence and the Practice of "Bolting"' Philip Ebert and Simon Robertson analyse a specific controversy in climbing ethics. Traditionalists claim that ascents ought to be free of the use of metal rungs, which are drilled into the climbing surface and are used to assist the climbers.

Effectively then, we have two climbing games: the bolted and the unbolted. Bolted climbing is one form of 'sport climbing' where bolting is deployed to produce safer climbs that are reliable and give greater access to climbers who wish to experience greater levels of technical proficiency without increasing the corresponding risk of harm. Although the different activity forms are spread geo-culturally, the labels themselves 'sport climbing' and 'traditional climbing' are hardly innocent. All forms, however, appear to offer and sustain an ethos of freedom, but one set against governing bodies, codes of conduct, and other rules that check behaviours of climbers in ways strongly analogous to athletics or football.

They argue that two factors may be used to compare and contrast the values of bolting: individual excellence and adventure. While bolting may support participants with a strong perfectionist tendency (achieving the highest levels of technical excellence they can requires bolting) it is an open question whether the bolts, once driven in, also support or detract the climber on the same surface who attempts to satisfy their aims in a traditional manner, or whether the value of sport climbing is in some way a derivative of traditional climbing. What, if anything, of value is lost by the sport climbers who adopt technical assistance in the form of bolting? Ebert and Robertson argue that the traditionalists' greater embrace of adventure (we might re-describe this in Suitsian terms as a more vital embrace of gratuitousness) includes the openness to exploration and risk. To find one's own route through to the end of a climb is an experience intrinsically valuable for the traditional climber, as is overcoming the dangers inherent in the climb. This experience and its value is, they argue, denied to the sport climber. On these grounds, and recognising that mountain climbing may afford all the values of sport climbing and more, they tentatively argue for the conclusion that the traditional ethos is to be preferred.

What is clear in Ebert and Robertson's essays extends to all sports ethics discussions regarding the uses of technology in sports. They make it clear that what is at stake in the issue of bolting is a complex amalgam, of 'individual ideals, the values and goals of different climbing practices and communities, as well as various aesthetic and environmental matters' (2007: 56). This amalgam surfaces in a novel way in Jesús Ilundáin-Agurruza's 'Kant Goes Skydiving' where the same spirit of playful gratuitousness leads people to run in front of bulls in Pamplona, or launch themselves down steep mountains on bikes, or – as is the object of his discussion – leap out of aeroplanes 13,000 feet (4,000 metres) above the ground. He argues that a consideration of Kant's (1991) discussion of the sublime can help us to understand better what experiences these activities offer from a conceptual point of view.

Ilundáin-Agurruza observes that skydiving and other activities like extreme sports are self-consciously chosen in rejection of the organised, commodified and commercialised fare of modern sports. He offers a historicised perspective of the European development of their mien in romantic attitudes to untamed nature, a world of the unknown, in relation to the modernist view of rational science and civilised society. Ilundáin-Agurruza introduces the aspects of the concept of the sublime – understood mathematically or dynamically – in relation to our judgment of a thing so absolutely great that we cannot fully comprehend it. He notes that both aspects combine to capture the two central features of extreme experiences like skydiving, mountain climbing and skiing difficult terrain: the transcending of boundaries and the courting of danger in the face of nature. This experience is to be understood as generated both by reason and imagination. In the face of the awesome power of nature, skydivers experience their own fragility or diminutiveness.

One key to understanding the felt satisfaction of the successful skydiver (mountain biker, extreme sportsperson, etc) is the courting of danger to a degree where the fear does not overwhelm the skilful execution of the activity nor one's sense of the situation. Elation, exhilaration and relief are the intrinsic rewards of the sublime experience. One feature that connects the aesthetic and the ethical is the playful spirit, which suffuses the pleasure and fear in activities like skydiving. Just as Best (1978) argued, not any way of rotating 360 degrees head-over-heels constitutes a somersault. There are criteria to satisfy, canons to measure oneself against in these activities too. Thus there is a trade-off between serenity (true of much aesthetic experience conceived of as contemplative) or mindfulness with its intensity in dangerous activities.

Thus writes Ilundáin-Agurruza 'The sublime is chaotic and dynamic and it brings about a tension between pleasure and pain that is resolved in a negative way. The extreme again partakes of this process for there we find a mixture of fright and exhilaration that is resolved in alleviation' (2007: 162).

This balance between the sought-for risk and subjective value found in jumping into the high air is extended in Gunnar Breivik's essay 'Can BASEjumping Be Morally Defended?'. While Ilundain argues that when fear becomes too great, jumpers cannot experience the sublime, Breivik argues it is difficult to disentangle the estimation of risks and questions of moral responsibility from the prudential value of egoism.

BASEjumpers project themselves from steep mountains or very high artificial structures that constitute a base. Despite being a heterogeneous group, they are all high-sensation seekers for whom the intense stimulation is in part a function of the risk-taking. Breivik summarises the arguments for and against BASEjumping combining factors both within and beyond the jumpers' experiences. Clearly, jumpers who are alone in life or who are terminally ill can estimate risks that largely affect only themselves. Those with families and dependents must weigh their own interests in engaging in activities that give their lives deep meaning and value with the potential loss or detriment to their loved ones. And both must consider the consequences if they incur a need for public healthcare resources. The metaphor of weighing interests seems to align itself with a consequentialist framework, but it is not clear that the subsequent harms to self and others can be evaluated in the same way as estimating the value of being free to live life according to one's endorsed risk-taking commitments.

Breivik marks out a distinction between being reasonable and being rational. He argues that BASEjumpers's actions may seem unreasonable to everyday prudent others, but are not thereby irrational. To the contrary he writes: 'People that are fully normal and rationally competent take unreasonable choices' (2007: 180). The mere fact that other sane persons would not jump because of their life plans or preferences, he argues, cannot be a basis for moral criticism. He concludes that BASEjumping can be morally defended along with the caveat of responsible risk-estimation and the balancing of other's reasonable interests in the life of the jumper.

The final essay of this Part, and the Volume as a whole, draws together themes scattered throughout these pages. And it may seem odd that it comes from a source reflecting on our lives in nature, both animal and geological. Raymond Gaita's essay 'Sacred Places' comes from his book *The Philosopher's Dog* where he reflects on some of the deepest attachments we have that bring meaning and sense to our lives. Gaita's reflections are autobiographical yet express important aspects of mountaineering that compare and contrast with broader sports experiences. He sets the activity of climbing within the broader context of a love of nature and speaks of his un-apprenticed initiation, and early (near disastrous) encounters with the sublime that Ilundáin-Agurruza depicts. He asks whether following an exploratory instinct – untutored by those more steeped in the practices of climbing – is irresponsible. He rejects the charge and draws us to themes explored by each of the authors in this Part: 'Mountaineering is degraded unless the prospect of death is lucidly accepted' (2003: 144). The depth of commitment experienced by some mountaineers is comparable to the kind of compulsion that is called 'volitional necessity' (Frankfurt, 1986). This is doubtless true of many athletes and even fans. But the price of their zeal is not always counted in the absolute costs that mountain climbers knowingly acknowledge they may pay.

Gaita considers whether the traits of character, vaunted by educationally minded sportspersons and coaches, are not mere simulacra in the contexts of mountain climbing (and by implication all sports). He asks this, since sceptical questions may reasonably be asked of the worthiness of the ends in which virtues are seemingly required. Courage in the pursuit of an unworthy end might not be a virtue in a person so disposed. Is mountaineering really worth all that? One point of contrast between mountaineering and the paradigmatic sports we find in Olympic sports, is made regarding the conventionalism of the latter. Nevertheless, he writes:

> Our interest in them is hardly ever just an interest in how a machine can perform,

but how a human being can overcome weariness, demoralisation, temptations to be a bad loser or even to cheat. Were this not so sport would be of no interest. But no sportsperson, I think, can say in his defence, when he has broken the rules of the game, that his conscience required him to play as he did.

(2003: 149)

Respect for the mountain forms the 'horizon of significance'[1] for mountain climbers – that is the background against which judgements are to be made. He suggests that what is needed here is some kind of authentic discovery rather than a decision, made by some institution or other, as to what is in the best interests of the activity. It will be argued by those who set great store in conventionalism that it too, when properly attuned to the best of a practice's history and traditions, can assist in the development of such attitudes when its leaders are sensitively, virtuously, inclined. Nevertheless, Gaita's point goes deeper: it is to undermine the claim, often made against the ethics of sports that they are mere conventionalism as opposed to morality proper. It is, he states,

> a moralistic conception of morality that would claim for itself all serious value that conflicts with it. We should resist its imperious claims. The need to climb can go deep and when it does its depth is not merely psychological. [...] Sometimes – at the best of times – the necessities of mountaineering, the reasons why mountaineers must climb, are like moral necessities, outward-looking, and also like moral necessities they are distorted when one tries to explain them by an inward-looking psychology.
>
> (2003: 150–1)

I hope not to overstate matters when I observe two related points at the end of this introduction to this, the last Part of the *The Ethics of Sports: A Reader*. First, much scholarship in sports ethics (as in other spheres) has rigidly observed the morality–prudence distinction, which elevates the former to a sphere of almost supra-human existence and relegates the latter, all self-regarding aspirations, strictly to second division status. Although metaethical considerations have been deliberately neglected here,

Gaita's essay, perhaps more than any other in the present volume, bridges the space between applied and metaethical considerations as they relate to sports. He observes the weakness of this moral economy and expresses how the relations between self- and other-regarding attitudes are constituted in and through human–human and human–nature interactions in a way that gives depth and meaning to lives. Secondly, and relatedly, sport is often derided as being hived-off from the everyday business of living. This point is even crystallised in Huizinga's canonical reflections which appeared in Part 1. Partly in contrast to his opening salvo in the philosophy of play, the essays gathered here also celebrate an athletic way of life and show, I think, how sports may not only adorn a life, but also transform it.

Note

1. To use Charles Taylor's (1992) apt phrase.

References

Best, D. (1978) *Philosophy and Human Movement*, Allen and Unwin: London.

Breivik, G. (2007) 'Can BASEjumping be morally defended?, in *Philosophy, Risk and Adventure Sports*, M. McNamee (ed.), London: Routledge.

Ebert, P. and Robertson, S. (2007) 'Adventure, climbing excellence and the practice of "bolting" ', in *Philosophy, Risk and Adventure Sports*, M. McNamee (ed.), London: Routledge.

Frankfurt, H. (1986) *The Importance of What We Care About*, Cambridge: Cambridge University Press.

Gaita, R. (2003) *The Philosopher's Dog*, London: Routledge.

Jesús Ilundáin-Agurruza (2007) 'Kant goes skydiving: understanding the extreme by way of the sublime', in *Philosophy, Risk and Adventure Sports*, M. McNamee (ed.), London: Routledge.

Kant, I. (1991) *Observations on the Feeling of the Beautiful and the Sublime* (trans. J. T. Goldthwait), Berkeley: University of California Press.

Russell, J. S. (2005) 'The Value of Dangerous Sport', *Journal of the Philosophy of Sport*, 33: 1–19.

Taylor, C. (1992) *The Ethics of Authenticity*, Boston: Harvard University Press.

The value of dangerous sport

J. S. Russell

If sport requires the development and exercise of physical skills for overcoming unnecessary obstacles, it is hardly surprising that physical danger is found in sporting activity. A moment's reflection, however, reveals that danger is not a necessary element of sport, although it is certainly a prevalent one. Bowling, golf, and billiards are all sports according to the standardly accepted definition (18), but they hardly involve any interesting degree of physical danger intrinsic to the activities of the sport. By contrast, baseball, boxing, cricket, downhill ski racing, football, free skiing, gymnastics, hang gliding, high diving, hockey, horse racing, judo, karate, lacrosse, marathon running, motor racing, mountain climbing, pole vaulting, polo, rodeo bronco riding, rugby, skydiving, skateboarding, steer wrestling, surfing, and wrestling are all sports that incorporate the presence of physical danger to a substantial degree. And the list could go on. Notice, too, that the entries cut across a division between contact and noncontact sports. Contact sports like boxing, football, and rugby have no special corner on danger. Noncontact sports like free skiing, gymnastics, motor racing, and mountain climbing can involve equally serious or greater threats to life and limb.

It is surely a puzzle why so many people so readily engage in activities that subject them to such risks. It is more puzzling when we recognize that those risks are unnecessary. After all, such activities take place in a separate, temporary world of play that people choose to enter. Moreover, it is not immediately obvious that there is any special direct or indirect value to participating in dangerous sports, per se. For it seems possible to realize the same values of athletic excellence, discipline, perseverance, sportsmanship, and so on by pursuing nondangerous or minimally dangerous sports such as badminton, golf, or tennis. And it is obvious that the risks taken today in dangerous sports are increasingly unrelated, even indirectly, to the satisfaction of any practical needs of the participants or of society more generally. That is, the risks taken in dangerous sports are now rarely connected to the preparation of skills that are useful means to satisfying individual or social needs. The ability to dish out a potentially bone-crushing body check in hockey has no evident utilitarian purpose outside that context. Even where there is such a connection, as in sports involving weaponry or martial training, for example, the need to learn such skills to hunt prey or for self-protection has for some

J. S. Russell 'The Value of Dangerous Sport' from *Journal of the Philosophy of Sport*, Vol 33, Issue 1, pp. 1–19, © 2005 J. S. Russell. Reprinted by permission of Human Kinetics.

time now ceased to be a practical necessity for virtually all participants.

In this context, dangerous sports can appear not only self-destructive but also utterly frivolous and anachronistic. Yet the interest in such sports is hardly waning. The 20th century saw the emergence of many dangerous sports as popular public spectacle (hockey, football, motor racing, etc.), and so-called extreme sports are emerging now at a pace limited only by the capacity for human invention. But there is nothing very new in this, for dangerous sports have always existed and held a fascination for both participants and audiences. One evident explanation for their prevalence and attraction is that more is at stake than in sports in which participants do not place themselves in physical danger. But while this undoubtedly explains a part of the draw of dangerous sports as public spectacle, it simply presses further the question of what their value is for those who freely choose to take unnecessary risks to their lives or bodies by taking part in them.

My aim in this article is to attempt a general defense of the institution of dangerous sports, if not all instances of them, for those who participate in them. Against this, I recognize that the attraction of dangerous sports to particular individuals is bound to be complex. There is unlikely to be a single, all-encompassing explanation for why each individual in fact chooses to participate in these activities. Nevertheless, I will try to show that some obvious reasons people might give for valuing these activities look partial at best and in need of deeper explanation and support. In particular, I will argue that defenses of dangerous sports based on pursuit of glory or honor, or as connected to the development of courage, or as an outlet for physical aggression or risk-taking impulses, or just for pleasure or satisfaction or thrills, are all significantly inadequate. I shall present a general argument for the value of dangerous sports that I believe represents a deeper explanation of the dominant, distinctive value of such sports. I find that value in an ideal of what I shall term "self-affirmation." Dangerous sport in its best exemplars, particularly those in which substantial bodily danger is an immediate and ever-present risk, represents an opportunity for confronting and pressing beyond certain apparent limits of personal, and indeed human, physical and psychological capacities in ways not

afforded by other normally available human activity. Thus, I say that the dominant, distinctive value of dangerous sport consists of an activity of self-affirmation because dangerous sport invites us to confront and push back the boundaries of the self by creating contexts in which some of the ordinary bounds of our lives can be challenged. Hence, we discover and affirm who we are and what we can be by confronting and attempting to extend these boundaries. In this sense, dangerous sport is perfectionist. It tests us by requiring us to make the most of our whole selves, of our bodies and our minds working together as a unity, when (or because) everything, or almost everything, is at stake.

These ideas will be developed further later. For now, it is important to recognize that there is a broad existential resonance about such extreme human exertions, because human activity in all areas of serious endeavor, in art and science, for example, can be aptly characterized as a confrontation with, and an attempt to push, the boundaries of our limitations as finite beings. This expresses a familiar response to the conditions of our existence, one that can be found both in myth and in history, from the exploits of Theseus taking the less-traveled road to Athens, to the various campaigns of Joan of Arc, to Kant confronting his dogmatic slumber. In this sense, dangerous sport is continuous with human realities and strivings that are well known to us. Sometimes those strivings can consume us—and not only in dangerous sport. For my purposes, however, the distinctive ideals of self-affirmation that are most directly relevant to dangerous sport can be found in the yearnings of romantic militarism that emerged in the 19th century as a response to the waning opportunities for expression of martial spirit amid the orderly comfort and security of modern civil society. This will undoubtedly seem a surpassingly odd source for defending the institution of dangerous sport, but in fact the parallels between romantic militarism and dangerous sport are striking and deserve to be explored.

It is not my purpose in drawing this parallel to argue that dangerous sport has an innately military character. I argue that the general ideals that motivate romantic militarism have obvious counterparts in dangerous sport. I shall argue that dangerous sport can and does appropriate those ideals to a more effective extent than does romantic militarism, which was doomed from the start by its inability to be reconciled with either modern civil society or the practice of modern warfare. By contrast, the expression of those ideals through dangerous sport poses no similar threat to civil society. Dangerous sport can civilize those ideals to constrain their worst excesses. Thus, dangerous sport represents a practical and morally defensible institution for realizing an important source of human value. It is an alternative to romantic militarism, not a paler version of it. If I am right, it is hardly surprising that dangerous sport has flourished in recent times whereas romantic militarism has become a mere historical curiosity.

I begin by describing what a dangerous sport is. I then examine various reasons people give for valuing such sports. This will lead to a consideration of my main thesis about the relationship between dangerous sport and self-affirmation.

What is a dangerous sport?

By "dangerous sport," I mean a sport that involves activity that itself creates a significant risk of loss of, or serious impairment to, some basic capacity for human functioning. Dangerous sports, then, range along a continuum of significant risks. They come in degrees of more or less danger as determined by their potential to harm basic capacities for human functioning and the probability of such harm occurring (that is, by the standard method of assessing risk as a matter of degree and probability of harm). There is a proviso here that must be marked, however. Because all physical activity undoubtedly involves some risk to basic human functioning, we must be careful to preserve some meaningful distinction between dangerous and nondangerous sport. It is likely, for example, that in rare cases badminton players will become paralyzed from injuries incurred from diving for volleys. Thus, there is some risk of loss of basic capacities for human functioning from playing badminton. Rare instances of losing an eye in this sport would be another example. This does not necessarily make badminton a dangerous sport. Thus, I have qualified the definition of dangerous

sport so that it must involve some "significant risk" of loss of, or serious impairment to, a basic capacity for human functioning. By this, I mean a risk that is substantial enough that it is, or should be, an expected outcome from time to time that is directly attributable to the specific activities involved in the sport itself and that exceeds the risk of such injury found in participants' day-to-day life outside of sport by more than a modest degree. Such an injury does not have to be permanent, although typically the potential is there for that.

This does not mark a boundary between nondangerous and dangerous sport with precision, but that is not necessary for my purposes. Even so, we can make this a bit clearer. A key distinction seems to be that in nondangerous sport no special provision is normally needed to protect basic capacities for human functioning (because the risks are modest at most) or that when such a measure is thought necessary or prudent, it can pretty much guarantee effective protection. By contrast, dangerous sports will usually acknowledge the need to take measures to protect basic capacities for human functioning, but precautions cannot guarantee such protection. Thus, serious head injuries can still occur in sports like football, amateur boxing, or motorcycle racing despite the required use of protective headgear.

There are, of course, elements of serious danger in all physical activity, but it seems right to say that sports like badminton, bowling, golf, and tennis, which are normally acknowledged to be nondangerous, expose their participants to only fairly modest physical risks beyond what might be found in everyday life, if they exceed them at all. Thus, the position I advance seems to conform roughly to our considered judgments about dangerous and nondangerous sport. For example, it is hard for me to imagine that bowling is more dangerous than a vigorous afternoon spent digging a new rose garden in the front yard. Golf is undoubtedly more dangerous, due mainly to the risk of having one's skull split by some duffer's slice peeling off the next fairway. But if those risks were more than modestly greater than the everyday risk of being hit by errant projectiles (or falling off the ladder while clearing the gutters), one would expect serious consideration to be given to head protection. It appears relevant, too, that the victim is a victim *incidentally* as opposed to receiving

443

his lumps as a result of his or her engagement in the sport's activities qua participant. Thus, my main interest here is with more immediately dangerous sports, particularly those in which serious temporary or permanent handicap, or death, is an expected and unpreventable result of direct participation in the specific activities of the sport.

To understand the notion of a dangerous sport we also need to describe more clearly the nature of the injuries that determine that the sport is dangerous. I have suggested that we use the notion of basic capacities for human functioning. A great deal of work has been done on this topic in the last 20 years by theorists of social justice who are interested in determining appropriate levels of basic human functioning for the purposes of measuring and promoting human development, in particular in impoverished countries where measurements of economic growth and gross national product might not accurately reflect improvements in human well-being. This also seems an appropriate metric to judge the harms associated with dangerous sport. It is better than, say, economic loss to an individual, because it measures the effect of injury on the person's physical and mental health, which is what is most directly and immediately threatened in this context. For purposes of this discussion, Martha Nussbaum's list of "central human functional capabilities" is helpful. These include

> being able to live to the end of a human life of normal length ... being able to have good health ... being able to move freely from place to place ... being able to use the senses to imagine, think, and reason, and to do these things in a "truly human" way.
>
> (8: pp. 80–82)

Thus, sports whose activities can reduce a normal person's life span, significantly interfere with a participant's general health or capacity to move about freely, or undermine cognitive abilities all count as dangerous sports by my account. Nussbaum also includes social capacities for affiliation on this list, but for our purposes here I would emphasize the physical and cognitive capacities of human functioning. For example, a sport can become an obsession for some to the detriment of their basic capacity for human affiliation, but I don't think this makes it a dangerous sport (or perhaps we

should say that any sport is dangerous in this respect).

Finally, it is important to distinguish dangerous sports from dangerous recreations or amusements. If sport involves the exercise of physical and mental excellences for overcoming certain physical obstacles (18), then some types of dangerous activities will not count as dangerous sport, even though they might claim to be sports. Take, for example, some of the main activities of the Oxford Dangerous Sport Club. Among other things, this club has for some time now been flinging people through the air from medieval-style catapults into strategically positioned nets. Accidents have occurred, including at least one reported death,[1] so there is evidently a significant risk to basic human functioning associated with this. Bungee jumping is another more common example of a so-called extreme or dangerous sport that is not a sport. As far as I can tell none of these activities requires physical skill (unless some physical dexterity is involved in deceiving one's health- or life-insurance carrier). These are amusements or recreations or mere play, perhaps, but not sport. I take no position on the applicability of this discussion to these other activities.

Attempts to explain the value of dangerous sports

Given the public fascination and spectacle that often surround dangerous sport, it is plausible to think that participants take risks to pursue glory or honors associated with participating in them. To use a more modern, inclusive term, I shall speak of pursuing "public recognition" as including glory, honors, adulation, etc. Certainly, pursuit of public recognition is a common enough motivation for engaging in many activities, and it can undoubtedly play some role here. But this looks like an inadequate explanation of the value of dangerous sport for many reasons. The most obvious one is that identifying the value of dangerous sport solely in the public recognition that can be derived from participating in it locates the value outside of dangerous sport in an important sense. That is, dangerous sport has no value whatsoever in itself or for its own sake if it is done for these reasons—it is a mere means to achieving what is of value. Of course, we might have to accept that dangerous sport has only such merely instrumental value, but there are good reasons to think otherwise.

To begin with, many people engage in dangerous sports with no hope or expectation of, or desire for, public recognition. For these athletes there must be some other value to dangerous sport, and it is plausible to think that it is found in the activity itself in some sense. We can support this argument by noting that undoubtedly many of those who do have an expectation or desire for public recognition would, nevertheless, participate in dangerous sports without any prospect of these benefits. Such individuals must recognize some other value of dangerous sport. All this is suggested in the following homage to wrestling:

> True wrestling is a sport apart from all others. It is a contest of strength, skill, and sheer will between two men. There are no balls, no goal zones, no roped rings. Just the mat, your opponent, and you. A wrestler is not often given the recognition or fanfare of more popular sports. Yet the demands of will, discipline, and commitment are extraordinary. While technically a team sport, the action is one-on-one, making self-reliance an inseparable component. Each match becomes a test of ability and character.
>
> (19)

According to this writer, wrestlers have little expectation of public recognition or fanfare, but they find its principal value in the test of ability and character that the sport provides. There is no reason to think that wrestling is unique in this respect, even among sports that receive greater public notice. At best, then, the argument to place the value of dangerous sport in public recognition looks as if it could represent the full value of dangerous sport only for some. If so, we should consider what intrinsic value dangerous sport might hold and whether the participant whose sole interest is the pursuit of public recognition might be overlooking something of important value in such activity.

Of course, the very fact of public recognition supports this position. After all, public recognition is itself a way of showing that some activity or accomplishment is valued. That raises the question of what it is that is valued. In the current context it is presumably a recognition of some value or excellence that the athlete has realized. In his classic work on play and games,

Homo Ludens, Johan Huizinga makes similar points:

> From the life of childhood right up to the highest achievements of civilization, one of the strongest incentives to perfection, both individual and social is the desire to be praised for one's excellence. ... *We want to be honoured for our virtues.* ... *In order to merit recognition, merit must be made manifest.* Competition serves to give proof of superiority.
>
> (3: p. 63, emphasis added)

Huizinga thus acknowledges what is obvious, namely, that pursuit of public recognition is a powerful motivator. But he is clearly aware that such recognition is *for* the participant's virtues or excellences and that such recognition is the result of having made those virtues publicly manifest. Thus, the existence of public recognition presupposes some value (or values) that is (are) the basis for such recognition. Of course, Huizinga goes too far in suggesting that we all want to be honored for our virtues. Undoubtedly, some athletes pursue their endeavors solely for the sake of public recognition. Such persons often appear to have a shallow commitment to their sports, and this is another reason to consider that they might be overlooking something else of value. In any event, it certainly seems plausible that many athletes pursue public recognition, as Huizinga argues, in order to be honored for virtues made manifest in the course of competition. Because the fact of public recognition presupposes this, as well, we should consider what those virtues or values might be.[2]

Another obvious candidate for the value of participating in dangerous sport is the subjective value that it realizes for the participant. I am thinking here of what might be described as proaffective psychological states such as pleasure, enjoyment, satisfaction, or contentment—in short, psychological experiences that human agents like to have. This is an initially plausible view of the value of dangerous sport. It is difficult to deny that experiences like pleasure or satisfaction are intrinsically valuable, and we seem to be wired biologically to take pleasure in various types of physical activity, particularly those involved in sporting games and play. As well, the pleasurable adrenaline rush of facing and coming through danger intact is a familiar, satisfying experience for many, and it is one that participants in dangerous sports normally acknowledge and often state as a goal, even a prime goal. Thus, subjective value, or the experience of proaffective psychological states, seems to describe at least part of what people value about participating in dangerous sport.

While I do not deny that subjective value is an important source of intrinsic value in dangerous sport (or sport generally), we should look more carefully at such arguments to consider whether these represent the only source of value in dangerous sport. Consider, however, that if they are, this will press the question even harder about why anyone would wish to participate in such sports, because dangerous amusements offer plenty of proaffective experiences without the effort that dangerous sports entail. The question is immediately raised as to why athletes should bother putting themselves through the rigors and frustrations of playing such sports when the preparation is typically arduous and success is a scarce commodity. Once more, identifying the value of dangerous sport in this way seems to locate it externally to the sport's activity in an important sense, so that the value of dangerous sport itself is simply instrumental. Again this seems at odds with common experience, because athletes who make even a modestly serious commitment to play a sport often appear to participate in it in part because they believe its activities are intrinsically interesting or valuable.

The main problem, however, with claims to make subjective value the exclusive basis for why people participate in dangerous sport (or any sport) is that they pretty clearly rest on a confusion about the role that subjective value often plays in our reasoning about value. The key question is whether people participate in these activities *simply for* the pleasure or satisfaction they get out of them or whether they get pleasure or satisfaction *as a result of* valuing certain activities involving physical excellences or accomplishments and then seeing those realized. If the latter is true at least sometimes, then other things are being valued besides subjective value. Moreover, this seems to represent a universal experience, namely, that of valuing something, say, justice or the well-being of another person or clear reasoning, and getting pleasure or satisfaction as a result of seeing that realized.

This sort of reasoning about value is apparently everywhere in sport, including in dangerous sport. The thrill of pleasure one gets in baseball of pitching a ball for a called third strike on a batter or hitting a home run or throwing out a runner on a steal seems clearly the consequence of believing that those activities have some value. If one did not believe that such excellences or accomplishments had value, then it would be difficult to see what special pleasure would be taken in them. I think this is particularly true of dangerous sport. If one did not think that there was some value in successfully climbing an especially technical mountain, in completing a tricky maneuver to gain an advantage in a hard-fought motorcycle race, or in knocking out an opponent in boxing, it would be difficult to see what pleasure or satisfaction could be taken in the activity. As I have already noted, it is puzzling what this might be, and because the experience of pleasure or satisfaction is often present in these contexts, it is natural to suppose that it is the end of action. I will develop the idea of what this other value might be in the next section, but let me further lay the groundwork for that discussion by presenting a concrete historical example, which I think compellingly demonstrates both the source of this confusion and why it is a confusion.

In *Touching the Void*, one of the classic survival tales in mountaineering, climber and writer Joe Simpson recounted his miraculous solo journey to safety after falling into a deep ice crevasse. In 1985, Simpson and his climbing partner Simon Yates became the first to climb the west face of Siula Grande in Peru. On their descent, Simpson broke his leg badly. This usually means death for a climber on an isolated mountain at high altitude. But Yates designed a way of lowering Simpson by rope down the mountain. Against all odds, this was apparently going to be successful, until Simpson was inadvertently lowered over the edge of a cliff. Yates made the decision to cut the rope suspending Simpson once it became clear that he could no longer hold Simpson's weight and that both of them would soon be pulled off the mountain to their deaths. However, Simpson fell into a deep ice crevasse and landed, still alive, on a small bridge in it. Simpson describes the harrowing despair he felt knowing that he could not climb up the crevasse and would die a slow, lonely death there. He decided to lower himself further into the crevasse, hoping either to find a floor or to die quickly by falling once he could no longer hold himself at the end of his rope. He found a floor a few dozen feet beneath the bridge and from there was able to undertake a difficult climb through a hole in the crevasse. Here is Simpson's recounting of the experience of exiting the crevasse and facing the challenge of descending the rest of the mountain alone:

> An excited tingle ran down my spine. I was committed. The game had taken over, and I could no longer choose to walk away from it. It was ironic to have come here searching out adventure and then find myself involuntarily trapped in a challenge harder than any I had sought. For a while I felt thrilled as the adrenalin boosted through me.
>
> (15: p. 141)

It is easy enough to read this passage and think that what Simpson finds valuable about "the game" is the pleasurable "tingle" or the adrenaline rush of the new challenge provided for him. But, in fact, if he did not value "the game" and in particular the hard challenge it presented, there is no reason that he would have felt any pleasure or elation. Moreover, Simpson himself implicitly recognizes this. The pleasure evaporates almost immediately and is replaced by a deeply unsettling sense of isolation and loneliness as he realizes the difficulty he faces. But this does not diminish his sense of the challenge's worth:

> It sharpened my perception ... to realize how vital it was just to be there, alive and conscious, and able to change things. There was silence, and snow, and a clear sky empty of life, and me, sitting there taking it all in, accepting what I must try to achieve.
>
> (15: p. 141)

Contrary to initial appearance, everything about this passage suggests ideas of value that can be realized in action; that is, it rejects a purely subjective conception of value by implicitly acknowledging objectivist or perfectionist components of value. Pleasure is not the principal goal here—it is the human capacity for willing and acting, that is, for consciously changing things and thereby for achievement, that seeks its own goals and challenges. If there is any

lasting pleasure here, it is likely to come from achieving chosen goals by surmounting the obstacles they present.

The arguments examined so far, then, make a compelling case that we should consider what specific value there may be in the activities connected with dangerous sport. There are a few further positions that are sometimes offered, however, to explain the attraction and value of dangerous sport. I will discuss these briefly before moving on.

It is sometimes argued that the desire to participate in dangerous sport is based in some deeply rooted or even genetically programmed impulse for risk taking that many have, much like a gustatory desire for sweet or fatty foods. Perhaps there is some truth to this. But this is, of course, an extremely weak reed on which to rest any defense of the value of dangerous sport, because if there are such primal urges to engage in dangerous activity, this does not yet show that they are valuable at all. Indeed, they may simply be a biological anachronism. Moreover, this hypothesis overlooks the psychological complexity of humans by ignoring the plausibility of the argument just canvassed, for it is evident that we reason about what gives value to sporting activities and take pleasure in realizing those ends, as well. We still need to consider what this value might be.

It is natural to suppose that this distinctive value is the promotion of a general virtue of courage, because courage requires a capacity to face and master physical danger and dangerous sport poses just that sort of challenge. Courage, like any virtue, is realized in action, so it can be realized directly by participating in dangerous sport. Perhaps this will do as a description of the distinctive value of dangerous sport. It is important to be careful about this, however, for a number of reasons. To begin with, the classic accounts of the general virtue of courage connect it with correct choice. Not just any choice to face physical danger will count as courage. Socrates makes this clear when he points out to Laches that a fearless readiness to stand firm in battle in all conditions involves taking foolishly needless risks that can hardly be described as courageous (10: p. 193 c7–e5). Certainly, a similar point could be made about taking unnecessary risks to one's body or mind in boxing or football or rugby or other dangerous sports.

There are other problems connecting participation in dangerous sports with the general moral virtue of courage. As Huizinga notes, games are "all temporary worlds within the ordinary world, dedicated to the performance of an act apart." He adds that "play as such is outside the range of good and bad" (3: pp. 10–11).

This is too brief a comment on complex matters, but it is true that game playing, including in sport, is separated from ordinary life and that that separation often involves a certain suspension of ordinary constraints of good and bad from everyday life. This is not to say that we completely suspend judgments about good or bad within sport. Certainly, we assess participants as good or bad sports on the field of play, and we often expect them to be role models away from it. Nevertheless, sport often permits opportunity for activities—assaults and deception, for example—that would normally be subject to criminal or other social sanction if they were not committed in games. Boxing is perhaps the clearest example, but there are many others. This raises questions about whether the character traits required in these temporary, separate worlds actually contribute to virtues that are transferable to the regular world once the game stops. This can be doubted. Research into the ethical development of athletes is not particularly encouraging. Some of the key research done in this area, by Shields and Bredemeier, has found that college and high school athletes of both genders had lower capacities for ethical judgment both inside sport and in ordinary life than nonathletes do (13, 14). They point out that this in fact coheres with anecdotal information in personal experience and media reports. This evidence is also readily found in memoirs, particularly of those engaged in contact sports. For example, in his clear-eyed, first-person account of amateur boxing, the author and playwright Robert Anasi frequently makes the point that people who are attracted to boxing tend to be people who like to fight outside the ring, as well as inside it (1). The courage that they acquire to face an opponent in the boxing ring is not necessarily a socially welcome excellence. It might encourage them to take liberties with people who cross them outside the ring, as it apparently did to Anasi and others with whom he trained.

Dangerous sport, of course, provides opportunities to face physical danger. Although such opportunities bear a connection to courage, it seems evident that there is no straightforward connection between physically dangerous sport and the development of the general everyday virtue of courage. In fact, there is no reason to think that people who play nondangerous sports are less courageous than those who play dangerous sport, and there is some reason to be concerned that physically dangerous sports may sometimes be socially counterproductive in their effects on courage. This should not be taken to imply that play is discontinuous with general moral obligations and virtues, as Huizinga's remark might suggest. As I have argued elsewhere, the opportunity for play afforded by sport is connected to the promotion of human flourishing and the requirement that participants in games participate voluntarily. This implies that games are moral institutions that are broadly continuous with basic moral commitments to human flourishing and respect for persons (12). The opportunities they provide for flourishing, however, are different than, and often at odds with, those permitted in ordinary life. Hence, it is not surprising that certain virtues that are required in this context are not readily transferable to ordinary life. This recognition, however, of how games can expand the opportunities for human flourishing will be important to understanding the value of dangerous sport, as we shall see later.

Another common, related idea about the value of dangerous sports is that they represent a relatively safe outlet for release of physical aggression toward others. Thus, dangerous sport is a way of containing antisocial forces. This is an empirical claim, of course, and I have already expressed some reservations about it in some instances of dangerous sport. But let us suppose that it is true. There are two things to be said about this. First, although this might explain some of the value of dangerous sport for society, it fails to explain the value of dangerous sport for the participant except in instrumental terms—it keeps them out of jail or other types of trouble. But we have already seen that we often reason about the value of sport as if it had intrinsic value in some sense, and this argument does not explain that value. Second, not all dangerous sport involves direct physical aggression toward others. Contact sports do, but mountain climbing, gymnastics, and motor racing do not, although they are certainly dangerous sports. Perhaps these noncontact sports discourage antisocial behavior by providing some sort of outlet or release, but it is not directly as an outlet for physical aggression toward others. A more general related good for participants in dangerous sports might then simply be the release of tension or stress that competition affords, including through the opportunity to best others. This may be a good for society, as well as the individual. There is undoubtedly something to this. But it seems inadequate to locate anything of special or distinctive value in dangerous sport. For non-dangerous sports and other play activities can, and do, serve the same purpose for many. If dangerous sports are preferred by some, we apparently need a reason why. And if some are only inclined to find such release in dangerous sport, medication (or self-medication) might be a more prudent option unless there is a more distinctive value to be found in dangerous sport.

The value of dangerous sport

The problems with each of these attempts to explain the value of dangerous sport press us to look for a better, or at least a further, defense of its value. Let me try to set the stage for this by drawing on discussions in political philosophy from an earlier time, when modern institutions of civil society were emerging. Although dangerous sport is certainly no modern invention, it is perhaps no accident that it flourishes to such an extent and with such diversity in modern times.

It is too seldom noted that the great architects of modern political economy, such as Adam Smith, Wilhelm Von Humboldt, John Stuart Mill, and others, although they welcomed and supported the orderliness and peaceful security of modern civil society and its capacity to increase wealth and improve living standards, were also acutely aware that these benefits came at the expense of other significant, established values. Smith in his lectures on civil security avers that "the heroic spirit is almost utterly extinguished" by modern

commercial society (17: p. 541), and he is quite clear that this is a regrettable loss:

> Another bad effect of commerce is that it sinks the courage of mankind, and tends to extinguish the martial spirit. ... Among the bulk of the people military courage diminishes. By having their minds constantly employed on arts and luxury, they grow effeminate and dastardly.
>
> (17: p. 540; see also 16: pp. 734–735)

Mill condemns similar aspects of modern society in equally strong terms in his essay "On Civilization":

> There has crept over the refined classes, over the whole class of gentlemen in England, a moral effeminacy, an inaptitude for every kind of struggle. ... This torpidity and cowardice, as a general characteristic, is new in the world: but ... it is a natural consequence of the progress of civilization.
>
> (6: pp. 180–181)

These were commonly expressed ideas in Smith and Mill's times. But it is not as if they occasioned no response. It is possible to see in the romantic notions of self-affirmation that were also prevalent a social reaction, and even a challenge, to the enervating, pacific effects of modern civil society. Nancy Rosenblum's insightful study of romantic and liberal values in her *Another Liberalism* (11) identifies a key aspect of that reaction as pitting "romantic militarism" against the "prosaic promises" of modern commercial liberal society. She traces this reaction through the works of major English, French, and German romantics including Wordsworth, Humboldt, De Musset, Sorel, Constant, De Vigny, and others.

Romantic militarism comes in many guises but it is defined primarily by its focus on war "as the experience of freedom from inhibitions and conventional constraints" and by militancy as an opportunity for "spontaneous self-display." Thus, romantic militarism "substitutes extravagant self-assertion and self-display for more benign forms of the pursuit of happiness" (11: pp. 9–10). Rosenblum argues that romantic militarism thus illustrates a fundamental dilemma of liberalism, namely, that at some level the ideals of personal freedom and self-expression, which are central to liberalism, will always be frustrated even by liberal rights and freedoms and promises of limited government. Thus, Wordsworth wrote in "The Convention of Cintra" that "the true sorrow of humanity consists in this;—not that the mind fails; but that the course and demands of action and of life so rarely correspond with the dignity and intensity of human desires" (20: p. 192). According to Rosenblum, the special arena provided by war answers these longings for romantic militarists (11: p. 9).

The general point here about the fettering of self-affirmation and personal freedom is a familiar enough romantic criticism of modern liberal society. Nietzsche's "last men," whose only aspiration is to a "pitiable comfortableness," and his alter ego Zarathustra's scolding remark that "Man is something to be surpassed. What have you done to surpass him?" (7) are perhaps the most familiar romantically motivated philosophical expressions of the same complaint about the enervating and constraining effects of modern civil society. For such thinkers, real heroism is reflected in casting aside everyday boundaries to discover and realize one's true self. But for our purposes it is especially interesting that the romantic-militarist reaction is ultimately traced to ideas of heroic self-affirmation in preparedness to face physical danger. In this respect, it is instructive that Rosenblum chooses to focus on romantic militarism because it reflects "the limits of romantic revolt" and can be used to bring into focus liberalism's openness to certain romantic claims (11: pp. 5–6). In so doing, she unsurprisingly passes over any examination of the challenges to the physical dimension of being that romantic militarism asserted. This is consistent with earlier liberal commentators' responses to such romantic yearnings. Mill regards them as an anachronism and (characteristically for him) encourages the development of more socially congenial character virtues (6). Humboldt, who is attracted by romantic-military ideals in a way Mill is not, ultimately recognizes that opportunities for self-affirmation in war and in other physical struggles that were present for the classical Greeks and others are no longer available and that, ultimately, this is an improvement. Thus, he concludes that "whereas physical variety has declined, it has been succeeded by an infinitely richer and more satisfying intellectual and moral variety" (4: p. 18).

Rosenblum follows in a similar path when she argues that romantics can "make their peace" with liberalism and help reform modern civil society, in particular by reconceiving the public sphere as a place for "heroic self-display" and the private domain as a scene for cultivating "beautiful individuality" through renewed respect for pluralism (11: p. 4).

What is strikingly absent from all these responses to romantic militarism is that they either entirely overlook or treat as an anachronism the romantic impulse to bodily self-affirmation represented in the willingness to confront and master physical danger. If these theorists of modern civil society are correct about its diminishing opportunities for self-affirmation through confronting physical danger, it is hardly surprising that dangerous sporting activities should emerge and flourish. The institution of dangerous sport can be seen as filling this void.[3]

Moreover, if Rosenblum is right that romantic militarism is founded on a will or desire to be free from conventional constraints and inhibitions and to have opportunities for spontaneous self-display, dangerous sports offer an obvious outlet for such longings that should not be overlooked. Like war and like all play, dangerous sport is a world apart from ordinary life as represented in the everyday activities of work, family, friendship, making plans, and generally getting on. Also as in war, there is a certain suspension of the moral constraints of ordinary life reflected in play. (Where else could one pursue world domination, even at the expense of one's closest intimates, except at the summer cottage playing Risk?[4]) The separate world of play is one that is in some respects beyond good and evil. Hence, it is a place where certain conventional moral constraints and inhibitions grounded in prudence can be discarded for the time being. This fits the description of dangerous sports perfectly. It is a place, indeed, where what would normally count as criminal behavior or plain and utter recklessness or poor judgment is not judged or constrained by the normal conventions or inhibitions of ordinary life. Thus, compare tripping someone at the mall as they break ahead of you to pick up the last unit of your child's coveted Christmas present (clearly a criminal assault) and tripping someone on a partial breakaway in hockey (a 2-minute penalty at most, unless committed in the third period or overtime by the home team, in which case it is just as likely to be overlooked).

Also, few institutions in society provide as rich an array of opportunities for spontaneous self-display as does sport, and this is especially true of dangerous sport. The field of play creates an obvious opportunity for spontaneous self-display for participants. Dangerous sports themselves frequently institutionalize the response to the moment, novel improvisation, and creation or exploitation of immediate opportunity that are all occasions for spontaneous and original self-display that challenge us mentally, physically, and emotionally in the heat of the moment. These opportunities can, of course, be made more demanding by the presence of physical danger as an obstacle to be overcome.

Clearly, then, there are important parallels to be drawn between dangerous sport and the aspirations of romantic militarism. One might still ask, however, how this justifies the value of such activity.

It is evident that these romantic-militarist impulses have a physical, intellectual, and emotional dimension. They strive to encompass and challenge the whole being of the person. Although political philosophers have debated whether romantic yearnings can be accommodated, they have done so at a conventionally social level because they have thought that the accommodation must take place in ordinary life within civil society. As a result, physical aspirations for self-affirmation have understandably been ignored or discounted because of the costs they can impose on others. But this overlooks the opportunity that sport can provide to accommodate what romantics sought along this dimension as part of a challenge to the whole being of the person. Thus, in her now classic writings on boxing, Joyce Carol Oates speaks of the attractions of boxing and other extreme sports in ways that resonate fully with romantics:

> Life outside the ring is real—but is it *really* real? Not public display as such but the joy of the body in its straining to its very limits of ingenuity and endurance underlies the motive for such feats of physical prowess as championship

boxing or aerial trapeze work. The performer is rewarded by his performance as an end in itself; he becomes addicted, as who would not, to his very adrenaline. *All of life is just getting through the time between acts.*
>
> (9: p. 142, original emphasis)

What the romantic spirit recognizes in such activity is release from the enervating safety, comfort, routines, and conventions of prosaic modern civil society, thereby expanding the boundaries of human experience and reality. Such intellectual and emotional release is perhaps possible for some in ideas and discourse; in poetry, fiction, art, nonsporting games, and all manner of creation of fantastic visions; in science, and so on. By contrast, dangerous sport can offer a missing, though parallel, opportunity for release for the physical body, but in ways that also directly challenge the other dimensions of our being. Dangerous sport is not quite unique in this sense; nondangerous sport can also offer such challenges. But these are not such that they challenge the body, and therefore all other of our basic human capacities, to remain intact while facing threats to its very being or to fundamental aspects of it. Arguably, then, participating in dangerous sport has the potential, in principle at least, to be more satisfying than pursuing nondangerous activity, which can often seem vaguely anemic by comparison, because it can incorporate a challenge to capacities for judgment and choice that involves all of ourselves—our body, will, emotions, and ingenuity—under conditions of physical duress and danger *at the limits of our being.*[5]

Facing physical danger in sport thus represents an opportunity for self-affirmation that challenges us distinctly along all the basic dimensions—physical, emotional, and intellectual—that constitute our being as practical, self-directed agents. It can extend those dimensions by challenging us to preserve ourselves physically while devising and willing action to overcome dangerous obstacles that would not, or should not, be present in ordinary life. The greater these obstacles and challenges, the greater the achievement in these respects. And so in confronting serious physical danger through our own choice and actions, we can be affirming our being by meeting and extending the boundaries of our existence.

In this sense, dangerous sport can often appear to challenge us to the very limits of what it is to be a certain type of embodied rational being. No other sports, games, or ways of transcending the boundaries imposed on us by ordinary life or play quite permit this, although perhaps war or protection of public safety does in some circumstances. This can explain the value of dangerous sport for its participants. It can also explain the special awe and fascination audiences have for such sports, their attraction to them as public spectacle, and the recognition those audiences bestow on participants. Oates again makes this point succinctly in discussing boxing—a (if not the) quintessential dangerous sport—although her remarks apply in different degree to all dangerous sport:

> Boxers are there to establish an absolute experience, a public accounting of their outermost limits of their beings; they will know, as few of us can know of ourselves, what physical and psychic power they possess—of how much or how little they are capable.
>
> (9: p. 8)

Let me conclude this section by noting that what I have described as self-affirmation obviously has a close connection to ideals of self-realization. There are of course many different accounts of self-realization, but a dominant theme sees self-realization as a perfectionist idea involving realization of distinctive human capacities. The classic view has Aristotelian and Platonist origins where self-realization involves mastery of capacities for choice and deliberation. Self-realization thus involves a sort of practical self-mastery, which in turn requires developing and exercising character and intellectual virtues, having good social relations with others, developing distinctive human talents, and having favorable external circumstances that will support these goods in a self-sustaining unity. There is no direct suggestion here that self-realization requires a testing and pressing of the very limits of the person, although it may do so at times along the way. It is easy to see why, for pressing the very limits of who we are can hold dangers, too, and threaten to upset the harmony and unity of a realized self. A common, and characteristically romantic, concern is that this sort of ideal can be too complacent and lacking in challenge. Perhaps this is an unfair criticism. I cannot argue it here. But what the

romantic asserts much more explicitly is that an important type of self-realization requires a confrontation with, and an attempt to surpass, the apparent limits of oneself. I have characterized this as a type of self-affirmation. In reaching and attempting to surpass our limits, we inevitably confront what we are. In doing so, we affirm or declare to ourselves who we are and what we are striving to make of ourselves. Dangerous sport, in its best exemplars—in, say, mountain climbing or boxing or bicycle stage racing—provides one avenue for such self-affirmation by challenging one's whole self at the limits of one's being. It is a particularly rich avenue of realization because it forces us to confront and overcome fear of danger and to face physical threats to those things that we cannot put a value on. Of course, all this makes sense only against a commitment to a perfectionist idea of value, but we have seen that our reasoning about value strongly reflects this sort of commitment. And this speaks to something deep in us. Testing ourselves against danger to see what we are capable of, and thereby affirming who and what we are, puts us on the same path as Theseus coming of age and choosing to take the longer, more dangerous route to Athens to present himself to his father.

Further considerations of value and practice

If I am right, this account shows why the elimination of all physical risk in sport would be a misguided goal and that something of important value would be lost thereby, specifically, the opportunity to test ourselves at the limits of our being. This, of course, does not mean that countervailing prudential considerations carry no weight, but it does mean that they cannot be presumed to outweigh these other considerations of personal value. As in other cases of assuming risk where competing considerations of personal value might be at stake, we should take a fairly standard nonpaternalist approach. That is to say, the decisions of competent persons should generally be respected if they are properly informed about the relevant risks. Dangerous sports as institutions typically add a mild paternalistic requirement that participants also be properly prepared to undertake such risks. In these circumstances, decision makers should normally be presumed to be in the best position to weigh competing considerations for themselves, and allowing them to do so respects them as persons.

In assessing the value of dangerous sport, it is also instructive to see that it is in many ways superior in realizing romantic militarism's own objectives and values. Romantic-militarist yearnings for self-affirmation seem utterly disconnected from the actual circumstances of military life. They are typically driven by mythic accounts of war[6] rather than the grimness, discipline, and the oppressive routines, rules, and bureaucracy of actual military activity. And, as the romantic militarists knew, with each advance in the art of war the opportunities for individual self-assertion and spontaneous self-display recede (4: p. 47). In these respects, romantic militarism was doomed from the start. By contrast, dangerous sport more successfully accommodates the yearnings of romantic sensibilities, the challenge to one's whole self, and the heightened experience of freedom and reality that comes from surpassing the boundaries of ordinary existence. It is not surprising then that romantic militarism waned and dangerous sport has flourished in recent times.

Another key success of modern dangerous sports is that they do not represent a direct challenge to civil society in the way that romantic militarism and 19th-century romanticism in general did. Dangerous sport represents a sort of accommodation with liberal civil society that romantic militarists yearned for but most knew was ultimately impossible. Indeed, romantic militarists often saw their outlook as an idealized vision of perfect freedom and self-expression, not as a practically realizable option (11: p. 9). The institution of dangerous sport is, then, superior to romantic militarism in that it has the capacity to be realized and, in that process, to civilize some of the worst excesses of the latter's aspirations. This is most obvious in the social costs of militarism, which are remarkable and are typically imposed on many others besides the participants themselves. Dangerous sport does not have anything like these costs; its costs by and large fall on the participants themselves. To be sure, dangerous sport cannot accommodate all of what the romantic militarist desires. It draws an important boundary to the romantic's yearnings to impose his or her will

on the real world of human affairs. But those yearnings undeniably require boundaries, and dangerous sport as play may even reinforce our awareness of them.

There are also more prosaic advantages of dangerous sport. As games, opportunities for realizing the distinctive values of dangerous sport can be ready-made with defined starts and finishes and do not have to wait on public events. Also, the institution of dangerous sports can ensure that their participants are properly informed about the dangers of such activities, that risks fall narrowly on those who genuinely consent to participate, that excessive risks are managed or eliminated, and that dangerous activities are undertaken only by those who are properly prepared to undertake them and who have the capacity to consent to them. There is room for debate here over whether some sports are so dangerous that consent to them would be such an uncertain matter that they should be forbidden altogether. Sometimes a ban on boxing is proposed on these grounds. I am, in the main, skeptical about such arguments, and although I cannot address this issue here, I will note that support for boxing is usually argued, rightly in my view, on antipaternalistic grounds (2). What is missing in these discussions, however, is a clearer appreciation of what sorts of values boxing might realize. It is not as if nothing of important value would be lost if boxing were banned, and this should have weight in the argument. It is not as if the antipaternalistic argument carries little weight because the sport itself has negligible or merely frivolous value, so that no one is really harmed by its elimination. Issues of consent, which are key in my view in dangerous sport, must be examined with this in mind, because the value of dangerous sports is important enough that it cannot be counted an anachronism or frivolous, and the suspension of the ordinary implied in play in general, and in dangerous sports in particular, means that we must be careful about importing considerations found in everyday morality to evaluate them.

A related ethical issue has to do with the involvement of children in dangerous sport, given in particular that the problems of informed consent are clearly present and some sort of paternalism is standardly thought to be acceptable. A different moral issue that is often discussed in this context is the effect that tragedies of dangerous sport have on loved ones who are left behind. This is another issue that deserves careful ethical treatment. Certainly, one can raise moral questions about the voluntary undertaking of serious, unnecessary risks when one has obligations to family, in particular to children, to fulfill. But such a debate should be conducted with a clear appreciation of the value of dangerous sport and why it is so important to some to pursue such activities. In any event, such a discussion does not challenge dangerous sports so much as it raises a question as to how, if at all, participation in dangerous sport can be reconciled morally with certain types of personal relationships. These are all issues that deserve further discussion in light of what has been presented here.

We have seen, then, that there is distinctive value in dangerous sport but that such value is continuous with strivings in other sport and in other areas of human activity. There are also certain practical advantages to dangerous sport over alternatives that pursue similar values. There is more here to be discussed and worked out, and it is possible that there are other sources of value that I have missed that help explain the value of dangerous sport. But enough has been said, I hope, to demonstrate certain distinctively valuable features of dangerous sport.[7]

Notes

1. "Man Killed in Catapult Stunt." November 25, 2002, *BBC News*. Available at http://news.bbc.co.uk/1/hi/england/2510573.stm. Accessed June 1, 2003.
2. I have been speaking of a certain type of skeptic about the value of dangerous sport itself who claims that public recognition counts as the sole source of value in such activity. It is worth noting, however, that those who steadfastly profess to have public recognition as their end do not have to reject the idea that there are other values to dangerous sport. I have previously referred to "sports amoralists" as those who pose an interestingly distinct skeptical challenge to the idea of moral obligation in sport (12: pp. 152–154). Sports amoralists recognize such obligations but are simply indifferent to them. We can extend the notion of a sports amoralist to include those who recognize the intrinsic value of participating in a sport but are indifferent to, and thus not moved by, such values. Such people, then, might be motivated to pursue other goods that are external to those found in sporting activities. This might well apply to some athletes who take public recognition as representing the sole source of value in their activity. They may pursue dangerous sport for public recognition and the benefits it confers, say, the status, the social opportunities, the adulation and respect of others, the money, etc. None of this, however, denies the preceding argument. Indeed, it accepts the argument that public recognition is still *for* certain types of excellence or accomplishment and that without a perception that these were valuable there would of course be no such adulation, respect, money, etc. Sports amoralists actually accept that there are such values, but they are simply not interested in or motivated by such values and are drawn to other goods instead.

   I have no doubt that sports amoralists exist (and sometimes come into existence once the benefits of public recognition are bestowed on them), and it is plausible to think that they would be a part of this odd group that would engage in sport just for its external benefits. But they do not represent a challenge to the idea that there may be intrinsic value to participating in dangerous sport. Their challenge is a different one, namely, that such values provide no reason on their own to engage in these activities. Whether they have reason to be motivated by those values, however, is a separate question from the question of whether such values exist and what their nature is. The latter is my main issue here, so I will not systematically address the special challenge posed by the sports amoralist, which, in any event, is a general one and does not apply only to dangerous sport. It involves demonstrating that the value of sport, including dangerous sport, is worth pursuing for its own sake. Before we can pursue that question, however, we need to be satisfied that there are such values and to know what they are about. Most of us are not sports amoralists, so we assume that such values do provide reasons for actions. That is the assumption I will work with here, and although I will have things to say about motivation. I will not directly address the challenge posed by the sports amoralist, and it is possible that more argument is necessary to fully answer this challenge.
3. Indeed, it seemed to do so even in the 19th century. See Robert McFarlane's tracing of the history of mountain climbing. McFarlane makes no reference to romantic militarism, but he sees the emergence of mountain climbing as a recreation and sport in the 19th century as having its source significantly in Nietzschean reflections about the value of confronting fear and also as a response to "cosseted urban living" (5: pp. 86–88). There was quite a bit of nonsense spoken at this time about

the value of confronting danger. McFarlane quotes a letter from John Ruskin that asserts that confronting and mastering danger produces "a stronger and better man, fitter for every sort of work and trial, and *nothing but danger produces this effect*" (5: p. 86, original emphasis). I make no such claims here.

4. For the uninitiated, Risk is a board game in which the object is for each participant to achieve world domination at the expense of all the others. There are no rules regarding the making—or breaking—of alliances to achieve this objective, so it models international relations on a state of nature free of moral constraints.

5. Thus, I am revising Oates's remark here slightly. It is not that dangerous sport challenges us to "the very limits of ingenuity and endurance" but that ingenuity and endurance can be challenged at the limit of our being.

6. Humboldt's views about the virtues of war are founded in classic Greek and Roman myths. See Rosenblum's remarks at (11: pp. 13–17).

7. I am indebted to an audience at The Ohio State University in June 2003 for many helpful comments on an earlier draft of this paper. I have benefited particularly from the comments of three anonymous reviewers for this journal and from nonanonymous colleagues Alister Browne, Murray Mollard, and Ted Palys.

References

1. Anasi, R. *The Gloves: A Boxing Chronicle*. New York: North Point Press, 2002.

2. Herrera, C.D. "The Moral Controversy Over Boxing Reform." *Journal of the Philosophy of Sport*. IXXX(2), 2002, 163–173.

3. Huizinga, J. *Homo Ludens: A Study of the Play Element in Culture*. Boston: Beacon Press, 1950.

4. Humboldt, W. von. *The Limits of State Action*. Edited by J.W. Burrow. Cambridge: Cambridge University Press, 1969.

5. McFarlane, R. *Mountains of the Mind: How Desolate and Forbidding Heights Were Transformed Into Experiences of Indomitable Spirit*. New York: Pantheon Books, 2003.

6. Mill, J.S. "On Civilization." In *Dissertations and Discussion: Political, Philosophical and Historical*. Vol. I. London: John W. Parker and Son, 1859, pp. 160–205.

7. Nietzsche, F. *Thus Spoke Zarathustra*. Trans. Thomas Common. In *The Philosophy Source* [CD ROM], Daniel Kolak (Ed.). Belmont, CA: Wadsworth, 1999.

8. Nussbaum, M. *Women and Human Development*. Oxford: Cambridge University Press, 2000.

9. Oates, J.C. *On Boxing*. Expanded ed. New York: HarperCollins, 2002.

10. Plato. *Laches*. In *The Collected Dialogues of Plato*, Edith Hamilton and Huntington Cairns (Eds.). Princeton, NJ: Princeton University Press, 1963.

11. Rosenblum, N.L. *Another Liberalism: Romanticism and the Reconstruction of Liberal Thought*. Cambridge, MA: Harvard University Press, 1987.

12. Russell, J.S. "Moral Realism in Sport." *Journal of the Philosophy of Sport*. XXXI(2), 2004, 142–160.

13. Shields, D.L., and B.L. Bredemeier. *Character Development and Physical Activity*. Champaign, IL: Human Kinetics, 1995.

14. Shields, D.L., and B.L. Bredemeier. "Moral Reasoning in the Context of Sport." Available at http://tigger.uic.edn/~Inucci//MoralEd/articles/shieldssport.html. Accessed December 20, 2004.

15. Simpson, J. *Touching the Void*. London: The Random House Group, 1997.

16. Smith, A. *The Wealth of Nations*. New York: The Modern Library, 1937.

17. Smith, A. *Lectures on Jurisprudence*. Oxford: Oxford University Press, 1978.

18. Suits, B. "The Elements of Sport." In *Philosophic Inquiry Into Sport*, W.J. Morgan and K.V. Meier (Eds.). Champaign IL: Human Kinetics, 1995 [1973], pp. 8–15.

19. "What Is Wrestling?" Available at http://www.geocities.com/Colosseum/Arena/6677/articles/WhatIsWrestling.html. Accessed June 1, 2003.

20. Wordsworth, W. "The Convention of Cintra." In *Political Tracts of Wordsworth, Coleridge, and Shelley*, R.J. White (Ed.). Cambridge: Cambridge University Press, 1953, pp. 117–193.

7.3

Adventure, climbing excellence and the practice of 'bolting'

Philip Ebert and Simon Robertson

In this chapter we examine a recent version of an old controversy within climbing ethics. Our organising topic is the 'bolting' of climbing routes, in particular the increasing bolting of routes in those wilderness areas climbing traditionalists have customarily believed should remain bolt-free. The issues this raises extend beyond the ethical, however, encompassing a wider normative field that concerns individual ideals, the values and goals of different climbing practices and communities, as well as various aesthetic and environmental matters. This makes any assessment of the acceptability of bolting a complex affair, requiring not only the identification of relevant considerations and arguments but also some way to evaluate their comparative significance.

Here, though, we limit our discussion somewhat. We begin by explaining what bolting involves and then introduce some of the general issues it raises by considering as a concrete example disagreements about the acceptability of bolting in what has until recently remained a bastion of the bolt-free ethos – Scottish winter climbing. Second, we examine the roles of excellence and adventure in arguments for and against bolting respectively, concluding that defensible cases can be made on both sides

of the debate. Third, we present a new argument for a presumption towards traditional climbing in the Scottish mountains, by implication arguing that the use of bolts should be restricted.

Bolting

Climbing comprises a multifaceted set of practices or games, each with its own methods, styles, goals and ideals.[1] Our focus is on two such games – those that deploy bolts and those that come into conflict with those which deploy bolts. We begin by explaining both 'bolting' and 'bolted climbing'.

Bolting is the practice of drilling into the climbing medium permanent metal rungs, which climbers then use to aid and protect their ascent. A climber clips one karabiner from an 'extender' (usually a short sling attached to two karabiners) onto each bolt reached and places the rope to which he or she is attached through the second karabiner. The climber is belayed by a partner, so that in the event of a fall the climber drops only the distance above the last bolt clipped plus the same distance below the bolt (if 2 metres above a bolt, the climber falls

Philip Ebert and Simon Robertson 'Adventure, Climbing Excellence and the Practice of "Bolting"', from *Philosophy, Risk and Adventure Sports*, Mike McNamee ed., © 2007 Philip Ebert and Simon Robertson. Reprinted by permission of Routledge.

4 metres in total). Bolted climbing is one form of 'sport climbing'; this being any form of climbing deploying fixed (pre-placed and/or permanent) protection. Because bolted protection is reliable, bolted climbing is relatively safe. With the element of danger reduced, sport routes facilitate climbing at an increased level of technical difficulty, this typically being one of its constitutive aims. What we shall call 'traditional' climbing, in contrast, involves placing one's own protection ('natural protection') to safeguard progression, the second climber on the rope removing it during ascent. Risk is part and parcel of traditional climbing. Not only is the availability of protection often sporadic, the quality of protection is only as good as the climbing medium allows and the climber's skill in placing it. These two factors increase the likely severity of a fall.

In many countries, bolting is an accepted and commonplace practice.[2] In others, like Britain (perhaps especially Scotland), there remains a default presumption against it. Despite this presumption, recent years have seen the development of sport climbing venues on crags and cliffs in Scotland. While many, if not most, traditionalists now at least tolerate established sport venues, they do oppose expanding the repertoire. A recent development they find especially worrying is the creation of sport venues for winter climbing in Scotland.[3] To give a flavour of some of the issues involved in the debate generally, we concentrate on the Scottish case, paying particular attention to the inadequacy of existing legislation.

One of the key issues concerns what would count as a suitable sport climbing venue. In its most recently drafted *Code of Good Practice* (2004), the Mountaineering Council of Scotland (MCoS) accepts 'that there is a place for both sports style and traditional style climbs in the future development of Scottish climbing, both in winter and summer' (Howett, 2004: 13). It suggests nevertheless that bolting be restricted so as to ensure that the 'highly regarded ethos of, and future development of, traditional climbing is not diminished by the development of new sport climbing venues' (ibid.). This seems initially ambiguous: whether the future development of new sport climbing venues is to be restricted on the grounds that it does, in fact, diminish the ethos and development of traditional climbing; or whether it is to

be restricted only *if* it were to diminish this highly regarded ethos and development. With respect to the first reading, we can note at least one source of conflict: protagonists of the competing climbing styles sometimes want to climb in the very same area and on the very same cliffs, though traditional climbers typically do not want to climb in areas with a proliferation of bolts. Mark Colyvan expresses the tension thus:

> the proper care of an oval on which football and cricket must coexist is a difficult matter. Unlike the cricket/football problem, though, sport climbers and traditional climbers can not come to some agreement on a temporal demarcation, as both wish to climb all year around and the removal and re-placing of bolts seasonally would not be practical anyway.
>
> (Colyvan, 1993: 20–1)

Given a scarcity of climbing venues within Scotland, we can see that sport climbing does have a damaging effect on the development of traditional climbing, since extensive bolting does, in fact, restrict the space available for the development of further traditional routes.

In order to alleviate such worries, however, the *Code* presents several criteria which it advises 'should be born in mind by climbers when deciding whether a crag is suitable for the production of sports routes in either summer or winter'. (What it is to 'bear in mind' these criteria is far from obvious – one might of course bear them in mind whilst openly flouting their recommendation.) The criteria focus on the 'character' or 'feel' of the prospective venue, for which a number of determinants are offered. The *Code* tells us that:

> The character of a venue is often typified as adventurous (and enhanced) by the wild nature of its surroundings, the imposing nature of the crag, the lack of protection, the seriousness of the approach or descent and the commitment needed from both members of the climbing team.
>
> (Howett, 2004: 13)

In contrast: 'If the potential quality of the route lies in the technical aspects of the climb rather than the stature or adventurous nature then they may give better quality as sport climbs' (ibid.). More specifically, the character of a venue depends on the availability of natural protection, the *Code* advising that 'If there is natural protection available then the route has clearly an adventurous nature and should remain bolt free' (ibid.). Similarly, 'If the crag has strong natural lines, whether some are well protected and others are not, then the character of the crag can be said to be more adventurous and would be best remaining bolt free' (ibid.). The *Code* also suggests that 'Some areas may have a strong local or historical anti-bolt ethic and this should be respected' (ibid.), and that the 'proximity' of a potential 'sport climb to naturally protected climbs' should not be such as to 'detract from the adventurous nature of the latter' – a criterion which, apparently, will 'determine whether currently unclimbed sections of a partially developed crag would be best left for future [traditional] advances' (ibid.).

These descriptions (the 'wild' and 'imposing' nature of a venue, the presence of 'strong natural lines'), as well as the tone of subsequent advice (that some routes '*may* give better quality as sport climbs', that 'a strong local or historical anti-bolt ethic should be *respected*', that some venues 'would be best remaining bolt free'), leave much to interpretation, indeed much to the interpretation of those with vested interests in precisely these practices. We should not expect an exact science when it comes to deciding on the suitability of a venue for one or other style of climbing. Yet the *Code* is not sufficiently explicit even to guide good practice in a context where most parties would quite reasonably hope to be offered a clear conclusion – the acceptability of bolts in the mountains. It ambivalently declares that 'Under *most* circumstances the placing of bolts is inappropriate on mountain cliffs ... *but there may be exceptions*' (Howett, 2004: 13, our emphasis). Instructions that explicitly permit exceptions yet fail to clarify what exceptions are acceptable do little – so the proponent of traditional climbing will fear – to protect the traditional ethos and its development.

Furthermore, the criteria offered in the *Code* quite easily permit conflict. On the one hand, the *Code* allows that bolting be permitted on routes lacking natural protection; on the other, it seems to want to restrict bolting to 'low-lying inland crags' – the obvious thought being that some relatively high-level lines in mountainous areas lack natural protection.[4] Similarly, the *Code* claims that sea-cliffs should generally remain bolt-free; yet some sea-cliffs are not suitable for natural protection and so satisfy one of the *Code*'s criteria for the acceptability of bolting, while also satisfying one criterion for remaining bolt-free. What to do in such circumstances is left open by the *Code* and no further criteria are given to provide practical guidance in these cases.[5]

This lack of specificity in turn gives rise to a further worry, namely that bolting, even on low-lying naturally unprotected crags, leads down a slippery slope to a more pervasive bolting culture. Though we are not wholeheartedly condoning slippery-slope *reasoning* the recent developments of winter sport venues to which we refer do at least indicate that such worries are not *in practice* unfounded.[6]

So far we have attempted to show that there is a genuine practical conflict between sport climbing and traditional climbing (one which current legislation does little to allay). A full examination of the conflict requires a wide-ranging discussion to which a single chapter could not do justice. But having introduced some of the issues, we now consider the role of two values in climbing, excellence and adventure, our aim being twofold: to assess what we believe to be the strongest arguments for and against bolting, and to diagnose perhaps the main source at the heart of the conflict between those on each side of the debate.

A perfectionist argument

For many, climbing provides opportunity to escape from the perceived mundanity and petty rules of day-to-day life. It offers a degree of freedom from the externally imposed duties and expectations that constrain us in societal life, freedom to pursue our own personal projects in a way unfettered by those constraints. The nature of the projects we do pursue of course shapes and structures how we are able to express such freedom; but given the ethos of freedom which climbing seems to offer, it might in turn be supposed that climbing not only permits individual expression but that it falls beyond the jurisdiction of *any* juridical authority or mandate. As a result, one may be tempted to conclude that if *I* want to bolt routes as part of *my* personal project, that is what *I* am permitted or even entitled to do (or, more interestingly, the issue of permission never even arises). There are a number of obvious worries with such an argument. For one thing, even if one's climbing projects are themselves neither morally perverse nor impermissible with respect to state law, this does not show that they fall outside the jurisdiction of all ethical constraint. The climbing world has its own governing bodies, one role of which is to implement 'rules' that guide and sometimes check practices in a way that protects the freedoms required for others to pursue their projects. The authority of such bodies may itself be open to dispute; but the issue remains as to whether the practices they rule against are practices one ought not engage in. And insofar as it is plausible to assume that not all climbing practices are acceptable, the question is whether bolting in particular is. To assess this, we need to show that bolting is something climbers have (good enough) reason to do.

We think the strongest pro-bolting argument lies in the suggestion that sport climbing is valuable in virtue of its facilitating the advancing of climbing standards amongst elite climbers. Because sport climbing is pre-protected and relatively safe, it allows climbers to move safely at the limit of their capabilities on routes they would be unable or unwilling to attempt with the less reliable protection traditional climbing affords (the limits in question typically concerning those of technique, strength and endurance). Climbing harder in turn improves the climber's abilities, fostering the qualities necessary not just to improve their own climbing but also, for those at the top end of the sport, to surpass existing levels or achievement by other climbers. Insofar as technical advances are valuable in their own right, or at least insofar as the kinds of excellence required to make such advances are valuable, the value of sport climbing that makes this possible provides (at least some) reason to allow it. We shall call this the 'perfectionist' argument since it seeks to justify sport climbing by its role in the development of climbing excellence at the elite end of the activity. We develop this argument in the rest of the present section.

An obvious assumption underwriting the argument is that climbing excellence is a valuable or worthwhile aim, at least relative to what

is valuable about climbing. While we cannot defend the claim fully here, we find it plausible that, just as the goals of climbing in its various forms are shaped by the climbing community and the climbers that comprise it, the values of climbing are shaped by standards internal to those practices and the climbing community. And one of these values is excellence. Certainly, climbers themselves value improving their own abilities, to which end they challenge themselves with progressively more testing climbs; and those within the climbing community typically regard as admirable those climbers who surpass existing standards of climbing excellence by pushing further the limits of achievement.[7] To this extent, we shall assume that excellence is one value of climbing.

An immediate complication emerges, though. Different climbing games, including sport and traditional climbing, each have their own internal standards by which excellence is measured; and what counts as excellence relative to the standards of one climbing game may not count as valuable by the standards of another. Traditional climbers, for example, may value the development of standards in traditional climbing yet, if they deride the value of sport climbing, regard its technical advances as valueless. Pro-bolters therefore require an additional assumption if they are to defend the value of bolting in such a way that does not turn solely upon their own pro-bolting preferences (preferences whose value may be in doubt). One way to do this is to show that the advances made through sport climbing are transferable in that they serve to improve the standards of difficulty and excellence achievable on traditional routes. This would demonstrate not only that excellence in sport climbing is valuable with respect to the goals internal to sport climbing, but that such excellence is valuable for traditional climbing too. If they can show this, then even the sport-antagonistic traditionalist, who values developments at the cutting edge of traditional climbing, has reason to value (advances made in) sport climbing. Whether or not these skills are transferable is an empirical matter. With rock climbing, the evidence indicates that they are: not only have standards in traditional climbing advanced in tandem with the progression of standards in sport climbing, the vast majority of the best traditional climbers train on sport routes precisely to develop their technical

459

abilities, power and endurance. With winter climbing, matters are less clear. One view is that winter climbing at the cutting edge requires certain heightened psychological qualities that only experience of leading winter routes traditional style can bring. While any form of climbing requires of the climber a degree of mental control in the face of physical insecurity, the especially insecure terrain and unreliable protection typical of extreme winter climbing requires a level of mental control exceeding that which could be provided through sport climbing. In defence of the perfectionist argument, however, we should note that the plausibility of this objection trades on the assumption that those doing sport routes in order to improve their traditional winter climbing abilities do not already possess, to a suitable degree, the psychological qualities in question. Even if practising winter sport climbs would not by itself cultivate the skills necessary to succeed at the forefront of traditional winter climbing, by combining the technical benefits of winter sport climbing with their existing experience on hard traditional routes, climbers would improve on the latter. In which case, at least for those already at the cutting edge of traditional winter climbing, the availability of sport routes may well support improvements in traditional climbing after all.

We want to consider two lines of objection to the argument so far, responses to which will serve to constrain its general application. The underlying claim of the perfectionist argument is that sport climbing, in either summer or winter conditions, is *instrumentally* valuable, valuable as a means to improving climbing standards and excellence. A first line of objection is that climbers who create and climb bolted routes, perhaps especially winter sport routes, regard sport climbing as a valuable end in its own right but *not* as a means to the development of standards in traditional climbing. This worry has two aspects. First, one might think that if climbers do not use sport routes as a means to develop their technical ability for traditional climbing, the perfectionist justification for the creation of sport venues, which relies on their being instrumentally valuable, fails. It would fail because the argument goes through only if sport climbing actually has the effect to which it is supposedly a means. (This may be a particularly pressing concern in the present

context of Scottish winter climbing, where those currently at the cutting edge of traditional climbing seem reluctant to use winter sport routes as a means.) This raises a number of complications both theoretical and practical, given that the creation of a sport route might prove justified only retrospectively, whereas we want to know whether it is now justifiable. Nonetheless, for practical purposes at least, the following line of response to this worry offers a relatively commonsense reply: if bolting is to be acceptable on perfectionist grounds, those intending to develop sport climbing venues must at least; have sufficient reason to believe that such venues will in practice facilitate improved standards at the forefront of traditional climbing. A lot more would need to be said to vindicate this suggestion fully on theoretical grounds. Nevertheless, insofar as it presents a plausible line of response, we now turn to the second aspect of the objection.

The second aspect of the worry is that the actions of somebody who appeals to the perfectionist argument to justify bolting, but who regards sport climbing as an end in its own right and not also as valuable with respect to traditional climbing, would not be justified in bolting. For the perfectionist argument we have presented requires that the justification for sport climbing is grounded just in the advancements it makes possible for traditional climbing. Not only might the motivations of someone who appeals to the perfectionist argument to justify bolts, but whose real goal lies elsewhere, be somewhat infelicitous, more significantly their actions would not he prospectively justified by the perfectionist argument to which they appeal, since the reasons for which they bolt are not the reasons sanctioned by the perfectionist argument. Together, these two aspects of the overall objection suggest that the perfectionist argument will work only if those who develop sport climbing venues have sufficient reason to believe that such venues will benefit traditional climbers *and* they sincerely intend this effect.

A further objection, however, may be raised. Even if sport climbing is instrumentally valuable, in the sense that it serves as *one* means to improvements in standards for traditional climbing, it does not seem to be a *necessary* means. There are, after all, other ways to develop climbing standards – with indoor climbing walls, bouldering, and so on. In which case, the perfectionist argument appears weakened, at the very least placing the onus on those who favour bolting to provide further argument to demonstrate its acceptability.

The most promising response, we think, is to show that although (outdoor) sport climbing is not the only available means to the advancement of climbing standards, it is nevertheless the best means. Indeed, it is plausible to suppose that climbing on real rock or mixed routes of technical severity similar to or surpassing the standards set at the upper echelon of traditional climbing is the most effective form of technical training. Although there may be other ways to develop general strength, for example, the specific kinds of power, endurance and technical skills required for extreme climbing are most effectively developed through climbing itself. Granting that this is so, the perfectionist argument, incorporating the earlier caveats, seems to us defensible. Nonetheless, we should emphasise the limitations of the argument. It does not by itself show that bolting is acceptable. Rather, it provides part of an explanation for why, if bolting is acceptable, it is so. For even if bolting is the best means to developing climbing excellence on traditional routes, the question remains whether that means is itself justifiable. We have been implicitly assuming, for sake of simplicity, that the end of excellence would justify sport climbing instrumentally; yet we have not ruled out the possibility that, despite its instrumental value, other considerations might render it unacceptable. So we think that, while the argument itself is defensible, by itself it yields at best a *prima facie* case for bolting, a fuller assessment of its acceptability requiring consideration of other reasons for and against the practice. In the next section, we introduce a set of arguments against bolting which emerge from considering the role of adventure in climbing.

Adventure

It is sometimes suggested, by climbing traditionalists, that in those areas where traditional styles of climbing are the norm, that norm itself supplies a default presumption against bolting. By itself this suggestion is inadequate if intended to justify prohibition; for the very issue is precisely whether the tradition reflected by that norm is a tradition worth defending. To assess this, we need to consider what it is about traditional climbing that is of value and then see how this might form part of an argument against bolting. We focus on one of the central values of traditional climbing – adventure. We first analyse the conception of adventure integral to traditional climbing, and then go on to examine the extent to which bolted climbing lacks adventure before evaluating how this contributes to a case against bolting.

The precise extent to which we think of climbing as adventurous depends on many factors, including not only the nature of the climb itself and the style of ascent deployed, but also its location. Our primary focus is climbing in mountain regions or other remote wilderness areas. In what sense, then, is traditional climbing in such areas to be thought of as adventurous? We begin by distinguishing two relevant components: exploration and risk.

The exploratory nature and value of traditional climbing has two main elements. On the one hand, there remains the possibility to discover new climbing routes, either by finding cliffs not previously explored or by exploring the potential for new climbs at more established venues. For many, a principal attraction of climbing is being in remote areas, areas where the climber is more likely to be alone – not just far from the madding crowds of other climbers all attempting (sometimes clogging up) the same route, but being able to enjoy the solitude itself. Exploratory climbing of this type serves those who desire remoteness. On the other hand, the process of climbing, whether pioneering a new route or repeating an established one, can itself be an exploratory process, one that involves route-finding, the assessment of alternative lines, finding suitable placements for protection, and so forth. Again, for many this is a fundamental attraction of climbing.

The other component of adventure comes from the fact that traditional climbing is dangerous (at least potentially) and thus typically involves an element of personal risk. While part of the appeal of traditional climbing is the risk involved, the climber typically seeks to diminish the danger and risk to an 'acceptable level', though without removing it entirely. Climbers do not generally climb under the description *doing something dangerous* but, rather, *overcoming the dangers inherent to the activity*, the aim being to control both the physical danger and one's reactions to it.[8] Although climbers know that injury and death are possibilities, they do not *intend* them, nor climb because it increases their probabilities. Climbing in remote areas is especially committing in that it heightens risk by magnifying the significance – the likely impact and effect – of mistakes. This idea of commitment has both a physical and psychological dimension. Physically, the risks involved in climbing in remote areas are greater, the event of injury typically requiring both greater self-reliance and effort to return safe, the success of self-rescue less assured. The climber of course knows this, his or her awareness of it adding an important psychological dynamic to the activity: not only can the feeling of risk, occurrent or underlying, be more intense, the degree of focus and mental toughness required to execute the climb is to that extent greater, with the success of achievement in turn more gratifying.

When combined with the kinds of gratification climbers experience upon moving fluently over their medium or else struggling to overcome its obstacles, the exploratory and risk dimensions of traditional climbing contribute to an aesthetic experience of sorts, at least for those suitably disposed.[9] With bolted climbing, however, certain elements of exploration and risk are either lessened or eradicated entirely, and traditional climbers often remark on how comparatively empty the experience of sport climbing is, even if it sometimes allows for more fluid movement and progression over rock.[10] So in what ways is sport climbing 'less adventurous'?

On the one hand, there is nothing to stop the sport climber from exploring remote areas and pioneering new (bolted) routes on previously unclimbed lines. Nonetheless, sport climbing is less explorative in two main ways. First, if the bolter climbing a new (previously unbolted) route faces a difficult section from which the traditional climber would retreat, he or she may simply drill a bolt, thereby either removing the obstacle or making it protected and thus safer.[11] Second, once bolts are in place and a bolted route exists, this removes the exploratory element of route finding, since one just follows the line of metal.[12] One could of course explore ways of linking different bolted routes on the

same face, so long as those routes are free of other climbers. Notwithstanding this, not only is this 'exploration' constrained by the availability of pre-placed bolts, the prevalence of bolts itself makes the climbing less adventurous by removing both the physical risk and a sense of what climbers often refer to as 'being out there on the sharp end of the rope'. Although it is possible that those committed to traditional tactics climb a sport line without using the bolts on it, not only would there be a constant reminder of the kind of item to which they object; the very presence of bolts, with the added security it offers, changes the nature of both the activity and experience. Climbing in such conditions is less committing, in terms of both the seriousness of the activity and the attitudes thereby required of the climber. For the climber would know that if he or she hits difficulty, reliable protection and/or a pre-established means of escape lie in wait. In these ways, bolted routes lack the adventure which many think is paramount to climbing itself.

We want now to examine three related arguments against bolting which the appeal to adventure might support. Each is successively less robust in terms of the substantive conclusions they seek to justify, though in turn more defensible. The first argument runs as follows: climbing is by nature (e.g. essentially) adventurous. If this is the case then climbing is valuable to the extent that it is adventurous. As bolted climbing is not adventurous, it cannot therefore be valuable.[13] There are a number of obvious problems with this argument. One worry is that it relies on the (disputable) assumption that bolted climbing cannot be adventurous in any respect. Under this view, sport 'climbing' is not actually climbing – since if adventure is an essential part of climbing, and if bolted climbing lacks the relevant sense of adventure, then it lacks a feature an activity must have if it is to count as climbing. This position is unsustainable. Insofar as those who use bolts are making movements identical in type to those made by traditional climbers, it is difficult to see why the use of fixed rather than natural protection renders the ascent something other than a climb.

Perhaps, though, we might just remove the problematic first premise, revising the argument as follows: climbing is valuable to the extent that it is adventurous; bolted climbing is not adventurous; so bolted climbing is not valuable.

Even so, the argument is problematic. It is worth drawing attention, first, to the phrase in the first premise 'to the extent that', which is ambiguous. On the one hand, it might mean that climbing is valuable *only if* adventurous; but this is a strong claim, which rules out the possibility that climbing could be a valuable or worthwhile activity in respect of features other than adventure unless it is at the same time adventurous (as we might put it: its being adventurous would *uniformly* have to serve as both *the* value-providing feature *and* a feature whose presence *enables* any other feature to have value).[14] We find it hard to see how an argument for this could be given. On the other hand, the locution 'to the extent that' might imply that climbing is valuable *in proportion* to the degree of adventure it involves. There is a weaker and a stronger version of this claim. The stronger version is that the value of climbing is determined *solely* by the degree to which it is adventurous. Yet this is again too strong since it excludes the possibility that climbing is ever valuable in respects other than adventure. Furthermore, it implies that the more adventurous (e.g. dangerous or risky) a climb, the more valuable it is – whereas we would generally expect there to be some rough threshold of danger or risk beyond which the value of a climb diminishes (one only has to think of climbs that turn into (near-) disaster scenarios). The weaker version of the claim is that the more adventurous a climb is the more valuable it is *qua adventure*, at least once possible thresholds at which value diminishes are factored in. This allows that climbing can be valuable in virtue of features other than adventure and that those other features can contribute to its overall value. Note that the second premise of the argument – that bolting is not adventurous – is not something we have argued for; nor are we denying that bolting can be adventurous, or that it can be valuable in further respects. What the anti-bolting argument has to say, though, is that traditional climbing is more valuable than bolted climbing *with respect to adventure*.

These considerations take us on to the third and, to our mind, most plausible of the arguments from adventure against bolting. It runs as follows: traditional climbing is more adventurous than bolted climbing; so, traditional climbing is more valuable than bolted climbing with respect to adventure. Obviously this relies on the suppressed premise that adventure, or at least adventurous climbing, is valuable. We shall not here question whether adventure itself is or can be valuable but shall take it for granted. Insofar as climbing is adventurous, then, it is or can be valuable. The phrase 'is valuable' in this context means something like 'is worthwhile' and it should be uncontroversial that traditional climbing is, in respect of adventure, a more worthwhile activity than bolted climbing – in the sense that traditional climbing is generally more conducive to an exploratory experience involving risk, with adventure generally being partly constitutive of the value of traditional climbing. We should nonetheless add a proviso here, to the effect that a traditional route is typically more adventurous than a sport route *of similar technical standard*. We are not committed to the view that bolted climbing is never as adventurous as traditional climbing (nor, therefore, that bolted climbing cannot be adventurous in some ways and to some degree); we make the weaker claim that, generally, traditional climbing is more adventurous, and therein valuable with respect to adventure, than bolted climbing.[15]

We find this third argument quite plausible; and few climbers would deny that, in respect of adventure, traditional climbing offers more than bolted climbing. Yet we also acknowledge its limitations. It presents only one way in which traditional climbing is more valuable than sport climbing, with there being many further considerations relevant to a proper assessment of the acceptability of bolting. In the following section we therefore develop a further line of argument in favour of traditional climbing – and, by implication, against bolted routes in the mountains.

An argument for the traditional ethos

The argument we advance in this section relies on the idea that valuable activities typically have certain preconditions that have to be in place for the valuable activity to be realisable. Insofar as there is a good reason to respect the valuable activity itself there will also be some reason to preserve the relevant preconditions. The mode of reasoning that underlies this argument is often found in so-called 'closure-reasoning' in epistemology. We briefly explain the idea behind 'closure-reasoning' and then transfer that idea to the evaluative context.

The idea is that knowledge is closed under known entailment. If you know that *p*, and if you know that *if p then q*, then you know or are in a position to know that *q*. For example, if you know that *it's snowing on the Buchaille Etive Mor* and you know that *if it's snowing on the Buchaille Etive Mor then it's snowing in Glen Coe*, you know or are in a position to know that *it's snowing in Glen Coe*. Most epistemologists accept (some version of) a closure principle; we shall now explore how a similar style of reasoning, in an evaluative context, would support anti-bolting intuitions.

First, let us assume that traditional climbing is valuable and that one way it is so is by virtue, of its being adventurous. Now for the value of climbing qua adventure to be realisable, certain conditions must obtain: in particular, there have to be suitably remote traditional climbing venues free from bolts. As an intermediate conclusion, we may say that the relevant realisability conditions for climbing being of value (by virtue of its being adventurous) are themselves valuable. This is the rough analogue of the closure reasoning about knowledge, here applied to the notion of value. The most plausible way in which such conditions are valuable is extrinsic[16] – the value of the mountains being bolt-free depends on the value of adventurous climbing. Now if two valuable courses of action are incompatible with one another in that the realisation of the value of either one excludes the realisation of the value of the other, the more valuable course of action is the one we have more reason to promote (to protect and/ or pursue). In which case, given that on any climbing venue the realisability of the value of traditional climbing *qua its being adventurous* is incompatible with there being sport routes, then assuming that the value of adventure that is part of traditional climbing makes it more valuable than sport climbing, there is a presumption in favour of traditional climbing and thus against sport climbing.

This argument clearly depends on the assumption that the value of adventure that is part of traditional climbing does make it more valuable than sport climbing. Although we have not argued directly for this, it is eminently plausible. For one thing, many sport climbers agree that traditional climbing is a purer and in some sense superior form of climbing to sport climbing. Furthermore, the perfectionist argument *for bolting* that we discussed in the previous section implicitly rests on the claim that the value of sport climbing *derives from* the value of traditional climbing to which it is a means – arguably suggesting that traditional climbing is the ultimately valuable form of climbing. We should add, however, that this reasoning, if defensible, generates only a *prima facie* presumption in favour of traditional climbing, one that may be overridden once other factors about the respective values of the two forms of climbing are factored in. Nevertheless, the argument places the onus on bolters to justify further development of sports venues, for if there is a presumption in favour of traditional climbing in adventurous climbing venues and thereby against sport climbing, the default presumption against bolting remains intact. Much more would need to be said in order to assess the ultimate cogency of the argument. An initial worry with the argument, as it stands, might be that analogous reasoning could be applied in defence of bolting. Insofar as any such argument would have to show that sport climbing is a more valuable or worthwhile activity than traditional climbing, we remain sceptical about its prospects.

If our argument is sound then it leads to the elevation of traditional climbing over sports climbing. It would thus call for serious revisions in the *Code of Practice* we criticised earlier; and it may provide the basis for a more instinctive and practically informative code which protects the traditional climbing ethos the *Code* claims to represent.[17] Let us stress again, however, that the argument as stated requires further consideration; we leave it in the hope that it presents food for further thought.

Conclusion

In this chapter we have discussed what we regard as the strongest arguments for and against bolting. These arguments focus on the pursuit of two different values – of excellence and of adventure – which underlie sport and traditional climbing respectively. We have shown that, though both arguments are defensible, they do not by themselves conclusively justify or forbid the use of bolts. The considerations in favour of the use of bolts in the second section provided a *prima facie* case for bolting, though without thereby justifying its use on all climbing venues. In contrast, the argument in the last section is best understood as providing a presumption in favour of traditional climbing at specifically adventurous climbing venues. There are of course other considerations relevant to a full assessment of the acceptability of bolting. Nevertheless, we hope that this chapter has helped to illuminate the disagreement about bolting by both connecting it to the values underlying the respective activities and identifying some of the arguments that can be advanced on each side.

Notes

1. See Tejada-Flores (1978) for classic discussion of these different games and the contrasting ideals they represent.
2. In many continental European countries it is the decision of the first ascencionist whether to place bolts instead of natural protection. For classic discussions of bolting in America (especially Yosemite), see the pieces by Robbins (1978), Harding (1978), Chouinard (1978), Drasdo (1978), each reprinted in Wilson (1978).
3. We have in mind Beinn Udlaidh (near Crianlarich), a reliable ice-climbing venue at an altitude of 850 metres, whose lower tier was bolted in 2004–5 for the purpose of training in relative safety for traditional winter climbing. For heated discussion amongst leading climbers, see for example the online climbing forums www.ukclimbing.com and www.scottishclimbs.com. In what follows, we use the description 'winter climbing' to include those forms of ice and mixed climbing (the latter on a possible combination of snow, ice, rock, frozen turf and the like) involving the use of specialist winter equipment such as ice axes and crampons.
4. The still contentious bolting in the early 1980s of unprotected lines in between some classic traditional routes at Creag a Bhancair (on Glen Coe's famous Buachaille Etive Mor) gives a concrete example of the kinds of conflict the *Code* leaves open. One explanation for the lack of clarity of the *Code* might be that it seeks to accommodate (and so legitimate) the continued use of this and other bolted venues.
5. The bolting of the Arbroath sea-cliffs was initially regarded as contentious but it has now become a more or less accepted sport climbing venue.

6. For more on slippery slope arguments, see for example Williams (1995).
7. Our thought here is analogous to Mill's claim that the only evidence for something being desirable is that people desire it (Mill, 1993: 36 [*Utilitarianism* ch. 4.3]); likewise, the only (or at least best) evidence that climbing excellence is valuable is that climbers value it.
8. The idea of overcoming dangers by controlling them is a recurring theme in climbing literature. See for example the interviews with Reinhold Messner, Walter Bonatti, Royal Robbins, Votek Kurtyka and Tomo Cesen in O'Connell (1993).
9. Interestingly, the vast literature on aesthetic experience typically focuses on the experience of the spectator rather than that of the performer. For some recent debate on what it is to have an aesthetic experience, see Carroll (2006) and Iseminger (2006).
10. In correspondence, the Scottish climber Alastair Robertson suggests that 'Sport climbing is the equivalent of McDonald's compared with Haute Cuisine. It tastes good initially but is quickly forgotten and you are left with a certain emptiness soon afterwards. That said, I quite enjoy going to McDonald's on occasion and it makes me further appreciate a fine dish!!'
11. Messner (1978) famously objects to bolting on exactly these grounds, claiming that it involves 'murdering the impossible'. A further consideration relevant in this context is the possibility that future climbers may be able to climb a sports route without bolts, due to which, it is sometimes claimed, bolts should not have been deployed in the first place and/or we have a responsibility to protect potential future climbing lines for future generations. This raises a number of interesting issues that we cannot pursue here.
12. There are also broadly aesthetic-environmental considerations relevant here – for many climbers, the very sight of metal (or other manmade items) on rock faces detracts from the beauty of the face and thereby spoils the aesthetic experience itself.
13. Messner (in O'Connell, 1993: 22) suggests something like this.
14. For more on enabling conditions, mainly in the context of normative reasons for action, see Dancy (2004: ch. 3).
15. The rider 'generally' need not be understood purely statistically. See for example Dreier (1990).
16. In roughly the sense intended by Korsgaard (1983).
17. This new *Code* might well render previous bolting venues illegitimate despite its current acceptance. We think that this is a bullet one may have to bite if, as pay-off, a clearer and more precise guide for *future* practice is gained.

References

Carroll, N, (2006) 'Aesthetic Experience: A Question of Content', in M. Kieran (ed.), *Contemporary Debates* in *Aesthetics and the Philosophy of Art*, Oxford: Blackwell.

Chouinard, Y. (1978) 'Coonyard Mouths Off', in K. Wilson (ed.), *Games Climbers Play*, London: Bâton Wicks.

Colyvan, M. (1993) 'Ethics, Morality and Rockclimbing', *T.H.E.* 6: 20–1, reprinted in *Screamer* (1993) 52: 3–5, and in *Redpoint* (1993) 14: 4.

Dancy, J. (2004) *Ethics Without Principles*, Oxford: Clarendon Press.

Drasdo, H. (1978) 'A Climb in Cae Coch Quarry', in K. Wilson (ed.), *Games Climbers Play*, London: Bâton Wicks.

Dreier, J. (1990) 'Internalism and Speaker Relativism', *Ethics*, 101: 6–26.

Harding, P. (1978) 'A Meeting with Dolphin', in K. Wilson (ed.), *Games Climbers Play*, London: Bâton Wicks.

Howett, K. (2004) 'The Code of Practice for Scottish Sports Climbing', *The Scottish Mountaineer*, 25: 13.

Iseminger, G. (2006) 'The Aesthetic Stare of Mind', in M. Kieran (ed.), *Contemporary Debates in Aesthetics and the Philosophy of Art*, Oxford: Blackwell.

Korsgaard, C. (1983) 'Two Distinctions in Goodness', *Philosophical Review*, 92: 169–96.

Messner, R. (1978) 'Murder of the impossible', in K. Wilson (ed.), *Games Climbers Play*, London: Bâton Wicks.

Mill, J. S. (1993) *Utilitarianism, On Liberty, Considerations on Representative Government, Remarks on Bentham's Philosophy*, ed. G. Williams, London: Everyman.

O'Connell, N. (1993) *Beyond Risk: Conversations With Climbers*, London: Diadem Books.

Robbins, R. (1978) 'Tis-Sa-Sack', in K. Wilson (ed.), *Games Climbers Play*, London: Bâton Wicks.

Tejada-Flores, L. (1978) 'Games Climbers Play', in K. Wilson (ed.), *Games Climbers Play*, London: Bâton Wicks.

Williams, B. (1995) 'Which Slopes are Slippery?', reprinted in B. Williams, *Making Sense of Humanity*, Cambridge: Cambridge University Press.

Wilson, K. (ed.) (1978) *The Games Climbers Play*, London: Bâton Wicks.

Kant goes skydiving

Understanding the extreme by way of the sublime[1]

Jesús Ilundáin-Agurruza

Taking off

> If the pain and terror are so modified as not to be actually noxious ... they are capable of producing delight; not pleasure, but a sort of delightful horror, a sort of tranquility tinged with terror; which, as it belongs to self-preservation, is one of the strongest of all the passions.
>
> T. Burke, *On the Sublime, and Beautiful*
> (Kant, 1951: 118)[2]

Some people jump out of airplanes 13,000 feet above the ground, while others leap off the edge of cliffs or launch themselves down impossibly steep mountains on bikes, and yet others run in front of bulls. The obvious question that arises in most people sane enough to remain spectators is: Why do these people engage in these activities that could cost them life and limb? There are many possible explanations, and the protagonists themselves have multifarious reasons that may or may not agree with what psychologists, sportswriters, and others come up with to elucidate such behavior. Rather than presenting a series of personal disclosures or the psychological analyses of these, I want here to answer the question from a conceptual standpoint that finds a common element to all

these experiences. And I want to argue that a specific aesthetic canon handed down from the Enlightenment, the sublime, allows us best to understand what is involved when someone pursues a genuinely dangerous activity that is undertaken as *divertissement*.

At first sight, it seems that the outrageous and untamed phenomenon of the extreme is worlds away from the calm and unruffled demeanor of Enlightenment intellectuals musing on the subject of the sublime. Imagine the following scenario:

> *The airplane, bouncing around, rapidly gains altitude as it slices through the clouds. Inside the loud cabin there are seven people. Pale faces and fidgety hands embody the tension. Six of them are seasoned skydivers, wearing special skinsuits that will enable them to soar while freefalling at 120 miles an hour – the 'high drag' material on top allows to change directions countering the pull from the skyboard, the bottom is silk smooth (Sydnor forthcoming). Dyed hairdos, some matching the skinsuit, and body piercings are common adornments. Yet it is the seventh person that seems the oddest looking one of the bunch. Without as much as a raised eyebrow they return the quizzical looks of the peculiar, quiet man sitting opposite them. They assume he is dressed in*

drag with his white curly wig, tight pants that end below the knee, pink stockings, and deep blue velvety jacket with ornate lacework popping out of the sleeves and neck. With the implausible phlegmatic assurance of a Briton, being Prussian, he breaks the silence, and extending his hand to a green-haired young woman introduces himself with a great impersonation he could not have been aware of 'My name is Kant, Immanuel Kant.'

But, what could Kant and the skydiver talk about? Indeed, apparently, not much. Nevertheless, the initial incongruence between the tranquil deportment endorsed by the sublime and the wild frolics embraced by the extreme disappears when the former and the world that came out of it are used to analyze the latter. Kant could prove to be an engaging and illuminating interlocutor to the skydivers: he might just teach them what it is about their activity that makes it so 'awesome.' Additionally, some of Kant's own chums, such as Dewey, Bullough, and Ortega y Gasset will further 'enlighten' Kant's insight so that he may soar with his skydiving companions:

'And my name is Anja,' she replies cordially, willing to entertain this endearingly eccentric man – she is well aware from her class in post-modern theory that Kant can't be around. 'Pray, do tell me,' asks Kant, with a worried look in his face. 'What is going on? I swear a moment ago I was having a jolly good time in Parnassus arguing about the allure of nonsense in the context of transcendence with my friends, and now I find myself in this diabolical contraption, flying! My goodness gracious, René's demon couldn't have dreamt up such a contraption! Though I must admit that there's some delight involved herein, as my friend Edmund would say.'

Amused, used to taking things at face value, she replies as if she were talking about the weather, 'We are about to jump off the airplane and kinda dance on the air!'

Kant's eyes pop out in disbelief, but being of a rather plucky nature he composes himself and, doing what he does best, reasons the situation: 'Unbelievable! Now, I think that such an experience, and ours gliding in the immensity of the sky, would be very nicely explained in a universal and a priori way if we resorted to ...'

Now Anja's eyes bulge out. '... the notion of the sublime.' Before long, they are both engaged in a lively discussion accented by the occasional bump in the flight. Anja fills Kant in on the

latest theoretical and cultural developments relevant to skydiving, extreme sports, and post-modernism, while Kant attempts to complement her ideas with a sound conceptual justification. The other skydivers shake their heads and place bets on whether he will jump or not.

The following is a possible account of the theoretical underpinnings that might have been gleaned from Kant's and Anja's conversation. Following this introductory takeoff, we jump into the world of extreme sports and sister activities in their postmodern context, to then resolutely freefall into the realm of the sublime, beginning first with its Enlightenment roots and then proceeding to frolic amidst the relevant ties to the previous section. After briefly managing to soar along a suggestive existential analysis that validates the experience of the extreme as sublime in our lives, we undergo a brief but jolting encounter with some possible problems and clarifications in our descent. The last section, a brief conclusion, lands us safely from our inquiry into the exhilarating.

The jump: our *extremely* postmodern world

> Between the seventeenth and eighteenth centuries in Europe this contradictory feeling – pleasure and pain, joy and anxiety, exaltation and depression – was christened or re-christened by the name of the *sublime*.
>
> (Lyotard, 1991: 92, his italics)

Contemporary *ménage-à-trois:* the postmodern, the extreme, and sport

1 *Postmodernity* mistrusts the grand metanarratives, such as Marxism or Freudian psychology, which so enthralled intellectuals and the masses alike last century. Life is seen as fragmented and lived at face value, on the surface, pastiche and pop culture being its trademark. Las Vegas, a city of simulacra where nothing is what it seems, is its 'cultural' icon. Postmodernist theory is not characterized by positive, novel claims, but is rather a self-reflexive and critical movement that crystallizes in its opposition

to other movements, in particular those that stand under the banner of 'modernity,' roughly mainstream intellectual thought in Western culture since the Enlightenment. Postmodernity for Jean-François Lyotard, one of its leading theorists, is 'the rewriting of some of the features claimed by modernity, and first of all modernity's claim to ground its legitimacy on the project of liberating humanity as a whole through science and technology' (Lyotard, 1991: 34). It embodies a critique and fragmentation of traditional Enlightenment 'dogmas': truth is not universal, but contingent; foundationalist epistemological positions on knowledge and reason are forsaken; there are alternative models to scientific truth, such as narratives; without a unified subject that gives coherence to our experience the self becomes dispersed; faith is lost in the ability of ideologies to serve mankind. To summarize this by paraphrasing and appropriating – a very postmodern practice – the title of one of Lyotard's essays: postmodernism is a 'rewriting of modernity' (ibid.).

2 It's popular. It sells. It's hot. The phenomenon of the extreme has taken over much of the limelight on and off the sports arena. Magazines and television commercials shower us with advertisements where particularly ordinary, even unattractive, products are promoted by mere association with the world of the extreme. Lately everything is 'extreme,' from magic shows to apple juice sold as 'extreme-cooler' under the license of Disney World, from Timex watches and Volkswagen beetles both advertised in conjunction with images of the running of the bulls to ... lip balm? Bonnebell launched a series of 'Xtreme flavors to go,' rappelling clip included. There are magazines whose *raison-d'être* is largely predicated on an active involvement of the outdoors centered on the adventurous. *Outdoor Explorer*, which highlights the slogan 'Real Adventure, Real People,' often runs articles and specials on extreme and adventurous enterprises, and *Outside Magazine* is famous for its guides to the ultimate extreme vacations. Yearly ESPN

broadcasts, very successfully, *The X Games*, which by now have a serious following. There is even an encyclopedia dedicated to the phenomenon, fittingly entitled *Encyclopedia of Extreme Sports*.[3] The extreme also showcases an awesome ability to use an aggressive and intense vocabulary that seeks to outrageously push the limits of the conventional over the edge as it dynamically courts the radical side of life. Both the extreme and postmodernism are rebellious teenagers that react against their 'faddy daddy' modernist culture.

3 Extreme sports and performances are the latest and the sexiest in the world of sports. And they come with an attitude. They are postmodern through and through: flirting with danger, based on a cultivation of risk, the excitement of the moment, the daring stunt, and sporting an aesthetic that seeks to transgress traditional sports mores, fashion, and ways of institutionalization. Fittingly in sync with the times they are individualistic rather than team oriented, defiant of conventions, and seek to outrage both within and without the 'field.' The adrenaline rush takes over tactics; the edge of the cliff is more appealing than the most monumental stadium. Riding on the crest of a tidal wave that acclaims the allure of danger and adventure, they have even begun to chip away at the hegemony of 'the big three' in the USA. As Bob Igial, director of the advertising agency Media Edge says, one has 'to look outside the traditional sports' to find the young male demographic, a population constituted by the 12–34-year-old segment that is crucial for advertisers, programmers, and business people (Greenfeld, 1998: 80–1). They also cultivate an aura of authenticity, particularly among its young followers, who eschew traditional sports heroes by seeing them as sold to the system. Many of them started from grassroots movements that originated with a few friends getting together to have fun off the beaten track, e.g., skateboarding. Pop culture thus performs its way into the world of sports. These endeavors hardly need a formal presentation. Besides the

usual suspects, there are a plethora of other sports that respond to the extreme moniker: skateboarding, deep cave diving, base jumping, free soloing boulders, street-luge, wake boarding, aggressive in-line, to name a few.

Before proceeding I note an important caveat. I am not interested in a taxonomy that determines the membership status of candidates. For the purposes of this chapter, when I write of 'the extreme' it should be understood that I include alongside the paradigmatic extreme sports other activities, like the running of the bulls, that court danger and share other central attributes with this fellowship of the extreme – be they mainstream sports or not. My interest lies not in the extreme sports *qua* sport, but, to say it with a Kantian flavor, in the conceptual conditions that make the experience of the phenomenon of the extreme possible, wherever it may be found. The premise of this exposition is that what enables the sublime to work is precisely mirrored by the frame of mind required of these pursuits on the edge, where the limits of one's world are transcended by confronting risk. In the process I hope some understanding of the implications and relevance of a somewhat obscure modernist aesthetic principle, life, and ourselves may be gained.

Freefalling: the realm of the sublime

Rosencrantz: Fear?
Guildenstern (in fury – flings a coin at the ground): Fear! The crack that might flood your brain with light!

(Stoppard, 1967: 15)

The changing outdoors: from terror to awe

If our adventure is to come to fruition, rather than recklessly leaping into the sublime directly and prematurely, I propose that we take as guides both modernism *and* postmodernism. Our gear: art, and the origin of certain modern sports, e.g. mountain climbing, that have been appropriated and 'reinvented' by the postmodern world in a rather brazen and

interesting fashion. From the terrifying dusk that preceded the Enlightenment to the exhilarating dawn of Romanticism there was a dramatic change in the perception and experience of nature by the European mind. Art as well as the outdoor enterprises of men and women living in those periods attest to this. Alongside the scientific and geographical discoveries of the eighteenth and nineteenth centuries, and with new concepts and artistic sensibilities brought about by the Romantic reinterpretation of the British Empiricists and German Idealists that preceded them, nature went from fearful hinterland to be avoided to wondrous realm to be discovered.[4]

Before the Romantic aesthetic and new scientific ethos came about, the mountains, the oceans, the forests were all seen as hazardous places where only the bravest or the most foolhardy ventured. Bears, wolves, avalanches, rogue waves, and monsters from the depths awaited the unfortunate few who were daring enough to leave the safety of cities and *Terra Firma*. Alexis D. de Fontanay's sinister painting *Seen on the Way to Maladeta* attests to the foreboding feelings associated with the mountains: in the immensity of a dark forest in the Pyrenees a hunter tries to help a petite shepherdess chased by a bear. With the exploration of the Alps first, trepidation changed into admiration. This process took longer to reach the Pyrenees, Briffaud points out, but eventually, those mountains also saw a blooming influx of 'visitors' (Briffaud, 1994: 40). What previously had caused dismay and terror became exhilaration, enjoyment, and wonder, a transformation detailed by Olivier Mesley (1999: 56–63). Caspar David Friedrich's paintings, such as his popular *Wanderer above the Mists*, illustrate this. Mary Shelley's *Frankenstein* reflects this new vogue when she places the meeting of Dr Frankenstein and his creature in the midst of cold and ominous mountains. To be sure, there was still anxiety, but it was channeled into awe. Artists, naturalists, and scientists, often one and the same, spearheaded this move. The initial rationales of science and art soon gave way to going up the mountains just to climb them. As Guttmann states, '[b]y the time that Edward Whymper conquered the Matterhorn in 1865, no such scientific justification was necessary' (Guttmann, 1979: 50). Already by the middle of the nineteenth century, first in England, occasional climbing and hiking were transformed into a more or less modern sport (ibid.). As the European landscape was tamed, the search for excitement of the same kind was expanded to the Poles, the 'Black Continent,' the Australian Outback, and the immensity of the American West.

The sublime, while unable to claim to be the sole protagonist for effecting these changes, was certainly instrumental in changing the sensibilities of the Europeans. Spanish painter Manuel Goya and his contemporaries loved being terrified by the new frontiers being explored, which included the open sky, as illustrated in his painting of an agitated crowd that has gathered to see a hot air balloon. The dreadfulness remained but, rather than provoking panic, it begun to be associated with excitement. This is a paradoxical feeling that those who engage in the extreme are very familiar with. The sublime was the hub on which this new sensibility spun. It helps us understand these changes in the relation between pre-Romantic Europeans and their post-Romantic heirs leading all the way up to us, their postmodern grandchildren. Although Kant could appreciate nature he found the actual aspect of 'the wild greatness of nature' as 'rather terrifying' (Kant, 1951: 40). He was not enthused by the Romantic spirit, but he provided the conceptual tools to find liberation from such terrors.

Sublimating the extreme by way of Kant

The distinguished lineage of the sublime can be traced back to Longinus. He was concerned with the sublime in literature, but he already singled out the fact that both 'horror' and pleasure were the lot of the sublime. Presently we shall follow the lead of Immanuel Kant, the most influential of thinkers on the sublime, although I acknowledge that others, most notably France Hutcheson and Edmund Burke in particular, introduced him to and showed the domain of the sublime. The latter in fact developed a very complex and original account that relied on an empirical psychology – Kant would instead rely on a transcendental philosophy since his judgment of the sublime is based on an a priori foundation (however, this may not be

completely unproblematic for Kant).[5] Burke distinguished the beautiful from the sublime, the former bringing positive pleasure, the latter a diminution or removal of pain (Beardsley, 1996: 194). For him the sublime centers around a feeling he calls 'delight,' which is present whenever we have an idea of pain or danger without actually being in such circumstances (ibid.).[6] The account of the sublime advanced here agrees with physiological explanations of the body's reaction to extreme situations, from the sympathetic to the parasympathetic systems' workings, and the concurrent experience of pleasure and pain, for instance. In addition, this account is also congruent with contemporary psychological theories about our responses to dangerous situations, such as those put forward by Michael Apter who, in *The Dangerous Edge: The Psychology of Excitement*, deploys an apparatus that concurs with Kant's views on the sublime.[7]

Kant's thoughts on the sublime are found in the first part of his *Critique of Judgement*, therein we find two distinct yet complementary theories, one of the beautiful and one of the sublime. The former is based on predicates of judgments of taste, and the latter is concerned with predicates of judgments of feeling. Kant himself favored the orderly, rational, and Apollonian beautiful over the unruly, irrational, and Dionysian sublime: 'we see that the concept of the sublime in nature is far less important and rich in consequences than that of its beauty' (Kant, 1951: 23). However, I focus on the latter since it has proved to be the more fecund for our contemporary world.[8] Kant analyses the sublime from two perspectives: the mathematically sublime and the dynamically sublime. Each aspect captures one of the two central features of the extreme experience: transcending boundaries and courting danger in the face of nature.

The feeling of the sublime lies in the limits of the capacity we have to comprehend, that is to put things together – thus works the mathematically sublime – which is soon overcome by the feeling that there is an inconceivably larger 'amount' which our imagination cannot even begin to fathom.[9] It is concerned with an 'enormous object' that cannot be encompassed, e.g. the size of the universe (Kant, 1951: 23). The judgment of absolute greatness is non-conceptual and beyond the senses.

One's understanding cannot subsume it, and the imagination is soon dwarfed. This is the key premise of the sublime. Thanks to this move Kant places the sublime in the realm of reason and beyond the reach of any possible experience. The nature of the sublime is found in phenomena whose intuition brings the idea of an infinity we cannot behold in the face of our reason, which demands a totality. The mathematically sublime enables us to go from the finite to the infinite, from the limited to the limitless. In the case of the extreme, the limits being overcome are those of perception and of what we think is physically possible. When skateboarders perform 'Ollies,' frontside 180s, take big air, or pull off the ultimate, the 900 – where the skateboarder twists and turns around his axis until he has completed a spin that adds to 900 degrees of rotation – they thwart our expectations by seemingly bending the laws of physics. It must be noted that the search to surpass current limits is done for the sake of the performance itself, not for an imprimatur 'so and so set this record.' In a radical sense, and for some activities, the ultimate limit being wooed is death itself: away from the airplane, and until the parachute deploys, one is virtually dead.

Kant's analysis of the dynamically sublime, focused on nature, is applicable to elements that seem to have an absolute power over us, e.g. the raging sea (Kant, 1951: 23). It seems that paradigmatic examples for both the sublime and extreme endeavors are particularly rich in this fashion. We experience the sublime when fear takes over as an 'intellectualized' response from our 'secure' vantage point as we feel the might and size of nature from the standpoint of our fragility. This brings the first characteristic of the feeling of the sublime: an unpleasant feeling that drives in the sudden realization of the limitations of our imagination and ability to sense. We are human, all too human, and very small at that. Nevertheless, this awareness also brings about the other essential element of the feeling of the sublime that makes it ultimately appealing: pleasure. The sublime gives us elation and delight because it reminds us that we have a faculty that is beyond any standard of sense or any such limitation. We are diminutive but endowed with a boundless ability. The uncomfortable feeling upon realizing the disparity between the imagination and reason turns to joy because we can, ideally, celebrate the unsurpassable superiority of reason. The extreme is generous in its courting of the greatness and threat of nature as we meet danger at impossible odds. We are emboldened by the fact that our physical skill and reason enable us to tame the forces of nature, whether it be jumping off or ascending an 'impossibly' steep mountain face.

Key to this process is a courting of danger that manages to remain safe *enough* to find some measure of enjoyment: This is the paradox of danger, which places us as close to danger as possible, but beyond harm or a lethal 'appointment.' The closer we get to the source of danger – the higher we jump above the edge of a half pipe, the U-shaped ramp in the skateboard ring – the higher the risk, and thus the greater the intensity and the pleasure. In turn, the temptation to avoid this intensifies because, as a corollary the pain, the fear, also increases. The margin of safety dynamically changes according to the particular situation. Some days we may choose to wait a little longer before pulling out the ring that opens the parachute. At the conceptual level this shielding framework enables us to distance ourselves sufficiently to stay in the danger zone without panicking. When the situation gets out of control and we are in harm's way, the sublime disappears, leaving fear and potential calamity as its signature.

Edward Bullough's concept of 'psychical distance' helps explain how the paradox of danger unfolds. For him this distancing has a negative aspect which inhibits our practical concerns, and a positive one which explores the experience created by the negation (Bullough, 1996: 165). Both of these ideas are at work in both sublime and extreme situations. He illustrates this with an example of the fog at sea (so feared by anyone offshore), and claims that through this distancing we can find 'a source of intense relish and enjoyment. ... just as every one in the enjoyment of a mountain-climb disregards its physical labor and danger' (ibid.). This distancing, however, involves a paradox: the antinomy of distance. For although we must have some inclination to enjoy or become engaged with the thing distanced, we must at the same time resist the inclination to become over-involved (ibid.: 166–7). His antinomy is the aesthetic counterpart of the paradox of danger. The goal is to be neither far behind the edge of the precipice nor over it, but right at it. The extreme demands that we get as close to danger as possible while staying right on the edge of safety, barely holding the temptation to take one more step. The antinomy, as an aesthetic principle of artistic appreciation, is not easy to develop. It requires a discriminating sense of taste – different arts placing particular demands – developed through attentive exposure to, and critical reflection on, art works. Likewise, mastering the paradox of danger of the extreme involves abilities that need to be developed to a high degree by means of practice and experience of the requisite skills for the given sport or activity.

I cannot boast to be an extreme sportsman 'proper' who indulges in any of the recently brewed extreme sports. Nevertheless, I ran with the bulls dozens of times in my hometown of Pamplona, an activity that some today experience as extreme sport (when it was first carried out, this 'extremist world' was still centuries away). The conceptual apparatus I use captures the subjective experience in a manner that corroborates the process and the motivation: there is an amalgamation of severe fear and joy ruled by the chaotic dynamics between them as one 'plays' at getting as close as possible to the two-pronged paradox of danger embodied on two horns and the might of nature incarnate in a bull, all of which is unraveled into an exquisite sublime moment – when all goes well, that is.[10]

The extreme 'artificially' generates the workings of the sublime encounter with fear and joy by means of a risk that is mastered by means of skill. Some are uncomfortable with this because fear and danger are part of the equation. Are they necessary? Stephen Davies states '[t]o ask if climbing would be more enjoyable for the person if she were always without fear is to ask a far from straightforward question' (Davies, 1996: 396). This fear is aroused by danger, understood as physical hazard, which is the real source of the discomfort. In the case of the sublime we need not be exposed to *actual* danger – although this would increase the intensity of the feeling – the risk may be merely *perceived* in order to feel the sublime overtake us. Neither is it sufficient: for being at risk does not guarantee it either. Sometimes a scary experience not grounded on the sublime can be more intense, but mere intensity is not all that counts. We may become too terrified for the interplay with

delight to successfully bring a feeling of awe, and then it will fail to produce the same subjective type of life-enriching experience for which we prize the sublime (and the extreme). However, risk as *actual* possibility is necessary for the extreme. After all, this is the premise of extreme activities, pushing matters to the edge of calamity: the chance to get hurt must be real and present if things do not go our way. Otherwise the event will be a mockery of such an experience, a mere simulacrum (which is what the bold soul wishes and sometimes gets).[11] Yet, being at risk is not sufficient in this case either. Merely being in danger neither guarantees nor justifies the kind of experience we are looking for. Awareness of the danger is prerequisite. In a sense the extreme follows the Aristotelian analysis of courage. If I undertake a real risk without thinking it so, I will be acting recklessly not courageously, and I will not be in a situation to experience the extreme because the fearful aspect is missing, e.g. if I run with the bulls because I think they are trained and harmless or I believe myself to be invulnerable. Both, fear and its overcoming, and actual danger consciously perceived unite sports and other activities into that brotherhood of the extreme. At the other end elation, relief, or exhilaration solve the equation that began as a challenge. Finally, although most sports involve the risk of physical damage – even snooker or pool can result in a black eye – this risk is not central in the way that danger is in mountain climbing. I could be badly injured in a tennis game, but it is not the risk of trauma that makes tennis interesting. On the other side, the constant danger of sustaining a fatal or maiming fall is an *integral* part of going up the steep side of cliffs using rope, a bit of chalk, and some remarkably gripping footwear.

I do not claim that there is or need be an exact one to one parallel between the extreme and the sublime, but rather that the apparatus that allows for the experience of the sublime – to see the tornado as a terrifying and exciting event – is also in place when one chooses to jump off a bridge and fall 300 feet tied to a rubber band while on steroids. And when the extreme is accompanied by the actual experience of the awe-inspiring sublime, life does not get much better than that, or at least more intense. It is this very intensity that I will now explore in greater detail.

Soaring: the value of the experience of the extreme

Such wonder and terror came on him that he stood still forgetting all else, and gazed as one turned to stone.

(Tolkien, 2002: 266–7)

An experience

John Dewey's concept of 'an experience' is particularly appropriate to make sense of the sublime with regard to its value and place in our lives. In *Art and Experience* he differentiates between the experiencing that takes place any and every moment in the lives of creatures, and those special experiences that are brought to a fruitful end. Dewey emphasizes the uniqueness of this way of experiencing by italicizing either the preposition 'an' that precedes it or the verb that implicates it. 'Experience in this vital sense is defined by those situations and episodes that we spontaneously refer to as being "real experiences"; those things of which we say in recalling them, "that; *was* an experience"' (Dewey, 1980: 36). This can be something very consequential, or something lesser, perhaps better suited to exemplifying what is to be an experience because of its very slightness (ibid.). For instance, it could be escaping unharmed from a terrible car accident or the encounter with that diminutive landscape by Corot in the Louvre, amid all the huge canvases by David and Delacroix, which changed the way we thought of Romantic art. Now, that was an encounter! The sublime is ripe ground for this concept of experience. At one point Dewey illustrates his exposition, saying:

> Then there is that storm one went through in crossing the Atlantic – a storm that seemed in its fury, as it was experienced, to sum up in itself all that a storm can be, complete in itself, standing out because marked out from what went before and what came after.
>
> (ibid.)

Well said. And experiencing the storm along the lines provided by the sublime will enrich both the experience and our lives, for one can feel *both* the terror in the storm and the exhilaration. Obviously, if we are about to drown then the protective framework will disappear, and it may all come to a sad end or a scarring event. But, if we have reason to feel confident that we will make it, then the pain and the pleasure will make of such occurrence an adventure worth remembering. Experience is aesthetic for Dewey, moreover. This parallels the aesthetic nature of the sublime and the role it plays in *enriching* an event so that it is no mere happening, but veritable experience.

The extreme shares in this aesthetic appreciation, largely because its allure lies in this fashion of engaging it as well – one attempts to snowboard or jump according to certain canons. More importantly the enjoyment can be argued to be of a sensuous and aesthetic nature as well. Additionally, for Dewey each of these complete and mature experiences also has 'an element of suffering, in its large sense' because 'otherwise there would be no taking in of what preceded' (Dewey, 1980: 41). He actually deals with the pleasure and the pain separately, yet it is telling that both elements are what constitute the character of the Deweyan experience. The sublime adds a layer of additional meaning to his views on the matter, and *vice versa*. In this regard, the extreme seeks to provide just *this* type of *experience*: we seek to replicate the 'sublime buzz' sometimes in the overcoming of limits, other times in the might of nature, but the goal remains to live these experiences that enrich the experiential and existential content of our lives. Of course all this will come to naught or little more if our nature lacks the required contemplative propensity, but then it is ourselves who are to blame. For the extreme and the sublime, by virtue of being this type of experience, also afford us insight into ourselves, that most Socratic of enterprises. Ralph Keyes writes:

> To the world at large the most famous rationale for scaling a peak is George Mallory's flip 'Because it's there.' But to his fellow climbers, Mallory's more insightful remark was made after conquering *Mont Blanc*. 'Have we vanquished an enemy? He asked upon returning. "None but ourselves."'
>
> (Keyes, 1985: 118)

Our fears can be a source of self-knowledge and a fountainhead to develop our characters: a process that can be very revelatory of who we are and why. But more relevantly, it presents us with a challenge to be met and it is one that has a very special reward of its own: an enhancement of life precisely because central things to our life, our *only* one, are put at risk.

Affirming life by way of the extremely sublime

Our lives are complex and rich in contradictory ways. We love and hate, fear and confront, enjoy and dislike, hope and despair. We try to avoid the negative side of life often enough; as Stephen Davies says, 'sensible navigators of the ocean of existence give rocky outcrops a wide berth. But also such things ... come unavoidably with life itself' (Davies, 1996: 394). Yet sometimes we also seek excitement precisely in those places. The sublime encapsulates this complexity of our lives in a concrete manner: it manages to capture the unpleasant; and the attractive in one single experience, with the result being *an* experience that we come to enjoy precisely for what it is. Davies ponders on why we listen to sad music, since it makes us sad, and along the way he realizes that he must answer deep questions about human nature and life at large. Why do we engage in dangerous, unpleasant, sad, uncomfortable, demanding things? Often, because it comes, like an uninvited guest, with the turf, but sometimes because we want and choose to. Overcoming difficulties and meeting challenges brings great satisfaction, and sometimes this depends not on *what* was achieved, but on *how* difficult it was to attain (ibid.: 395). For Davies, the kinds of activities he mentions and under consideration here are 'engaged in for fun!' And as he rightly points out, sometimes the inconveniences, the dangers are integral to the activity itself. We engage in dangerous activities precisely because they *are* dangerous. Take the danger away and you change the nature of the activity. The point of climbing a mountain is to climb it; otherwise we would take a helicopter, as Davies points out (ibid.: 396). If we replaced the fighting bulls in the running of the bulls for a bunch of harmless steers, or better yet ducks, the activity would lose its *telos*, its nature and defining purpose. Furthermore, I argue, the way to make the dangerous enjoyable, fun, and enriching, is by way of the sublime, by being able to relish and thrive on the chaos of fear and joy of which Burke, Longinus, Kant and company have long

been aware. *That* is what makes it fun, and that amounts to *an* experience. The extreme is a wonderful way to enrich and concurrently experience some of the most complex yet basic emotions proper to life, and in intensities that are barred from our mundane lives.

Ortega y Gasset's reflections on the origins of the sporting state inspire the title and some key insights in Klaus Meier's 'An Affair of Flutes.' In his essay Ortega argues that the origin of the state is not found in a utilitarian ethos, but in a youthful surplus of creative vigor fond of hazardous enterprises (Ortega y Gasset, 1962: 27ff.). His views effectively complement the account of Deweyan experience. Meier contends that in opposition to a too orderly, pragmatic, rational, and *secure*, Apollonian consciousness we should resurrect the elements of, and celebrate, the capacity for Dionysian consciousness, which 'will alter the barrenness of life, grant transcendence of servitude, dependence, and utility, and radically transform man' (Meier, 1995: 129). The Sublime is utterly chaotic and Dionysian. Furthermore, much of this transforming Dionysian spirit he favors is captured by the extreme sports and events we choose to engage in. To pursue extreme experiences with the right disposition is to transform our lives. Meier quotes Ortega:

> Life is an affair of flutes. It is overflow that it needs most. He who rests content with barely meeting necessity as it arises will be washed away. Life has triumphed on this planet because it has, instead of clinging to necessities, deluged with overwhelming possibilities.
> (Meier, 1995: 128)

Indeed, the sublime and the extreme certainly qualify as some of the fittest ways to indulge in these overwhelming possibilities. Meier quotes Ortega anew – and he might as well be thinking of the sublime or the extreme: for him play is a most exceptional mode of being, '"a humus from which man surges creatively forward toward a horizon full of 'the lure of infinite distances"' (ibid.). This lure of infinity rings in consonance with the limitlessness of the sublime, and in turn this chord is in harmony with the extreme endeavor as a way to challenge our limits whether facing the infinite or the immensity of our world. What Meier says of play can also be applied to the sublime as I understand it, '[i]t is *a joie de vivre*, and adventurous, festive undertaking that reduces man's provincialism and enlarges his experience by embracing, and penetrating to, the heart of life' (ibid.: 129). The sublime is playful, orgiastic, Dionysian, chaotic, creative, just in this fruitful manner. And the appeal of the extreme is based on a joy that celebrates *being alive* precisely in the willful and 'frightfully-fun' courting of danger. What a cocktail!

Turbulences and tribulations

> A rush that resembled passion crept from the insides of his guts and somehow drew the skin from every part of his body toward the center of his joy and fear, so tight that when he smiled it made his cheeks burn ...
>
> (Keyes 1985: 34)[12]

The convoluted relationship between the sublime and the extreme

In this section I attempt to elucidate the relevant senses in which the sublime and the extreme interact. Two key attributes characterize the type of chance-ridden ventures we are concerned with presently: a courting of physical danger, preferably encountering the awesome in one of the many grand manifestations the natural world affords us, and a quest to overcome limits. These may occur concurrently or separately. The fascination of the extreme is predicated on, and replicates, the dynamics that constitute the breathtaking experience of the sublime. In both instances the intensity of the feeling aroused by the interplay between pain and delight is the vital element that brings about their respective attractiveness. The rush Webb describes above comes from the interaction between these two ingredients. Both are jointly necessary to deliver a sublime or extreme experience, inclusively speaking, and neither alone is sufficient. If the fearful and painful aspect becomes too dominant the feeling of awe becomes terror: the parachute tangling or the hiker lost in the foggy mountains and unable to see the chasms in his path exemplify this. If the joyful aspect eclipses fear, the exuberance of the moment quickly deflates into the uninteresting, we get a happening rather than *an* experience.

A ski slope with a mean reputation leads one to muse about a veritable challenge only to find it lacking, the run is fun but the prevalence of the pleasurable aspect decaffeinates matters. If neither is present then obviously we need not speak of anything sublime or extreme taking place; the anticipation and trepidation are aborted into mere regret.

Further honing the foregoing analysis, the sublime is not sufficient to bestow the seal of 'extreme' to a particular activity. Many activities that regale one with the experience of sublimity are not of the extreme kind, much less are they an extreme sport. For example, simply standing next to the wave breakers as the gale blows the crests of the waves over the parapets induces the sublime feeling as one wonders about one's safety while the sense of awe sets in. Analogously, some 'prudent and ordinary' sports may also deliver an encounter with the sublime, e.g. a night dive in the ocean with a Mako shark encounter, matches the intensity of deep cave diving, fin stroke by fin stroke. Nonetheless this does not work with all non-extreme sports. I doubt that table tennis could bring on the encounter with the larger than life aesthetic feelings.

Is the sublime essential to the extreme? The answer is not straightforward. If 'extreme' here is shorthand to designate certain sports the sublime is not necessary. Otherwise any given failure to engage the sublime would disqualify the activity as extreme *sport*. The sport still is, taxonomically speaking, an extreme sport, only that in this case the performance itself fell short. A bad game of tennis is still a game of tennis; a below-par extreme performance as one tries to work the pipeline of a 30 foot wave with a body board is still a token performance within *extreme* sport. If 'extreme' denotes the *quality* of a special 'sports' experience then any time we have a *genuine* extreme occurrence the sublime will be in place. The 'awesomeness' of the extreme moment is a synonymous manifestation of the sublime (this is etymologically warranted in a deeper sense than most who use the epithet realize, since the sublime is about the awesome in nature). The extreme in its paradigmatic sense is about intensity, the sublime instrumentally enriching it. Nevertheless, this does not entail that every time we engage in an extreme endeavor it will be intense and a full-blown confrontation with the sublime. The pleasure or the pain, or both, may be absent, or present, but in too low a degree to effect a veritable encounter with the awe-inspiring. Moreover, merely partaking of the combination of fright and pleasure renders the process neither sublime nor extreme. All goal-oriented activities involve the possibility of failure while many replicate the process ascribed to the sublime yet are not extreme (much less sports), e.g. an entrepreneurial business venture or presenting a paper at a conference. The risks are not physical (unless the presentation is *that* dreadful perhaps), but pain and pleasure are present as one faces the possibility of bankruptcy or ridicule. What is unique to the sublime is not the mere mixture of delight and pain, but *how* this takes place: facing the awesomeness of nature or an immensity that escapes our ability to think it. In a parallel fashion the extreme benefits from the natural context within which it unfolds to court the domain of the sublime concurrently.

Some readers may remain reticent about the purported cohesion I articulated as the chapter took off between the serene demeanor of the sublime and the outrageous behavior of the extreme: the very intensity (so valued by seekers of the extreme) gets in the way of the sublime, does it not?[13] For them the sublime moment is embodied in the 'Romantic trekker' who, reflectively and calmly, gasps in awe as he looks onto an unbelievable canyon. There is little in the way of activity if we contrast it with the turbulent experience of the skydiver as she hurls down performing acrobatics in 'the void.'

First, we must realize that the view of the Romantic wandering in the mists as simply delightfully quiet is so to our twenty-first-century eyes. Such a person would have approached the outdoors with much more trepidation than we imagine nowadays. Second, Kant himself contrasts the case of the beautiful which 'maintains the mind in *restful* contemplation' with the sublime which brings *a movement of the mind*' (Kant, 1951: § 24, his italics). Whereas in the feeling of beauty there is a harmonious interplay between the imagination and the understanding, in the feeling of the sublime there is a *conflict* between imagination and reason. It is worth quoting Lyotard, our postmodern paladin, again, '[t]his dislocation of the faculties among themselves [imagination and Reason] gives rise to the *extreme tension* (Kant calls it agitation) that characterizes the pathos of the sublime, as opposed to the calm feeling of beauty' (Lyotard, 1991: 98). The sublime is chaotic and dynamic, and it brings about a tension between pleasure and pain that is resolved in a negative way. The extreme again partakes of this process for there we find a mixture of fright and exhilaration that is resolved in alleviation. Still, the happening could be termed 'contemplative' in so far as Kant is talking about the mind being active not the body, this being the case of the physically extreme. Yet the point stands that the sublime is not *restful* contemplation. Third, even if we wish to preserve a certain meditative state, the way to the sublime is more complex than the model of passive reflection suggests. We must consider *how* we get to face the greatness of nature, which varies on an individual basis depending on the activity. Engaging in some sort of extreme sport or endeavor will enhance such momentous encounters in ways and to a degree that the passive approach cannot fathom. In some instances, the possibility to absorb and appreciate the sublime will be intensified after the activity in question comes to fruition. In other cases this will happen both during and after, and at other times solely or primarily while, one is engaged in it. Climbing to the top of a Himalayan peak will reward the mountaineer as he straddles the narrow rim at the peak with an awe-inspiring view of a horizon filled with mountain range after mountain range. Had he taken Davies's helicopter ride he would still have been awestruck, but I deem *ceteris paribus* that getting to the same spot after climbing the face of the mountain and overcoming numerous challenges will deliver the more intense, richer, and deeper experience. All along the way he will have been exposed to that fear and delight *as* he made his way up, and moreover the resulting feeling of exhilarating awe will be increased manifold courtesy of the accumulation of tension. In skydiving the extreme comes hand in hand with the sublime preponderantly *as* one performs the activity: once on the ground there is exhilaration, but there is not an encounter with the sublime, the chance to take in the outrageous interplay between the largesse of the horizon and the awareness of the fast approaching ground lies in those precious few seconds before the parachute deploys. In this instance one 'meditates' in the very intensity of the activity.

To further validate this last point I resort to the figure of the expert, someone with ample experience and skill in the pertinent adventurous pursuit. To an outside observer the performance may look fast, chaotic, disordered. By contrast, skilled practitioners of sports know that sometimes a sort of *Zen* state can be achieved wherein time decelerates and one feels the situation unfold in slow motion, even as a disembodied observer. In those moments one can contemplate and sense the sublime in a fashion foreclosed to the 'quiet wanderer': for it is intense yet meditative. We can contrast the veteran with the novice. His lack of ability means that likely the first few, or many, times the element of fear will overpower anything else, thereby excluding enjoyment and ultimately awe in favour of post-activity relief expressed with exaggeration.[14] It is not that the old hand does not experience fear, sometimes more than the 'new hand,' for she may take things further and is more aware of what is at risk, yet her ability and experience enables her to perform 'feats' unthinkable for the newbie. On rare occasions, once my skills had developed sufficiently, as I ran right in front of a bull there was a dream-like quality to the run soaked in trepidation and exhilaration: I was able to react to the movements of the bull as if I anticipated them, managing to dodge the thrust of the horn at the last moment instinctively yet deliberately.

Landing

> And I want to say anything is possible. Comma. You know.
>
> (Frank Bruno in Sherrin, 1995: 317)

I have proposed that the sublime sheds light on the conceptual framework and 'postmodern sensibility' that is at work behind the appeal of the extreme. After the Enlightenment, the sublime placed itself at the heart of a modernist outlook showing a novel and enriching way of relating to the natural environment, both aesthetically and physically. The West became enthralled with the might and dangerousness of nature. With it came an attitude of daring exploration of limits: those of nature and our own. This behavior is mirrored nowadays by 'the extreme.' Just as the initial pain and fear felt when facing the sublime mix with pleasure and turn to elation, so is the process replicated in the experience of the extreme and risky activity. Central to both is a paradoxical stance that seeks an encounter with danger that is risky *and* safe. Nature appears as sublime when its overwhelming might makes it appear fearful yet we feel secure. The extreme also depends on this ability to securely court peril. Along with this comes an enriching understanding of life and of what is an intrinsically rewarding activity – regardless of what is at stake.

Let's return to the airplane for an impossible moment; a last peek, before we lose sight of it:

> *The time to jump has come: one by one the sky-divers are seemingly 'sucked out' the open door. Anja has explained to Kant how the 'chute' works.*
>
> *Spitless and speechless for once he stands there, frozen.*
>
> *'Hold on to your wig,' she yells, leans out of the door and disappears.*
>
> *Kant sighs, and, thinking that he really never did do much outside of Königsberg, approaches the gate, intensely scared yet feeling the intimations of a promised exhilaration ('I promise, Immanuel,' she had told him, 'the biggest rush, – er joy,' she had amended in answer to his puzzled look, 'of your life'). As he holds on to his wig with one hand, and the parachute ring with the other, Kant jumps out.*

The reader is now equipped to understand the conditions, the how and more importantly *why*, of what Kant is about to experience: *the* rush of his life.

Notes

1. I am grateful to the attendees of the conference session where I presented an earlier version of this chapter during the 30th Annual Meeting of the International Association for the Philosophy of Sport, State College, Pennsylvania, in October 2002.
2. As quoted by Bernard (Kant, 1951: 118, n. 20).
3. R. Rinehart and S. Pope (eds.) (2003) *The Encyclopedia of Extreme Sports*, ABC-Clio Inc.
4. As Allen Guttman (1979: 50), and Monroe Beardsley (1996: 182), point out this process and the ensuing theological controversy have been documented by Marjorie Hope Nicholson in *Mountain Gloom and Mountain Glory: The Development of the Aesthetics of the infinite* (Cornell University, 1959).

5. The sublime is a culturally emergent property that enables us to interpret a certain phenomenon so that pain and pleasure expand the realm of what is possible for us to experience. Contrary to Kant's own sense, it seems that its universality is conditional at best: all rational beings do not experience the world in the same way *de facto*, sublimely in this case, but are capable in *principle* of experiencing the sublime. Consider the Japanese appreciation of nature wherein, as Yuriko Saito explains, there is a complete and utter lack of sublime objects. The focus is on an emotive identification with nature and the transient, best exemplified by falling cherry blossoms rather than terrifying mountains (Saito, 1996: 141ff.).

6. Burke's and Kant's assertion that we are not actually in danger seems to contradict my stance. However, this is only apparently so. Below I will draw some distinctions between the extreme and the sublime that address this satisfactorily, I deem. Even in the stronger case, the extreme, I do not argue that the danger need be *actualized* it only need be an actual *possibility*.

7. For him there are three basic zones: (1) a safety zone where we are nowhere close to being harmed; (2) a danger zone where there coexist the risk of the danger being actualized and the dangerous phenomenon itself, e.g. a fall and the risk of falling; and (3) a trauma zone, where the danger becomes actualized as injury, loss, or even death (Apter 1992: 23). In addition, there is the dangerous edge, that invisible line that makes all the difference between enjoying the experience safely and being hurt. Last he presents the protective frame, a psychological barrier that we imagine along the dangerous edge. It is dynamic and can move further or closer from the edge depending on the circumstances, our level of confidence, the availability of others to help us, the materials at our disposal, etc. (ibid.: 23–4).

8. The analytic of the sublime largely resembles the one of the beautiful, but also evinces striking differences. First, the similarities: both types of predicates of aesthetic judgments are singular in form and claim universal validity; second, they both implicate a pleasure that is independent of sense or from a particular concept of the understanding (Kant, 1951: § 23) To these we can add that both are aesthetic reflective judgments, they arise out of our own subjectivity and they are 'independent' from the sensuous properties of objects. Next, the differences: first, whereas beauty is concerned with form and limits, sublimity is concerned with limitlessness; and second whereas beauty depends on a purposiveness of an object of nature, the sublime is 'an outrage on the imagination' (ibid.).

9. Kant uses the term 'comprehension' in a special manner lost to modern English readers. Cassirer illuminates the sense in which the concept is in be taken. 'Comprehension' in this context should not be taken to mean 'to understand,' but 'to put things together' (Cassirer 1970: 230–1). It is in this sense that Kant intends that there is a limit to our comprehension, wherein he grounds the feeling of the sublime.

10. I delve into the experience of the running of the bulls via an existential analysis in 'Between the Horns: A Dilemma in the Interpretation of the Running of the Bulls,' work in progress presented at the 32nd IAPS conference in Grapevine, Texas, September 2004.

11. In our postmodern world simulacra, the *appearance* of risk and resulting fear in this case, are often embraced as the real thing because we are not supposed to be able to tell the difference experientially. I beg to differ. The thrill is simply *apparently* as intense: a confrontation with and *awareness* of actual danger intensifies matters in a way precluded to a virtually dangerous scenario. Awareness of the replacement of the fierce lions in a safari by domesticated doppelgangers surely renders the encounter as less powerful. Moreover, choosing a replica (in this case disowning awareness so that we are ignorant of the appearance of danger) is tantamount to choosing a fake diamond: its intrinsic value, what we precisely appreciate it for, is gone. In our case the existential price we pay is an impoverished life experience. The extreme, this very postmodern phenomenon, ironically brings a measure of authenticity to this postmodern world infatuated by the replica.

12. Quoted in Keyes (1985) from *Fields of Fire*, a novel on Vietnam written by James Webb, who is a veteran.

13. I am grateful to Simon Eassom who pointed this out.

14. Thanks are expressed to Gunnar Breivik who brought this to my attention.

References

Apter, M. J. (1992) *The Dangerous Edge: The Psychology of Excitement*, Place. Free Press.

Beardsley, M. C. (1996) *Aesthetics from Classical Greece to the Present: A Short Introduction*, Tuscaloosa: University of Alabama Press.

Briffaud, S. (1994) 'Une mémoire du regard,' *Pyrénées Magazine*, Special Issue 'Les Pyrénées par les peintres,' 40–65.

Bullough, E. (1996) 'Psychical Distance,' in K. M. Higgins (ed.) *Aesthetics in Perspective*, Fort Worth, TX: Harcourt Brace & Co, 164–67.

Cassirer, E. (1970) *A Commentary on Kant's Critique of Judgment* (reprinted), New York: Barnes and Noble.

Davies, S. (1996) 'Why Listen to Sad Music if it Makes One Feel Sad,' in K. M. Higgins (ed.) *Aesthetics in Perspective*, Fort Worth, TX: Harcourt Brace & Co., pp. 389–96.

Dewey, J. (1980) *Art as Experience*, first printing, 23rd edn, New York: Wideview/Perigee Books.

Greenfeld, K. T. (1998) 'A Wider World of Sports,' *Time*, 80–1.

Guttmann, A. (1979) *From Ritual to Record*, New York: Columbia University Press.

Kant, I. (1951) *Critique of Judgement*, trans. J. H. Bernard, New York: Hafner Press.

Kant, I. (1991) *Observations on the Feeling of the Beautiful and the Sublime*, trans. J. T. Goldthwait, Berkeley: University of California Press.

Keyes, R. (1985) *Chancing It: Why We Take Risks*, Boston: Little, Brown, and Company.

Lyotard J.-F. (1991) *The Inhuman: Reflections on Time*, trans. G. Bennington and R. Bowlby, Palo Alto, CA: Stanford University Press.

Meier, K. (1995) 'An Affair of Flutes: An Appreciation of Play,' in W.M. Morgan and K. Meier (eds.) *Philosophic Inquiry in Sport*, Champaign, IL: Human Kinetics, pp. 120–35.

Meslay, O. (1999) 'Nouvelles Frontières,' *Beaux Arts Magazine*, 183: 56–63.

Ortega y Gasset, J. (1962) *History as a System and Other Essays toward a Philosophy of History*, trans. H. Weyl, New York: W.W. Norton & Co.

Saito, Y. (1996) 'The Japanese Appreciation of Nature,' in K. M. Higgins (ed.) *Aesthetics in Perspective*, Fort Worth, TX: Harcourt Brace & Co., pp. 140–7.

Sherrin, N. (1995) *The Oxford Dictionary of Humorous Quotations*, Oxford: Oxford University Press.

Stoppard, T. (1967) *Rosencrantz: and Guildenstern are Dead*, New York: Grove Press.

Sydnor, S. (2003) 'Soaring', in S. Sydnor and R. Rinchart (eds.) *To the Extreme: Alternative Sports, Inside and Out*, Albany, NY: State University of New York Press (referenced from manuscript).

Tolkien, J. R. R. (2002) *The Return of the King*, reissue, London: HarperCollins Publishers.

Can BASEjumping be morally defended?

Gunnar Breivik

Introduction

Modern society puts more and more weight on security and safety. In some ways life has become much safer and more secure, at least in Western societies. At the same time there arc new dangers imposed by our industrialized society (Giddens, 1990). There are new sources of risk like nuclear weapons, chemical pollution and radioactivity. The increased perception and awareness of risk has lead Beck (1992) to call modern society 'the risk society'. These authors talk about imposed risks that threaten our lives and therefore should be considered as negative factors in modem society. This line of argument is in keeping with most of the literature on risk related to risk management in business, technology and economy. Risk is normally considered as something negative and unacceptable that should be avoided (Yates and Stone, 1992). On the other hand risks also come as freely chosen risks in risk sports or extreme sports (Cashmore, 2000; Rinehart, 2000). Innovation and modern technology open up possibilities for new types of sports and activities. This type of risk often has a positive flavour for those who are involved in the activities (O'Connell, 1993).

Most sports are relatively safe. They havc low or medium risk levels. The high-risk sports can be defined as sports where you have to reckon with a possibility of serious injury or death if you are not doing the right things. Such sports are downhill skiing, rock climbing, sky diving, Formula 1, white-water kayaking. In the following I will simply use the term 'risk sports' to refer to these high-risk sports. The questions I will raise here are: Can risk sports be considered valuable? Do they represent good value? Can risk sports be morally defended? Are they morally and legally acceptable? I will try to answer the questions by presenting some prima facie arguments that are based on what I take to be shared intuitions. I will first not use a definite and specific ethical theory, but rather test and sharpen our intuitions and common arguments *pro et con*. I will then bring in two theories, first Amartya Sen's theory of goal rights and then Feinberg's analysis of the moral acceptability of personal risk taking.

Forms of risk taking

Risk taking can be a part of different actions and projects. We can distinguish between three forms of risk taking:

1 pro-social risk taking where risk is taken for the sake of others (typical are

situations encountered by firemen or policemen who try to save or protect other people under risky or dangerous circumstances);

2 anti-social risk taking where people act in ways that can hurt or endanger other people (typical are situations produced by smugglers, burglars, violent criminals, soldiers); and

3 ludic risk taking where the risk is taken for the sake of one's own interests and satisfaction (here we find situations produced and encountered by sky divers, climbers, gamblers).

This is in accordance with Gomà-i-Freixanet (2001) who defines three groups of risk takers or risk taking:

> Thus, the antisocial physically risky activity is one in which the activity can result in harm to others, the prosocial physically risky activity is one in which the behaviour can result in benefit to others, and in the physically risky sports group, the behaviour may only harm oneself.
> (Gomà-i-Freixanet, 2001: 1,402)

Gomà-i-Freixanet finds interesting personality differences between the three groups, while they have in common a sensation seeking profile; they like to experience novel, intense and complex sensations and experiences and are willing to take risks to acquire such experiences. These different forms of risk taking are normally considered to have different moral status in our moral space.

The moral space

In our lives we operate in a moral space exemplified in the illustration in Figure 7.5.1, We seek positive values and we avoid negative values. In between there is a grey zone which the Greek philosophers called the *adiafora*: those things that are neither good nor bad but indifferent to the good life. There are different ambitions in the moral space. Some norms in the Christian ethic are very ambitious as, for instance, in the Sermon on the Mount. The ambition goes vertically upwards when demanding 'You shall be perfect as your heavenly Father is perfect.'

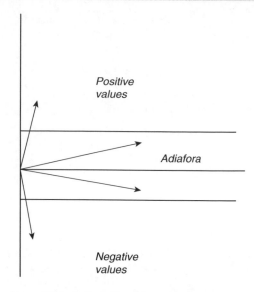

Figure 7.5.1. An illustration of the moral space.

Similarly there can be extreme negative values attained by people like Hitler who caused the Holocaust. Both in the positive and negative moral space there are actions with varying degrees of goodness and badness. The adiafora zone can be drawn broadly or narrowly depending upon the ethical worldview of the society. Some types of ethics have very precise and encompassing norms leading to few and narrow neutral zones. Others leave more space to ludic risk taking which involves play, experimentation and actions that are neither good nor bad.

In relation to the three forms of risk taking one could very easily imagine that pro-social risk taking is placed among the positive values in the positive moral space. The anti-social risk zone is to be placed in the negative moral space and the ludic risk raking is to be placed in the adiafora zone. Or is this too simple?

Risk taking and risk sports

Risk taking can take place in a lot of sports. Based on the type and amount of risk taking, I distinguish between three groups of sport in relation to risk:

1 high-risk sports where as part of the activity one mast reckon with a possibility of

serious injury or death if things go wrong in one way or another (examples are sports like Formula 1, downhill, sky diving, climbing, white-water kayaking);

2 medium-risk sports where serious injury or death can be the result, but only under unfortunate circumstances (examples here are soccer, ice hockey, diving, gymnastics); and

3 low-risk sports where it is almost impossible to get seriously injured or to die (examples are tennis, golf, running).

Inside the three groups there are differences in relation to performance level, specific type of the activity and so on. There is a difference between ordinary sky diving and BASEjumping, or between indoor climbing and climbing in the Himalayas. To test our moral intuitions it is relevant to look at some extreme cases like solo climbing, Formula 1 racing, Russian roulette (where one has a one in six chance of dying) and BASEjumping.

BASEjumping is one of the most dangerous and extreme risk sports and is probably the sport that intuitively looks strangest and most extreme to the general public.[1] In many ways BASEjumping is taking place around a boundary situation, a situation at the edge, not only physically but also mentally and culturally. Lupton (1999) uses Hunter S. Thompson's concept 'edgework' to describe activities that 'take place around cultural boundaries: such as those between life and death, consciousness and unconsciousness, sanity and insanity and an ordered sense of self and environment against a disordered sense of self and environment' (Lupton, 1999: 151). BASEjumping is such an activity, especially since it

is also characterized by an emphasis on skilled performance of the dangerous activity, involving the ability to maintain control over a situation that verges on the complete chaos, that requires, above all, 'mental toughness', the ability not to give in to fear.

(ibid.: 151–2)

By definition BASEjumping is jumping off from solid objects like bridges, antennae, spans and earth. It started in its modern form on 18 August 1978 when Carl Boenish and three friends made the first modern leaps from El Capitan in Yosemite National Park in the USA.

Since then BASEjumping has spread worldwide (www.baseclimb.com/BASE_history.htm).

A test case: BASEjumping in Norway

In the discussion below I will use material from the history of BASEjumping in Norway, whose steep mountains make it a popular place for the sport. The Troll Wall in Romsdalen and Kjærag in Lysefjorden are well-known and attractive places for BASEjumpers. Both have 1,000 metre vertical walls. In Norway the first BASEjump from Bruraskaret in the Troll Wall took place on 23 July 1980 by a group of Finnish jumpers. A month later the first two Norwegians jumped. In 1986 it was prohibited by law to jump in the Troll Wall. At that time 352 jumps had been performed. After 1986 the jumping continued secretly and illegally, often in the dusk or at dawn. In the period since 1986 around 50 illegal jumps have been performed every year. In total around 5,000 BASEjumps have been performed each year since the mid-90s. From 1980 to 2002, 13 persons have died, 8 in Kjærag and 5 in the Troll Wall. When BASEjumping started, a conflict broke out between ordinary sky divers and BASEjumpers which led to the exclusion of BASEjumpers from the skydiving federation. Subsequently, the BASEjumpers started their own federation.

The media focus on BASEjumping has been strong since the start. First of all it was incomprehensible to the public that some people, of their own free will, would jump off mountains. Then came the accidents and the rescue dramas. The secret jumping in the Troll Wall made good stories in the media. Because of the media focus there has been a continuous debate about whether jumping should be legally prohibited both in the Troll Wall and also at other places like the most popular jump site, Kjærag. Presently it is prohibited to jump in the Troll Wall although it is allowed in other places.

The media often portray risk sport people as young irresponsible bohemians who travel around with a high-risk sporting lifestyle. In Norwegian BASEjumping the fact is almost the opposite. Mæland (2002) conducted an in-depth study of Norwegian BASEjumpers, their background, motives and characteristics and

483

found that many were academics, family people, even doctors. Nine of sixteen informants had girlfriends or boyfriends. Four jumpers out of sixteen had children. These jumpers said the risk profile changed once they had children. They became even more careful, but could not stop. The jumping was essential for their quality of life.

Even if many Norwegian BASEjumpers are resourceful people they constitute a heterogeneous group. And some of their characteristics appear to be paradoxical. As a group they are high sensation seekers who love intense stimulations and are willing to take risks. On the other hand they characterize themselves as control freaks. Because BASEjumping is very dangerous they have to be obsessed with control and safety. Probably because of the extreme character of the sport these strong individualists feel that they constitute a group with strong bonds of friendship. According to Mæland (2002) they look at themselves as a distinct community: BASEjumpers are a spontaneous, emotional and often ecstatic group of people.

Similarly, the descriptions of risk takers are often contradictory. On the one hand they are serious people trying to build character and gain deep insights. O'Connell (1993), describing some of the leading climbers in the world, says:

> As a group, then, they should not be seen so much as thrill seekers but as truth seekers. They climb not just for the adrenaline or exercise, but for the opportunity to gain insight into themselves and the world around them. Long, exhausting, nervy routes serve as purgatories through which they must pass to test and perfect their character.
>
> (O'Connell, 1993: 11)

On the other hand BASEjumpers have a 'relaxed attitude' to regulations and rules. And some of them are very egoistic and show lack of empathy.

Ture Bjørgen is the leader of the alpine rescue team in Lysefjorden who rescue BASEjumpers who have had accidents at Kjærag and other places. He is not against BASEjumping as such but has a dislike for parts of the BASEjumping subculture. He has found BASEjumpers cynical and cold in their attitudes towards other jumpers who have had accidents. Some of them continue to jump while dead jumpers are carried out from the wall. Bjørgen thinks many of them are egoistic adrenaline junkies who are only interested in their own goals. They do not pay respect to other jumpers and the rescue team. Some of them look at jumping as a survival game where the weakest are taken out by accidents and only the best survive. Bjørgen (1999) cites the brother of a dead BASEjumper: 'We have a right to be pissed off. The jumpers think they do their things with full safety. This is bullshit! And then they talk about a beautiful death! What is beautiful about death?' (Bjørgen, 1999: 177).

In contrast, Simon Jakeman (a pioneer in BASEjumping) talks vividly about the strong feelings of ecstasy, the eternal 'now', the fear, and the dangers of BASEjumping (Jakeman, 1992). Mæland (2002) thinks BASEjumping is in many ways a sublime experience. It has all the elements of the sublime – the enormous nature, the attraction and repulsion, the feeling of freedom, the aspect of eternity and the unending. Jumpers tell how the tension builds up in the days before the jump, how they are scared to death when standing at the edge. The experience they have is almost beyond imagination. In the first few seconds after jumping off they feel that time stands still. It is an 'eternal now'. Then speed picks up and they get the feeling of falling, the big wall, the pressure of air. After speed and action and the landing comes the period of the warm comforting 'emotional high'. The experience of BASEjumping is so special and so extreme, according to the jumpers, that they get hooked. But they get hooked on something that is very different from what the public imagine.

For many people cannot understand why others, of their own free will, choose BASEjumping. It is simply incomprehensible to them. Some consider BASEjumpers selfish, irresponsible and stupid. This is reinforced by the fact that BASEjumpers constitute a small minority group, in some countries a deviant subculture that is regarded with suspicion. Many people feel sympathy with the rescue teams, who, they think, have to put their lives in danger. Some rescue operations are not only dangerous but also expensive. There is also a considerable amount of sympathy with the family of the jumpers who are anxious and afraid of accidents and who suffer deeply if the jumpers die. How good and relevant are these arguments?

Arguments for and against BASEjumping

There are several types of ethical argument that can be used against BASEjumping. First there is the paternalism argument which implies that individuals do not know what they are doing. They need to be guided by those who know better what is in their deeper interests. Against this BASEjumpers might maintain that they are not irrational, what they are doing is not unreasonable from their point of view, that they choose this freely, and it is part of their idea of a good life. A second argument is a moralistic one. It says that BASEjumpers are egoistic and selfish; they present a bad example for others. Here the BASEjumpers could say that they think they are not. But if they are morally weak and bad role models then that is an argument that also can be made against performers in other risk sports.

Many arguments are of a more intuitive type and rely on feelings. One strong intuitive argument from many people against BASEjumping is that it is too risky. It is not morally right to experiment in this way with one's life. On the other hand there is a strong feeling among many of us that people must have a right to live their lives in the manner they choose. They must be allowed to follow their own values. Freedom to lead the life one wants is an important value.

One special follow-up to the argument about risk, is that the risks entertained must be appropriate. One could argue that people must be able to enjoy the climbing but the risk should be eliminated or made as small as possible. There are two arguments against this: one is an empirical one and the other is normative. In many cases it is not possible to enjoy the climbing, for instance in the Himalayas, without having the risks. The other argument is more about the goal one seeks. For some people the risk is part of the experience one seeks. To be able to control one's body and mind and perform complicated and difficult things under stress, knowing that things can go wrong, is part of what they seek. In the case of BASEjumping the experience is impossible to have without the risk and for most BASEjumpers the risk is an intrinsic and valuable part of the experience itself.

Another type of argument is that the experience must be worth the risks. Also here the BASEjumpers most probably will answer that they continue with BASEjumping because the experience outweighs the risks. They cannot find other ways to have the same strong experience and with lower levels of risk. But have they tried hard enough to find other arenas, other activities? Or did they stay with BASEjumping because this is where they happened to land, and they stayed because the rewards were high enough and worth the risk?

Yet BASEjumping is not only about the jumpers and their jumping. The surroundings are affected; families, friends and rescue personnel to mention a few. BASEjumping is inherently dangerous and some jumpers die. This is a loss for the family. But, in the case of a death, it is not only about the grief and sorrow in case of a death; it is also the constant apprehension, the stress and fear of possible accidents. Against this one can argue that the harm to families must be weighed against the benefits to the jumpers. Families understand that if this is a very important activity for the BASEjumper, this is the life she wants to lead, they are more willing to accept the fear and anxiousness they feel.

The extreme Himalayan climber Reinhold Messner answers the question about the balancing of the need to take risks and the relation to families and loved ones in the following way: 'I think we have the right to do it. I think it's fair.' Messner maintains:

> it's never a tragedy for the one who dies, because the one who dies is not living the tragedy. The tragedy is only with those who survive. But a climber who is married or who is growing up in a family is evolving like this, so the family sees and lives with it.
>
> (O'Connell, 1993: 26)

On the other hand there are people who find that the need to take personal risks is performed without the proper attitude, without consideration of the consequences for family and friends. The brother of a dead BASEjumper said:

> In the ecstasy of joy and in clouds of adrenaline after a jump some of them completely take off, lose all inhibitions and forget the world around them, including their good friend who lies smashed in the scree, the girlfriends, the mothers and maybe the kids who are left behind. That the jumper 'died while he did what he liked best' is a meagre comfort.
>
> (Bjørgen, 1999: 177, my translation)

If one accepts a weighing of the interests then the situation and the context must be analysed further. How many family members are scared? How close are they? How deep and strong is the fear? Are they properly informed about the probability of accidents? Do they overestimate the risk? One could also ask whether it would be better if they did not know about the BASEjumping. But then what about honesty and trust as important values in close human relations? Does this mean that it is more acceptable to BASEjump if you are (1) alone in life; (2) old; and (3) terminally ill? Is the number of people who will suffer and the amount of suffering relevant? There is also a further aspect here which merits consideration. If the BASEjumper dies the family may lose economic support. Perhaps more importantly, there is the loss of emotional support, the loss of a father or a mother who are the basis of family care, life and identity. This means that BASEjumpers with small children have both an emotional and economic obligation that applies over and above those cases where one simply affects parents or brothers and sisters.

The deeper question here is whether concerned and worried families can cripple a person's right to flourish and live a life that is rich for him/her, a life where BASEjumping is a central part. Questions like the ones we have been discussing are very often asked in relation to people who are involved in activities that are considered to be extreme, strange, or incomprehensible to most people. BASEjumping is such an activity. People cannot understand that such an activity can be valuable, enjoyable and of central importance in a person's life. And in addition the risk of the activity is overestimated. But questions that are asked of BASEjumpers could also be asked of people involved in risky activities that are more common and understandable, like heavy drinking, fast driving and unprotected sex.

One of the arguments often used in the public debate is that BASEjumping leads to unnecessary risks for the rescue people. BASEjumpers get injured and need to be rescued from steep mountain faces by helicopter pilots and climbers who place their lives at risk trying to save injured jumpers. Very often they become the heroes in the eyes of the public. Against this one could argue that the rescue teams are not obliged to risk their lives.

They are involved in rescue of their own free will. Many of them are themselves risk takers. They too need challenges. It is therefore unfair when the BASEjumpers alone get the blame while the praise is reserved for the rescue people. It should be added here that in some cases the rescue personnel are professionals and therefore there is a pressure on them to do the job. In addition rescue personnel may feel the strong silent 'ethical call' from an injured or even dying person being stuck in a vertical wall. This makes it difficult to say no and not risk one's life.

Some of these problems can be solved by making clear contracts with BASEjumpers about what they can expect if they happen to get stuck in the wall and become injured. But the possibility of risky rescue operations can never be eliminated. The conscience of a society cannot tolerate the fact that badly injured BASEjumpers may hang helplessly in a vertical wall, even if they have no insurance or clear contract about rescue. But the same sort of reasoning should then apply to people in less heroic situations, for instance on ski trips in the mountains. In Norway a lot of people spend their Easter holidays in the mountains and dangerous rescue operations are sometimes the result of bad planning, stupid decisions or a sudden change in weather conditions. These people, too, should then be blamed, but rescued.

Rescue operations may be dangerous for the rescuers but they are also expensive for society at large. Against this argument there are several counterarguments. First there should be insurances for BASEjumping. If this is impossible the jumpers could be asked to pay for rescue operations themselves. This has already happened in some cases. In a broader picture BASEjumping is a commercial success through films, videos, entertainment for the public. This means that for society at large the economic benefits far outweigh the costs.

Backing our intuition with theories

To varying degrees our intuitions can be backed by more general theories. This is often made in an *ad hoc* way, where the weight in the end is on the intuitions and not on the theories. Two main theoretical approaches are often drawn in as support for our intuitions. According to deontological reasoning it must be possible to universalize our moral judgements. Could one wish BASEjumping to become an activity for all? The BASEjumpers would probably say yes – at least some of them. I am not sure whether people that are not BASEjumpers are willing to accept BASEjumping as an activity for all. But is this the relevant question? We should rather ask: could one wish BASEjumping to be an activity open for those people that want to be BASEjumpers? An anti-paternalistic view would imply that people should have freedom to live the kind of lives they want. There are good reasons to look at BASEjumping as morally acceptable and as having specific values. There are not good enough arguments to prohibit BASEjumping by law.

If we use a utilitarian background and look at BASEjumping in a cost-benefit perspective, I think the results are positive. For the jumpers themselves there is a positive result. The joy, the mastery, the friendships, the conquering of fears, the breaking of limits and so on, more than outweigh the fear, the risk, the bad conscience for worried parents, children, partner. For the families of the jumpers the result: to varying degrees may be negative. For the public the result is positive. BASEjumping has become good entertainment through films, commercials, TV, magazines. This more than outweighs the costs and risks of rescue operations and hospitalization.

One could put BASEjumping to a sort of existential test by asking: Would I like to BASEjump myself? For my part the answer is yes. I would have liked to do it. Would I have done it when I was young rather than old? If I die when I am young I lose much more, many years of experiences. However I would have been fitter, more capable, have stronger sensations and positive emotions. I may be more scared when I am old, and less capable of coping.

Would I prefer to BASEjump when or if I was terminally ill? Would that give me a beautiful death if I failed? Would it be acceptable for me to take my life during a beautiful BASEjump? I can commit suicide by placing myself in a situation with good chances of dying, like a difficult BASEjump. But is that not cowardice? If I want to die, it might be argued, I should do it simply and properly. This does not mean that

BASEjumping *per se* is fuelled by a secret death wish. The BASEjumper wants to live life to its fullest extent, controlling herself, mind and body, facing a possible death. BASEjumping could rather be considered the ultimate confirmation of life.

The next question is then: Would I like my son or daughter to BASEjump? My own answer is no. But would I stop them? The answer is no. My concern and fear should be kept in place. If they have a strong desire to jump they should be free to do it. Human beings should have the freedom to choose the good life, even if for others that is a life that is full of risks and actions that are difficult to understand.

Instead of developing further the intuitions and the arguments for and against, backed by general moral theories, I now turn to a couple of approaches that are more specifically designed to solve some of the problems related to the right to take risks. In this way I hope to progress further in my effort to find a consistent and satisfactory answer to the moral problem of BASEjumping and other risk activities.

Amartya Sen's theory of 'goal rights'

In the discussion so far, I have tried to balance the rights of BASEjumpers against the interests of other parties: the family, rescue teams, the public. This could be regarded as an unclean mixture of deontological and utilitarian (cost-benefit) procedures. People have rights. If people have a right to take personal risks, and BASEjumping is such a personal risk, then people have right to BASEjump. But what then about other considerations, the interests of other parties, are they irrelevant? Not necessarily. Amartya Sen (1986) argues for a position that I find relevant here. He acknowledges rights-like considerations that are purely instrumental. They can be advocated because they have favourable consequences. But they are not really rights according to Sen; they are, rather, rules with a moral justification. We find such rights argued by utilitarian philosophers who will not accept moral rights as such.

Philosophers like Nozick however think that moral rights do exist. These are 'rights that are intrinsically valuable, irrespectively of whether they also have instrumental justification'

(Sen, 1986: 155). This means that if there is a moral right to take a personal risk like BASEjumping it would he morally wrong to stop the person from taking such a risk, no matter how good the consequences of stopping the person would be.

Sen instead advocates what he calls a goal-right system where 'the right to take personal risks can compete with other goals' (Sen, 1986: 167). Only in cases like that of Robinson Crusoe is it relevant to see personal rights in isolation from other persons and their interests. The right to take personal risks is an important right. Sen considers rights as capabilities to do this or that or to be this or that, such as the freedom to move around or to know freedom from hunger. Other persons and their interests, however, can come into conflict with such rights or capabilities and they must therefore he weighed comparatively.

Sen (1986) discusses the case of seat-belts and the right not to use seat-belts. This right must be weighed against how others are affected. Sen lists five types of effects, similar to the ones we have discussed in relation to BASEjumping. These are injury effects, psychological effects, opinion-offending effects, medical effects, economic and social effects. Sen finds good reasons in most cases to accept seat-belt regulations because the importance in people's lives is relatively small whereas to prohibit climbing would limit people much more in an important activity in their life.

The dynamic approach that Sen takes opens up new problems for our moral appraisal of BASEjumping. Rights seem to be unstable or not robust enough, and vulnerable to *ad hoc* interference. For instance if a BASEjumper has a large family of emotionally unstable persons will the added psychological suffering of these hysteric people outweigh the right of the jumper to live the risky life he or she wants? Sen will not accept the simple adding up of consequences like these but looks instead at how serious and important they are, what place they should have in a broader picture.

Another problem is related to interindividual variations. Sen draws our attention to differences between individuals. This means that if BASEjumping is very important for a person, the central goal in life, and the person has few relatives, then he is in a better position to have his right to BASEjumping accepted than

a person for whom BASEjumping is a hobby and who has many relatives who are concerned and apprehensive about the jumping. Sen thinks that people have the right to take personal risks but that they must be weighed against other interests. 'The Importance of the right to take risks varies with the nature of the activity involved. It also varies from person to person' (Sen, 1986: 167). Sen's theory thus becomes dynamic and flexible but may in many cases lack the clear direction that many people feel they need when it comes to guiding risky behaviour. A theory that goes many steps further in giving clear guidance based on a classification of cases through inherent principles is presented by Feinberg (1986) in his discussion of possibilities and limitations of personal liberty.

Feinberg and the discussion of personal liberty

Feinberg sees four principles that can be used to limit personal liberty and which can legitimize the coercion of people in certain directions:

1 the Harm Principle states that we need to prevent harm to persons other than the actor;
2 the Offence Principle says that it is necessary to prevent hurt or offence (as opposed to injury or harm) to others;
3 Legal Paternalism means that it is lawful to prevent a person from hurting or harming herself; and
4 Legal Moralism states that it is necessary to prevent inherently immoral conduct whether or not such conduct is harmful or offensive to anyone.

Feinberg will only accept the first two of these principles. It is only our relation to others and the concern for the welfare of other people that can be used to limit or coerce people. Feinberg argues that if a person wants to hurt herself this should not be criminalized. A consequence should then be that smoking cigarettes or BASEjumping in the Troll Wall should not be prohibited by law. This is in line with John Stuart Mill's view and the liberal position which implies that 'the attempt even of a genuinely benevolent state to impose upon an adult an external conception of his own good is almost certain to be self-defeating' (Feinberg, 1986: 58).

Some decisions and actions are relevant only to oneself; other decisions are relevant to others. Since no human is an island, most actions are other-regarding to varying degrees. One must therefore speak about directly, chiefly or primarily self-regarding actions. The question is to what degree BASEjumping is self-regarding. I would maintain that it is directly and primarily self-regarding since the jumping as such is an individual act that does not interfere with other people during the jump itself. It is however other-regarding in relation to family, friends and rescue personnel, especially if accidents occur. As we have already seen, the problem is how much weight should be put on the indirect relation to other? How strong are the other-regarding aspects?

Many philosophers, in addition to Feinberg, think that human beings have goals that are built into our lives, a potential or a life project that should be realized. The talents we have should unfold, our skills should develop and blossom, our ideals and goals should be fulfilled. A person does not always know what the good life is. According to the liberal tradition, however, no one is in a better position to know what is best for an actor than the actor herself. Philosophers like Plato, Aristotle, Rousseau, Hegel and Mill identify the highest good with self-fulfilment. Other versions of personal good are achievement or perfection, contentment, happiness.

People not only have the right to choose which goals and highest goods to pursue, they also have a right to pursue it in the way they want. People have a right to autonomy and sovereignty, the right to make their own decisions. What is the relation between autonomy and the good life? Are they in accordance with each other? Do we use our freedom to fulfil our lives? According to Feinberg there are four views on the relation between freedom and the good life. A first view states that they are always in accordance with each other and therefore the best way to forward a person's own good is to give her unlimited freedom in self-regarding matters. A second view says that they are usually in accordance, but in rare cases where they are not, the person's own good has priority over self-determination. A third possibility is that they are usually in accordance, but in the rare

cases where they do not correspond, the person's right to take her own decisions has priority over the good life. The fourth view states that they are usually in accordance, but, in rare cases where they are not, one must balance the person's right to her own decisions against her own good, weighing them intuitively against each other. This last view is close to that of Amartya Sen which we discussed earlier.

Feinberg opts for the third solution. It means that in certain situations we must accept that people act against their own best long-term interests. There may be many reasons for such acts. Sometimes people act without enough information. On other occasions short-term interests may determine personal actions. I agree with Feinberg's position here. In relation to BASEjumping this view entails that we should allow BASEjumpers to perform their acts without stopping them, even if BASEjumping is not a fulfilment. Their acts may even be in their own deeper interests. BASEjumping may be part of their own self-fulfilment.

Reasonable risk

One of the central problems in relation to voluntary risk taking is whether the risk is reasonable or not in relation to what one wants to achieve. Could BASEjumpers not have achieved the same, reached their goals, through less risky acts? There are five aspects that according to Feinberg need to be looked at. First we need to find the degree of probability for harm or injury as a result of the action. Then we must ask how serious the harm that may be the result of the action is. How probable is it that I will reach my goal through the action? And what is the value of the goal? How important is it to me? Finally we must ask how necessary the risk is. Could I have reached my goal through other, less risky, alternatives?

These points could be considered before a course of risky action is taken – if there is time. And one could see that an increase in the probability of harm and/or in the seriousness of the harm renders the action less reasonable. What is harder to judge, at least from the outside, is how important the goal is and how closely the action is connected with the goal. How important is BASEjumping to me? And is it only through BASEjumping that I can get what I really want? Are there less risky alternatives? And is it only through jumping at the really difficult, dangerous spots that I fulfil my deeper wishes, reach my goals? In many cases there seems to be a developmental process where BASEjumpers need new challenges, more difficult and demanding places to jump from. The goal itself moves me: it becomes deeper as one reaches new levels of mastery, experiences qualitatively richer emotions or the ultimate high. And one finds oneself needing new and more difficult challenges to reach these deeper goals. It is a dynamic interplay of goals and ways to reach the goals and it is not stable. For some people BASEjumping and the deeper goals are tied together in such ways that there are simply no alternatives to BASEjumping. For others there may be alternative roads. We know that high sensation seekers generally experiment and get involved in several and even many high-risk activities. One may even, as one progresses in life, acquires a partner and perhaps children, find that one should reduce the probability of risk, the seriousness of possible harm and injury, and take up other sports than BASEjumping, see if there are alternatives that are less risky. Others, however, will then feel that the goal slips away, the rewards diminish, they do not reach deep levels of satisfaction.

Feinberg maintains that the state should not prevent people from committing risky actions, not even extremely risky actions, simply because they are risky. If the state should prohibit taking such risks, it must be on the ground that the risk is extreme 'and, in respect to its objectively assessable components, manifestly unreasonable to the point of suggesting impaired rationality' (Feinberg, 1986: 103). As I have argued earlier, BASEjumpers are not in this category and BASEjumping should not be prohibited.

Irrational versus unreasonable

Nevertheless some may think that BASEjumpers perform actions that are unreasonable. Some go further and think they are irrational. There is, however, an important distinction to be observed here. People that act irrationally perform actions that are:

> inappropriate means to his own ends, invalid deductions from his own premises, gross

> departures from his own ideals, or actions based on gross deductions from own premises, gross departures from his own ideals, or actions based on gross delusions and factual distortions.
>
> (Feinberg, 1986: 106)

It would be very hard to argue seriously that BASEjumpers are irrational even if they may seem (or even are) unreasonable. People that are fully normal and rationally competent take unreasonable choices. When we say that choices are unreasonable we do it in a relation to a standard that we think is better. And we indicate that we would not have performed the action had we been in the other person's shoes. In this sense many or even most people think that BASEjumpers act unreasonably. They would not have done the same. Another important aspect here is that unreasonable does not mean unaccountable. We hold unreasonable persons responsible for their actions whereas irrational persons are not fully responsible but 'exculpated'. Irrationality seems to be connected primarily with the person, whereas unreasonableness is connected with single actions. Actions are irrational when they are performed by irrational persons. Unreasonable actions are performed by persons that are usually reasonable and rational. In relation to BASEjumping this means that BASEjumpers are not irrational even though many (or most) people think that BASEjumps are unreasonable actions. If this just means that they would not have done the same themselves, then this is merely a matter of individual preference. It cannot be used as a good reason for moral criticism.

Rational and unreasonable

We should remember that most people can be rational, yet perform actions that are unreasonable:

> Thousands of eminently rational and responsible persons, however, judge that it is not worth the inconvenience to fasten their seat belts in automobiles, or that reducing their risk of getting lung cancer does not justify foregoing the pleasures of cigarette smoking, judgements that I, for one, with all due respect, find unreasonable.
>
> (Feinberg, 1986: 106)

Therefore, we could say that BASEjumpers are rational yet perform actions that are unreasonable. This may however, be too weak. From their own point of view, from the perspective of their deeper life goals, they may thus act reasonably. If the experiences and the performance I seek in life is so intimately connected with BASEjumping that I see no other way to reach my goal or no way that is so satisfying, then it may be reasonable to be involved in BASEjumping.

However, we also have in our intellectual tradition an ideal of what philosophers and economists call 'the perfectly rational person', 'practical rationality' or 'economic rationality'. The perfectly rational actor has harmonious goals, weighs them against each other, maximizes his expected utility, chooses means with deliberation, and does not make choices with high costs that make actions unproductive. He does not make impulsive decisions, invest broadly, weigh short term and long term benefits, this year against next year. If such a person does something unreasonable, for instance drinks too much at a party, it is due to an intellectual mistake, a miscalculation.

In reality, however, we have individuals that are very far from such an ideal. They are not prudent and do not like long-term planning. They think the prudent life is boring, Feinberg says:

> Imprudence may not pay off in the long run, and impulsive adventurers and gamblers may be losers in the end, but they do not always or necessarily have regrets. Hangovers may be painful and set back one's efforts, but careful niggling prudence is dull and unappealing. Better the life of spontaneity, impulse, excitement, and risk, even if it be short, and even if the future self must bear the costs.
> (Feinberg, 1986: 109)

Feinberg thinks that such adventurers should not be denied the possibility to lead the type of life they want by saying that their preferences are not voluntary and not in the person's own, deep interest and so on. Even worse would be to admit that the person's preferences were genuine but not in accordance with prudence and the idea of a rational life project. That would mean not respecting autonomy and the right of people to lead the lives they want.

Feinberg made the now classic distinction between hard and soft paternalism. It is not clear that the soft version is paternalistic at all.

It is close to Feinberg's own views and implies that 'the state has the right to prevent self-regarding harmful conduct (so far it *looks* "paternalistic") *when but only when* the conduct is substantially nonvoluntary, or when temporary intervention is necessary to establish whether it is voluntary or not!' (Feinberg, 1986: 12).

Hard paternalism, on the other hand, means forcing people who are irrational or unreasonable in their actions. Feinberg rejects hard paternalism. He thinks instead that we should open up the moral space to the romantic and irrational in people. We are too much governed by the ideal of 'economic man'. If we can force people to become rational that is ethically a much bigger problem than allowing or enabling people to engage in actions that are irrational or imprudent. Feinberg sees rationality as did Hume and Rawls: rationality is related to choices of means to reach our goals and realize our preferences. But there is not only one way, but a variety of ways and means through which we can reach our goals. Different sets of life plans and lifelines can be developed. Some of our life goals are based on deep preferences tied to genetic makeup, early experiences, relationships to special persons and so on. We should accept diversity both in life goals and also in ways to reach our goals:

> Some people quite naturally prefer adventure and risk to tranquillity and security, spontaneity to deliberation, turbulent passions to safety. Instead of being ostracized as 'not rational', these givens should become part of the test for the rationality of subsequent wants that must cohere with them.
> (Feinberg, 1986: 111)

This means that a person who wants to live her life in strong colours must be judged according to that. For this person it is rational and reasonable to choose actions that cohere with these deep preferences and goals. This would lead to an acceptance of BASEjumping as a possible life project, a goal in a life that needs BASEjumping for fulfilment.

Concluding remarks

I started by asking whether risk sports could be valuable, whether they are morally acceptable or whether some of them should be prohibited by law. I used BASEjumping as a test case since it is one of the most extreme and risky sports. In order to answer the questions I presented some of the intuitive arguments that are most often used in the debate for and against BASEjumping. I then went on to discuss the more developed and systematic views of Sen (1986) and Feinberg (1986) on the right to take risks.

My conclusion is that BASEjumping should not be prohibited by law, as is the case now in many places. I think that people who BASEjump are not irrational. They need not be protected against themselves. There is no need to interfere in a paternalistic way. I also think that BASEjumping can be morally accepted provided the jumpers behave in a responsible manner. This means that the right to jump must be balanced against the interests of their families, friends, rescue personnel and so on. I think Sen's idea of goal-rights makes sense here. BASEjumping can be morally accepted provided the jumpers are aware of other responsibilities they have in their lives. This means that BASEjumping as such is not to be placed in the negative part of the moral space of Figure 7.5. 1. BASEjumping may, depending upon circumstances, be among the adiafora, in some cases in the negative space, but it can also represent important and worthwhile values in the lives of BASEjumpers. BASEjumping may for some people be an important part of a life project. It may be an important way to realize deeper life goals. Or rather it is a specification of the kinds of ends they pursue at the deepest level of meaningfulness for them.

This positive evaluation does not mean that the problems are dispelled. We have seen that even if many jumpers are resourceful and responsible people there are also selfish and cynical jumpers with a big narcissistic ego. The jumpers need to be aware of their responsibilities towards families and friends. There are problems related to risks and costs of rescue operations that need to he provided for through careful arrangements. But these are problems that can be solved in various ways and they do not as such stop BASEjumping from being an acceptable and even valuable activity.

Note

1. BASE is an acronym for the four categories of fixed objects BASE jumpers launch from – Buildings, Antennas, Spans (bridges) and Earth (cliffs). (See www.baseclimb.com/BASEjumping.htm.)

References

Baseclimb (2006) available online at http//www. baseclimb.com/BASE_history.htm (accessed 31 October 2006).

Beck, U. (1992) *Risk Society. Towards a New Modernity*, London: Sage Publications.

Bjørgen, T. (1999) 'Holdninger blant basehoppere' ('Attitudes among BASEjumpers'), available online at http://www.brv.no/sikkerhet-artikkel. asp?id=177 (accessed 31 October 2006).

Cashmore, E. (2000) *Making Sense of Sports*, 3rd edn, London and New York: Routledge.

Feinberg, J. (1986) *Harm to Self* (*The Moral Limits of Criminal Law*, vol. 3), New York and Oxford: Oxford University Press.

Giddens, A. (1990) *The Consequences of Modernity*, Stanford, CA: Stanford University Press.

Gomà-i-Freixanet, M. (2001) 'Prosocial and Antisocial Aspects of Personality in Women: A Replication Study', *Personality and Individual Differences*, 30, 1401–11.

Jakeman, S. (1992) *Groundrush*, London: Jonathan Cape.

Lupton, D. (1999) *Risk*, London and New York: Routledge.

Mæland, S. (2002) *B.A.S.E. En studie i samtidskultur. Ekstremt friluftsliv. Eksistensielle dilemmaer. Sublime opplevelser* (*B.A.S.E. A study in contemporary culture. Extreme outdoor life, existential dilemmas, sublime experiences*, Master thesis), Hovedfagsoppgave, Bø: Høgskolen i Telemark.

O'Connell, N. (1993) *Beyond Risk. Conversations with Climbers*, Seattle, OR: The Mountaineers.

Rinehart, R. E. (2000) 'Arriving Sport: Alternatives to Formal Sport', in J. Coakley and E. Dunning (eds.) *Handbook of Sport Studies*, London: Sage Publications.

Sen, A. (1986) 'The Right to Take Personal Risks', in D. MacLean (ed.) *Values at Risk*, Totowa, NJ: Rowman & Allanheld, pp. 155–70.

Yates, F. and Stone, E. R. (1992) 'The Risk Construct', in F. Yates (ed.) *Risk-Taking Behavior*, Chichester: John Wiley & Sons.

Sacred places

Raimond Gaita

Almost thirty years before I began to write this I thought of writing about human beings and their relation to nature by way of writing about my experiences in the mountains. Now, after so many years, I will do it in this chapter. It would be a strange bond with animals, I think, that was not at the same time an expression of a love of nature.

We were all exhausted. None of us, I think, had carried a pack before. I hadn't walked further than the corner shop since getting my driving licence five years earlier. Now we needed to rest after carrying packs of around thirty kilos for three days up and down steep tracks high in New Zealand's mountainous and densely forested Fiordland. We were there because a New Zealand friend had convinced me to go tramping, as they call it in New Zealand. While my companions were resting in the hut, I went alone for a short walk towards the ridge that defines one side of the Hollyford Valley. It was raining, but the wind was high and clouds swirled dramatically, parting every so often to reveal blue sky, encouraging my hope that when I reached the ridge I might be able to see across the valley—but when I got there, I could see nothing. Disappointed, I turned to return to the hut, but had taken only a few steps when something prompted me to turn around.

Through a break in the clouds, across the valley, I saw a mountain of dramatic nobility, trailing a snow plume. Her name was Mount Christina. Moved almost to tears by her beauty, I resolved I would become a mountaineer.

As soon as I returned to Australia I bought a climbing instruction book (the famous Blackshaw), boots, a rope, karabiners and slings, and with some anxious friends went in search of cliffs to climb. I recall vividly the first time when, on a beautiful early summer's morning, the same friend from New Zealand and I stood at the base of a cliff some eighty metres high in remote and dense Australian bushland, and with our hearts in our mouths tied on to the rope. As I laid my hands on the cliff face I experienced a sensation that I was to savour in years to come—the sensual feel of hands on warm rock, fingers tracing its contours to find a safe hold. I climbed the first ten metres or so and knew that we were committed. Pride alone would ensure that we would get to the top or fall.

Just as vividly I recall the comic scene that occurred only a month or so later when I was standing on a small ledge, some eighty metres above the ground, on a sheer and sometimes overhanging face. It was again a beautiful summer's day and I was enjoying the shade of an overhang as I surveyed the golden wheat fields of the Wimmera. I had tied myself to the rock face and was belaying my friend from New Zealand. From the amount of rope I had paid out I estimated that he was six or seven metres above me, but the overhang prevented me from seeing or hearing him. It seemed to me that it had been a long time since he had started the pitch, but though it was the first time he had led, the day was so glorious, the scenery so entrancing, and the adventure so exhilarating, that anxious thoughts had no room in my mind.

I think I had just started whistling a tune when a flake of rock fell past me. I hardly saw it disappear when I saw my friend plummeting silently behind it—because, he told me later, he was too terrified even to scream. Climbing the overhang had drained the strength from his arms, which began to feel like wooden blocks and he peeled off backwards, dislodging the flake as he did so. When I saw him flying past I was too shocked to do anything but hold the rope tight. I don't know how much rope slid through my gloved hands, but when it stopped, and I realised that he and I were still tied to each end of it and still high on the face rather than at the bottom of it, I whooped so loudly and repeatedly with pleasure that I must have been heard for miles across the wheat fields, perhaps all the way to Natimuk. Everything—the bowline knots which tied us to the rope, the figure-of-eight knot which anchored me to my belay, the chocks we placed in the crack to secure the belay—worked just as Blackshaw said it would if we did it properly. I could hardly believe it. The cost was merely a bone chipped in my friend's ankle as he crashed back into the face when I stopped his fall.

We were accused of being irresponsible, climbing like that without first serving an apprenticeship with experienced climbers. Perhaps we were, but climbing clubs were uncongenial to our anarchistic temperaments. And instinctively we knew that to face the challenge by ourselves, with only Blackshaw and the great climbers we had read about as companions, would yield to us an adventure of a kind and intensity we would surely miss if we had the comfort of someone experienced beside us. We would not have missed the adventure for the world.

Even so, I have often reflected on the accusation that we were irresponsible. I have never

taken it seriously when it comes from the kind of person who would weigh down young climbers with so many spare socks and emergency supplies that they are bound to be caught out after dark because their packs are too heavy. Nor by those—often the same people—who would wish the mountains always to have the appearance of danger but never the reality. Mountaineering is degraded unless the prospect of death is lucidly accepted. To discover after one has come close to death oneself or after a climbing partner has died that one climbed only because one never really believed that one would be killed is a demeaning experience for anyone who has climbed for any length of time. This is because, for most mountaineers the risk of being killed is integral to the experience that attracts them to the mountains. If we were immortal, mountaineering would not exist or only in a form unrecognisable to us. The risk that one might be killed is inseparable from the intensity of the joy that mountaineers sometimes experience and crave to experience again. It is a joy they cherish, but only insofar as they believe they really are prepared to die. If they should discover that it was an illusion, that in their hearts they never believed they would die, then those intense experiences would become worthless.

One can, of course, have experiences whose intensity depends on the risk of death soloing on a six-metre boulder or sky diving or driving a racing car. For most mountaineers however the intense joy is joy in the beauty of the mountains which they experience as a gift granted to them only because they have risked their life for it. This is romanticism, of course, with all that is suspect in it, but it is romanticism tempered by the disciplines of skill and concentration necessary to stay alive for more than a season in the high mountains.

Vulnerable to that romanticism, I never yielded entirely to it because for all the years that I climbed I was conscious of how deeply it upset my father. He never properly understood the reasons why I climbed and insofar as he did he scorned them. He would climb mountains too, he said, if it were necessary to secure food or seek medical help for his family, or for any other necessity presenting itself under the guise of duty. His attitude was one that dominated the European poor for whom necessity—especially the necessity to provide for one's family—could redeem and give dignity to a life whose crushing burdens would otherwise drive one to despair.

Of itself, that attitude was enough to make it offensive to him that I should choose to do what no sane person would do unless they had to. More deeply even than that, however, he was offended—sometimes I think he found it obscene—that I could (as he saw it) hold my life so cheap. Certain experiences in his life had brought him to look upon suicide as something terrible even when it caused no harm to anyone else or showed no obvious vice, such as cowardice in dealing with one's problems. I doubt that he would have thought it morally terrible. Schopenhauer caught something important in the attitude to suicide of people like my father when he said that the problem of suicide is too deep for morality.

My father believed the death of mountaineers to be terrible in much the same way as the death of someone who had committed suicide. The virtues of character that I praised in the great mountaineers were for him false virtues. In circumstances of genuine necessity, he said, the courage shown by mountaineers would be a virtue, but exercised in the reckless lack of regard for one's life and for one's responsibilities to others it was a counterfeit virtue. In this he reminded me of a philosopher who had commented on the ancient doctrine, to be found in Plato, Aristotle and later in Aquinas, that the virtues formed a unity, that one could not possess one unless one possessed at least many of the others. The philosopher argued that a person who risked his life for an evil cause might show courage, but courage was not a virtue in that person. My father's anger at my mountaineering exploits was in part fuelled by his fear for my safety, but it was also informed by the belief that it went against everything that had deepened his life and for which he was grateful.

Many mountaineers do of course bring what they do under various concepts of necessity. They say that they must climb, that they cannot give it up. Bonatti says in the passage I quoted earlier that he curses the need to prove himself, wishing he were free of it as most people are. For him, the need was not to prove himself to others, but to prove to himself that he possessed certain virtues even in the face of death—not death in the mountains but in the face of death period.

Most people live their lives without worrying about whether they would have the courage to face death. For others it can be very important to know what they would do if they were sitting on the train next to a person whose safety was threatened by a gang of thugs. Would they intervene, or would they sit quietly hoping to be left alone? What would they do, they ask themselves, if they lived in a country in which a neighbour might disappear in the middle of the night at the hands of the secret police? Physical courage has been devalued in most western democracies where people are lucky that moral courage seldom needs physical courage to support it. Most of the peoples of the earth are not so lucky.

It is not therefore because they are morbid that men like Bonatti are tortured by doubts about their courage. In the mountains they seek to know not what kind of mountaineer they are, but what kind of human being. That is why it is so shaming to know that one has proved a coward even when no one has suffered the consequences of one's cowardice. But the knowledge that cowardice led one to abandon one's partner is devastating. Friendships developed in the mountains between the most unlikely people may be sustained for a lifetime because each knew they could rely on the other's courage. And, of course, close friendships have been broken when one climber proved a coward. But though it is devastating to learn that one is a coward, to have been brave in the mountains is not a good reason for believing that one will be brave elsewhere. It is one thing to risk death, to face it courageously in a blizzard or when someone has fallen, and another thing to face it in the guise of a slowly degenerative illness, and another thing again to have the courage to remain human in a concentration camp.

Most mountaineers do not, I think, treat the mountain as merely a preferred environment in which to learn about themselves what racing-car drivers learn just as well. Most mountaineers (though perhaps not all rock climbers) love to be in the mountains and, though they may much prefer the mountains over the low country or even over the sea, their love of the mountains is an expression of their love of nature. Their love of nature shows itself in their love of the mountains just as a love of humanity can show itself in the way one loves one's friends, or a love of womanhood in the faithful love of one's wife. Their love of nature does not just add a further reason why they need to climb—it generally transforms that need. The self-knowledge they are compelled to seek is no longer just whether they have this or that virtue or failing. They seek to understand themselves through an understanding of the human condition and in the mountains they seek an understanding of that in its essential relation to nature.

Writing in a climbing journal in response to acrimonious arguments about climbing ethics—about when one may use a piton or a bolt, or when, in the Himalayas, one may use a ladder and so on—a distinguished British mountaineer pointed out that if one were to judge by the passions the argument aroused, one might be misled into thinking that it was not about climbing ethics, but about 'real ethics', by which be meant about morality, about rules (as he put it) that: govern our relations to people rather than to cliffs and mountains. Mountaineering literature is, of course, filled with heroic and noble stories of people sacrificing themselves for others, but debates about 'mountaineering ethics' are usually about the relatively artificial constraints that are now imposed on how one can legitimately get up a mountain or a rock face.

Though rock climbing may become an Olympic sport, the big arguments in mountaineering have not been about standards that might govern mountaineering practice as the rules of a sport govern the players. That is because all sports are artefacts, as it were, created by their rules and the rules can be made and modified by a committee. I do not mean to trivialise sport by saying that. Concern with character is fundamental to most sports. Our interest in them is hardly ever just an interest in how a human machine can perform, but how a human being can overcome weariness, demoralisation, temptations to be a bad loser or even to cheat. Were this not so sport would be of no interest. But no sportsperson, I think, can say in his defence, when he has broken the rules of the game, that his conscience required him to play as he did.

Mountaineers may be competitive and vain to an astonishing degree, but reflection about how one may legitimately climb a mountain is not intended to enhance the competitive dimensions of the practice. It is to alert the climbing fraternity about how advances in climbing techniques and in the technology of climbing equipment can threaten the respect for the mountain, a respect that at its best is deepened by a love of its beauty. That, rather than the fact that mountaineers tend to be an anarchistic lot, is the reason why disputes in mountaineering ethics can never be settled by a committee. Like morality, mountaineering ethics looks to be a matter of discovery rather than decision, and to some degree always a matter of conscience.

When a fine mountaineer climbed a peak in the Andes with a pneumatic hammer with which he inserted bolts and, I think, aluminium ladders, there was widespread anger that he had made it easy for himself. Deeper, though, was the outrage that he violated the mountain and betrayed the love of nature that should be at the heart of mountaineering.

The writer who distinguished between real ethics and mountaineering ethics was more wrong than right. It is an old ruse of morality to make it seem that only moral value can go deep with a morally serious person, and that such a person could never, except through confusion or self-deception, think that any other value could compete with moral value. The ruse has been remarkably successful. Because the need to climb is sometimes so transparently in conflict with family obligations—death may deprive a family of a parent—it is sometimes turned into a moral need in order to make it look more respectable when it conflicts with other moral obligations, Thus the mountaineer who is torn between his need to climb and the responsibilities to his family begins to look like someone who is merely torn between conflicting moral obligations. Either that or he is plainly irresponsible or in the grip of pathological needs.

It is, I think, a moralistic conception of morality that would claim for itself all serious value that conflicts with it. We should resist its imperious claims. The need to climb can go deep and when it does its depth is not merely psychological. For though it may be true that the climber's need is in part a need to be true to himself, the values in whose light he understands what it is to be true to himself are not reducible to a value-neutral psychology. Sometimes—at the best times—the necessities of mountaineering, the reasons why climbers must climb, are like moral necessities, outward-looking, and also like moral necessities they are distorted when one tries to explain them by an inward-looking psychology.

Like other values the deepest values in mountaineering can show themselves in what seem to be trivial details. Even when the need to climb is justifiably called a spiritual need, in which other needs for, say, self-knowledge are transformed by an almost mystical love of the beauty of the world realised in the mountains, that need can show itself in one's attitude to the use of pitons or bolts, or even in how one climbs. Shame that one allowed oneself because, for example, one is unfit or because one lacks the climbing skill, to be dragged up the face, second on the rope, like a sack of potatoes, can go well beyond personal pride. It can be an expression of respect for the mountain. No one who climbs a mountain because of its beauty could climb it like that. Climbing it properly, with some grace and without excessive use of aids, can be an expression of love for the mountain, rather than an expression of the need always to perfect one's standards, to climb harder, more elegantly as an ideal in itself.

Many mountaineers speak of their relation to the mountains in words more normally used in speaking of relations to persons—they speak of respect for the mountain, of gratitude that though they were reckless in their climbing, the mountain had let them off lightly. Sometimes they speak obsessively of it as a foe to be vanquished. But of course, no mountaineer believes that mountains are persons. Mountaineers speak in metaphors that enable them, sometimes in powerful ways, to express the fact that their will is limited by necessities that are nothing like the rules of a game and seem like nothing that a group could impose, and that they are driven by necessities whose nature is to be explained by things external to themselves.

If is of course true that one cannot rationally feel guilty towards a mountain. No one rationally feels remorse for placing more pitons than he should have. Mountains cannot be wronged. And if someone feels ashamed for making an ascent with unnecessary aids, then he is not ashamed in front of the mountain. But this should not lead to the conclusion that the outward-looking references are illusory, that the shame is self-regarding, a function of the standards of achievement and of character that one has set oneself.

A different kind of example might help to clarify what I mean. I remember an occasion walking with my father's friend Hora when he stopped, the expression on his face transformed by wonder. 'Look,' he said, 'how amazing life is'. He was pointing to a blade of grass that had reached to the sunlight through a small crack in the concrete. He knew, of course, that there was a perfectly natural explanation of why this blade of grass had managed to grow there, an explanation that anyone could accept without responding as he did. And that same explanation would reveal that, considered only as an event, this was not one to wonder at. Hora knew all that. He wasn't expressing puzzlement or even astonishment. He was expressing his reverence for nature, a reverence that always existed in him, but which the sight of that blade of grass had brought again to a pitch of intensity.

Suppose now that someone had been with us and that, when he heard Hora's exclamation of wonder, he crushed the blade of grass with his foot—perhaps because he was angry with Hora—scraping his foot up and down over it until nothing was left, just a green smear on the concrete. There is more than one reason why this person might later be ashamed of himself. He might be ashamed for the way his action was directed against Hora whom he knew to be a good man. He might be ashamed because of the pettiness and coarseness that his actions revealed. But, in addition to this, he might feel humbled by Hora's reverence for life and come to see in what he did not just the expression of petty and base motives, or an offence against Hora, but an offence against the life that Hora revered. Hora could not have done what the other person did and an account of that impossibility should not look to Hora but to the world his wonder revealed.

So it might become for the person who crushed the blade of grass. And so it sometimes is for the mountaineer who cannot continue a climb when he knows he could do so only by driving in bolts. To understand why he cannot, one should look not to his psychology, but to an understanding of how it can see this as a defilement. Love is everywhere distinguished from its false semblances by the way in which one respects the independent reality of what one loves. This is obvious in the case of human beings, but it is also true of animals and nature.

So much talk of the love of nature may seem an example of the romanticism I had earlier claimed to keep at a distance. The great tradition of mountain romanticism focuses on the European Alps. Grand, noble and savage though they may be, when one climbs in the Alps one is never far from civilisation. Only half an hour or so before one reaches a barren landscape of rock and ice, one was walking through a summer field. Descending from the bleak world of the glaciers and peaks, lifeless and intimidating, the roar of crashing stones and avalanches still in one's ears, it is hard to describe the joy of lying in the high, soft, green meadow grass, amongst the wild flowers, listening to the bells around the necks of the goats and cows and dozing for perhaps an hour before going down to the village. For a time after the intensity of the glories and the miseries of an Alpine ascent, the return to the village is unsettling, even alienating, but a large tub of French ice-cream followed by a steak with salad and olives, on a sidewalk café surrounded by ordinary people, gradually restores one to the human world and an ambivalent acceptance of its everydayness. In every Alpine village one sees young men and women whose faces radiate the joys of their adventures or, sometimes, betray the terrors of avalanches and lightning in the high mountains or the bitter exhaustion of their efforts to accept that their climbing partner is dead, Nowhere else in the world, I think, can one experience such dramatic contrasts as in the European Alps. They have nourished romanticism in generations of mountaineers.

In Australia it can be different. Though the mountains are not dramatic they are remote and their flanks are covered in often impenetrable scrub. In the winter of 1971, well before eco-tourism and even before the widespread popularity of ski touring, I went with three friends to the Cradle Mountain National Park in Tasmania. We went looking for ice-climbing in the gullies that cut the vertical precipices of Mt Geryon. As far as I know we had the entire park to ourselves. Certainly we saw no one in the two weeks we were in it. As well as heavy climbing equipment and clothes we had to carry enough food to last the fortnight. Our packs weighed just under forty kilograms. When we

fell over, as we often did, stumbling over the slippery roots of beech trees, or over the infuriating button grass, we could not get up without help.

We left the end of Lake St Clair later than we should have and dark caught us as we emerged from the forest, with less than a kilometre to go to the hut. In the dark we lost the path and found ourselves wading, sometimes waist-deep, in a swamp, frustrated that we were close to the hut yet knowing we had almost no chance of finding it. When we came upon a little island in the swamp, we decided to pitch a tent for the night.

Our clothes were never dry again for the entire time we were in the park. Never before or since have I been in terrain, not even in high alpine regions, where I felt nature to be so remorselessly hostile. Though it yielded almost every day vistas of matchless beauty, never once did I feel it offered them in friendship. After only five or six days, we were becoming demoralised, especially since we found only soft snow and no ice. We thought of little else but good food and warm, dry clothes. I remembered Bonatti's account of the Italian ascent of K2. After a time, he said, the climbers dreamt not of sexy young women, but of motherly fat ones who served them salads, pastas and fresh meat.

One day we decided to climb a mountain just above the hut. We decided to go directly to its main face, which meant first trekking through scrub. It took us nearly three hours to cover a kilometre or so, as we fought our way through the tangle of trees, branches lashing our faces, snow going down the sleeves of anoraks as we raised our arms to push the branches aside. Cursing nature for not allowing us even on this day, after a wet and cold night, the relatively simple pleasure of climbing a nearby mountain, we made our way to the face and were on the summit in late afternoon. There we enjoyed some chocolate and a cigarette rolled painfully and slowly with frozen fingers. The view of the park and its peaks, bathed in the crimson light of the late afternoon sun, was one of heartrending beauty.

We headed down. The slope was steep but the snow was soft, freshly fallen the night before, so we didn't rope up. My good friend, Dave, with whom I had climbed many times, and who had held me more than once when

I fell on rock climbs, was perhaps fifty to sixty metres ahead of me. He was having a pee near a bush that protruded a metre from the snow. As I came down I slipped, and started sliding a little in the snow, not dangerously because I would not slide far in such soft snow. But because the snow was fresh it was sticky and soon formed a small avalanche. When it came near to Dave, I could see that it was already high enough to sweep him off his feet. Not more than twenty metres behind him was a cliff eighty or more metres high.

I sat and looked as the avalanche gained momentum and height. Almost certainly, I thought, it would sweep Dave off his feet and over the cliff where he would plunge to his death. Yet I looked on, seeing it all as in slow motion and with detached amusement, thinking what a way for him to go, with his climbing trousers down. He grabbed the bush and the avalanche passed.

Not long after I saw a film on a climb of Everest by a British team. Two climbers were making a bid for the summit, without oxygen. The lead climber dropped onto the slope from exhaustion. His friend, who had climbed with him for many years, thought he was dead. He searched the pockets of his fallen comrade, looking for cashew nuts. Since he was dead, he thought, he may as well have his nuts. That's all. He thought nothing and felt nothing else.

When I spoke of the need that many mountaineers have to seek through climbing an understanding of their humanity I expressed sympathy for that need. My own sensibility has been profoundly shaped by it and by the effects of the landscape of my boyhood. I do not, however, believe that an interest of any kind in nature or animals is essential to a full development of one's humanity. In the modern celebration of nature and wilderness we are sometimes in danger of condescending to, even having contempt for, people who have no interest in nature, and who are in various ways physically incompetent. We are always vulnerable to the ideal of a full human life being a life in which, as Marx said, we read philosophy in the morning, work with our hands in the afternoon and fish in the evenings. But there are people who want only to work in philosophy, who never leave the city, who are completely incompetent when it comes to doing anything with their hands and who cannot bear animals. In a very important sense, their lives need be lacking in nothing. The English philosopher Stuart Hampshire said that anyone with some knowledge of other cultures and with an imaginative sense of human possibilities must realise that there are many but incommensurable ways of living. In a memorable phrase, he remarked that we all go lopsided to the grave. That's half true.

Norman Malcolm reports in *Wittgenstein: A Memoir* that when the philosopher was on his deathbed he asked his housekeeper to tell his friends 'that it has been a wonderful life'. Malcolm says he found it deeply moving that Wittgenstein should say this in the face of the evident misery that had marked much of his life. He did not, however, suggest that knowledge of that misery might give one reason to challenge what Wittgenstein said. Wittgenstein was not in any ordinary sense expressing an *assessment* of his life. He was expressing an unconditional gratitude for it. No one has the right to challenge him to qualify his gratitude.

There is no human being of whom we have the right to say that he or she could not express the same gratitude as Wittgenstein did. Only arrogant folly could make one think that someone who had all her life been estranged from the natural world could not, with lucidity, say that she had had a wonderful life.

Index